THE MARITIME HISTORY
OF RUSSIA 848-1948

The
Maritime History
of Russia
848-1948

BY

MAIRIN MITCHELL, F.R.G.S.

*

WITH MAPS SPECIALLY DRAWN BY
J. F. HORRABIN
and others selected by the Author,
some from original sources

SIDGWICK AND JACKSON LIMITED
LONDON

MGE

FIRST PUBLISHED IN 1949

PRINTED AND BOUND IN ENGLAND BY
HAZELL WATSON & VINEY Ltd
AYLESBURY AND LONDON

DEDICATED TO

G.E.M., E.P.H.M., E.T.P., and S.M.

CONTENTS

LIST OF ILLUSTRATIONS

CHAPTER I

CHAPTER II

SUPPLEMENTARY SECTION

ACKNOWLEDGMENTS

AMONG the sources consulted for this book, many have been made available to the author through the courtesy of the Department of Naval Information, also of the Library and Press Division, the Admiralty. The Libraries of the Royal Naval College, Greenwich, the Royal Geographical Society, and the United States Embassy have provided indispensable material, as has also the Reading Room of the British Museum. Appreciation is recorded of the facilities for the selection of maps granted by E. Lynam, Esq., D.Litt., M.R.I.A., F.S.A., Superintendent of the Map Room, the British Museum.

The Author's thanks are also expressed for the courtesy of the Trustees of the British Museum in permitting reproductions of maps and illustrations. The encouragement and the help given by A. I. Ellis, Esq., C.B.E., Keeper, Department of Printed Books, is recalled with gratitude.

In the collection of material, Miss E. M. L'E. Cartwright has generously collaborated.

The author here recalls with gratitude the late Mr. Francis E. McMurtrie, A.I.N.A., Editor of *Jane's Fighting Ships*, for his highly valued criticism and advice, and also for his kindness in favouring her with the summarised account of the Russo-Japanese War on pp. 321-323.

To Mr. Brian Tunstall, formerly Honorary Secretary of the Navy Records Society, she is indebted for the inspiration to write this book, and to Mr. Christopher Lloyd, Lecturer, the Royal Naval College, Greenwich, for his helpful commentary and suggestions.

Numerous individuals, publishers and societies have given their permission for quotations made in this work. In particular the author is under obligation to the Hakluyt Society, to the Department of the Archives of Hudson's Bay Company, to *The Navy*, official organ of the Navy League, and to the Society for Cultural Relations between the Peoples of the British Commonwealth and the U.S.S.R. She wishes also to record her appreciation of Lady Mackinder's kindness in permitting extracts to be made from the late Sir Halford Mackinder's *Democratic Ideals and Reality*. Her thanks are due as well to Lady Corbett for the inclusion of passages from the works of the late Sir Julian Corbett. Gratitude for similar help is here expressed to R. C. Anderson, Esq., D.Litt., F.S.A.

For kind permission to quote from *Jane's Fighting Ships, All the*

World's Fighting Fleets, and *The World's Warships*, the author tenders her sincere thanks to Messrs. Sampson Low. To Messrs. William Clowes, as the publishers of *Brassey's Naval Annual*, and to Lloyd's Register of Shipping for references to *Lloyd's Register Book, 1947-48*, she is much indebted for the same favour. Acknowledgments are due as well to Odhams Press, Ltd., for their consent to reproduction of passages from *The World Crisis, 1915*, by the Rt. Hon. Winston S. Churchill, M.P., and also to Messrs. Cassell, London, and the Houghton Mifflin Company, Boston, for quotations made from Mr. Churchill's book *The Second World War*, Vol. I. For passages reproduced from the works of certain Russian and other writers, the author has to thank in particular Messrs. Gollancz, and Messrs. Hutchinson, also Messrs. Secker and Warburg for references to *Hitler and His Admirals*, by Anthony Martienssen, and to H.M. Stationery Office for extracts from *Fuehrer Conferences on Naval Affairs, 1939-1945*.

For the reproduction on the cover of this book of the Viking Ship (ninth century A.D.) from a model in the Science Museum, acknowledgments are made to Crown copyright. The writing of the sections on the Soviet development of Inland Waterways has been much facilitated by illustrations and diagrams kindly lent by Mr. Hugh P. Vowles, M.I.Mech.E. Indebtedness to various other sources is acknowledged in the Supplementary Section of this book.

The late Mr. Hugh Carrington, F.R.G.S., is remembered with gratitude, not only for his counsel but for his introduction to the publishers of this book, whose helpfulness throughout the various stages of its production has been cordially appreciated.

Note.—The use of Russian characters for the titles of Russian books has been preferred in general; in the few cases where transliteration occurs, the forms adopted have been based on the Glossary published in 1942 by the Permanent Committee on Geographical Names for British Official Use (House of the Royal Geographical Society, Kensington Gore, London, S.W.7).

THE MARITIME HISTORY
OF RUSSIA 848-1948

I

THE BACKGROUND

RUSSIA has a greater length of coastline than any other country in the world. But her only undisputed sea is that sector of the Arctic Ocean on which she has 15,000 miles of shoreline. To the Black Sea, the Caspian, the Baltic, she has never held sole title, and on the Pacific Ocean she has never been unquestioned mistress. Yet the geographical situation and the physical character of the land-mass known as the U.S.S.R. makes it inevitable that Russia should not only find her way to all the oceans, but that her strength at sea should become considerable. We are witnessing in the U.S.S.R. an effort to change the navy from one mainly defensive to one of Ocean Fleets, in all of which the real strength lies underseas. At the time of writing, the Soviet submarine strength exceeds that of any other Power, and it is the under-water vessel rather than the atomic bomb that would be the greatest menace to sea-bound countries aligned against the Soviet Union in any future war. The naval ambitions which Imperial Russia had nursed at the opening of the twentieth century were shattered in the Russo-Japanese War, but now, Russia has broken through again in the Baltic as she has broken through the ice-barriers in the Arctic. She is vigilant on the Pacific and efficient on the Black Sea. An expanding future lies before her on the two oceans and twelve seas that wash her shores.

Just half a century ago a remarkable passage was written by Mr. Fred T. Jane in his study of Imperial Russian sea power: "Every Russian feels himself a member of the empire that will be the world-empire of the future. And that empire will be a great sea-empire, since the sea is now what the land once was in the matter of communications. At some future date that great struggle between the British Empire and the Russian, between the Anglo-Saxon and the Slav, that so many prophesy, may come off. The day is probably yet far distant ere this new Punic War comes about. When it comes it does not do too hastily to assume that England is its Carthage and Russia its Rome. . . . neither nation is likely to crush the other as Rome crushed Carthage. Yet the war of the future, when it comes, is none the less likely to be absolutely decisive, for one mighty empire or the

3

other will in all human probability split into fragments."[1]   The fact that the American Empire has now replaced the British as the most powerful, does not affect the potential validity of F. T. Jane's forecast. In a third world war Britain itself could become the Spain of the Second—experimental target for the newest long-range missiles—but in the view of many, the two chief protagonists in all probability would be the United States with the British Commonwealth, and Russia. In other words the conflict would be one between the Anglo-Saxon and the Slav as envisaged by F. T. Jane. Today, when the term sea power is only valid if it has co-efficiency of air power, and when atomic fission adds unknown possibilities to the naval weapons of the future, it is still the hope of multitudes that such a danger as F. T. Jane foresaw, may at least have one chance of receding now that Russia has gained several of her most urgent maritime objectives as a result of the second world war. "It must be recognised that free and effective access to the oceans and broad waters of the world is a natural claim for so vast a land Power as the Soviet. I have myself always favoured this aspiration," wrote Mr. Churchill in 1947. Nevertheless, in the minds of many, the fulfilment of that aspiration could provide Russia with vantage points for any offensive rôle which she might in future wish to assume. Certainly the fact that one of her chief aims is to become a great Sea Power, and that, in submersible ships, she has already gone far in that direction, is a fact whose influence on the future of a shrinking British Empire will be profound.

Within twenty-five years Britain has changed from a Two-Power naval standard to one which time alone can reveal to be adequate or otherwise for security. For, although America and the lands of the British Commonwealth will take the place once held by Britain, as guardians of the oceans, and the future rôle of the United Kingdom may become increasingly that of a continental land-and-air Power, yet her first duty as a member of the Atlantic Alliance will be to hold the Channel, and the home waters which, viewed strategically, are so important. Certainly she is engaged on revolutionary naval technical developments, and her forthcoming submarines will, one may be sure, embody the results of the most advanced research, and will indicate the character of Britain's new navy. But to whatever extent she develops her naval power, the maritime relations between herself and America are complementary. In the

[1] *The Imperial Russian Navy, Its Past, Present, and Future.* (Thacker & Co., London.) First published 1899; pp. 605, 606.

last war, before America became a belligerent, it was at once apparent that but for the British Navy the ocean lay open to Germany from Bremen to Brooklyn. The Atlantic, which once divided Britain and America, now unites them. There is as yet no underlying unity of oceanic interests linking the British Empire and the Soviet Union, no maritime nexus such as binds Britain and America, and Britain with the members of the Commonwealth and Empire.

The foundation of that Empire is a maritime one, and its existence today depends upon its sea-and-air communications. Challenged as it has been in different areas of critical location by the Russian imperium, we may recall the speech made by President Kalinin to shipyard workers on 2 July, 1938: "We, the greatest socialist country, must outmatch England." The first step, he said, was to build a great navy, and to build one rapidly: "The mighty Soviet Union must have the strongest navy in the world." Less than twelve months later the period of naval service was raised to five years, and men who wished to serve longer were not to be accepted for a further period of less than three years. This decree, it was calculated, would increase by more than twenty-five per cent. the number of men serving with Russia's naval forces. It was in operation at a time when many British Sea Cadets were being sent to the mines by ballot. Referring to the Russian decree, *The Times*' Special Correspondent wrote from Moscow:[1] "The most important provision, however, is that those who have had secondary and higher education must serve the full five years; hitherto they have been able to obtain release after two years. *This means that the Navy will be favoured at the expense of other professions with the services of the educated classes.* These already enter it later than others to allow them to complete their studies, but the decree will delay for a further three years the beginning of a professional career. Obviously civilian enterprise will suffer; *but the Navy's need of expert personnel is presumably considered more urgent.*"[2]

Such advances towards the fulfilment of Russia's maritime ambitions will naturally affect also the United States, to whom the trident passed in the second world war. America has moved nearer to Russia now that she has acquired a succession of island bases which bridge the Pacific, and her relations with Russia will be governed increasingly by the question of sea power. In this connection the geopolitical theories of Sir Halford Mackinder are of paramount interest today. Those theories were used

[1] 19.5.1939.　　　　[2] Italics ours.

by Hitler as the groundwork of his plans for world conquest, and the extent to which the German effort nearly succeeded, went far to demonstrate the validity of Mackinder's thesis. The latter briefly described the continents of Europe, Asia, Africa, as the "World Island", for the insular nature of this land mass had become apparent when Nordenskiöld, by his voyage in the *Vega*, had shown that ships could sail from the North Atlantic to the North Pacific by the Arctic route. The region stretching from north-east Siberia to the middle of Europe, Mackinder described as the "Heartland" of this World Island, and he gave emphatic warning that once a great land Power got control of that vital "Heartland", there was a danger that it would advance from its interior bases and capture the littoral regions. When that was accomplished the land Power would prove its superiority over such island peoples as Americans and Australasians, by developing from its strategic vantage points a sea power mightier than that of the islanders. "What," he asked, "if the Great Continent, the whole World Island or a large part of it, were at some future time to become a single and united base of sea power? Would not the other insular bases be outbuilt as regards ships, and outmanned as regards seamen? The fleets would no doubt fight with all the heroism begotten of their histories, but the end would be fated." [1]

When Mackinder wrote his *Democratic Ideals and Reality* he visualised the possibility of a renascent Germany as the land Power, advancing eastwards, likely to capture the "Heartland". Today the greatest pressure from a land Power comes from the east and is exerted west, far into the heart of Europe, and even beyond to the North Atlantic littoral. Here, verging on the Arctic seas, this pressure impinges on American strategic requirements. Polar projection brings the next meeting point to the Bering Strait, the extreme north-east fringe of Mackinder's "Heartland". This Strait at its narrowest point is only fifty-six miles wide. The Alaskan Cape—Prince of Wales, and the Russian Cape—Deshniev, are separated by less than sixty miles of water, and less than nine miles divide the Big Diomede Island, which is Russian territory, from the Little Diomede, which is American. The boundary between the U.S. and the U.S.S.R. runs through the water that separates these two islands. [2] And,

[1] *Democratic Ideals and Reality.* (Constable & Co., 1919); p. 91.
[2] The Meridian of Longitude 168° 49′ 30″ W. runs between these two islands, and was the line agreed upon in 1867 when Alaska was purchased by America from Russia.

northward, the race for the Polar air routes with their Arctic bases takes its rapid course.

Russia is the country which possesses by far the greatest share of the "Heartland", while America has a greater preponderance of sea power than any country has ever yet achieved. Consequently the maritime aims of Russia are profoundly concerns of the United States. Across the Pacific Ocean the chain of island bases and the acquired administration of the ex-Japanese mandated islands, have brought America closer to the Siberian seaboard.

Since the opening of the twentieth century the Pacific has superseded the Atlantic in world importance.[1] Its basin will become the centre of world currents, for round its western edge is settled one of the largest shares of the earth's population; the vast natural resources of that region remain to be developed. This century has already seen a steep rise in the volume of foreign trade of the Pacific countries, and a corresponding increase in the mercantile services of those lands.[2] In the case of the United States and Russia it has also seen an expansion of naval power in the Far East. America, by the creation of her mighty navy, may achieve the position envisaged eventually for his country by President Theodore Roosevelt, who said, half a century ago : "to the United States must belong the dominion of the Pacific." Russian aims also were given explicit expression in the speech of Admiral Kuznetsov, Commissar of the Navy, at the 18th Conference of the Communist Party, March 1939. "We have now," he said, "started on a programme of further naval expansion in order to create a big, powerful fleet representative of the Soviet Union as a great naval Power." With a naval base at Port Arthur, the use of Dalny as a free port, the reversion to her of southern Sakhalin, her acquisition of the Kurile Islands, and with other gains resulting from her entry into the war against Japan in 1945,[3] Russia can become a maritime Power of the first rank in the Far East. The second world war has seen the emergence of America as the greatest naval Power; the strength of these two countries in the Pacific is a factor that will from now on determine the course of world history. A century ago Tocqueville wrote of Russia and America as "two

[1] Even the formation of the Atlantic Union has not altered that fact.

[2] For tables of increase see Bienstock, *The Struggle for the Pacific*. (Allen and Unwin, 1937) ; p. 23.

[3] The Soviet Union's participation in the war against Japan lasted only six days; never, perhaps, have greater territorial gains resulted from so short a period of conflict,

THEATRUM ORBIS TERRARUM ORTELIUS

(Reproduced by permission of the Trustees of the British Museum)

THIS World Map of Ortelius (dated 1587) is reproduced from the edition of his *Theatrum* of 1592—just one hundred years after Columbus had made his first voyage across the Atlantic—and is of special interest in showing the vast land mass representing the "Unknown Continent", embracing the extreme southern latitudes of the globe. It was due to the second voyage of Captain Cook in 1772 that this widely held belief in an immense continent occupying those regions came to be shaken. The expedition of the Russian explorer, Commander Bellingshausen, in 1819-1821, was made with the intention of supplementing Cook's voyage. During his circumnavigation of the Antarctic Ocean in the *Vostok*, Bellingshausen, who was accompanied by Lieut. Lazarev in the *Mirny*, reached latitude 69° 52', and within the Antarctic Circle he had sailed over 42° of longitude.

great nations which seem to tend towards the same end, although they start from different points . . . each of them appears to be marked by the will of heaven to sway the destinies of half the globe." In our century, Stalin was reported as making a forecast whose probability of fulfilment seems remote. But it is quoted for the temptation it may afford many to substitute "Russia" for "England" in the battle of the giants. Speaking on 13 July, 1928, Stalin envisaged a hostile situation developing between the two chief capitalist Powers, America and England. "What," he asked, "is this basic conflict fraught with? It is fraught with war. *When two giants collide with each other, when this globe is too small for them, they try to measure their strength, they try to solve the vexing question of world hegemony by means of war.*"[1]

To Stalin the importance of sea power in any such war is forcefully clear. Some of his utterances suggest that he has studied the works of the maritime historian Nicolas Klado, a writer little known in England, and yet one who might without exaggeration be called the Russian Mahan. Klado, who was Professor at the Naval Academy, St. Petersburg, and served as Flag-Captain in the Second Pacific Squadron in the Russo-Japanese War, held very definite views about the importance of educating the Russian people to realise the need for a strong navy. "During more than two centuries of the history of our much-suffering fleet," he wrote,[2] "we have not shown ourselves capable of firmly deciding, not only what kind of fleet we need, but absolutely whether we need one at all." Though Peter the Great, he added, had shown why a fleet was indispensable, the lesson was not learnt by the nation, and "up to the time of Catherine the Great the navy was merely tolerated, and consequently fell into decay." It need hardly be said that an impressive navy is not necessarily an indication of a sea-minded people. Catherine the Great, like Peter the Great, had no illusions about the lack of sea sense in her subjects as a whole, yet after her war with Turkey, 1787-89, her fleet outnumbered the combined Swedish and Danish navies. As the naval historian, Dr. R. C. Anderson, has pointed out, "the Russian superiority to the other two Baltic Powers had been more or less assured ever since the days of Peter the Great, but after this war with Sweden [1790] it had become far more marked than before,

---

[1] Quoted by D. J. Dallin, *Russia and Post-War Europe*, translated by F. K. Lawrence. (Yale University Press, New Haven, 1944), 3rd impression; p. 85.
[2] *The Battle of the Sea of Japan*, translated by J. H. Dickinson and F. P. Marchand. (Hodder & Stoughton, 1906); p. 278.

and it was not until quite modern days that the rise of the new German Navy deprived Russia of her position."[1] There is a tendency today to regard the rising creation of Russian sea power as a new portent, and to forget that it was only after her losses in the Far Eastern war of 1904-05 that Russia's navy fell to a place of comparative insignificance among the world's principal fleets.

The essential difference in the contemporary naval drive in Russia and those of periods between the deaths of Peter I and of Nicholas II, is the fact that the Soviet rulers are endeavouring to make the peoples of the U.S.S.R. sea-minded. The recent efforts to popularise the study of maritime subjects throughout the Soviet Union—the great output of seafaring literature, the number of nautical lectures and of naval exhibitions—all testify to this intention. Much that Stalin himself has said might have come from a chapter entitled "Our Future Duty" in Klado's principal work, *The Battle of the Sea of Japan*. Here the author urges his countrymen to study the maritime history of England, where "the whole nation very early understood the need and importance of sea-power, inasmuch as this is the best guarantee for the prosperity of maritime commerce."[2]

The nature of Stalin's pronouncements about the necessity of Russia obtaining new bases, is in the direct line of, if it does not actually derive from, the teaching of Captain Klado. "It suffices us to look attentively at the system of English seaports and stations spread all over the terrestrial globe," wrote Klado, "in order to convince ourselves that we are in the face of a well-thought-out and definitive plan—carried out indeed by various individuals and different generations, varying also in the development of details, but it is evident that all these men kept before them one clearly conceived and firmly established aim."

That same aim is one which Stalin and his colleagues are not only themselves pursuing, but towards which they are turning the minds of their fellow countrymen. The change of Russia from a "land animal" to an amphibious one, is a process rapid even for these days. How long may it be before the organ of the Central Committee of the Communist Party, Moscow, can point to the validity of its claim—more than doubtful when made in 1946—that "in armament and durability our ships have proved superior to ships of similar classes produced by

[1] *Naval Wars in the Baltic, 1521-1850.* (C. Gilbert-Wood, London, 1910); p. 293.
[2] *The Battle of the Sea of Japan*, p. 283-4.

capitalist countries"? Certainly no sceptical attitude can be
adopted towards the statement of Vice-Admiral Abankin on
Red Navy Day, 1946, that the Soviet Union "has her interests
on the sea, and she will always defend them," and that " in the
interests of her security and independence she will continue to
build up a strong navy and to consolidate her naval power."
Progress in this direction was accelerated by the second world
war, which brought Russia within visible distance of achieving
her old ambition of gaining a free seaboard on all the chief trade
routes adjacent and near to her territories. This much good the
war did Russia—it ensured for her a future on the seas such as
Peter the Great had once promised his people.

At the time when that promise was made, more than a
hundred years were to go before the first railway was laid in
Russia, so that the importance of the sea for the expansion of
commerce was the more considerable. But, as George Borodin
and other Russian writers have pointed out, the sea was not
Russia's natural medium, and more than two centuries were to
pass before she came near the fulfilment of the promise made by
Peter I. When the railways came, their development was for
some time directed to making them not only the chief instrument
of transport, but one which need fear no rival in the shipping
industry, particularly in the Far North. This statement must be
qualified however, by the reference, which will be made in
more detail later, to the Russian Government's concessions to
an English Company founded in 1896 with the object of
developing a commercial sea route to Siberia. And subsequently
the Government itself became the sponsor of efforts made to
that end by its own nationals. The fact remains however that
the rail magnates, fearing rivalry, had succeeded in thwarting
Admiral Makarov's plea for the opening of a northern seaway
to link Archangel with Vladivostock, and had pressed instead
for the construction of the Trans-Siberian Railway to the Far
East. As few other outlets to the sea had been gained, it was by
the Trans-Siberian that grain from the south of Russia found
its way overseas from a Pacific port, once the branch line
through Manchuria was completed. The use of the sea for transport from the Far North to the East had been frustrated earlier
still by the fur trading companies which held monopoly rights
on the caravan routes from the fur regions of Siberia. (As late as
1913 Russia's trade distribution by the northern and eastern
ports combined was only 8 per cent. of the total, whereas from
the southern ports it was 44 per cent., and from the Baltic 48 per

cent.—a disparity too great to be accounted for by the sole factor of the Arctic climate.) Another reason why Russia's maritime enterprise in the Arctic was restricted as much by some of her rulers as it was encouraged by others, was the fear of certain of her ministers that, once it became known that a North-East Passage could be used as a channel of communication, it would be likely to encourage foreign invasion.

One more reason must be added to these just given for the late development of the Northern Sea Route—and that is, the Russians themselves. The great Plain which stretches from the Baltic to the south of the Urals, and thence across Siberia right to the Lena, has determined that the main migrations of the Slavs have been riverine and landward, not maritime ones. And the outlook of these peoples has been correspondingly conditioned by the land, not the oceans. Another factor which has helped in the past to keep the Russians continental-minded has been their subjugation for more than two centuries to the Mongols—people of the plains to whom the seas were unknown. One of the foremost Russian geographers of today, N. N. Mikhailov, has testified to the numerically insignificant contributions made in the past by his countrymen to the eastward exploration of the Arctic Seas. "The northern seas between Novaya Zemlya and the Bering Straits, which intimidated people because they were ice-covered and had never been investigated," he says, "were seen only by ships of extremely rare scientific expeditions which were mostly foreign and not Russian." [1] This statement, however, cannot apply to the intensive work directed by the Emperor Alexander I, who commissioned von Wrangell to survey the Siberian coast between the Yana and Kolima Rivers, nor can it relate to the encouragement of exploration given by the Tsarist Governments from the time of the expedition of Baron Toll, 1900, up to the outbreak of the 1914-1918 war. And geographical names such as Cheliuskin, Laptev, Malygin, Litke, and many others, testify to the earlier achievements of numerous Russian explorers in the easterly sector of the Arctic, though by no means all of their voyages would come within the definition of "scientific expeditions". Mikhailov's assertion regarding the rarity of such maritime excursions on the part of the Russians was one which Baron von Wrangell had also made in 1820, when he wrote that "with the exception of the voyage of Cook and Billings, none afforded any

---

[1] *Soviet Geography*, translated by Natalie Rothstein. (Methuen, 1937); pp. 192, 193. By permission of the Publishers.

precise determinations as far as geography and hydrography are concerned".[1] It was, as he says,[2] the scientific researches of the English in the region of the Bering Straits, that induced the Russian Government to try to learn more about the remote parts of their empire, and for this purpose the expedition of the Englishman, Joseph Billings, had been commissioned.

In a chronology of the principal excursions into the Arctic from A.D. 870 to 1918, given by Dr. Louis Segal,[3] we find the following lists: British, 59; American, 21; Russian, 18; Danish, 11; Swedish, 9; Norwegian, 8; Dutch, 5; Canadian, 4; German, 3; Italian, 1; Austrian, 1; Icelandic, 1; Swiss, 1. The figures possibly underestimate the outstanding contributions made by the Dutch, but they are interesting in showing that for over a thousand years the peoples with shores on the Frozen Ocean were yet eclipsed in the realms of Arctic adventure by the much remoter British.

Despite however, the land-minded character of her people, Russia for many centuries in her history has manifested an instinctual and also a conscious political urge *towards* the oceans. That urge was thwarted in the Baltic by the Teutonic Knights and by the Poles, and in the fourteenth century by the Kingdom of Lithuania which, in 1386, after its union with Poland, stretched right from Memel on the Baltic to the territory between the mouths of the Dnieper and the Dniester on the shores of the Black Sea. Beyond that, to the east, spread the Khanate of the Golden Horde which blocked Russia from the Caucasus and Crimean coasts of the Black Sea, and for long restricted her intercourse with Byzantium. But under Peter the Great the map of Russia was changed. "The land army has one arm," said that monarch, "but the Government which possesses an army and a fleet, is a body with two arms." And it was Peter's efforts to give his empire a navy, that more than anything else changed the face of Russia. His almost obsessional *drang nach Westen* drove him to war with Sweden, which then ranked as a leading naval Power. His victory at Narva in 1704 over the armies of Charles XII, was a turning point in Russian history. Narva, a river-port of strategic value from its position on the Narova, had, in the reign of Ivan the Terrible, figured

---

[1] *Narrative of an Expedition to the Polar Sea in the Years 1820, 1821, 1822, and 1823 by Lieutenant now Admiral Ferdinand von Wrangell*: Major Edward Sabine. (James Madden, 1844). 2nd edtn., p. 1.

[2] *Ibid.*, p. 474.

[3] *The Conquest of the Arctic.* (Harrap, 1939); Appendix, pp. 271-6.

prominently in dispatches from the King of Poland to Queen Elizabeth. "The Muscovite sovereign," he complained, "is daily augmenting his power by the acquisition of objects imported through Narva, for they import by this route not only merchandise but weapons." In the eighteenth century this port was a centre of shipbuilding, and did a considerable export trade in timber with merchants from England and the Netherlands, as well as with those of the German and Baltic Hanse cities. When Peter captured Narva he got not only that fortress-town but its port of Hungerborg on the sea coast. His victories over the Swedish armies brought him Karelia and the port of Viborg, and so established Russia at the head of the Gulf of Finland. The acquisition in 1720 of Livonia (eastern Latvia) gave to Russia the Gulf of Riga; and when the province of Ingria (between St. Petersburg and Novgorod) passed to the Tsar, his empire now extended westward as far as Oesel Island in the Baltic. The conservation of his fleet to maintain his hard-won position on that sea, was thereafter the task to which Russia's remarkable, shrewd, and eccentric ruler applied himself with undeflected zeal.

Catherine the Great, who ruled Russia from 1762 to 1796, continued the seaward drive of Peter the Great, and in that last year of her reign her acquisition of the duchy of Courland increased Russia's Baltic littoral by the addition of territory from Riga to Memel. From Catherine's accession till twelve years before her death, Russia was engaged in warring for possession of the Crimea—territory which the Tartars held under suzerainty of the Ottoman Empire. In 1777 General Suvorov defeated the Tartars, and in 1783 the Crimea finally passed into the Empire of the Tsars. But Russia's position on the Black Sea was to be seriously threatened from another direction; less than a century later she was at war with Great Britain in the Crimea, while in the Mediterranean as on the Persian Gulf, her seaward ambitions were thwarted by the same western oceanic Power. The recovery of Russia's Black Sea Fleet after the Crimean War, and its later growth under the Five-Year Plans, forms the subject of another chapter in this book, but here it may be said that the real test of that fleet has not yet come. The possibilities of such a test invite speculation, as, for instance, a future westward movement of Asiatic peoples such as once brought the Mongolians into Europe. In the days of the Tartar invasion of the Crimea there was no Black Sea Fleet to meet that menace from the east. Today whether the threat be from east

or west, the Soviet Union aims at making the Black Sea a powerful zone for the defence of her frontiers in southern Europe. It is
also her intention to gain Mediterranean bases for that fleet,
until she eventually creates a squadron for the Middle Sea.
"For centuries the destinies of the civilised world had seemed
to turn about the Mediterranean. Each Power that had in its
time dominated the main line of history had been a maritime
Power." [1] The truth of this statement by a great English naval
historian, Sir Julian Corbett, has been apparent to the rulers of
contemporary Russia no less than to such of their predecessors
as Peter I, Catherine II, and Alexander I.

On the Pacific seaboard, Russia's development of her position
has been one comparatively recent in her history, owing to lack
of communications across Siberia. Until the Trans-Siberian
Railway was constructed there was practically no direct route
from west to east. If the rivers of that region had flowed west-
east instead of south-north, the Russian settlements on the
Pacific seaboard would have been larger and more easily
accomplished. A scarcity of ships retarded the transport of
colonists to the Far East in the days when the long Cape route
had to be used, and even when the Suez Canal was opened. The
laying of the Trans-Siberian meant the linking of the Atlantic
with the Pacific. Russia had begun looking to the east, however,
as early as the days of Ivan IV, and during the seventeenth
century the Slav colonists after fighting their way through
Siberia, had reached the Pacific. The shrewd and strong-willed
Golovin, Voivod of Yakutsk, had backed the adventurous ataman Vasili Poyarkov, who ploughed his way from the Lena to
the Amur in search of fabled wealth of grain, and in 1643 had
struck the sea in his trail down the Amur. From Yakutsk he had
set sail in his birch-frame boat of deerskins and sailed up the
Lena, forced to use paddles in wet weather; braving the rapids
of the Aldan he had left that river to trek across the Stanovoy
mountains of eastern Siberia. These he and his fellow Cossacks
had to cross on skis, dragging their equipment on hand sledges
over the heights until they descended by the river Seya, a tributary of the Amur. Of the twenty-five men whom he sent thence
to explore the Sungari, all but two were murdered by natives.
Poyarkov finally reached the mouth of the Amur river, and he is
the first recorded Russian to have done this. The following
spring he had sailed to Okhotsk, and by the time he returned to

[1] *England in the Mediterranean, 1603-1713.* (Longmans, Green & Co., 1917,
2nd edition); Vol. I, p. 4. With acknowledgments to Lady Corbett.

Yakutsk this fearless hunter had voyaged 4,000 miles.[1] Five years later the Cossack chieftain Yerofei Khabarov and a band of hunters, crossed the Yakutsk territory in search of a short route to the Amur, slaughtering the "Daurians" east of Lake Baikal, plundering their villages and leaving such desolation behind them that the cry "the Cossacks are coming" would for years to come ensure a clearance of the countryside of all inhabitants.

On the Upper Amur the Cossacks were well established by 1682, and further east their choice of Albazin as their chief fortified settlement proved a sound one, that place becoming the base for their expansion to the Pacific seaboard, and one which they kept till the ill-fated Treaty of Nerchinsk, 1689. The historian Müller, writing in 1741, stressed how desirable it would be to gain the right of free navigation on the river, and to use this for sending supplies to the Russian settlements on Kamchatka; later the Governor of Siberia had drawn up plans for provisioning in this way the Russian settlers on the Pacific coast.

In their *kochi* (light sailing boats), undaunted by raging rivers and the Arctic climate, intrepid hunters continued to push across Siberia eastwards in search of furs and of the ivory tusks of frozen mammoths. The advances eastward made after Bering's time by trading expeditions fitted out by merchants of Yakutsk, have been unforgettably described in Coxe's *Account of the Russian Discoveries between Asia and America*, published in 1780. His chronicle tells how the merchants, banding together as small trading companies, sent cordage and sails from Yakutsk to Okhotsk for the building of their boats—known as *skitiki* from the use of stitched thongs for binding together the planks. In these days when the question "Private enterprise or State-planned economy?" is a major one still in many countries, it is interesting to find Coxe claiming that "within a period of ten years, more important discoveries were made by these individuals, at their own private cost, than had been hitherto effected by all the expensive efforts of the crown."

But by the time the dominions of the Tsar stretched across the

---

[1] See Prince Lobanov-Rostovsky's account of Poyarkov's voyage, in *Russia and Asia*. (The Macmillan Company, New York, 1933); p. 57. Reference by permission of the Publishers.

A detailed history of the Amur and of the pre-Poyarkov attempts to reach that river will be found in *Le Fleuve Amour*, by C. de Sabir. (Georg Kugelmann, Paris, 1861.)

ADMIRAL OF THE FLEET NIKOLAI G. KUZNETSOV

APPOINTED Navy Commissar in 1939, and at the age of 38 he was the youngest supreme naval chief in the world. Under him, particular regard has been paid to the Far Eastern Flotilla whose augmentation commenced in 1939.

North Pacific, the story of the Russian trader and trapper on the north-west coast of America might have been a very different one if these *promyschleni*, or early speculators in seal skins and otter pelts, had not persuaded certain of the most skilled seafarers in the world to join in their ventures on a profit-sharing basis. From the Aleutian Islands came natives in their *baidarkas* —canoes made of walrus and seal skin stretched over a frame of light wood or whalebone, and having joints lashed with thongs of hide. Paddling such craft, in some cases no larger than the *kayak* of the Eskimo, the Aleuts for hundreds of miles pursued the sea otter, seal, and black whale along the coasts of Alaska, and in and out of the maze of their own fog-shrouded islands.

From the days of the *promyschleni* who derived much of their profits from the skill of these Aleutian Islanders, and from the days of the Cossack adventurers, begins the divided east-west outlook which has dominated so many chapters of Russian history. Indications are, that in the future the eastward orientation will be stronger than the western. Today the maritime position of Russia in the Far East is a factor whose importance will be very high in the emergence of new economic and social forces around the Asian Pacific seaboard. Even in the second world conflict, although the Soviet fleet was not called upon to undertake any major operations in the Pacific, the fact that Russia had, in the Far East, a fleet in being (though numerically very small, and comprised mainly of submarines) was not without its effect upon the ocean war in that area of the globe. In this sense the Russian fleet was a recognised factor in the struggle at sea.

The expansion of the U.S.S.R.'s navy in the Pacific from one purely defensive to one whose long-cruising submarines provide it with offensive power, is one of the most remarkable developments in the recent history of Russian maritime enterprise. (It is in under-water craft, not in surface-ships, that the future Russian navy must be looked for.) The Soviet Union has frontiers which total 60,000 kms. in length, and three-fourths of this is sea-washed. The realisation of the implications of this—that Russia must be strong at sea—though it is a recent realisation, has been responsible for an expansion of her navies; and of her four fleets, the Baltic, Black Sea, Northern, and Far Eastern, none has shown a more speedy advance than the last. Admiral Kuznetsov, Navy Commissar, has stated that even up till five years before the outbreak of the second world war (at the very time when Japan had just denounced the Washington Treaty limitations on her own navy) the Soviet Far Eastern Fleet consisted of only one warship—a submarine. From that solitary ship the Russian Pacific Fleet has grown, till today the humming shipyards of Nikolaievsk are building vessels whose numbers point to a progressive sea-consciousness. The Russians, who are living in the past as well as the future, recalling their heroes of other centuries, are remembering that they once had a record of exploration in the Pacific which, though markedly eclipsed by those of the leading maritime nations, and lasting for a time comparatively short in the annals of seafaring, was yet a gratifying record. That period might not have been such a brief one but for the priority given to the development of railways when these came to Russia.

The first three decades of the nineteenth century saw an almost phenomenal wave of Russian maritime enterprise in the Pacific, north and south, for reasons (as we shall later see) partly connected with the Russian-American Fur Company, partly with the desire of successive Imperial governments to open up trade with Japan. From the Bering Strait to Antarctica Russian mariners ploughed the waters of the Pacific. In the encouragement of long-distance navigation Alexander I was ahead of many of his naval staff. The Tsar saw the necessity of his seamen learning this art, as the eastern outposts of his empire were dependent on supplies from his dominions in the west (except for those brought in the Russian-American Company's ships from Alaska.) There was then no North-East Passage, and so the Russian vessels had to sail from the Baltic to the Far East via the Cape. The captains of these early expeditions were in nearly every case men who had served for a time with the English navy, and so were not unfamiliar with long cruises. Between 1803 and 1849, says M. A. Sergeyev,[1] there were thirty-six Russian voyages round the world. The first of these was the joint one undertaken by Captain Krusenstern in the *Nadezhda* and Captain Lysiansky in the *Neva*. Accounts of their expedition have been given by each of those commanders, and have been enriched by the publication in 1944[2] of the diary of N. I. Korobyzin, a clerk of the Russian-American Company,

[1] Introduction to *Russian Voyages Round the World*, by N. Nozikov. Edited by M. A. Sergeyev and translated by Ernst and Mira Lesser. (Hutchinson, 1945); p. xv.

[2] Russian (All-Union) Geographical Society. Edited by A. I. Andreyev. Academy of Sciences, Moscow and Leningrad.

who sailed on that voyage. And absorbing narratives they are, with their colourful descriptions of native life in the South Seas, in particular of Nukahiwa in the Washington Group (though much of their information there was gathered from an English sailor Roberts, living on the island.)

The first thorough-going investigation of the Northern Kuriles and of the Strait of Korea was the work of Krusenstern, but his ethnographical and social studies of islanders in the Washington and Sandwich groups have earned for him recognition equal to that derived from his work in oceanography. It is but fair however, to point out that his entire scientific staff were Germans, and his chief officers, though Russian-born, show a high percentage of German names: Krusenstern himself was, like Bellingshausen the Antarctic navigator, of German Baltic origin. The nautical instruments used in his expedition were obtained in England. When Krusenstern made his first voyage round the world, his country was still young in the art of seafaring, for when his ship crossed the Equator it was the first Russian one to do so. "Up to this time, Russian ships had not been farther than the Tropic of Cancer."[1] Nor had the crew of Lysiansky's *Neva* ever seen a shark till that voyage, and the incompetency of the naval officers sent out from St. Petersburg to Alaska in the early days of the Russian-American Fur Company had drawn contemptuous remarks from the great Governor, Alexander Baranov (who was visited by the *Neva*). Up till that time—if we except the merchant adventurers who ploughed the North Pacific in unseaworthy ships in pursuit of the seal and the otter—the Russians, partly because they lacked overseas bases, had never, elsewhere than in the Arctic, displayed the maritime enterprise of the English, Dutch, Portuguese, Spanish, or French. Until the time of Krusenstern and his contemporaries Russia was still a land-minded sub-continent.

The Pacific discoveries of Lieut. Kotzebue rank with those of Krusenstern and Lysiansky in the annals of Russian seafaring. When Kotzebue sailed north in 1815, the question of the relation of the Siberian and American mainlands was still undetermined. "Are Asia and America separated? And is the sea into which you penetrate through Beering's Strait to the north the great Icy Sea itself? Or is this basin a Bay of the Southern Ocean, bounded and surrounded by the coasts of the two uniting

---

[1] See also N. Nozikov, *Russian Voyages Round the World.* Edited by M. A. Sergeyev and translated by Ernst and Mira Lesser. (Hutchinson, 1945); p. xv.

quarters of the globe in the north?" wrote the naturalist[1] of that expedition. And when Kotzebue himself, sailing in the *Rurik* in search of the North-East Passage, reached the bay on the American coast later to be called Kotzebue Sound, he believed at first that he had ended the search of centuries by finding a way to the Arctic Sea. He was to learn later that it was only an inlet of the great Frozen Ocean. It was possible for the Russian Government, he believed, to establish settlements along the coast of the Bering Strait northwards, in much the same way as Hudson's Bay Company had done along the shores of their own territory. In his introduction to Kotzebue's book, Krusenstern mentions as among the discoveries yet to be made, the northern coast of the Sea of Okhotsk with its vast frozen bays, and the greater part of Kamchatka. The possibilities of the latter suggested, as Krusenstern pointed out, that this peninsula might be of considerable influence for the expansion of Russian trade.

But it was from the more southerly latitudes that Kotzebue's chief claim to distinction derives. He had instructions to make particular investigation of the islands discovered by the Dutch in the seventeenth and early eighteenth centuries, notably those found by Jacob Roggeween.[2] The small size of his ship enabled him to do this satisfactorily. Rurik's Chain has been so named after his vessel, though possibly the eastern part of these islands was seen by Cook from his third island of the Palliser Group. The Krusenstern Islands, discovered by Kotzebue, were named by him in honour of his maritime predecessor and compatriot. On his way from the Sandwich Islands to the Radack Group Kotzebue discovered New Year's Island: at Guam he found in La Calderona a place of safe harbourage, and earned the thanks of succeeding mariners by charting it. The Romanzov and the Kutusev Groups, and the true longitude of Christmas Island were also his discoveries: Tahiti was surveyed by him, and he gave a more detailed description of the Coral Islands than any which then existed. But it is principally for his interest in the life and customs of the South Sea Islanders that the *Voyage of Discovery*, compiled by his naturalist, makes enthralling reading. Nearly all these nineteenth-century Russian voyagers show an intense interest in ethnography—

---

[1] L. C. A. Chamisso de Boncourt, *A Voyage of Discovery into the South Sea and Beering's Straits, etc.* (Longmans, Hurst, Rees, Orme and Brown, 1821); Vol. III, p. 265.
[2] Discoverer of Easter Island.

a characteristic too of modern Russian pioneers among such Arctic littoral peoples as the Chukchis and Yakuts. De Boncourt, the naturalist of Kotzebue's expedition, has left accounts almost as interesting as those of the better-known Langsdorf, and of Steller (who accompanied Bering.) Sadly he observed that the once-famed maritime knowledge and skill of the islanders of Guam had gone; the natives had ceased to be either sailors or swimmers. Readers of his work will remember de Boncourt's description of a South Sea Islander whom Kotzebue took to fog-ridden Unalaska, and who expressed surprise at finding no coconuts or bread-fruit there. More forcibly did the tropical visitor express his dislike of the underground life of the Aleuts, and asked if the citizens of St. Petersburg lived in that way too. Not only did Kotzebue take a naturalist on his expedition, but he also had the services of the famous painter, Ludovic Choris, whose beautiful drawings of South Sea Islanders and of North American Indians give a wealth of detail illustrating the social life of these peoples.

Admiral Litke and Captain Golovnin are the names of more Russian pioneers in Pacific exploration in the nineteenth century, and reference to their work will be made later. Other names such as the Russky and Predpriaty Groups in the South Pacific, and the Bellingshausen Sea called after the explorer who discovered territories in Antarctica which he named Alexander I and Peter I Land—show the activities of mariners from the Tsar's dominions at that time. It was not to be wondered at that such penetration of Pacific areas on the part of an aspiring land Power, was viewed with disfavour by the United States. American interest in Pacific trading had heightened ever since the first Boston brigs had crossed the ocean from the Alaskan port of Sitka to Canton, after New England merchants had found they could trade Alaskan furs with the Chinese. Round the Horn had sailed others of these adventurous traders, bringing in the course of their passage firearms to the Sandwich Islanders and taking from them sandalwood, which they shipped to Canton. In the Chinese markets the Americans undersold the Russians not only in the furs which they brought from Sitka, but in those which their Salem ships carried from Oregon. (The American motive for the later treaties of 1846 which ended the dispute with Britain over the rivalry for Puget Sound and its control of the eastern Pacific, was the desire to gain a monopoly of the fur trade with China. These treaties had established America's right to California and Oregon, all the Columbia

Valley and the harbours of Puget Strait, while Britain was confirmed in possession of Vancouver Island.)

The round-the-world voyages in 1803-1806 of the Russian ship *Nadezhda* and her consort the *Neva* were, as we have said, part of the maritime policy of Alexander I, who was anxious not only to ensure a regular sea service from the west to his outposts in the Far East and on the American mainland, but to extend Russia's trade in the Pacific areas. The failure of the Russians to establish commercial relations with Japan when Ambassador Rezanov voyaged in the *Nadezhda* to the court of that country, had made the Tsar the more anxious to promote trade with China, and the *Nadezhda* and the *Neva* as part of their mercantile mission had brought furs to Canton. The news of this was received unfavourably by the American Government, who saw in it another sign of a coming clash of interests in the Pacific. A crisis was averted however by a Convention between the United States and Russia in 1824, defining their relations in the Pacific and on the north-west coast of America. Reciprocal freedom of navigation and of fishing was guaranteed, and the Convention was strengthened eight years later by a treaty of commerce and navigation. None the less the Nantucket whalers were frequently engaged in disputes with Russian pelagic seal-hunting vessels, and the Baltimore clippers racing for the China tea trade made no secret of their desire to keep the Tsar's ships out of Chinese seaports.

Russian vessels were by that time feeling their way over fresh tracks across the ocean, gaining by their new departure into pelagic whaling a closer knowledge of the Pacific than the trading exploits of the Russian-American Fur Company had brought them. The profits made by other whalers had led to the formation of the Russia-Finland Whaling Company, who sent out the *Suomi*, *Tusko* and *Anjou*; their work in the Sea of Okhotsk and elsewhere, however, was of but short duration, being ended by the Crimean War. But in the North Pacific the Russian-American Fur Company increased in stature and profits. From the seal rookeries at the Pribylov Islands the market became so overstocked that it did not pay to sail with skins as cargo, so hundreds of thousands of them were thrown back into the sea. It has been estimated that in one year two million seals were killed. Rezanov, Imperial Chamberlain, on his arrival in Alaska ordered this slaughter to cease for five years. The substantial advantages derived by these Russian traders from their posts in the far North-West, had made Hudson's Bay Company anxious to establish a post above the Russian boundary on the

HONDIUS HIS MAP OF RUSSIA

(about 1620)

FROM *Purchas His Pilgrimes*, Third Part, edition of 1625. (Note: The map, which is paged in *Purchas* as "200", lies actually between pages 219 and 221.)

The map is undated, but it was probably executed about 1620. It is one of the few of its period which show in some detail on the same plate both the Murman Sea and the Gulf of Ob. Little advancement in the cartography of those regions was made by the Western nations between the time of the early seventeenth-century Arctic voyages of the Dutch and English whalers and the expedition of Captain John Wood in 1676, for it was in 1620—the probable date of the Hondius map—that the Emperor Michael Feodorovitch interdicted Arctic navigation to foreigners. Hence the Hondius Map was of particular interest for half a century.

Russia cum Confinijs

Stikine River. To prevent this the Russians set up a blockhouse on the mouth of that river near Fort Wrangell. The watershed of the Stikine nearly caused some fighting between Hudson's Bay and the Russian-American Companies, but in 1839 a settlement was reached when the English company secured a ten-years' lease of the shore-line from Portland Canal to Mount Fairweather.

"Politics should be studied with large maps," said Lord Salisbury. To few regions is this truth more applicable than to the north-west coast of America, where events today have been determined not only by the territorial and maritime rivalries in the past of three great mercantile organisations—the Russian-American Fur Company, Hudson's Bay Company, and the Boston Marine Society, but by the geographical factors which affected the policies of the respective Governments towards these organisations. That period of adventurous expansion moves like a tapestried pageant, whose colours are heightened by contrast with the sombre scenery of the White North. For those who read Russian, that period will be incomplete without a study of Tikhmenev's vividly detailed history of the Russian-American Company.[1] In it we shall read that tale of wonder, the story of Alexander Baranov, Governor of Alaska, whose portrait magnetises the reader on opening that book. There we may try and unravel the tortuous maze of Agreements which led up to the Anglo-Russian boundary convention of 1825, only to be queried later, after the Americans had purchased Alaska from the Russians. (The discovery of gold in the Klondike district, and the claims made by Canadians to ports on the Lynn Canal and the Yukon River, made urgent a final interpretation of the boundary question as between the United States and Britain, and so in 1903 a tribunal met to deal with the matter. Its decision was that the 1825 treaty had given to Russia the shore-line from the head of the Portland Canal to Mt. St. Elias, and to Britain had been awarded Pearse and Wales Islands at the entrance to the Portland Channel. In effect, America, by her acquisition of the territory formerly Russian, was now established in her title as mistress of the North Pacific seaboard in the western hemisphere.)

From Kodiak Island, Alaska, to Fort Ross in California, Russia's overseas possessions in the days of the Russian-American Fur Company had ranged down the Pacific shores of the United States. To find the Russians established so far south, and at

[1] *Историческое обозрение образования Российско-Американской Компании.* С. П., 1861-63; 2 ч.

a point which appeared to menace San Francisco Harbour, dismayed the Spanish colonists of Mexico and Nueva California. At that time the Spaniards were powerless to resist the depredations of the Russian otter-hunters, and Ludovic Choris, the artist who accompanied Kotzebue's expedition, estimating in 1816 the number of otters which the Russians were obtaining yearly from the waters round Fort Ross, stated that they were fast exterminating the animal.[1] An open clash did come a little later between the Slav and Spanish settlers when the *Ilmen* sailed with supplies to Fort Ross, and was attacked by the Spaniards. The Russian captain, Tarakanov, was taken prisoner, and sent to Sta. Barbara prison. In the eyes of the Spanish seamen the *Ilmen* was nothing more than a raiding vessel. But not till 1823 at Sonoma did the Spaniards succeed in checking the Russian drive southwards; after that no further penetration on the part of the Slav colonists was possible. Less than twenty years later the Russians had abandoned their settlement at Fort Ross altogether, selling it to Capt. John Sutter of the North-West Company. (To that Company there passed also the establishments and property of the John Jacob Astor's Pacific Fur Company which had kept the Russian settlers supplied with primary necessities.)

After the sale of Alaska in 1867, when Russia lost her interests in the North Pacific, "the Colossus of the North" turned south, and eventually succeeded not only in gaining a twenty-five-year lease of the warm-water base of Port Arthur and the commercial port of Talienwan, but of the whole Peninsula of Liao-tung, which runs out for 120 miles between the Bay of Korea and the eastern part of the Gulf of Pechili. America did not intend that Russian ambitions should be fulfilled beyond that. In the crisis before the outbreak of the Russo-Japanese War, the American Government's attitude showed that it was not in the interests of the United States that Russia should increase her strength, or even—in Manchuria—consolidate, her position in the Far East. So President Theodore Roosevelt had sent a Note to France and Germany informing those Powers that if they entered the coming war in support of Russia, America would go to the aid of Japan.

It was Russia's encroachment on Korea, bringing her farther south on the Sea of Japan, and her drive from the Liao-tung Peninsula to the Yellow Sea, that chiefly alarmed Japan.

[1] *Voyage Pittoresque autour du Monde.* (Firmin Didot, Paris, 1822); pt. III, p. 7.

Russia now possessed the best parts of the Manchurian coastlands, and a sea war between the two Powers appeared to the
rest of the world an inevitability. The subsequent victory of
Japan over the Russian fleet at Tshushima, halted for a long
time this expansion of Russia in the western Pacific. But the
defeat of Japan in the second world war has reversed that position.

Until the advent of the atomic bomb it was at sea that Japan
could be broken most easily, because her life lines cross the sea.
Of the two most vital of these, one concerns Russia closely:
crossing the Yellow Sea from China, it brought Japan the coal
and strategic ores of Manchuria. The second vital sea line for
the Japanese is the one that crosses the South China Sea, which
brought oil from the Netherlands East Indies and rubber from
Malaya. For cutting these sea lanes in the event of any future
conflict with Japan, the bases on Russia's Far Eastern seaboard
along the shores of her Primorsk Territory are potentially of
the greatest value. "We regard the Far Eastern Territory as
a mighty outpost of Soviet power in the East which must be
strengthened in every way," declared M. Molotov in 1939, at
the 18th Congress of the Communist Party of the U.S.S.R.
Though the Japanese armed forces were rendered impotent by
the Allies, following their defeat of Japan, Russia will never rule
out the possibility of a renewed attack directed from that
country, and whatever the weapons to come, the Soviet Union
continues to develop as naval and air bases such places as
Vladivostock, Khabarovsk, and Komsomolsk (on the Amur
River), Alexandrovsk and Nikolaievsk (on the Gulf of Tartary),
Okha (on Sakhalin Island), Petropavlovsk (on Kamchatka),
and Gizhiga (near the northern extremity of the Sea of
Okhotsk.) On all four sides of that enclosed Sea of Okhotsk,
Russia has now been made secure by her acquisition of the
Kuriles and of the southern part of Sakhalin Island. In addition
to their use in any war of the future, Russia's bases north of
Gizhiga and Olyutorskoye are important because they are the
guardposts of her shortest sea communications with America.
The Pacific route from Vladivostock to San Francisco via Yoko-
hama is approximately 6,200 miles, but from Anadir on the
Gulf of that name to Nome in Alaska is but 500 sea miles.

Vladivostock is not by nature an open port; even with the use
of ice-breakers it has until recent times been ice-bound for an
average of three months in the year, and it has a further disadvantage in its position on the Sea of Japan—a sea which is
practically an enclosed one. Hence, as the last war showed,

Vladivostock can become virtually isolated; as a port for the reception of supplies from America it could be used very little from the time that Power became engaged in the struggle at sea with Japan. It was surely a strange situation which determined that though Russia owned half the Asian continent, she could not, till recently, send a single ship, naval or mercantile, from one of her own Asiatic ports in the winter months. The value of Port Arthur as a warm-water port (which, by the terms of the Russo-Chinese Treaty, 1945, Russia acquired jointly with China for use as a naval base) is thus of the highest order to the future sea strategy of the Soviet Union. More than a hundred years ago the U.S. Secretary of State, Van Buren, noting the naval facilities which advances in the Far East had brought to the Russians, predicted that these must in time "give them a preponderance in the naval concerns of the world".[1] Van Buren had not foreseen the emergence of his own country as the mightiest naval Power in history, but no one would be rash enough to deny the possibility of ultimate fulfilment of his prophecy.

The greatest naval writer that America has yet produced—Admiral Mahan—drew attention to the inevitability of Russia's maritime expansion, by pointing out that as only relatively small areas of Russia did at that time benefit from seaborne commerce, that country was bound to extend her seaboard and develop in a maritime direction. The more territory Russia acquires, the more the diversity of her products increases, and the more imperative becomes her need for warm-water ports and an expanding mercantile marine to reach overseas markets (e.g. for the sale of her cotton from Central Asia.) It is just because they are primarily landsmen, knowing little of the limits imposed by the sea, that the Russians are capable of infinite experimentation.

With their sea lanes in the Pacific we will deal in a later part of this book: it is sufficient here to say that they are now directly connected with their Northern Route, owing to the work of icebreakers in the Bering Strait, and of meteorological observations on the peninsulas of Kamchatka and Chukotsk. A most significant development in this direction is the Soviet Government's intention to construct a canal through a promontory of north-east Siberia into the North Pacific. This could change the normal westward flow of the ice and reduce by a small extent the ice of the eastern Polar Seas.

[1] MS. U.S. Minister's Instructions, XIII, No. 12, 16 June, 1830.

"Our destiny lies in the East," said Lenin. But only when the western ambitions of Peter the Great were attained by Stalin as a result of the last war, could the words of Lenin become clear to all. From the days when the Muscovites drove the Poles back from the banks of the Dnieper, Russia has, at intervals, enlarged her territory by the absorption of parts of Poland. Both the Russo-German Pact of 1939, and the Potsdam Agreement of 1945, in their arrangements for the partition of Poland, advanced Russia along the course dictated by her *Drang nach Westen*. The break-up of the German State as a result of World War II, brought the Slavs still further across the great plain of Northern Europe. The end of the German dreams of Baltic domination had come with the defeat of the Third Reich, and the political victories of Stalin ensured for his country a position of primacy on that sea when, having already incorporated the coasts of the Baltic States in the U.S.S.R., he secured Koenigsberg for the Soviet Union. Russia could now look east without fear that her western shores were imperilled. She has become the greatest Power on the Baltic, and her coastline has been brought farther south than it has ever been since General Fermor's short-termed capture of Koenigsberg and Elbing during the Seven Years War.[1] In 1758 Fermor's Russian troops had taken those Prussian ports from Frederick the Great, but they were soon recovered by German forces at the decisive battle of Korndorf.

Russia's new dominance of the Baltic means that she will suffer less from that divided outlook which has characterised her history. Security and the opportunity for expansion in the west means that the U.S.S.R. can turn with undivided energies to the realisation of her destiny in the east. Writing fifty years ago a Russian historian made this significant statement: "For the future history of the world, the conquest of Siberia will be more important than most of the modern history of European Russia."[2] The demographic centre of Russia has shifted in the former direction within the last thirty years, and more than one Soviet scientist has predicted that Omsk in Siberia will become that centre. That eastward orientation is an ancient one, as we shall see when recalling the Cossack migrations to the Yenesei and the Lena, the Pacific advances made by Muraviev, and

[1] It is true, however, that the Byorussi who inhabited the coastal regions of Prussia in the tenth century were a Slav people.
[2] Vladimir, *Russia on the Pacific*. (Sampson Low, Marston, 1899); Introd. p. vi.

when realising how the building of the Trans-Siberian Railway and its extension through Manchuria to Port Arthur under Tsar Nicholas II, was actuated by Russia's historic urge to the ocean.

The most easterly point of the U.S.S.R. lies on the Bering Strait, and that is the passage that leads to the world of the future. The narrow channel between the two desolate fog-shrouded islands of Nunabook and Iganalook,[1] leads to the north of Siberia, a land of the future. Polar air routes bring Alaska and Siberia into the forefront of the picture of tomorrow's world. It is sufficient here to recall these facts mentioned earlier: two continental land masses face each other across a strip of water less than sixty miles wide. Part of one land mass, Siberia, is potentially one of the richest areas in the world; vis-à-vis that territory is a chain of radar stations sited on land once owned by Russia—for before its purchase by the United States, Alaska and the coastline to a point less than sixty miles north of San Francisco were part of the Russian Empire. A key position is occupied by St. Lawrence Island, which, though it lies nearer to Asia than to America,[2] was acquired by the latter Power when she took Alaska. It is the largest island between the Aleutians and the Bering Strait.

The area of that Strait is a grand junction of the world's chief skyways: its importance is high and its future unpredictable. Yet the voice of the well-known American strategist, Brigadier-General W. B. Mitchell, was a lone one when in 1929 he asserted that Alaska was the most central place in the world for aircraft. "Alaska," he also said, "is the key-point of the Pacific Ocean; it almost touches Asia." Outside the United States proper, Alaska was the vital point of protection against Asia. "If there is an attack on this country it will not be against the Panama Canal: the enemy will come right here from Alaska. I therefore

[1] The names in the native Eskimo tongue, of the Krusenstern and Ratmanov Islands in the Diomede Group. The existence of the latter was known to natives on the Chukchi Peninsula at least by 1711, as in that year a Russian, Popov, trading among these tribes, brought back from them vague accounts of the Diomedes. The actual discovery of the archipelago is generally credited to Bering, who named it after the saint on whose day the islands were found. The international date-line passes between the Big and Little Diomede Islands, so that the natives sometimes refer to the former (Russian) as "Tomorrow" and to the latter (American) as "Today". As neither of the islands have natural harbours they are unsuitable for naval bases, but by 1943 the Russians had established a scientific station on the Big Diomede.

[2] St. Lawrence Island is only 40 miles from the Siberian coast, but 118 from the nearest mainland point of Alaska.

think that Alaska is the most important strategic area in the world."[1] Events proved the correctness of General Mitchell's forecast. The enemy came from Japan to the Aleutians, with the intention of forcing the Alaskan back door to America. But thanks to American preparation the Aleutians, from the Alaskan coast to the most westerly island of Attu, eventually became the back door to Japan.

When we recognise the fact that this zone is, for all common strategic purposes, a vital one no less for the U.S.S.R. than for the U.S., the importance of the Alcan Highway as a supply line to Russia is evident. That Highway, over 1,600 miles long, was constructed east of the Rockies "because (1) it is less exposed to air attack: (2) it follows the line of strategic air bases already established by the Canadian Government, and (3) the snowfall is less than on the seaward side of the ranges."[2] The Road commences at Dawson Creek, cuts across the north-east corner of British Columbia, and runs to Whitehorse in Yukon territory, then almost due north to the seaport of Fairbanks in Alaska. The Highway, continued to the port of Nome on the Seward Peninsula, strengthened Russia's Pacific defences in the second world war by providing her with a supply route to East Cape, Siberia, the terminus of her own highway system.

East Cape is also the eastern extremity of Russia's Northern Sea Route, whose value as a link between North Pacific and North Atlantic is obvious. The Soviet Union in the years devoted to Arctic exploration and scientific investigation, had carved herself a "cut" for naval reinforcements for her ships in the Pacific. She can bring units of her Northern Fleet along her North-East Passage, through the Bering Sea to Vladivostock. She can even (since the construction of the White Sea Canal) bring her Baltic Fleet that way. What that means to her will be understood when we remember what happened in the Russo-Japanese War, 1904-05. In October 1904 the Baltic Fleet had left Libau to join the Vladivostock Squadron. Those Baltic ships, under Admiral Rozhdestvenski, had to sail through the North Atlantic, and by the Indian Ocean to the Sea of Japan. The passage however, owing to fear of British intervention in the Mediterranean, was made even longer by using the

[1] Quoted by Philip Paneth, *Alaskan Back Door to Japan*. (Alliance Press, Ltd., 1943); p. 26.
[2] Jasper H. Stembridge, *The Oxford War Atlas*. (Oxford University Press, 1943); Vol. II, Section 42. Reproduction by permission of the Clarendon Press, Oxford.

Cape route. "The voyage from Tangier to Port Arthur is about the same as the voyage from the Cape to Port Arthur," wrote the chief engineer in one of the vessels. "What a much longer distance we have come by going round Africa!"[1] And when the Baltic Fleet Commander reached Madagascar, it was to learn that Port Arthur had fallen. By failing to send at once to Admiral Makarov at Port Arthur the five 18-knot battleships which she possessed in the Baltic, disaster for Russia had been made doubly certain. Rozhdestvenski's fleet was reinforced by a number of ships sent from the Baltic under Admiral Niebogatov, and these, which had taken the shorter route by the Suez Canal, had joined Rozhdestvenski's at Camranh Bay in Indo-China. But as the Niebogatov squadron was composed of old and slow ships, Rozhdestvenski was deprived of the last chance of putting up a good fight against the Japanese. When the united Baltic Fleet did reach the Sea of Japan, it was to find that Japanese warships under Admiral Togo had by that time cut off the Russian battleships from their naval base of Vladivostock. The ensuing annihilation of the Baltic Fleet near Tsushima was therefore hardly surprising. The opening of Russia's North-East Passage ensures that such a disaster is not repeated.

And in the west also it gives her strategic safety. If the Baltic is ever closed to her by the Kattegatt or Kiel, her ships in the Atlantic can retire to Arctic bases by way of the Northern Route. That route is one of primary concern to America as well as to the Soviet Union. Communicating as it does with the Bering Sea, it enters a zone in which America has always been vitally interested. Before the Russo-Japanese War the United States had considered the construction of a North Pacific Railway from Yukon, taken by tunnel under the Bering Strait to Siberia, and thence to the Lena and Lake Baikal. Russian alarm was understandable—was the Bering Sea to become an American *mare clausum*? Today however, apprehension is mutual. "The time may come when Russian activities in the Far North will constitute a threat of which we must take notice," said George Fielding Eliot (formerly of Military Intelligence Reserve, U.S. Army),[2] speaking of the maintenance of Russian communications along the Arctic seaway. The defence of

[1] Eugen S. Politovsky, *From Libau to Tsushima*, translated by Major F. Godfrey, R.M.L.I. (John Murray, 1906); p. 65.
[2] *The Ramparts We Watch*. (Reynal & Hitchcock, New York, 1938); p. 165.

communications between her Northern and her Far Eastern
Fleets will be Russia's principal consideration in determining her
sea strategy in the North Pacific. In his fascinating story of *Forty
Thousand Against the Arctic*,[1] H. P. Smolka says of the Northern
Sea Route, that it has "a great strategic significance, which
I think is probably one of the reasons why the Soviet Govern-
ment pushes ahead so energetically with its developments".
When Mr. Smolka wrote that, the route was open only for three
months in the year, but in the second world war it could have
brought considerable relief to the trans-Siberian transport sys-
tem had the Soviet Union been engaged in the war against
Japan for any length of time.

The mercantile as well as the strategic advantages of such
a route are obvious. Ships can bring cargoes from San Francisco
and Seattle across the Bering Sea, and piloted by Russian icebreakers, can steam through the channels to unload at the
northern Siberian ports. There the cargoes can be trans-
shipped to river craft and taken up the rivers to the industrial
centres of Siberia, and they can also be sent by sea to Murmansk and thence transported by rail or by the White Sea
Canal to the Baltic and western Russia. Timber ships can now
pass from the Yenesei delta to the Arctic ports east of Cape
Cheliuskin and west of Dickson Harbour. In this way the
thriving timber town of Igarka can send its sawmill products
and its graphite down the Yenesei to the new coastal settlements, and so help in the building of the towns that are arising
out of the wastes of the Siberian Area. Similarly the forest
products of Yakutia can be brought westward to Europe, where
they are likely to be in increasing demand, for as Professor
Mikhailov has pointed out,[2] the larch of those forests is as dur-
able in water as is metal. Hence the work of icebreakers in
keeping open the mouths of the Siberian rivers for the passage
of timber ships to the Northern Route, is almost as important as
their work in the Arctic Seas for the passage of warships.
"Soviet icebreakers discovered the forests of Siberia. The timber
is floated along the Yenesei to the Arctic Ocean. Every year it is
met by the caravan of the Kara Expedition—timber-carrying
ships accompanied by icebreakers and aeroplanes. They carry
the timber to Europe via the Kara Sea."[3]

[1] Hutchinson, 1938; p. 251.
[2] *Soviet Geography*, translated by Natalie Rothstein; p. 169. By permission
of Messrs. Methuen.
[3] *Ibid.*

The future importance of the Arctic regions was foreseen by the Soviet Government soon after the Revolution, and in 1926 when Amundsen had arrived at Leningrad for his trans-Polar flight in the dirigible *Norge*, Russia had laid claim to all lands and islands (known and unknown) which were not already in the possession of other Powers between her own shores and the North Pole.[1] Thus any territory which might be discovered by Amundsen during his flight was decreed to be Russian. (This claim was based on the principle known as the "Sector Theory", about which there has been considerable controversy at different times.) The development of these territories is part of the work of the Central Administration of the Northern Sea Route (Glavsevmorput) established in 1932 at that time primarily to make the North-East Passage a practicable commercial route. The scope of the Administration was extended to the opening up of the Arctic regions as an economic area, and in this it is served by such specialised organisations as the Arctic Institute, and the State Institutes of Hydrography and of Oceanography. The magnitude of the work already successfully carried out by the Central Administration, is the result of one of the most thoroughly planned, carefully executed of undertakings on a vast scale. In this it differs from the pre-Revolutionary enterprises, daring and vigorously pursued though many of these were. As Dr. Taracouzio rightly remarks: "It was left for the Soviets to prove that the taming of the Frozen North is not a one-man job."[2]

No Introduction to the sea power of the Soviet Union would be complete without some reference to the riches of these northern regions, in the development of which the Northern Sea Route is to play such an important part. "There is enough timber in northern Siberia to supply the whole world. That is not a guess, but the result of sober survey."[3] The discovery of uranium near Kandalaksha on the Kola Peninsula, and also in Karelia, will make the White Sea region one of Russia's valuable areas in the age of atomic energy. In the oil-bearing region of Ukhta in the Komi Peninsula, is found a principal source

[1] This is defined as lands between the meridians of long. 32° 4' 35" E. and 168° 49' 36" W. It, however, involves the complicated and disputatious subject of Water Domain.

[2] *Soviets in the Arctic.* (Copyright 1938 by the Bureau of International Research, Harvard University and Radcliffe College.) Reproduction by permission of The Macmillan Company, New York. Pub.; p. 72.

[3] George Borodin, *Soviet and Tsarist Siberia.* (Rich & Cowan, 1944); p. 149.

of radium in the U.S.S.R., and in the same republic, along the banks of the Pechora River which flows into the Barents Sea, are sources of radio-active material. The Kola Peninsula helps substantially to supply the Leningrad ship-building yards with iron ore, and from the Khibin Mountain in this Arctic peninsula the apatite may one day make the U.S.S.R. independent of imported phosphates. There is oil at Inostrantsev Bay, Novaya Zemlya, and on Begichev Island; oil from the Khatanga and Pechora Basins provides part of the fuel for the Northern Fleet. At Norilsk is the Northern Polymetallic Combinat where the production has enabled Russia to increase her supplies of various metals, including mercury and molybdenum. The salt of Khatanga can now be shipped via Nordvik for the Far East, which formerly had to be supplied with salt coming all the way from Odessa. The fish-canning industries along the Siberian coasts are in their turn greatly helped by the salt-ships that come from Nordvik through the Laptev Sea. Near Nordvik, and near the shores of Kozhevnikov Bay, is the oil deposit, which is the richest yet discovered on the Arctic littoral; it can supply fuel for polar aviation and for maritime transport. The coal of the Tunguz field in the Yenesei Basin, of Franz Josef Land, of the Pechora Basin, and the non-ferrous metals of Vaigatch Island, the oil of the Taimir Peninsula, the asbestos of Novaya Zemlya—these are only some of the products of the Far North, with whose development the Arctic Sea Route is indispensably connected.[1]

Agriculture has been fostered no less than industry along the northern littoral. The Arctic experimental station known as the All-Union Institute of Plant Culture, has raised special types of crops—wheat, barley and oats—and potatoes, lettuces, spinach, and tomatoes, suitable for cultivation in the Arctic climate. On the shores of the Kara Sea, greens can now be grown in the open. The most northerly gardens in the world are the hot-houses of Tranquillity Bay, Franz Josef Land (81° N.).

The Northern Route is thus of economic importance. Some idea of the progressive development of the northern territories will be gathered from the figures published at the end of the First Five-Year Plan. Whereas in 1914 the total goods turnover of Kara Sea transport was 5,614 tons, in 1933 it was 102,900 tons. For the sake of the development of these Arctic regions, therefore, it is well that the explorers of the northern seas did

[1] For further details of materials in the Far North see N. N. Mikhailov, *Soviet Geography*, p. 20.

not pay too much heed to the Russian proverb: "Where there is a lot of water, there you may expect disaster." Rather are they proving true the words of Stefansson: "There is no northern boundary beyond which productive enterprise cannot go till north meets north on the opposite sides of the Arctic Ocean as east has met west on the Pacific."[1] Today the blue flag of the Northern Sea Route Administration (Glavsevmorput) flies not only on the shores of the Polar seas, but on the banks of the great rivers. In opening up the Arctic for navigation, that Administration has always borne in mind the fact which was early proclaimed by Vilhjalmur Stefansson: "The shortest link between Moscow and San Francisco, or between Chicago and Calcutta, is over the Pole."

The Arctic coast of Russia-in-Asia will, in the age of super-submarines, no longer be regarded as an area comparatively safe from enemy seaborne invasion, yet that Arctic littoral will still be safer than those of most countries which have land frontiers with potentially hostile peoples. Certainly it is more secure than the Trans-Siberian rail route, which at its eastern end is always exposed to any Power operating from Japanese bases. The Trans-Siberian has been worked to capacity, hence the Northern Sea Route has become a necessity for relieving the traffic of that railway. The seaway is an all-Russian route, and intending invaders would have difficulty in getting icebreakers there without help from Russian radio stations.

Towards securing these advantages, the efforts in Arctic exploration have been directed, but more than the actual advances themselves, such achievements are remarkable for the fact that they have been the work of a people comparatively young in the history of *open* sea navigation. Apart from certain exceptional periods, such as the first thirty years of the nineteenth century, the lack of maritime enterprise elsewhere than in "the Cold Ocean", shown by Russia in the past, has been a fact widely accepted, and in the first printing of the collection *Great Sea Stories of All Nations*,[2] Russia is not included. We find sea sagas from Ancient Greece, Ancient Rome, stories from Biblical literature, Arabia, and Persia, Celtic legends, maritime deeds of Great Britain, Canada, Australia, the United States, and of fourteen other countries, but there are no Russian epics of the ocean. The zest for ocean adventuring which the Russians displayed in the early years of the nineteenth century was not

---

[1] *The Northward Course of Empire.* (Harrap, 1922); p. 19.
[2] Harrap, 1930.

maintained for long: with the sale of Alaska in 1867 their interest in the north-east Pacific ended. Their subsequent expansion on the south-west seaboard of that ocean and along the Manchurian littoral to the head of the Yellow Sea, was undertaken from the land, not the ocean. The more noteworthy, therefore, is Russia's evolution after the Second Five-Year Plan from a land-minded to a land-and-sea-minded Power.

"Soviet warships will police the Seven Seas" declared Moscow radio on Red Navy Day, 1946. Russia's sea-sense, if it has come to her relatively late and as an acquired characteristic, is a fact which will be one of influence in the changing of the world-map. In temperate latitudes, as well as in the far north, her efforts to attain thalassic power have been consistently maintained. The recurring Russo-Turkish wars have been inevitable; the frequency with which these occurred in the eighteenth century was due to the fact that Russia was a land-locked Power while the Turkish Empire, occupying an area of critical location could deny Russia access to southern waters. Danilewski, the pan-Slavist writer, however doctrinaire many of his assertions, was profoundly right when he said that his country could not remain a continental Power only, she must become a maritime one too. For this, the possession of Constantinople was necessary, for only then could Russia acquire dominance in the Black Sea. Possession of that city on the Bosphorus would, moreover, reduce the long line of defences on her southern frontiers by giving her command at this vitally strategic point.[1]

We may note how closely events today in the Near East conform to the pattern set by Catherine II. The aim of that empress was to give Russia sea power, and this she could only then do at the expense of Turkey. The break-up of the Ottoman Empire (under her pretext of championing the cause of Christendom), was accordingly one of the chief aims of Catherine, who planned to make Bessarabia, Wallachia, and Moldavia an appanage of Russia. This territory, embracing roughly present-day Rumania, would have given her all the north-western shore of the Black Sea. The whole of the western shore would have fallen to her if Catherine's plans for a virtual annexation of Bulgaria had materialised. Russian control of the Aegean too, would have been assured if her intentions with regard to Greece had been fulfilled. In sending Admiral Orlov to promote a rebellion there, she had hoped to gain Thrace, Mace-

[1] *Russland und Europa*, edited by Karl Nötzel. (Deutsche Verlags-Anstalt, Stuttgart und Berlin, 1920.)

donia, and Northern Greece. These were to be merged into a single region with Constantinople as the capital, and one of her grandsons had been thoughtfully named Constantine in anticipation of his sovereignty over these lands. Her aims as regards the Bosphorus were well known outside her dominions, and some time before war broke out between Russia and Turkey in 1769, Voltaire had slyly remarked in a letter to Catherine that hostilities between these two countries might result in Constantinople becoming a new Russian capital. Two of the Aegean islands were to be taken over for use as Russian naval bases. On the Adriatic too, Russia was to gain a dominant position by the acquisition of territory roughly approximating to present-day Albania.

The determination of Britain and France to prevent Russia from gaining control of the eastern Mediterranean and their resolve to keep Turkey as guardian of the Bosphorus, was the root cause of the Crimean War. Russia's defeat in that war did not deflect her from her maritime aims. Writing in 1885 Alexander III said: "In my view we ought to have one principal aim, the occupation of Constantinople, so that we may once for all maintain ourselves at the Straits and know that they will remain in our hands. That is in the interests of Russia and it ought to be our aspiration. Everything else that is in the Balkan Peninsula is secondary for us." That aim is not an end in itself; it seeks the wider issue of the emergence of Russia as a great maritime Power.

One of the shortest cuts to that end would be the possession of the Straits. "If anything in this world is sure, it is certain that Russia will eventually obtain Constantinople," was a prediction made by F. T. Jane in 1899.[1] To speculate on the probable accuracy or otherwise of his forecast is not a purpose of this book. But, as we have said, the vital role of sea power in global warfare has always been recognised by Stalin. That is why in 1940, when Ribbentrop tried to get Russia to join in the Tripartite Agreement, Moscow stipulated that Bulgaria should be recognised as belonging to Russia's sphere of influence. Bulgaria, at some points within a hundred miles of the Straits, can give domination of the latter by air power. And command of the Straits is a pre-requisite for supremacy of sea power in the Near East. Of the Allied invasion of France, 1944, Stalin said that the achievement was one which taught Germany that no wide-scale war could be waged without a navy. But more significant

[1] *The Imperial Russian Navy: Its Past, Present, and Future*; 2nd edition, p. 583.

from the point of view of a changing map of the world, is the fact
that in the Order of the Day to the armed forces on Red Navy
Day, 1945, he said : "Our people will create new fighting ships
and new naval bases." That last objective has directed the policy
of Russia towards the Baltic, the Mediterranean, the Red Sea,
and the Persian Gulf, as it has done towards the Aegean and the
Dardanelles. Indeed, a *cordon sanitaire* through the acquisition of,
or control over, neighbouring States has been a motive not more
compelling with the Kremlin than its desire for uninterrupted
communication from the Arctic Ocean to the Middle Sea. From
naval bases in the Far North, on territory formerly Finnish, to
ports on the Adriatic, the Soviet Government has aimed—via
Esthonia, Latvia, Lithuania, Poland, Czechoslovakia, Hungary,
Yugoslavia, Albania, and Greece—to secure an unbroken line
from the Northern Ocean to the Aegean. (See Map, p. 284.)

The geographical imperative is determining Russia's maritime advancement in a still more important region—the Pacific
—and to that region we will briefly revert in concluding this
Introduction. It is in that vast expanse of ocean whose area is as
large as the moon's, that the shape of the world to come will be
determined. Here the mighty sea power of the great republic of
the west meets the nascent sea power of that Euro-Asiatic empire which, like America, stretches now from the Atlantic to the
Pacific seaboard. When by the decision of UNO in 1947, the
United States was granted "sole and paramount trusteeship" of
the formerly Japanese-mandated islands in the Pacific, she
gained 3,000,000 square miles of ocean territory, which included over 600 fair-sized islands and an uncounted number of
atolls and reefs. With the Marianas north of her own major
base of Guam she gained Saipan as a useful secondary naval
station; in the Carolines she acquired Truk with its unrivalled
harbour, and Ponape (of proved value to the Japanese in the
last war.) From Midway north to Samoa south, and from
Palmyra east to the Philippines west, America now contains
a vast circle of the mid-Pacific area, and by gaining the Marshall Islands with the important base of Jaluit, she controls
from the centre all that this great circle embraces.

Another zone of power lies within the Pacific; in the southern
stretch of that ocean is the island continent marked as the future
arsenal of the British Oceanic Commonwealth. "The history of
mankind began with a Mediterranean epoch, it continued in
the Atlantic period, and now it is entering into the Pacific era"
—words which naturally have a special meaning for Australia

with the new grouping of World Powers and the new consolida-
tion of areas of primary defence. But for no Powers more than
America and Russia has this utterance of Theodore Roosevelt's
greater significance.

Remote from reality now is the view of John Quincy Adams,
U.S. Minister to Russia, who in 1811, even at the crest of
Russia's maritime adventures in the Pacific, could tell Count
Romanzov, St. Petersburg Minister for Foreign Affairs, that
Russia never could be a great naval Power, since nature in so
large a measure had denied her that possibility.[1] What, on the
other hand, will be the verdict of the future on the prophecy
made by U.S. Secretary of State Seward, who more than any
other man, was responsible for the purchase by America of
Alaska from the Russians? Speaking in Minnesota in 1860, he
said: "Standing here and looking far off into the north-west,
I see the Russian towns and fortifications on the verge of this
continent . . . and I can say, 'Go on, build up your outposts all
along the coast, up even to the Arctic Ocean—they will yet
become the outposts of my own country—monuments of the
United States' civilisation in the north-west.'" When those
words were uttered, the Aleutian Islands formed no part of the
dominions of America. If the latter had not acquired them
when she did, it is more than likely that she would have been
obliged to take them today, or even in 1940 (just as Russia felt
compelled to take the strategic Baltic islands of Oesel and
Dagoe). The Aleutians form an almost continuous chain with
the Russian Kommandorski islands off Kamchatka,[2] and thus
bring America so near the east Siberian mainland that they are
valuable also as offensive no less than defensive outposts in the
event of any clash between the United States and the U.S.S.R.
Dutch Harbour, the American naval base on Unalaska Island,
lies in the zone where the Arctic and the North Pacific ocean
fronts meet, and this island, like others in the group, is well
provided with inlets for under-water vessels. The warm
Japanese currents flowing up from the south provide some ice-
free harbours, hence it was not surprising that on the expiration
in 1936 of the Washington Naval Treaties, America availed
herself of the right to develop naval defences on the Aleutians.
When war came between herself and Japan five years later,

[1] MS. Despatches, Russia. II, No. 53, August, 1816. United States State
Department Archives, Washington, D.C.
[2] The Russian naval base of Petropavlovsk, Kamchatka, is only eight
hundred miles from Kiska, one of the most westerly of the Aleutian Islands.

the importance of these islands was at once made clear: their capture by the Japanese made it impossible at that time for the Northern Route to be used by America for the transport of supplies to Russia—an idea for which the United States had invited Vilhjalmur Stefansson to draw up plans.[1]

If a conflict of interests arose in this region, then the volcanic nature of the Aleutian-Alaskan formation would be instantly manifested as a chain-reaction encircling our globe. And who today would venture to assert that echoes from the salute fired by order of Generalissimo Stalin on Red Navy Day, 1946, in the Far-Eastern port of Khabarovsk (in latitude nearly as northerly as the Aleutians), will not one day reverberate over oceans far from the Pacific?

[1] See Emil Lengyel, *Secret Siberia*. (Robert Hale, 1947); p. 229.

II

EARLY EXPLORATIONS

THE RIVER ROUTES

THE growth of populations, the expansion of industry, and discoveries of metals, coal, and oil—many of the fields near her
coasts—have made it inevitable that Russia will before long
change her character from that of a partially land-locked sub-
continent to that of a Great Power enjoying the freedom of all
the seas. What we have witnessed in the last war has been the
gaining of significant stages towards that final achievement. It
is a curious fact, but one well known to students of Russian
history, that so often Russia's losses have turned out to be her
gains. At the price of incalculable suffering and uncountable
losses she has been brought many long milestones nearer to
her traditional goal. When that goal is reached, it is no over-
statement to say that it may mark the greatest epoch in her
history. Much that, on the face of it, may have seemed difficult
of interpretation, can be understood if we take the sea as the
key to certain Russian enigmas.

But before we can reach the sea on all sides of that country,
we have many thousand miles of European and Asiatic rivers to
traverse, for it was by her rivers, long before her railways, that
Russia found her way to the oceans. Apart from certain exceptional periods of maritime activity however, the sea, as the ultimate objective, remained with the Russians a dream rather
than an element of substance which at all costs must be reached
and used as a means to progress. Indeed the observation made
by Hegel in his *Philosophy of History*, that for certain countries in
Asia which border on the ocean "the sea is only the end of the
land, they have no direct relations with it," is a statement which
could well be applied to Russia for a long period of her history
in the Far East.

When she did reach the seas, it was unfortunate for her that
they were enclosed ones. Her river most favourable for navigation—the Volga—flows into the Caspian Sea, which, till the
construction of the Manych Canal, had no outlet via the Black
Sea into the Mediterranean. Ice barred Russia's passage
through the Arctic to the warm waters of the Great Southern

Ocean. Japan blocked her ingress to that ocean from the Sea of Japan, and even the great advantage which Russia gained from control of the Amur River was to some extent offset by the fact that the sea which this brought her to was the (at times) icy one of Okhotsk—though by using the Tartary Strait she did also have access to the warm Sea of Japan. Of the Siberian rivers the Yenesei is the best as an approach to the Arctic Ocean, since it is influenced by warm currents. The Lena has a delta full of shoals and sand-bars, and the mouth of the Ob is often blocked with ice. The two great rivers Syr Daria and Amu Daria which flow into the Aral Sea, are not much better for navigation seawards, for they are too shallow for any but low-draught vessels, and such ships are of litle use on that water. The river which is the most serviceable to Russia is the Volga, whose delta, deep compared with other rivers', opens on the Caspian. As the latter is now linked with the Black Sea, the Volga provides the longest part in the chain of navigable waterways from Moscow to the Mediterranean.

The rivers were the main routes of communication in early times, and it was by these that boats came to the Caspian and the Black Sea in ancient days. The riverways were also the main invasion routes, and brought at different times the many streams of Asiatic, Scandinavian, and Germanic peoples, who penetrated deep into lands settled by the Slavs. The very flatness and monotony of the landscape are primary causes of that restlessness in the Russians which today as of old, impels them to be for ever on the move. (A common form of Russian salutation is still "Putiem dorojki"—"Going the road," and the reply "May you do the same".) The rivers were "the roads that run" —the tracks that nature had laid in a land where space was too vast for those early travellers to have built roads for any great distance within the region now European Russia. The chief watershed of the Russian European system is in the Valdai hills, a region which the Scandinavian invaders of the ninth and ten centuries held as the hub from which their riparian trade highways radiated. R. J. Kerner even goes so far as to describe this region as a single grand portage in itself, and hence the key portage of the world.[1] "The head-waters are so near together," says another writer, "that it is relatively easy to drag boats overland, across the watersheds, from one river to another; excellent water roads thus being provided from the Baltic to both the

[1] *The Urge to the Sea: The Course of Russian History.* (University of Californian Press, Berkeley and Los Angeles, 1942); p. 1.

Black Sea and the Caspian Sea."[1] It was the Volga and the Dvina which, with the growth of commerce, became the main arteries of trade, and it was along their banks that the most populous parts of Russia were to be found. To the Scandinavians indeed, sailing down these waterways, Russia was *Garderyk*, the Kingdom of the Towns.

Scandinavians living then in Constantinople travelled in this way in A.D. 839 as envoys from the court of Byzantium to Louis the Pious, where on the discovery being made that they were Northmen, they were for a time kept in prison. But the true pioneer among the riparian adventurers was Rurik, of the royal Swedish line of Skiöldung. From Jutland he had ravaged not only the coasts of France, Friedland, and the Elbe, but had directed one of the expeditions against Chatham and London. Holding all the sea-passages from the North Sea to the Finnish Gulf, he was able to bring Danes, Swedes, and Frisians to Novgorod, the Holmgard of these Vikings. According to the twelfth-century chronicle of Nestor, the monk of Kiev, the warring Slavonic tribes—who had radiated out over Russia from the lands of the Vistula—had invited these Varangians over from Sweden to settle disputes among themselves. Exploratory penetration of "Russia" by the water routes had been made by the Northmen between 785 and 820, i.e., before the arrival of Rurik, and the name Varangian Sea had been given to the Baltic which the Northmen crossed later in answer to the call of the Slavs, "our country is large and abundant, but there is no order; come over and be our princes and govern us". Sailing up the Gulf of Finland to the place where Leningrad now stands, the Northmen had followed the Neva to Lake Ladoga, thence by the Volkhov they had reached the spot on which in A.D. 862 they chose to found the settlement later to be known as Novgorod the Great. By using the rivers of the east Baltic lands, the Swedes made themselves masters of that territory; about this time too they formed the stronghold of Seeburg at the mouth of the Dvina, and Northmen then penetrated up to the coast of Murman, whose name is equated to "Norman".[2] The Nestorian Chronicle relates that some of these Vikings from Great Novgorod, turning north-eastward to collect tribute, had even reached the Pechora coast on the Arctic by A.D. 1095.

---

[1] Hugh P. Vowles, M.I.Mech.E. *Ukraine and Its People*. (W. R. Chambers, 1939); p. 20.

[2] See *Saga Book of the Viking Society*, Vol. X, 1929.

In the south-east of Europe the first raiding expedition against the territories of Byzantium was led by two Varangian *boyars*, Askold and Dir, who had left Rurik's service, and who (in the Nestorian account) had collected two hundred boats for the occasion. We may imagine the panic which seized the citizens of Constantinople when suddenly, on a morning in A.D. 860[1] there descended upon them a fleet manned by the fur-clad, blonde-haired men of the far north. Nestor, often referred to as the first historian of Russia,[2] introduces the miraculous element into his account, describing how the Patriarch Photus took the robe of Our Lady of Blachernes and plunged it into the waves, whereupon a tempest arose and destroyed most of the boats. But for this the Varangians would have attacked Constantinople. They did so, again led by Askold and Dir, in 867, but the assault was unsuccessful. Forty years later another attempt was made by Oleg, a kinsman of Rurik's, when legend has it that his ships were put on wheels, dragged on shore, and the wind, catching their sails, carried them forward. Then it was that the cry went up from the Bosphorus, "Who can resist God and Novgorod?" And this time the Greeks paid ransom money.

Nestor for this occasion gives the very improbable number of ten thousand Viking ships and eighty thousand warriors.[3] The bogey had grown even bigger in the account which his literary successors gave of the next raid under Rurik's son Igor in A.D. 941, but one in which the Greeks, nevertheless, managed to reverse their previous defeat. Their use of "Greek fire" in the Black Sea so terrified the Northmen that many, preferring death by drowning, jumped overboard, when the weight of their helmets and cuirasses dragged them to the bottom. According to Gibbon, "instead of the single tube of Greek fire, usually planted on the prow, the sides and stern of each vessel were abundantly supplied with that liquid combustible".

With their maritime background these Scandinavian settlers not unnaturally founded their chief trading centres at such places as Novgorod on Lake Ilmen, at Kiev on the Dnieper, and at St. Eleutharia (Berezan) on the Black Sea. Among them were the *druzhinas* or warring bands centred at Kiev, who were

[1] The Nestorian Chronicle places it a few years later.

[2] Actually, his chronicle exists only in an abridged form which is the compilation edited by Abbot Silvester of Kiev, about A.D. 1116. See T. D. Kendrick, *A History of the Vikings*. (Methuen, 1930); p. 145.

[3] The Langobard chronicler Luitprand gave 1,000 as the figure for the ships.

known as "Rus", and from them it is thought that the name "Russia" derives.[1]

In the opinion of Mr. T. D. Kendrick, there is reason to think that the Viking infiltration had advanced far in a south-easterly direction many years before the Scandinavian foundation of Novgorod. It is probable, he thinks, that Swedes had settled on the upper Volga and on the Dnieper at Kiev by the beginning of the ninth century.[2] He also thinks it possible that a Kievan State controlled by these inland voyagers may have been in existence by about A.D. 840. The Emperor Constantine Porphyrogenitus has left a detailed description of the trading fleets which passed down the Dnieper in the great days of Kiev —"The Mother of all Russian towns". As the starting-point of the voyage down the Dnieper to the Bosphorus, Kiev was known in those days by the old Scandinavian name of *Sambat*, "the place of assemblage of boats" ;[3] the flotilla increased its numbers downstream when joined by other trading ships at Vitichev. The 'Rus' names for the seven great rapids, which the Emperor recorded, are of Old Norse or Old Swedish origin.[4] The feats of the Vikings in crossing the Dnieper have been somewhat over-rated, for in spring, when water covered the rocks, the boats could be towed by slaves through all the rapids except that of Nenasytets. Here the voyagers unloaded the boats and carried the latter on their backs to a place where they could be launched again for the journey to Byzantium : the real danger was not so much the rapids as the war-like Patzinaks who roamed the river banks.

The Varangian axe-armed warriors, men "tall like palm trees", had, on the word of Masudi the Arab, established themselves so strongly on the Black Sea, that from about A.D. 900-1223 it was known as the Russian Sea "because none but the 'Rus' navigate it".[5] About 914 a fleet of Scandinavian ships

[1] *Ruotsi* is a Finnish name for the Swedes of a northern province, probably cognate with *Rothsmenn* or *Rothskarlar*, meaning "rowers" or "seafarers". See W. R. Morfill, *Russia*. (Fisher Unwin, 1880) ; p. 19. Also Fr. Miklosich, *Летопись по Лаврентиевскому Списку*. Издание археографической коммиссии. Санктпетербург, 1872; стр. 18, 19.

[2] *A History of the Vikings*, p. 146.

[3] A. Rambaud, *L'Empire Grec au dixième siècle*. (A Franck, Paris, 1870) ; p. 365.

[4] Dr. Vilhelm Thomsen, *The Relations between Ancient Russia and Scandinavia*. (James Parker, Oxford and London, 1877) ; p. 67.

[5] Quoted by Dr. Vilhelm Thomsen, *The Relations between Ancient Russia and Scandinavia*.

RIVER ROUTES AND PORTAGES USED BY THE VARANGIANS IN THEIR VOYAGES FROM THE BALTIC TO THE BOSPHORUS

THE rivers of Russia brought the trade of Byzantium and of Persia to the west from the time of the ninth century and earlier. The numbers of Persian and Arabic coins dating from the ninth to the eleventh century which have been found along the waterways of Russia, and thence right up to Scandinavia and even to Iceland, testify to the traffic on these routes.

The Varangians in their early trading voyages to the Bosphorus had often, when sailing down the Dnieper, to withstand the attacks of the warlike Pechenegs, who fell on them at the portages. But in spite of all difficulties this river continued to be the highway principally used by these Scandinavians in their descent on Byzantium, and the Dvina–Dnieper route remained "the Road from the Varangians to the Greeks".

RIVER ROUTES AND PORTAGES USED BY THE VARANGIANS IN THEIR VOYAGES
FROM THE BALTIC TO THE BOSPHORUS

appeared on the Sea of Azov, and before the end of the tenth
century Varangians had settled on its shores and occupied the
Taman Peninsula opposite that of Kerch, but the Russian
chronicles make no reference to them there after 1094. Sailing
down the Volga they had even penetrated to the Caspian, and
according to Masudi they appeared with five hundred ships,
each manned by a hundred Varangians, whose voyage to Baku
was followed by the plundering of that place. There are records
of 'Rus' vessels raiding the Persian shores of the Caspian five
times between A.D. 880 and 1041. We have the word of another
Arab writer, Khordadbih, living in the time of Askold, that
Russian traders used to bring their merchandise from regions as
remote as the Baltic, to the Greek colonies on the northern
shores of the Black Sea, and that they would proceed thence to
the Volga and the Don and so to the Caspian. From that sea
they would even journey on by camels to Baghdad. "This
information," observes Kluchevsky,[1] "is the more important in
that it refers to a period as early as the first half of the ninth
century—to a period not later than the year 846, or twenty
years before the date assigned by the Chronicle [Nestorian] to
the coming of Rurik and his brethren."[2] An account in the
chronicle of an early Armenian writer, Mosè Caghancatov,
however, describes the arrival of Northmen on the Caspian in
914, as their first expedition to that sea.[3] The nineteenth-century historian, Soloviev, mentions that they captured the city of
Karabagh from the Arabs. Ibn-Fodhlan, sent by the Abasside
caliph as companion to an ambassador to the "Sclaves" in 921,
provides one more early Arab source of information about the
'Rus'. This writer, during his journey, met Russians of the
Volga regions who had sailed down the river to trade with the
south. His account of these merchant travellers was for long
preserved among the archives of Yakutsk.

The long, undecked boats of the 'Rus' were fashioned out of
tree trunks, and had two rudders, but the masts were often too
slender for the sudden storms that whipped up the great rivers.
These vessels were sent down the Dnieper with furs and tallows,
amber and slaves, to be bartered for the gold, wine, and fruits

---

[1] *A History of Russia*, translated by J. C. Hogarth. (Dent & Sons, 1911);
Vol. I, p. 52.
[2] The Nestorian date of A.D. 866 is regarded by most authorities as about
six years later than the actual time of Rurik's arrival on the Neva.
[3] See С. М. Соловьев: *История России с Древнейших Времен*. С. Петербург, 1894; 5 том; Том I, стр. 129.

of Byzantium. When the 'Rus' set sail again for Kiev, they were provided by the Greeks with free equipment such as sails, cordage, and anchors, for their ships. For by this time Igor was a power whom Byzantium preferred to have for friend than for foe: he now had control of the Russian waterways from the Baltic to the Black Sea, and made them the tradeways between Sweden and the Empire.

On the Black Sea the Rus had shown skill in manœuvring their small ships against the more formidable ones of Byzantium, though in 1043 when the Varangian prince, Yaroslav, was at war with Byzantium, his vessels, outmatched by the Greek triremes, had suffered defeat. In a doubtful passage Theophanes gives A.D. 774 as the year in which Rus ships served in Greek seas as auxiliaries to the Byzantine navy. The year ante-dates the arrival in Russia of Varangians in any numbers. (The Langobard chronicler Luitprand, records in 986 that two Rus ships were with the Greek fleet, but this was more than two hundred years later than the date mentioned by Theophanes.) Rus mariners certainly played a part in the Mediterranean wars between Greeks and Arabs. By that time they had become the allies of the Emperor in whose service was the famous Varangian Guard, believed to have been founded by the Norseman, Harald Hardrada. Scandinavian seamen were recruited to help the Greeks in their attempt to recapture Sicily from the Moslems. It is more likely that those mariners mentioned by Theophanes, like the sixth-century settlers in the Caucasus (also known as Rus), were a non-Scandinavian people.[1]

In their penetration of Russia to the extreme south-east, the Vikings followed two main river routes: (1) To the Black Sea, from Lake Ladoga via the rivers Volkhov and Lovat to the Western Dvina and thence to the Dnieper; (2) To the Caspian, (a) from Ladoga, and (b) from the Northern Dvina and thence to the Volga. The first route is referred to in the old chronicles as "The Road from the Varangians to the Greeks", and before the rise of Venetian sea power this waterway from the Baltic to the Bosphorus certainly rivalled the Mediterranean as a trade route. In nothing more clearly than in his determination to make his countrymen take to the sea, did Peter the Great, in his day, break with the past. In siting his new capital of St. Petersburg on the eastern arm of the Baltic, he was forsaking Moscow, the traditional centre of the river system of the

[1] See Kendrick, *A History of the Vikings*; p. 148, footnote 2. (By permission of Messrs. Methuen.)

Russian empire. That ancient capital has been described by
R. J. Kerner as "the crossroads of two great waterways, trunk
lines of trade, the Caspian-Baltic axis of rivers and portages, and
the west-coast route from the Western Dvina to the Volga".[1]

Much of the history of Russia indeed, during the fourteenth
and fifteenth centuries, is the story of the struggle between the
rulers of Novgorod for the domination of the route to the
Northern Dvina, the outlet to the Arctic. Those were the days
when "the Braves of Novgorod" descended upon the Volga in
their canoes, "fighting mad".

Few things are clearer in the story of Russia than the extent
to which her watercourses have shaped her history. The reason
of her rise in the thirteenth and fourteenth centuries was, as
Gregory and Shave[2] have explained, the fact that the State of
Muscovy "had extended to control the heads of the waters
giving access to the four seas around the East European Plain,
and no trader could send goods from one part of the plain to
another without passing through the lands of this small State".
From its favoured position in relation to the waterways it could
stretch north to the Arctic, south to the Black Sea, east (by portages to the Siberian rivers) to the Pacific Ocean, west to the
Baltic, and from it came "the Russian urge to the sea". Mr.
Horrabin's maps in this section, showing the river and portage
system of Russia, illustrate how the Cossacks in their eastward
migrations followed the rivers, using the easy connections
formed by tributaries between the main waterways. In the
seventeenth century they were continually raiding the Black
Sea ports. These men, after sailing in their pirate galleys, had
settled on stretches of the Lower Don, Dnieper, and Volga, and
had become famous as rivermen as well as riders. The Don and
the Zaporozhye Cossacks of the Lower Dnieper were sea and
river raiders "on Mother Volga . . . on the blue sea, on the
Caspian sea," in the words of their song. (Gogol, in *Taras
Bulba*, gave a stirring story of the life of these Zaporozhye Cossacks in a river camp.) On the Sea of Azov they were to be
found too, rowing in *tchaikis*, their coracles.

In 1613 the Don Cossacks captured Azov from the Tartars,
and offered it to Tsar Michael Romanov. The importance of
the place was obvious to the Emperor; whoever held it controlled the water communications between Middle Russia and

---

[1] *The Urge to the Sea: The Course of Russian History*; p. 36.
[2] *The U.S.S.R.: A Geographical Survey.* (Harrap, London, 1944; John
Wiley and Sons, Inc., New York); pp. 146, 147.

the Black Sea. But Michael was in no position to face a war with the Ottoman Empire, and had to decline the offer made by the Cossacks. The latter, a year later, sacked Sinope on the Black Sea; the next year they set fire to the outskirts of Constantinople and raided the Turkish ships which had come out against the Cossack vessels in the Danube delta—events which curiously foreshadowed the Russian annihilation of the Turkish squadron at Sinope in the Crimean War. But the Turks were avenged for the 1614 attack on Sinope, for ten years later they destroyed the whole Cossack flotilla which was about to raid Constantinople.

The Kazan Kingdom had dominated the Volga and the Don, and the Tartar occupation of lands bordering on the Lower Volga had checked the Russian expansion in the neighbourhood of the Caspian Sea. So in 1552 the Volga river had carried the infantrymen, and along its banks had ridden the cavalrymen, in the forces which Ivan the Terrible sent to Kazan. When they captured that city the Russians got command of the Middle Volga. Four years later, when they secured Astrakhan at the mouth of that river, they gained the most important port on the Caspian Sea. "For the first time the Volga became a Russian river", and from that time on, the rulers of Russia were determined to keep it so. Ivan the Terrible however, in his desire to foster mercantile relations with the west, adopted a different policy in this respect from that of his successors. He granted transit trade with Persia to English merchants, and protected them when, to this end, they tried to get up the Volga, and he even banished to Siberia the Cossacks who had set upon these traders. We find in Hakluyt a passage which shows that at this time the Russian rivers were used freely by English merchants, for, he says, "Neither hath our Nation been contented onely throughly to . . . view the Northren, Southerne, and Westerne frontiers, but also by the rivers of Moscua, Occa, and Volga, to visit Cazan and Astracan, the farthest Easterne and Southeasterne bounds of that huge Empire." Anthony Jenkinson for instance, the noted English traveller, on his visit to Persia in 1558, used an all-water route from Moscow to Astrakhan by voyaging on the Okha and the Volga. From Astrakhan he sailed to the eastern shore of the Caspian, and remarked that "the fewe shippes upon the Caspian seas, the want of Mart and port townes, the povertie of the people, and the ice, maketh that trade naught". On another occasion he journeyed from Derbend to other parts of Persia, and on his return to Moscow so impressed the Tsar with the information he gave about the Caspian and the Trans-Caucasian regions, that Ivan granted to English merchants the liberty to establish themselves at such trading centres on the Volga as Kazan and Astrakhan. We have too the account in Hakluyt of the voyage of Christopher Burrough down the Volga and across the stormy waters of the Caspian Sea (on which compass-reckoning was then unknown) on his way to Persia.

But the successors of Ivan IV made no such exception in favour of Elizabethan merchants. And when later, in 1614, John Merrick had come from England to demand for his fellow countrymen the right to use the Volga waterway in order to trade direct with Persia, Russia had refused.[1] Requests made subsequently by the French and the Dutch were unavailing: the Volga led to Persia, and with that country the Tsars aimed at a monopoly of trade.

The river routes became matters of international concern once more when Napoleon and Tsar Paul laid their plans for a combined march on India. French troops numbering 35,000, led by Masséna, were to sail from the Rhine down the Danube, and at its delta to embark in Russian ships and make for Taganrog on the Don. Up the Don they would voyage to Isbanskaya, then cross the Volga to Astrakhan. There, once more in Russian vessels, they were to sail on the Caspian Sea to Astrabad. Joined by 35,000 Russians, these French troops would then proceed via Herat and Kandahar to India.

The importance to Russia of her rivers not only in Europe but in Asia, was clear to many foreigners as well as Russians, in the eighteenth century. "There are a number of navigable rivers, the course of which is in so advantageous a direction, that from Petersburgh to the frontiers of China, there is a water-carriage for everything to within the space of about a hundred wersts. . . . This convenience much facilitates the transport of provisions and merchandise."[2] But earlier accounts are contained in *Purchas His Pilgrimes*[3] of the way in which Russians in

---

[1] A servant of the East India Company, Giles Hobbes, however, succeeded in making his way down the river to Astrakhan, whence he sailed across the Caspian and reached Persia in pursuit of the silk trade.

[2] *Memoirs of Russia, Historical, Political, and Military, From the Year 1727 to 1744.* Edtd. by David Hume and translated from the Original Manuscript of General Manstein (Officer in the Russian Service). (T. Becket and F. A. De Hondt, London, 1770.)

[3] Edtd. by S. Douglas Jackson. (Jackson, Son & Co., Glasgow. And James MacLehose, Glasgow, 1905); Vol. XIII, Chap. 7.

the beginning of the seventeenth century used the rivers of western Siberia. The numerous tributaries of the great rivers of that region and the lowness of the watersheds which they drained, made it possible to cross that region in boats, using only short portages till the Lena was reached. By using the affluents of the Ob and the Yenesei the Cossacks could take their boats by water for the whole distance—with the exception of about five miles—between these two rivers, and similarly could cover all the distance except for a stretch of ten miles, between the Yenesei and the Lena.[1] But there were times when these Cossacks had to follow the example of one of their earliest leaders in Siberia, Yermak Povolski, who, in using the streams that connected the great rivers, had sometimes to dam them with his sails at the shallow reaches in order to collect enough water to drag his boats through. After the Lena came the mountains, and the real difficulties began.

The seventeenth century saw the penetration of Siberia by bands of Cossacks from the west. One such adventurer was Vasili Poyarkov who had heard tales of a wonderful river, the Black Dragon, flowing through China and into the rich country bordering on the Great Ocean. So in 1646 he had made his way eastwards to the Amur River, and after sailing down it returned to Yakutsk with curious tales of his travels through lands of fabled wealth and mythical beasts. From his enterprise followed the real development of Russian settlements along the Amur, until the Aigun treaty with China in 1858 confirmed Russia in her conquests and gave her the Amur lands stretching to the Pacific. Other rivers in eastern Asia which have aided the Russian advance to the Pacific are the Lena and its tributary the Kut, which played an indispensable part in the First Kamchatkan Expedition, led by Bering, for here Lieut. Chirikov had boats and barges built for the attempted voyage for the North-East Passage. By the Aldan, too, another tributary of the Lena, supplies went on rafts, and thence to the River Urak, which flows into the Sea of Okhotsk. Riverine transport was a method of conveyance to which the Russians of Bering's time were not only accustomed but in which they were skilled.

But these river routes, in spite of the work of Peter the Great, who commissioned the First Bering Expedition, and notwithstanding the labours of others after him, were not more than partially developed as sea-to-sea routes until the time of the

[1] Vladimir, *Russia on the Pacific*. (Sampson Low, Marston, 1899); pp. 72, 76, 77.

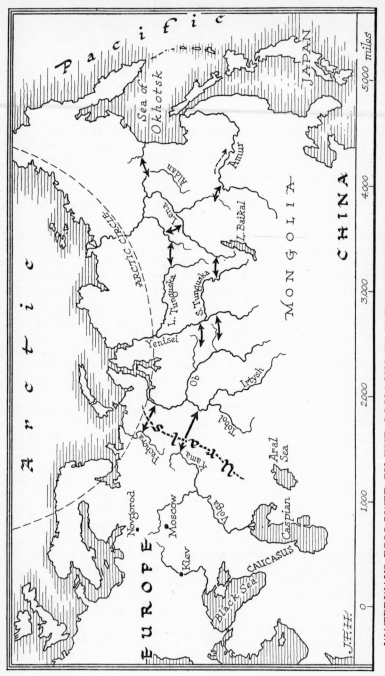

WATERWAYS FOLLOWED BY THE COSSACKS IN THEIR EASTWARD ADVANCE ACROSS SIBERIA
IN THE SEVENTEENTH AND EIGHTEENTH CENTURIES

THE expansion of Muscovy across Siberia, which commenced in the last two decades of the sixteenth century, was the work of two forces: on the one hand was the enterprise of individual bands of Cossack hunters and of merchants taking part in the great sable quest (roughly embraced by the period 1580–1820), and on the other hand (though very often encouraging and making use of these adventurers) was the State-directed drive from the Urals to the Pacific. The unity of the Euro-Asiatic territory embraced by Russia could not be achieved until that country had reached the Pacific. This fact was perceived by the rulers of Muscovy, from the time of Ivan the Terrible till the climax of rapid expansion in the Far East was reached under the pro-consul Muraviev, Count Amurski.

The seventeenth century saw the establishment of *ostrogs* or forts on all the great rivers of Siberia and on most of their principal tributaries. In the setting up of these blockhouses, the Russians showed the same regard for strategic advantage across a continent, as the British, by the establishment of naval bases, showed in their advance along the ocean trade routes of the world. Only by their settlements and their outposts along the rivers of Siberia could the Russians extend their fur trade eastward; the advances they made had to be held in face of attacks from Buriat Mongols and from Manchus. At the beginning of the seventeenth century, Tomsk was built at the confluence of the Ob and the Tom, and was the most important of the *ostrogs* in the basin of the Ob. From Tobolsk on the Irtysh, the Cossacks reached the Yenesei by their rivers Tura, Ket, and Narim, and on the last named there rose the fort of Makovsk. On the Lower Yenesei the settlement of Turukhansk was founded in 1607, and on the Upper Yenesei, Krasnoyarsk and Yeneseisk were established. By 1625 Muscovy controlled much of the Yenesei basin.

The pursuit of furs drew the Cossacks on to the Lena, by use of the Upper, the Stony, and the Lower Tunguska Rivers: on the Lena, the *ostrogs* of Yakutsk and Kerensk rose up as guardposts of the regions which the adventurers had brought within their control. From this time—the third decade of the seventeenth century—commences the real advance to the sea, undertaken through voyages on the great rivers of eastern Siberia. This is the period when the Cossacks and merchant explorers set sail on the Yana, Indigirka, Kolima, and finally the Anadir, whose mouth Deshniev in 1648 is believed to have reached by sailing through the Strait dividing Asia from America. The story of the advance eastward from the Lena by the Aldan to Okhotsk, as also of the advance farther south to the Pacific along the Amur, is the story of great hardship and of ruthless warfare in which Manchus and Buriat Mongols were the fiercest resisters of the Slav penetration. The Russians, as they pushed ever eastward, were getting farther away from such aid as Moscow ever did send them; like the Germans in their march across the Ukraine and down to the Crimea in 1942, the Russians were going " beyond their depth". It was not till the conquests of Muraviev after 1860 that the Slavs consolidated their earlier gains east of the Lena, and it was not till 1945, after the end of the second world war, that Russia regained the strategic vantage points for maritime expansion which she had lost to Japan after the war of 1904–05. Her gains of 1945 indeed, have placed Russia in a stronger position than she held at the beginning of this century, as today she holds all the Kurile Islands and the whole of Sakhalin.

Will this "Century of the Cossacks" envisaged by Napoleon, bring her still farther into the Pacific?

Five-Year Plans. In 1815 the first steamer, built by a Scotsman, appeared on the Neva, and was followed by two Russian-built steamers on the Kama. In these days when vessels can sail right up to Moscow—since the building of the Moskva-Volga Canal—it may be difficult to remember that at one time such boats could not get beyond Kazan. Goods carried by vessels of that size were trans-shipped to smaller ones before they could proceed north-west. Large boats could not reach Nizhne Novgorod at any seasons except those of the spring floods; in the late summer and autumn the water was too shallow for such vessels to traverse all the Middle Volga. Today, dredging, and the system of canals which has made Moscow a port, has enabled steamers to reach the capital.

PETER THE GREAT

It is usual to regard Peter the Great as "the Father of the Russian Navy", and it was certainly his maritime ambitions which took Russia farthest in the direction which geographical, economic, and other factors had made it inevitable that she should move. His father Alexis however, had made consider-able efforts to secure all the Neva and such Baltic ports as Narva and Orieshk. But the Imperial Chancellor of that time, Nastchokin, realised that such gains would not be enough. Russia must get Livonia from Sweden in order to acquire Riga, the best Baltic port for the trade of western Europe, and though as Kluchevsky[1] points out, the efforts which Nastchokin made in this direction were unsuccessful, Peter the Great did succeed wholesale to the ideas of his father's Minister.

About this time the Muscovite Government, convinced of the benefits derived by other countries from their overseas trade, began to revive the interest in shipping which had been mani-fested much earlier by Ivan IV. On the advice of a Dutch merchant, Andrew Vinnius, founder of the ordnance works at Tula, they brought into the country Dutch shipwrights and seamen. A fleet of barges was to be built on the Caspian Sea, and in 1669 at Diedinovo on the Okha river, the *Orel* was built, her constructor being the famous Karsten Brandt. She was launched at Astrakhan, but had only a year of life, as in 1670 the Cossack rebel, Stenka Razin, burnt her to a skeleton.

Ivan IV had extended Russian enterprise from the small State of Muscovy to the White Sea. To that extent he had anticipated Peter the Great in his efforts to secure a trade route

[1] *A History of Russia*; Vol. III, p. 355.

with the west. It was with the hopes of advancing those efforts that Ivan had given a most cordial reception to Richard Chancellor when the latter visited the Muscovy court for commercial negotiations between England and Russia, and the Emperor had promised to English merchants "a free Marte with all free liberties through my whole dominions" if Edward VI would send trade envoys to Moscow.

It was at this time that the Company of Merchant Adventurers was formed for the discovery of "regions, kingdoms, islands and places unknown and unvisited, by the highway of the sea". The Company was under the direction of the navigator Sebastian Cabot, and its vessels were welcomed on their visits to Muscovy. A letter of King Philip and Queen Mary, written in April 1555, refers to the favour shown by Ivan Vasilivich to "our right well beloved Richard Chancellor", to whom the Royal letter was entrusted for delivery to the Tsar. It also mentions the grant made by Ivan "that all such marchants as shall come forth of anie of our realms of England or Ireland with al maner of wares, if they will travel or occupie within your dominions, the same marchants with their marchandises in al your lordship may freely and at their liberty travaile out and in without hinderance or any maner of loss". A letter sent two years later to the Company's agents, Killingworth, Gray, and Lane, specifies the cargoes of English cloth and cottons as merchandise for bartering with the Russians for wax, flour, tallow, and oil. Samples of rope, and of steel from Tartary, are to be sent back to England in the Company's ships; "yew" is to be felled from the banks of the Arctic River Pechora for the making of casks, and a special man to "cut and cleve" this wood is being sent out from London. And—how little does habit change—the ship's officers are charged "not to suffer any of our nation to send any wares to their wives or friends in any of these ships".

But the long voyage and the fact that the Northern Sea Route taken by Chancellor was frozen for part of the year, made that route impracticable. So Ivan turned to the Baltic. Here, after his war with Livonia, he was successful in getting Dorpat and Narva, but efforts to gain more territory on the Baltic were blocked by Poland and Lithuania, as well as by Sweden, and his Livonian conquests had to be abandoned at the end of his reign. By that time Sweden was in possession of territory round Lake Ladoga, of all Esthonia, and part of Karelia; in this way Russia was barred from the Baltic. Peter the Great, in his time, had no option but to challenge the sea power of Sweden; blocked by the Tartars in the south from access to the Black Sea and the Caspian, his country would have remained a land-locked dominion. Ivan had proclaimed himself "Tsar of all the Russias"; his territories however, were less than those of Peter I, and Russia remained at the death of Ivan to all practical purposes a sealess country.

In those days, the English sovereigns had been anxious not only to foster commercial relations, but to gain the monopoly of trade with "the Russe Commonwealth", and Elizabeth had fre-quently complained to Ivan of the growing number of Dutch vessels which called at White Sea ports. By 1565 the Dutch had established a trading post on the Kola Peninsula, and Chan-cellor, on his voyage to Muscovy in 1553 had noted that in Novgorod they had a Staplehouse; significantly the reply to the letter which he brought back from Ivan IV to Edward VI had been accompanied by an interpretation in Dutch. At the end of the sixteenth century the Netherlands States-General had begun to act on advice which it had received to the effect that sea-borne trade with Russia might be as profitable to Dutch mer-chants as was their trade with America (through Spain). And by 1638 the Dutch were sending more ships to Archangel than the English were.

Commercial rivalry had long been bitter between the two peoples, for we read in Hakluyt that "these Flemings, hearing of the arrival of our men in those parts, wrote their letters to the Emperor against them, accusing them for pirates and rovers".[1]

Not till it was under pressure from the Muscovite merchants to secure for them the monopoly of middlemen, did the Tsar's Government attempt to restrict the trading of foreigners as retailers. Under Boris Godunov definite prohibitions were made, but these in time were everywhere evaded. Even when Peter I came to the throne the position was such that, as Alexei Tolstoi has written, "the foreigners had their paws on every-thing". The establishment of English traders on the White Sea had begun that commercial rivalry with Germany for Russian trade which was to continue up to the first world war. Tolstoi, in his novel of Peter the Great, describes a young merchant as saying: "I'm from the coast. I went for blubber. I came back as I set out—with empty carts. The Germans have bought up all the blubber for ten years ahead, and all the whalers are

[1] *The Discovery of Muscovy.* (Cassell & Co., Ltd., 1886); p. 44.

hopelessly in debt to them. The Germans give them a quarter of the right price, and forbid them to sell to anyone else. And the whalers are beggared, and now they're no longer going to sea—they've scattered to other parts. We Russians can't even go north now." Later we read of "how you could not sell to your own folk—they were too poor. Wares could not be taken abroad—there was no seaport. All foreign trade was in the hands of foreigners."[1] Tartars held the Black Sea coast, the Baltic was inaccessible. Commerce there was dominated by the Hanse merchants whose control extended from Novgorod to the White Sea. In the North Sea the Swedes were masters, and in the Mediterranean the Turks.

It was the work of Peter to attempt an economic revolution. He was no Free Trader; "according to the laws, no foreign merchant has even leave to buy, in the seaports, goods of another foreign merchant; he must buy them of a Russian".[2] The same inclination to create a trade monopoly for Russia in her own seaports, is marked in the maritime policy of Catherine, of whose attitude to the British Maritime Code we will speak later.

If Peter the Great was eccentric he was also practical. He would know all the business of shipbuilding before setting out to make Russia a mercantile Power. On his first visit to Archangel in 1683 he noticed how all the ships moored there were foreign ones, and how ridiculous by comparison appeared the Russian barges which had accompanied him in his sail down the Northern Dvina. So at Archangel he started to work on the wharves, eagerly questioning English and Dutch seamen about their craft. He had launched a flotilla of small ships on Plesht-cheyevo, and afterwards wrote in his Maritime Regulations: "For some years desires were satisfied by this lake, but in the end it got too narrow for me. So I went to Kubensky Lake, but that was too shallow. I then decided to make for the open sea, and often used to beg my mother to let me go to Archangel." His love of the sea nearly cost him his life, for he all but perished on a stormy voyage to Solovetski Island in the White Sea—that sea upon whose frozen waters he was the first Tsar to ever gaze. His robust adventurous life contains such periods as those spent as a deck-swabber on the ship of the Dutch skipper Musch, then as a cabin boy waiting at table, and

---

[1] Translated by Edith Bone and Emile Burns. (Gollancz, 1946); p. 57.
[2] General Manstein (Officer in the Russian Service), *Memoirs of Russia, Historical, Political, and Military, From the Year 1727 to 1744*; p. 385.

later as a seaman running up the shrouds to the mast. For a short time he worked as a shipwright in the yards at Saardam, a town then noted for its building of medium-sized ships, where he was known as *Min Her* Peter Mikhailoff the shipwright. "We labour," he wrote to the Patriarch Adrian, "in order to master thoroughly the art of the sea"; but learning that the best boats were built in England, and that the *science* of navigation was understood there as nowhere else at that time, he left Holland for Deptford (saying that he thought it a happier life to be an admiral in England, than a Tsar in Russia.) Seeing from the King's wharf the shipping on the Thames, as he had done too at Amsterdam, the Tsar realised that the wealth of the world could never come to Russia as it did to Britain and Holland, unless Russia had access to the oceans.

Later Peter sent some of his nobles to Britain to get trained both in navigation and shipbuilding; some of them also he sent (much against their will in many cases) to Holland, Venice, and Leghorn, for his own people had no sea traditions. When, more than a hundred years earlier, Boris Godunov had tried to advance Russia's maritime position, he had had to call on seamen from abroad, mainly from England and Holland. Despite their historic urge to the oceans, and the high praise which the Russian explorers Krusenstern and Kotzebue later bestowed upon their particular crews, there was much to justify the despairing cry of Peter the Great: "My people will never be a nation of sailors." And there was much evidence to support the view of an eighteenth-century writer: "The Russians, in general, have an aversion to the sea".[1] The author of this passage was almost certainly an Englishman in the service of Peter I, and his name is believed to have been John Deane. Of Russian sailors, turned from doing several years' land service to the sea, he says that the crews, "thunderstruck with the terror of an approaching engagement", are under many disadvantages, "in an element disagreeable to far the major part of them".[2] But the writer pays tribute to the defence which the Russians generally put up when attacked in their own roads, "provided there is smooth water". He rates highly the quality of those

[1] *The Russian Fleet under Peter the Great.* By a Contemporary Englishman, 1724. Publications of the Navy Records Society, Vol. XV. Edited by Vice-Admiral Cyprian A. G. Bridge, K.C.B. (Printed for the Navy Records Society, 1899); p. 102.

[2] *The Russian Fleet under Peter the Great.* By a Contemporary Englishman, 1724. Publication of the Navy Records Society, Vol. XV, p. 116.

Russian ships which were built after Peter's visits to foreign yards; few in the world, he says, are better equipped, but there is neither good navigation nor speedy sailing. And the Tsar's successes led him to send to sea more ships than could be manned by seamen of experience.

When Peter I decided to set up a school of navigation in Moscow, he persuaded British engineers and mathematicians to form the principal part of the staff, and when, for enabling his Volga ships to join the Don flotillas in their attack on Azov he conceived the idea of constructing a Volga-Don Canal, it was the Englishman, Captain John Parry, whom he asked to undertake that work. Nor as regards the efficiency of Russian seamanship did the Tsar show any more confidence in his countrymen. His order during his wars with Sweden, was that no admiral was to attack the Swedes unless he was certain he had half as many ships again as his adversaries. And although some of the British sea captains who, as exiled Jacobites, took service in the Tsar's navy, were far from competent, of not many could it be said, as of the generality of Russian officers, that "in the quality of lieutenants foreigners ever desire to leave 'em ashore . . . in bad weather, or any extremity, sick abed, when they should be serviceable".[1]

It was scarcely surprising therefore that Peter had gone further afield than Russia for the officering and even the manning of his navy. Of a list of officers commanding the Russian warships in his Baltic Fleet in 1713, only two out of eleven ships will be found with Russian commanders. And of the total number of officers serving with that fleet, which sailed from Kronslot and Reval during Peter I's campaign against Sweden in 1713, only nine out of a total of eighty-one will be seen to have Russian names. Almost one-quarter of the list consists of officers from Britain.[2] The preference shown for British (particularly Scottish) officers in Peter's fleets had its parallel in shipbuilding. Though many Danes and Dutchman were engaged by the Tsar for that purpose, we are told of Peter "justly giving the preference in building and equipping ships to the method used in England". The author of *The Russian Fleet under Peter the*

---

[1] *The Russian Fleet under Peter the Great.* By "A Contemporary Englishman". Navy Records Society, Vol. XV, p. 114.

[2] British names were not confined to personnel, they were not infrequently given to Russian ships; in the case of those built in England, the English name was sometimes retained. In Peter the Great's Baltic Fleet, 1714, for instance, will be found *Randolph, Portsmouth, Devonshire, Marlborough.* For other British names, see Navy Records Society, Vol. XV, p. 68.

Great[1] writes: "To give the Russians the better insight, it is usual when an English master begins a ship, to order a Russian master to set up one of the same dimensions, near at hand; and the Russian must be indulged the liberty of observing and measuring the Englishman's work." The writer of this passage (probably John Deane) had met Peter I at Deptford, and had been persuaded by him to go to Russia, where he became superintendent of the shipyard at Voronezh, and here English craftsmen were in the majority. They, with Dutch shipwrights too, had settled in this fortress city of the Upper Don in the time of Tsar Michael, Peter's predecessor. Native labour was largely forced, but more than the workers were in resentment over Peter's dynamic drive for ships—*boyars* and merchants bitterly complained of the levy of ship money. But the Emperor won his way and Voronezh developed as a centre of shipbuilding, yards being built on an island in the river, and boats were constructed of timber from the neighbouring forests. Voronezh indeed, became the cradle of the Russian navy. It was only when Russia had stretched west to the Baltic and east to the Black Sea, when the land around Voronezh, denuded of its forests, had become a treeless waste, that the great port not only ceased to be the principal one of Russia, but its shipyards lost their life.

The Tsar himself lived among the workers at Voronezh, and James Keith, who became famous later as a Marshal of Prussia, wrote of him: "He loved more to employ his money on ships . . . than sumptuous buildings, and was always content with his lodging when he could see a fleet from his window." Alexei Tolstoi, in his novel *Peter the Great*, gives a vivid picture of him in a dirty white shirt and canvas apron, his face haggard, covered with sweat, standing before the furnace with his long tongs. He and his workmates were forging flukes of the anchor for the battleship *Fortress*, and all were in a rush to get the ships down to the Don estuary while the floods lasted. No less than twenty-nine of these ships had been built in a single winter, and were launched in the spring of 1696.

As Captain P. Alexeivitch, Peter commanded the Don galley flotilla from the *Principium*, which he had helped to build. He had raised an imposing number of small ships, but many of his earlier vessels had proved unseaworthy; made of green fir, a number of the hulls suffered from shrinking timbers. Of those

[1] By "A Contemporary Englishman", 1724. Publication of the Navy Records Society, Vol. XV, p. 104.

on the Caspian, all of which had been built at Kazan on the
Volga, a contemporary writer[1] says: "In a word, little is to be
said in favour of the ships built before the Tsar's return from
his travels; to pass them by in silence is the highest compli-
ment." Many of the Kazan vessels were of a Flemish type,
snows. On the Dnieper too the Tsar built vessels, and he had
founded the shipyards at Briansk to take Russia south.

It was after his first attack on Azov failed that Peter had
determined to build a fleet capable of preventing the Turks
from relieving it by sea. And on his main expedition against
the enemy, eighty-six ships of war—two-decker ships, galliots,
brigantines—and five hundred barges, had sailed down the Don.
His capture of the fortress in 1696 had given him a firm foothold on the Sea of Azov; Russia's aim to dominate the Black
Sea had been brought a little nearer achievement. But even
complete control of the Sea of Azov could never of itself, before
the days of icebreakers, mean even partial supremacy on the
Black Sea, because Azov, as well as the Strait of Kerch which
connects the two seas, is frozen for several months in the year.
The ports of the Don were thus of only qualified use to Peter.
To consolidate his position on the shores of the Sea of Azov, he
built Taganrog as a new naval fortress,[2] and set up an arsenal
at Azov. The Treaty of Carlowitz, which confirmed him in his
conquests, established him still more securely on Azov by giving
a strip of the hinterland.

The Sea of Azov, however, was not Peter's principal objective. It was the Black Sea to which his far-sighted eyes were most
often drawn. That the Russians were late in establishing themselves on its shores and its waters was due to the early inroads of
Asiatic hordes. In the hopes of getting freedom of navigation for
his ships on the Black Sea, Peter sent Prince Dmitry Golitsyn to
Turkey to broach the matter with the Sultan. (Unfortunately
for the Tsar, the Sultan gave it to be understood that he would
sooner open his harem to the Russians than open the Euxine to
them. But he did consent to their merchandise being carried
through the Straits, provided this was done in Turkish bottoms.)
In sending many of his nobles to Venice for instruction in the
arts of shipbuilding, the Tsar's aim of creating a fleet in the
Black Sea is evident, for only in Venice could those nobles be
taught how to make the galliots which would be suitable for the

[1] See Footnote [1] p. 62.
[2] For the toll of life taken in building the harbour here, the Tsar seems to
have shown as little concern as he did in the case of Kronstadt.

Straits and the Euxine littoral. But Peter's gains in the region of
that sea were lost in 1711, when, after more engagements against
the Turks, his forces were defeated on the Pruth. He had to
surrender Azov, destroy Taganrog and, worst of all, the Black
Sea was interdicted to his ships. Turkey also now gained control
of all the river mouths. Pruth was not only a severe setback to
Russia's drive to the sea: it was a disaster. It meant that
"Turkey could once more command the Delta of the Don, not
to add the whole river system of Southern Russia—the Dniester,
the Don, and the Kuban. Russian trade was thereby throttled".[1]

The ships which Peter had built with such cost and care were
almost totally destroyed, and for a time it looked as though
Russia's advance in the south was ended. The Azov Sea and the
delta of the Dnieper remained Turkish till 1738, when Russia
recovered Azov, but by the Treaty of Belgrade the following
year she was prohibited from fortifying the place, and still more
serious, from maintaining a fleet not only on the Sea of Azov,
but on the Black Sea.

Though Peter's losses to Turkey were, as we have said, more
than a setback to Russian aims on the Euxine, his gains on the
Caspian remained considerable at the time of his death. In
1722 he had started his campaign against Persia, recruiting
forces from those Cossack bands who, since the time when
Yermak's comrade Andreya Shadrin had set up a fort at the
mouth of the Terek River, had steadily gained ground until
"The Cossack Line" was extended to the Sea of Azov. Admiral
Apraxin had won over many of them for service with the Tsar,
and they held for Peter, against the native tribes, part of the
northern shore of the Caspian. Using Astrakhan as his base, the
Emperor had a small fleet of boats called *evers* built, but it was
never launched. He himself went to the port of Derbend, where
he "broke with his own hands a window through the wall of
the room he occupied in the Khan's palace that he might
watch the waters of the Caspian, over the city at his feet, for
the coming of his transports".[2] But though a storm wrecked
most of his flotilla and he failed to advance that time in his
intended campaign on Persian territory, he did later capture
both Derbend and Baku, and in addition, certain of the Caspian
provinces. Astrakan he had made the centre of the silk trade,

[1] Sir J. A. Marriott, *Anglo-Russian Relations, 1689-1943*. (Methuen, 1944);
p. 39. By permission of the Publishers.
[2] John F. Baddeley, *The Russian Conquest of the Caucasus*. (Longmans,
Green & Co., 1908); p. 28. Quotation by permission of the Publishers.

and for this purpose had encouraged Armenians to settle there. As regards the Caspian Sea itself, the most detailed chart of it ever made till that time was the work of the Englishman, Captain Bruce, commissioned by the Tsar to survey all the gulfs, harbours, and rivers on the eastern shore. Of his Persian policy, Peter said to the Moldavian prince, Cantemir: "It is not the land I want, but the sea."

As well as on these thalassic waters of the Caucasian region, his mind was much on the Middle Sea, and the creation of a Mediterranean squadron was certainly one of his aims. "Just before the conclusion of the late peace [of 1721] it was hotly talked of that the Tsar would send a squadron of men-of-war through the Sound and British Channel up the Straits into the Mediterranean."[1]

To follow the Emperor in all his main maritime tracks, we turn now from south-east Europe and go north-west to the Baltic, where he was called upon to defend his frontiers against Charles XII of Sweden. The wars of Charles IX—undertaken primarily to ensure Swedish supremacy in the Baltic—had been continued by Gustavus Adolphus, which had brought the latter into conflict with Tsar Michael Romanov. By the Treaty of Stolbovo, 1617, Russia had regained Novgorod and all other territories previously conquered by Sweden. But Sweden had got Ingria, and with it both Narva and the fortress of Nöteborg on the Neva. She had also recovered her former rights in Livonia, and Russia had renounced her claims on Esthonia. At a meeting of the Estates at Stockholm, Gustavus Adolphus had given a detailed report of the treaty: "From now on," he said, "the Russians are denied entrance to the Baltic at any point, and neither in time of war nor for peaceful trading can their ships use its harbours without our special permission." Pointing to a map, the King had shown the assembly how Russia was entirely excluded from the Swedish Sea. "And that, we will hope, by God's help, will always prove too wide a jump, even for a Russian!"[2]

But in the following century Peter the Great faced that jump. He was determined not only to get "a window on the west", but a wide one. His aim was to turn the Baltic from a Swedish to a Russian lake. In the northern part of that sea he succeeded in doing this. (The window was opened a

---

[1] *The Russian Fleet under Peter the Great.* The Navy Records Society, Vol. XV, p. 108.

[2] W. R. Morfill, *Russia*; p. 107.

good deal wider when, after the second world war, Russia acquired the former Prussian naval base of Koenigsberg—now Kaliningrad.)

In the Middle Ages, Russia's way to the Baltic was via Novgorod at the head of Lake Ilmen, thence by the River Volkhov, Lake Ladoga, and the Neva to the sea. Peter the Great used much of the course of the modern Baltic-White Sea Canal when he took two frigates and part of his army to attack the Swedish forces then in Finland. St. Petersburg was built to give Peter his western window, and from his "city on stilts" he was to look far out over the west, where he felt Russia's destiny lay. "He had need of a port on the east of the Baltic Sea for the execution of all his ideas", wrote Voltaire; and so in 1712 the Tsar declared St. Petersburg the capital of all the Russias. The tower of Rastrelli's Admiralty now soared above the banks of the Neva, and on that river rose Nöteborg—which Peter had taken in 1702—to become the fortress of Schlusselberg, i.e. the "key" town. The harbour of Kronstadt was built, and the fort of Kronslot was constructed on Kotlin Island to protect the mouth of the Neva. Peter himself could have been seen at that time with a sounding lead examining the depth of water off a sandbank near the island. The first foreign vessel to call at Kotlin was a Dutch boat with provisions from Saardam; the Tsar went out to meet it and acted as its pilot up the Neva.[1] He was so pleased at the arrival of this ship at his newly founded capital that he declared it to be exempt from dues then and thereafter. This concession he made also in favour of other Dutch and also English vessels in order to attract trade to St. Petersburg.

That city was to be a key to force a passage for Russia to the open sea, and at the same time to lock that passage against intruders. So strongly did Peter feel about his new capital that, when his dissolute eldest son Alexis let it be known that when he became Tsar he would give up that city, return to Moscow, and pay no concern to the navy created by his father, Peter regarded him as a traitor and deprived him of succession.

The first overseas action ever fought by Russia (if we exclude raids on Constantinople) only took place in 1713, when Admiral Apraxin took Åbo and Helsingfors. There was, how-ever, no Swedish opposition to the seizure of the first town. His ships were to carry his troops across the Baltic to Sweden, and

[1] G. Dobson, H. M. Grove, and E. Stewart, *Russia*. (A. & C. Black, 1913); p. 67.

Apraxin was to raid the coast up to a point only seven miles from Stockholm, and to burn the port of Umea. This new phenomenon of a Russian fleet of efficient ships in the Baltic, challenging the well-established sea power of Sweden, may be reckoned among the forces which led the Swedes to accept the Treaty of Nystadt in 1721. (The terms of the settlement as regards the Russo-Finnish frontier are curiously similar to those of the Agreement of 1940—and yet not perhaps so curious after all, when we realise that Stalin as much as Peter the Great, appreciated the strategic and the commercial value of the water routes afforded by the rivers and lakes from Ilmen northward through Karelia.) By the time the Peace of Nystadt was signed, Peter the Great had made Russia a first-class Power and had given her control of nearly all of the northern Baltic. The coast of that sea from Viborg to Riga was now Russia's; over most of the Gulf of Finland she had command, and the Province of Viborg was hers. The Treaty did not, however, deprive Sweden of the right to trade freely in the Baltic, and it was not till 1809 that the whole of Finland, and the consequent control of *all* the north-east Baltic, passed to Russia under Alexander I.

The earliest commercial treaty that Russia had ever con- cluded was with England, in the time of Elizabeth Tudor. We may recall how Ivan instructed his Ambassador: "Present this gift to our sweet sister, Elizabeth of England, and with these chessmen explain to her how her English ships can sail to us by the White Sea and outwit both Germans and Livonians. And remind her that Tsar Ivan of Muscovy is the sole merchant here." But as regards the Baltic, it was Peter the Great who opened that to Russia, and a year after the Treaty of Nystadt had been signed he expressly prohibited the carrying of goods by sea to Archangel (except for use locally). As only one voyage a year to that White Sea port was possible at that time, the Tsar had no difficulty in getting merchants to favour St. Peters- burg rather than Archangel, once he had overcome at the latter port the opposition of the long-established Dutch traders. Archangel, which arose from a tenth-century settlement, had been one of Russia's earliest trade ports, and till Peter the Great obtained part of Finland and all Livonia it was almost the only known port that Russia possessed in the north. But after the Tsar's conquests Russia had eight chief ports—Riga, Pärnau, Reval, Narva, Viborg, Frederikshaven, Kola, and St. Peters- burg. (In the south there was Astrakhan.) Archangel's growth from the monastery settlement of St. Michael's to the chief port

on the White Sea was largely due to English help; its later
decline was attributable not only to Peter's mercantile schemes,
but to his realisation of the impracticability of using any port on
the White Sea as a naval base: it was to the Baltic he must turn
for that. Between 1717 and 1719 the value of the annual import
trade of Archangel was 2,344,000 roubles, and that of St.
Petersburg was only 269 roubles. But in 1726, a year after the
death of Peter, the imports of Archangel had fallen to 285,000
roubles, while those of St. Petersburg had risen to 2,403,000.[1]
In 1724 the total number of vessels reaching Baltic ports
(excluding Pärnau and Reval) was 914.[2]

In the latter half of the seventeenth century many English
shipwrights had become employed on Lake Ladoga; at Olonets,
where Peter was later to establish a dockyard, an Englishman
made anchors for the entire Russian Navy.[3] The reason for the
presence also of English shipwrights on the shores of Lake
Peipus was that the Tsar, whose Esthonian conquests had given
him that lake, was determined to create a flotilla here as on
Lake Ladoga. Peter was aware that if his countrymen had only
had a fleet on Ladoga in 1612, they could have prevented
Swedish troops from reaching Narva, and that city might never
have fallen. The origin of the Ladoga flotilla can be traced to
Archangel, whence the Tsar had two small frigates, the *Holy
Spirit* and the *Courier*, dragged overland from Onega Bay to
Onega Lake. From there they were sent by the River Svir to
Lake Ladoga, and during the overland stage, in the necessary
work of making roads and of moving these ships on rollers
placed under the keels, Peter himself had helped. This nucleus
of the Ladoga fleet was increased by a number of ships made by
an English firm, and when these, in addition to a fleet of Cossack
vessels under Colonel Tirtov, were called into action against
Swedish vessels, they proved their worth. Ladoga was won for
Russia.

On Lake Peipus, Peter's efforts to build a fleet capable of out-
matching the Swedish ships were so successful that in 1711 one
hundred Russian vessels attacked the small number of enemy
ones which were on that water.

[1] Gregor Alexinsky, *Russia and Europe*, translated from the Russian by
Bernard Miall. (Fisher Unwin, 1917); p. 81.
[2] V. O. Kluchevsky, *A History of Russia*, translated by J. C. Hogarth.
(Dent & Sons, 1911); Vol. IV, p. 125.
[3] The practice of engaging Englishmen to build ships and dockyards
continued right into the nineteenth century.

His capture of Nyenskans at the mouth of the Neva had regained for Russia that access to the Baltic without which his empire could never be a world Power. His enemy Charles XII, had in 1701 been able to land a force of 60,000 at Reval, and Peter realised the urgency of creating a strong Baltic fleet to make a renewal of such invasions impossible. His establishment of Kotlin as a fortress proved to be tactically sound, for it was by this island-garrison that the Swedish efforts in 1705 to destroy the Tsar's new fleet were frustrated. Not till 1711 however, were Russian ships of the line seen in the Baltic. Their names, given by Dr. R. C. Anderson[1] are: *Vyborg, Riga, Dumkrat, Shtandart, Hobet*,[2] *Liseta, Munker.*

The first warship constructed overseas for his new fleet was the *Samson*, built in Dutch yards. It is proof of the rapid advance towards Sea Power made by Russia under Peter the Great that, of the Baltic Fleet of fifty-three ships, twenty-four were built in the Tsar's dominions, Archangel providing seven. After the removal of many from the list of the Russian Navy, the latter in 1722 had twenty-nine serviceable battleships.[3] Russian secondary ships of the line did not make their appearance on this sea till 1719. In that year they sailed from Reval under the command of Van Hofft, an event which coincided, as Anderson remarks,[4] with the first victory of the Russian deep-sea fleet, which took place off Oesel Island.

In his capacity as Rear-Admiral, his triumph over the Swedes in an engagement in the Baltic in 1714, probably gave Peter more pleasure than anything else in his life. The extent to which he did take part in that event, however, has been a subject much debated. It was the Tsar's creation of a Baltic Fleet which had made it possible for Admiral Apraxin on this occasion to command a fleet of about a hundred galleys against the Swedish Admiral Wattrang. Peter himself organised the line of battle,[5] but whether he was actually in action or followed the operations from an island has not been finally determined. The capture of Åland by his ships brought the Tsar great rejoicing, and at a public dinner in his new capital he had asked his nobles, "Brothers, is the man among you, who twenty years ago could have conceived the idea of being employed with me in

---

[1] *Naval Wars in the Baltic, 1521-1850:* (C. Gilbert-Wood); p. 146.
[2] But see Anderson's note.
[3] R. C. Anderson: *Naval Wars in the Baltic, 1521-1850*; p. 207.
[4] *Ibid*; p. 195.
[5] For diagram see *Ibid*, p. 158.

shipbuilding on the Baltic?" More than one writer[1] has spoken of the citizens of Moscow of those days having an aversion to maritime affairs. Their ruler was determined to show them that it was to the sea they owed the greatly improved position of their country after Nystadt. And so he made his triumphal entry into Moscow like the one into St. Petersburg—a maritime fête. A small yacht, fully rigged, was drawn on a sledge through the snowy streets of the city, mounted with small brass guns from which salutes were fired. (Its picture is in this book, on p. 90.) It was the first time those astonished citizens had seen a model ship of war. But it was not till more than three hundred years later, when Moscow became a "port of five seas", that the people of that city began to be sea-minded.

The expansion of Russia under Peter I was made possible because Charles XII, like Charles XI, failed to carry on Sweden's traditional policy of maintaining her status as a naval rather than a military Power. Charles XII tried to make his country supreme in both spheres, and failed. His ambitious enterprises on the continent spent the power of Sweden, and it was this fact, even more than the emergence of Russia as a country equipped with fleets, which brought such substantial maritime gains in the west to Peter the Great.

In the east the Tsar was ever alive to the great advantages which would be gained by his country if a North-East Passage could be discovered. Before sending Bering on his first Kamchatkan expedition for this purpose, Peter had commissioned two of his officers, Luchin and Evreimov, to sail up the fog-covered coast of Kamchatka and find out whether Asia and America were separated. Their reports, made in 1723, were indecisive, so came the turn of the great Danish navigator, about which more will be said shortly.

> *Dauntlessly ploughing through ice and snow,*
> *Forward the Russian Columbuses go,*
> *Braving all dangers, until they attain*
> *Their ultimate goal of the Eastern main,*

wrote Lomonosov in his poem *Peter the Great*.[2] Certainly the Emperor himself was inclined to believe that a passage did exist between the two continents, but he was ignorant of the extent of

---

[1] cf. John Bell, *Travel from St. Petersburg to Divers Parts of Asia*. (Glasgow, 1763); 2 vols.

[2] Author's rendering of the Russian lines in Lomonosov's poem *Петр Великий*; (St. Petersburg, 1770) [?].

the Pacific, and of the length of the coastline of North America. Under the impression, as he was, that the whole ocean was far narrower than was the case, he imagined that trade could be opened up with *Central* America via north-east Asia. That so serious a student of maritime history (and moreover one who had founded "the Chancery of the Military Marine" for the training of geodesists and hydrographers) should not have had a truer concept of the geography of the North Pacific, is rather remarkable. And the more so when we recall that the Barents Map, published by Pontanus in 1611, draws approximately correctly the position of Siberia vis-à-vis the extreme north-west of the American continent, and shows the two land masses to be separated by a strait, at that time called Anian. (Nordenskiöld believed that the Barents Map was based on charts still older.) Martin Waldseemüller's Inset Map of 1507 had also shown the conception of America as a separate continent. So too, had the Zaltieri "Nova Franza" Map of 1566 (or earlier), and those of the Gemma Frisius series, from 1537. But as regards the Pacific coast of North America, this had only been charted as far as Cape Blanco, 43° N., by the time of Peter's death.

The Peace of Nystadt would have left Peter with sufficient security to further his maritime schemes, but by that time his health was failing. In his lifetime he had seen the advantages that might be made "of every port, and every river in his Empire. . . . It was he who taught his people to triumph by land, and opened them a passage to the sea; in short it was he that conceived and executed the amazing project of making them a maritime Power, and this in a surprising extent".[1] And at his death there were, according to Kluchevsky,[2] 48 ships of the line, 800 galleys and minor vessels, and a man-power afloat of 28,000. It must be said, however, that other authorities give much lower figures; in one case the numbers mentioned are 41 ships of the line and a complement of 14,900 seamen.

THE NORTH-EAST PASSAGE

The opening up of a North-East Passage that would lead his ships from the White Sea to the coasts of China had been one of the dreams of Peter's life. The search for such a passage was a long one in the history of navigation. A tradition that the ocean encompassed the northern and eastern limits of Siberia was well established as early as 1246, the year in which Johannes

[1] Harris's *Collection of Voyages;* Vol. II, p. 1,017.
[2] *A History of Russia;* Vol. IV, p. 66.

de Plano Carpini, a Friar Minorite, travelled with three companions to Tartary at the behest of the Pope. Hakluyt's account
of that astonishing journey is based partly on Carpini's "litle
historie" of it, and partly on the report of one of the other friars,
Simon de Sanct Quintin. Though both accounts have received
some embellishments from Vincent de Beauvais and Sir John
Mandeville, it was certainly the expressed belief of Friar
Carpini that Siberia on its northern and eastern sides was
"invironed with the Ocean Sea"—Siberia in those days being
described as "Tartaria, that part of the worlde which is thought
to be most North Easterly".[1] The Strait of Anian (later known
as the Bering Strait), and the "Big Land" to the east of it, were
known by hearsay to Marco Polo, but whether that land was
America was not then known. The map-maker Gastalde, in
a pamphlet published in Venice, 1562, entitled *La Universale
Descrittione del Mondi*, had based much of this essay on the narrative of Marco Polo, and in his writing Gastalde described the
Strait of Anian as connecting the Pacific and the Arctic Ocean.[2]
(See the Wright-Hakluyt map.)   The Portuguese navigator
Gaspar de Cortereal in 1500 had purported to give confirmation of the existence of the Strait, though actually the one he
had sailed through was on his voyage north of Labrador, and
later became known as Hudson's Strait.   More than one sixteenth-century map gives the name of "Anian" to a passage
separating Asia from America, and among such maps is the one
of 1578 based on the work of George Best, known as "A true
discourse of the late Voyages of Discoverie for finding a passage
to Cathaya by the Northwest under the Conduct of Martin
Frobisher."[3] (But in the general map accompanying Hakluyt's
Voyages it will be seen that the name "Anian" is given not to
the Strait, but to coastland on a land-mass opposite Siberia.
So too, in Sir Humphrey Gilbert's map of 1576 and in his
"Discourse", where we find him speaking of the people "which
inhabit Anian".)

Sir Humphrey Gilbert was never converted to the belief in
the existence of a North-East Passage, though he was convinced
that a North-West one could be found, and that the strait

[1] *Hakluyt's Voyages*, edited by S. Douglas Jackson. (Jackson, Son & Co.,
Glasgow; J. M. Dent & Sons, London, 1907); Vol. IX, p. 2.
[2] L. C. Wroth: "The Early Cartography of the Pacific". (Published in
The Papers of the Bibliographical Society of America, New York, 1944; Vol.
XXXVIII, pp. 87-268.)
[3] Reproduced in Dent's edition of *Hakluyt's Voyages*, Vol. V, p. 171.

bordering on that coast of Anian led to such a passage. In his "Discourse of a Discoverie of a new passage to Cataia" he tells of how the English traveller, Anthony Jenkinson, had heard "a Fisherman of Tartaria say in hunting the Morce, that he sayled very far towards the southwest, finding no end of the Sea: whereby he hoped a thorow passage to be that way". Gilbert ridicules the Siberian fisherman's tale, but the man, if he did exist and did make such a voyage, knew better than Gilbert, even if his story of finding "Unicornes on the coast of Tartaria" was taller than most fishermen's. There were many who believed the word of Marco Polo, who "affirmed that he sayled 1,500 miles upon the coasts of Mangia, and Anian, toward the North-east; always finding the seas open before him".[1] Numerous fabled expeditions followed, such as that of Juan de Fuca, who claimed to have found "gold, silver, pearls" in the Arctic regions when on his apocryphal voyage through the North-West Passage. Other legendary ones, though exposed by the historian Navarette, kept alive the tradition of a passage from the Frozen Sea to the Great Southern Ocean.[2]

Among those to which a greater degree of veracity is attached are certain of the accounts collected by Baron Sigismund von Herberstein, and for those who enjoy rare literary curiosities his two volumes of travellers' tales about Russia, entitled *Rerum Moscoviticarum Commentarii*, will provide much entertainment. The Introduction to this work with its references to old Hebraic, Latin, Portuguese, and Italian manuscripts, offers much of interest to readers of early discoveries. Baron von Herberstein, who was born in 1486, became ambassador for the Emperor Maximilian to Moscow, and had exceptional opportunities for getting information about different parts of Russia. He relates how, when at the Court of Muscovy, he heard from an interpreter, Gregory Istoma, an account of his journey to the King of Denmark in 1496, and of how a much longer route than the usual one had to be taken from Great Novgorod, owing to the revolt at that time of Sweden from Denmark. So Istoma and his party had gone by the mouths of the Dvina and then by boats to the coast of "Finlapeia"; rounding Sviatoy Nos (Holy Cape), they had passed the Rock of Semes, and were told by one of the sailors that "unless we appease it with a gift we shall not easily

[1] *Hakluyt's Voyages*, Vol. V, p. 102.
[2] The subject of the Strait of Anian has been discussed by G. E. Nunn in *Origin of the Strait of Anian Concept*. (Privately printed, Philadelphia 1929. Copyright George H. Beans, 1929.)

pass it". Baron von Herberstein was told of Indians at sea being driven round the north to the coasts of Germany—a story which we find repeated in several of the chronicles of voyages during this period. Blazius, also an interpreter at the Court, was another from whom von Herberstein learnt more about these sixteenth century Arctic voyages. In the house of an Italian poet, Hieronimus Frascator, a learned fellow-countryman had discoursed on the possibility of navigation through a North-East Passage. Then, "takyng the globe in his hande, he made demonstration that this voyage should bee very shorte", and that the one Prince above all others who by reason of the geographical position should discover the route "with greater commoditie", was the Duke of Muscovy. It is related by Herberstein that an ambassador at the Muscovy Court had talked with Paulo Centurione, Genoese ambassador from Pope Leo, and that this man had come to try and interest the Tsar in the opening up of a passage to Cathay. Centurione (who in 1525 put the same proposition to Henry VIII) is reported as saying that "no man ought to doubt of that sea, but that it may be sayled sixe monethes in the yeere, forasmuch as the dayes are then very long in that clime, and hot, by reason of continuall reverberations of the beames of the Sunne, and shorte nyghtes".[1] It is interesting to find von Herberstein giving a fairly true account of the nature of the ice both at the deltas and out at sea, from these reports which he collected of the different attempts to penetrate the frozen waters of "the Great White Sea". Supporters like von Herberstein, of the belief in the possibility of a Northern Sea Route, had little to encourage them in the productions of the cosmographers of those days. Even in the *De Orbe Novo* map of Petrus Martyr (published in Paris, 1587)—in many ways the most advanced map of its time—a great frozen land mass joins Asia to America, and stretches far north of the true configurations of these continents.

The story of the Cossack migrations across Siberia to the Far East is linked with the later discoveries of the passage from the Northern Seas to the Pacific. In the middle of the sixteenth century a Tartar chief, harassed by enemies, had sent envoys to Ivan the Terrible asking the Tsar to take Siberia under his protection. Ivan, an expansionist by ambition, was by no means averse to such a proposal, and in a letter to Edward VI of England he styles himself "Lord of all Sibir". To Grigor

[1] Sigismund von Herberstein, *Rerum Moscoviticarum*. (Antwerp, 1557); Vol. II, p. 189.

Stroganov and his family he gave charters to exploit for a period of twenty years the regions of the Ob, Irtysh, and Tobol rivers. Tobolsk, at the confluence of the rivers Tobol and Irtysh, was founded by Cossack enterprise, and was the earliest Russian town in Siberia. The principal trading centre, however, was Sibir, the Tartar settlement on the Irtysh, and the merchants of Novgorod, long before the arrival of the Stroganovs in Siberia, had known the traders who came from Sibir to the Fair on the Volga. Under Ivan III indeed, traders from Moscow had reached Siberia, and in 1499 had sent armed forces to take over lands on the Ob; these Muscovites later came into conflict with the traders from Novgorod. It was however the latter who made the most headway in Siberia, and the descendants of Anika Stroganov did so largely through their family securing the services of Yermak Timofeyevitch, who came originally from one of the Cossack settlements at the mouth of the Volga. Yermak[1] had become a Cossack officer in the service of the Government at Perm, but in 1579 he had crossed the Urals and made his way into Siberia, where he was to leave his mark on Russian history. He and his fellow-adventurers penetrated the regions between the Ob and the Yenesei, and on the latter river between 1625 and 1630 were founded such settlements as Krasnoyarsk, which grew up from an early *ostrog* or fort. Buriat Mongols had checked the advance of these Russians along the Upper Tunguska, and this had made them push on to the Yenesei. That river however had been reached by Russians earlier, for in 1595 the Dutch admiral, Cornelius Nai, had been told by Russian sealers in Yugorski Shar that from Kholmogori on the White Sea some smacks sailed annually "right past the River Obi to another river, the Gillisey."[2] The latter is clearly the Yenesei, and Nansen says that this reference to it is the first one he knows of to be recorded in literature. In the beginning of the seventeenth century the Russian settlement founded at Mangaseya on the Gulf of Ob, was moved to Turukhansk, and from here, in 1610, Cossacks had descended the Yenesei to "the Cold Ocean".

In recalling the achievements of great voyagers like Bering and Cook in the North Pacific, it must not be forgotten that the pioneers of exploration in the seas of northern Siberia which led

[1] This nickname, meaning "the millstone", he gained for grinding corn for his parents. His real name was Vasili, and he was the son of a Volga trapper.
[2] Fridtjof Nansen: *Through Siberia, the Land of the Future,* translated by Arthur G. Chater. (Heinemann, 1914); p. 441.

to the Great Southern Ocean, were the intrepid Cossacks—men
like Yermak and his bands who continued the eastward trek,
and indomitable but ruthless adventurers such as the ataman
Khabarov who made his way down the Amur to its confluence
with the Ussuri. There was Postnik who discovered the Indigirka, and there were Goreloi and Buza who on separate
occasions voyaged to the mouth of that river from Yakutsk; of
the same doughty company was Buldakov who sailed from the
Lena to the Kolima, beating his way through the ice there in
1647. His vessels after being frozen in, had to be abandoned, and
parts of them were broken up and used as sledges. Well did he
and his companions, living according to their own accounts on
"larch-prickles" for a month, know the truth of the Russian
saying "Who has not been at sea has not known trouble." Two
years earlier Michael Stadukhin too had found his way to the
delta of the Kolima, and there had built an *ostrog*. His difficulties in sailing in the Arctic Sea in vessels built originally only for
use on the rivers, can be well imagined. To Issai Ignatiev is due
the first known attempt to navigate the waters east of the
Kolima; this redoubtable Cossack is believed to have reached
Tchaun Bay, opposite Arautan Island. And there were the
Cossacks Amosov and Vilygin from the Kolima delta, who gave
the first authentic information about Wrangell Island. To
Kosirevski, who had made an expedition from Kamchatka to
the Kuriles, Bering owed some of his early knowledge of the
North Pacific. Kosirevski was a most remarkable man, and the
story of his life would make a gripping play. He had been
a Cossack who had fought against the native tribes in north-
eastern Siberia; after sailing up the Kamchatka River he had
built a fort at its headwaters. He was then directed by the
Governor of Yakutsk to explore and report on Kamchatka Cape
and its islands, and to get all the news he could as to the
possibility of navigation from that region to Japan. Acquain-
tance with the delta of "the Big River" on the Penjinsk Sea
enabled him to set up an *ostrog* there and also to establish a
port. In 1712 Kosirevski had sailed from Kamchatka for the
Kuriles, and of these islands he had gained quite a lot of knowledge. This he passed on to Bering when the latter was in
Yakutsk. By that time the Cossack had turned monk.

But while, as before said, due recognition must be given to
the Cossacks as the earliest known of the Russian voyagers in
the waters round north-east Siberia, it must be realised that
these reckless rovers were in general no seamen. Of knowledge

of navigation they had practically none; they made no surveys, and in their later voyages as fur hunters in the north-west Pacific they sailed simply from island to island, sometimes without any idea as to course. Golovnin records how one ship of such adventurers sailed so far south that the pitch melted in the seams before they turned north again and found the islands they were making for. Those Governors of Yakutsk who encouraged them in their enterprises, were unrealistic in expecting these untrained navigators to bring back reliable information. Of maps they knew little or nothing; when Gvosdov sailed along part of the American coast in 1732 he thought it was that of an island. For making any observations of a scientific nature these Cossack voyagers were totally unequipped.

One of these bands of roving adventurers known as *promyschleni* set out in 1647 to search for the mouth of the Anadir river. This they failed to find, but one of them, Semeon Deshniev, partly from that voyage, partly from one made in the previous year by the same company, was able to give the first detailed description of the Chukot Peninsula, and by his report he showed himself to be a navigator in advance of his fellows and something of an exception to their failure in general to keep any precise account of their seafaring exploits.

Though the Bering Strait has taken its name from the Danish discoverer Vitus Bering, who in 1741 ascertained that water separated north-east Siberia from north-west America, probably the first authentic sailing from the Arctic Ocean to the Bering Sea was that achieved by this Cossack leader, Deshniev, in 1648. His name has been revived in the Cape on the Bering Sea formerly known as East Cape. He left an account of his voyage down the Lena to its delta, and of his sail thence round a cape which in the opinion of some authorities—Coxe[1] among them—can be identified with the promontory later described by Captain Cook in his voyage to the North Pacific, and for long known as East Cape. Deshniev, it is known, went from the Kolima nearly to the mouth of the Anadir, but did he and his two companions, Alexeiev and Ankudinov, go all the way by water? This question has been critically examined at great length by F. A. Golder,[2] who gives his verdict against the

[1] *Account of the Russian Discoveries between Asia and America.* (Cadell, London, 1780); Supplement, p. 12.

[2] Reprinted by permission of the Publishers, The Arthur H. Clark Company, from *Russian Expansion on the Pacific*, by Frank A. Golder; Chap. III.

achievement claimed for Deshniev by such writers as Müller and Baron von Wrangell.

Another discussion on the subject of that voyage was given by Capt. James King in his third volume of *Capt. Cook's Voyage to the Pacific*. Deshniev's own account of his adventure, claiming that three of the seven boats reached a point south of the Anadir estuary, lay unread for over eighty years in Yakutsk.

But whether his route was an all-water one or not, Deshniev certainly reached the Bering Sea, and the outstanding fact is the rapidity with which the Cossacks had made their way across Siberia between the time when in 1579 Yermak had crossed the "Stony Girdle" of the Urals, and 1648 when Deshniev rounded the north-east extremity of Asia and reached the Anadir Gulf.

The Cossacks had frequently reported that inhabitants of the coastal regions had told them that women had rowed the native boats, *baidarkas*, across to the "Big Land", and when Popov —sent in 1711 to exact tribute from the Chukchi tribes— returned from Cape East, he brought back stories of islands beyond that cape, and of the continent to the east. (This had sharpened still more Peter I's thirst for knowledge of an all-sea route from his Far-Eastern outposts to his domain in the west.)

It was the Cossack exploits which led to the conquest of Kamchatka by Vladimir Atlasov, who with his followers had set out at the end of the seventeenth century from Anadirsk, the fort on the Anadir River founded by Deshniev. Atlasov found that the inhabitants already had some knowledge of the Russians, and that a companion of Deshniev's was said to have landed there after the voyage through the Bering Strait. But the stories he heard of his fellow countrymen suggest that their existence on the Peninsula was of a somewhat legendary character. Atlasov's description of the Kamchatkans, and of the beavers, foxes, and otters which they hunted, shows keen powers of observation, and as a contemporary chronicle it is certainly informative. But it was not till 1716 that Kamchatka was reached by crossing the Sea of Okhotsk. It was natural to the Russians to use the land rather than the sea whenever possible for the conquest of new territory. One can hardly imagine the English of that time deferring for so long, a seaward assault on Kamchatka from the port of Okhotsk. Peter the Great however, was the exception to the Russian rule. In his maritime approach

to problems of expansion he was almost English. Kamchatka he
regarded as the starting-point for Russian expansion in the
Pacific—particularly in the northern area of that ocean—
though even he could hardly have foreseen the immense advantage this was to bring the Russians (over all other traders except
the Spanish), in having bases on the North Pacific when the
fur trade came to be developed along the north-west coast of
America in the next few decades. Aware however of its obvious
geographical importance, the Tsar had opened navigation between the Peninsula and Okhotsk, thus saving the longer, more
difficult distance from the Anadir. It was Peter who ordered
that vessels should be built at Okhotsk when he heard that none
there were fit for the open sea, and it was he who introduced the
use of the compass at that eastern Siberian port where it had
hitherto been unknown. By his western conquests of Finland and
Karelia he was able to send prisoners of war to work on building
ships and yards in Kamchatka, and on the neighbouring
Siberian seaboard.

To find out whether "The Big Land" to the east of Siberia
was really separated from the Russian mainland, had, as we
know, been one of the most compelling wishes in the last years
of the Tsar's life. That question, of course, was inseparable from
the feasibility or otherwise of a North-East Passage. "You are to
go to Kamchatka and beyond . . . and find out whether Asia and
America are joined," he had told those two officers, mentioned
earlier, Yefreimov and Luchin. And one of the Tsar's last acts
was to give directions by his own hand for the First Great
Northern Expedition which the Danish sea captain, Vitus Bering,
was to lead. The instructions are explicit : "You shall endeavour
to discover, by coasting with these vessels (two were to be built)
whether the country towards the north, of which at present we
have no distinct knowledge, is part of America or not." Peter
was far-seeing enough to realise how valuable the outermost
parts of his empire would become. By his voyage Deshniev had
proved that Asia and America were continents divided from
each other, but his enterprise was known to comparatively few
people, and his actual passage through the Strait was credited
by fewer people still. Peter the Great although he did once write
that "the coast running north of Kamchatka seems to be part
of America," was, as we remarked earlier, inclined to accept
Deshniev's achievement as proof of the existence of a strait between the two continents. But he sought final confirmation on
the matter. He had seen the map drawn by Guillaume

Delisle,[1] "Premier Géographe du Roi", in which the compiler had shown a range of mountains stretching across Siberia, and suddenly coming to a stop with the words, "It is not known whether the range ends here or continues into another continent." So Peter's instructions to Bering were to start from Kamchatkan waters and sail north till he reached the land where Asia and America were popularly supposed to join one another. He was carefully to record his observations. The Tsar however, died before the results of the expedition were made known. It was unfortunate for him that one of the greatest questions in his life remained unanswered at the time of his death.

The Government of his widow, the Empress Catherine I, continued in the Far East the projects of the late Tsar, for by this time the era of free enterprise exemplified in the exploits of the Stroganovs, was changing to one of planned expansion, whose motives were the absorption of vast new territories, and the acquisition of a Pacific seaboard. Even Deshniev had been prevailed upon to "attend to the interests of the Crown" in his voyage made the year before his actual passage through the Bering Strait in 1648. Maps of the position of the monasteries founded during the seventeenth and eighteenth centuries suggest that the Orthodox Church too, played its part in the Government-directed eastward march of the Slavs.

In 1725 Bering had left St. Petersburg and gone to Kamchatka, where at Okhotsk he was directed to establish docks and to found a nautical school. On the Kamchatka River his men found timber suitable for shipbuilding, and at Nizhne Kamchatsk, twenty miles from the shores of the North Pacific, they built the renowned *St. Gabriel*. With this ship and the *Fortuna*, Bering set sail on 8 June, 1730, following a course north to the Gulf of Anadir, and thence eastwards, but he found that only water lay to the east, and that water separated Asia from America. It was when he reached latitude 67° 11′ N. on the north-east coast of Siberia, that he decided that the two land masses were not joined.

Near Yakutsk where he had set up an iron foundry for supplying anchors for his ships, Bering had access to little-known

[1] His brother, Joseph Nicolas Delisle, who lived in Russia from 1726-1747, founding there a school of astronomy and geography, had published in 1752 *Carte des nouvelles découvertes au nord de la Mer du Sud*, accompanied by a Memoir in which he quoted reports made to him verbally by Bering after his voyages. (English translation 1754.) See further, L. Breitfuss, *Early Maps of N. E. Asia and of the lands around the North Pacific : controversy between G. F. Müller and N. Delisle (Imago Mundi, III, p. 87)*.

maps of a much earlier date, based on the voyages of Cossacks. But it was only in 1736—too late, as we have said, to be of use in the first Bering expedition—that Deshniev's own account of his voyage round the north-east corner of Asia was discovered by the German historian Gerhard Friedrich Müller. (The Danish navigator himself regarded as reliable, however, the information he received in Yakutsk concerning that voyage which possibly had covered the whole distance from the Kolima to the Anadir.) Too late also for Bering's first expedition was the publication in 1739 of a map of eastern Siberia, partly based on an earlier one of eastern China made by the Jesuits.

Few maps however were as correct as the Barents one of 1611, referred to on p. 73. In most of the pre-Bering maps the Icy Cape is shown as the most easterly part of Asia, but Bering ascertained that this cape lay farther to the east, i.e. Siberia stretched farther towards America than was formerly believed. Indeed, the empire of the Tsars was found to extend forty-eight degrees farther in this direction than had been supposed.[1] Nevertheless much remained to be corrected by cartographers long after the Danish discoverer's time, for even by 1754 a Russian map of that year shows the American continent with a great promontory advancing towards Kamchatka in the region of latitude 50° to 60°.[2] This map, published under the auspices of Müller, and preserved at the Imperial Academy of Sciences, St. Petersburg, is believed to have been based chiefly on the discoveries of Bering and his Russian fellow-voyager Chirikov. Müller, however, later acknowledged the grave error in the 1754 map, and it was not repeated in the one of 1773 made by the Russian fur traders. What is particularly interesting in this connection is the fact that a map printed nearly two hundred years before Müller's first one, and known as the "De Orbe Novo of Peter Martire", shows a superior knowledge of the contour of the north Pacific shore of America. (A copy of the 1587 edition of this Map is in the library of the Royal Geographical Society.) Again, Francisco de Gualle, Spanish captain and pilot, reported after his voyage from Acapulco, Mexico, to the islands east of Japan, that the ocean between Japan and America was broader by many hundreds of leagues than contemporary maps suggested. But the belief that the North American continent bulged far out towards

---

[1] See Harris's *Collection of Voyages;* Vol. II, p. 1,024.
[2] See also Wm. Coxe's *Account of the Russian Discoveries between Asia and America.* Appendix I, p. 280.

Kamchatka persisted for long, and for this the Spaniards were no doubt partly responsible. Their early maps after Magellan's voyage deliberately represented the Pacific as being much narrower than they knew to be the case, in order that the Philippines might appear to fall within the Spanish imperium. (In general however, the weaknesses in showing longitudinal distances were mainly due to imperfect instruments and methods of observation.) Even in the Mercator and the Ortelius Maps the ocean area was distorted by the western coast of America being drawn so far in the direction of Japan. In the Venetian map of North America by Zaltieri, in 1566, Cipangu actually appears nearer the American than the Asian littoral, and part of the American coast takes a great sweep towards the "Golfo Chinan". Peter the Great was no exception to the majority of his contemporaries in believing that the distance across the North Pacific Ocean was much less than was really the case.

Bering's first expedition fell short of its full purpose, which in addition to finding out whether a sea passage connected the Pacific Ocean with the Frozen Sea, was to explore the northeastern coastline of Siberia. Bering, who in passing through the Strait had discovered the island of St. Lawrence, had turned back before reaching the mouth of the Kolima River. But in his report he said he concluded he *had* ascertained that Asia and America were separate continents, since "there was no more land to the north, nor did any land join the Chukchi or East Capes, and so I turned back." After rounding Chukotski Noss he had reached latitude 67° 18'. His fellow-voyager Chirikov however, had taken the view that unless they reached the mouth of the Kolima River they could not establish for certain the question as to whether the two continents were really separate. Bering pointed out that to continue on the ship's course would mean that the ice would close in before they could get back to Kamchatka, and the counsels of those who supported him in pressing for immediate return had prevailed.

On none of his expeditions was Bering fortunate in his crew, and for officers he had to rely much on non-Russians. According to one authority,[1] over half of the officers, many of the mates, and all the doctors were foreigners. "It had been the intention to recruit the expedition through the voluntary service of Russians, but the native officers showed but little inclination in this direction, and it was found necessary to fill the vacancies

[1] Lauridsen, *The Discovery of Bering Strait*. (Griggs Co., Chicago, 1889); p. 77.

by draft."[1] The most important part of the second expedition—the surveying of the north-east Arctic coast and the charting of the Bering Peninsula—was the work of Lassenius, a fellow Dane. From his fellow-countryman Spangberg too, Bering received great help. It was well for him that so many foreigners did enlist in his service, for the incompetency of some of the Russian officers was such that even in crossing the Okhotsk bar one of the vessels was stranded, and all the ship's bread was lost. The loss of any stores at all was a serious matter, considering that so many of the supplies had been sent right across Siberia, shipped on the Lena and Yudoma, dragged across the Stanovoy Mountains, and thence conveyed by the Urak River and by sea to Okhotsk. Indeed the preliminary parts of Bering's expeditions are, as feats of organisation, to be admired no less than his voyages.

His second expedition had been still more specific in purpose than his first. To start with, more definite data were to be given regarding the relations to each other of the American and Asian continents. His instructions show that his first report had failed to convince the Imperial Cabinet and the Empress that a sea passage really did divide the Old World and the New, for he received directions as to what should be done if the two continents were found to be joined. It is strange how long the Russian governments remained doubtful as to the reality of the separation of Siberia and America, despite the reports of Bering and others. As late as 1764 the Empress Catherine commissioned Lieut. Syndt of the British Navy to undertake a voyage to settle this question.

But when for the second time Bering had left Avacha on the Kamchatka River and sailed north, he had also instructions to investigate a good deal more than the feasibility of a North-East Passage. It is true that the Danish captain himself had proposed that the Siberian coast should be charted from the Ob to the Lena, but the Government had extended the scope of the enquiry to the mouth of the Anadir River. The western shores of North America and of Mexico, the Kurile Islands and Japan were also to be explored by Bering. Sakhalin he was to take in his stride, so to speak, and such minor undertakings as the opening up of new industries in the unexplored regions of the Siberian littoral were expected of him too. This one-time commander in the Baltic Fleet indeed thought himself lucky that he

[1] Lauridsen, *The Discovery of Bering Strait*. (Griggs Co., Chicago, 1889); p. 78.

was not required to annex large areas of Central Asia, in which the Russian Government was then much interested. Russian ambitions seemed limitless; imperial expansion was a primary motive of the Government's concern to open up a North-East Passage. Projected acquisitions of territory in the Far East and on the western coast of North America could be maintained much more cheaply if a seaway were opened from the White Sea to the North Pacific. And so the second Bering expedition was to be conducted in a scientific spirit; geographical and astronomical observations were to be made, particularly as aids to navigation along the difficult coast of eastern Siberia. On this voyage the Danish explorer had the assistance of Lieut. Walton in the *Hope*.

Bering's third expedition commenced in 1740 when, under instructions from the Empress Anne, he sailed from Okhotsk to Petropavlovsk on Kamchatka. Here, in the *St. Peter*, accompanied by Commander Chirikov in the *St. Paul*, he saw for the last time the snow-capped volcano Avacha rising above Petropavlovsk, the harbour which under him had grown into Russia's premier port in the Far East. In July he sighted the volcano known as St. Elias in Alaska. After landing on St. Elias Island Bering started to make the return voyage, but died on an island later to bear his name in the Kommandorskis, the group which also commemorates in its name the commander of the expedition. It had also been the wish of his fellow voyagers to give the name of "New Russia" to that part of the American coast which they had mapped (and to a point farther north— 59°—than any up to that time truly recorded.[1])

During Bering's second voyage, Shestakov, the Cossack provincial Governor in Siberia, had sent out a force by sea to subdue the Chukchis. This company, sailing in Bering's ship *St. Gabriel*, led by Gvosdov, and Ivan Fedorov, had passed Cape Chukotski and landed on the Little Diomede, where they had sighted the coast of America. This is said to have been the first expedition to do so. But neither in this case, nor in that of Bering, did the Russian Government make public till long afterwards the accounts of these voyages. In this respect the Russians differed from the British, who, quite soon after the expeditions made by Cook and Vancouver, published reports of both. The sea-otter pelts brought to Kamchatka by the survivors of the last

[1] See letter 15.11.1742 of Lieut. Waxel, Officer in Command after Bering's death. This was sent to Admiralty College, St. Petersburg, from Petropavlovsk.

Bering expedition, had opened the eyes of the Russian Government to the great potential wealth of the fur-bearing regions, a fact which that Government was anxious should not be revealed to others. The first recorded price of a cargo of skins taken by the *promyschleni* was 122,000 roubles. The report also of the merchants Golikov and Shelikov on the immense field for exploitation on the American mainland and the Alaskan islands, came at a time when the near islands of Siberia were no longer profitable to seal hunters. More ambitious enterprises were needed.[1] Hence the Siberian merchant Serebrennikov in 1743, organised the first voyage for the specific purpose of carrying the "fur belt" from Siberia to North America.

The policy of Catherine the Great (who ruled Russia in the time of Shelikov) was not so far-sighted in the Pacific as in the Mediterranean. Of the Amur River it is true she did say "if it were useful only as a convenient route to supply our possessions in Kamchatka and on the Sea of Okhotsk, its possession would be important." But she did nothing about it. And she refused to press for the Chinese to open a port to her fur traders; of these speculators in Russian-America she said "they may trade where they like, but I will provide neither ships nor money." The opening of a Chinese seaport would have been a boon to the Russian merchants, as will be seen from the following brief description of the complicated route they had to use to reach the market at Kiatcha. Their wares were sent from Petersburg and Moscow to Tobolsk, and thence down the Irtysh to its confluence with the Ob. From there the goods were shipped up the Narim to the Ket, and taken thence by portages to the Yenesei. Up that river they were conveyed to the Siberian waterways of the Tunguska and the Angara to Irkutsk, then ferried across Lake Baikal, and up the Selenga River. The wonder is that anything ever reached Kiatcha market. The journey often took more than one summer, as many of the rivers are only navigable in spring. The use of a Northern Sea Route, and facilities at a Chinese port, would surely have lengthened the lives of some of those fretted merchants!

But the attempt to find that "passage from the Pacific to the Atlantic"—in the words of the contemporary Admiralty sailing

---

[1] The earlier prosperity of the seal fishing off Siberia would appear to have been revived later, for Gerrare, writing in 1903, stated that "the Russian Company to whom the fishing is leased take about 30,000 head annually." See *Greater Russia*. (Heinemann, 1903); p. 194.

directions—made by the English explorer Captain James
Cook, had added knowledge to that existing of the Bering
Sea and Bering Strait. In 1777 in the 962-ton *Resolution*, Cook
started on his voyage from New Zealand, and sailed north up the
coast of the American continent, his highest latitude attained
being 79° 29'. His discoveries there included the gulf which
he christened Bristol Bay, on the north shore of the Alaska
Peninsula, and the cape that he described as "this point of land
which I named Cape Prince of Wales, the more remarkable by
being the western extremity of all America, hitherto unknown."
This was in latitude 65° 46' N., which he reached in 1778. He
also found the inlet later to be christened Cook River, which he
had first believed might lead him to the Polar Sea. On the Asian
side he reached latitude 65° 56' N. and he called that point
Cape North. As far as is known no Russian had ever reached by
sea—coming up from the south—a point as far north on this
littoral. On the return voyage, when his ship called at Unalaska,
Cook met Russians who showed sufficient knowledge of the
Alaskan coast to be able to point out to him some errors on
his charts. The scientific nature of this, his third and last
voyage, is clear from his Journal, which describes his soundings in the Arctic, and gives much information about the
currents.

One of the main advances in knowledge resulting from
Cook's expedition, was the confirmation of the discovery made
earlier by Bering that the Old World and the New were much
nearer each other across the Bering Sea than had commonly
been supposed. Even on a map of 1773, preserved in St. Petersburg Academy of Sciences, twenty degrees marked the narrowest point in the Bering Strait.[1] We have remarked how long
prevailed the doubts of governments and individuals as to the
validity of Deshniev's and Bering's conclusions that they had
found the way from Polar to Pacific waters. Even James Burney,
who voyaged with Cook through the Bering Strait, was not
convinced that Asia and America did not join somewhere north
of the point they had reached. Cape Shalagaski, he suggested,
was an isthmus linking the Old and New Worlds, and he read
a paper to that effect before a learned society in London. It is
surprising too, that (even allowing for the fact that he lived long
before the time of Burney) so learned a man as Samuel Purchas

---

[1] Reprinted by permission of the Publishers, The Arthur H. Clark
Company, from *Russian Expansion on the Pacific*, by Frank A. Golder;
p. 149.

should have thought that America was joined to Asia, as he states in *Hakluytus Posthumus.*[1]

After Cook's death, Capt. Charles Clerke took the *Resolution* up to the Bering Strait, but was unable to get through the ice. Ten years later the Russian navigator Gerassim Pribylov, sailing through the Bering Sea, discovered the two islands now known as St. Paul and St. George, which, together with three smaller ones, bear the name of the Pribylov Islands. When their discoverer first heard through the fog the barking of the seals, he little knew that he had stumbled on the greatest seal grounds in the world, and that when these islands were eventually ceded to America with Alaska, the seal herd was "estimated to have been about 2,000,000 animals."[2]

The island of St. Matthew had already been found by Lieut. Syndt, R.N., but this was not properly charted till Feodor Litke, one of the most celebrated of the nineteenth-century Russian navigators, explored the coasts of the Bering Sea.

From the other end of the Siberian Sea Route attempts had been made to find a north-east passage before the days of Bering, before even the days of the early Cossack migrations. Some of the earliest accounts of these efforts are to be found in the Novgorod Chronicle[3] which tells how the Russian nobles penetrated the region of the Ob and made their way to the sea from the beginning of the twelfth to the middle of the fifteenth century. "Perhaps," say the authors of *Russia from the Varangians to the Bolsheviks,* "as early as the time of Cnut the Great, the Novgorod pioneers had penetrated to the White Sea,"[4] and they remind us how, about the year 1096, Novgorodians had "come into touch with that corner of Asia between the Urals and the Ob estuary which was known to the Russians of that age as *Yugra.*" Maps of the Ob region were in existence before the Stroganovs had left Novgorod to adventure in Siberia, and shortly after, by 1593, the Cossacks had established a post at Berezob on the Ob, in latitude 64° N. The idea of using the Arctic route as a trade-way to the timber and fur regions at the deltas of the great rivers of the north, had stirred the minds of

---

[1] Jackson, Son, and Company, Glasgow. James MacLehose, Glasgow, 1905; Vol. III, p. 192.

[2] C. L. Andrews, *The Story of Alaska.* (Lowman & Hanford Co., Seattle, 1931); p. 134.

[3] Новгородская Лѣтописъ.

[4] R. Beazley, N. Forbes, and G. A. Birkett. (Oxford University Press, 1918); p. 47. Reproduced by permission of the Clarendon Press, Oxford.

ENGRAVING OF THE ROYAL PROCESSION,
MOSCOW, 1722

(Reproduced by courtesy of Messrs. T. Werner Laurie, Ltd., from "Peter the Great," by Georges Oudard)

THIS depicts the Nautical Masquerade which, by order of Peter the Great, continued for five days in Moscow, the Tsar's intention being to make the citizens believe that the victory of Nystadt had been won for them by their fleet. In the three-masted ship, drawn by fifteen horses, and mounted with guns, can be seen the Emperor, and during the actual procession ship's exercises were carried out under his command. The Tsar even climbed the mast, to the astonishment of the crowds thronging the streets of the capital. A pinnace in which seamen were heaving the lead into the snow, was another attraction in this fantastic pageant.

English traders as well as Muscovite merchants and Cossack hunters. Even in the time of Henry VIII two English merchants, Robert Thorne and Roger Barlow, had written a treatise called *The Declaration of the Indies* intended to be sent to the king, proposing that his country should find a way along the northern coast of Asia to Cathay—a way which, once discovered, should be an exclusively English route. Of the new lands to be found, the authors remarked: "To which places there is left but one way to discover, which is into the North, for that of the four partes of the worlde, it seemeth three parts are discovered by other Princes." The document, written in 1530, points out that if the Arctic sea be navigable, then "there is no doubt, but sayling Northward and passing the Pole, descending to the Equinoctial line, we shall hit these [Spice] islands." Thorne and Barlow in representing to King Henry that his realm is "the nearest and aptest of all other to the North partes," were considering only the kingdoms of Spain and of Portugal— the former having claimed "all the Indies and Seas" to the "Occidentall", and the Portuguese to the "Oriental" of the Papal Line. It does not appear to have occurred to them that the Emperor of Russia was the prince most favourably situated for the promotion of a northern sea route to the East.

In 1553 the expedition of Hugh Willoughby and Richard Chancellor had opened the sea-way to Muscovy. In the *Buonaventura*, Chancellor, who was acting as Pilot-General, had reached St. Nicholas Bay, and had landed near the site of the present Archangel. Here he had astonished the natives "with the strange greatnesse of the shippe," which, though so small a one for such a hazardous voyage, was to men accustomed only to boats, a terrifying spectacle. Chancellor had thence made his way overland to the Russian capital. His fellow-voyager, Hugh Willoughby, in the *Bona Esperanza*, had perished off the coast of Lapland, and a third vessel, the *Bona Confidentia*, had been lost. But in those days of Cabot, in whose service many of these brave mariners were engaged, so confident were such men of finding the way to the Indies by a Polar passage, that they had their ships protected by an outer casing of lead, having heard that in the tropics certain worms "were destructive of wooden sheathing." In Willoughby's expedition the three little ships, of 160, 120 and 90 tons respectively, had braved ice which even specialised Soviet icebreakers of 10,000 tons have sometimes found formidable. On his return voyage to England, Chancellor had taken with him the Russian ambassador who was visiting the English Court to arrange for treaties of commerce. In a storm off the north of Scotland the ship was lost, and Chancellor, in his successful efforts to save the life of the ambassador, lost his own.

Stephen Burrough, who had been master of Chancellor's ship, on a later voyage in the pinnace *Searchthrift*, got almost to the Kara Sea. A mariner in a passing vessel told him that he (Burrough) had reached Novaya Zemlya; he certainly did sail among its satellite islands, and he is believed to have been the first foreigner to have sighted this archipelago.[1] Later he anchored in those off Vaigatch; for long the passage now known as Vaigatch was called Burrough Strait. These Englishmen were the first known venturers to cover the initial stage of the North-East Passage. With the end of that route ever in mind, the promoters of an expedition of 1555, undertaken by Gray and Killingworth in the *Edward Buonaventura*, had in their Articles of Commission, the following order: "It is to be had in mind that you use all ways and means possible to learn how men may pass from Russia, either by land or by sea, to Cathaia."

Anthony Jenkinson, the celebrated traveller, who acted as ambassador-at-large for Queen Elizabeth through the Tsar's dominions, was convinced of the feasibility of such a Passage, and over the heads of the Muscovy Company—of which he was also a servant—he appealed direct to the Queen that a voyage of exploration should be launched. In a debate in Council with Sir Humphrey Gilbert, he assembled the reasons for his proposal, and though no voyage resulted from his efforts, he had, while in Russia, aroused the interest of Ivan IV in the project, also in the promotion of commerce between England and the Tsar's territories. Ivan had asked him to urge Elizabeth to further trade with Muscovy, and to send out English craftsmen in the Company's ships. Jenkinson, in a letter during his first visit to Russia, has left a quaint account of happenings at St. Nicholas, which these early merchant venturers made their principal port and where, says the writer, on the headland called Swetinoz at the entrance to the bay, was a statue at which mariners made offerings of "butter, meale, and other victuals, thinking that unless they did so their barkes or vessels there should perish."[2] Sir Humphrey Gilbert in his map of 1576,

---

[1] See also T. A. Taracouzio, *Soviets in the Arctic*. (The Macmillan Company, New York, 1938); p. 43. Reference by permission of the Publishers.

[2] *Hakluyt*, Vol. I, p. 411. See also this book, pp. 75, 76.

which illustrated his *Discourse of a Discoverie of a new passage to Cataia*, describes the voyage of Ohthere[1] in the time of King Alfred the Great, by which "it appeareth that he went the very same way that now doe yearly trade by St. Nicolas into Moscovia, which way no man in our age knew for certaintie to be by sea, until it was since discovered by our English men in the time of King Edward the sixt."[2] Nils Nordenskiöld is among the authorities who believed that this Norwegian mariner got to the estuary of the Dvina, or at least to the Mezen.[3]

More than twelve hundred years before the voyage of Ohthere, latitude 65° N. was certainly reached by the Greek navigator Pytheas of Massalia; it is quite possible that he crossed the Arctic Circle. This Phocean mariner who was a learned geographer and astronomer, left Marseille probably about 327 B.C. on a voyage to "Ultima Thule"; the Greeks of his day had felt the pull of the Magnetic North and knew the lure of the Northern Lights and the Midnight Sun. So leaving the tideless Mediterranean, Pytheas passed through the Pillars of Hercules, set his course north for the stormy seas ahead, and made his way round Britain till he reached the Shetland Isles. The land which he found after that was for long believed to be Iceland, but in Nansen's view it was Norway.[4]

Bjarmaland, about which Ohthere had given many details, is generally believed to have referred to the south side of the Kola Peninsula, by the river Varzuga, and in Nansen's view Norwegians must have reached this part of the White Sea before the visit of Ohthere. We know that the Rus via Novgorod and Ladoga had made their way to its shores before the end of the ninth century, and we find an Arab writer, Ibn Ruste, referring in A.D. 912 to Rus trading with the 'Wisu'—people dwelling

[1] Ohthere, a whaler from northern Norway, in a year variously dated between 871 and 889, sailed from Halgoland to the shores of the White Sea, and on to the delta of the Dvina, in search of ivory and skins. He gave King Alfred, in 890, an account of his voyage, and in the first chapter of Alfred's Anglo-Saxon translation (*Hormesta*) of the History of Orosius —the work of a Spanish Christian of the fifth century—the narrative of Ohthere is incorporated. Ohthere's exploit however, was eclipsed by that of Erik, son of Harald the Fair, who, when only twelve, set out as leader of five small ships and reached Bjarmaland on the White Sea in A.D. 960.

[2] *Hakluyt*, Vol. V, p. 97. (With acknowledgments to Jackson, Son & Co., Glasgow, and to J. M. Dent & Sons, London.)

[3] *The Voyage of the Vega Round Asia and Europe*, translated by Alexander Leslie. (Methuen & Co., 1883.)

[4] *In Northern Mists*. (Heinemann, 1911); Vol. I, p. 60.

on the coasts of the White Sea. In an old Novgorod document dated 1137, Professor Platonov has found a reference to a Russian settlement on the shores of the White Sea. Russian chronicles tell of hostile expeditions by sea between Norway and the Kola Peninsula a century before Willoughby and Chancellor reached the White Sea. In 1555 Stephen Burrough had counted thirty Russian ships fishing for salmon, and others hunting walrus, off the Kola Peninsula, so that even if the Russians had only made short voyages as opposed to the long ones of the Dutch and English, at least they were not strangers to the Northern Ocean at the time of the Tudor voyages of exploration. But that they were not then settled on the Kola Peninsula is clear from the visit there in 1553 of Sir Hugh Willoughby, who when he wintered at the mouth of the Varzuga found no inhabitants. When he and his companions later perished off Kegor on the coast of Lapland, it was Finnish fishermen, not Russians, who discovered their ships. The fact of most importance is however, that it was the voyage of the English navigators which brought Russia out of her isolation and opened for her a new, though brief, era of maritime trade by the western Arctic routes.

Among the many Englishmen who continued the quest for a short sea-road to Cathay was the tragic figure of Henry Hudson, who, though he was most closely associated with the North-West Passage, was yet, like all explorers of his time, set upon finding the North-East one to the lands of spice and silk. In 1608 when engaged by the Muscovy Company in the *Hopewell* he had reached 81°.[1] On his second voyage on this quest Hudson had touched Spitzbergen and had explored Hakluyt Headland, but pack-ice stopped him from passing between that island and Novaya Zemlya. Had he only sailed southwards he could have worked his way to the Kara Sea.

According to Dr. Taracouzio[2]—outstanding authority on the work of Arctic explorers—the first man to ever reach the river Ob by passing through the Yugorski Strait and across the Kara Sea was the Dutchman, Oliver Brunel, who had first voyaged thither in 1579 on behalf of the Stroganov family of merchants. Seven years later he made an attempt on his own

[1] *Purchas His Pilgrimes.* (James MacLehose, Glasgow, 1905.) Edtd. by S. Douglas Jackson. Vol. XIII, p. 11. Acknowledgments to Jackson, Son and Co., Glasgow.

[2] *Soviets in the Arctic.* Copyright by the Bureau of International Research, Harvard University and Radcliffe College, 1938. Reference by permission of the Publishers, The Macmillan Company, New York; p. 43.

account to reach the East by the Arctic route, but was stopped by ice at Novaya Zemlya. This remarkable man was one of the foremost promoters of Dutch mercantile enterprise on the White Sea.

Efforts to reach the Gulf of Ob were of the most determined nature; at the end of the sixteenth century some of the Cossacks who found their way to the shores of the Arctic were even using the rivers across the Yamal Peninsula to take them from the Kara Sea to the Ob. Using the Mutnaya River and the three linked lakes of Nei-te, they dragged their boats thence overland to Lake Yambu-to and then by the Zelyonnaya River to the Gulf of Ob. The estuary of the latter was described in a letter to the Muscovy Company by one of their agents, Giles Holmes, in 1558, and an account given of the Samoyeds who dwelt along the coasts of that region. Another of the Company's factors, Anthony Marsh, received a letter compiled in 1584 by four Russians whom he had commissioned to find the way to the delta of the Ob. These men by their detailed guide to the route given before starting, show themselves already familiar with that region. And English men, they tell Marsh, have been there already, but were slain by Samoyeds.[1] By sea the route passes Vaygats Island and Novaya Zemlya, they say, "and assure thy selfe that from Vaygats to the mouth of Ob, by Sea, is but a small matter to sayle." Alas that so many mariners found it otherwise.

That same year Bodan, a Russian servant of Marsh's, had led a party to discover the mouth of the Ob from the land. If they did not find the delta they certainly found sables, and so many that the Emperor's wrath was roused; Bodan was seized and thrown into prison. When Marsh protested, and reminded the Tsar of the privileges granted to English traders, it was clear that he was encountering a determined opposition to foreign penetration of the region east of the Ob. "Beyond that river is a warm sea" was a tradition that had become a belief with many Russians. "This Sea," it was said, "pierseth farre into the south parts of Asia."

The privileges pleaded by Anthony Marsh were extended after his time when, in 1605 the Emperor Boris Godunov granted to "the Merchants of England" (named) the right "to come with their ships into our Dominion the County of Dwina, with all manner of Commodities, to trade freely from the Sea side and within our Dominions to the Citie of our Empire of

[1] *Purchas His Pilgrimes*, Vol. XIV, pp. 292, 293.

Mosco."[1] But though they are not to be subject to any "kinde of Custome . . . for passing by any place by water; nor for Customs of their Boats or Head money," they are expressly prohibited from acting as commercial agents for other foreigners.

Boris Godunov, though he had certain sections of the Arctic seaway charted for the first time, discouraged foreign navigation lest the suspected wealth of Siberia should be laid open to other countries. However, until the voivods of Tobolsk and other Siberian settlements, alarmed at the penetration of northern Siberia by foreign traders, persuaded Tsar Michael Fedorovitch to interdict Arctic navigation to foreigners, there was a considerable amount of commercial activity in the region of the Gulf of Ob. An impetus was given to the traffic in furs here by the establishment of a trading post at Mangaseya on the Gulf of Tas, which is part of the Gulf of Ob. The English in particular were actively engaged here. From reports of the voivods of Tobolsk, and from the Novgorod Chronicle, it is, says Nansen, "sufficiently clear that in the latter half of the sixteenth century there was a well-known trading communication along the coast from the Pechora and the White Sea to the Gulf of Obi."[2] But the ukase of 1620 resulted in a complete decline in sealing and trapping along the shores of the Arctic. Despite the reversal of this restriction later by the unconditional promotion of Arctic voyages of discovery, it was not till 1879 that the North-East Passage was made in its entirety.

An important stage on the route had been reached with the discovery of the Strait between Vaigatch Island and the mainland—now known as Yugorski Strait. For long this was attributed to the English voyager Arthur Pet, who had been sent by the Muscovy Company in 1580 in command of the *George*, accompanied by Charles Jackman in the *William*, with special instructions to try and discover a possible "northeast strayte." If there be "a strayte in the passage into the Scithian Seas, the same is specially and with great regard to bee noted as a thing that doeth much import." Pet's name was given to the strait whose discovery made possible the later advances on the North-East Passage, but actually the channel through which he had sailed was probably the Kara Strait. Pet's ship, which was only forty tons, managed to enter the Kara Sea, but was prevented by heavy pack-ice from passing through it. This was the first English expedition to that sea. Later came the Dutch, who, not

---

[1] *Purchas His Pilgrimes*, Vol. XIV, p. 152.
[2] *Through Siberia, the Land of the Future*; p. 440.

wishing to encounter the Spaniards in the southerly latitudes in which they had voyaged on their eastward quests, were driven to seek a new way to the Indies. So in 1594 the United Provinces sent Cornelis Corneliszoon, with William Barents as chief pilot, on an expedition to find the North-East Passage to the Spice Islands. Corneliszoon, having passed Vaigatch Strait, and finding open water beyond, was convinced that the way lay open to the east, but instead of pursuing his course he returned to the Netherlands to report the possibility of doing so! Certain merchants of Amsterdam were impressed enough to fit out two ships with Barents as navigating officer, and sent them under Cornelis Ryp on the same quest. From Bear Island, which was their discovery, these explorers sailed eastward till they found land in latitude 80° 11', and named it Spitzbergen. "This," says the maritime historian Levinus Hulsius, "is unquestionably the first discovery of Spitzbergen."[1] (But the latter was more than probably the land named Svalbardi—Cold Coast—by the Icelandic mariners who discovered it at the end of the twelfth century.) Barents is related to have "met with much ice and abundance of Sea-Monsters, at which the seamen, being much discouraged, they resolved to return home."[2] On his third voyage to those regions, Barents, in 1598, spent the winter on Spitzbergen, but after reaching Novaya Zemlya, in latitude 77°, he died on the voyage back to Lapland as a result of extreme hardship.

After the "rediscovery" of Spitzbergen by Henry Hudson, the Muscovy Company sent Captain Jonas Poole there, and as a result of his visit in 1610 the first whale fishery to be set up by the Company on that land was opened the following year. Scoresby, whose account of Spitzbergen, published in 1820, is a detailed work and provides much of scientific interest, gives in his second volume the history of whaling enterprise there by British, Dutch, Basques, French, Danes, and Hamburgers, but makes no mention of the Russians. The first volume however describes the Russian whalers who had been employed on the island by the White Sea Fishing Company, and who, on the termination of that concern, carried on the fishing by private enterprise, sailing from Archangel, Onega, and other White Sea ports to Spitzbergen. They took with them huts in sections, and stayed the winter on the main island.

[1] *The Collection of Navigations Published by Levinus Hulsius.* (A. Asher, London and Berlin, 1939); Part III, p. 28.
[2] *A Collection of Voyages and Travels.* (Compiled by Awnsham and John Churchill, London, 1704); Vol. I, Introduction p. xviii.

The Muscovy Company in 1613 had obtained a Royal Charter for the monopoly of the Spitzbergen whale fishing. The only exception made was in favour of the French, and from them a special tribute was exacted. Anyone else venturing there was intercepted by the armed vessels of the English. The Dutch, who had set up their first fishing station on Spitzbergen only the year before, naturally continued to defy the prohibition. But despite the clashes between the seamen from Britain and from Holland in these waters of the Far North, they were never slow to help one another in adversity. In 1646 four Englishmen were discovered on an ice floe by a Dutch crew off Spitzbergen, where John Cornelius of Muniken had been sent to catch whales. In the galliot *Delft* he had reached the shores of Spitzbergen, but was unable to anchor in the bay owing to the vast ice-shoals. On one of these his crew spied what they first thought were white bears, but which proved to be sailcloth held up as a distress signal by four Englishmen. These men were all who remained out of an original company of forty-two; the survivors had dug themselves a hole in the ice for shelter, and all they had to eat for some time was a leather belt between them. When rescued by the crew of the Dutch galliot, they "upon their bended knees express'd their Joy and Thankfulness for so unexpected a Deliverance from the Jaws of Death."[1] But only one of the four lived to reach his native land. *6 1589*

The exploits of Barents and of the Dutch whalers above mentioned were followed by those of other voyagers from the Netherlands who in 1670 sailed round the north-east extremity of Novaya Zemlya. (They anticipated by ninety years the Russian voyager Savva Lozhkin for whom the distinction of being the first to sail round Novaya Zemlya has sometimes been claimed. The data given about the latitude of this alleged visit to the north-eastern extremity of this island group is too inconclusive to warrant any definite verdict here.) Though it is true that Stephen Burrough did meet several Russian vessels near these islands in 1556, it is also true that there is no record of any such vessels ever having passed round Novaya Zemlya, as Coxe points out in his history of Russian Arctic Voyages.[2] (Even the celebrated explorer Admiral Litke in 1821 could not make his way round the most northerly of the two main islands, and two hundred and seventy-five years were to pass before Ice Haven was visited again after Barents had anchored there.) Purchas in

---

[1] *A Collection of Voyages and Travels*, Vol. II, p. 429.
[2] P. 371.

His Pilgrimes takes the view that if only the Dutch would give up the idea of trying to get through the Waigatz Strait in ships, and stay instead for two or three years in some haven on the island, making explorations in small boats with native Russians as pilots, they would get to know the whole coastline in this way.

The expedition of Captain John Wood with the *Speedwell* and the *Prosperous* in 1676, was really the last English voyage of importance on "The Cold Ocean" for a hundred years; until Cook's final voyage most of the northern exploration was undertaken by Russians, though, as we have said earlier, few of their expeditions could be called scientific. Wood was convinced of the existence of a North-East Passage; one of the reasons he gave was the story of dead whales cast up at a bay on Korea with English and Dutch harpoons attached to the carcases. It would be profitable, he argued, to trade by sea with Japan, where English cloth would find a ready market. But between the warm seas of the East and the dales of the Yorkshire wool combers stretched the Ice-Way of the North, and brave Wood and his crew failed to get farther than Novaya Zemlya. To them we owe much of our early knowledge of the latter, though Wood had to admit that it was not known whether it was an island or "joyneth to the Continent of Tartaria." His voyage there was commemorated in such names on the island as "King Charles's Snow Hills" and "Point Speedwell". Thereafter the ice remained a seemingly impassable barrier to the stout purpose of intrepid seamen of the British Isles, of Holland, Scandinavia, and Russia. As more than one early eighteenth century geographer pointed out, although the distance from Northern Europe to India via a north-east passage could be much less than the distance involved in the sea route via the Cape, yet the fact that the Arctic seas were frozen would make a voyage by such a passage actually much longer. The age of icebreakers had not yet arrived.

One reason why the Russians felt impelled to push ever eastwards was the knowledge that the farther they went in that direction, the more valuable were the furs they found. In 1640 no less than 6,800 sables were collected, and even the less affluent Cossacks could line their coats with such furs. The opening of a North-East Passage would have made the fur trade an even more profitable one. And the discovery of a northern seaway to the east would have brought to Archangel—so much nearer the Arctic Ocean than was St. Petersburg—a renewal of the prosperity which it had lost after the Baltic ambitions of

Peter I had given the leading place to St. Petersburg. And so continued the struggles of seamen and straining of ships to break through the Frozen Sea.

In the time of Bering, Arctic expeditions (promoted by the Admiralty College, St. Petersburg) were undertaken in sections, viz. : Archangel-Ob ; Ob-Yenesei ; Yenesei-Cape Taimir ; Lena-Anadir. Two Russian vessels, the *Expedition* and the *Ob*, leaving Archangel in 1734, had got through the Kara Sea, as it was then ice-free, and nearly reached the mouth of the Ob. Three years later Lieut. Malygin and Skuratov succeeded, having sailed into the Bay of Ob and anchored off Berezob. At the same time Oftsyn mapped the coastline between the Ob and the Yenesei.

Between the time of the first and second Bering expeditions, a remarkable voyage was made by Lieut. Prontishchev, who, in command of an expedition to the Yenesei-Lena section of the Siberian coast, reached Cape Cheliuskin, the most northerly point on the Asian mainland. With him sailed his young wife, who shared all the privations of the voyage until she died from these hardships. Until the visit of Mme. d'Aunet to Spitzbergen in 1839, Mme. Prontishchev was the first known non-native woman to have reached latitude 77° 48′ N. Two years after the Prontishchev excursion, Selifontov went in 1737 by reindeer sledge along the west coast of the Yamal Peninsula, and from there he later surveyed the mouth of the Ob. But along the whole distance between the Murman coast and the delta of the Lena, there were large tracts which remained uncharted, and in Coxe's work previously mentioned, written in 1780, the author states that from all known evidence "we must conclude the whole space between Archangel and the Lena has never yet been navigated."[1] This view is endorsed by a modern American authority, Commander Greely, U.S.N., who has pointed out[2] that barely two centuries ago more than half of the Arctic coasts were unknown to geographers. Baron von Wrangell too had pointed out how unfavourably the exploration of the north-easterly shores of the Arctic compared with the researches of Franklin and Parry along the North-West Passage.[3]

Knowledge of the hazardous coast beyond the Lena delta, however, was advanced when Cheliuskin, the pilot of Laptev's expedition of 1741, sailing from the Khatanga delta round the east of

[1] P. 309.
[2] *The Polar Regions in the Twentieth Century.* (Harrap & Co., 1929); p.1.
[3] *Narrative of an Expedition to Siberia and the Polar Sea in the Years 1820, 1821, 1822 and 1823.*

theTaimir Peninsula, reached the cape that now carries his name. But still the ice held the ships, and the idea that a perpetual barrier of ice barred the way to vessels seeking a North-East Passage, persisted widely. So too, the view that the North Pole was beyond the reach of man. But in 1774 the Hon. Daines Barrington read a paper[1] at a meeting of the Royal Society in London, in which he assembled many convincing arguments to show that the North Pole could be reached. He pointed out that in 1694, English mariners had proceeded farther than 78°, on the east coast of Spitzbergen,[2] and that earlier still, in 1676, Captain John Wood had reached the west coast of Novaya, Zemlya in latitude 76°. And the Russians, he added, had not only discovered "but lived several years in the island of Maloy Brun, which lies between Spitzbergen and Novaya Zemlya, and extends from latitude 77° 25' to 78° 44' N." (Though Barrington does not mention them, the monks of Solovetski Island had materially assisted several Russian walrus and seal hunting expeditions to the Spitzbergen archipelago in the early eighteenth century.) Dutch settlements had been founded on Amsterdam Island much earlier, i.e. between 1633 and 1643. Barrington gives a list of twenty-two occasions on which latitude 80° had been passed, and it will be noted that of this total, twenty were achieved by Englishmen.

But the failure later of the *Resolution* and the *Discovery* to pass beyond latitude 65° 56' N. in longitude 179° 11' E., revived the belief that a permanent ice-barrier placed an Arctic sea route in the category of chimaeras rather than possibilities. The expedition of Lieut. von Wrangell confirmed the separation of America and Asia, and added considerably to the knowledge of the Arctic coast east of the Kolima. Yet his voyages and those also made in 1821-24 by Admiral Litke, who mapped the coasts of Novaya Zemlya and the Strait of Matochkin, seemed only to prove the impossibility of forcing a passage through the uncharted waters that lay between the Kolima and the Lena.

With one Siberian at least, however, the conviction that the North-East Passage could be made, was a compelling one. Sidorov it was who persuaded the navigator Ivan Krusenstern to investigate the Kara Sea with this objective. Of that voyage, however, nothing further came, and getting no more help from his own countrymen, Sidorov had gone to Sweden and there

[1] *The Possibility of Approaching the North Pole.* (T. & J. Allman, London, 1818); 2nd edition.
[2] See Supplement to Wood and Martens Voyages (1694); p. 179.

had enlisted the support of Baron Nils Nordenskiöld. Sidorov
had offered a reward to any vessel which should reach the
mouth of the Yenesei from Europe, and this was gained by the
English mariner Wiggins, captain of the *Diana*. In 1875 Wiggins had joined Nordenskiöld in the walrus-hunting sloop
Proeven, and had passed the delta of the Yenesei. He indeed,
had sailed many hundreds of miles up the river, to the point
where it is joined by the Kureika. Nordenskiöld started from
Tromsoe in the following year in the *Ymer*, and again reached
the mouth of the Yenesei. Two years afterwards he left Karls-
krona in the *Vega*, a stoutly built whale-steamer, with a strong
team of scientists on board; sailing through Yugorski Shar, at
a time when the Straits were ice-free, Nordenskiöld had passed
through the Kara Sea, and anchored in Taimir Sound. He
had corrected many erroneous beliefs about the Kara Sea—
"the ice-box" to unnumbered mariners—and stated that as
regards the nature of the ice here it was completely different
from that to the north and east of Spitzbergen. Off Tunat
Island, near the delta of the Lena River, the vessel *Lena*, which
had accompanied the *Vega*, now parted from the latter and
went up the river to Yakutsk; she was the first ship which, in
the words of Nordenskiöld, coming from the ocean, reached
the heart of Siberia.[1] Two other Swedish sloops, *Express* and
Fraser, were the first to bring cargoes of grain and tallow from
the Yenesei to Europe, but it was a Russian merchant captain,
Schwannenberg, who brought the first vessel of all from the
Yenesei to the Atlantic in 1877. This was the sloop *Dawn*, built
at Yeneseisk by the Siberian seaway enthusiast, Sidorov.

It was only when Nordenskiöld sailed east of Cape Cheliuskin
that he found the ice became a real obstacle. Finally he had
arrived at a point near the Irpaiki promontory[2] only a few miles
from the open water of the Bering Strait. Nordenskiöld had
almost succeeded in completing the voyage in one season, but
the *Vega* became ice-locked and had to winter in Koliuchin
Bay off the Chukot Peninsula. On 18 July, 1879, she was
released, and made her way through the Strait—the first ship
to make the whole route of the North-East Passage. The next
attempt was not made till 1900, when Baron Toll perished in
the Zaria expedition. Nordenskiöld's success was largely due to
the fact that he realised that the Siberian rivers bring warm

[1] *The Voyage of the Vega Round Asia and Europe*, p. 4.
[2] This was the "North Cape" at which Cook had turned back to the
Bering Strait, 1778.

water in summer to the Arctic seas, and he timed his voyage to take advantage of this. Thus he was able to get round the Bering Sea and to sight the Pacific on 27 September, 1879. In honour of this explorer, Nansen gave the name "Nordenskiöld" to the sea east of the Kara Sea, but in Russian maps it appears as "Laptev" in commemoration of the two navigator brothers for their voyages in that area, 1736-39.

Nordenskiöld's achievement in making the Passage from west to east, was a spur to the Russian Governments of later years to open the Siberian Sea Road from east to west. Their chief aim was to provide north-east Siberia with a cheaper route than the one down the Lena and thence overland by sleighs to the Polar port of Kolima. After the exploration of the Kara Sea route to the Yenesei River, it did become possible to consider a commercial waterway as a means of transport complementary to the Siberian railroad. The Government saw that Siberia would remain a sparsely populated region unless a seaway could be developed for the export of her timber and surplus harvests The cost of rail transport for the first item would make the dispatch of that commodity unprofitable. Hence the administration of that time reversed the tendency of many of their predecessors to favour transport by road, and of some of their successors to favour carriage by rail at the expense of the sailing routes. They gave all possible encouragement to the English company which in 1896 was formed for Arctic trading, and which had managed to get three steamers as far as Turukhansk, six hundred miles up the Yenesei. When the company established an agency on that river at Krasnoyarsk, the Russian Government, gratified by these English efforts to create a regular sea service from the West to Siberia, reduced by one half all the customs dues on the English goods, and granted the company various mining concessions. In 1905 a fleet of twenty-two ships reached the Yenesei by the Northern Sea Route, and all the vessels returned safely to their western destinations.

The next important step taken by the Government was to organise the Russian Hydrographical Expedition to the Arctic, a most important event, but one to which surprisingly little reference is made in contemporary accounts of modern Russian Arctic exploration. Preliminary voyages were made in 1911 when the steamer *Kolima*, of the Volunteer Fleet, sailed from Vladivostock to the Kolima River and back, and this marked the commencement of a regular steamship service between these points. In the same year the icebreaker *Vaigatch* carried

THE CHELIUSKIN

On August 10th, 1933, the specially designed ship *Cheliuskin* left Murmansk with a picked crew and a scientific staff, some of whom were women, in an attempt to reach Vladivostock by the North-East Passage. The expedition nearly succeeded in its venture, and was indeed able to send out a radio message "We are in sight of the Bering Strait." But the ship became crushed in the ice, and had to be abandoned in latitude 68° 18' N., in longitude 172° 50' E. The life of the voyagers for two months in an ice camp, and their final rescue by Soviet fliers, is one of the epics of the Arctic.

It has been natural, for reasons connected with the geographical situation of the U.S.S.R., to regard the Russian interest in ice-breakers as one almost exclusively concerned with northern latitudes. But the exploratory voyages of the Russian commander, Captain Bellingshausen, in the South Polar Seas, 1819–1821, are not forgotten in Russia today. Bellingshausen's cruise was intended to supplement the expedition made in 1772 by the English navigator, Captain James Cook, whose work was always held in the greatest esteem by the Russian sea captains. "Should anyone possess the resolution and the fortitude to elucidate this point [the existence or otherwise of a vast Antarctic continent] by pushing yet further south than I have done," wrote Cook, "I shall not envy him the fame of his discovery, but I make bold that the world will derive no benefit from it."

Only the future however, can decide whether the presence of minerals on the Antarctic continent is as negligible as is believed to be the case. Meantime, for reasons widely different from each other—the extension of whaling ventures, and the investigation of strategic possibilities—interest in the future of icebreakers is likely to increase.

out a survey of the coast from Cape Deshniev to the mouth of the Kolima, and charted part of Wrangell Island, of which little was known since Captain Kellett's time. One look at the map will reveal its strategic value today. Its name derives from the explorer who in 1820 had sailed into the Arctic from the mouth of the Kolima, but his expedition came only within forty or fifty miles of the island. The discovery of this important place is credited to Captain Kellett, R.N., after his voyage in search of Sir John Franklin, 1849, but the first news of its existence was probably that brought to Yakutsk by the Cossack Stadukhin in 1645. However, as Stefansson has said,[1] there seems to be no record of any Russian ship having actually reached the island before 1911. Known for long as "Kellett Land", the island was taken over in 1881 in the name of the United States by Captain Hooper during his search for the Arctic voyager, Commander De Long, U.S.N. The Canadian flag was raised here in 1914 and the British in 1921. But Ramsay MacDonald's Government had decided to renounce British rights here, and meantime an American company, the Carl Lomen Trading Corporation, had prepared to buy on Wrangell the holdings of Stefansson's Arctic Exploration and Development Company. But that same year, 1924, the Russian ice-breaker *Krasni Oktiabr* landed a party of Soviet explorers who took over the island, and in 1926 Russia formally included it among the lands claimed by the "Decree on the Territorial Rights of the Soviet Union in the North."

In the view of Stefansson, who had been interested in the question of the ultimate sovereignty of Wrangell, British owner-ship had been made good by occupation; America had the next best claim. "But Russia seems to realise the value of Wrangel Island better than any other country".[2] The island is rich in furs and fishes, but it was not only for economic reasons that Commander Davidov, leader of the *Krasni Oktiabr* adventure, rated it highly. To keep it out of the hands of British and Americans was to him a first necessity, for, in his own words, "the island would have made an ideal aerial base because it possesses a natural plateau".[3] Certainly the United States, had she taken that territory, would now be in possession of a place

---

[1] *The Adventure of Wrangel Island.* Copyright 1925 by V. Stefansson. Reference by permission of the Publishers, The Macmillan Company, New York; p. 395.

[2] *Ibid.*, Quotation by permission of the Publishers, p. 292.

[3] Vilhjalmur Stefansson, *The Adventure of Wrangel Island*, p. 309.

of considerable strategic value. The wisdom of the Soviet acquisition of the island is obvious today.

In 1913 Boris Vilkitski had discovered the large island formation to which he gave the name of Nicholas II Land, but which is now known as Severnaya Zemlya, "Northern Land"—territory about which nearly all the knowledge we possess is due to the Russians. But no scientific expedition visited the archipelago till 1930; in that year the icebreaker *Sedov* arrived with a team of Soviet scientists and the island group was surveyed for the first time.

During the period of pre-Revolutionary activity in the Arctic, the expedition to Franz Josef Land was made in 1912 by Georgi Sedov in his attempted excursion to the Pole in the *Sv. Foka*. The Russian flag was set up on Cape Flora by Captain Isliamov two years later. The Austrian explorers Weyprecht and Payer in the *Tegethof*, 1872, had discovered satellite islands of the group; eight years passed before the main islands were visited, when Leigh Smith in the *Eira* made investigations there and returned with valuable data. Nansen during his drift in the *Fram* discovered fresh islands in this archipelago.

Early descriptions of Spitzbergen had been given by Friedrich Martens as a result of the Wood-Martens voyage of 1676. Then came those of the Scottish whaler, Scoresby, in 1820, and were followed by the accounts of Parry in 1827. It is interesting to recall that in 1773, when Captain J. C. Phipps in the *Racehorse* had reached the north-western extremity of that land in latitude 80° 48′ N., his coxswain, a lad of fifteen, was none other than the future Lord Nelson, who, in a daring but foolhardy encounter with a Polar bear narrowly escaped death. Phipps, during this voyage, made with the intention of reaching the North Pole, had surveyed some of the north-westerly islands of Spitzbergen, and Greely, in his *Handbook of Arctic Discoveries*,[1] describes him as having reached "a higher latitude than any of his predecessors", but the writer has also said of the Dutch skippers, that "hundreds of them passed annually for a century the eightieth parallel".[2] Scoresby however passed beyond any authenticated northing when he and his father in the *Resolution* reached 81° 30′ N. in 1806. That same year Captain Broke, sailing in the *Shannon* with the English whaling fleet, recorded much of interest about the coast of Spitzbergen in the neighbourhood of Hambro Creek, where he referred to the small settlement of Russians. The latter had been engaged by the

[1] Sampson Low, Marston, & Co.,1896; pp. 65, 66.   [2] *Ibid.*, p. 166.

factors of Archangel to hunt the walrus and the whale, and they had, says Broke, reached this creek in "small brig-rigged vessels of about seventy or eighty tons burthen of a clumsy construction".[1]

The last notable expedition to Spitzbergen was undertaken in 1890 by Gustaf Nordenskiöld, who sailed there from Tromsoe in the yacht *Lofoten*. In barely thirty years Sweden had sponsored eight well-equipped voyages to Spitzbergen[2] for purposes of scientific discovery which, in the case of the 1890 visit, had brought to light many facts hitherto unknown about Large Red Bay. Thus, step by step, new light was thrown on the lands that lay along the routes of circum-Polar navigation. How much has been accomplished since Scoresby wrote his *Account of the Arctic Regions* is apparent when we remember that even as late as 1820 the author opened his book with a discussion on the "Celebrated Question of the Existence of a Sea Communication between the Atlantic and the Pacific Oceans of the North"— a question whose resolution has been primarily one of such immense strategic gain to the Soviet Union.

As the charting by Baron Nils Nordenskiöld on his voyage along the North-East Passage had been incomplete, the ice-breakers *Taimir* and *Vaigatch* were sent to take part in the 1914-15 Hydrographical Expedition from Vladivostock to Archangel, with instructions to survey the seaboard from the Chukot to the Taimir Peninsula, i.e. half the extent of Russia's Arctic coast. The voyage was definitely undertaken as one of a scientific nature, and not, as in the case of the *Kolima's* effort in 1911, a commercial venture. The two vessels, each of 1,500 tons displacement, had the advantage over ships of an earlier day in being equipped with wireless. They did not however make the passage to Archangel in one navigational season, being obliged to winter off the Taimir Peninsula.

The favourable report on the prospects of developing the Northern Route as a commercial channel, given by Fridtjof Nansen after his voyage in the *Correct* from Tromsoe to the Yenesei delta, is discussed in a later section of this book. That the route was not developed much earlier than has been the case, was due to the intervention of the first world war. In 1912,

---

[1] Rev. J. G. Brighton: *Admiral Sir P. B. V. Broke, Bt.* (Sampson Low, Son, & Marston, 1866.)

[2] Gustaf Nordenskiöld, *Report of the Swedish Expedition to Spitzbergen, 1890,* translated by R. Dunn-Gardiner, F.R.G.S. (The Eastern Press, Ltd., London, 1933); p. 7.

realising that in the event of a world conflict there was a probability that Turkey would close the Dardanelles, the Imperial Government saw that Russia might in this way be cut off from foreign sources of supply, and it would therefore be essential to secure delivery from Siberia. This would involve the development of the Northern Sea Passage. The benefit of that route had already been demonstrated in 1893, when metal for construction of the Trans-Siberian Railway had been brought to the mouth of the Yenesei, and then shipped up the river. The advantage of a northern seaway was quite clear to the Tsarist Government before the end of the nineteenth century, but its urgency had for a time been less apparent after the opening in 1869 of the Suez Canal. The latter passage could provide a shorter supply route to Russia than a voyage via the Cape could. So for the next half century only two men had performed Nordenskiöld's feat—Boris Vilkitski in 1914 took the icebreakers *Taimir* and *Vaigatch* from Vladivostock to Archangel, and Roald Amundsen in the *Maud* succeeded in making the North-East Passage from west to east in 1918.[1] But both explorers had to make breaks on their voyages and spend the winter on the ice. Not till 1932 was the North-East Passage made in one season. That year Professor Schmidt in the icebreaker *Sibiriakov* went from Murmansk to Vladivostock. This was a hazardous expedition, for at one stage every blade of the propeller had gone and the crew had to fit new blades; this involved raising the ship's stern, which meant moving four hundred tons of coal from stern to bow. Later the whole propeller was lost, yet by use of sails the expedition got through the Bering Sea just before the ice closed. Of the voyage of the *Cheliuskin*, which made world news in 1933 with her passage from Murmansk to the Bering Strait, we will speak later.

But for the second world war, the programme of the Third Five-Year Plan for the Northern Sea Route would have been carried out by 1942, and a regular shipping service would then have been operating between Murmansk and the ports of Russia's Far Eastern Territories. The naval bases of Murmansk and Vladivostock also would have been linked by the ocean route. But that the seaway did play a strategic part in the U.S.S.R.'s wartime defences was, despite Russian official

[1] There had been some talk in the Russo-Japanese War of trying to send the Baltic Squadron to Vladivostock via the Arctic Route, but nothing had materialised.

secrecy, the view commonly held in some British naval circles. It was stated in *Jane's Fighting Ships (1944-45)*[1] that most of the Soviet Fleet based on Vladivostock was believed to have proceeded to that base via the North-East Passage, and that some of the ships might have returned by that route. That same year the Japanese reported that Russian submarines had gone from the Barents Sea by the Northern Route to join the flotillas at Vladivostock. The Germans themselves in 1940 during their Pact with Russia, had sent by that seaway an auxiliary cruiser, *Komet*, to a port in Japan. This raiding ship left Bergen, rounded the northern coast of Norway, made use of the anchorage at the Soviet Arctic base of Poliarnoye, and in July passed through the Kara Sea. Through the Bering Sea the *Komet* went on to the Pacific to raid the shipping route between Vancouver and Japan.

The Soviet Government, according to its own statements, expected a war in the North Pacific. It knew that its Trans-Siberian Railway was unequal to the transport problem, and felt it could not rely upon a southerly route for vessels—the Suez or Panama Canals, or the passage round the Cape of Good Hope or the Horn. Therefore the Government had no alternative but to consider the use of a seaway from the Atlantic to the Pacific round the north of the Old World, which gave "a powerful motive for the discovery of warmth where cold had been thought to be, of open water where ice was thought to be".[2] The importance of that route to the U.S.S.R. was emphasised at the beginning of this book. The ability to bring her ships from the Barents Sea to the Bering Sea would mean everything to Russia any time she was involved in a naval war in the Pacific. The alternative—to bring her Northern or her Baltic Fleet to the Far East via the North Atlantic and Indian Ocean routes—could involve the cutting of a life-line as serious in her case as the loss of the Mediterranean would have been to Britain in the second world war.

In the history of the search for a North-*West* Passage few references will be found to the Russians, but the expedition of 1765 led by Captain Chichagov, must not be overlooked. His attempt to reach the Indies and Japan by following the coastline of North America with his three ships, was however a sad failure. Thereafter Russian efforts in this direction were rather in the nature of individual attempts to follow in the wake of

[1] Sampson Low; p. 373.
[2] Vilhjalmur Stefansson, *Ultima Thule*. (Harrap, 1942); p. 367.

British navigators. Some of these enterprises were made by Siberian settlers on the Alaskan coast in the days of the Russian-American Fur Company. The voyages of Sir John Franklin and others had prompted the Company to send the Russian navigator Kasharov in the *Polypheme* to explore the Arctic coast of North America, and he had reached a point about forty miles east of Cape Barrow. But the achievement of Kasharov was regarded as late in the history of North-West Passage seekers, in the minds of those who did accept the claims made for Andres de Urdaneta, a friar of Mexico, as long ago as 1560. According to the exaggerated report of Salvaterra, a Spanish traveller of that time, Urdaneta had sailed round the north coast of America and on to Germany, and had shown Salvaterra "a Sea Card" he had made of that voyage. "This Frier," declared the Spaniard, "was the greatest Discoverer by Sea that hath been in our age."[1]

For the English, the quest for a North-West Passage to the Pacific was the search for a short cut from Europe to China and the East Indies, and also one which would lead round the "back side" of Newfoundland—the territory which had been discovered by Sebastian Cabot. That navigator himself, having entered Hudson Bay, had believed that he had sailed along the entire sea route north of the New Found Land, and that to have proceeded farther would have brought him to Asia. In the reign of Henry VIII the petition by Roger Barlow and by Robert Thorne—previously mentioned—was addressed to the King, urging that an expedition should be fitted out for this purpose. In 1595 the Arctic navigator John Davis had published *Worldes Hydrographical Discription*,[2] one chapter of which he had devoted to proving "that America is an Iland" and "may be sayled round". The efforts of Henry Hudson to sail round the north of that continent had taken him into the great inland sea later called by his name. In 1669 Charles II had granted all the territory round Hudson Bay to Hudson's Bay Company with the understanding that they should try to discover a northern passage by which ships could sail from the Atlantic to the Pacific. And in 1745 a reward of £20,000 was offered by Parliament to those of "His Majesty's subjects who

---

[1] *Hakluyt*. (Dent's Edition, 1907); Vol. V, p. 111.

[2] Printed by Thomas Dawson, London, 1595, and published in *A Selection of Curious, Rare, and Early Voyages, and Histories of Interesting Discoveries, Chiefly Published by Hakluyt*. (This Collection was printed for R. H. Evans and R. Priestley, London, 1812.) p. 57.

might find a passage for ships from Hudson Bay to the Pacific."

Yet though it was to be long before east met west on the Arctic Sea Route, the belief persisted among seamen of different nations that the discovery of a North-*West* Passage would eventually be made by an Englishman. It had been an Englishman, Samuel Hearne, who, searching with an Indian as guide for the reputed copper mines in the Far North, had been the first known white man ever to have seen the Arctic Ocean north of the American continent. The Russian sea captain, Krusenstern, in his introduction of Kotzebue's *Voyage of Discovery*, written after more than three centuries of effort had failed to establish a sea route, paid this tribute to the greatest seafaring people of his time: "In this, as in all other maritime enterprises, the English were they who chiefly distinguished themselves. To them we are indebted for the first attempt; with the most laudable perseverance they continued their exertions . . . and to them we shall, in all probability, be obliged for finally and satisfactorily ascertaining the existence or non-existence of this remarkable passage." It was, however, fated that a Norwegian, Roald Amundsen, should crown with success the pursuit of earlier adventurers. But nearly a hundred years were to pass before that happened, and in the meantime Captain McClure in 1850 had sailed through the Bering Strait with the *Enterprise* and the *Investigator* in an attempt to make the Passage from west to east. The voyagers, after returning in the *Phoenix*, received an award of £10,000 for covering the whole distance of the North-West Passage. But they had spent four winters in the Arctic, and their original vessel had grounded off Banks Island.

Not till 1903 was the North-West Passage traversed from east to west when Roald Amundsen in the 47-ton sloop *Gjöa*, after spending two years on King William Land (above the North-West Territory, Canada) passed through Peel Strait and made his way west till he sailed through the Bering Strait and into the North Pacific Ocean.

Nearly forty years were to pass from the time of Amundsen's voyage till a ship, without relief, succeeded in making the Passage from west to east. What Frobisher in 1576 and Franklin in 1845 had so courageously endeavoured, but failed to do, what Parry and Ross with unsurpassed endurance had but partially accomplished, the *St. Roch* achieved under Captain Henry Larsen—the ploughing of a passage from the Pacific to the Atlantic. This police patrol vessel, manned only by a crew of eight members of the Royal Canadian Mounted Police, sailed

10,000 miles from Vancouver to Halifax, on a voyage which took her two years and four months. Yet until the publication of *Plowing the Arctic*,[1] four years after the commencement of her expedition, little was heard in Britain of that tale of proud and high adventure. It is true that the voyage was made in wartime, but it is strange that while the Russian papers had spared no space in recording the voyage of the *Cheliuskin* (4,000 tons) through the North-East Passage in 1933, many English papers should have given less notice to the achievement of the little 80-ton *St. Roch* than they usually give to some crisis in the life of a film star. Her perilous journey, undertaken to relieve the sufferings of native Eskimos, had started on 21 June, 1940, from Vancouver, and had taken her to Dutch Harbour, Unalaska Island, thence along the north Alaskan coast rounding Cape Bathurst, and on through the Drake Strait between Victoria Island and the mainland to Queen Maud Gulf. Northward through the Bellot Strait and thence past Cape York she sailed on between Bylot Island and Baffin Island; from there her course took her through the Davis Strait and down the coast of Labrador to Cape Breton, and finally to Halifax. Though much of the way had been covered (in reverse) in 1903-06 by Amundsen in the *Gjöa*, Larsen's voyage was one which will rank as a classic adventure for all time. In 1944 the return voyage was made by a more northerly route, viz., through the Lancaster Sound and along the southern shores of Devon, Bathurst, and Melville Islands, through the Prince of Wales Strait, into the Amundsen Gulf. "This," wrote Larsen, "had never before been completed by any vessel, although many had tried in vain. . . . Thus we became the only vessel to complete the Northern route both ways, and the only vessel to complete the Lancaster Sound route."[2]

As a result of that Canadian-manned voyage through the North-West Passage, and of the Russian service through the North-East Passage, the way has been opened for a sailing route round the top of the world. Regarding the Russians' share in that achievement, and their development of their Arctic coastlands, Professor Otto Schmidt has said: "The opening up of Northern Russia can be compared in importance with the opening up of America."

[1] J. G. Tranter. (Hodder & Stoughton, 1944.)
[2] "The Conquest of the North-West Passage: the Arctic Voyages of the *St. Roch*, 1940-44." *The Geographical Journal*, Vol. CX, July, 1947. (The Royal Geographical Society; John Murray, 1948.)

III

THE MEDITERRANEAN

IMPERIAL aims in the Mediterranean became clearly defined in the second half of the eighteenth century, and thereafter they have remained among the chief ends of Russian diplomacy. If Peter the Great was the father of the Russian Navy, Catherine the Great was its mother. Her grasp of the principles of sea power was remarkable. Recognising that Peter, by concentrating for the most part on the Baltic, had made enemies of the chief Sea Powers—Britain, Holland, and Sweden—Catherine, except for a comparatively short period of intensive activity in the north, directed her main efforts to the south. Nevertheless the Maritime Confederacy which she formed was aimed sharply against England : her declaration of 1780 laid down that free ships make free goods (except contraband) ; that neutral ships were to have the right of free navigation, even to ports of belligerents ; that blockade to be legal must be effective. An impulse to oceanic rivalry—which will materialise in the not distant future—was stirring in the mind of that unusual woman. Of her many notable achievements none was more bold, more far-sighted than Catherine's maritime policy with regard to the Mediterranean.[1] The first serious entry ever made by Russia into the Middle Sea was directly due to that Empress, who in pursuit of Russia's age-old ambition to gain command of the Straits, sent in 1769 a squadron from Kronstadt under Admiral Spiridov. (Supreme command of the expedition was vested in Admiral Orlov.) The route taken was from the Baltic through the Middle Sea. That voyage was more than a surprise to most of the other Powers ; it was a shock. When it was known by which route this squadron of seven battleships and eight smaller vessels was sailing, the Mediterranean States made various difficulties about harbourages, Venice going so far as to deny the Russian ships the use of her ports altogether. But the Baltic squadron had passed through the Sound, the North Sea, down the English Channel, and that it did sail on to Greece was entirely due to British aid. It is a curious fact that Britain,

[1] In the Pacific she was less interested and showed less foresight.

almost consistently suspicious of Russia's southward and
eastward moves, should at this time have placed her dock repairing yards, both at Portsmouth and Port Mahon, at the disposal
of the Russian ships (so soon in need of repairs after leaving
Kronstadt.) The most likely explanation is that the ships
appeared to be in such poor condition that the Russian navy,
despite its numerical strength, could hardly be regarded as
a serious maritime rival. At the end of the eight months which
it took this squadron to sail from Kronstadt to Minorca, only
eight of the fifteen ships had reached their destination. Catherine
dismissed Spiridov and asked England to send one of her
admirals to replace him. Elphinstone accordingly took command. If there had not been British officers on the vessels it is
doubtful whether they could have reached the Levant, according to a contemporary naval writer. A second squadron of three
battleships and five other vessels came to reinforce the first one.

At Greece the squadron made an ineffective attempt to
start a rebellion against the Sultan. Admiral Orlov took
Navarino in 1770, and in sending the news to his Empress
wrote this: "The fleet is not worth a pinch of salt. . . . If we
had to do with any but Turks, there would soon be an end of
the fleet." The Russians indeed played an undistinguished part
in this first Turkish war; the destruction of the Turkish fleet in
the Bay of Tchesimé that year was the work of the fireships of
Greig and Dugdale. Fourteen enemy battleships had been
attacked in the Bay by the Russians, and the following night the
entire fleet, except for one captured vessel, was destroyed by the
'brulôts'. "The name of Tchesimé is now borne by a Russian
battleship; but the fact that the victory thus commemorated
was due to Elphinstone, Greig, Dugdale, and Mackenzie, is
altogether forgotten."[1]

During the war in the Mediterranean Admiral Greig seized
several islands in the Aegean, and the Turkish campaign gave
to Russia the control of the Levant. It enabled her to blockade
the Straits and to do considerable harm to Turkey's trade. Her
advances in the Crimea had increased Russia's desire to obtain
a Mediterranean station for her fleet, and so Catherine's
Minister, Count Potemkin, had suggested that in return for an
offer to aid England against her insurgent colonists in America,
England should be asked to cede Minorca to Russia. Dissension
among Catherine's Ministers over this proposal caused it to be

[1] Colonel Sir George Sydenham Clarke, *Russia's Sea Power, Past and
Present.* (John Murray, 1896); p. 34.

dropped. By then however, France, Austria, and Prussia were as alarmed as Turkey at Russia's entry into the Mediterranean, and at her efforts to get control of the Straits. Of the Russo-Turkish war which ended in 1774, Sir George Clarke pertinently remarks: "The Russian Navy, under British auspices, had found its way to the Mediterranean, and Russian frigates had anchored before Constantinople."

Admiral Nelson had his own, and definite, ideas about Russia's advances into the waters of the Middle Sea. When Napoleon went to Egypt to try and seize the route to India, Russia (for once) was allied with Turkey, and by the latter power her Black Sea squadron under Admiral Feodor Ushakov was allowed to sail through the Dardanelles, while these were kept closed to other Powers. To Nelson, commanding the British Mediterranean Fleet co-operating with the Russo-Turkish squadrons, it was quite clear that the main object of the Russians was not to beat the French at sea, but to seize bases in the Mediterranean, e.g. the Ionian Islands. Ushakov did capture Corfu in 1799, and this was the last Ionian Island to be freed from Napoleon. Russia, who gained a base on the Adriatic when Montenegro became her protectorate, strengthened her position on that sea when Ushakov set up a "Republic" in the Ionian Islands under Russian control. Nelson, who had not much opinion of the Russian navy—and said so plainly elsewhere—wrote congratulating Ushakov: "I assure you that the glory of the arms of a true ally is as dear to me as the glory of my Sovereign."

But Nelson spoke his true mind to Lord Spencer. The Russians, he wrote, "seem to me to be more bent on taking ports in the Mediterranean than in destroying Bonaparte in Egypt". He was quite sure they wanted to get Malta, and told Captain Ball by letter:[1] "The Russians are anxious to get to Malta, and care for nothing else." Subsequent events proved him to be not wide of the mark; not long afterwards they demanded the island, but in 1800 Britain stepped in and took it. The great naval enterprise of Catherine II had exhausted itself, and under Tsar Paul Russian ambitions in the Middle Mediterranean were for the time checked. They were blocked at the eastern end of that sea when, just over half a century later, Britain declined the proposal made by Tsar Nicholas for a condominium of Constantinople. Similarly British control of Cyprus, which commenced after the Russo-Turkish war, 1878, and was designed not against the Sublime Porte but against

[1] 5 September, 1799.

the ambitions of Tsar Alexander I, checked the Mediterranean aspirations of Russia for another period.

In a new direction however, but one yet linked with the Mediterranean, the Russians began to take soundings, and though these were ostensibly the work of individuals, they had the stamp of official approval. In 1889 Achimov, a Cossack, led a small band of people across the Indian Ocean to French Somaliland, opposite British Aden, and erected his country's flag at the fort of Sagallo. The fort was duly regained by the French under Admiral Orly, but it was not the last Russian venture into Red Sea territory. Lieut. Mashkov had followed by making a journey to the court of the Emperor Menelik, and with the object of getting a Russian colony established in Ethiopia, attempts had been made to win over to the Orthodox the Abyssinian Church, then in communion with Alexandria. A mission had next been conducted in Addis Abbaba by Captain Leontov, and during the Fashoda Incident between Britain and France, Colonel Artamontov was found to be in command of Abyssinian forces on the side of the French. To threaten British sea communications with India was then, as earlier, a persistent aim with the Russians. The Red Sea was the vital artery that linked the Mediterranean with the Indian Ocean.

These nineteenth century instances of Russian interest in a zone near the Indian Ocean, were not however their earliest. Ubiquitously Peter the Great had cast his eyes in this direction. During his reign buccaneers of the West Indies had fled from the British and French, and had taken refuge in Madagascar. From here they sent word to Charles XII of Sweden, asking him to become their protector. Peter, hearing of this through one of the pirates, who by that time had joined the Russian Navy, laid plans for capturing Madagascar, and for that purpose invited to Russia a Swedish sea captain, Ulrich, with whom Charles XII had previously planned an expedition to the same island.

The Mediterranean aspirations of Russia never stop at the Straits, but are always projected to the Indian Ocean. Checked by Britain in the time of Tsar Alexander I, they have never been relinquished, they have only been dormant, and in 1909 in the secret treaty made between Russia and Italy at Racconigi, Russian interest in the Mediterranean received a fresh impetus; in return for a promise of Italian support should Russia press for a revision of the position regarding the Straits, the Tsar's

Government agreed to back Italy in her claims for Tripoli.[1]
(In 1945 she was to ask for that port herself.)

Three years later when Italy and Turkey were at war,
Italian ships attacked the Dardanelles; though this was only
a short-lived operation, Russia suffered severe economic losses,
and this increased her desire to prevent the future possibility of
a blockade of the Straits by foreign warships. Before the outbreak of these Turkish-Italian hostilities, Russia had vainly
pressed the Sublime Porte to open the Straits to Russian warships, and to close them to ships of all other Powers. But though
she showed in this as in other ways, that she was anxious for
a change from the *status quo* which governed the closure of the
Straits, she was equally anxious that Turkey should remain in
control of the Straits rather than that a maritime Power like
Britain should have any voice in their administration. Hence
Russia opposed Britain's suggestion that Constantinople should
be neutralised and internationalised. For the same reason at
the Treaty of London, 1913, Russia pressed for the strategic
islands of Lemnos, Samothrace, Tenedos, and Imbros, to be put
under Turkish control.

It was the second world war which brought the biggest
opportunity for open revival of Russia's Mediterranean aspirations. The Soviet Union's interest in that area increased as the
result of the damage which her southern railways suffered
during the war. The Mediterranean route offered her a new
(though obviously much longer) means of communication from
Leningrad to the cities of the Ukraine and the Caucasus. The
roads too, still make urgent an alternative means of transport.

So at the Berlin Conference (Potsdam), 1945, Russia made
proposals that part of the former Italian colonies in North
Africa should pass under a trusteeship of the United Nations,
which should include the Soviet Union. She also pressed for a
naval and air base in the Central Mediterranean, at Tripoli.
Agreement could not be reached on this matter at Potsdam, so
it was later referred to the Council of Foreign Ministers in
London and in Paris, when M. Molotov recommended that
Tripolitania should be governed by an advisory Commission
having a Russian administrator. He insisted that the Soviet
Union which had a sea outlet in the north, required one in the
south, "especially so since we now have the right to use Dairen

---

[1] *Un Livre Noir*. Diplomatie d'avant-guerre d'après les documents des
archives Russes, edited by René Marchand. (Paris, 1922-34); Vol. I,
pp. 357-58.

and Port Arthur in the Far East". He also urged that his country "should have bases in the Mediterranean for its merchant fleet".[1] The proposal also that Eritrea should be ceded to her, revealed Russia's desire to extend her power to a maritime sphere entirely new (if we except the isolated instances recently mentioned)—that of the Red Sea. The Power which holds Eritrea holds also the port of Massawah, almost half way between Port Sudan and British Aden.

A change in the whole strategic set-up of the British Oceanic Commonwealth would at any time result from the establishment of Russian control on the Red Sea, that sea which is "the throat of the British Commonwealth". The fact that in future the use of narrow channels such as the Suez Canal will be ruled out in time of warfare, does not diminish the importance of the Red Sea to British Commonwealth strategy. The decision to make East Africa the location of some of the principal bases in the Empire's scheme of defence, means that the Red Sea will have a new significance to the members of the Commonwealth. It was the Russian demands concerning this sea that prompted Mr. Bevin to declare in the House of Commons on 7 November, 1945: "We have met territorially almost every demand that we ever thought we should be asked. Warm water ports, everything has been conceded. I must say that having conceded all this and not taken one inch of territory or asked for it, you cannot help our being a little bit suspicious if a great Power wants to go right across the throat of the British Commonwealth."

Needless to say, the British Government during the 1939-45 war was in no doubt as to the importance of the Red Sea route to the Commonwealth, and the relation of this route to the "land bridge" of that pivotal part of the Middle East which links three continents. In all the complexity of modern foreign politics, one thing remains clear: whatever the leaders of Britain, be they Conservative or Socialist—and whatever the rulers of Russia—be they Tsarist or Communist—their policies with regard to the eastern Mediterranean and the Red Sea, remain in essence unchanged.

The Red Sea is not, any more than the Mediterranean, contiguous to Soviet territory, hence Russia's foreign policy with regard to these two regions must be considered from the point of view of long-term, and global, rather than immediate, and

[1] James F. Byrnes (former United States Secretary of State), *Speaking Frankly.* (Copyright by Donald Russell, Trustee of the James F. Byrnes Foundation, 1947.)

local, objectives. Upon those aims the far-sighted eyes of the American Government were fixed when in 1947 President Truman made his appeal to Congress for the dispatch of immediate financial and military aid to Greece and Turkey, whose strategic position in relation to the Middle East and to the focal waterways of that region, has now an importance for the United States as considerable as for the British Commonwealth. By 1949 the United States planned to have completed the longest pipe-line in the world, and certainly marked as one which by its strategic location would be the most sensitive. Starting from Dhahran on the Persian Gulf, this pipe, laid by the Trans-Arabian Pipe-line Company, was to run through the desert of Saudi Arabia and terminate on the coast of Lebanon, near Sidon. For 1,000 miles it will run parallel to, though some distance from, the eastern shore of the Red Sea. Its termination at a port on the eastern Mediterranean can give America greater commercial interests than any other Power in that area of the Middle Sea, and her maritime strength there will become proportionate to those interests.

In the Middle Mediterranean the attitude of Britain and America to Soviet aims was reflected by their policy with regard to Yugoslavia. Serbia had been marked as a vassal state in the Russian plans of 1914-18 for an advance to the Adriatic; outlet to that sea was to be secured by a corridor from Bohemia, then through Austria-Hungary to Serbia. These projects were not forgotten after the second world war by the two Atlantic Powers. Their opposition to Marshal Tito's occupation of Trieste in 1945, and to the Russian demands in Paris a year later that Trieste should be given to Yugoslavia, was based primarily on the unwillingness of Britain and the United States to see Russia, already the most influential Power in Yugoslavia, in a dominant rôle on the Adriatic. The Anglo-American proposal that Trieste, in which Yugoslav influence had become preponderant, should cease to be an international port and should revert to Italy, was designed to hold back the Slav drive on the Mediterranean. The choice of Belgrade as the first location of the Communist international organisation (Cominform) for the States within the Soviet orbit, could be regarded as following the direction of that drive. Already, as a result of the Italian Peace Treaty, 1947, the cession of Pola on the Istrian Peninsula to Yugoslavia had meant that one of the main seaports of the Adriatic had passed to a country whose political ties were closest with the Soviet Union. On the small island of Sasseno, off

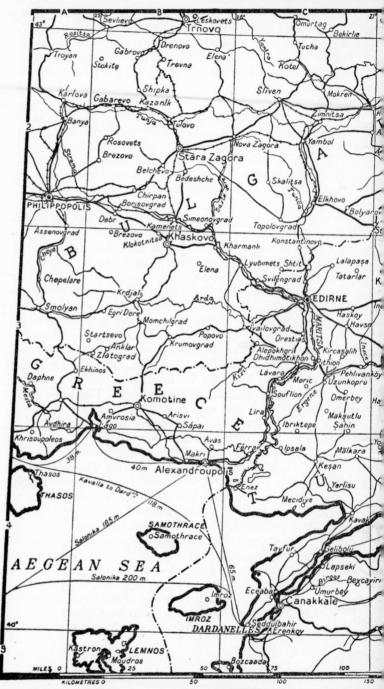

(*Reproduction by permission of Serial Map Service, from "Serial Maps", Vol. V, No. 4, Map 228.*)

SHOWING the passage from the Black Sea to the Aegean.

Valona, Russians were helping Albanians to build a submarine base early in 1947, according to reports from Rome.[1]

The British and American Governments were aware that Marshal Tito's proposals for a federal Yugoslavia had included Macedonia, and that this would bring Russian influence to Salonika and the head of the Aegean Sea. Soviet support of Communist elements in Greece was designed with one end in view—the capture of Salonika. Once that city fell, unless American intervention was sufficiently powerful, surrender of the Straits to Russia would not be long delayed. Such a change would vitally affect Britain's maintenance of sea communications via the Suez Canal with the Dominions of the southern hemisphere, and it would be regarded by America as a menace to her own vast oil interests in the Middle East. A shifting of the balance of power in the eastern Mediterranean would inevitably result.

With regard to the western Mediterranean, the British attitude towards Russia here was shown by certain events during the Spanish Civil War. Between 6 August and 9 September, 1937, twenty-seven ships of various nationals had been attacked in the Mediterranean by submarines and planes of undisclosed identity. France had proposed that a conference should be called of the Powers which had suffered from these attacks, including Italy and Spain. Britain agreed in principle, but objected to the inclusion of Spain, and also of Russia, yet required the inclusion of Germany, although the latter was not a Mediterranean Power and had suffered from no attacks on her ships.[2] British reluctance to witness the arrival of Russian influence in the western Mediterranean was manifest when in 1945 the Soviet Union requested that she should be represented at the conference on Tangier, concerning the reversion to the pre-war international status of that zone. Russia, like America, was not a signatory to the original Statute of Tangier (though she was a party to the Act of Algeciras) but America was interested in Tangier as an Atlantic port, while Russia regarded it as a Mediterranean question. And it is with the Mediterranean that so much of the future of Russia will be concerned.

RUSSIA, TURKEY, AND THE BLACK SEA

Russian relations with Turkey have as their guiding principle the unchanged objective of a free passage from the Black Sea

[1] *The Daily Mail*, 8.1.47.
[2] See also *Labour Research*, Vol. XXVI, No. 10, p. 230.

to the Mediterranean, and the question of the control of the Straits is one that determines today the Kremlin's policy with regard to Ankara no less than this question for centuries shaped Imperial policy concerning Constantinople. From the far-off days of the Varangian voyagers a belief had arisen that on an equestrian statue in the square of Taurus, a secret prophecy was inscribed that "in the last days the Russians should be masters of Constantinople".[1] In some of the older Russian maps that city is marked as "Tsargrad". But though various writers have used this as a proof of Russian aims, it implies actually, the city of the Byzantine emperors, not the Russian tsars.[2] From the days however of the splendour of Byzantium under Porphyrogenitus, 'Rus' and Russians have at different periods tried to capture that city on the Bosphorus.

The first attack, as mentioned earlier, came in A.D. 860 when the Northmen known as Varangians passed through the Straits with two hundred wooden ships; but the superior size of the Byzantine vessels prevented them from taking Constantinople, and they were successfully repelled. In 907 a more menacing assault on the City of the Caesars was made under Oleg, kinsman of Rurik the Swede, who sailed down the Dnieper and pillaged the land round Constantinople for four years. By a trade treaty, however, signed later, the Northmen withdrew. The year 941 saw them back, and this time with more ships than Byzantium mustered, but once again the Varangians were defeated —on this occasion by the use of "Greek fire", which destroyed almost the entire Russian fleet. A fourth attempt was made in 1043, only to meet with worse failure than before: Greek fire was responsible for the total loss of the Russian fleet. More than seven hundred years later Russia was still uninstructed in the use of fire-ships; it was the British officers mentioned earlier, serving with the Imperial Navy in 1770, who by use of eighteenth-century "Greek fire", won for the Russians the Battle of Tchesimé, one of the most notable sea-fights in their history.

Four years later the Treaty of Kutschuk-Kainardji concluded one phase of the long series of Russo-Turkish wars. Russia restored the provinces of Bessarabia and Georgia to Turkey, and in this way lost the Black Sea port of Batum, but she kept the ports of Azov and Taganrog, also Yenikale and Kerch,

[1] W. S. Lindsay, *History of Merchant Shipping and Ancient Commerce.* (Sampson Low, Marston, Low & Searle, 1874); Vol. VIII, p. 231.
[2] See also N. Dascovici, "La Question du Bosphore et des Dardanelles." (Georg et Cie., Geneva, 1915); p. 85.

which gave her on those Straits passage from the sea of Azov to the Black Sea. The Treaty also gave her the right to Kinburn on the mouth of the Dnieper, and consequent control of the Dnieper delta. The two Kabardas also went to Russia, who thus "obtained for the first time a firm grip upon the northern shore of the Black Sea; the Kabardas would give her a footing on the eastern shore".[1] More important still, Russia gained the right of passage for her merchant ships through the Straits. She could now trade freely in the Black Sea, and to her merchants were granted "Most-Favoured-Nation" privileges in Turkish ports and waters. Seventy years earlier when Peter the Great had tried to secure those privileges for his trading vessels, he had sent a squadron from Azov to accompany his envoy, Emilien Ukraiintsov, to Constantinople. Peter himself went with his emissary as far as Kerch in the *Kriépost*, and this warship had subsequently entered the waters of the Bosphorus. Ukraiintsov however failed in his mission; he had received the reply that "the Ottoman Porte guards the Black Sea like a pure virgin whom none will dare to touch". Russian goods destined for the Porte must cross the Black Sea in Turkish vessels. But Russia's trade development depended on the freedom of the Straits to her ships—this was the achievement of the Treaty of Kutschuk-Kainardji—it gave her a passage to the west.

The work of Catherine the Great in annexing the Crimean Peninsula was the fulfilment of the earlier efforts of Peter the Great. The policy of her Minister Potemkin had been to instigate a revolt among the subjects of the Khan of the Crimea. Russian forces thereupon invaded the Peninsula in 1783, the Khan was deposed, and "the world notified that the independent Tartar State had been annexed to Russia".[2] Catherine then built dockyards at Kherson, and Sevastopol was developed as a naval dockyard by Samuel Greig, the Scottish admiral in her service. With ostentation calculated to inflame His Sublime Highness, Catherine proceeded by the Volga to Simbirsk, and continuing her journey to Kherson she here viewed her formidable arsenal, and at Sevastopol saw her warships riding at anchor. All the same there was, as one writer has truly said, an element of farcical comedy about this review of the fleet.

[1] Sir John Marriott, *Anglo-Russian Relations, 1689-1943*; p. 50. By permission of Messrs. Methuen.
[2] S. P. H. Duggan, Ph.D., *The Eastern Question. A Study in Diplomacy.* (The Columbia Studies in History, Economics, and Public Law, No. 39. The Columbia University Press, New York, 1902); p. 48.

Catherine in a confidential letter to Panin, complained that she had seen the fleet "fire all day at a target without once hitting it, and that it manœuvred more like a fleet of herring boats than a naval squadron".[1]

The encroachments of the Empress on the Black Sea and her demand that Turkey should give up Bessarabia (in order that Russia might control all the northern shore of the Black Sea) led to the Russo-Turkish war of 1787. In that conflict surprisingly good work was done by the Russian fleet, considering that it was numerically small: for though Russia now possessed fifty-four battleships, only six belonged to the Black Sea Squadron.[2] They were, however, all ships of good account, due to the resolution of Potemkin to create an efficient Black Sea fleet. In 1792 the Treaty of Jassy between Russia and Turkey reaffirmed the terms of Kutschuk-Kainardji, but also gave the former Power increased territory so that the Dniester became her western boundary on the northern shore of the Black Sea. By her control of the estuary lands of the Dnieper, Dniester, and Bug, Russia was still more securely established on the Black Sea. In defiance of the long series of preventive measures on the part of the other maritime Powers, she signed with Turkey a Convention in 1798 which gave her warships free passage through the Straits.

Alexander I continued the expansionist policy of his predecessors, one of his chief aims being to make his country supreme on the Caspian and the Black Sea, for only so could she be safe on the one hand from Persia, on the other from the Porte. So on the Caspian Sea a flotilla had been launched against Baku, but the attack had been repelled by the Khan of Khouba. As far as the Straits were concerned the Tsar never lost sight of the ultimate goal of their capture, and with that incentive his agreement to the Treaty of Tilsit was given to Napoleon. In a secret annex to that treaty Russia, in return for promising to join Napoleon's planned offensive against England, was to get, among other territories, Moldavia and Wallachia from Turkey, which would give the Tsar complete control of the Danube delta. In the event of certain contingencies the Russians were to join the French in driving the Turks out of nearly all their possessions in Europe.

When Alexander's troops did enter Moldavia, the British,

[1] Francis Gribble, *The Comedy of Catherine the Great.* (Eveleigh Nash, London, 1912); pp. 169-170.
[2] See R. C. Anderson, *Naval Wars in the Baltic, 1521-1850*; p. 241.

fearing the effect of this on Danubian navigation, and also unwilling to see Russia brought nearer the Straits, sent Admiral Duckworth to the Dardanelles. Here the Turks with the aid of the French had strengthened the fortifications, and but for British intervention, Russia could have passed her warships through the Straits to aid Napoleon in his intended invasion of Egypt and Syria. The English admiral destroyed a squadron of Turkish frigates and anchored just off Constantinople, but he found the Porte's defences too strong and had to retreat.

The Tsar was persuaded by Napoleon to join his "Continental System," which had been founded principally to counter British maritime power. But unfortunately for the Russians this move did not work out in their favour. Their Emperor had said to Napoleon that the key of the Tsar's house was the Dardanelles, and Alexander was to have cause to remember that. Napoleon's order for the closing of Russian ports to American trade became a particular hardship to Russia, as the latter, then at war with England, was dependent entirely on the United States for all but luxury imports. America was supplying Russia with West India products, trading tea, coffee, rum, from Massachusetts to the Baltic ports. A powerful British fleet under Admiral Gambier had sailed for the Baltic and had bombarded Copenhagen; Russian sea power being no match then for the British, the Tsar's fleet had to remain inoperative in the Baltic till 1812. Imports were vital then to Russia, so Alexander connived at the release of American ships in Russian ports. It was the Tsar's subsequent evasion of the "Continental System" that was mainly responsible for Napoleon's march on Moscow. That invasion was ruinous for Russia, although she was victorious, because as her ports were ice-locked she was denied the free flow of imports to make good the ravages from which she had suffered. And during the later years of the Napoleonic war, though Russia was then allied with Britain she had been unable to get supplies from her ally, as the Turks had closed the Straits to British ships. "The key of the Tsar's house" had been turned against him.

To justify his campaign against Russia, Napoleon had said to his intimate friends beforehand: "If ever Russia gets possession of Constantinople, then, with her flanks on the Baltic and the Bosphorus she will enslave Europe and Asia under the same yoke."

The long history of attempts to exclude Russia from the Black Sea were the more bitterly opposed by that Power when

her industries in the coastal regions showed promise of development, and Nicholas I was no exception to his predecessors in
striving to break through the barriers. By the Treaty of Akerman, 1826, his Government did succeed in gaining for Russia
complete freedom of navigation for merchant ships in all the
waters of the Ottoman Empire. But the greater part of the
Black Sea littoral was still held by the Turks; the whole
Russian frontier from Mount Ararat to the sea and along its
shores to Sukhum Kaleh, was exposed to Turkish attack.
Nicholas therefore directed Prince Paskievitch to secure that
Caucasian frontier, and for this the conquest of the vilayet of
Kars and the capture of the Black Sea fortress of Anapa were
necessary. As a result of the campaign undertaken by the prince,
these two objectives fell to Russia. Her position with regard to
the south-eastern shore of the Black Sea was thereby considerably strengthened, and the fact that the Turks still held the
Taman Peninsula farther north, was now of much less account
to the Tsar.

In 1829 Russia was to surprise the other Powers, when her
fleet passed through the Dardanelles. And while the Black Sea
Fleet came out in this way, Russian troops which had crossed
the Pruth advanced through the Balkans. Their ensuing victories over the Turkish land-forces were due mainly to their
command of the Black Sea. For the first time the Russians
dominated that sea, and in that war they justified the maritime
efforts of Peter the Great and Catherine II by proving that
Varna and Poti could be used as ports of supply and for the
transport of troops.

The Treaty of Adrianople ended, in favour of Russia, the
Russo-Turkish campaigns begun in 1827; the gains of Akerman
were re-confirmed, and Russian ships were now exempted from
inspection before passing through the Straits. Moreover
Georgia was formally ceded to the Tsar's dominions, thus
equipping them with east coast ports on the Black Sea. (The
value of those ports was one reason why Russia, after the
Revolution, compelled Georgia—whose independence had
been recognised—to become a Republic of the Soviet Union.)
Adrianople also gave Russia a third arm of the Danube, i.e. the
St. George. The effect was, that she now became mistress of
navigation on that river. In later years the Germanic Powers,
Austria-Hungary in particular, were to resent this Russian
control of the Danubian delta: difficulties had been created by
St. Petersburg about navigation on the Sulina branch of the

Danube through Russia's ambition to develop Odessa. The Central Powers feared that her command of Oczakow would give her even greater control of the Black Sea region occupied by the mouths of the Danube. "A cette époque, le Danube était réellement la base stratégique de l'équilibre politique en Orient."[1]

The Treaty of Unkiar-Skelessi, 1833, by which Russia promised to defend Turkey against all attacks, and (by a second Article) Turkey undertook to close the Dardanelles against any country with which Russia might be at war, and to give Russia exclusive right of passage for her warships "au besoin",[2] was a treaty, as Skrine points out,[3] which made the Black Sea a Russian lake, and brought Russia nearer to establishing her long-desired protectorate over Turkey than she had ever been before. In the eyes of Britain, this treaty was a repudiation of that of Constantinople made between England and Turkey in 1809, and it was denounced by Lord Palmerston. But the first Power to put to a real test the conflicting clauses in these treaties was the United States, who in 1835 sent a frigate to the Bosphorus and asked for passage into the Black Sea. The Porte referred the question to Russia, who, fearing that consent would create a precedent of which Britain and France might take advantage, withheld permission. Again, in 1858 a large American frigate Wabash, ostensibly for the service of the U.S. legation, was sent to the Bosphorus, but Turkey denied her ingress. The Russians, who had protested against the passage of the Anglo-French Squadron to the Sea of Marmora, themselves tested the principle of closure by sending the corvette Sokol through the Straits in 1863. In 1902 they were successful in getting the permission of the Porte to send through the Dardanelles four torpedo-boats for the Tsar's review of his Black Sea Fleet. In some naval quarters in Britain it was considered that this ingress had been planned as a test for egress in the event of units of the Black Sea Fleet being required to reinforce the Pacific Squadron. This did occur in 1904 when seven ships with coal cargoes at Odessa were directed to join Admiral Rozhdestvenski's Second Pacific Squadron in the Russo-

[1] G. Demorgny, La Question du Danube. (Société du Recueil Sirey, 1911); p. 191.

[2] For analysis of the secret Article see Phillipson and Buxton, The Question of the Bosphorus and the Dardanelles. (Stevens & Haynes, 1917); p. 66.

[3] F. H. Skrine, The Expansion of Russia, 1815-1900. (Cambridge University Press, 1903); p. 138.

Japanese War. They were only allowed conditional passage through the Straits, and the principle of closure placed Russia at a severe disadvantage in her struggle at sea with Japan. In the 1914-18 war, Turkey, in giving passage to the *Goeben* and the *Breslau*, was held by the Allied Powers to have acted in contravention of the Treaty of Paris, 1856.

All the length of this tedious chain of conventions and treaties—and how long that chain is, anyone who has worked through Noradounghian's exhaustive collection of documents[1] will know—one question recurs: in the words of Sergei Gorianov, "de quelle autorité dépendent les détroits de Bosphore et des Dardanelles? Qui en est le détenteur? Pour la Russe," he says, "toute la fameuse question l'Orient se résume dans ces mots".

When in 1838 Turkey had been seriously threatened by the Khedive of Egypt (Mehemet Ali) Russia was ready to step in on the Bosphorus to "defend" the Sultan. Britain, apprehensive of a menace to her route to India, had forestalled the Russian move by calling a Conference in London to settle the Egyptian-Turkish question. This was a diplomatic victory for Britain, as the outcome was the "Protocol des Détroits," 1841, which practically reversed the favourable position gained by Russia through the Treaty of Unkiar-Skelessi. "So long as the Porte is at peace," the Convention declared, "His Highness will admit no forces or ships of war into the said Straits."

In 1853 Russia was again at war with Turkey. The chief engagement in that conflict took place at Sinope on the Black Sea, when a Russian fleet attacked the Turkish squadron, and shell-fire was used for the first time. It was this demonstration of the power of shell-fire by the Russians which expedited the building of ironclads by France and Britain; for the attack by Admiral Nakhimov's fleet of five ships of the line and three steamers, had resulted in the almost total destruction of the enemy. But the fruits of the Tsar's victory were lost, as the commander, Menschikov, who was Governor of Sevastopol, gave orders for most of the Black Sea Fleet to be sunk, so as to block the harbour entrance. What was left of the fleet was destroyed by fire when the Russians withdrew at the end of the Crimean War.

In that war England and France had joined, because both Powers feared that Russia's efforts to gain free access from the Black Sea to the eastern Mediterranean might seriously affect

[1] *Recueil d'Actes Internationaux de l'Empire Ottoman.* (Pichon, Paris, 1897-1902); 3 vols.

their own maritime interests. Lamartine writing on the very eve of war said: "Russia at the Dardanelles means the Russian frontier at Marseille and Toulon", and he pointed out[1] that Russian control of the Straits would mean that the Mediterranean became a Russian lake. Before Russia had attacked Turkey, the former Power had been told by the British Government that a state of war would not arise so long as the Tsar's fleet did not pass the delta of the Danube, or did not attack any Black Sea port. Russia had replied by attacking the Turkish squadron in Sinope harbour. "It is difficult to resist the conclusion that Great Britain was impelled for the first time to wage direct war with Russia for reasons mainly naval" is the opinion of one English maritime historian.[2] Over this question of Russian power in the Black Sea, the policies of Pitt and Fox were at variance, Pitt favouring active opposition to the Tsar, and Fox advocating Anglo-Russian collaboration as the best safeguard for British interests in the Near and Middle East.

It is interesting to recall that in the defence of Sevastopol, 1941-42, the Russians drew inspiration from the defenders in the Crimean War, who more than made up for the cautious conduct of Mentschikov. (In accordance with a not unusual practice in the Imperial Russian Navy, he, as commander-in-chief of the Russian Army, had authority over the naval leaders, in this case Admirals Kornilov and Nakhimov.) In the earlier war it was not till Malakov[3] fell that Sevastopol fell, after a siege of nearly a year, during which Russia lost a quarter of a million men. And even after the capture of Nikolaiev and Kinburn, the Isthmus of Perekop held out. (These events were to be closely paralleled nearly ninety years later, though the enemy then were Germans and Rumanians instead of British and French.) When in 1855 the Black Sea Fleet was sunk in the harbour of Sevastopol by order of Admiral Kornilov to block the British and French seaward assault, the sailors had rallied under Admiral Nakhimov, the victor of Sinope, and had worked at the trench defences on land (which had been organised by Colonel Todleben) just as the seamen of the Black Sea Fleet came ashore to fight in the defence of the Crimea in 1941. To hold the Crimea had been a Russian aim ever since the days of Ivan IV, the first Russian ruler to attack the Peninsula. He had secured

[1] Preface to *Histoire de la Turquie*.
[2] Sir George Sydenham Clarke, *Russia's Sea Power, Past and Present*; p. 184.
[3] Malakov Tower dominated the main defences of Sevastopol.

Perekop, and would have put an end to the Khanate of the Crimea, but for the difficulty of holding territory so far removed, in those days, from the centre.

The Treaty of Paris which followed the Crimean War, confirmed Russia in possession of the Crimea, but she lost Bessarabia, and her monopoly of interference in the Danubian provinces came to an end. The Danube was henceforth to be a free highway under international control. Russian coastal defences on the Black Sea were to be dismantled. The fortifications of Sevastopol were to be razed, and the harbour was to be kept open to the merchant ships of all nations. Worst of all from the Russian point of view was the fact that the Black Sea was to be closed to all ships of war (except a strictly prescribed number for Russia and Turkey); it was to be open to ships of all nations for commerce.

Although Turkey was prohibited from maintaining any naval arsenals on the shores of the Black Sea, the treaty terms placed her at an advantage over Russia, who now had no seaway in the south for the transport of her troops in wartime, and for supplies had to depend on the Danubian port of Galatz. For action against the Turks in the Black Sea, she would have to rely upon mine-laying and torpedoes, sending torpedo launches from Kronstadt to the Danubian ports by rail. "The broad result of the war was, then, to deprive Russia of almost everything she had laboriously obtained by a century of consistent diplomacy and several wars: to thrust her back from Constantinople; to repudiate her quasi-protectorate over Turkey, and to close the Black Sea to her ships of war."[1]

Before the expansion of Peter I and Catherine II, that sea had been a Turkish lake. The Treaty of Unkiar-Skelessi had changed it to a Russian one, and now the Treaty of Paris had virtually internationalised it. "To the existing notions of free sea and territorial sea . . . a new conception was added, viz., that of a *neutralised* sea; thus the principle of continental neutralisation, adopted in the interests of political equilibrium, was applied to a maritime sphere with the same object."[2] In effect, therefore, a new principle of international maritime law had been added to the classifications of Grotius.

The position established by the Treaty of Paris was such that,

---

[1] Sir J. A. R. Marriott, *Anglo-Russian Relations, 1689-1943*; p. 97. By permission of Messrs. Methuen.

[2] Phillipson and Buxton, *The Question of the Bosphorus and the Dardanelles*, p. 99.

while Turkish ships could command the Bosphorus and British ships controlled the eastern Mediterranean, the Russian Navy was consigned to impotence even on the Black Sea. It was natural that such a state of affairs could not continue. The confusion which prevailed after the Franco-Prussian War gave the Russians (who were supported by Bismarck) their opportunity to denounce the demilitarisation clauses, and at the Black Sea Conference, 1871, these were abrogated. The right to fortify Sevastopol was re-established, and Russia lost no time in availing herself of this. Nothing shows more clearly than those prohibitory clauses of the Treaty of Paris, the British concern with Russian expansion in the Near East. Five years later, when Turkey was again in trouble, Britain helped her, so as to head off Russia from Constantinople; apprehensive as to the Tsar's designs on the Straits, England made it clear she would oppose any attempt to alter the *status quo*. Russia accordingly assured Britain that she had no intention of annexing Constantinople, but actually it was only the presence of British ships at Besika, ready to pass through the Dardanelles, that made Russia halt before her intended march on the Turkish capital. Her conduct also during the peace negotiations with Turkey, so far from allaying British misgivings, intensified these, and resulted in England threatening to send a squadron under Admiral Hornby to Constantinople. The matter however ended in a compromise.

By the Treaty of Berlin, 1878, Russia retrieved Bessarabia which she had lost to Rumania after the Crimean War, and she gained from Turkey the Black Sea port of Batum. (It was stipulated that Russia should not make Batum a naval station, it was to be used only as a commercial port, but the Russians later repudiated this prohibition.) The Treaty of Berlin had also deprived Turkey of the Provinces of Bosnia and Herzegovina, which were assigned as mandated territories to Austria. The new strength of the Central Powers was directly due to Britain's mistrust of Russia: it brought the Germanic Powers into the Balkans. In 1908 Austria annexed Bosnia and Herzegovina outright. The Austrian Government then announced its intention to build the Mitrovitza railway, the real purpose of which was the economic exploitation of the Balkan peninsula. Russia thereupon made public her own plan for building an east-west railroad to the Adriatic; the incursion of the Central Powers into Balkan territory only gave fresh impetus to Russia's Adriatic aims. Support of the southern Slavs to this end had been the policy of Isvolsky, and the same aim was apparent now when the Tsar's Government gave diplomatic encouragement to the Serbs in their protest against the annexation of Herzegovina (as it also supported them in 1914 against the Austro-Hungarian demands made upon Serbia, following the murder of the Archduke at Serajevo.) By this time Russia had come to regard the Teuton menace as more formidable than the Turkish.

In an annex to a secret agreement made at Reichstadt in 1876, Russia had consented, in the event of the dissolution of the Ottoman Empire, to the partial annexation of Bosnia and Herzegovina by Austria-Hungary. This was to be the price of Austro-Hungarian neutrality in Russia's intended march on "the road to Byzantium". But when Austria-Hungary did seize the two Turkish provinces, Russia demanded, this time as the price of *her* neutrality, that the Article in the Reichstadt Treaty, concerning the closure of the Straits, should be abrogated. To St. Petersburg the question of the Dardanelles remained outstanding. For just as the Baltic Sea and Leningrad can be isolated from the Atlantic if an enemy Power closes the Kiel Canal and the Kattegat, so the Black Sea and Odessa can be cut off from the Mediterranean if a Power actively hostile to Russia controls the Dardanelles. To few statesmen had this been more clear than to Nelidoff, Russian ambassador to Turkey during the Turco-Armenian conflict at the end of the nineteenth century. Nelidoff, at a time when the Ottoman Empire appeared to be disintegrating, had proposed that Russia should occupy the Straits. He had reckoned that even Britain would not at that time interfere, and that Russia would be able to establish herself permanently on the Upper Bosphorus, at whose northern end, he advised, the Black Sea Fleet should be stationed. The proposal had the personal approval of Nicholas II, but the opposition of de Witte, the Finance Minister, prevented the plan from going through. Nevertheless the Black Sea Squadron had been kept in readiness till the outbreak of the Russo-Japanese War, and Russian troops had been kept on the heights of the Upper Bosphorus.

It was with the object of getting aid to Russia, isolated by the closing of the Straits, that the Allies attempted to force the Dardanelles in the first world war. Without some knowledge of the strategic significance of the Dardanelles in World War I, it is not possible to understand very much about Russia's attitude to Turkey during World War II. At a meeting of the British

War Council, 26 January, 1915,[1] Mr. Balfour had pointed out that the Dardanelles, if forced, would have given the Allies control of Constantinople, enabled Russia to resume her exports, and opened a passage to the Danube. Mr. Churchill's plea for an operation off the Dardanelles was approved by Russia, but Sir Edward Grey was informed by Sir George Buchanan that "Russian Dreadnoughts were not finished; they had no submarines of modern type and only an insufficient number of destroyers. Their Fleet was, therefore, not more than the equal of the Turkish Fleet, and that only when all the ships were together. Russian ships carry only four days' coal, and coaling at sea in the Black Sea was rendered impossible in the winter by bad weather. . . . Guns of the Bosphorus batteries as compared both in number and power with those placed in Russian ships were such as to give little hope of a successful attack by the latter."[2]

The weakness of the Black Sea Fleet was admitted by the Russians themselves. Two Dreadnoughts, *Rechad I* and *Rio de Janeiro* had reinforced the Turkish fleet in the autumn of 1914. The Russians expected to have their own fleet strengthened by three Dreadnoughts in 1915 and a fourth later; two cruisers were also to be added. But until these additions could be made the situation was such that one of the secret documents at that time made the admission: "Nous ne pouvons pas malheureusement leur opposer un seul dreadnought dans la Mer Noire, et la supériorité passera donc à la flotte ottomane."[3]

The Turkish fleet was largely officered and manned by Germans. Admiral Louchon led the fleet through the Straits to the Black Sea, and prepared to bombard Sevastopol. The Russians succeeded in repelling the attack, but their destroyers were no match for the *Goeben*. Some German and Turkish ships attacked Odessa harbour, and the *Breslau* bombarded Novorossisk.

It was now the turn of the Anglo-French naval forces to enter the Straits. Between 19 February and 2 March the successful naval bombardment of the outer forts of the Dardanelles took place. On 15 October Mr. Churchill wrote: "The one great prize and reward which Russia can gain is Constantinople."

[1] See The Rt. Hon. Winston S. Churchill, M.P., *The World Crisis, 1915*. Vol. II, p. 163. By permission of Odhams Press, Ltd.

[2] *Ibid.*, Vol. II, p. 158. By permission of Odhams Press, Ltd.

[3] Emile Laloy, *Les Documents secrets des Archives du Ministère des Affaires Étrangères de Russie.* Publiés par les Bolcheviks. (Bossard, Paris, 1919); p. 95.

The surest way of re-equipping her, the one way of encouraging her efforts, was, he said, the opening of the Dardanelles and the Bosphorus. "With the evacuation of the Gallipoli Peninsula that hope dies." Four months earlier Mr. Churchill had pointed out that the capture of Constantinople would multiply the resources and open the way for the re-equipping of the Russian armies. That was the purpose of the Battle of the Beaches on Gallipoli Peninsula, when the 29th and 42nd Divisions of Anzacs, the Royal Naval Division, and two French Divisions, played their imperishable part.

Of the subsequent evacuation of Suvla, Anzac, Helles, and the close of the Dardanelles campaign, Mr. Churchill wrote: "There ended with the Dardanelles all hope of forming direct and continuous contact with Russia. A railway 1,200 miles long might be built to Murmansk; Vladivostock might continue to pass supplies across a distance of 4,000 miles; but the intimate co-operation of men and munitions, the vast exportation of South Russian wheat, the expansion of a vitalising trade which could alone spring from the opening of the Black Sea, was for ever denied us. The abandonment of Gallipoli dispelled the Russian dreams. In her darkest hours, under the flail of Ludendorff, driven out of Poland, driven out of Galicia, her armies enduring disaster and facing death, often without arms, the cost of living rising continually throughout her vast, secluded Empire, Russia had cheered herself by dwelling on the great prize of Constantinople."[1] That prize she had been promised by secret agreement in 1915, conditional on her helping Britain at the time of the projected naval attack on Turkey. She had also been promised the Asiatic shore of the Bosphorus and Dardanelles, with the stipulation that the Straits should be open to merchant shipping of all nations.[2] The Aegean Islands of Tenedos and Imbros were also to pass to Russia.

The aim of the British Navy, as conceived by Mr. Churchill, was to have entered the Sea of Marmora and destroyed the German-Turkish Fleet; when this was done the Russian army would have been free to cross the Black Sea and attack Constantinople from the north. The Russians however had profound misgivings about the projected British occupation of the

[1] *The World Crisis, 1915;* Vol. II, p. 510. By permission of Odhams Press Ltd.

[2] Russia, for her part, had undertaken among other things, to acknowledge the Suez Canal and the Persian Gulf as England's special sphere of influence.

Straits, although their own co-operation in this had been asked for. The suggestion that the Greeks should also take part in the Dardanelles campaign made matters worse in the eyes of the Russians, and open rift followed.

The 1915 secret agreement was later repudiated by Lenin in accordance with his declared policy of no territorial annexations by the Soviets. But Trotsky took a different view. When he was Commissar for Foreign Affairs, he had asserted that the Straits and Constantinople provided one of the rare instances in which Imperial Russia had pursued a reasonable policy. He said that the world must be given to understand that "Red Russia" regarded them as essential to her. He added a lot more to the effect that even though France and England went back on the secret agreement made with Russia during the war, he firmly believed that sooner or later the Straits would be hers. Other Russian spokesmen had been no less insistent on the importance of the Dardanelles and of the Bosphorus. Addressing the Duma in 1916, M. Miliukov (who became Foreign Minister after the Tsar's abdication) had said: "We shall not end the war without securing an outlet to the open sea. The annexation of the Straits will not be a territorial annexation, for vast Russia has no need of new territories, but she cannot prosper without access to the open sea."[1] Had the 1915 secret agreement been implemented, Russia would not only have had such access, but, with control of both shores of the Straits, and having Bulgaria within her orbit, she could today have dominated the Aegean—a strategic area of the eastern Mediterranean.

Russia had pursued her traditional aim of strengthening her position on the Black Sea when in 1921 by the terms of her treaty with Turkey, she had regained Batum from that country. Once again she was in possession of a strong port at the south-eastern extremity of the sea: it remained for her now to work for the achievement of her long-standing aims at the south-western end. At the Convention of Lausanne, 1923, which dealt with the question of the Straits, it was clear from the attitude of Chicherin, Russian Minister for Foreign Affairs, that the Russian proposals for the Straits regarded the Black Sea as a *mare clausum* against the ships of other Powers.[2] Chicherin took the

---

[1] See André Chéradame, *The Pan-German Plot Unmasked*, translated by Lady Frazer. (Murray, 1916); p. 173.

[2] *The Lausanne Conference on Near Eastern Affairs, 1922-1923.* Cmd. 1814. (London, 1923); p. 129.

standpoint that the Black Sea should be closed to all foreign warships, and that fortifications should be constructed on the Bosphorus and the Dardanelles. Any other settlement, he contended, would place the Black Sea States at the mercy of the principal naval Powers. So strongly had Chicherin felt on this matter that at one meeting of the Conference he had ignored the Turkish delegates, and had appealed through the Turkish press to the people direct. Russia failed to get her way, but actually the demilitarisation of the Dardanelles was not absolute, inasmuch as Turkey was allowed a garrison of 12,000 men, a naval base, and an arsenal at Constantinople. (The strategic islands in the Aegean and in the Sea of Marmora, however, were totally demilitarised.)[1] Further, by the terms of the Convention, the Soviet Union gained a certain nominal safeguard in this matter, since it was arranged that in peace-time no Power should send into the Black Sea a naval force greater than that of the most powerful fleet of the littoral countries at the time. But as each of the Powers, including the non-riparian ones, had the right to send into the Black Sea ships not exceeding three in number and each of a tonnage not exceeding ten thousand, the proviso was in effect of theoretical rather than practical advantage: the Soviet Union was handicapped here, as at that time she had no fleet worth its name in the Black Sea.

Chicherin to some extent regarded the Convention as a gain for his country in its implication of the granting of *de jure* recognition of Soviet Russia by at least certain of the signatory Powers. Russia reserved the right to press for amendments to be made later to the terms; her policy at that time, as in 1947, had been consistent with regard to the Straits. She must have free access for her imports and exports, and there must be no possibility of any attack on her via the Dardanelles or from bases on them. (This policy was equally clearly directed in the reigns of Catherine the Great, of Alexander I during the Crimean War, and of Alexander II in the Turkish wars.) The Bosphorus was the egress to the Mediterranean and the Suez Canal for the commerce of four great rivers, the Danube, Dnieper, Dniester and Don. The extent to which Russia depended on the Straits for her commerce will be seen from the following table for 1913:[2]

[1] See J. T. Shotwell and F. Deák, *Turkey at the Straits.* (Copyright 1940 by The Macmillan Co., New York. Reference by their permission.); p. 116.
[2] Figures taken from *L'Europe devant Constantinople*, by Max Hoschiller. (Rivière et Cie., Paris, 1916); p. 99.

		Exports *(In 1,000s of tons)*	Imports *(In 1,000s of tons)*
Black Sea and Azov	..	11.086	921
Baltic	.. .. ..	5.857	7.515
White Sea ..	.. ..	1.506	315
Pacific	.. .. ..	61	128

The first decade of the twentieth century had seen a great industrial expansion in South Russia, resulting in an increase of metallurgical exports from the Donbas, naphtha and oil from the Caucasus, and the real force behind Russia's drive to the Straits was supplied by the industrialists of those areas. Agriculturists too had played a part in the Russian impulse to the Bosphorus. In the Black Earth region an immense increase in crops was responsible for a total export of corn of 47,265 (in 1,000s of tons) in 1919. During the blockade of the Straits the following year, the corn exports fell to 3,282 (1,000s of tons). The question of the Dardanelles was thus one of first importance to Russia, and after the *Goeben* and the *Breslau* had passed the Bosphorus into the Black Sea, public opinion in that country was widely reflected in the declaration that "*les Détroits doivent appartenir à la Russie. Il ne peut y avoir d'autre solution*".[1]

During World War II the Turkish Republic was the Power which controlled the Straits, consequently few countries could have meant more to Russia as a belligerent ally than Turkey. Such an alliance would have meant that the ships of the chief maritime nations could have passed through the Straits—protected by their own warships—to bring supplies to Russia. Another important advantage would have been the fact that Turkey and the U.S.S.R. could have undertaken joint operations in the Black Sea, based on a unified strategy. During the course of the war, Turkey had promised to give Russia facilities for the passage of her Black Sea Fleet in the event of the position becoming worse for the Soviet Union. Actually however, the use of the Straits by Russian warships in the last resort was already provided for by the Convention of Montreux, which under Article XIX permitted the passage through the Straits of warships cut off from their base. (Hence there was a way of escape for Russian units of the Black Sea Fleet, and actually three Soviet ships were evacuated from the Black Sea to the Mediterranean, with the active aid of Turkey.[2])

[1] *Russk. Vyedomosti*, March 1915, translated by Max Hoschiller, *L'Europe devant Constantinople*, p. 89.
[2] Admiral Sir Howard Kelly, *The Sunday Times*, 3.11.1946.

The Straits had been neutralised by the Convention of Lausanne, 1923; freedom of passage was from then up till 1936 maintained by the International Straits Commission of the League of Nations. During the period when the U.S.S.R.'s naval policy was mainly defensive, the Russian view had been that it was better even that Turkey should fortify the Dardanelles than that the latter should be open to any ships which might wish to go to the Black Sea. Here the continuity of aim is clear; Isvolsky at the beginning of the century and Sasonow at the beginning of the first world war, had taken the same view that the Soviet spokesman did in 1923. To all of them it was better that Turkey should be empowered to close the Straits than that the principle of free navigation should be established there. So the Treaty of Lausanne, which demilitarised the Straits, had been unpopular with Russia, and indeed was never ratified by that country.

The subsequent Convention of Montreux, 1936, however, had empowered Turkey to fortify the Dardanelles and to replace the International Straits Commission in regulating the passage of ships through the Bosphorus. But when later Moscow's policy changed to one directed to making the Soviet Union a first-class Sea Power, she showed that she desired a revision of the Montreux Convention, which had settled for a period of ten years the position of the Powers with regard to the Straits. By its terms the Dardanelles were to be closed to naval fleets in war-time, and also under a "general or special threat of war", so long as Turkey herself was not a belligerent. Britain and France however were already bound by treaty with Rumania to assist her in the Black Sea against aggression by any Power, and by the terms of the Montreux Convention Turkey must give passage through the Dardanelles to the British and French fleets if coming to the aid of Rumania. It had also been agreed that warships might pass through the Straits if in pursuance of obligations under the League of Nations, or in fulfilment of a pact of assistance to which Turkey was a party.[1] We have noted also the provision guaranteeing passage to ships of war which would otherwise be isolated from their base.

Russia's position was now improved, because, as a Black Sea Power, she gained the right to send warships through the Straits irrespective of numbers or tonnage. Warships

[1] G. M. Gathorne-Hardy, *A Short History of International Affairs, 1920-1939*. (The Royal Institute of International Affairs, Oxford University Press, 1942); p. 424. Reproduced by permission of the O.U.P.

of the non-Riparian States suffered a restriction in being allowed to remain in that sea for twenty-one days only, and they were required to give longer notification for their transit.

The passage of *armed* merchant ships in wartime was interdicted to all Powers. (There is nothing in the Treaty to indicate that its makers realised that in wartime practically all merchant ships would come to be armed.) A limitation to the passage of merchant ships during a period of war was imposed when they were neutral ships carrying supplies to an enemy of Turkey's: enemy merchant ships were of course without rights if Turkey was a belligerent. Otherwise unarmed merchant vessels had the right to pass through freely in time of war as in peace. Hence the terms of the Convention did not preclude ostensibly unarmed German cargo vessels sailing from the Danube in the last war and bringing such supplies as Rumanian oil to Italian bases in the Aegean, and to Rommel's forces in North Africa. Had Russia succeeded in her own efforts to get Turkey to keep out any ships except those of the Black Sea Powers (and thus to contravene the provisions of Montreux), she would have been the loser thereby, for early in 1945 American ships carrying supplies to the Soviet Union passed through the Dardanelles for the first time. In thus taking cargoes direct to Russian Black Sea ports via Istanbul, they saved the distance involved in the earlier route to the Persian Gulf.

Through Turkey's respect for the Convention of Montreux, Russia was helped to maintain her control of the Black Sea during the most critical period of the German advance on the Crimea; despite much that has been said to the contrary it was Ankara's policy of firmness which prevented Italian ships of war from sailing through the Dardanelles to operate against the Red Fleet. And the Turkish Republic refused passage to ships seized by the Axis which were intended to be used as auxiliary vessels for war purposes.

In August 1941, Russia addressed a Note to the Turkish Government, with assurances that the Soviet Union had no claims concerning the Straits, and would respect Turkey's territorial integrity. In March 1945, she made it clear that she desired a revision of the Treaty of Montreux[1], with the object of getting a share in the control of the Straits, and establishing

---

[1] Provision was made in the Treaty whereby its signatories might propose every five years that the Convention be amended. Revision was not till July 1946.

bases for that purpose. Mr. Churchill subsequently[1] disclosed that America and Britain at the time of the Potsdam Agreement, had offered to the Soviet Union a joint guarantee of complete freedom of the Straits in peace and war, whether for merchant ships or ships of war. But, said Mr. Churchill, Russian aims went further. "Russia must have a fortress inside the Straits from which she could dominate Constantinople. This is not to keep the Straits open, but to give the power of closing them to a single nation. This is out of harmony with the principle urged by United States representatives, of the freedom of the great waterways of Europe, the Danube, Rhine and other rivers which run through many countries." British and American spokesmen declared that at the time when the Soviet Union was pressing for control of the Straits, she was opposing the Anglo-American demand for free navigation on the Danube,[2] Russian aims on the Bosphorus had been apparent at the outbreak of the second world war, when the Soviet Union had asked the Turkish Republic for military bases on the Dardanelles. (This had been refused by Turkey.) And during his talks with Hitler and Ribbentrop in Berlin, 1940, M. Molotov had made the same demand. On 26 November, 1940, he had notified Count von Schulenberg that Moscow would accept certain proposals made by Berlin on condition that, among other things, Russian requirements concerning the Straits were fulfilled.

Dominance of the Dardanelles would place Russia at a decisive advantage in the eastern Mediterranean, and enable her to secure that position which Nelson had foreseen and feared. This aim has been the over-riding factor in Soviet policy in the Balkans. Moscow's desire to obtain right of passage through Adrianople, has been due to the fact that the railway which runs through that city leads to the port of Dede Agatch at the head of the Aegean. Similarly the "Greater Macedonia" movement was supported because its achievement would bring Russian influence to the Aegean. This support was viewed with misgiving by London; the prospect of a Russian advance on Salonika to aid any "Liberation Movement" among the Slavs

[1] At New York, 15.3.1946.
[2] The Soviet Government no doubt had in mind the fact that Russia once had a privileged position as regards Danubian navigation. In 1922 the Russian mouths of the river had been declared exempt from the operations of the European Commission of the Danube—a Commission on which however, she had not been represented, as her loss of Bessarabia after 1918 had meant that she was no longer a Riparian State.

of Macedonia, recalled the fact that Tsar Nicholas II had for a time a squadron stationed at the Greek harbour of Poros; the possibility of a Russian return to the Aegean after 1948 was one which could hardly be otherwise than of concern to the Power whose oil interests in the Near East and whose short sea route to Australia and New Zealand must remain unchallenged. For Pan-Slavism is not an end in itself with the Kremlin; it is linked with Russia's traditional march to the oceans.

IV

THE BLACK SEA AND ITS FLEET

STRATEGIC IMPORTANCE

INEVITABLY the Euxine has been an area of contest all through history, as any land-locked sea having on its shores more than one State, is bound at some time or another to become the subject of dispute. The general principle that all riparian States have equal right of navigation on their common sea, is a principle which has rarely been followed in practice, and one of the most outstanding examples of this is presented by the Black Sea. The control of the latter is of first importance in the defence of South Russia because it means the denial of the seaway supply route to an enemy, and it ensures the delivery of Caucasian oil to the naval ports of Sevastopol and Kherson, to the harbour of Odessa, and to the shipyards of Nikolaiev. Such importance does Russia attach to the Black Sea that at the Convention of Lausanne, as we have seen, she opposed the Treaty's provision for the entry of non-Russian warships to that sea. "Even defensively armed merchant ships, if their guns exceed six-inch calibre, were not to be allowed passage."[1] She has always regarded the Black Sea as her own.

The Germans have been no less alive to its importance, and that is why, even before the first world war, their geo-politicians were marking the Black Sea as belonging to the Ukrainian zone. For Ukraine, they had decided, was to be annexed by Germany —an aim which they pursued as fixedly in the years preceding the second world war—financing to that end movements among certain disaffected Ukrainians for the separation of their country from the U.S.S.R. The following extract from *Germany's Annexationist Aims*,[2] is but one of many examples of the thought pursued by those writers who were urging that Germany should close the Black Sea to Russia:

"The aim of the Peace Settlement must be to preserve Russia's Asiatic character and to destroy its position as a

[1] H. C. Ferraby, "Nazi Naval Approach to Oil"; *Serial Maps*, Vol. II, No. 12. (Serial Map Service, Letchworth.)

[2] Translated and abbreviated by J. Ellis Barker, from the work of S. Grumbach. (John Murray, 1917); p. 72. Note.—A fuller version will be found in *Welche Strafe soll die treffen, die Schuld am Weltkrieg tragen?* by A. Oetzelt Lewin. (E. V. Mayer, Leipzig, 1915.)

143

European Great Power. That can be done only by cutting off
its western parts which culturally and economically are most
valuable, and at the same time keeping Russia away from all
European seas. The latter cannot be achieved by mere treaty.
The separating line should be drawn from Kronstadt via
Brest-Litovsk and Taganrog to Baku. Finland would, of course,
be separated from Russia. All fortresses, especially those on the
sea, would have to be destroyed, and Finland, Esthonia,
Livonia, Courland, Poland, Volhynia, Podolia, Bessarabia, and
parts of Little Russia and Lower Russia, Taurida and Caucasia
would have to be ceded."

Such a "Peace Settlement" would have meant the annexation by Germany of the whole of the Black Sea and the Sea of
Azov, since a line drawn from Taganrog on the Sea of Azov
to Baku on the Caspian Sea, brings all the area of the first two
seas, as well as the Caucasus, within the German imperium. It
was part of the traditional policy of Germany to deprive Russia
of an outlet to the sea—a policy clearly pursued earlier by
Count Mirbach, German Ambassador at Moscow.

The same intention was apparent in the Treaty of Brest-
Litovsk. When the Russians signed that Treaty in 1918, they
ceded to Germany the eastern shores of the Black Sea from the
Kuban to the port of Batum (the latter actually was given up to
Turkey), also all the Sea of Azov. Russia recognised the
"Independence" of Ukraine, which meant the German suzerainty of that region. Following the Treaty, the Germans occupied not only the Crimean ports but Baku on the Caspian.
The division of the Dobrudja between Bulgaria, Germany, and
Austria-Hungary, established the Germans in a central position
on the western coastline of the Black Sea. Soviet Russia, however, did not allow herself to be placed at such a disadvantage
for long. The ports of the Black Sea were essential for the exports
of the Union, and so in 1920 she signed with the Ukraine a
treaty of military and economic alliance.

That same year, at Versailles, the Treaty of Bucarest was
annulled. Its terms had made the German position on the Black
Sea a dominant one from Odessa to Varna. It had left Rumania
with no seaboard, the only concession here being the use to her
of Constanza as a free port, and she was allowed to have "a free
hand in securing from Russia the province of Bessarabia."[1] Not

[1] *The Treaty of Brest-Litovsk and Germany's Eastern Policy*, John W. Wheeler-
Bennett. Oxford Pamphlets on World Affairs, No. 14. (Oxford University
Press, New Edition, 1940); p. 14. Reproduction by permission of the
Clarendon Press, Oxford.

THE PORTS AND THE NAVIGATIONAL ROUTES OF THE BLACK SEA

(Reproduction by arrangement with the London Geographical Institute, from their "Mercantile Map of Europe, 1948")

THE Black Sea, on whose shores lie the coastal frontiers of four countries, has inevitably been an area of recurring conflict since the days when the Rus Northmen first attacked the Greeks on the shores of the Euxine, and the Bulgars in the delta of the Danube. One of the most formidable of such raids was made in A.D. 907 by Oleg, when with his company of Varangian warriors he sailed down the Dnieper to the sea, where he reached a point on the coast of the Crimea between Ochakov and Kinburn, and advanced to Constantinople, inflicting sufficient damage to cause the withdrawal of the Emperor's troops.

Rus princes, Byzantine emperors, and Turkish sultans, realised the importance of the Black Sea to the trade with Persia and the Levant, as did the tsars of Russia from the time of Ivan IV. Peter the Great's intention to link the Black Sea with the Caspian in order to secure that trade, is well known; not so well known, however, is the fact that long before him, in 1569, the Turkish Emperor Selim II had the same idea. Jealous of Russia's commerce with the west, Selim was bent on taking Astrakhan from the Russians; he therefore ordered work to commence on the plan of his grand vizier, Mohammed Sokolli, for linking Azov and Astrakhan by a canal. In this way the Don would be connected with the Volga, and the canal could be used for the transport of troops to the Caspian Sea with the object of capturing trade with Persia. Although the Sultan's forces were routed by the Russians at Astrakhan, the Black Sea remained a Turkish lake. Under Selim indeed the zenith of Turkey's sea power was reached, and this was the period of her great sea captains.

Peter I's project of uniting the Black Sea with the Caspian was formed by the time he visited Amsterdam, for on a chart belonging to the learned Burgomaster Nicolas Witsen, the Tsar sketched his plan. With his mind set on the advantage of launching a Russian fleet on the Black Sea, he sent plenipotentiaries to the Hague to ask for at least 70 warships and 100 galleys, pointing out that not only was it in the interests of all Christian countries to support Holy Russia against the Turk, but that his country, if she had control of the Black Sea and Azov, could supply Holland with grain in time of emergency.

Today, not only grain passes through Black Sea ports (in particular Odessa and Mariupol), but the chief shipping routes on that sea carry from Kherson the iron ore of Krivoy Rog and of Kerch; zinc, lead, and magnesium from the region east of the ports of Sukhum and Tuapse, manganese from Chiaturi and copper from Ordzhonikidze (exported from Poti), coal from Azov, salt from Perekop (via Odessa), timber from White Russia, cement from Novorossisk, molybdenum from Azerbaijan, oil from Grozni and Maikop (exported from Tuapse), cotton from the trans-Caucasian Republics, which, with oil from Baku, is shipped from Batum.

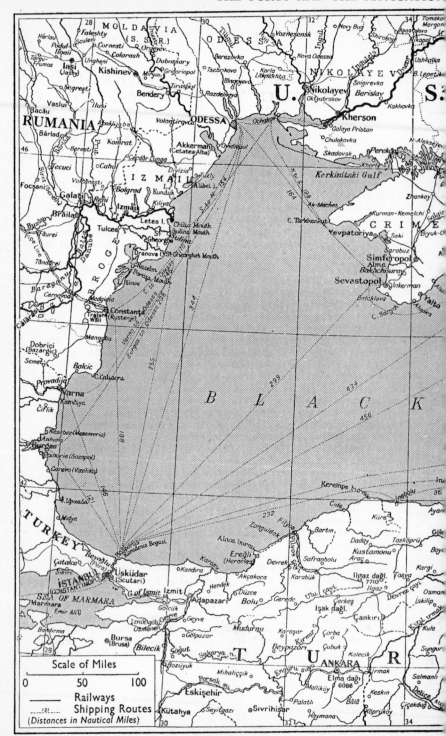

only had the delta of the Danube passed under German control, but the whole of the lower reach of that river, and with it the Rumanian town of Giurgiu. Steamers from here can go to Ruschuk, the Bulgarian port which is linked by rail with Varna[1] on the Black Sea. As a port for the export of grain and oil, the importance of Giurgiu to the Power which commands the delta of the Danube is considerable. In the second world war, as in the period immediately following the Peace of Bucarest, the controlling Power of this Danubian port was Germany. In the last war Germany's canal system, linked with the Danube, enabled her to send the sections for a certain number of ships to the Black Sea via Rumanian and Bulgarian ports. In this way too a number of German submarines and motor torpedo boats built for Rumanian use against Russia, found their way to Constanza and Galati. (Here was a reverse of fate, for Constanza and Ruschuk had been the ports to which the Russians had shipped oil for the Reich during the Russo-German Pact.) Command of the Danube also enabled the Germans to send supplies down to their U-boats, and when these were pressed at sea they were able to make use of bases up the river. These demonstrations of its value for wartime transport have made the Russians anxious to secure control of this river.

Constanza, if we exclude Odessa in the extreme north-west, is the largest port on the western shores of the Black Sea. Two breakwaters protect the harbour, which is not a good natural one, owing to the constant need for dredging. Cruisers however can berth here, and there are repairing docks. In the protocol to the Russo-German Treaty of 23 August, 1939, the interest of the Soviet Union in Bessarabia had been specified. In 1940 that territory was recovered by Russia from Rumania, and with it the port of Sulina at the end of the central channel of the Danubian delta. The depth of the delta approach here enables it to be used by deep-water vessels. On the right bank of the Dniester is Cetatea Alba, not deep enough for large vessels, but useful for small cargo ones and light coasters. This port was also regained by Russia, and in 1940 she was back on the Black Sea from Odessa to the delta of the Danube.

The area of the Black Sea is an extensive one, and involves considerable distance for the passage of supply ships which have to cross it; the passage to be made by even the most direct route from east to west averages seven hundred miles. (From

---

[1] This port was enlarged for the shipping of oil to Germany by Russia during the Pact between those two countries in 1940.

Batum to Constanza it is 1,230 miles.) From north to south the voyage from Odessa to the Bosphorus is 344 miles.

Reference to Odessa in any maritime history of Russia would be incomplete without some account of the revolt of the *Potemkin*. Seamen have so often been in the vanguard of revolts; it will be recalled that many of the Kronstadt sailors who had led the attack on the Aurora Palace in 1917, mutinied four years later against the Bolshevik Petrograd Soviet. It was the Black Sea, however, which was the scene of the first impressive revolutionary movement in the Fleet, and this began in 1903. Conditions in the Fleet were bad, and they were aggravated by the appointment of Tchunin as commander; partly in order to dispense with hired labour he got sailors to do dockyard work, and here they met agitators and political-minded workers. Corruption was widespread, and the food was bad. Discontent came to a head two years later, when the immediate cause of the outbreak of revolt was the discovery that there were maggots in the meat and the crew were expected to eat it. Men and officers were killed on board, and into Odessa went many of the ratings to join a demonstration of the shore workers. Owing to the number of new hands who had come to the warship straight from villages where there was little or no revolutionary activity, *Potemkin* was not the most obvious ship to lead a mutiny of the fleet. Nevertheless after the overthrow of the ship's officers, the crew steamed for Odessa and shelled the town, aiming at the theatre, in which a military council of generals was being held. Instead, the shells hit the soldiers' barracks. "The fire of revolution broke in and consumed the whole edifice of military discipline, and the last relics of loyal feeling. And their deafening report echoed all over Russia from the Black to the Baltic Sea, from the Caucasus to Siberia, and everywhere it awakened the slumbering Russian soldier from the unbroken sleep of ages."[1]

A proclamation addressed "to all European Monarchs" was sent out by *Potemkin's* crew with the object of enlisting the help and support of democratic peoples against those of their Governments which were reactionarily inclined. It declared that "The crew of the Squadron ironclad *Prince Potemkin Tavritcheski* has opened war upon the autocracy. While acquainting all European Governments with this fact, we think it is our duty to declare that we guarantee absolute security to

[1] Constantine Feldmann, *The Revolt of the "Potemkin"*, translated by Constance Garnett. (Heinemann, 1908); p. 94.

all foreign vessels navigating in the Black Sea and all foreign ports situated therein."[1] But the revolt was short-lived. When the *Rostislav, Sinope, Three Bishops* and *George the Victorious* approached Odessa a few days after the shelling of the port, *Potemkin*, calling on the ships to surrender, hoisted the Red Flag. The crew of *George* signalled that they were with *Potemkin*, but later deserted her. *Potemkin* herself, after soldiers had fired on her crew when she called for coal at Feodosia, steamed to Rumania and there surrendered.

Conditions in the Black Sea Fleet improved but little in the next fourteen years; Russian sailors were still poorly fed, their clothing was inadequate for cold climates, and they worked in cramped, ill-ventilated quarters. But the main cause of the revolt which broke out in 1919 was the continuation of the war after the Armistice. French ships were in the Black Sea, and among their crews were many sympathisers with the Russian Revolution. Those in *France* and then in *Jean Bart*, revolted in Sevastopol roadstead. Eventually the French squadron was compelled to leave Sevastopol before the end of April, and all warships except *Jean Bart* steamed for France. It had been a political victory for the Black Sea Fleet.

That Fleet, as we said earlier, had been in no position to meet alone the Dreadnoughts of the Turkish Navy, still less the combined Turkish-German squadron (which included the *Goeben* and the *Breslau*) when in 1915 it steamed through the Straits, and proceeded to bombard Odessa, Sevastopol, Novorossisk. The mining of the Kerch Strait prevented several of the Russian steamers from retreating to the Sea of Azov, and some of them were sunk. Grain badly needed by the Allies lay in the warehouses of the Black Sea ports; the situation became critical. The condition of the Russian Black Sea Squadron by 1918 was such that when the warships were about to fall into the hands of the Germans, the Bolshevik Government asked, through the British Commissioner at Moscow, that British naval officers should take charge of the Black Sea Fleet. "If those officers," Trotsky said, "find they can do nothing else, they can at least sink the fleet before the Germans get it."[2] It is curious after

---

[1] Constantine Feldmann, *The Revolt of the "Potemkin"*, translated by Constance Garnett, (Heinemann, 1908); pp. 158-59.

[2] William Hard, *Raymond Robins's Own Story*. See reference to letter from R. H. Bruce-Lockhart to Robins, May 5, 1918, which states that Trotsky had invited the Allies to send a Commission of British naval officers to save the Black Sea Fleet. (Harper Bros., New York, 1920); pp. 201, 202.

this to find that a belief was current in Germany that British
naval officers commanded part of the Russian Black Sea Fleet
in the second world war.[1]

[1] See *The Daily Telegraph's* report, 11 June, 1942.

V

THE CASPIAN SEA

Russian expansion towards the Middle East in the early part of the eighteenth century had two principal motives—to obtain control of the Caspian, and to acquire an outlet on the Persian Gulf. Alexis Mikhailovitch, father of Peter the Great, had tried to follow the example of England in opening trade on the Caspian, but his efforts had failed owing to the rebellion of the Don Cossacks, and the Caspian Sea remained a Persian lake. Nothing short of bringing Persia under Russian domination could change that position, was the view of Peter the Great. One of his ambitions was to open up trade with India, and, aware of the necessity of gaining control of the Caspian first, he directed Kojni, a naval officer, and Prince Bekowitsch, to erect forts on that sea for his expedition against the Khanate of Khiva— a venture which was designed to take his forces eastward. In 1722 he had invaded the Caspian Province and had gained by enforced treaty the ports of Baku and Derbend. This to some extent changed the political character of the Caspian Sea. Two years later Russia acquired more territory on that sea by the treaty signed at Constantinople. When Peter I died, his empire embraced the north shore of the Caspian from Guriev on the Ural River to Kizliar on the delta of the Terek.

His aims had also been pursued by his successors; in 1816 Baku, which had meanwhile been lost by Russia, was regained from Persia, and in 1811 by the Treaty of Gulistan which ended the Russo-Persian war, Russia got all Persian Caucasia. Further successes gained for the Russians not only the right to sail their ships on the Caspian Sea, but the exclusive right for warships; and gradually that sea which had once been a Persian *mare clausum* became a Russian one. Having gained certain islands, the Russians began to increase their flotilla on the Caspian, and in 1852 had steamers sent in sections from Sweden to St. Petersburg and transported to the Caspian by water. They also set up a naval station at Ashurada on the Gulf of Astrabad, and one on Sara Island. These measures were necessary for the protection of their trading vessels crossing from Astrakhan, and for the safety of their fishermen against attacks by local tribesmen.

The Russians enforced the registration of trading ships at Ashurada, and made them submit to examination as a safeguard against the piratical raids of the Turcomans. The Persians, prohibited from keeping a fleet on the Caspian, could make no contribution to defence. It was, indeed, not till 1921 that Persia, by treaty with Russia, was free for the first time for nearly a hundred years to maintain a naval force on that sea.

To her capture of Krasnovodsk in 1869, Russia owes her possession of all the eastern shore of the Caspian Sea, for she made that port a base for the conquest of Persian territory, and her Trans-Caspian Railway, commencing at Krasnovodsk and running to Merv near the north-east frontier of Persia, was designed to help Russia in her advance to the Gulf. As long as Persia's northern frontier remains the southern shore of the Caspian, that sea separates Soviet territory in Europe from Soviet territory in Asia; only by sea-transport can Krasnovodsk be reached from Baku. Hence the control of the Caspian north of Astara and of Chikishlar is most important to the U.S.S.R. The whole sea indeed is geographically important to Russia as it affords the shortest means of communication between Caucasia and Turkestan, between the alluvial delta lands of the Volga and the Don, and the arid steppes of Kirghiz.

The Soviet Union, even before the north Persian oil concessions of 1945, possessed the second greatest oil resources in the world. The addition of the Galician fields had further increased her supplies, hence need for oil was not Russia's first consideration. It was the Caspian Sea from Astara to Bandur Shah, more than any increase in petroleum production, that the Soviet Union was seeking.

That sea was given a new strategic value when plans to link it with the Black Sea by a canal system were first made. Peculiar problems arose in work over the Canal, owing to the low level of the Caspian, but now destroyer flotillas there are linked with those on the Black Sea. To save the Caspian from slow evaporation, the Greater Volga Project has provided for the creation of two large dams which will raise the level of the northern rivers Pechora and Vychegda till they spill south at a certain point and eventually join the Volga. The fulfilment of other plans by the construction of the Don-Volga Canal will give fresh importance to Astrakhan. This is the principal centre of shipbuilding for Kazakhstan. Situated on the left bank of the Volga, and fifty feet below sea level, it is frozen sometimes for

[continued on page 156

RUSSIA IN 1725

From *The Cambridge Modern History Atlas*, Map 52

(Reproduction permitted by the Cambridge University Press)

THE acquisitions of Peter the Great on the Caspian Sea and the Baltic are shown by the solid black portions in this map. On the Caspian the Tsar gained not only the whole of the southern coastline, which included Astrabad, but on the western shore he acquired the ports of Derbend and Baku. Holding already the northern coast from Guriev on the Ural River to Kizliar on the delta of the Terek, Peter's gains in the south brought Russia nearer her intended domination of the Caspian Sea.

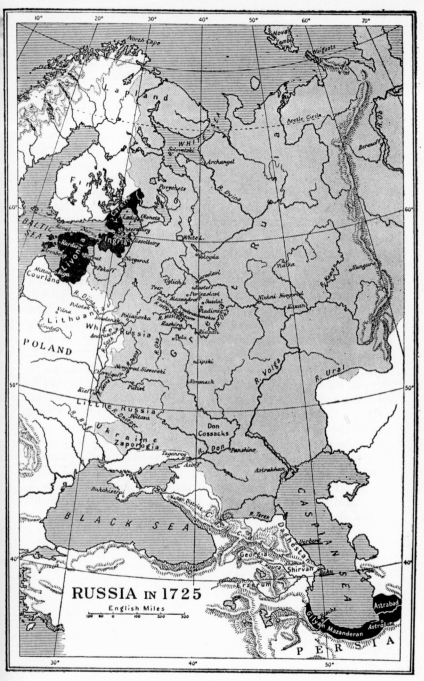

RUSSIA IN 1725

English Miles
100 50 0   100   200   300

four months in the year, but in its ice-free period it receives oil from Baku, cotton from Turkestan, and rugs and wool from Persia. Its chief exports are grain and salt.

Between the Aral and Caspian Seas, surveying of subterranean waters has been undertaken extensively to help the rise of new industries, which must be sited near water. The port of Krasnovodsk has become of greater value since hydrologists revealed that supplies of subterranean water were on the Krasnovodsk Peninsula. Formerly this port—the only one of any size on the east Caspian shore—was almost entirely devoid of fresh water, which had to be brought from Baku across the Caspian, a voyage of nearly two hundred miles. The provision of new shipyards at Krasnovodsk was the work of the First and Second Five-Year Plans. Another port enlarged under these plans was Makhach-Kala, the port for the oilfields of Grozni. Drilling for oil is in operation under the sea off Baku, and today nearly three-quarters of the cargo carried on the Caspian consists of oil. The sea routes crossing the Caspian from Astrakhan and from Baku with tankers and grain ships, are an essential part of the transport system for supplies to and from Central Asia. The State Caspian Boat Company has linked Trans-Caucasia with the Central Asian Republics, for the construction of the deep channel connecting Karabugaz Bay with the Caspian Sea has made it possible for cargoes destined for Turkmenistan to be shipped direct to Karabugaz, instead of, as formerly, having to be unloaded in the Caspian Sea and trans-shipped in barges.

Will a time ever come when the legend (derived from Greek and Arabic geographers) that the Caspian Sea was once linked to the Northern Ocean, becomes a reality? By no very great stretch of the imagination we can conceive of a canal running from the Caspian through the Kirghiz steppes, and then following a course parallel with the Urals, till it joins the Pechora River and finds its way into the great "Storm Kitchen" of the north—the Barents Sea.

VI

THE PERSIAN GULF

EFFORTS to reach the Persian Gulf have been made by Russia throughout many chapters of her history, and British reactions to these efforts, in view of their suspected relation to the Indian Ocean, have always been unfavourable. Britain, as Sir Halford Mackinder has emphasised,[1] has in the past made it a declared principle of her policy that no sea-base should be established on either the Persian or Turkish shores of the Persian Gulf. Internal strife in Afghanistan had led to British intervention in 1838; Russian intrigues with the Amir Dost Mohammed were actuated mainly by the desire to bring Russia nearer to the Arabian Sea.

In pursuance of her eastern aims, Russia had established a new shipping line to the Persian Gulf at the end of the nineteenth century. A few years later, by the Anglo-Russian Agreement of 1907, Russia recognised Afghanistan as the special concern of Britain, and one outside the Russian sphere of influence. The latter, it was agreed, embraced north Persia; the fact that Teheran and Tabriz were specifically mentioned is not without interest today in view of Russo-Persian relations, and events connected with these places in 1946. It is significant that the Agreement gave Russia no rights on the Persian Gulf and no warm-water port. The Agreement was, indeed, a diplomatic victory for the western Sea Power. Between Odessa on the Black Sea and Vladivostock on the Sea of Japan, Russia had no ship-repairing establishment for the equipment of her Volunteer Fleet which had been founded in 1876. Hence her continued sense of frustration after a treaty which deprived her of the possibility of gaining a coaling station, still less a naval base, on the Persian Gulf. It is interesting to see how this subject of Russia's attempted rivalry with Britain in the neighbourhood of the Persian Gulf was viewed by a leading Japanese naval writer only three years before the commencement of World War II. The following passage is from *Japan Must Fight Britain*, by Lieut.-Cmdr. Tota Ishimaru, I.J.N.:[2]

"Every expansion of Russian influence in Persia increased

[1] *Democratic Ideals and Reality.* (Pelican Books, 1944); p. 49.
[2] Translated from the Japanese by Instr. Captain G. V. Rayment, C.B.E., R.N. (Hurst & Blackett, 1936); p. 235.

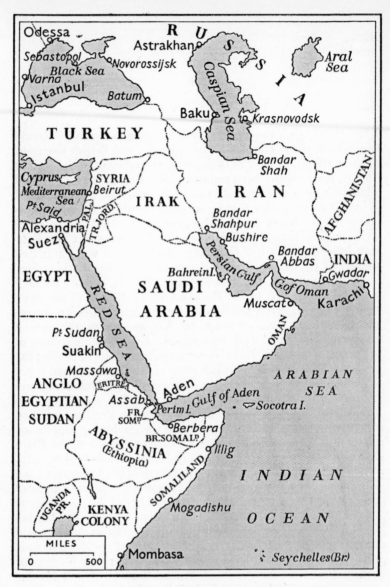

THE PERSIAN GULF

THE Persian Gulf is a region of critical location, and is the
centre of a zone containing seven seas.

*(Illustration by permission of Messrs. Hutchinson and the Grout Publishing Company,
from "We Can Keep the Peace", by Mairin Mitchell. Map drawn by "Geographia" Ltd.)*

THE PERSIAN GULF

British anxiety. For, if Russia came out into the Persian Gulf she would be in a position to attack the trade routes across the Indian Ocean and also to threaten India itself. England was compelled to uphold the independence of Persia so that she might, like Afghanistan, serve as a buffer state. When, then, Sir Edward Grey made a Treaty with Russia in 1907, he included in it an Agreement for a divided control of Persia. The part on the Indian side was to be regarded as the British zone and the rest as a Russian one. By this means the safety of the Indian frontier was secured. The whole of the Persian Gulf was not included in the British zone. That was where British diplomacy was so clever. After preventing Russia from obtaining an ice-free port in the Far East by means of the Anglo-Japanese Alliance, it would have been unreasonable to deny her one in the Middle East. So England gave up the Gulf and made it into a neutral zone with which neither Power was to interfere. In effect, she prevented Russia from coming out into the Gulf, a diplomatic victory." Russian efforts in that direction were pursued in 1940, when, during his talks with Hitler in Berlin, M. Molotov demanded for his country the recognition of her right to expand southwards towards the Persian Gulf.

De Witte, when Finance Minister of Russia, had established the Persian Loan Bank as much to bring his country to the Gulf as to advance commercial aims. Had he succeeded, the projected Russian railway via Ispahan to Bandur Abbas at the entrance to the Persian Gulf would then have materialised in the reign of Nicholas II. This line would have been open to Russia during the last war. It was however the routes from Bandur Shahpur and from Basra on the Persian Gulf, to Pahlevi and to Bandur Shah on the Caspian Sea, that saved Russia from isolation during some of the most critical periods of that war. Up the ancient way of the Tigris and Euphrates, whose banks are fringed with the grey-green date palm, Indian paddle steamers sailed on the first stage of the journey to the Caspian. Basra, near the head of the Gulf, has rail and river communication with Baghdad; from here supplies were taken by road over the Paytak Pass to the Caspian port of Pahlevi.

Another supply route to the U.S.S.R. was served by the port of Bushire on the eastern shore of the Persian Gulf. The use of this route for supplies to the southern armies of Marshal Timoshenko in 1941, became additionally valuable as the Germans increased their advance down the Don. Here the importance of

Russian sea power is clear; the supplies could not have been shipped across the Caspian Sea to Baku and Astrakhan if the Red Navy flotillas had lost command of that sea. It is equally clear that supplies could never have got through Iran to the Russian Caspian ports but for the Royal Navy's command of the Persian Gulf; it was British naval and air co-operation which had made possible the landings of troops at Abadan and Bandur Shahpur, and which destroyed the German raiding ships that had already reached the Persian Gulf.

The movement in 1945 for the incorporation of Iranian Azerbaijan with Soviet Azerbaijan was viewed with apprehension by Turkey, as such a change threatened to cut off that country from direct communication with Persia, and also to extend Russia's frontiers to the borders of Irak. The Soviet Union already had approximate connection with the *southern* frontier of Irak by means of the Trans-Persian Railway. Russia's actions with regard to Persian Azerbaijan were determined not only by her desire for security in the regions bordering on her pipe-line from Baku to Batum, but also by her ambition to extend her control over areas on the south-western shore of the Caspian Sea.

Gains in that direction were made when the Russo-Persian oil agreement, giving the U.S.S.R. oil concessions in land bordering on the Caspian, was signed in 1946. The territory of the new oil company stretched from the Turkish frontier in the west to the border of Afghanistan in the east—an area which embraced the whole of the southern shore of the Caspian, and included the ports of Astara and Bandur Shah. Though the Persian parliament later refused to ratify the agreement, Russia had gained ground here for the time being. Her objectives in the region south of Baku and Batum had been underlined by M. Molotov in his discussions with Ribbentrop in 1940, and on 26 November of that year he had informed von Schulenberg that the Soviet Government would accept certain proposals made by Ribbentrop on condition that, *inter alia*, "the area south of Batum and Baku in the general direction of the Persian Gulf is recognised as the centre of the aspirations of the Soviet Union." These aims were made forcefully clear when Moscow later pressed Turkey for cession of the provinces of Kars and Ardahan. These would not only give Russia an additional strip of coast on the Black Sea, but would bring her nearer her march to the Persian Gulf. These provinces are regarded by the Turks as "the backbone of Turkey", and the Russian claim for their possession led to a call that the Republic should seek an alliance with a strong Middle Eastern bloc to check Soviet expansion seawards. "Russia", declared Çumhuriyet,[1] "is trying to extend her frontiers to the Dardanelles, the Mediterranean, the Red Sea, the Persian Gulf, and the Indian Ocean."

These aims can be traced in the railway systems of Asiatic and Caucasian Russia. The line through the Caucasus was designed partly to give Russia an overland route to the Straits; the Trans-Caspian Railway was directed to bring her through Persia to the Gulf, and the line from Merv in Turkestan was planned with the intention of eventually taking her to the Arabian Sea and thence to the Indian Ocean.

THE INDIAN ROUTE TO RUSSIA

The joint operations of English and Russian naval forces in the first world war, and the development of the Indian supply route to Russia during the second world war, provide two of the very few instances in which there has ever been co-operation between the two countries in this region. One of Peter the Great's ambitions had been to build up trade with India, not only by way of the Caspian and Bokhara, but by an all-sea route; he did not however live to attempt such a project, which would certainly have brought about opposition from England. Ever since the days of Catherine II, who wanted to overthrow British power in India, relations between the two Powers have been strained at this point. Catherine's successor Paul had intrigued with Napoleon to break up the British Empire by conquering India, and plans had been discussed for a combined march on that country from Astrabad on the southern shore of the Caspian Sea. Russian intrigues during the Afghan Wars had the same objective. Tsarist interest in trying to find a Russian trade route to India would, had that objective been fulfilled in the reign of Alexander I, have brought Russia into conflict with Britain.

The desire of the Imperial Government at that time to consolidate and extend Russia's eastern possessions, and also to open up new markets, was well known to some of her sea captains, and certain of the more adventurous ones lent themselves to these projects. In 1865 officers in Russian ships visiting Singapore, reported on the possibility of opening trade negotiations with Siam, and later when a Russian squadron called at Bangkok definite steps in this direction were taken, resulting eventually

[1] 28.12.1945.

in the conclusion of the first commercial treaty between the two countries in 1899. Another instance of the part played by Russian naval officers in their country's eastward expansion had been provided earlier by Ivan Krusenstern, the first Russian to command a round-the-world expedition. He had followed the custom of those days by serving for a time with the British Fleet, and voyaging through the Indian Ocean and the Bay of Bengal, made it the occasion for recording observations useful for the projected rival Russian sea route to India.

But the first world war saw a temporary change in the Indian scene. Units of the Russian Navy co-operated with those of the Royal Navy in the Indian Ocean. There the Russian cruiser *Askold*[1] and the light cruiser *Zhemchug* did escort duty for a time, being in charge of transports bringing in British regiments from Singapore, Hong Kong, and Tientsin, to Calcutta.[2] Later the *Zhemchug* patrolled the waters round the Andaman and Nicobar Islands, searching for the German light cruiser *Emden*. Eventually, when in harbour at Penang, she herself was attacked by the *Emden* and sunk "as though," says Corbett,[3] "the curse of the ill-fated Baltic Fleet, in which during the Russo-Japanese War she had seen her first service, still clung to her."

In the second world war, India became a vast Allied base for the whole of the war effort in the East. The importance of that country as a supply base for Russia was shown in the course of the war, when from India the north-east route to the U.S.S.R. was developed from the most elementary of roads into a system of communications along which could pass lorries laden with supplies for the Soviet Union. The rail route is the one to Zabedan in Iran, which by way of Meshed, connects with the Turkestan system at Merv; from here freight continues by rail to the Caspian port of Krasnovodsk. This became one of the main supply routes from Britain to Russia, a fact which could not have been foreseen three-quarters of a century ago, when, on the inclusion of Krasnovodsk in Russian territory, explanations were demanded by the British Ambassador at St. Petersburg. In 1943 was opened the new railway linking India with Irak; by this route too, supplies were sent to the U.S.S.R. But neither of these main ways from India to Russia, so vital

---

[1] The name perpetuates one of the early Rus leaders mentioned in Chapter II.

[2] See Sir Julian Corbett, *History of the Great War*. (Longmans, Green & Co., 1938, 2nd edition); Vol. I, p. 282. With acknowledgments to Lady Corbett.

[3] *Ibid.*, Vol. I, p. 337.

to the latter, could have been kept open if Britain had not maintained command in the Persian Gulf and in the Indian Ocean.

The wartime demonstration of the importance of the Indian route to Russia has enhanced its value in the eyes of Moscow, and the indications are that Russia aims at making her influence felt in those sea areas. From her oil concessions on the Persian-Afghanistan border an important advance towards the Persian Gulf may be said to have commenced in 1946, and further progress in that direction would bring a conflict of interests. For Britain has considerable interests in the Iranian wells of Khuzistan, near the head of the Persian Gulf, oil from which supplies the navy. The projected pipe-lines for Anglo-Iranian oil production from Haifa on the eastern Mediterranean to Ras Tamura and to Abadan on the Persian Gulf, will increase for Britain the importance of the Gulf. Persia, with its southern shores washed by the Arabian Sea, has a coastline from Yekhuni to Gwatar. Hence any advance southwards of the Russian sphere in Persia, or any encroachment in Afghanistan, affects Commonwealth communications across the Indian Ocean. But any threat on the part of Russia to British sea communications from here to Australia and New Zealand, would require an increase to Russia's surface navy.

For long it was an axiom of British policy that Britain could not afford to have the borders of the Persian Gulf become the territorial base for the navy of a potential enemy—and in the mind of most British statesmen in the past that "enemy" would be Russia. Subsequently there was a tendency to pay less attention to Soviet aims in this direction—aims which would place Russia upon the flank of India—because India was no longer a British possession. This view was a short-sighted one, for India by her geographical situation will continue to exert great influence on the course of Commonwealth relations. Dominating as she does the great basin of the Indian Ocean, India must be grouped among the maritime, not the continental states. The safeguarding of the ocean routes is vital also to India no less than to the members of the British Commonwealth, for her future industrialisation must depend on ocean commerce.

Another factor has today however entered into the situation. American, as much as British sea power, is now affected by Russian policy in the direction of the Persian Gulf—the Gulf which is the north-west arm of the Indian Ocean. Nearly fifty years ago Admiral Mahan pointed out that Americans must become familiar with the fact that by their inevitable entry into world politics they had an interest in the Persian Gulf. United States oil concerns in that area have given Americans additional reason for assenting to the truth of Mahan's words, for the oil reserves in the United States are now within a predictable period of exhaustion; those in the Middle East on the other hand, may well be the richest in the world.

VII

THE FAR EAST

GENERAL MURAVIEV

IT was through Central Asia, and also in the Far East, that Russian expansion was most successful in the nineteenth century. It received its greatest impetus under Nicholas I (1825-55), to whose far-sightedness present-day Russia owes many of her advantages in the East. His choice of the remarkable young General, Nicholas Muraviev, as Governor of Siberia, and his support of this soldier against numerous attacks by politicians, achieved for Russia the realisation of ambitions more than a century old. At that time the country, involved in the Crimean War, was weak in the Far East. The Russian posts on the Bays of Aniwa and De Castries on Sakhalin Island had been abandoned, and on the Amur River it was only at Nikolaievsk and Mariinsk that any garrisons remained. Muraviev saw that if his country could get control of the Amur she could hold her Far Eastern possessions against any likely assault on them by the British or French. To him possession of that river had become imperative, since the blockading of the Black Sea Fleet by Britain and France had made it impossible for supplies to be sent from southern Russia to Siberia by the usual sea route. The only vessels available for defence in the Pacific at that time were three frigates, *Diana, Aurora, Pallas*, and some smaller ships. These, Muraviev feared, might be left without provisions now that Russia was fighting in the west. He had to victual the Russian settlements on the Pacific coast, and he saw therefore that navigation on the Amur was essential. That river was the best outlet to the ocean from Siberia, as Okhotsk, which at the time when Muraviev became Governor of Siberia was Russia's principal port in the Far East, was often blocked by the sandbars of its own shallow river. So Muraviev sent Lieut. Nevelski to explore the mouth of the Amur, and it was found that despite shoals and sandbars it was navigable from the estuary. To ascertain how far China was able to keep Russian troops off the river, Nevelski, acting on his own initiative, took a force down it, and from the delta sailed across the Sea of Okhotsk to southern Kamchatka. It was this exploit which drew from the

165

Emperor Nicholas his famous declaration: "Where once the Russian flag has been raised, it must never again be lowered." Nevelski twice more sailed down the Amur, and Muraviev, as a measure against possible Chinese opposition, created a flotilla. He himself, with a force of eight hundred men, then went down the river. "For the first time since the days of Poyarkov and Khabarov, the Amur was travelled by Russians in its entire length."[1] From that voyage dates the foundation of the river port of Khabarovsk, now one of the principal towns in the Russian Far East for industries ancillary to shipbuilding.

The Chinese Commander-in-Chief, deciding that resistance was useless, signed with the Government of Siberia the Treaty of Aigun in 1858. This gave to Russia all the region between the Yablonoy Mountains and the north bank of the Amur; the land east of the Ussuri—i.e., between that river and the coast of the Sea of Japan—was to be jointly controlled by Russia and China. By the supplementary treaty of Peking the demarcation lines were further defined, and to the advantage of the Tsar's Government. The Amur, up to its junction with the Ussuri, was to be the frontier between Russia and China. In effect Russia now gained all the north (left) bank of the Amur, and the whole seaboard between the rivers Amur and Ussuri. For the first time "the Amur served to convey colonists and provisions to the possessions of the Russo-American Company."[2] And Muraviev, who had impressed upon the Government the advantage which the Amur would bring as a shorter route to the Pacific, had now been justified in his claim. He also gained for his countrymen navigation rights on the Sungari[3] and the Ussuri—rivers which were to be open only to Russian and Chinese vessels.

China had acquiesced in this transfer of the Amursk region partly because she thought it wisest to make an ally of Russia at that time; memories of the Anglo-French attack on Peking, when the Son of Heaven himself had been put to flight and the Imperial Palace fired, inclined the rulers of the Celestial Empire to regard its northern neighbour as an element more tolerable than the foreign devils of the west.

In a sense the gains which brought his country to the Pacific

[1] Prince Lobanov-Rostovsky, *Russia and Asia*. Copyright 1933 by The Macmillan Company, New York. Quotation by their permission; p. 141.

[2] E. G. Ravenstein, *The Russians on the Amur*. (Routledge & Kegan Paul Ltd. 1861); p. 139.

[3] The right of navigation was confirmed by later sanctions, but actually the Russians were hardly able to enforce their privileges, owing to the opposition of the mandarins.

THE SOVIET FAR EAST

(From Vladivostock to the ports of Ayan, Eastern Siberia, and
Okha, Sakhalin)

SHOWING the strategic advantage which the Russian acquisition of southern Sakhalin has brought to Vladivostock. The
Soviet ports of the Primorsk coast, and those of the Amur delta
region, have gained a similar advantage on the sea of Japan
and on the Gulf of Tartary respectively.

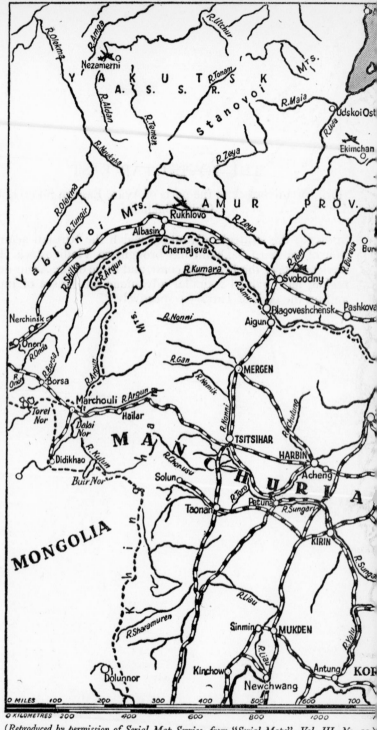

coast were the price received by Muraviev for his promised protection of the Chinese against third-party attack. But these gains
were not enough for the great Russian pro-Consul. The war in
the west was now over, and Muraviev, no longer restrained by
events in the Crimea, quickly seized all the Manchurian coastline between the Ussuri and the sea. He needed both banks of
the lower Amur, since the ice there restricted navigation.
Chinese failure to populate the country east of the river had left
it almost inevitable that this region should fall to Russia. In
1857 a regiment of Transbaikal Cossacks went to settle the new
Russian lands along the Amur, and four years later the emanci-
pation Acts freed many potential colonists, a considerable number of whom went to the Far East. Between 1859 and 1914
about 250,000 Russian peasants, exclusive of the Cossack
populations, settled in the Ussuri province.[1] In 1883 the Government paid 1,300 roubles, or about £130, to each family volun-
teering to settle in the maritime provinces,[2] and Russians
resident in America were encouraged to go there. But in accordance with St. Petersburg's determination to keep foreigners
away from Russian Pacific territory, the latter was closed to
non-Russian subjects, except such people as the Chinese who
were engaged to work in developing that area.

The defeat of his country in the West had made it clearer
than ever to Muraviev that it was to the East that Russia must
now devote her energies. So he instructed Nevelski to establish
trading posts at Nikolaievsk and Mariinsk for the Russian-
American Fur Company, and he also had a line of fortresses set
up along the Russian bank of the river. Having seized the
Maritime Provinces from the Chinese, he created a single
administrative area of the region, embracing Kamchatka, the
shores of the Sea of Okhotsk, and the delta lands of the
Amur. This now became known as Primorsk, and realising the
strategic necessity of linking this Far Eastern territory with St.
Petersburg, Muraviev gave his support to the project of a
trans-Siberian railway. Aware too of Siberia's need for a good
harbour, he decided that the best place for one was on the bay
which he christened Peter the Great, near the Korean frontier,
and there he founded Vladivostock. The port was settled partly
by traders from Nikolaievsk, and when later the Russian Volunteer Fleet was created, a quay was built here for it. Muraviev
lived to see the first English warship, the *Winchester*, enter

[1] Fridtjof Nansen, *Through Siberia, the Land of the Future*; p. 360.
[2] Wirth Gerrare, *Greater Russia*. (Heinemann, 1903); p. 202.

Vladivostock when searching for the Russian Pacific Squadron in 1856. In his time Petropavlovsk came to supplant Okhotsk as a primary naval port, for Muraviev had been impressed by the fine harbour on Avacha Bay, Kamchatka, climatically more favourable than Okhotsk.

"Ere his retirement in 1860, this great pioneer had laid a solid foundation for an Empire in the East which, in the twentieth century, will revolutionise the Asiatic continent," wrote F. H. Skrine.[1] But credit must also be given to the policy of Tsar Nicholas I, whose clear sense of Russia's destiny in the Orient brought the boundaries of the empire to be extended to new parts of the Pacific. From the north-east shores of the Caspian to the coasts of China, Russia had moved eastwards.

At the other end of Asia, Russia had earlier got control of the rivers Syr Daria and Amu Daria, and after General Chernaiev's capture of Tashkent in 1864, Alexander II had proclaimed the whole territory between the Aral Sea and Lake Issik Kul—comprising the province of Turkestan—to be under the Governor-General of western Siberia. Lake Issik Kul itself, and Lake Balkash, were gained for Russia by Muraviev, who thus made substantial additions to the already extensive area of inland seas possessed by his country.

PORT ARTHUR

For a long time the authenticity of the Agreement between Russia and China, known as the Cassini Convention of 1895, was a debatable question, but it is now established that this secret understanding had existed between the two countries. One of its main points was that Russia, lacking in the Far East any convenient ice-free bases, must be conceded one or more ports which she could share with China.[2] There followed another agreement the next year which gave Russia the right to use Port Arthur, and the free use of any other port in China. This understanding, known as the Li-Lobanov Secret Treaty, shows the importance attached by the Russians to Chinese ports, for the latter were to be open when necessary to the warships of Russia. And by a subsequent Convention of 1898, it was expressly stated (Article VI) that "Port Arthur shall be used solely by Russian and Chinese vessels and shall be considered as a closed

---

[1] *The Expansion of Russia, 1815-1900.* (Cambridge University Press, 1903); p. 132.
[2] See B. L. Putnam Weale, *The Reshaping of the Far East.* (The Macmillan Company, New York, 1905); p. 263.

port to warships and merchant vessels of other States."[1] But
during the period of the lease the only time when the Chinese
had tried to dock (with two cruisers), the Russians had refused
them the right. The following year the Tsar's Government sent
five warships to the Liao-tung Peninsula and announced they
would winter at Port Arthur, after which it compelled China to
agree to a lease of that peninsula for twenty-five years. Actually
this aggression was precipitated by the ambitions of Muraviev,
who persuaded the Tsar that a British squadron was about to
seize Port Arthur as a reply to the German occupation of the
Chinese port of Kiao-Chow.[2] (De Witte, in his Memoirs, quotes
the Tsar as saying "You know I have decided to occupy Port
Arthur. . . . If we do not do it the British will.") It was far from
the wish of England to see Russia in exclusive possession of Port
Arthur. Russia, however, not only entered upon sole occupation of that base but fortified it, and announced that only
vessels manned entirely by Russian or Chinese sailors would be
allowed to trade there, although she had given an assurance to
Britain that the port would be maintained as an open and commercial one. In the dispute which followed with England on
the "open port" question, the Russian Government declared
that it had never promised to open Port Arthur to foreign trade.[3]

A year after their acquisition of this harbour the Russians had
also gained a part of Talienwan for naval purposes; one inner
bay was to be reserved exclusively for Russian and Chinese
fleets. This produced from the British Foreign Minister the
statement that: "Her Majesty's Government regard it as most
unfortunate that it has been thought necessary, in addition, to
obtain control of a port which . . . will give to Russia the same
strategic advantage by sea which she already possesses in so
ample a measure by land." How far Russia was at the end of
the nineteenth century from the idea of the "Open Door" for
trade with China, is shown by the view taken by the Russian

---

[1] See *Treaties and Agreements With and Concerning China, 1894-1919.* (Oxford
University Press, American Branch, New York, 1921); Vol. I, p. 120. The
terms of the treaty, though intended to be secret, were seen by M. A.
Gérard, and published in *Ma Mission en Chine, 1893-1897.* (Plon Nourrit,
Paris, 1918.) The document was also copied by Yakhontov from the original
found in the archives of the Ministry of Foreign Affairs, Moscow, and
translated from the French. See Yakhontov's book *Russia and the Soviet Union
in the Far East.* (Allen & Unwin, 1932); Appendices, p. 365.

[2] *The Memoirs of Alexander Isvolsky,* edited and translated by C. L. Seegerd.
(Hutchinson, 1920); p. 124.

[3] See *China,* No. 1 (1898); pp. 47-8; No. 114.

ambassador in London that if the British Government insisted on Talienwan being an open port (which actually had been agreed upon in the Sino-Russian Convention, 1898), Britain would be encroaching on the Russian sphere of influence.

The secret memorandum from Mr. Chamberlain, dated 3 February, 1898, to Mr. Balfour, in which he complains that Russians "have induced us to let our ships leave Port Arthur" and have "forced us to withdraw our proposals to make Talien Wan (Dairen) a free port," and are "ousting us from influence in Corea,"[1] showed how far apprehension as to Russia's maritime objectives was the basis of British policy at that time. Britain, fearing Russian domination of China would threaten her own East Indian possessions, had tried to get an understanding with America on the "open door" policy in China. Russia's control of Port Arthur gave her the chance to dominate the China trade up to Pekin. That England had not interfered when Russia established herself on the Liao-tung Peninsula is very strange, seeing that the Tsar then got a naval base six hundred miles nearer to the sphere of Britain's interests in the Far East.[2] Britain did however take the precaution of obtaining the lease of the bight of Weihaiwei on the north-east coast of the Shantung Province. This ex-Chinese naval station, on the Gulf of Pechili, was only eighty miles from Russia's new naval base. Recognising that such a good harbour as Weihaiwei could, in British occupation, neutralise their own gain of Port Arthur, the Russians protested to China. But the Chinese had themselves asked Britain to lease territory around Weihaiwei in order to counter the Russian occupation of the Liao-tung Peninsula. The lease was to remain in effect "for so long a period as Port Arthur shall remain in the occupation of Russia."[3] The British Far Eastern Squadron continued to use Weihaiwei, and when Russia was supplanted by Japan in the Liao-tung Peninsula China did not ask Britain for the restoration of Weihaiwei. Broadly it may be said that in China England sought trade, Russia territory. England wanted treaty ports for commerce, Russia huge areas to dominate politically, and eventual supremacy on the Pacific seaboard. "In her descent on Asiatic waters, Russia has been impelled neither by the need of extended territory nor by the desire for commercial relations with

[1] See Dugdale. Balfour, pp. 252-53.
[2] See also Alexis Krausse, *The Far East.* (Grant Richards, 1900); p. 115.
[3] *Occidental Interpretations of the Far Eastern Problem*, H. G. W. Woodhead, J. Arnold, and H. N. Norton. (University of Chicago Press, 1926); p. 149.

other countries. Indeed, Russia's trade with China was and is insignificant . . . Her ambitions were political and her absorptions have been prompted partly by a craving for a seaboard, partly by a political instinct of expansion, and partly by the personal ambitions of a few statesmen."[1]

The Li-Lobanov Secret Agreement of 1896 had permitted Russia to construct the Chinese Eastern Railway, across the provinces of the Amur to Vladivostock, and with control of this line for a period of eighty years. By the later Convention (1898), Russia gained the right to extend this railway southwards to connect Harbin with Port Arthur and Talienwan.[2] (For the purpose of the construction of this new railroad the Russo-Chinese Bank was created.) This line now gave the Trans-Siberian an outlet to the Pacific. For the first time Russia could break out of her ice-locked prison of Siberia to the warm waters of the Southern Ocean. But further implications than these were in the minds of certain British naval strategists, who feared that the Chinese Eastern Railway could be used to transport troops for attacks on the British Coastal Concessions. And the Tsar's appeals for world peace they interpreted as a policy of necessity until the completion of the Trans-Siberian Railway, after which Russia would have secured communication from the Baltic to the Pacific, and from her eastern ocean front could then embark on a policy of aggression. It is to be noted that in the Report of the Technical Committee on the Chinese Eastern Railway, given at the Washington Conference in November 1921, Dr. Hawkling Yen, the Chinese representative of the sub-committee dealing with this line, stated that "the construction of this Railway by the Russians was obviously for a strategic purpose, and therefore political in nature."[3]

The Trans-Siberian Railway, with its terminus at Vladivostock, had been opened in 1902; this line, six thousand miles long, had been projected as early as 1866, when General Bogdanovich had proposed to Alexander II that a railway should be constructed to connect Moscow with the Far Eastern naval base. About the same time McDonough Collins, who in the United States had urged the laying of a cable from America to

[1] T. W. Overlach, *Foreign Financial Control in China*. (The Macmillan Company, New York, 1919); pp. 69, 70.

[2] For terms of the Convention see *American State Papers, Foreign Relations, 1900*; p. 383.

[3] Quoted by W. W. Willoughby, *Foreign Rights and Interests in China*. (The Johns Hopkins Press, Baltimore, 1927); Vol. I, p. 437.

Siberia across the North Pacific, was pressing for a railway from Irkutsk to Chita in order to link that region with the Pacific by use of the Amur River. An interesting exception to the traditional tendency of the Imperial Government to favour rail development at the expense of water transport was now shown, somewhat unexpectedly, by de Witte, who, writing in his Memoirs[1] about that section of the Trans-Siberian which was to be constructed from Lake Baikal to Vladivostock, pointed out that to have run the line along the great curve of the Amur "would have competed with the steamship companies operating on the river."

The first years of occupation of Vladivostock were disappointing to the Russians; existing icebreakers were not strong enough to make the harbour as useful as they had hoped. Port Arthur was found to be much better, as, except for Korea on the east flank, it opens on to the Pacific, whereas Vladivostock is almost an enclosed port on the Sea of Japan. The outlets from the latter are the Soya Strait (500 miles N.E.), the Tsugaru Strait (424 miles E.), and the Korea Strait (600 miles S.). All three are geographically dominated by Japan; it was natural therefore that Russia should move south through Manchuria to get to the freer waters of the Yellow Sea, as well as to blue-water ports.

Port Arthur is the only part of the short coastline of Manchuria which is ice-free all the year round. The hills give the harbour good defence, but at the same time prevent much expansion of the port, and its situation at the extremity of the narrow peninsula has certain drawbacks. The natural approach to the harbour is much narrower than the one to Vladivostock, and the water in the inner harbour is shallow. Ships of deep draught have in the past been compelled to lie in the outer roadstead.

Dairen (Dalny) had the advantage of being nearer than Vladivostock was to the great trading ports of Hong Kong, Shanghai and Newchang. Before 1888 it had been a tiny fishing village, and then, from six thousand miles away, came the Imperial decree that Dalny should become a great Russian port. In its fulfilment of this it became a witness to the policy "that sought to accomplish in less than a decade what in other parts of the world centuries of civilisation have not achieved."[2] No more rapid development has yet been seen on any part of

---

[1] P.74.
[2] Lancelot Lawton, *Empires of the Far East*. (Grant Richards, 1912); Vol. II, p. 1,274.

the Manchurian coast, and the transformation of this port in so
short a time showed that the same feverish haste which under
the Soviet regime has aimed at accomplishing in thirty years
what in some other countries has taken three hundred, could
also, on occasions, be displayed in the times of the Tsars.

During the negotiations between Russia and Japan which
preceded their war of 1904-05, one of the Russian Notes to
Tokyo had stipulated that the Tsar's Government required
recognition by Japan of "Manchuria *and her littoral* as being
outside her sphere of influence."[1] For this, Russia stated herself
willing to concede Japan's special rights to the Korean coast.
The importance attached by Russia to the Manchurian seaboard was not lost on Britain, who saw in it a potential threat
to her own influence on the China coast. To her it was ominous
too that Russia, in the Li-Lobanov Treaty, had demanded the
right to train Chinese sailors in the Chinese navy.

The acquisition of Port Arthur made it clear that the Colossus of the North was gradually descending to the mid-latitudes
of the world. The Premier of New Zealand, Sir Julius Vogel,
had accordingly urged that the Dominions should take control of the South Pacific islands in order to forestall Russian
encroachment. Three years before the outbreak of the Russo-
Japanese War, the Bertie Memorandum[2] had been drawn up,
dealing with the position in the Far East. The Memorandum
pointed out that Russia, in addition to her control of Port
Arthur and of the Liao-tung Peninsula, was now extending her
influence into Korea. This, it was certain, would produce a collision with Japan, and war would result. The Memorandum
drew attention to the Russian menace to British interests in the
Far East, and the possibility of a combination of Russia, France,
and Germany—Powers which had acted jointly in compelling
Japan to give up Port Arthur after she had seized it from China
in 1894. To counter such a combination, the Memorandum
discussed how Japan might play a part. If Japan proved the
victor in the coming clash, she might prove equally dangerous
to the British position. But there would be no fear of her
retaining such a conquest as for instance the Liao-tung
Peninsula, as sooner or later Russia would set out to recover it.
Clearly it was implicit in the Memorandum that the real
danger to British interests in the Far East was Russia. Earlier

[1] *Nichi-Ro.* Dispatch No. 38. Tokyo.
[2] 11.3.1901. (Lord Bertie was Assistant Secretary of State for Foreign
Affairs at the time when the Anglo-Japanese Alliance was made.)

than this however, British statesmen, concerned with the Russian threat to England's own interests in the maritime provinces of China, had felt it imperative to have a naval base on the Yellow Sea. So in 1885 Britain had taken Port Hamilton on the southern shores of Korea. Within reach both of Vladivostock and the Amur delta, it gave her a vantage point for any offensive action she might be called upon to make against the Tsar's territory on the Pacific. And it provided an excellent defensive base against any Russian attack from the north on British trade with the Chinese ports. England however had only retained Port Hamilton for two years, but had taken care to get a guarantee from China that the latter would not permit Russia to occupy any part of Korea. It was the extension of Russian influence in Manchuria, particularly in the coastal area near Korea, that led Britain to ask China for a guarantee of non-alienation of the Yangtze Valley. If Russian influence became paramount in the Peninsula, it was felt that she could exercise such pressure on the Chinese Government that the British position in the Yangtze region would be threatened. For the same reason, when the Tsar's Government was trying to secure for a Russian national the office of Inspector-General of Maritime Customs—which had for so long been in English hands—Britain in 1898 got an assurance from China that this post should continue to be held by an Englishman as long as Britain maintained her position of commercial supremacy in China.

Up to 1902 British sea power alone barred Russia's way to the oceans. After that the task of keeping Russia from the Pacific was divided by the partners of the Anglo-Japanese Alliance, England actually withdrawing her Pacific Fleet from Eastern waters and sending it to the North Sea. Henceforth Britain was to guard against Russia's exits to the Atlantic and Indian Oceans, and Japan was to close Russia's exits to the Pacific.

The same year that the Anglo-Japanese Alliance was formed as a defensive union against Russian advances in the Far East, Kaiser Wilhelm II sent his sensational telegram to the Tsar. The German Emperor had been present at the Russian naval manœuvres held that year, and he had telegraphed to Nicholas II, "The Admiral of the Atlantic greets the Admiral of the Pacific," thus defining their respective spheres. In other words the Tsar was not to encroach in the West. The complexity of Russo-German relations at this period becomes intelligible only when it is understood that it suited Germany to let

Russian energies be devoted to expansion in the east because
Germany wanted a free hand in the west. "In Russia," Bismarck is reported to have said to Prince Von Bülow, "there is
a serious amount of unrest and agitation for territorial expansion which may easily result in an explosion. It would be best
for the peace of the world if the explosion took place in Asia,
and not in Europe."[1] But at the same time Germany herself had
designs in the Far East. She had, as before mentioned, aided
China in securing the withdrawal of the Japanese from the
Liao-tung Peninsula, 1895, and had obtained in return the
lease of the Chinese port of Kiao-chow. The very day that the
convention for the lease was signed, Russia demanded the lease
of Port Arthur, and just one month later she occupied that port.
She made Kiao-chow her partial pretext for doing this, though
actually the Tsar had agreed to the German acquisition of that
harbour.[2] Nicholas II had given as additional justification for
the Russian acquisition of Port Arthur the necessity of fore-
stalling the intentions of an English squadron to take that naval
base.[3]

An instance of England's traditional mistrust of Russia
occurred then, for Britain showed no concern at the German
occupation of Kiao-chow, but, as we recall, was sufficiently per-
turbed about the Russian one of Port Arthur to secure for herself the lease of Weihaiwei. She was later also concerned about
the action of Russia in using the opportunity provided by the
Boxer Rebellion to occupy large areas of Manchuria. It was
clear to Britain that Russia, with land frontiers in the Far East,
was potentially a greater danger to her in that area than
Germany was.

THE RUSSO-JAPANESE WAR

When Russia gained control of Port Arthur, it brought her
on to the Pechili Gulf, and marked an important stage on that
seaward advance which the Russians, no less than the Americans,
regarded as their "historic destiny". This was proclaimed by
Admiral Alexeiev, who had not only been given supreme command of the naval forces in the Pacific, but had been created
"Imperial Lieutenant (Viceroy) of the Far East"; he was

[1] See K. Kawakami, *Japan and World Peace*. (The Macmillan Company,
New York, 1919); p. 4.
[2] See E. J. Dillon, *The Eclipse of Russia*. (J. M. Dent, 1918); p. 347.
Reference by permission of Mrs. E. J. Dillon.
[3] *Ibid.*, De Witte to Dillon; p. 250.

a determined expansionist, and after blustering at the Chinese with demands tantamount to a Russian claim for all Man-churia, he carried out a provocative display of naval force at Port Arthur.

When the Russo-Japanese War broke out, Rear-Admiral Mahan was almost alone among American naval strategists in taking the view that it would be to Britain's interest for Russia to keep Port Arthur, "for it will exhaust all her surplus energy and will withdraw her from the Persian Gulf"—an area which Mahan regarded as far more vital to Britain than any interests in the Far East. When the war started, the Russians for the first time had the advantage of two bases, Port Arthur and Vladivostock, though unfortunately for them these were separated by 1,200 miles. According to the figures given by Captain Nicolas Klado, I.R.N.,[1] Russia's First Pacific Squadron consisted of seven battleships, nine cruisers listed as first-class, two as second-class, two auxiliary cruisers, two torpedo cruisers, twenty-six destroyers, seven torpedo boats, sixteen torpedo vessels and a number of gunboats. Her Second Pacific Squadron at that time was composed of seven battleships, five cruisers listed as first-class, and three as second-class, five auxiliary cruisers, twelve destroyers and 35 sea-going torpedo craft. The Japanese had six new battleships (eight in all), eleven armoured cruisers, fourteen protected cruisers, seventeen destroyers, seventy-one torpedo boats, seventeen gunboats. The First and Second Pacific Squadrons of the Russians together certainly outnumbered the Japanese battle-fleet, but as Admiral Skrydlov (Commander-in-Chief of the Pacific Fleet in succes-sion to Admiral Makarov) wrote in his report on the naval forces in May 1904, "the Port Arthur and Vladivostock squadrons are much weaker than the Japanese fleet." The Black Sea Fleet was unable to supply any support to the war in the Far East, as under the modified treaty which followed the Crimean War, Russia was prohibited from ever taking her fleet out of the Black Sea without the permission of Turkey.

The strategic advantage of a base on the Korean Peninsula was proved at the very outset of the Russo-Japanese War, when Admiral Togo was able to place twelve of his armoured ships at Masampo, whence he could exercise control of the Straits and protect the transport of troops from Japan. Actually the first shot in the war was fired by a Russian cruiser at a Japanese

[1] Figures as given in *The Battle of the Sea of Japan*, by Captain Nicolas Klado, I.R.N.; pp. 291-98.

troopship on its way to Korea. This occurred off Chemulpo, and was followed by an attack by the Japanese squadron on the Russian cruiser *Variag* and gunboat *Korietz*.

In the main Japanese assault on the Russian fleet, Admiral Togo concentrated on Port Arthur first. Japanese destroyers without warning fired torpedoes at Russian battleships, putting out of action two of the best, the *Tsesarevitch* and *Retvisan* and the cruiser *Pallada*. (The damage inflicted would probably have been less if many of the Russian officers, instead of being at their posts, had not been attending a ball ashore.) Togo waited through storm and icy blast outside Port Arthur, his aim being to blockade the Russian squadron in the harbour till the fortress surrendered to the besieging Japanese army. Had that army been in a position to attack immediately, Port Arthur might have fallen sooner, as the fortifications were incomplete. The position of the Russian fleet was made worse by the Japanese blockade; except for a few Chinese junks which managed to sneak through this, the British ship *King Arthur*, which brought provisions, and the *Foxton Hall*, which arrived with coal, the garrison received few supplies from the seaward side. It was indeed so badly equipped that at one time it had to draw for supplies on the squadron it was sheltering. After the complete defeat of the Russian Port Arthur Squadron, Admiral Kamimura dealt with the one at Vladivostock, an operation in which he was completely successful.

From the Baltic meanwhile, the main battle fleet had sailed from Libau under Admiral Rozhdestvenski to reinforce the First Pacific Squadron. The commander, fearing that the British would attack him in the Mediterranean, took the Cape route. (Under Admirals von Felkerzam and Wirenius, the smaller, older vessels, however, sailed through the Mediterranean.) The timidity of Russian naval policy at that time was matched by the poor work of Russian Naval Intelligence, which belied its high reputation in this instance. Rozhdestvenski's ships, passing through the North Sea on their outward voyage to the East, had sighted some English trawlers off the Dogger Bank, but, panicked into believing them to be Japanese boats, had fired on them. With more haste than discretion the Russians had even failed to stop in the English Channel after this incident. (But they were to hear more of it later.)

At Madagascar the admiral heard of the fall of Port Arthur, yet he continued his voyage, reinforced at Camranh Bay by units under Rear-Admiral Niebogatov, who had come by the

Mediterranean route. But disaster awaited the Russian fleets. At Tsushima they were annihilated in a day, and only one of Rozhdestvenski's ships reached Vladivostock. Actually the over-riding factor in Japan's victory was that the idea of offensive sea warfare was almost non-existent with the Russians.[1] "To the St. Petersburg authorities, a fleet was merely an assembly of armed ships with men on board to work the guns and engines."[2]

The underestimation of the importance of the naval staff was another factor highly detrimental to the Russians. When General Kuropatkin became Commander-in-Chief of land and sea forces, the naval staff diminished until it was reduced to a mere committee. So it was inland from Mukden, not from the naval base of Vladivostock, that the most important directions concerning the operations of Rozhdestvenski's ships as well as the Vladivostock cruisers were given.

The Treaty of Portsmouth which followed the war was disastrous to Russia's naval ambitions in the Far East; Port Arthur was surrendered, and its lease, together with that of Dairen, was transferred to Japan. (The original lease was for twenty-five years,[3] but Japan succeeded later in getting this extended to ninety-nine years.) The southern half of Sakhalin Island was also ceded by Russia, who now recognised Korea as Japan's sphere of influence, and was obliged also to evacuate Southern Manchuria. With this she lost the line from Changchun to Port Arthur, which, when taken over by the Japanese, became known as the South Manchurian Railway. Russia also lost the railroad she had laid as a branch of the Chinese Eastern Railway from Tashikcha to the Treaty Port of Newchang.

Thus thwarted in Manchuria, she had turned to Mongolia, and in 1907 by an Agreement with Japan, Russia's right to "special interests" in Outer Mongolia and part of Inner Mongolia was recognised. After the Civil War however, when in 1922 Red soldiers entered Khabarovsk and advanced up the Ussuri to Vladivostock, Russian ambitions in the maritime provinces of China were actively renewed. With the aim of eventually reducing British naval supremacy in the western Pacific,

[1] (An exception to this was the Sinope attack in the Crimean War.)

[2] Vice-Admiral G. A. Ballard, C.B., *The Influence of the Sea on the Political History of Japan.* (John Murray, 1921); p. 201.

[3] It was only with reluctance that China agreed to the transfer of these leases from Russia to Japan. Her nominal consent had been required by the Treaty of Portsmouth.

the Russians began to take part in the anti-British movement in the Chinese coast towns, particularly in Canton and Hankow, where they helped to drill soldiers for the Nationalist Army commanded by General Chiang Kai-shek. These agitations came to a head in 1925, and resulted in Britain later giving up the coastal Concessions at Amoy, Chin-Kiang, and at the river port of Hankow, rather than have open war with the Wu-han National Government. (The return of Weihaiwei had already been agreed to at the Washington Naval Conference.)

The part played by the Russians during the birth of the young Chinese Republic showed that between 1923 and 1927 they were looking southwards for at least a sphere of influence on the East China Sea. This urge was almost inevitable, owing to Japan's virtual exclusion of the Soviet Union from the Pacific in the north, also from the Sea of Japan, and the Amur delta. It was clear to the Russians that to protect their own eastern littoral they must always have control of the Trans-Baikal region, and hold the few mountain passes that exist in the formidable ranges of the Baikal territory. So an experimental "Buffer State", known as the Far Eastern Republic, had been created. It comprised Trans-Baikala, the Amur region, Primorsk, Northern Sakhalin, Kamchatka, and the zone of the Chinese Eastern Railway. It embraced of course Vladivostock and the inland port of Blagovyeshchensk. Early in 1921 however, a revolt, centred at Vladivostock, but believed by many to have been inspired by Moscow, furnished the latter with a pretext for absorbing the Buffer State. The continued independence of that State would, it was now felt, deprive Russia of power on the Pacific.

The Russo-Chinese Treaty of 1945 has regained for Russia that access to the eastern ocean and that prospect of maritime security which had been hers before the rise of Japan as a formidable Pacific Power at the beginning of the twentieth century. By that treaty it was agreed that Port Arthur should be used by both Russia and China as a naval base. The port was also to be open to both nations for use by merchant vessels. It is significant however, that the chairman of the Military Commission which was to be set up to deal with problems concerning the joint use of Port Arthur, was to be a Soviet citizen, and three out of the five members of that Commission were to be Soviet representatives.[1]

(Since Port Arthur commands the naval approaches to

[1] Clause 3 of the Agreement.

Peiping, and indeed to all North China, the joint control of this port by two Powers whose interests have so often conflicted, is a venture which has tempted speculation. It has been asked, will China, who has permitted herself to be embraced by a former foe, come to recoil from "the lethal hug of the Polar bear"?) Under the Agreement Dalny (Dairen) was to be a free port administered by China, but the Chief of the port was to be a Soviet citizen. Certain of the port installations and equipment were to be leased to Russia. The main trunk lines of the South Manchurian and the Chinese Eastern Railway were to be jointly owned and operated by China and Russia for thirty years, after which they were to revert to the former Power, but without compensation. The Chinese were to be responsible for guarding the railway, and only in time of war with Japan might the line be used for carrying Russian soldiers.

In this Sino-Russian treaty there is an echo of an earlier agreement in 1924, known as the Agreement for the "Provisional Management of the Chinese Eastern Railway," whereby it was laid down that the Manager of the Road was to be a Russian. Professor Willoughby pointed out that "Russia, under this arrangement, exercises a dominant influence in the actual operation of the Railway."[1] In order to settle certain outstanding disputes with Japan, Moscow sold the Railway to the Japanese in 1935. The Chinese Government protested that while it was conceivable that Russia might have some right to sell her own interests in this line, there was no possible justification for her selling China's too. The Soviet Government's reply was that at that time Japan, not China, was the real master in Manchuria.[2]

The question has been asked, are there aspects of the Russo-Chinese Agreement of 1945 which recall the words of Prince Menschikov: "Our time-honoured policy from the days of the Variags down to the reign of the Emperor Alexander III, was founded on the axiom that Russia needs territorial expansion at the expense of her neighbours."[3] Even now, with her

[1] *Foreign Rights and Interests in China*; Vol. I, p. 445.

[2] For a detailed account of the Chinese Eastern Railway, see Harriet L. Moore, *Soviet Far Eastern Policy, 1931-1945.* Issued under the auspices of International Secretariat, Institute of Pacific Relations. (Princeton University Press, 1945); Chapter 3. See also *Problems of the Pacific.* Proceedings of the Third Conference of the Institute of Pacific Relations, 1929. (University of Chicago Press, 1930); p. 516.

[3] *Novoe Vremya*, April 1912. Quoted by J. O. P. Bland in *Recent Events and Present Policies in China.* (Heinemann, 1912); p. 342.

greatly improved maritime position in the Far East, there remain coastal areas outside her own territory which the Soviet Union will always regard as menacing to her security unless under the ownership of a strong and friendly Power.

JAPAN

The earliest news of the existence of Japan reached the west through Marco Polo, who on his return from China in 1295, reported that he had been told of the island of Cipangu. When, almost two hundred years later, Columbus sailed west, hoping that way to reach the Spiceries of the East, on the map that he took with him Cipangu was marked. (The only fifteenth-century map before Behaim's to show Japan, was that of Fra Mauro.)

The first known western discoverers of Japan were three ship-wrecked Portuguese who in 1542 landed on the shores of that kingdom. Three years later one of their fellow countrymen, the navigator Ferñao Mendes Pinto, came here too, landing on the island of Kiushiu, and secured an agreement whereby every other year a Portuguese ship with merchandise was permitted to call at the island.[1] Other Portuguese traders from Macao and Goa followed: in 1549 came Francis Xavier and his fellow-missioners. Spaniards were then asked to come to Japan as naval architects, but Spain, unwilling to face the possibility of a maritime rival in the East, declined the invitation. The Dutch, the first of whose ships to reach the Island Empire was the *Liefde*, arrived in 1600. The Pilot-Major was an Englishman, Will Adams, who remained in Japan and placed his knowledge of shipbuilding and navigation at the service of the Shogun. Then in 1613 appeared the ships of the East India Company with Captain John Saris in command, calling at Hirado with letters from James I to the Emperor, and Will Adams acted as interpreter. The reply given by the Emperor was, that he would welcome Englishmen in any port of his dominions "for their worthiness in the admirable knowledge of Navigation, having with much facilitee discovered a countrie so remote." But the period of trade relations which did follow between England and Japan was a brief one.

Again comes the name of that dynamite Tsar, Peter the Great, during whose reign Atlasov, in his travels through Kamchatka, had discovered a shipwrecked Japanese called

[1] Some of Mendes Pinto's stories however were so "tall" that Congreve in *Love for Love* makes a character say "Ferdinand Mendes Pinto was but a type of thee, thou liar of the first magnitude."

—see over

"KING PETER THE GREAT
LEARNING SHIPBUILDING
AT DEPTFORD"

"KING PETER THE GREAT LEARNING SHIPBUILDING AT DEPTFORD"

Reproduction of an oil-painting presented by Mrs. E. Beddington Behrens (née Princess Obolensky) to the Deptford Borough Council, by whose courtesy this picture appears.

AVID for more knowledge of the art of shipbuilding, Peter the Great had left Saardam where he had worked as a carpenter in the building of a Dutch galliot, and had come to England. Here, for a time, he was lodged by the Thames in a mansion belonging to John Evelyn, paying frequent visits to the shipyards at Deptford and the gun foundry at Woolwich.

Early in his reign the Tsar had realised all that the acquisition of sea power could mean to a land-locked dominion such as his own. He knew too that the primary reason why his countrymen lacked sea-consciousness was the fact that, unlike the leading maritime nations—Britain, Holland, Portugal, Spain—Russia had no possessions along the great trade routes of the world. Peter must acquire seaports on such routes if his country was to enjoy the mercantile advantages of the maritime Powers. But he needed ships to get such ports, and so he was to be found at Deptford, intent, as in this picture, in studying from a model the English art of shipbuilding.

Denbei. Peter, hearing of this, had ordered the man to be sent to St. Petersburg, and after being taught Russian there, Denbei was questioned all about Japan. His information was to be given to Spangberg before the latter sailed with the Bering expeditions, during which Spangberg was to try to discover a sea route to Japan. What is of still more interest is the fact that the Tsar gave certain secret instructions to Bering to find out all he could about the Amur route. This is clear from the "secret information" of the contemporary Russian Ambassador to China, Sava Vladislavich, who stated that "an attempt to seize this route is being prepared. For this a strong fleet is needed, and that is what Bering must secure".[1] This was the Tsar's view also, for he held that there were three points of primary importance to Russia—the mouths of the Don, the Neva, and the Amur. The third, he was convinced, was the gateway to trade with Japan.[2]

But right up to the beginning of the nineteenth century foreign vessels entering Japanese harbours did so at their peril. And even later, trade was proscribed to all but the Chinese, who were confined to Nagasaki, and to the Dutch, who were restricted to Deshima, the small island in Nagasaki harbour—where incidentally they were treated with marked contempt and subjected to public humiliation. The arrival of Commodore Perry, U.S.N., at Yokohama Bay with two frigates and two sloops in 1853, caused consternation among the Japanese. (Perry's object was to try and get permission for the use of a port of supply for American whalers, and also the use of a coaling station.) Panic seized Tokyo, but the Commodore's visit eventually opened the ports of Nagasaki and Hakodate to America. Shortly afterwards similar concessions were obtained by Britain, and Russia too got the right to trade with those ports and also with Shimoda. Evidence of Russia's anxiety to open up relations with Japan was given when the Commander of the Russian Fleet approached Perry and suggested that they should take joint action to force Japan to open her doors. The same year, 1854, Putiatin, a Russian shipwrecked naval officer, settled in Japan, and to his instruction in the building of vessels of European design, the Japanese owed to some extent their impulse to build trading schooners.

[1] Gaston Cahen, *Histoire des Relations de la Russie avec la Chine sous Pierre le Grand (1689-1730)*. (Librairie Félix Alean, Paris, 1932); Appendix of Documents, pp. lxxi-lxxii.

[2] C. de Sabir, *Le Fleuve Amour*. (Georg Kugelman, Paris, 1861); p. 38.

Perry, who had declined the proposal to act with the Russians against the Japanese, viewed with extreme suspicion the attempts of the former to gain a foothold in Japan. He pointed out to his Government that the Russians were at that time established on every side of the Japanese Empire but the south. "With harbours on the coast of western Asia and western America, opening on a sea which must be the seat of an immense and lucrative commerce," he stated,[1] Russia "might aim to be a great maritime power, and to rule mistress of the Pacific. If she possesses Japan, she would have an abundance of harbours, unrivalled in the world for excellency, and with her resources, would control the commerce of the Pacific. It is not, therefore, to the interest of any part of the commercial world that Russia should ever own Japan; but Russia has, doubtless, seen the importance to her of its acquisition."

The trading concessions gained by the Tsar from Japan in the middle of the nineteenth century were reciprocated during the first world war, at a time when Russia was dependent on Japan for supplies of war material in the Far East. For by a secret agreement signed between the two countries behind the backs of their allies, the Russians gave to the Japanese the right to settle in eastern Siberia (over which Japan gained virtual control), to engage in trade there, and to extend their fishing rights along the coasts of the Maritime Territory. The right of shipping on the Sungari, the great tributary of the Amur, was also granted. These concessions however, were far from satisfying Japan's ambitions, one of which was to remove Russia from the coasts of the Yellow Sea. The Treaty of Portsmouth, following the Russo-Japanese War, had helped her in this direction by giving her control of the southern section of the Chinese Eastern Railway, whose Company, in addition to its railroads, maintained a shipping service between Talienwan and Shanghai. Under Japanese organisation a monopoly of coastline services for South China was achieved. Further, Japan announced that Japanese products (in Japanese vessels) intended for distribution in Manchuria, would be carried on the Chinese Eastern Railway free of charge. The freight in Japanese ships was to be free, or at half the usual rate.[2] Total discrimination against

---

[1] Official account of the Perry expedition, prepared by Francis L. Hawke. Quoted by Felix Riesenberg, *The Pacific Ocean.* (Museum Press, 1947); p. 240.
[2] For full details of terms see T. F. Millard, *America and the Far Eastern Question.* (Moffat, Yard & Co., New York, 1909); p. 207.

foreigners was one of Japan's objectives. Another of her aims was to exclude Russia from the shores of the Sea of Japan. This she accomplished after 1918 by her occupation of the Maritime Territory, of the Amur region, and of northern Sakhalin. From the latter it would have been within her power to make an attack on the Soviet seaboard by transporting troops across the frozen Strait of Tartary during the winter months. Control of the Tartary Strait gave her also control of the passage to the Sea of Okhotsk, which is even more important to Russia than is the Sea of Japan, since it commands the approaches to Siberia. At that time Japan also contemplated seizing Kamchatka, and with this last misfortune Russia would have lost all hope of becoming a Pacific Power. It is not easy to understand why Russia, who had for so long smarted under her losses to Japan after the war of 1904-05, should have been so apparently ready in 1917 to assent to Japanese expansion in the Pacific. A note from the Russian Embassy to the Japanese Ministry of Foreign Affairs (20 February, 1917) gave the assurance that they could count unreservedly on Russian support for Japanese desiderata "concerning the eventual surrender to Japan of the rights belonging to Germany in Shantung and of the German Islands occupied by Japanese forces, in the Pacific Ocean to the north of the Equator."[1]

Japan's ambitions however were for the time frustrated by America, who had never lost sight of the fact that the axis of world politics had shifted to the Pacific. So at the Washington Naval Conference she had compelled Japan to disgorge most of her gains. These included the German base of Kiao-chow, which along with other rights in the coastal Province of Shantung, had been transferred to Japan by the Allied Powers in 1919. (To that Treaty however, China had refused to give her signature, and had not ceased to press for Shantung until Japan was compelled to relinquish it.)

When, to retrieve these enforced losses Japan overran Manchuria in 1931-38, it meant that Russia lost an important section of the Trans-Siberian Railway; from Harbin to Vladivostock the line was now closed to the Russians, who were compelled to go a long way round to reach their naval base. So on 12 July, 1938, Soviet troops, following "incidents", crossed the Manchukuo border and occupied Possiet Bay, in the neighbourhood of Vladivostock. The Bay also commands the Korean port

[1] Translated from *Conflict of Policies in Asia*, by Thomas F. Millard. (Appleton-Century-Crofts, Inc., New York and London, 1929); p. 61.

of Rashin which is the terminal of a railway to Hsinking. That line is important, as in Japanese hands it could be used for bringing troops to the interior of Manchuria. Fighting between Japanese and Russian forces continued near the south-west shore of Lake Khassan, where the volcanic range, which forms part of the frontier between Russia and Manchuria, is only six miles from the Pacific coast. If the Japanese had won in that clash they could have commanded the two peaks, Zoozernaya, and Bezmyannaya, which dominate Possiet Bay. In this way they could have threatened Vladivostock. But Soviet artillery settled the issue, and a truce was arranged between the two Powers. Chang-ku-feng was Russia's.

KOREA

South of Manchuria, and separating the Yellow Sea from the Sea of Japan, is the Korean Peninsula. Only late in the history of exploration had that territory become familiar to the western nations. The islands off the west side did not appear on the early Chinese charts, nor on those made by the Jesuits who visited Korea from Pekin. Only in 1816 was a map of the archipelago published from the survey made by Captain Basil Hall in the *Lyra* and Captain Maxwell in the *Alceste*. On the Peninsula, Basil Bay is named after the first explorer, and Broughton Bay on which is the principal port of Gensan, is called after Captain Broughton who had surveyed the north-east coast in 1797. The Russians next had a share in exploring Korea when half a century later they surveyed the fine harbour now known as Port Lazarev. Strategically placed on the Sea of Japan, and the nearest Korean port to Vladivostock, Lazarev was coveted by the Russians as a terminus for their Trans-Siberian Railway. Their next move was in 1861, when in an attempt to get a port in the southern part of the Peninsula, Admiral Likhachev sent, in the frigate *Possadnik*, a detachment of marines who landed at Tsushima Island. Here they had attempted to establish a settlement and to hold the Japanese naval base, but a British man-of-war had compelled them to withdraw, and the island was restored to Japan. Marauding bands of Cossacks had been coming in from bases along the River Tiumen, which formed the frontier between the Russian Maritime Province and north Korea. This Russian advance towards Korea was but the logical development of the policy of Muraviev, who had so clearly seen that occupation of the Peninsula by any hostile Power would mean the isolation of Vladivostock. Equally clear to the British was the fact that a Russian occupation of Tsushima—an island of great strategic value commanding the southern entrance to the Sea of Japan—constituted a threat to the balance of power in the Far East. Thereafter Britain's relations were strengthened with Japan.

The struggle between the latter and Russia for control of this territory was perpetual between the two Powers. After the Japanese had invaded Korea, overrun South Manchuria, and destroyed the Chinese fleet in 1895, China had been compelled to sue for peace. By the Treaty of Shimonoseki which followed, Japan, in addition to getting the Liao-tung Peninsula (which gave her Port Arthur and Dairen), gained also Formosa, the Pescadores (with their excellent harbour facilities), and Korea. The latter gave the Japanese an immense strategic advantage over their neighbours, and Russia now had to face the rise of Japan as a new Pacific Power.

Accordingly St. Petersburg resorted to diplomatic procedure of a most tortuous character, persuading France and Germany that Japan's gains could make the "Yellow Peril" a formidable menace. She succeeded so far that the Western Powers saw to it that the Treaty of Shimonoseki never became fully operative. Had it done so, Russia would have been kept back from the sea by Japan.[1]

It had always been clear to Russia that an occupation of the Peninsula by her rival would mean that Japan could enter Kirin city from north-eastern Korea, and thus imperil Russia's communications via the South Manchuria Railway with Vladivostock and Port Arthur. Occupation of Kirin would also threaten Russian navigation on the Sungari, exclusive right to which had been acquired by the treaty of Aigun with China. By the Convention of Seoul, 1896, the Russian position in Korea had been slightly improved, and soon there had followed an Imperial decree that all railways built in that country should be laid to the same gauge as the Russian one. St. Petersburg never lost sight of her aim to secure uninterrupted communications from the Baltic to the Pacific, and the Korean ports would give her easier access to the ocean than Vladivostock did. But for her pre-occupation with Port Arthur, Russia would have carried out her railway schemes in Korea (where the same policy has been revived under Stalin since 1945.)

Just before the outbreak of the Russo-Japanese War, Russia

[1] See also Le Roy-Beaulieu, *The Awakening of the East*. (Heinemann, 1900); p. 62.

pressed for free navigation of the Strait of Korea so as to have direct naval communication between Port Arthur and Vladivostock, and Russian officers urged the Government to secure a naval base on the ice-free shores of the Hermit Kingdom. As soon as the Korean Government opened the port of Masampo to foreign trade in 1899, Admiral Makarov, commanding the Eastern Squadron of the Russian Navy, had surveyed the coast in detail, and had chosen the most strategic site on the shore. This the Russians intended to purchase and there to establish a naval station, but when they came to land they found the Japanese had already forestalled them by buying the foreshore; their attempts to lease the port of Yongampo were also thwarted. The Russians did however, secure the lease of Pankumi and whaling rights on a strip of north-eastern Korea, but Japan had established herself in a far stronger position in the Peninsula. Russian occupation of Masampo would have meant control of the Pechili Gulf, an advantage too great for Japan to concede to the Power whom she regarded as an obstacle to her own maritime ambitions.

It is true there were certain economic reasons for Russia's desire to gain ports in Korea; it would have been cheaper for her to trade with China by sea. (Just before the Russo-Japanese War the freight rate for bulky articles was half that of the rail rate.)[1] On the other hand it cannot be said that the mercantile motives were compelling ones, for the Russians had hardly any trade with the Peninsula, and except in the extreme north there was no territorial connection between Korea and Russia. It was to secure a dominating position on the eastern side of the Sea of Japan that Russia risked a clash with her rival by penetration into the Land of Morning Calm.

The value of the Korean Peninsula was proved, as we have said, in the Russo-Japanese War, when the Japanese Fleet had two *points d'appui* in the deep Korean inlets. But the strategic location of the peninsula gives it a wider importance; control of Korea means control of the Sea of Japan and of the approaches to Vladivostock. Communication between the latter and Port Arthur has to be made via the Korea Strait, aptly described by a Pacific historian, Mr. Lancelot Lawton, as "the Dardanelles of the Far East". This fact, together with a realisation that the Power in occupation of Korea, by capturing the port of Auntung on its north-east border can command a principal entry into Manchuria, has always made Russia nervous of Japanese

[1] See U.S. Consular Reports, 24 February, 1903.

designs on the Hermit Kingdom. Most disturbing of all, from the point of view of Russia, has been the thought that any Power hostile to her, could, if in possession of Korea, endanger her access to warm waters and threaten her trade with the south.

This was most forcefully apparent to the Russian naval commander in the Far East, Admiral Alexeiev, who did all in his power to try and prevent his Government from yielding anything on the Korean question. If Japan gained control there he saw it would mean that "the Russian Far East would be split into two component parts—Manchuria and the Pacific Province—by the out-jutting boot of land, and the possibility of dominating the eastern seas with a powerful Russian fleet thus made very faint. With both sides of the Strait of Korea in Japanese hands, Port Arthur and Vladivostock bore but little relation to one another".[1]

The impact of Russia on the bastion of Korea has been vividly summarised by a French historian of the Pacific: "Dans son rapide glissement vers l'Océan, 'le glacier Russe' se heurtait à un énorme rocher, la Corée".[2] Russian aims in Korea, much more than in Manchuria, had brought on the Russo-Japanese war. The importance which Japanese industrialists attached to Korea was such that the Russian Minister in Tokyo, Baron Rosen, knowing that Japan would fight for Korea, had recommended (unavailingly) his Government to accept the Japanese proposal that in Manchuria Russia should even have a free hand, provided that Korea was left to Japan. Only fifty miles from Japanese territory, the Peninsula was vital for the food and raw materials obtained in exchange for Japanese manufactures. Thus the commercial interests of Japan in Korea far exceeded those of Russia, who indeed, had only sent goods to the northern part of the country, and these had been carried by sea from Vladivostock. It was Japan who felt there was sufficient economic reason for a railway to be laid through the Peninsula. There was a political motive too; the line which she built from Kirin to the free port of Chhongjin in north-eastern Korea, was partly designed to divert freight from the Russian-controlled Chinese Eastern Railway, and this would inevitably lead to the decline of Vladivostock. It was but the logical sequence to the policy of Japan that, after her victory in 1905, she made

[1] B. L. Putnam Weale, *The Truce in the East and its Aftermath.* (Macmillan & Co., 1907); p. 388.

[2] René Pinon, *La Lutte pour le Pacifique.* (Librairie Académique, Didier, Paris, 1906); p. 16.

Korea her vassal state, and outright annexation soon followed.

Writing some six years before the second world war, the naval authority, Lieut.-Commander Tota Ishimaru, said that Russian designs on Korea were fairly widely known, and that if the Peninsula were taken by the U.S.S.R., neither Japan nor the position of Britain in China would be secure any longer.[1] In the opinion of Count Hayashi, "sooner or later it would have to be decided whether the country was to fall to Russia or not. The Japanese would certainly fight in order to prevent it, and it must be the object of their diplomacy to isolate Russia, with which Power, if it stood alone, they were prepared to deal."[2]

At the modern port of Rashin, in the north of Korea, the Japanese had established naval air bases to avoid the long distance by sea to Dalny and Port Arthur. Rashin is a warm-water port, and is connected by rail with Manchuria's chief industrial centres; it is only one hundred miles from Vladivostock. For these reasons the Soviet Union showed no inclination to remove its troops from northern Korea after the defeat of Japan in World War II. Five days after the Russians had entered the war against the Japanese in August 1945, their naval forces had captured Rashin, and the neighbouring harbours of Seishin and Yuki, thus removing the danger of a combined sea and air attack on Vladivostock.

It was in northern Korea that, by decision of the Moscow Conference, 1945, representatives of the Soviet Command were delegated to take their part in the work of the Four-Power trusteeship of the Korean Peninsula, whose future independence was agreed upon at the Conference. Russian control in northern Korea became predominant, and was almost a natural corollary to the instrument of surrender formulated by General Mac-arthur, whereby the Japanese were ordered to surrender to the Russians, not only in Manchuria, the Kuriles, and southern Sakhalin, but in northern Korea. The fact that Russia is to share with China in controlling the railways of Manchuria, means that the Korean ports, linked by rail with Mukden, Hsinking, and Harbin, will be developed with due regard to Soviet sea and rail transport. Today, the Soviet Government by the pattern of its railway construction designed to ensure

[1] Lieut.-Commander Tota Ishimaru: *Japan Must Fight Britain*. Translated from the Japanese by Instr. Captain G. V. Rayment, C.B.E., R.N. (Hurst & Blackett, 1936); p. 27.

[2] British Documents ii, 80-3. Quoted by Sir J. A. Marriott. *Anglo-Russian Relations, 1689-1943*; p. 155. By permission of Messrs. Methuen.

uninterrupted land and sea communication, gives evidence of the continuity of Russia's Pacific aims.

THE SOVIET FAR EAST

The Trans-Siberian Railway today is not only double-tracked, in some places it is treble-tracked. Something of the strategic conception of this railway—a great supply route—will be understood by the following facts: Taishet,[1] half way between Novosibirsk and Yakutsk on the Trans-Siberian, is connected with the Lena port of Ust-kut by the 'B.A.M.' Railway which is extended east through the Chita and Amur regions to the naval port of Sovietskaya Gavan. This means that the industrial region of Krasnoyarsk, two hundred and seventy miles west of Taishet, has direct communication with Russia's Pacific ports. It also means that the Lena and Tunguska Rivers have an all-Russian connection with the Sea of Japan.

Running for a distance of 1,500 miles from Tashkent in Turkestan to Semipalatinsk on the Irtysh, the 'Turk-Sib.' Railway was built to link the lines of Central Asia with the Trans-Siberian Railway. An interesting offshoot of the latter is the 'B.A.M.' (Baikal-Amur-Magistral) which we have just referred to as the line starting from Taishet. Although it is widely regarded as the creation of the Soviet Government, credit for its original conception must be given to the Tsar's Government, which in 1908 had planned to build the Amur Railway. At that time China (by the Agreement of 1896) had the option of purchasing from Russia and Japan by 1939 the whole of the Manchurian Railway system, or, alternatively, of taking over in 1983 all the lines without compensation.[2] If she did this it would isolate the Russian Maritime Territory and the railway linking Vladivostock and Khabarovsk. The projected Amur line was designed to forestall such a situation. It was to be about 1,300 miles long, and by joining it to the Trans-Siberian Railway, and constructing an extension through Trans-Baikala from Khabarovsk to Nikolaievsk, an all-Russian route from St. Petersburg to the Pacific would be completed. Plans for this were advanced by 1912, but opposition from Count de Witte and others, on the grounds of expenditure, prevented fulfilment of the plan.

The 'B.A.M.' Railway passes through the shipbuilding city

[1] Taishet is on the air line from Moscow to Vladivostock.

[2] See K. Kawakami, *American-Japanese Relations*. (Fleming H. Revell Co., London and Edinburgh, 1912); p. 49.

of Komsomolsk, and terminates, as we have said, at the naval base of Sovietskaya Gavan. The disadvantage of having its terminal on water that is ice-free for only part of the year, is outweighed by the fact that Sovietskaya Gavan is a port which can be used to defend the Maritime Province if ever this should be attacked from the seaward side, and the 'B.A.M.' is the supply line to that harbour. Even by 1948 few details had been published about the 'B.A.M.' Railway, during the building of which close secrecy was maintained. Strategically it is a most important line, as in the event of the Trans-Siberian railroad to Vladivostock being cut, it provides alternative transport from the great industrial region between Novosibirsk and the Seas of Okhotsk and Japan.

The industrial centre of Yakutsk is now linked with the Sea of Okhotsk by the highway which runs from Skovorodino, the northernmost point on the Trans-Siberian Railway. Hence the chief inland port of the Lena—Yakutsk—has direct communication with the Okhotsk ports of Nogayevo and Magadan. Ayan also, on the southern shore of Okhotsk, has been developed to provide the Yakutsk Republic with an outlet to the Pacific, but this port is ice-free for only six months in the year.

The last war gave considerable impetus to Russia's Far Eastern development on account of the necessity of that area becoming independent of supplies from the West. Indeed, the pre-war process of West supplying East was to some extent reversed—Siberia became the Eastern arsenal of the Western Front. For so important an area as the Far Eastern region, the need for the U.S.S.R. to have undisputed access to the Pacific is clear. At this point of her Empire she is very sensitive, and it was her awareness of this which in 1910 made her oppose the American scheme for financing a railway to be constructed from Chinchow on the Liao-tung Gulf, to Aigun on the Amur. Russia interpreted this proposal as one designed to facilitate American penetration into Soviet territory on the eastern Siberian seaboard. To the suggestion that the Chinese Eastern Railway should be internationalised, St. Petersburg replied that this line constituted the principal one of communication "between the Russian possessions in the Far East and the rest of the Empire; it is also the great artery by which these possessions are supplied with Russian merchandise."[1]

[1] *Problems of the Pacific.* Proceedings of the Third Conference of the Institute of Pacific Relations, 1929. (University of Chicago Press, 1930); p. 483.

From the mouth of the Amur at Nikolaievsk to Cape Deshniev on the Bering Strait, Russia has 9,000 miles of coast. She has two principal sailing routes, and both commence at Vladivostock. The first one follows the western shore of the Sea of Japan, then running north it goes through the Gulf of Tartary to Alexandrovsk, thence through the channel separating Sakhalin Island from the Russian mainland to Nikolaievsk. Following a northerly course up the Sea of Okhotsk to Obdorsk, it proceeds east to the port of Gizhiga.

The second sailing route from Vladivostock approaches the Soya Strait, through which it passes on a north-easterly course between Sakhalin Island and the Japanese island of Hokkaido; thence it continues to the northern part of the chain of the Kurile Islands. From here, between two of the islands, it goes to the port of Petropavlovsk on Kamchatka, and through the Kamchatka Sea it proceeds in a north-westerly direction to Olyutorskoye. Part of this route has been of proved value to Russia in the past. In the Russo-Japanese War, 1904-05, a number of ships,[1] mainly British colliers, broke the blockade, and passed through the Soya Strait to Vladivostock with coal for the Russian squadron.

A third route takes a course through the Tsugaru Strait which separates the main Japanese island of Honshu from the northerly island of Hokkaido, but all these routes have been threatened at different times by the Empire of Nippon, and the whole complex of Russo-Japanese relations in this area resolves itself into the question, is there room on the Sea of Japan for two Powers?

Japanese expansion at the expense of Russia featured in the works of many leading German geopoliticians, notably Otto Richard Tannenberg. If we look at a map of Asia, drawn for his *Grossdeutschland, die Arbeit des 20. Jahrhunderts*,[2] we shall find Japan in possession of eastern Siberia, and Germany of the eastern Chinese seaboard from the Gulf of Pohai, and inland from Peiping to the Hwang-Ho basin. (In the south, Germany holds the Netherlands East Indies.) Karl Haushofer in his *Geopolitik des Pacifisches Oceans*[3] advocates Russia conceding northern Sakhalin to Japan, and agreeing to Japanese control in Manchuria. Japan, in alliance with Germany, could in this

---

[1] W. B. Whall, in *The Romance of Navigation*, puts the number at thirty-eight. (Sampson Low, Marston, 1925); p. 215.

[2] Bolger, Leipzig-Gohlig, 1911; p. 254.

[3] Vowinckel, Berlin, 2nd edition, 1938.

way, said Haushofer, ensure for herself a position unchallenged in the western Pacific.

Grandiose proposals such as these were by no means unrealistic, because the population of Japan is approximately twelve times that of Far Eastern Russia, though the area of Japan is seven times less. It is computed that a population of about six million Soviet citizens faces a Japanese population of over seventy millions. The policy of settling Russian territory in the Far East had begun in 1906, when the immigration figures there were 180,000; two years later they were 500,000.[1] This policy has been continued also by the Soviet Government, which in 1933 devised special means for attracting its citizens to the Far East; these included increased wages for workers and tax exemptions for collective farms. In addition to this planned settling of pioneers from the west, the care of indigenous peoples from the Chukchis in the far north, to the fisher folk of the Amur River and the miners of the Sikhota Mountains in the south, forms part of the Russian attempts to meet the population menace of Japan.

"In the 1914-18 war, Russia and Japan were allies, but after the Russian Revolution of 1917, that did not prevent Japan from occupying a considerable part of Russian territory in the Far East. Though she retired in 1922 from Vladivostock and East Siberia, this occupation is instructive concerning Japanese aims."[2] The region is one to which the Island Empire attached almost as much importance as Russia does, and as early as 1859 we find in the writings of Yoshida Shoin, leader of the Chosin Clan, that the Military Party had plans for annexing Eastern Siberia, as well as Manchuria and Korea. A recent instance of this Nipponese determination to oust Russia from the Pacific coast, was provided in 1942. With an effrontery only matched in degree by stupidity, Japan suggested that, as a corollary to the Russo-Japanese Neutrality Pact, Japan during World War II should have control of the Russian seaboard territory known as Primorsk, and of the whole of Sakhalin Island (which would have given Japan the oil wells in the northern half of the island), and the strategic Peninsula of Kamchatka. After the war these regions were to be ceded outright to Japan! It need hardly be said that Moscow's reply did not encourage Tokyo to make further honourable proposals.

The same may be said of the American treatment of the

[1] Thomas F. Millard, *America and the Far Eastern Question*; p. 287.
[2] *Soviet Russia in Maps*. (George Philip & Son, 1943); p. 8.

proposals made by the Japanese Minister M. Kato, who on a visit to Washington in 1940, assuring the White House of Japan's peaceful intentions, suggested that the U.S. Navy should be removed from the Pacific, where, he maintained, its presence was not only unnecessary, but was wounding to the feelings of his countrymen. Russia, which at that time had no more foreknowledge of Pearl Harbour than America had, was none the less anxious that the U.S. Pacific Fleet should be maintained at full strength, for it was not then from America that she feared attack, but from Japan. A strong American Navy in the Pacific was at that time Russia's best guarantee of security against a seaborne invasion until she herself could increase her own Pacific Fleet to safety strength.

Even more astonishing than the suggestion made by M. Kato to Washington was the proposal made by M. Matsuoka to the well-known American writer, Hallett Abend. Matsuoka, who was at that time managing president of the South Manchuria Railway, in a private talk with Abend at Mukden in 1938, requested him to transmit certain proposals to President Roosevelt. In his book *Pacific Charter*,[1] Abend gives an account of this remarkable interview, in which Matsuoka told him that he believed another world war was imminent, and that his aim was to ensure that Japan should be free of the menace of Soviet air attacks and Soviet armies from the frontiers of Manchukuo and of Korea. So he proposed that Japan and the United States should make Russia a joint offer for the purchase of all Siberia east of Lake Baikal. The purchase price suggested was from thirty to fifty billion yen spread over thirty years; an initial payment of ten billion yen would be made. So much importance did the future Japanese Foreign Minister attach to the timber, minerals, oil, and fishing of Siberia, that while he told Abend that if he became Foreign Minister or Premier he would even arrange to have the Japanese army withdrawn from South China, the Yangtse Valley, and Shantung, if the deal went through, he made it clear Japan would never give up the territories she had acquired in *North* China. These territories were limitrophe with Siberia, and their proximity to the Russian Maritime Territory, Primorsk, would in enemy control, endanger Soviet security on the Pacific. (Japanese aims to this end had been apparent to many American observers before the first world war. "Strategically the preparations which the naval authorities are steadily organising at Port Lazareff, Dalny, and

[1] The Bodley Head, 1943; pp. 148-53.

other places," wrote J. O. P. Bland, "are unmistakably intended to enable Japan, if necessary, to envelop Vladivostock and the Primorsk.")[1]

Matsuoka's proposals were taken secretly to President Roosevelt early in 1939, but according to Hallett Abend they were not regarded seriously in Washington. "It was, of course," said Abend, "never possible for the American Government to consider any kind of proposal which would betray China to the extent of leaving Japan in possession of four provinces in North China." Nevertheless the suggestion that Japan should purchase the Russian Maritime Region was actually made in the Japanese Diet that year.[2] Molotov is reported as having drily countered the proposal by remarking that he was sure that purchasers for southern Sakhalin could be found in the U.S.S.R. The affair is interesting not only as showing that Japan's desire to get Siberia was as strong in 1939 as it ever was in the past, but in revealing the ideas which Japan entertained, or professed to entertain, as to the strength of Russia's defensive forces in her Eastern Territories.

Certainly the Far Eastern territories of the Soviet Union are such as to call for strong defences. They include the coalfields of Cheremkovo, and the coke-forming coal deposits in the basin of the Burei—a tributary of the Amur—assets for the development of communications and for the expansion of harbours in the Maritime Province. This coal too is useful for the extension of the Amur-Yakut highway via the Yablonoy mountain passes, a route designed to link the Okhotsk Sea with the Siberian Sea. The high grade coal of the Sutchansk mines north of Nakhoda Bay in the Maritime Territory, assists the development of the metallurgical industries springing up in the valleys of the Sikhota Alin mountains, as well as the needs of Vladivostock. Other resources of which increased production will mean an expansion of Russia's mercantile marine in the Far East, are the oil and mica of Kamchatka, the tin and zinc of Yakutia east of the Lena, and the great coalfield of the Lena basin. In the Chukot Peninsula on the Bering Sea there are coal, zinc, lead, gold and silver mines. In the Anadir Basin there are coal deposits, and ships call at the port of Anadir for local fuel. Tungsten is mined near the inland port of Blagovyeshchensk. From the latter town to Khabarovsk the dark soil of

---

[1] *Recent Events and Present Policies in China*; p. 35.

[2] Harriet L. Moore, *Soviet Far Eastern Policy, 1931-1945.* (Princeton University Press, 1945.)

the Amur Valley makes that stretch of country a valuable one for the development of timber for the shipyards of Nikolaievsk, on the Strait of Tartary.

The value of navigation on the Amur had become clear after the conquest of Kamchatka. The river can be used by vessels for nearly half the year, and during the open season it conveys oil which has been shipped from Moskal-vo, the western port of Sakhalin, to Komsomolsk on the mainland. The Amur is one of the only two great rivers of Siberia which do not flow into the Arctic. It is 3,000 miles long, and is navigable for nearly half that distance. In 1937 the Soviet Government gave orders for the channel on the north side of the islands near Blagovyeshchensk to be dammed, to prevent the Japanese from sending their ships up to that part of the river to spy on Russian defence works. A dispute with Tokyo followed, as Manchukuo claimed some of the islands on which the Russians had set up fortifications.

At the confluence of the rivers Amur and Ussuri is the large inland port of Khabarovsk. It is also situated on the junction of two branches of the Trans-Siberian Railway, one of which runs due south to Vladivostock, the other due north to Komsomolsk. From Khabarovsk, too, runs the highway to the north, constructed, as previously stated, to link the Sea of Okhotsk with the Sea of Siberia, and the navigable Kolima with the Arctic. The city is important as well for its large oil refinery, which takes the new grades of oil from the Sakhalin wells. Timber of the Ussuri region is floated to the Pacific for shipment overseas. The basin of the Ussuri promises to become a miniature Ukraine, with its fine crops of wheat, oats, sugar beet, soya bean, and vegetable oil plant. East of the river is the tongue of land known as Primorsk, the Maritime Territory, situated between the Ussuri River and the Sea of Japan. The coastline of that Territory is protected to some extent by the Sikhota-Alin range; the latter has manganese, molybdenum, tin, lead, zinc, and iron ore.

North of Khabarovsk and also on the Amur River, is the shipbuilding city of Komsomolsk in whose shipyards "the first warships (probably destroyers) built by the Russians in the Far East were launched in the summer of 1939."[1] The building of such ships was undertaken here because Komsomolsk is by its situation much better protected than Vladivostock. It has the advantage of being far from the open sea, and well away from the Manchurian frontier. It is therefore a rapidly rising maritime city. "The largest of the new engineering enterprises is the

[1] R. A. Davies and A. J. Steiger, *Soviet Asia*. (Gollancz, 1943); p. 154.

shipbuilding yard now under construction at Komsomolsk" wrote two American authors[1] in 1936. "They were," says William Mandel,[2] "quite modest in defining the Komsomolsk shipyard as the biggest in its field in the East. Although its capacity has never been stated, its cost was six times as large as that of the Marty shipyard at Nikolaiev in the Ukraine, which was built at the same time, and which had six slipways. Moreover, its cost was greater than that of any other manufacturing plant of any type ever known to be erected in the Far East."

From Komsomolsk a coastal railway has been constructed to run right up to the Chukot Peninsula on the Bering Sea. This was planned to link the ports of the Sea of Okhotsk—Ayan and Okhotsk—with those on the Gulf of Kamchatka—Gizhiga and Kamensk—and these in turn with the Polar station and northern shipping centre of Anadir on the Bering Sea. The line will continue thence round Providence Bay to Cape Deshniev, the nearest point in Asia to Alaska.

South-east of Komsomolsk, and on the Primorsk coast, is the naval base of Sovietskaya Gavan, built to deter Japanese expansion along the Amur. It is not an ice-free port, but it has a floating dock, and so, before the last war commenced, risks were distributed by sending some of the ships here, instead of sending them all to ports on the Sea of Japan and thus exposing them to the chance of attack from Honshu. Sovietskaya Gavan is on the west shore of the Gulf of Tartary; in the extreme north of that Gulf at the delta of the Amur is the harbour of Nikolaievsk, frozen from November to June. It has good depth of water at the roadstead, but the harbour entrance has a bar. Near this port are valuable deposits of coke-forming coal.

With all its natural wealth and its rising industries, it is no wonder that such a region as the Amur Valley is formidably defended, and this was one of the main reasons why Japan signed the Pact of Non-Aggression with Russia in 1941.[3] That Neutrality Pact later enabled American ships to have unimpeded use of Russian ports on the Northern Pacific, and also made it possible for a certain number of Soviet ships to bring in supplies from the United States to Siberian seaports. The value of those ports to America as well as to Russia, in the event of a war

[1] E. Raikhman and B. Vvedensky, *The Economic Development of the Far East.* (Institute of Pacific Relations, New York, 1936); pp. 13, 14.

[2] *The Soviet Far East.* (Institute of Pacific Relations Inquiry Series, New York); p. 54.

[3] The Pact was denounced by the Soviet Union on 4 April, 1945.

undertaken by those two Powers jointly against Japan, and the value of Siberia as an ally, had been stressed by Mr. Thomas Millard, American adviser to the Government of the Chinese Republic, during the Peace Conference at Washington, 1919. His opinion was justified by events in the Far East in the second world war.

The blow to American sea power at Pearl Harbour was deplored at the time by Russia, and there was nothing neutral in the tone of the contemporary article on this disaster which appeared in *Pravda*. "December 7, 1941, will go down in history as the beginning of the great war in the Pacific Ocean," stated the paper. "On this date the Japanese naval and air forces predatorily and without warning attacked American possessions in the Pacific. . . . The negotiations being conducted by the Japanese representatives in Washington clearly had the object of concealing the preparations for this predatory attack. Japan acted on the lines so well known to the Soviet Union from her experience in the war against Hitler, who similarly, in a predatory and piratic fashion, attacked the Soviet Union. And so it is quite clear that in this instance Japan is undoubtedly the aggressor and the United States and Great Britain have been the victims of a premeditated and previously planned act of aggression."[1]

The more intently therefore, did Russia go about her business of strengthening her possessions in the near neighbourhood of Japan. On the eastern side of the Sea of Okhotsk and flanking it for 750 miles, stretches the Peninsula of Kamchatka, whose southern extremity Cape Lopatka, is but a short distance from the Japanese base of Paramushiro, and only seven miles from the northerly tip of the Kuriles. The principal port of Kamchatka is Petropavlovsk[2] on Avacha Bay, 1,500 miles from Vladivostock. It is sheltered by high mountain ranges and has excellent harbourage. During the Crimean War Russia's Pacific Fleet had been based on this port, and had defeated a joint attack by the British and French. Petropavlovsk under Soviet rule has been developed as a naval base and has a floating dock; part of its function is to guard the oilfields of Kamchatka, also the pipe-line which brings oil from Okha on the Sea of Okhotsk, to Nikolaievsk. The harbour, because

[1] Published in *Soviet War News*, 13 December, 1941.

[2] Its name derives from *St. Peter* and *St. Paul*, the ships from which Vitus Bering in 1740 led his expedition from Kamchatka to the Bering Sea. On a northern arm of the bay, some of his men formed a small settlement.

it is ice-free, was used during the second world war as a supply
port for lend-lease exports from America, and is now the
winter station for that part of the Northern Fleet which does
service in the Eastern zone of the Arctic Ocean.

It was at Petropavlovsk that in 1938 the floating dock
ended its voyage of 11,000 miles, after taking four vessels from
the Black Sea to Kamchatka. The dock, which was towed by
the steamer *Kharkov* and the tug *Typhoon*, was equipped with
electrically driven engines, and the dockyard deck was fitted
with wave-breakers.

THE KURILES

South of Kamchatka the Kuriles stretch in a long arc to
Nemuro Bay on Hokkaido, one of the four main islands of
Japan. They cross the seven-mile wide strait of Chishima-
Kaikyo, and are physically part of the Kamchatka formation.
For eight hundred miles they form a barrier between the Sea of
Okhotsk and the Pacific Ocean, a formation of which the
Japanese took advantage in the second world war by building
strong forts on most of the islands. The prevalence of fogs on and
around the Kuriles made it possible for them to work out their
naval and military preparations in secrecy here. The proximity
of these islands to Russian mainland territory makes it imperative for the Soviet Union to maintain powerful naval and air
forces around this group. That American naval authorities were
alive to the strategic significance of the Kuriles is clear from the
Report of the House Naval Affairs Committee, 18 August 1945,
which (unaware of the decisions reached at Yalta) urged that
the United States should establish defences on these islands, as
well as the Ryukyus, after the peace settlement in the Far East.
The news that Russian paratroops had landed in August 1945,
on two of the Kurile islands—Shumshi and Paramushiro (the
Japanese naval base)—was not altogether welcome in certain
naval quarters in America. It had, however, been agreed at the
Yalta Conference, that Russia, on condition that she entered
the war against Japan, should receive among other territory,
the Kuriles. These islands give her more direct communication
by sea with her naval base of Petropavlovsk.

VLADIVOSTOCK

When the Chinese Eastern Railway had been opened, the
Russians had developed Port Arthur at the expense of
Vladivostock and freight discrimination had been marked
against the latter. But with the loss of Port Arthur after the

Russo-Japanese War, Vladivostock began to receive favour. The Russians then aimed at making it a port of entry for Manchuria, so a shipping service between Vladivostock and Shanghai was started. From the former, goods were transported on the Russian railway to the interior of Manchuria. Vladivostock in this way expanded its trade as a result of Japanese "closed" policy as regards her own ports in southern Manchuria. At the time of its establishment as a naval harbour in 1874, the overseas ambitions of the Russians were moribund. Vladivostock, by its geographical location, was not a port from which to embark on conquests; from its enclosed position it was a harbour primarily defensive in character. Today that is no less true; as the base for the Russian Far Eastern submarine flotillas Vladivostock is naturally a place where intensive labour has been devoted to fortifications. Before the outbreak of the second world war it was known that it had twenty-inch guns or even larger.[1] The defensive system stretches northward to Lake Hanka on the borders of Manchuria and Russia's Far Eastern Territories, the seaboard Province of Primorsk. Such powerful fortifications, particularly round Vladivostock, are most necessary considering that the Japanese after their seizure of that base at the end of the first world war, acquired a first-hand knowledge of it. It was not till 1922 that they were obliged to surrender it. From its situation Vladivostock is, indeed, "Lord of the East"; a radius of seven hundred and fifty miles from this base includes Tokyo, Kobe, also the pre-war main Japanese naval bases of Kure, Sasebo, and the secondary bases of Ominato and Maizuru. In addition Vladivostock is but 300 miles from Harbin—focal point of the Manchurian railway system. Its importance had been manifest in the 1914-18 war, when owing to the blockade of her western ports, much of the supplies which Russia purchased from America had to be shipped across the Pacific to Vladivostock. During the first six months of 1915, the imports here from all sources amounted to over 200,000 tons.[2] The difficulties of transport were due not to limitations in the port itself, but to those of the Trans-Siberian Railway. By the end of 1915 accumulation of munitions and war material was estimated at no less than 2,000,000 tons.[3]

[1] W. P. and Z. K. Coates, *Why Russia Will Win*. (Eldon Press, Ltd., 1942.) Quoted by these authors from the writings of the Japanese military author, Yasuo Mishima, extracts from whose works were published in *Parade*, November 1938 (published by the Periodical Press, Ltd.).
[2] C. E. Fayle, *Seaborne Trade*. (John Murray, 1920); Vol. II, p. 121.
[3] *Ibid.*, p. 351.

As long as Russia maintains a fleet in being, Vladivostock remains a potent check—as regards Japan's communications with Manchuria and Korea—on any revival of Japanese naval ambitions. In addition to the submarines, it is the base for the Far Eastern units of the more recent destroyers of the *Stremitelny* class.

Vladivostock is used to some extent as a commercial harbour, particularly for the export of timber, soya beans, and canned fish, and a growing shipbuilding industry is established here. "The Golden Horn", the land-locked bay on which the harbour stands, has a double turn in the navigation channel; this provides a natural defence, inasmuch as it exposes incoming enemy vessels to fire. It is not by nature an ice-free harbour, a fact which in the past caused Russia to look south, especially to Korea and the Liao-tung Peninsula. To overcome the previous difficulties caused by ice conditions, the Russians had set up a supply base on the ice-free Possiet Bay, south of Vladivostock: this also served the naval base of Postovoy. The "Golden Horn" can now however be kept open by icebreakers and this has changed Vladivostock into an open harbour. According to a statement made in *Trud* in 1941,[1] the difficulties of weather conditions had then been so far mastered that regular winter shipping could be undertaken between Vladivostock and the ports on both the east and west side of the Kamchatka Peninsula.

SAKHALIN

Sakhalin Island, now entirely in Russian hands, is an important gain for the Soviet Union's defensive system in the Far East. It has changed hands many times. The Japanese, who had once occupied the northern half of the island, gave up this territory to Russia later in exchange for certain islands in the Kuriles. But in 1887 Sakhalin was divided between the two Powers, the northern part (i.e. above 50° Lat.)—comprising three-fifths of the island—going to Russia. After the 1914-18 war Japan had seized again that northern area of Sakhalin. She had also stationed troops across the Tartary Strait at Nikolaievsk and on De Castries Bay.

This Japanese aggrandisement had reactions in America, whose Government was anxious for the balance of power to be maintained in the Far East and the Pacific. Apprehensive that Japan would no longer observe the policy of the Open Door for trade with China, and aware that Japan must not be allowed to

[1] 22 March, 1941.

obtain a dominating position on the coast of Russia's Far-Eastern Territory, the United States brought pressure to bear on her, with the result that Japan withdrew from that region. Twelve months after the signing of the Naval Limitation Treaties of Washington, 1922, she had given up her occupation of the Russian Maritime Territories. Three years later she withdrew from north Sakhalin; in the southern part of the island however, Japan remained until Russia declared war on her in August 1945, soon after which Soviet forces made amphibious landings at the coastal towns of Anabestu and Esutoru. The whole of southern Sakhalin and the islands adjacent to it, have since been acquired by the Soviet Union, in accordance with the terms of the Yalta Agreement.

In 1941 the oil wells under Russian control were reported to have a total output of 700,000 tons. "That figure appears suspiciously low to people who have observed the island carefully,"[1] and who point out that it would not be in the interests of the Soviet Union at that time to make that northern section appear too desirable, especially as the Okha wells supplied fuel for Russia's Far Eastern flotillas. Oil and coal concessions had been granted to Japan; these were due to expire in 1970, but when the Russo-Japanese Neutrality Pact was signed in 1941, an undertaking had been given by M. Matsuoka to settle in the near future the question of the liquidation of the Northern Sakhalin concessions.[2] When these were surrendered in 1941, Japan was limited to receive 50,000 tons of oil over a period of five years, but only after the war in the Pacific was over. This, together with the surrender of fishery concessions, showed that Japan wished at all costs to maintain the Neutrality Pact. Any breach on her part would mean she was faced with the probability of action by the Russian Pacific Fleet, and of attack by Soviet naval planes on her harbours—the main ones as we have seen, being within comparatively easy reach of the Vladivostock base.

The surrender by Japan of the Sakhalin concessions not only meant that she was unable to get any more oil from Okha during the war, but also the cancellation, twenty-six years before expiry was due, of the oil and coal concessions granted in 1925 for a period of forty-five years. By a cash settlement all Japanese coal and oil properties were transferred to the Soviet

[1] Emil Lengyel, *Secret Siberia*. (Robert Hale, Ltd., 1947); p. 207.
[2] See also article by James Aldridge from Moscow: *The Evening Standard*, 3 April, 1944.

Union. The value of the island's coal to Russia's Pacific Fleet is considerable, for about half that produced in the eastern territories of the U.S.S.R. comes from the Alexandrovsk field in north-west Sakhalin.

The 1944 Agreements also related to the fishing concessions. Japan was now prohibited from fishing in certain prescribed areas, e.g. around Vladivostock; and twenty-four fishing lots leased by Japanese fishery organisations were withdrawn. The lease of fishing grounds to Japan on the east coast of Kamchatka and in the Olyutorsk district was renewed, but Japan was prohibited from exploiting them till the end of the war in the Pacific. The significance of this fishing protocol lies, of course, in the Russian mistrust of Japanese designs in Far Eastern waters, and Russia's determination to safeguard her own shores against any attempted seaborne invasion from Japan. The Soviet Government had sent to its own fishing grounds off Sakhalin men whom it could rely on not only to develop the fisheries, but to keep their watchful eyes on Japanese activities in those waters. Volga fishermen were sent to join the Collective on Black River; their boats went to the southern part of the Tartary Strait where they worked the herring shoals. In this fishing they were helped by the new Soviet motor fishing boats,[1] for navigation in the Strait is very difficult, the passage being full of rocks and subject to sudden storms. In one part it is so narrow that there is no difficulty in making it impassable to submarines and destroyers. For five months in the year the Strait is closed by ice.

The port of Okha on north-east Sakhalin is one of value to Russia as it is ice-free, benefiting from the warm currents of the Sea of Japan. It is however subject to breakers and has no natural screen against gales. Unloading is often difficult, and sometimes ships have to return to the mainland with undischarged cargo. Alexandrovsk on the north-west coast of the island is a port of some activity owing to the nearby coalfield. Moskal-vo is the chief oil port of Sakhalin, oil being shipped thence across the Tartary Strait to Nikolaievsk. North of the latter is the port of Nogayevo; it is the best equipped harbour on the Sea of Okhotsk and can take several ocean steamers. Gold is exported here from the Kolima River region. Another port which has grown up of late years is Magadan: it lies some way

[1] For some account of the lives of these fishermen see Vladimir L. Kontorovich, *Soviet Sakhalin*. (Co-operative Publishing Society of Foreign Workers in the U.S.S.R., Moscow and Leningrad, 1933.)

inland, is rarely ice-free for more than five months in the year, but is important as being used like Nogayevo, for freight directed to the development of the Kolima district. The future possibilities of these Far Eastern ports have never been lost sight of by Russia. When by the Treaty of Portsmouth, 1905, she was obliged to give to Japanese subjects the right to engage in the fishing trade along the Siberian coasts, Russia took care, two years later, to apply restrictions to certain bays, all river mouths, and to particular coastal areas on the Sea of Okhotsk. The use of ports there for the reception of supplies from America during the second world war, fulfilled the expectations of earlier Russian governments as to the future importance of these harbours of eastern Siberia.

VIII

THE NORTH PACIFIC

THE BERING SEA

FOR only four months in the year, from June to October, is the Bering Strait ice-free, hence Russia's icebreakers are indispensable for maintaining communications between her Northern and Far Eastern bases. The Bering Sea is bounded on the south by the Aleutian Islands which stretch in a semi-circle nearly to the Russian Kommandorski Islands off Kamchatka. On Unalaska Island in the Aleutian group the Americans have their important harbour at Fort Mears, and the Russians have established a correspondingly powerful base at Medni in the Kommandorskis, where they have submarine stations. During the last war these bases were used to protect the sea communications between the United States and the U.S.S.R. across the Bering Sea. It was disclosed by the United States Lend-Lease Administration in 1943 that the North Pacific had become one of the chief supply ways to Russia. The Soviet mercantile marine had grown by then, as "nearly one-third of all American shipments to the U.S.S.R. were being sent in Soviet vessels from our [U.S.A.] West Coast to ports in the Soviet Far East".[1]

The report that Russia had a maritime base on the American mainland in the second world war received partial confirmation from Mr. James V. Forrestal, Secretary of the U.S. Navy. *Post Intelligence*[2] "which obtained its information from Representative Warren Magnusen, member of the House Naval Affairs Committee, told of 'an American port under Russian command, operated by the Russian Government under terms of Lend-Lease for trans-shipment of cargoes and refuelling of armed vessels'."[3] The port was said to have been handed over to Russia in July 1943.

One of Japan's principal reasons for coveting Russia's Far Eastern seaboard was to be able to dominate the North Pacific, and when she did seize certain of the Aleutians, that ocean supply route was gravely threatened. So too was the summer supply route of the North-East Passage. This menace to the sea

[1] William Mandel, *The Soviet Far East*. (The Dial Press Inc., 1944); p. 20.
[2] 30.9.1944.　　　　　　　　[3] *The News Chronicle*, 2.10.1944.

lanes made air transport a matter of first importance as between
America and Russia. The air route from Nome in Alaska to
Markovo in eastern Siberia—a distance of 620 air miles—was
used for supplies from the United States to the U.S.S.R. during
the last war, when also the Russian airport at Olyutorsk was
connected with the airport at Fairbanks on the Alaskan Highway. That highway, the Alcan Route, was of real strategic
value to Russia's Pacific defence system in the war. The railway
running from Edmonton to Fairbanks and Seward Harbour,
and linked by ferry with the Siberian railway to Irkutsk,
follows fairly accurately what navigators term 'a Great Circle'
connecting the terminal ports.

Though Alaska, including its islands, has a coastline of
26,000 miles, there are only a few ice-free ports. Among these
are Juneau, the Alaskan capital, and Seward. Teller is the
nearest port to the Russian mainland, but Anchorage, though
ice-locked for part of the year, is the one more frequently used.
Harbourages on the Russian side of the Bering Sea are being
developed as fast as the conditions of the Arctic climate will
allow. Inseparable from the expansion of Russia's Arctic and
Pacific Fleets is the realisation by the Soviet Government of the
fact that the coastline on the Russian mainland from Cape
Lopatka (Kamchatka) to Cape Deshniev (on the Bering Strait)
is, like the Alaskan shore from Prince of Wales Island to Prince
of Wales Cape, strategically one of the most important on the
globe. Six months before the outbreak of the last war, Admiral
Kuznetsov, Commissar for the Red Navy, proclaimed that
Russia had a formidable fleet in Far Eastern waters. Two years
later, after the Soviet-Japanese Pact of Neutrality, Japan complained of the mines being laid by Russia in the Kamchatka
Sea. The reality of Russia's proclaimed defensive measures was
thus soon attested by the naval War Lords of Japan.

THE NORTH-WEST COAST OF AMERICA; EARLIEST EXPLORATIONS

In 1816 the U.S. Secretary of State, Monroe, writing to the
American Ambassador at St. Petersburg, had said: "In looking
forward even to a distant period, the only circumstance in which
a difference of interest is anticipated between the United States
and Russia, relates to their respective claims on the Pacific
Ocean. . . . Remote, however, as the danger of collision is, it had
better be provided against."[1]

[1] *The Road to Teheran*, Foster Rhea Dulles. (Princeton University Press,
1944); p. 30.

Will the danger of a collision always be remote? For the sake of some 2,174,000,000 beings it is to be hoped that the agreement signed between Russia and America in 1942 may prove an exception to the rule that pacts made today are but scraps of paper tomorrow. The fact however that the Soviet Union emerged after the last war a first-class Power, sharpens considerably the question of "respective claims on the Pacific Ocean" as between herself and the United States.

The first overseas possession of Russia was on the American continent; Alaska and the seaboard as far south as Fort Ross (less than sixty miles from San Francisco) were once part of the Russian Empire. But this coastline had been explored long before Tsar Paul chartered it for development to the Russian-American Fur Company. The "Oval World Map" of Battista Agnese, 1558 [?], shows not only a strait running through part of the North American continent (at approximately 52° N., however), but it also traces the outline of the Californian Peninsula.[1] Writing three and a half centuries later, a Russian seaman described the expeditions thither of Bering and Chirikov as recalling "the supreme daring and self-reliance of those arch freebooters, Drake, Cavendish and Dampier". The mention of Drake is certainly apposite here, for that world-minded mariner, after plundering Spanish ships in Callao and loading his own with hauls of treasure all up the coast of Peru, had landed with some of his men on the North American continent in 1579. Here the Californian natives, venerating the visitors as gods, had offered Drake their land, and in the name of New Albion he had taken it for his sovereign. His own name is perpetuated in Port Sir Francis Drake.

As the question of the territory discovered by the Elizabethan navigator was to become—exactly two hundred years later— a cause of conflict between the respective mercantile interests of Britain and Russia in the North Pacific, it is worth while stating briefly what is known of Drake's voyage up the north-west coast of America. The most northerly point which he reached has been the subject of much controversy. The authorities who maintain that he sailed as far north as latitude 48° base their belief mainly on the notes of Francis Fletcher, who had voyaged with Drake as a preacher, and whose diary of that expedition

[1] See *The Manuscript Atlases of Battista Agnese*, edited by Henry R. Wagner. *The Papers of the Bibliographical Society of America*, Vol. XXV. (University of Chicago Press, 1931.)

was published later in the work known as *The World Encompassed by Sir Francis Drake*.[1] The account in Fletcher's journal is regarded as reliable by Captain James Burney (the first real historian of the Pacific), and, in our own time, the naval writer, Sir Julian Corbett, claims latitude 48° for Drake. Purchas in *His Pilgrimes* however (Vol. I, p. 52), says "Sir Francis Drake sailed on the othe side of America to 43° of northerly latitude, and with cold was forced to retire." Hakluyt in his *Voyages and Navigations of the English* includes "The Famous Voyage of Sir Francis Drake", by William Pretty, who takes the view that Drake after 5th June, did not advance far north of latitude 43°. This view is supported by George Davidson in his study on "Francis Drake on the Northwest Coast of America".[2] The Dutch cartographer, Jodocus Hondius, writing in 1595, states in his note about New Albion that Drake reached latitude 42°; his map of 1590 is a primary one on this subject.

While some writers believe that the English navigator did not anchor in San Francisco but in Trinidad and Bodega bays, and it is fairly generally recognised that the first real exploration of the Bay of San Francisco was made by the Spaniards in their Portola expedition of 1769, it is also widely accepted that Drake did reach that Bay exactly 190 years earlier. William Camden (contemporary historian), records Drake as landing at 38°. Certainly he was the first known European to have landed on the Farallon Isles (which he called the Islands of St. James); the South Farallon lies only twenty-three nautical miles from "The Golden Gate". Seeking to escape the vengeance of the Spaniards who would surely attack him in the Magellan Strait after his great haul of treasure from Valparaiso and Santiago, Drake on his return voyage in the *Golden Hind*, had vowed he would seek "the Englishman's streight", viz. the Pacific entrance to the North-West Passage. Even five years after his voyage, the legend was current that this strait, called Anian, "continues to, and ends near, Ireland".

The territory which became known as "Drake's Bay" had actually been taken thirty-seven years earlier by the Portuguese seaman Cabrillo, with the Spanish galliots *San Salvador* and *La Vittoria*. In 1542 he had discovered the harbour of San Diego which the members of his expedition had christened San Miguel. His ships, commissioned by the Government of Spain, were poor, smaller than contemporary coasting schooners, ill-

[1] Nicholas Bovine, London, 1628.
[2] *Transactions and Proceedings of the Geographical Society of the Pacific, 1908.*

equipped, and manned by natives and conscripts; "he went not beyond the forty-fourth parallel".[1]

The name of a Greek pilot, Juan de Fuca, had been given to a strait whose ownership was to be contested later by Russians, Spaniards, and British. By some historians however it is believed that this eighty-three-mile-long strait into which de Fuca took a caravel in 1592, may have been the fabled one of Anian. Cortereal claimed to have sailed from the coast of Labrador through a narrow strait to the Indian Ocean in 1500, and Maldonado made the same claim in 1588. It is not to be wondered at that the appropriation of the whole Pacific Ocean made in the name of his sovereign by the Spanish navigator Balboa, from his peak in Darien, was to be contested by the settlers of different nationalities who for the next three hundred years were busy colonising its eastern shores and islands. For the discovery of the Aleutian Islands, credit must be given to the Russians, but the map made by Bodega, commander of *La Señora*, shows the old Spanish place-names from Puerto de Acapulco to Alaska.

Neither the voyages of Bering and Chirikov along the north-western shores of America, nor the Aleutian chart made by the Russian trader Glotov in 1759, had made clear the question as to whether or not Alaska was part of the mainland or only a large island. It was not till 1790, by the discovery of the English navigator Captain George Vancouver, that it was finally demonstrated that no other passage except the Bering Strait linked the Pacific and the Arctic Oceans. The Russian explorer Lieut. Chirikov, who accompanied Bering on his North Pacific Expedition of 1741, had sighted the American continent at latitude 55° 21′. The land which he saw lay off Prince of Wales Island.[2] Part of the Alaskan coast he explored and charted, and he discovered the cape on Sitka which later was named in his honour. An island in the Aleutian chain also bears his name, though Mikhail Novodchik, who had sailed with Bering, is usually credited with the actual discovery of the whole group on his voyage in the *Eudoki* in 1745. Glotov, a pioneer among the Russian merchant adventurers in these regions, was the first to explore the Fox Islands in the Aleutians, and in this

---

[1] Étienne Marchand, *A Voyage Round the World Performed During the Years, 1790, 1791, and 1792.* (Longman, Rees, Cadell & Davies, 1801); Introd. Vol. I, p. v.

[2] See Bertholf's map, based on the log books of the voyages of the *St. Peter* and the *St. Paul.*

group is Unalaska, on which the Russians made their earliest settlement. Shumagin Island takes its name from a member of the crew who died here on Bering's final expedition.

In the chapter entitled "Early Explorations" in this book, we reviewed briefly the Russian voyages of the Cossacks. For those hunters it had become, during the late decades of the eighteenth century, a necessity to find "The Big Land" across the North Pacific, because the Siberian sables were almost exhausted. And it was the enterprises of such expansive adventurers as Shelikov, "the Russian Columbus"—leader of an expedition which left Okhotsk in 1783 and was to last four years—that caused alarm among the Spaniards in their settlements to the south. Shelikov had not been content merely with surveying the islands and coast between the southern extremity of Alaska and Prince William Sound, nor with bestowing his own name on the strait on the western side of Prince William's Island. Spurred on by the ambitions of his strong-willed spouse Natalie —the first European woman known to have crossed the North Pacific—Shelikov aimed at getting a monopoly of the fur trade in Alaska, not only as against foreigners but other Russians, and to this end he petitioned Catherine the Great. But he wanted more than that, too: his mind was set on his Company eventually embracing the whole of the North American coastline down to California.[1] This would inevitably have brought the Russians into conflict with the Spaniards.

CALIFORNIA

The story of the Spanish exploration of the coasts of California and of north-west America had reached an important chapter when the first definitely commissioned Spanish expedition to North Pacific waters was undertaken in 1774. In that year Juan Perez in the corvette *Santiago* had set out to explore the coast up to 60° N., and thence to survey the shore-line south to Monterey. He was instructed to proclaim the Spanish ownership of territory south of latitude 60°, and to turn out from the islands any Russians he might find in those parts. Perez, who succeeded in making a general investigation of the coast from 42° N. to 54° 40', had sighted Prince of Wales Island, and named it Santa Maria Magdalena. He also discovered Nootka Sound, later the scene of much activity among the pioneers of

[1] Many of Shelikov's own reports appeared for the first time in 1944, when the Russian (All-Union) Geographical Society published them under the editorship of A. I. Andreev. (Academy of Sciences, Moscow and Leningrad.)

the Russian fur traders on the American continent. In a subsequent voyage, known as the Second Bucarelli expedition, this renowned Spanish sea captain sailing again in the *Santiago*, left Porto San Blas (Mexico) and reached 57° 57′ N., viz., a point north of the landing-place of the Russian voyager Chirikov, and named by the Spaniards Porto de los Remedios. He sighted the mountain which three years later was to be christened Mount Edgcumbe by the English navigator Cook, and which was to be a landmark on so many of the Russian expeditions up the Alaskan coast. *Santiago* had been accompanied by *La Señora*, in which the second pilot was Don Antonio Maurelle, who left a long account of this expedition. The voyage had been made not only with the purpose of exploring further the northern coast of California, but of finding out how far the threat of Russian encroachment from the north was a reality. Along the Californian coast explorers had continued to plant the flag of Spain, the country whose navigators had probably been the first to discover the seaboard—in 1535—though the earliest Spanish settlement there which could properly be called a colony, was not formed till 1769, when a community was started at Port San Diego. The Franciscan Missions strung out along the shores of Nueva California served a double purpose. Not only were the Russians expanding southwards, but the English were creeping up the coasts in their search for a North-West Passage; the early Missions had therefore a military character. San Francisco for instance was definitely founded to protect the Californian coastline.[1] Rumours of armaments in preparation at Kamchatka had alarmed the Spaniards, who, to head off the Russians in their southward drive, had strengthened their own settlements at San Diego and Monterey, relying for provisions on their supply ships *San Antonio* and *San Carlos*. Their main concern was to consolidate their possessions north-west of Mexico, and at the port of San Blas they built ships and sent them north on scouting voyages. One of such vessels, the *San Carlos* just mentioned, was the first vessel to sail through the Golden Gate. Another Russian-hunting expedition had been conducted along the Alaskan coast by Artega and Bodega, but though its members approached the post on Kodiak Island, they saw no sign of the Russians.[2]

[1] Before the Russian advance southward was known however, José de Galvez had intended founding a Spanish settlement here.
[2] F. B. Eldridge, *The Background of Eastern Sea Power*. (Phoenix House, London. Georgian House, Melbourne, 1948); p. 182.

The Hon. Daines Barrington, in his preface to Maurelle's Journal, says naïvely: "The Spaniards should, after our late voyage of discovery . . . be convinced that the English Nation is actuated merely by desiring to know as much as possible with regard to the planet which we inhabit, and to which our geographical inquiries are necessarily bounded. This distrust on the part of Spain would more wisely be directed against the Russians, who from Camskatka might easily establish themselves on the West coast of America, and from thence perhaps in time shake their unwieldy and already tottering Empire."[1] Barrington says he has in mind here the projected expedition of the Empress Catherine who is reported to be fitting out four vessels "on the coast of Camskatka which are to be employed in discoveries during the proper season of 1781".

Despite Barrington's strictures the Spaniards continued to mistrust English and Russians alike, and their voyages northward were still undertaken as much for defensive reasons as for the wish to extend their trade. When the Spanish Government heard rumours of Russian intentions to occupy Nootka Sound, it sent an expedition to defend that water as part of His Catholic Majesty's dominions. It also sent a memorial to the Empress of Russia stating that Prince William Sound was to be regarded as the limit between the dominions of the two sovereigns. This was the first instance of an admission by Spain of the right of any other Power to occupy a part of America bordering on the Pacific. Names such as Cordova, tide-water terminus of Copper River, and Port Valdez on the northern arm of Prince William Sound, show the extent to which the Spanish were creeping north. The farthest point of their exploration in the north-west Pacific was reached in 1792, when they sailed to Cape Camaano. About these voyages, however, the Spanish Government kept very quiet. For instance, it was not till 1802 that they gave any information about the *Santiago* expeditions previously referred to. None the less the fact that the Spaniards had reached latitude 58° N. had been no secret to Russian or to British traders.

Spanish trading interests were mainly connected with the search for sea otters, which the home Government had started about 1786 on the advice of their agent Vasadre, who had pointed out that quicksilver, needed by the New Mexican miners, could be obtained from China if otter pelts were offered in exchange. But so great was the fear entertained by the

[1] *Journal of a Voyage Northward of California*; p. 4.

THE NORTH PACIFIC REGIONS

As they appear in the *Zaltieri Map*, "Nova Franza", of the undated issue, 1566 or earlier.

(Reproduced by permission of the Trustees of the British Museum)

This is the earliest map remaining to show the name "Strait of Anian" given to the passage separating Asia and America. (There were of course however, antecedents of the conception of the separation of those continents.) Marco Polo had alluded[1] to a "Strait of Anin", though this was probably the Gulf of Tong-king. The Italian cartographer Gastalde, who had plotted Marco Polo's journey in his map of 1561—*Tertia Pars Asiae*—had elsewhere misplaced the "Strait of Anin" so that it appears far to the north of Marco Polo's passage of that name. In 1507 Martin Waldseemüller had printed at Strasbourg an Inset Map which shows he was familiar with the concept of a strait between North America and Asia, and the Gemma Frisius series of maps (from 1537) shows the water between the continents as "The Strait of the Three Brothers".

Another feature of special interest in this *Zaltieri Map*, is the island of "Giapan", representing Japan as being nearer the American than the Asian mainland.

[1] This allusion was the discovery of Dr. Sophus Ruge, whose monograph on this subject was published under the title of *Fretum Anian* in *Abhandl. u. Vort. z. Hesch. der Erdkunde*, Dresden, 1888. (It was also published earlier in *Die Geschichte der Beringstrasse vor ihren Entdeckung*, 1873.) See George E. Nunn, *Origin of the Strait of Anian Concept*. (Privately printed, Philadelphia, 1929. Copyright by George H. Beans, 1929.)

AMON

ΕΝ RVTLANDIA

CN

MARE
COGELATO

DE CLO

MARE DELVERI

Spaniards of Russian encroachment south, that they were ready
to risk losing an offer made by the Russians to hunt the otter on
a profit-sharing basis. This offer the Spanish colonists were only
prepared to accept at that time on condition that the Russians
withdrew from California. However, in 1823 the first Mexican-
Russian contract for otter hunting was signed. This did permit
the Russians to hunt the otters from San Francisco to San Diego
on condition that they sold their share of skins to the Mexican
Government; in return they were to receive wheat at a low
figure.[1]

CAPTAIN COOK

Of all the names associated with the exploration of the north-
west seaboard of America, Captain Cook's of course is pre-
eminent. His charts constituted the first accurate survey of the
Alaskan seaboard, and though Cook had made it clear to the
British Government that considerable commercial advantages
would result if trade were opened with the natives on the shores
of the northern Pacific, and remarks in his Journal that unless
a North-West Passage could be found, the fur trade which
Britain would otherwise develop with north-west America
would hardly be profitable, yet his own voyage was undertaken
in an exploratory rather than a mercantile spirit. It was the
ventures of his successor in these regions, the voyager John
Meares, definitely commercial in aim,[2] which helped to bring
about the restrictive policy adopted by the Russians later as
regards the trading of foreigners with Alaska.

The Admiralty instructions to Captain Cook on his last
voyage directed him to proceed northward from the Russian
port of St. Peter and St. Paul in Kamchatka, or from wherever
else he thought fit, and to coast northwards to latitude 65°, and
thence to sail "in further search of a North-East or North-West
passage from the Pacific Ocean into the Atlantic or North Sea".
He was certainly given wide enough latitude. The instructions
as to soundings, observation of currents, and surveys of coasts
as an aid to future navigation, show the importance attached
by the British Government to the desired discovery of a sea
route which would carry the ships of their traders from ocean
to ocean.

[1] Adele Ogden, *The Californian Sea Otter Trade, 1789-1848*. (University of Calfornia Press, 1941); p. 96.
[2] Meares, *Voyages Made in the Years 1788 and 1789 From China to the
North West Coast of America*. (J. Walter, London, 1790); Introd. p. lxix.

And so in the *Resolution* Cook made his northward voyage, in the course of which he learnt much about the Russian expeditions in the North Pacific. The voyages of Bering, Chirikov, and Spangberg were well known to the Russians whom he met on Unalaska Island, and one, Gerassim Imylov, had accompanied Lieut. Syndt of the Royal Navy. Syndt had been commissioned by the Empress Catherine to follow up Bering's attempts on the North-East Passage. But from the accounts given by the old Russian seaman Imylov, Cook surmised that Syndt at that time had not sailed farther north than the Bay of St. Lawrence. Where he got to after that, Cook never found out. "A sensible, intelligent man" was Cook's description of Imylov, though their conversation had perforce to be carried on by means of signs, figures, and charts. Imylov had traded for many years between Kamchatka and the Aleutian Islands; "the information thus received from him however, was only so far valuable to the English navigator as it proved the inaccuracy of the ideas of the Russians with regard to the American continent".[1]

Cook had found Müller's accounts of Bering's voyage incomplete, especially in the region of Mt. St. Elias. From the latter point he observed that the shore turned westwards instead of continuing north, as marked in the Russian charts. Nevertheless after passing the 58th parallel, Cook, with customary fairness frequently acknowledges his indebtedness to the records of Bering's expedition, as well as to those of earlier Russian voyagers. At the river later to be called "Cook's," the English navigator sent an expedition to find out if that river led to a north-east passage, but it was reported to him that land extended over the right of the whole line surveyed, although in Russian charts that area had been marked as ocean. "Cook Inlet," which had also proved a vain hope, was renamed "Turnagain River" by the captain himself. Not only were there serious inaccuracies in the Russian charts of the American side of the Bering Sea, but, as Cook had surmised, on the Asiatic shore too. In his opinion indeed, the north coast of Asia from the Indigirka eastwards, had been drawn more than two degrees too far to the northward.[2]

Imylov had told Cook that the Russian settlers on Unalaska Island had often tried to get a footing on the Alaskan mainland

---

[1] Robert Greenhow, *North-West Coast of North America*. (Wiley & Putnam, New York, 1840); p. 82.

[2] Coxe's *Account of the Russian Discoveries Between Asia and America*; Supplement, p. 22.

adjacent to the near Aleutian Islands, but that they had been repelled by natives. ("Alashka" was the name then given by the Russians to the American continent as a whole.) Before Cook's Journals were published, the Russians were getting from English ships at Unalaska all the information they could about Cook's latest discoveries. Less than nine years after the English navigator's voyage up the north-west coast, Imylov, with a Russian fellow-seaman, Betscharev, sailed as far eastwards as Mt. Edgcumbe, taking possession of the land in the name of the Empress. The latter had engaged Captain Joseph Billings, one of Cook's lieutenants, to make a scientific expedition to the North Pacific: he was to determine the latitude and longitude of the mouth of the Kolima River, and to chart the coast from its delta to Cape Deshniev. The islands in the North Pacific were also to be charted, and Billings was given very detailed instructions for getting information about them. But provisions had run out when the vessel reached Mt. St. Elias, and one writer observes, "no evidence exists that his labours were of any service to Russia or to the world, either in the field of discovery or the departments of science".[1] Coxe, on the other hand, in his account of the Russian discoveries in these regions, asserts that Billings must be credited for the information he gave about certain islands in "the Frozen Ocean".

Up to this time the Russians were the only people who had sailed for any distance along the coast of north-eastern Siberia: Capt. Clerke, fellow-voyager of Cook, had failed to get beyond latitude 67° owing to the ice. The sailors of Clerke's expedition had however collected furs which they had sold in Chinese ports for about ten thousand dollars, and had nearly mutinied when told they could not make a return trip to the lands of the blue and the silver fox, and the islands of the seal. The indefatigable adventurer John Ledyard, who had sailed with Cook on his last expedition, wrote that in Nootka Sound "was a species of Weazle called the glutton", and that "the skin of this animal was sold at Kamschatka, a Russian factory on the Asiatic coast, for sixty rubles, which is near twelve guineas, and had it been sold in China it would have been worth thirty guineas".[2] This was a fact which not only made the Russian hunters and trappers anxious to gain access to Chinese seaports, but also to keep all other nationals out of the fur trade on the

[1] Jared Sparks, *Travels and Adventures of John Ledyard.* (H. Colburn, 1834); p. 363.
[2] *Life and Travels of John Ledyard.* (H. Colburn, 1839); p. 97.

American mainland and the North Pacific islands. The French had by now shown themselves interested in these regions when in 1785 they gave instructions to their renowned navigator La Pérouse, "particularly to explore those parts of the north-west coast of America which had not been examined by Captain Cook, and of which the Russian accounts gave no idea". He was to obtain information about the Russian fur trade, and also to find out whether any river led to Hudson Bay or Baffin Bay.

The extent to which Russian influence was gaining ground on the littoral of the north-west Pacific can be judged from the following passage written in connection with Vancouver's expedition of 1793 and with his map of the north-west coast:

"The Russians, who now occupy the whole west coast of America and the adjacent islands north of the parallel 54 degrees 40 minutes, appear to have excluded, as far as possible, the appelations bestowed by the subjects of other States. Thus, on their charts of the North Pacific, *Cook's Inlet* is termed the *Bay of Konay*; *Prince William Sound* is the *Gulf of Tschugatsch*; *Admiralty Bay* is the *Bay of Yakutsk*; *Norfolk Sound*, the *Port Guadelupe* of the Spaniards, is the *Gulf of Sitca*. The territory called by Vancouver *King George the Third's Island* has been since found to be divided by channels into four islands which are severally distinguished by the names of *Chichagof*, *Baranof*, *Jacobi* and *Krooze*. The *Prince of Wales Islands* are *Tschrikof's Islands; Admiralty Island* is *Hoosnoof;* and *Stephen's Passage* is the *Strait of Acco*." It is improbable, says Greenhow,[1] that the names given by the members of Vancouver's expedition and earlier will ever be used by the Russians. From Vancouver's own account of his voyages we know that the Russians whom he met near the mouth of the Columbia River did their best to convince him that the mainland of America and the islands as far east as Kayes Island belonged to Russia.

But as we know too, the Russians were threatened by commercial rivalry urged upon the British Government by such English adventurers as Meares. The latter had pointed out that the "gewgaws" of the first British traders on the north-west coast had been followed by British wool, and "whole villages of American natives were seen clad in blankets and decorated with every article of English dress".[2] Envy of the Russian fur trade

---

[1] *North-West Coast of North America.* (Wiley & Putnam, 1840); pp. 137, 138.
[2] John Meares, *Voyages Made in the Years 1788 and 1789 from China to the North-West Coast of America.* (J. Walter, London, 1790); Introduction, p. lxix.

which crossed the North Pacific had led Meares to press for a British settlement on an island of the Korean group. He even said this would "enable us to annihilate, in a great measure, this profitable branch of Russian commerce". And so from the Merchants Proprietors came these instructions to John Meares, commanding the *Félice* and *Iphigenia*: "Whereas it appears that a very beneficial trade may be carried on between China and the North-West coast of America, part of which was discovered by Sir Francis Drake in the year of Our Lord 1579 . . . you are hereby required and directed to proceed with both vessels with the utmost dispatch, to the North-West coast of America."

So it was that in 1788 Meares started on his voyage in the *Félice* across the trackless ocean, his log recording such events as "a small piece of wood seen", and that in mid-Pacific was observed the "trunk of a large tree". In the name of the English sovereign he took the strait known as Juan de Fuca, the same strait which Vancouver was commissioned to investigate for a possible route to a North-West Passage to the Atlantic. Meares, who charted the coast from Cook River (near the Russian settlement on Kodiak Island) to Shoal Water Bay, affirmed[1] that the Russians by 1789 had navigated Cook's River farther than anyone else had.

Borne on the tide of exploration which, on the north-west shores of the Pacific, reached one of its highest levels about this time, Captain William Douglas in the *Iphigenia*, undertook the detailed exploration of the coast between Cook River and Nootka Sound. In the journal of his voyage he states that he had heard from the Spanish Commander in that region that the Russians on Unalaska were expecting two frigates to sail from St. Petersburg round Cape Horn to Nootka, and against their arrival the Spaniards were erecting forts. The clash of nations was already pending in this remote part of the earth, and the shadow of war was creeping up the Alaskan coast when in 1789 Spaniards seized some British trading vessels in Nootka Sound (Vancouver Island), over which Spain claimed jurisdiction. Her claims rested on the Papal bulls of 1493, and in the following century her seamen had taken advantage of that licence to beat their way up the coasts of California.

THE RUSSIAN-AMERICAN FUR COMPANY

The Russians, as we have shown, had become an increasing menace to the Spanish possessions on the western shores of the

[1] *An Answer to Mr. George Dixon, late Commander of the "Queen Charlotte"*; p. 16.

New World, but at the outset of their Pacific expansion their activities were confined to the northerly latitudes of that ocean. Ever since the days of Bering they had indulged in sporadic trading with Aleuts and Alaskans. Trading companies had arisen from the enterprise of men like Gregor Shelikov who, with the seafarer Golikov, had, as mentioned earlier, explored some of the Aleutian and Alaskan islands in the *Tri Svyatitelya*: the Andreanov islands in the Aleutians had been taken by a Russian trader too in 1760. Along the Alaskan coastline the English were regarded by the Russians as a greater danger than the Spanish. A rumour that Vancouver was coming with an expedition to reclaim for England all the territory which Drake had claimed for his sovereign as "New England", had disturbed the Siberian merchants, and orders were sent to their Alaskan governor, Baranov, to withhold from English seafarers any information which they came seeking. Already the ships of the East India Company had come trading up the coast, and England had seized from Spain a base on Nootka Sound.

The establishment of a Russian colony on the American mainland was indeed partly due to the realisation that English mariners had the advantage of a post such as Hong Kong based on the China trade, with outposts on the South Sea Islands. If Russia wished to draw level with that trade she must set up bases on the North American coast. So, as the Golikov-Shelikov Company (now amalgamated with the Miulnikov Company) formed a strong combination against English interests, it was granted a charter in 1799 for twenty years' development of this region. The monopoly rights of exploitation comprised not only all Russian possessions on the American mainland, but in the North Pacific Islands and the Kuriles. Under the new name of the Russian-American Fur Company, the heirs of Golikov's original enterprise were empowered to occupy as Russian possessions new territory on each side of the 55th parallel provided that such land was not already occupied by nationals of any other country. These measures were also aimed at checking the corrupt competition of rival traders which was threatening to exterminate the fur-bearing animals.[1] Traffic in ivory too was on a scale likely to lead to a serious reduction in the number of "sea-horses". The Governor of

[1] A full account of the foundation of the Company, and its activities up to the time of the Convention with England, 1825, will be found in Dr. Hans Pilder's work, *Die Russisch-Amerikanische Handels-Kompanie bis 1825.* (G. J. Göschen'sche Verlagshandlung, G.m.b.H, Berlin u. Leipzig, 1914.)

Hudson's Bay Territories in North America, in his Journals of 1841, described how even at that time 20,000 "sea-horse teeth" were collected in a year (each tooth weighed on an average 1 lb.), and that as the animal only produced two, 10,000 head had to be destroyed.[1]

The expansion of the Company until its activities embraced a wide area of the North Pacific was largely the work of Alexander Baranov, one of the most remarkable men of his time. How he had ever reached Unalaska, on taking up his appointment as colonial Governor of the Russian territories in North America, is a matter for wonder. When the galliot *Tri Svyatitelya* (The Three Holy Bishops) in which he had sailed reached Unalaska, "her timbers but for the grace of her three heavenly protectors, should long since have fallen apart".[2] Such were the Company's vessels in those days. But under Baranov, whose reputation in time caused him to be styled "Lord of Alaska", the Company's ships came to sweep the seas. Under him New Archangel (Sitka) grew to be regarded as the centre of Russia's Pacific empire stretching from Fort Ross on the coast of California to the Bering Strait opening on the Arctic Ocean.

Baranov was responsible for the building at Sitka of the first Russian ship on the Alaskan coast, and it was in 1794 that this vessel, the three-masted *Phoenix*, sailed with furs to Okhotsk. Even that port relied much on shipyards in far away European Russia for such important items as cables and anchors. The former were sent in sections, and then spliced together at their destination. The practice of assembling indeed, was as much the custom on the shores of the Okhotsk as on the Caspian. At the time the Company was founded, the Okhotsk flotilla had only four galliots and the frigate built by Baranov, but when it came to an end its fleet consisted of fourteen good-sized steamships and some dozens of sailing vessels.[3] The development of the Company's fleet under Baranov can mainly be attributed however to the arrival of the English seaman James Shields, who had broken the record by sailing across the Pacific in the *Eagle* in six weeks. Arriving with material for the building of

---

[1] Sir George Simpson, *Narrative of a Journey Round the World during the Years 1841 and 1842*. (Henry Colburn, London, 1847); p. 222.

[2] Hector Chevigny, *Lord of Alaska*. (Hale, 1946); p. 30.

[3] M. A. Sergeyev, Introd. to *Russian Voyages Round the World*, by N. Nozikov. Translated by Ernst and Mira Lesser. (Hutchinson, 1945); pp. x, xi.

ships, he taught Baranov how to construct vessels, showed him where on the Alaskan mainland he could get good strong timber, and soon shipyards were built at Sitka and Kodiak. But for the help of Shields the projects of Baranov would never have been fulfilled. Much of the Russian-American Company's success in finding the best otter creeks all down the Yakutat Bay territory was due to the exploration of this English sailor, who by that time had entered the Governor's service.

The early shortage of ships had compelled Baranov to accept the offer made by the Boston traders of a share in their seal catches and the transport by the Americans of Russian furs to Canton, if the Russians provided the hunters. So in 1803 Baranov had made an agreement with the New England traders whereby he supplied to an American vessel, the *Eclipse*, a hundred and fifty expert Aleutian hunters of sea otter, and all the necessary equipment, in return for a half-share in the proceeds of the expedition. Not only was the Russian-American Company in this way able to get their furs sold in Canton—the Americans being the only traders to whom the Chinese seaports in general were open[1]—but by the bartering permitted in Sitka harbour of American rum and British broadcloth for sea otter pelts the Russians extended their trade, till the field of their exploits stretched far southwards, and brought Baranov nearer his ambition of establishing a great Russian trading empire in the Pacific.

It was then, with deep interest, that the Governor of Alaska had heard for the first time of the possibilities of the Sandwich Islands through two Irishmen—Moore, of the India trade, and his first mate, O'Cain. The chief purpose of their voyaging was to gain advantages for the Boston traders as against the Spaniards, but they realised that to do this they must get allies. So when their ship *Phoenix* had put into Prince William Sound and they had met Baranov, O'Cain had pointed out that a contract system of trade would be profitable to Bostonians and Russians. He also told Baranov that he had Hawaiians in his crew, and that their islands could become profitable sources of supply. But there was one great obstacle to the Russian-American Company seeking supplies from any distance by sea. The difficulty they experienced in bringing supplies across from the Siberian to the American mainland was "a serious drawback, ... in view of the fact that the Russians were poor sailors. Many ships started and only few reached their

[1] The English were restricted to trading at Hong Kong.

destinations".[1] Sir George Simpson, Governor of Hudson's Bay Company Territory at this time, speaks of the yards at Okhotsk being always at work preparing to make good "the next vacancy"; the timber, he says, is good, the carpenters efficient, and the losses can only be due to the incompetency of officers and men.[2] Capt. Golovnin, himself a Russian and a renowned voyager, speaks of the "unskilfulness of the Company's seamen".[3] Often the vessels, for the most part ill-provisioned, were unable to make the crossing from Alaska to Okhotsk with their cargoes of furs, and had to spend the winter in Unalaska or some other island in the Aleutian chain. A young Russian officer, Davidov, stated that there were instances of ships from Okhotsk taking over three years to reach Kodiak, and he recorded that fifteen thousand sea otter pelts and other furs had accumulated for five years because no vessel had arrived in that time which was fit to take away such a valuable cargo. Davidov described the company's galliots as being built at Okhotsk under the direction of "a hunter or a cabin-boy who has not the smallest knowledge of ship-building". In the barren country of Alaska and its islands, the problem of supplying their colonists with food was taxing the resources of the Russian Government. Attempts to introduce agriculture on Kodiak had failed, and it had become necessary to send food cargoes from Okhotsk. But "the wretched construction of the vessels" and "the ignorance of most of their commanders"[4] had resulted in heavy loss of ships. The crews were not professional sailors but, according to Langsdorf (naturalist of the *Nadezhda* expedition), they were men who, despite the fact that they had sailed from Okhotsk to Kamchatka the year before, "had to learn anew the names of sails and ropes: they were always standing in each other's way, and in case of a change of wind, fifteen men could scarcely perform the services which would ordinarily have been performed by ten ordinary sailors".[5]

[1] Frank Golder, Ph.D., *Proposals for Russian Occupation of the Hawaiian Islands: Early Relation with England, Russia, France.* Official Papers read at the Captain Cook Sesquicentennial Celebration, Honolulu, 17.8.1929. (Published by the Captain Cook Sesquicentennial Commission and the Archives of Hawaii Commission, 1930); p. 39.

[2] *The Letters of John McLoughlin from Vancouver to the Governor and Committee.* Edtd. by E. E. Rich. (Hudson's Bay Record Society. Published for the latter by The Champlain Society, 1941-44); Series II, p. 253.

[3] *Recollection of Japan.* (Colburn, 1819); p. 266.

[4] Krusenstern, *Voyage Round the World.* (Murray, 1840); Introd., p. xxix.

[5] C. H. von Langsdorf, *Voyages and Travels.* (Henry Colburn, London, 1813); pt. II, p. 12.

Facts such as these, in addition to the great difficulties of land transport across Russia to Okhotsk, led the Imperial Government to issue a ukase permitting officers of the Russian navy to enter the Company's service. The Government also decided to embark on the new policy of sponsoring long-distance voyages with the object of finding fresh sources of food for the Alaskan Russians, and of discovering other markets for their furs. It was felt too that if American ships were to be kept out of the North Pacific, Russia must establish naval forces near her settlements in America. Such forces would guard the ocean trade routes from Siberia to Alaska. The well-known Russian naval officer, Captain Ivan Krusenstern, had impressed on the Government the advantage of bringing back valuable furs in Russian rather than foreign ships, and in view of the superiority of the shipyards in the Baltic over those at Kamchatka, he had urged that vessels whose home ports were in north-western Russia should be used for the fur trade. Finally the publication of a paper by Krusenstern pointing out how important was the Cape Route to Russia's communications with the Far East, impelled the Government to put its resolution to practical test.

Accordingly in June 1803, the first Russian round-the-world expedition, with Krusenstern commanding the *Nadezhda*, and Lysiansky the *Neva*, sailed under Imperial orders from Kronstadt via Cape Horn and returned by the Cape of Good Hope. When the commander of the *Neva*, after sailing to Hawaii and across the North Pacific, brought his frigate into Sitka Sound, he was called upon to help Baranov to recover the important base of Old Sitka, which had been captured from the Russian colonists by the Kolosh Indians. Its restoration to the Russians, who re-named it New Archangel, stirred Baranov to such emotion that he composed an ode setting forth the triumphs of his country in the New World. The poem, set to music, was sung whenever the Russians set up a new fort along the coast.

Lysiansky, after mapping Sitka harbour and surveying the surrounding region, returned to Russia via the Cape with an impressive cargo of furs. His fellow-voyager, Krusenstern, got a promise of delivery of food supplies to Sitka from natives, but in the end he had to sail on to Petropavlovsk, the main Russian base in the Far East. From there in his ship *Nadezhda*, he made for Japan, taking with him the Russian Chamberlain Rezanov who made a fruitless effort to open Japan's doors to Russian trade. Those doors were closed to all but the Dutch.

Rezanov was a son-in-law of the merchant Shelikov, and his

ambitions were even more far-reaching than those of the pushful *promyschlenik*. One of his aims was to make Okhotsk a great base for the North Pacific, from which Russian ships should sail to the ports of Japan, China, South America, and Britain, and it was across those trade routes which he had mapped, that he now sailed in the *Nadezhda*. Like Baranov, Rezanov realised that Alaska could give Russia control of the North Pacific. But his aims went far beyond that. The unsettled state of Europe during the Napoleonic war provided Russia, in his view, with an opportunity to expand over the whole Pacific area. His avaricious eyes were turned now on the Sandwich Islands, now on California.

Rezanov had tried in San Francisco Bay to get the Spaniards to send supplies to the Russian colony farther north, and in 1805 Baranov had sent the *Juno* to San Francisco for the same purpose. The failure of these efforts, as also of the attempt to expand Russia's sources of supply along the eastern shores of Siberia, had led Governor Baranov to send out two vessels to survey the coast from Washington to California. They were to find out the possibilities of developing part of that seaboard as an agricultural larder for the Alaskan Russians. The *St. Nicholas* was wrecked on the voyage, but the *Kodiak* sailed to Bodega Bay, and on her return the commander, Kuzkov, reported that the coastal region would be admirable for Baranov's purpose. In the *Chirikov* he sailed again to California, where he established Fort Ross as the southerly headquarters of the new colony. (The name "Ross" became to the Spaniards an almost nightmarish reminder of "Rossia", suggestive of intentions on the part of that country to embrace California in its dominions.) The supply problem was to some extent relieved when in 1810 the Pacific Fur Company was formed by John Jacob Astor to establish trading posts on the Columbia River and its tributaries. The Astor Company's vessels undertook to furnish the Russian colonists with the goods they required in exchange for furs, and the Company gained the right under certain conditions, of exclusive trade with the Russian-American possessions.

The Russians had now established a secondary trade post not only at Bodega but at the Farallon Islands, where the Aleuts were engaged by them in capturing the seals in large numbers. From Bodega the Russians sent a ship once a year with the furs they had collected to the principal depot at Norfolk Sound, and from here they were shipped to Kamchatka. In a letter dated

14 October, 1839, by James Douglas, a factor of Hudson's Bay
Company, to the Governor and Committee, the writer reports
that the Russians at Bodega "sail their vessels under cover of
licences taken out in the name of a citizen, which relieves them
entirely from the more onerous charges levied exclusively on
foreigners".[1] Meantime the agricultural prospects on the mainland, held out by Captain Kuzkov, had failed to materialise;
farming had proved far from profitable. So Baranov, whose resolution was only increased by adversity, had sent the *Attawelpa* to
the Hawaiian Islands on a sealing expedition. The King of those
islands, Kamehameha II, had already traded salt with the Russian
seal hunters, and some of that salt had not only gone to Alaska
but across the Pacific to Kamchatka for curing skins and fish.
The *Attawelpa* had been wrecked with her cargo: Schäfer, a German, was then sent by Baranov to retrieve the boat, and this adventurer told the Company that Russia should take the Sandwich
Islands which were, he said, the keys to China, Japan, the Philippines, India, the north-west coast of America, and islands of the
Pacific. Schäfer's efforts to get the Russians established on the
Hawaiian Islands cost the Russian-American Company
230,000 roubles.[2] Already four years earlier the King of Kauai
Island in the Hawaiian group had offered Alexander I the
suzerainty of his island, but neither this offer nor Schäfer's more
ambitious plan for a Russian seizure of the Hawaiian Islands as
a whole was followed up by the Tsar. Nor did the latter yield to
the objurgations of Peter Dobell, consul-at-large in the Russian
service, to take the Sandwich Islands and from them get the
Philippines. Alexander I was not unmindful of the probable
English reactions to the fulfilment of any such projects, and
deemed such adventures hardly worth the inevitable clash with
his more powerful rival in the Pacific.

Following Schäfer's expedition to Hawaii, the Russian ship
Discovery sailed there with Kodiak Indians aboard, then followed the *Myrtle*, whose crew landed at Honolulu, ran up the
Russian flag, and started to set up a blockhouse. King Kamehameha was prepared to resist, but the Russians then sailed for
Kauai Island, where at Waimea they erected a fort. Schäfer
had plotted with the native king to get Kauai separated from
the dominions of Kamehameha, but the latter had Schäfer

---

[1] *The Letters of John McLoughlin from Vancouver to the Governor and Committee.*
Second Series, Appendix A, p. 206.
[2] N. Nozikov, *Russian Voyages Round the World.* Edited by M. A. Sergeyev
and translated by Ernst and Mira Lesser. (Hutchinson, 1945); p. 117.

expelled, and the Russians left the island. When later the
navigator Kotzebue visited Hawaii in the *Rurik*, he told the
King that the Imperial Government had had no part in Schäfer's
acts. Nevertheless Kamehameha suspected the Russians of
aiming at annexing his dominions and went to London to ask
for British protection. (This was but in keeping with earlier
events, for in 1794, after Vancouver had re-visited Hawaii to
try and settle inter-tribal disputes there, the chiefs had decided
to ask that the islands should become a British protectorate.)
Actually the English colours were hoisted on Hawaii. But in
1845 the British Government, which was most unwilling to
annex the island, disclaimed responsibility for this incident, and
recognised the independence of Hawaii. Of the potential
economic resources of the islands, Russia was well aware : the
production here of sugar, tobacco, coffee, rum, could have
rivalled Britain's West India trade.

But the activities of the Russian-American Company in the
Pacific were by that time so extensive as to have made Russia
a considerable commercial Power in that area. The Company,
which in the first decade of the nineteenth century had shipped
from Sitka furs to the value of over twenty million roubles, also
exported steel, iron, copper, glass, china, ropes, timber, tobacco,
tallow, furs, fabrics; it imported wheat, barley, fats, salt, raw
hides, and meat.[1] This trade was carried on with America,
Canada, China, Japan, the Hawaiian Islands, and Chile. It is
clear from the despatches of the Russian Minister Rumiantsev
in 1803, that his Government regarded the Company's settlements on the American continent as bases from which to extend
her influence even as far as the East Indies. The far-reaching
enterprise of their traders at this time brought the Russians
much nearer the commercial level of the English and the Dutch
in the Pacific.

On the China coast however, they were definitely at a disadvantage compared with the Americans, who were permitted
to sell their furs at Canton, from which Russians, as we know,
were excluded. Foreign merchants had received limited privileges for trade with the Celestial Empire under a special edict in
1720. But those merchants were representatives of the British
East India Company and of American concerns: Russians were
not included in the foreign settlement at Macao to which these
traders were virtually confined. The Americans had gained

[1] See also N. Nozikov, *Russian Voyages Round the World*. Edited by M. A.
Sergeyev and translated by Ernst and Mira Lesser. (Hutchinson, 1945) ; p.117.

much more advantageous trading privileges with China after 1788, in which year they had sent from Boston the *Columbia* and the sloop *Washington* to Nootka Sound, whence the *Columbia* had sailed with a cargo of skins to Canton. Here America now brought from the isles of the South Sea the incense which the Chinese used in their temples, and from the Hawaiian Islands traded sandalwood for the silks and teas of the Chinese markets. Americans also, as we have mentioned, came to do most of the shipping between the Alaskan and north Californian coasts and China—a fact which at one time was viewed by the Russians as an encroachment on the monopoly claims of their Fur Company. Krusenstern, who sailed in a merchantman to China in order to learn the navigation of the China Sea, believed that Russia would benefit greatly if she could open up a maritime trade with the Celestial Empire: "the chief obstruction to trade how-ever, with these distant regions is the want of people capable of commanding her merchant vessels".[1] Lysiansky, fellow-voyager of Krusenstern observed too, that once commerce had opened with China, the Russian settlement of New Archangel, Alaska, would become valuable for timber trade. Accordingly Krusen-stern had received instructions to open trade at Canton, where he did succeed in selling a cargo before the order came from Pekin to detain his vessel. "Though barbarians are accustomed to frequent the port of Canton," wrote the Chinese Emperor, "the name of the Russians has never appeared among them. . . . How have the Russians who trade by way of Kiatcha, and have never visited Canton, been able to navigate their ships, or how have they become acquainted with the shoals and islands on their way from Russia?"

The earliest of the "barbarians" referred to in this passage were the Portuguese, the first of their ships having arrived on the coast of China in 1514. Three years afterwards Fernao Perez came with eight ships to Canton, and later got permis-sion to build a factory on Shangch'wan Island: Perez opened trade with the north and a depot at Ningpo. As regards the Spaniards, they, after their occupation of the Philippines, had visited Amoy, and had for a time gained a monopoly of trade there.[2] The Dutch were the next to arrive off the coasts of

[1] Otto von Kotsebue, *Voyage of Discovery into the South Sea and Beering's Straits.* Introd., p. xxv.

[2] English efforts to reach China had been made before this, however. Queen Elizabeth had commissioned three ships, under command of Benjamin Wood, to open up trade with the Celestial Empire, but the vessels were all lost on the way out.

China, and in 1622 they had made settlements in the Pescadores. Then came the East India Company, which since the end of the seventeenth century had been represented by a "President" and Council at Canton. But the decrees of the Chinese Commissioners had practically compelled the British to withdraw from Canton, and this led them to acquire Hong Kong, in order to set up a trading station with South China. Not so well placed were the Russians. They had obtained commercial conventions with China by the treaties of Nerchinsk (1689) and Kiatcha (1727), but these had given them no right of trade by sea. Hence when in 1806 the Russian vessels called at Canton, the Chinese Government decreed that as Russia had only the privilege of trading at the land frontier and not by sea, she was excluded from coastal trade with China.[1] (Later, when the Russian admiral, Putiatin, tried to get right of maritime trade at Peiho he failed for the same reason, so went to Hong Kong, where he aligned himself with representatives of Britain and France who also were trying to gain coastal trading privileges.)

The Pacific voyages of Krusenstern and Lysiansky were followed by those of other Russian circumnavigators, among them Feodor Litke. His work showed how seriously these explorers regarded the scientific side of their undertakings. "His observations on the magnetic needle and on the swing of the constant pendulum are particularly noteworthy," says N. Nozikov. "As a result of these experiments the amount of shrinkage of the earth was determined; exact knowledge of the phenomena is of the greatest importance for geodesic work and for an exact investigation of certain complex movements in the solar system." The first *detailed* description of the Caroline Islands was the work of this scientific navigator, and the members of his expedition discovered one group here to which the name of his ship, *Senyavin*, was given. "Altogether they discovered twelve and described twenty-six groups or separate islands in the Caroline archipelago."[2] In the North Pacific, too, Litke's name is another link in the chain of North-East Passage seekers. In 1826 he received Admiralty instructions to chart the Kamchatkan coasts, which he did from the sloop *Senyavin*, making many corrections in existing charts, and discovering too the Aramchechin Island. He also charted much of the

[1] See M. J. Bau, *The Foreign Relations of China.* (Nisbet & Co., 1922); p. 5.
[2] N. Nozikov, *Russian Voyages Round the World.* Edited by M. A. Sergeyey and translated by Ernst and Mira Lesser. (Hutchinson, 1945); p. 138.

G. F. MÜLLER'S MAP OF THE
NORTH PACIFIC
1754,

in English, edited by T. Jefferys. Accompanying a paper by
L. Breitfuss, "Early Maps of North-Eastern Asia and of the
Lands around the North Pacific", published in *Imago Mundi*,
No. III, edited by Leo Bagrow and Edward Lynam.

(Reproduced by courtesy of Henry Stevens, Son & Stiles, London, 1939)

In common with several contemporary and earlier maps,
this one shows the exaggerated projection of part of the American continent into the North Pacific. Müller later acknowledged
this error, and it was not repeated in the map of 1773 made by
the Russian fur traders.

Siberian coastline of the Bering Sea up to Cape Deshniev, and among the several places which bear his name is Cape Litke on the Bering Strait.

JAPAN AND THE KURILE ISLANDS

The successive Russian Governments in the first three decades of the nineteenth century, in their efforts to expand their trade in the Pacific, had naturally to take into account their relations with Japan. In the previous century Peter the Great had dwelt on the possibility of entering into commercial relations with the Island Empire; these he had tried to establish by sending a trade emissary from Kamchatka to open up definite sea routes to Japan. Though Catherine the Great showed far less enterprise in the Pacific than in the Mediterranean, she had, on the advice of Laxman, sent an expedition to Japan in 1792, when for the first time a Russian ship sailed into Hakodate. The visit however had brought only the promise that "one great ship of the Russian State" would be permitted to call at Nagasaki to re-open talks.

It was from Kamchatka that the Russians had made their way into the northern Kuriles at the beginning of the eighteenth century. Little was then known of the islands, and earlier, when the Dutch navigator Vries, in the *Castricum* had sailed among them in 1643, he had thought that one of them formed part of the American continent. Nor did the visits of the Jesuits in the latter half of the same century do much to clarify the confused ideas about this island chain. Little more successful were the results of the inquiries of Peter I, who had charged two of his officers, Yefreimov and Luchin, to explore the Kuriles; from them he had received only a very imperfect map of the chain as far as they had been able to chart it. Bering, as we reported earlier, had learnt something about the islands from the monk Kosirevski in Yakutsk, but it was left to Spangberg, a member of the Bering expeditions, to throw new light on this foggy region by his voyage in 1738 round the islands, to twenty-nine of which he gave names. Up to the time when Lieut. Walton in the *Hope* charted the most easterly of them, it was believed by many that Jezo (Hokkaido)—the most northerly of Japan's islands and adjacent to the southerly Kuriles—was a vast land mass lying between Asia and America. Walton and Spangberg showed that it was but a moderately sized island. A Russian name was given to the group, "Kurile" being derived from "Kooreetch", to smoke, by association with the

volcanic nature of the islands. Errors in existing charts of the
Kuriles were pointed out later, in 1821, by the voyager and
traveller John Cochrane, R.N.: "I should," he said, "feel
greatly pleased if I could draw the attention of the Russian
Government to the propriety and necessity not only of surveying generally the Kurile Islands, but particularly those extending from Cape Lopatka to the lat. of 46".[1]

Krusenstern and Golovnin at different times charted these
islands, and in Russian maps Golovnin's name is perpetuated
in a strait between two of them. Their survey formed part of the
work that he had been instructed to undertake in his special
mission to the Sea of Okhotsk—a region which he was required
to explore with a view to eventual maritime relations with
Japan. Golovnin, who was the first European to investigate the
channel between Kinaschier Island (the twentieth in the group)
and Matsumai, owed something to the reports of the English
mariner Captain Gore in his stormy voyage in the waters round
Paramushiro, 1779. In the sloop of war *Diana*, Golovnin was
able to observe the trade in beaver skins and otter pelts carried
on by the Kurile Islanders and the Japanese, and his log book
contains most instructive accounts of the lives of the former
people. Writing of his captivity in Japan in 1811-13, he
stressed the advantages that might result from opening up
Russian trade relations with Japan, and especially the benefits
which would be gained by the Russian-American Fur Company,
as sea otter pelts bought from the Company at Kamchatka by
Siberian merchants, had been taken by a long and expensive
route to the Chinese frontier town Kiatcha, where traders
purchased them to send to Pekin, and thence to Japan—a land
journey of over 2,100 miles.

Golovnin was not only a great sea captain, but a man of
shrewd political insight. He was well aware of his Emperor's
wish to bring Japan within Russia's orbit as a market for the
furs of the Russian-American Company, and also as a source
for supplying the Russian Alaskan colonists with grain. He was
careful when in Japan, to refute accusations that his Government had taken any part in the raids made by the Company's associates, on the shores of the Island Empire. The
directors were not, he said, "persons of great consideration in
Russia, but even they had never sanctioned that illegal proceeding which was wholly attributed to the captains of the

[1] *Narrative of a Pedestrian Journey Through Russia and Siberian Tartary.*
(Knight, London, 1825); Vol. II, p. 81.

vessels, and that His Imperial Majesty had ever entertained a wish to establish friendly compacts and commercial relations between Russia and Japan". The opening for any such commercial relations was a particularly narrow one, as the Dutch at that time were the only foreigners allowed to trade with Nippon. Only at Nagasaki were Russian ships permitted to call, and even here the landing of their crews was made as difficult as possible. It is not therefore surprising that at the time when Captain Krusenstern visited Nagasaki in the *Nadezhda*, there was no strictly accurate information as to the latitude and longitude of that harbour. Details of this were given later by Krusenstern himself. He was not permitted by the Japanese to visit their western coast, but he was able to make a thorough exploration of the channel of La Pérouse between the Japanese island of Matsumai and Karafuto (southern Sakhalin), and inquiries made during his visit to Nagasaki brought Krusenstern to believe that a good trade opening with Korea was possible.

Despite the fact that the Russians had for so long inhabited Kamchatka, they remained surprisingly ignorant of the islands to the north of Japan. What knowledge they had of the waters surrounding them was partly derived from the English mariner Captain Broughton, who in the *Providence* had voyaged in Japanese seas in 1795-97. For long the Russians entertained the most strange ideas about the islands of Jezo and Kunashiri, sometimes taking the view that they were part of a vast mid-Pacific island, sometimes regarding them as smallish members of the Kurile group. It was the French, not the Russians, who found out whether large ships could pass through the strait between North Jezo and Tartary. Earlier still it was Spangberg the Danish explorer and Walton the English navigator who in the sloop *Nadezhda* showed the Russians the way to Japan. But that way did not become fully open to them till after the second world war, when Russia gained the Kuriles and southern Sakhalin.

SAKHALIN

Concerning the exploration of Sakhalin, "Russia deserves", says the Pacific historian F. A. Golder,[1] "the chief credit for bringing this work to a successful end", though, as he points out, England, France, China, and Japan, had also made their contributions. Krusenstern had explored the east coast of the

[1] Reprinted by permission of the Publishers, The Arthur H. Clark Company, from *Russian Expansion on the Pacific*, by Frank A. Golder; p. 253.

island, adding data to that collected earlier by the English explorer Broughton and the French navigator La Pérouse. Sailing through the Tartary Strait, La Pérouse had been stopped by sandbanks from finding the true geographical character of Sakhalin, and he had reported the strait to be non-navigable beyond the fifty-second parallel. That Russia was late in discovering the insular nature of Sakhalin was due partly to the Treaty of Nerchinsk, which her defeat by the Manchus had compelled her to sign with China in 1689. That treaty was the first one ever signed by the Celestial Empire with a European Power; by it the Argun had been fixed as the boundary between the two countries, and the Amur region was held to be outside Russia's sphere. This was a disastrous chapter in the history of Russia in Asia, and its effects run through that chronicle for nearly two centuries, cutting off the Slavs from the sea.

Up to the time of Krusenstern's voyage it was believed that southern Sakhalin (Karafuto) was separated from the northern part. In an attempt to find the mouth of the Amur River, Krusenstern had rounded the northern shore of Sakhalin, which he surveyed. But though he voyaged on through the Tartary channel he failed to discover the estuary of the Amur, and this led him to believe, as others had done before him, that Sakhalin was joined to the mainland. Even Golovnin alludes to Sakhalin as a peninsula. More than one map at the end of Peter the Great's reign however, had shown a large island off the coast of Asia, not far from Japan, and this was undoubtedly drawn from reports based on the existence of Sakhalin. In 1644 the hunter Poyarkov had reported Sakhalin to be insular, while Jesuits who had sailed down the Amur in 1709 were told by natives about a near-by island of considerable size. Reference to a large island at the delta of the Amur is found in more than one Russian seventeenth-century manuscript—as for example, that of the Dutch geographer Witsen, instructor of Peter the Great,[1] and the map published by D'Anville in 1753 definitely shows Sakhalin as insular. It is interesting to find Sir George Simpson, Governor of Hudson's Bay Territory in North America, describing in 1841 the delta of the Amur as being "bounded in front by the Island of Sagalin".[2] Yet it is commonly

[1] N. Witsen, *Noord en Ost Tartarie* (F. Halma, Amsterdam, 1705); Vol. II, p. 825.
[2] *Narrative of a Journey Round the World during the Years 1841 and 1842*; Vol. II, p. 237.

asserted that until Nevelski's discovery in 1853 this fact was not known. Actually Sakhalin's true nature had been ascertained at the beginning of the nineteenth century by the Japanese voyager Mamia Rinso, exploring the estuary of the Amur. Voyaging through the Tartary Strait from Jezo, the most northerly of the Japanese islands, Rinso had entered the mouth of the Amur in 1808, and the chart he made had been used by various cartographers for the next fifty years. It is surprising therefore that the Russians had not availed themselves of this map.

Krusenstern observed that it would be easy for England to establish herself on Sakhalin from the East Indies, and that it should be still easier for his own countrymen to settle on it from Kamchatka, but he also realised that the length of the sea communications between the Tsar's territories in Europe and his possessions in north-east Asia was a drawback to this. Yet an establishment on Sakhalin was necessary as being possibly the only means of sharing in Japan's trade.

The earliest Russian settlement[1] of any size on Sakhalin had been made in 1805, when seamen, led by two lieutenants, Davidov and Khavostov, landed at Aniwa Bay. Commanding respectively the *Yunona* and the *Avos*, ships of the Russian-American Company, these two officers were commissioned by the Russian Chancellor Rezanov to undertake an occupation of Sakhalin. Khavostov, in carrying this out had even issued a proclamation to the effect that Alexander I had taken possession of the territory—a proceeding which, as we have seen, Golovnin found extremely embarrassing when he came to try and persuade the Japanese to open up commercial relations with his country, and an act with which his Emperor was in no way associated. A serious view of the action was taken by the Japanese, whose Prime Minister, M. Sadanobu, spoke in a secret Memorandum of the possibility of his country attacking Russia, and of "an unexpected descent by sea" on Kamchatka.[2] Khavostov's principal object in seizing Aniwa Bay had been to use this as a base from which to advance on the mouth of the Amur, a course which had always been advocated by Captain Krusenstern. An official of the Russian-American Fur Company had pointed out that 14,000-15,000 pack-horses were required to carry provisions to Russian settlements on the Pacific

---

[1] This was, however, but a temporary one.
[2] E. J. Harrison, *Peace or War East of Baikal?* (Kelly & Walsh, Ltd., Yokohama, 1910); p.10.

seaboard, and that navigation of the Amur would save that great cost.

Muraviev, who was the driving force behind the later advances on the Amur, feared that the trade agreements which England was then making with South China would place Russia at a disadvantage. The Amur Route would be the best one into China, therefore it was imperative to get control of that before England did. Muraviev had a further object in sending an expedition to explore the delta—he wanted to secure for the Russians a share in the whale fishing in the Sea of Okhotsk in which the other Great Powers were then all engaged. The wide expanse of water known as the Liman, opposite the mouth of the Amur, had already been explored by Lieut. Gabrilov in the *Constantine*, but the actual investigation of the mouth of the river was made by Lieut. Orlov of the Russian-American Company. Later Nevelski had left Petropavlovsk in the brig *Baikal*, had sailed up the west coast of Sakhalin, and as a result of his voyage had told Muraviev that the Amur estuary could be navigated by open-sea vessels of 15 ft. draught. As long as Sakhalin was regarded as non-insular, the Amur could only have been navigated from its delta by vessels coming in from the north, i.e. from the Sea of Okhotsk, whose coasts are frozen for part of the year. But the discovery that ships could sail up the delta from the south, i.e. from the Strait of Tartary, meant that they could take a course more favourably conditioned.

The fact that the Strait of Tartary did separate Sakhalin from the mainland, affected the course of England's operations against Russia in the Far East. In 1855, during the Crimean War, Petropavlovsk was bombarded by an Anglo-French squadron, but the reinforcements which Muraviev brought down the Amur saved the garrison, and a second assault by the Allied ships was beaten off. Petropavlovsk, except for a small remaining force, was then evacuated by the Russians, and under direction of Admiral Zavoiko a passage was carved through the ice in the harbour to enable the ships to reach Avacha Bay. The Russian vessels then sailed for De Castries on Sakhalin. In the fog, the English vessels *Barracouta* and *Encounter*, which had been watching the southern entrance to the Tartary Strait, but believing there was no northerly escape, i.e. no through channel to the Amur River, failed to find the Russian ships, six of which escaped down the Strait and into the Amur.

Up to the time of Nevelski's discovery, Russia, by the terms

of the Nerchinsk Treaty, was deprived of any satisfactory
communication between Lake Baikal and Kamchatka; that
treaty had fixed the Stanovoy "range of mountains extending
to the sea" as the *ne plus ultra* for Russia's eastward advance.
To Muraviev, as we have said earlier, it seemed imperative for
Russia to control the Amur. But to get control of the delta it
was also necessary to get Sakhalin. Accordingly the Russian-
American Company was appointed to carry out an occupation of the island; their ship *Nikolai* had landed arms and
men at Aniwa in 1854, and Nevelski had founded the post of
Alexandrovsk on De Castries Bay. This marked the final stage
of the great trek across Siberia to the Pacific, which Yermak
and his fellow Cossacks had started when they crossed the Ural
Mountains three centuries earlier.

IX

ALASKA

RUSSIA had reached the Pacific coast more than thirty-three years before America did. But not until the middle of the nineteenth century did Russian expansionist aims begin to show the same successes on the Asiatic shores of the Great Ocean as they had done on the American littoral. On the American continent the Russians were so well established that, as Mr. B. H. Sumner has stated in his *Survey of Russian History*,[1] with an outpost nearly as far south as San Francisco, and with their activities in the Hawaiian Islands, it seemed almost possible by 1820 that North America would be divided between the United States, Great Britain, and Russia. In 1824 an Agreement was signed between America and Russia whereby the parallel of 54° 40′ was to mark the southern frontier of Russian America;[2] and neither party was to impose restrictions on shipping or fishing in North Pacific waters. The necessity for the last-mentioned terms arose from the ukase of Tsar Alexander which in 1821 had prohibited non-Russian ships from coming within the limit of a hundred Italian miles of the Alaskan coast. Writers have sometimes represented that ukase as conflicting with the Monroe Doctrine, formulated two years later. But that Doctrine declared that the United States would not permit any interference in the American continent by any foreign Power *not already holding possessions in America*. The Emperor had let it be known that he would only enforce the ukase against American ships if these were engaged in contraband trade, but he none the less sent a fleet to the North Pacific with a show of readiness to enforce his proclamation. He had made claims too for Russia on the American mainland as far south as the 51st parallel, and also from the Aleutian Islands to the east coast of Siberia, "as well as above the Kurile Islands from Behring Straits to the south cape of the Island of Urup, viz., to the 45° 50′ north latitude". But the Russians were now to suffer for their long unbroken secrecy regarding their early

[1] Duckworth, 1944; p. 33.

[2] The most southerly point at which the Russians had settled on the American continent had been 38° 33′ N.

discoveries in the North Pacific. The claims they were making were discredited by the Americans, who now heard many of them for the first time. Such few reports as *had* been published in the past, had only in the rarest instances appeared in English.

When the Russian Minister Poletica suggested that his country had the right to exclude foreigners from the sea north of 51° on the American side, and 45° on the Asiatic side, he based his claim to this closed sea on the fact that Russia possessed territory on both sides of it. Whereupon Secretary of State Adams drily observed that the distance between the two shores on the 51st parallel, N., was only about four thousand miles! Popular feeling in America on the matter found expression in the following lines:—

> *Old Neptune one morning was seen on the rocks,*
> *Shedding tears by the pailful and tearing his locks;*
> *He cried, 'a Land Lubber has stole, on this day,*
> *Full four thousand miles of my ocean away:*
> *He swallows the earth (he exclaims with emotion),*
> *And then to quench appetite, slap goes the ocean;*
> *Brother Jove must look out for his skies, let me tell ye,*
> *Or the Russian will bury them all in his belly'.*[1]

The Tsar's declaration in respect of the 51st parallel, suggested that he had designs on the coast of Oregon—at that time claimed jointly by Britain and America. The Russians were already claiming territory right to Columbia River, although by the Convention of Nootka Sound, 1790, their claims had been limited to a point north of Lat. 60°. Hence at this time we find the Governor and Committee of Hudson's Bay Company writing that they "think it is desirable to extend our trading posts as far to the West and the North from Fraser's River in Caledonia as may be possible", and adding that they think it advisable "to keep the Russians at a distance".[2] Baron von Wrangell, Resident Governor of the Russian-American Company, had prepared a fort at the mouth of the Stikine, and here stationed the brig *Chichoff*, which, though not a ship of war, carried fourteen guns.[3] In a letter to the Governor and

[1] Published in *Niles's Register*, 10 May, 1823, and taken from the *Baltimore Chronicle*.

[2] *Fur Trade and Empire*. Sir George Simpson's Journal, 1824-1825, edtd. by Frederick Merk. Harvard Historical Studies, Vol. XXXI, Appendix A, p. 175. (Harvard University Press, 1931.)

[3] *The Letters of John McLoughlin from Vancouver to the Governor and Committee*. Introd., p. civ. First Series, 1825-38.

Committee of Hudson's Bay Company, dated 14 March, 1833, the Company's representative McLoughlin, reported that the Russians had prevented a British establishment being set up on the Stikine as had been planned, and complained that as well as loss of trade the British were suffering loss of prestige with the natives. P. S. Ogden, the Company's principal factor, took the view that the Treaty of 1824 between Britain and Russia gave the former every right to navigate the Stikine, but in view of the combined opposition of natives and Russians he thought it prudent not to force the issue.[1] Despite the fact that relations between Hudson's Bay Company and the Russian-American Fur Company remained, on the whole, remarkably friendly (the former doing all it could to meet the repeated requests of the Alaskan Russians for shipments of wheat and flour), protests against the southward encroachments of the Slavs were not unnaturally made by Britain as well as the United States. The result was that treaties were made by Russia with these two countries whereby the Tsar's maritime ukase was revoked, and the Convention of 1824 had, as before mentioned, placed the southern boundary of the Emperor's possessions in America at 54° 40′ N. Lat.

Soon afterwards however, Baron de Tuyl for the Russian Government, insisted that his country did not interpret the treaty as giving sanction to U.S. citizens to trade on the Siberian coast or in the Aleutians. Friction between the Russians and Americans had been frequent in this region north of the 54th parallel. Complaints had been made by Count Romanzov, Russian Minister for Foreign Affairs,[2] that American vessels had been carrying on clandestine trade with Alaskan natives, and that the destruction by the latter of a Russian fort had been due to the possession of American firearms.

ALASKAN CABLE PROJECT

Relations between America and Russia concerning the North Pacific became less strained however during the proposal for laying a cable from Alaska to Siberia. A grant was obtained from Russia by Percy McDonough Collins (commercial agent of the American Government for the Amur River) to construct a telegraph from the Amur to the Russian possessions in North

[1] *The Letters of John McLoughlin from Vancouver to the Governor and Committee.* Appendix A, pp. 317-319.
[2] See letter from Romanzov to Levett Harris, *American State Papers Foreign Relations*; Vol. V, p. 439.

America. The Russians had stipulated that the line should connect the European system with the Pacific Ocean. It is usual to give entire credit to Collins for the project, but actually he had only revived the plan of a Russian, Romanov, who had proposed to the Amur Company that a cable should be laid to the Kuriles and Kamchatka and thence across the Bering Strait to America. In 1862 Collins had petitioned the American Government to enable him to complete the enterprise. (The British Government at the same time authorised the construction of a line of telegraph across the intervening territory of British Columbia.)

"There is much in the North Pacific," says the Memorial of Collins, "valuable to us as a nation in a commercial point of view. . . . Our Pacific whaling fleet resort in considerable force to the seas, bays, and sounds, not only of the Pacific but of the Arctic; in one year more than seventy American vessels have passed through Bering Strait, and largely over one hundred have visited the waters adjacent, and the Okhotsk Sea. The commerce of Japan and of the Amoor region, increasing from year to year, makes it requisite that we should have a more perfect knowledge of these interesting regions of the Pacific."[1]

In the U.S. Senate, Mr. Latham, reporting on matters concerning the Collins cable proposal, pointed out that American vessels had lately entered Amoor, that "the Russian Government has also had constructed several sea-going and river steamers in the U.S. and in Europe for service here and in the North Pacific. Several American commercial establishments have found permanent place within the Amoor at the seat of Government, Nikolaievsky; American engineers are employed in this so recently unexplored region; American steam-engines, saw-mills and machine shops have also found in the wilds of Tartary a new field of practical occupation. Thus, independent of the consideration of telegraphic communication, the proposed survey of the North Pacific would be of much value to commerce in those regions, our whalemen and merchant ships would be guided by certain and reliable information; safe anchorage ground would be revealed; depots and deposits of coal, new bays and harbors, would be sought and sounded, and generally much information obtained, serviceable and interesting alike to commerce and science."[2] Regarding Mr.

[1] *Memorial of Percy McDonough Collins, upon the subject of an Intercontinental Telegraph connecting the Eastern and Western Hemispheres, by way of Behring's Strait.* (Government Printing Office, Washington, 1864); p.9.
[2] *Ibid.*, p. 46.

Latham's reference to steamers entering the Amur from the Pacific, the first of such vessels to do so was the s.s. *Constantinople*. Concerning the Alaskan fisheries, Collins predicted they would serve as "a nursery for first-class seamen, which in the growing commerce of the Pacific, will be just what we want there in the future, in order to give us the supremacy of that great ocean."[1] But though work was begun on the cable in 1865 and was continued for three years, Collins's efforts, and those of his sponsors, were in the end unavailing, for the Alaskan project fell through when the Atlantic cable was laid.

SALE OF ALASKA

It was to save Alaska from becoming English territory—the Tsar was particularly anxious not to have the British in that region—that it came to be sold to America for so small a sum, represented by "less than one-half its present annual output of canned salmon."[2] At the same time, the Russian-American Company which had colonised that region, was far from being in a strong financial position then; indeed it was only solvent by subsidies received from the home Government, and the Company had earlier vainly petitioned the Russian Government to take over control of its possessions. In 1839 it had even leased a large strip of coastal territory to Hudson's Bay Company. "The lease of this trail to the British Company marked the beginning of the end of Russian domination in America."[3] Fear that this territorial acquisition by the English would lead to a development of British maritime strength in the North Pacific, was the primary motive for the Russian sale of Alaska to another Power.

Actually the earliest proposition made by the Russians, in 1844, was that the United States could have Alaska for nothing beyond the mere cost of transfer, if the U.S. line were kept at 54° 40' and the English were shut off from any Pacific seaboard. A thousand miles of British coastal territory lay south of Alaska in British Columbia, and just as it was fear of English sea power that had led the Tsar to issue his ukase in 1821 excluding

[1] 40th Congress, 2nd Sess. H. Doc. No. 177, pp. 25-8.
[2] Reprinted by permission of the Publishers, The Arthur H. Clark Company, from *History of Alaska under the Rule of the United States*, by Jeannette P. Nichols; p. 21.
[3] Benjamin Platt Thomas, Ph.D., *Russo-American Relations, 1815-1867*. See Johns Hopkins Univ. Studies in Historical and Political Science, Series XLVIII, No. 2. (The Johns Hopkins Press, Baltimore, 1930.)

non-Russian ships from a considerable area of the Bering Sea, so it was the question of sea power which determined the fate of Alaska. In view of this it is somewhat ironical that the great North Pacific Empire of the Russians should have been ceded to America, the country then nearly as advanced in seafaring as Great Britain, and today the only great maritime Power in the world.

In 1863 units of the Russian Fleet, including the flagship *Alexander Nevski*, had arrived at New York and San Francisco during the American Civil War. Russian-American relations, particularly in the maritime sphere, were generally most cordial when one or other of these two countries was having trouble with Britain. By many Americans the arrival of the Tsar's ships was interpreted as a sign that Russia was going to give active aid to the North. However, as a recent historian[1] has pointed out, Russian ships did not come to America at a crucial time, but when the crisis was past and danger of intervention was over. (In any case the vessels were too antiquated to have been capable of any major engagement. The entire fleet at that time consisted of only two squadrons, the first of which comprised seven ships based on Kronstadt, and a frigate in the Mediterranean, and the second was a small and obsolete squadron in the Pacific. All the vessels were of wood and mainly dependent on sails for power.) Actually Russia's motive in sending her ships into U.S. harbours was to get them to neutral ports before her fleet could be attacked by Britain or France, who were then hostile to Russia over the Imperial Government's suppression of a Polish rising. Russia knew her navy was too weak to stand up to either the British or the French fleets, still less to these in combination, so, as her relations with the United States were then good, she ordered her ships to make for U.S. ports. All the same the Russian Government had feared that this very act might incite a British advance through Canada and Alaska to Siberia. Indeed some years earlier during hostilities in the Pacific in which Britain and France were ranged against Russia, the Russian possessions on the North American continent were declared neutral, and vessels of the Russian-American Company had crossed from Ayan and other ports on the Sea of Okhotsk to take refuge in Alaskan harbours.

The Crimean War had exposed Russia's maritime weakness; she had no desire to risk attack by Britain in the North Pacific, either off her Alaskan or her Siberian shores. It was better to

[1] S. F. Johnson, *American Foreign Relations*; Vol. II, p. 46.

sell while Alaska was hers. There were contemporary suggestions in the United States that the real reason why Russia sold out, was the hope of thereby having the United States as a buffer between Siberia and the British navy. One thing is certain—Russia at that time thought it worth while to make a considerable territorial sacrifice in order to avoid a conflict with Britain in the North Pacific. By this time the Tsar had not only to take into consideration the advanced mercantile power of England in the Far East, and the progressive strength of America at sea, but the rising maritime power of Japan. The link which bound the Russian Empire in America to the homeland was an uncertain one—the hazardous sea route from Okhotsk to Alaska could hardly be regarded as other than a dubious lifeline by a non-seafaring people. Even the great Governor, Baranov, for all his ambitions on the American side of the Pacific, had realised that unless Russia could get control of the Amur and strengthen her position on the Asian shores of the Great Ocean, her future in the Pacific would be extremely precarious.

Nevertheless the sale of the strategic territory of Alaska with such defensive key points as North Pacific islands, for the sum of $7,000,000, shows a singular lack of maritime ambition on the part of Russia, in strange contrast with her oceanic enterprise of forty years earlier. It is interesting to note that in 1860 too, Rear-Admiral Popov[1] stated that, while Russia must retain the Kuriles and the Kommandorski Islands, since cession of these would bring America too close to Russia, he would not object to a transfer of the Aleutians—yet these islands run from the Alaskan Peninsula to the Kommandorski group off Kamchatka. In early proposals (1857) made for the sale of Alaska however, Gortchakov, Russian Minister for Foreign Affairs, did state that the Russian-American Fur Company should retain the Aleutians for the Company's operations in Siberia. But no mention was made of the *strategic* value of these North Pacific islands.

Secretary of State Seward, who was responsible for the American purchase of Alaska, gave as the official reason for the "deal", the desire to improve Russo-American relations which had been endangered by disputes over fishing in Alaskan waters. But Seward's own expansionist philosophy may suggest to others that the reason so far as the American side of the transaction was concerned, was to be found elsewhere.

Seward regarded Alaska as a naval outpost vis-à-vis north-east Asia: "The Pacific Ocean," he said, "its shores, its islands, and

[1] In a Memorandum dated 6 February, 1860.

the vast regions beyond, will become the chief theater of events in the world's great hereafter." He foresaw that the Aleutian Islands would one day become American stepping-stones across the North Pacific. But few other men of his time took that view; to them Alaska was "Seward's ice-box", "the land of short rations and long twilights", "Walrussia", and they deplored the payment of two cents an acre for land which is now to be crossed by some of the most important trunk airlines of the globe—a region once remote but now a focal one in the sea-air strategy of the Great Powers. Alaska today figures prominently in the joint plans for Arctic defence undertaken by the United States, Canada, and Britain. Opposite its shores lies the Bay of Lavrenty, which marks the terminal of the Soviet Arctic air route[1] stretching from the Siberian side of the Bering Strait to Krasnoyarsk. A short flight from the Bering Strait Boundary with Russia is the air base at Mile Twenty-six, south-east of Fairbanks, which was planned as one of the largest bomber bases in the United States. A short air-distance too from the boundary line is Sitka, the principal U.S. naval base on the Alaskan coast. Not only do the shores of Alaska form a front line of defence for the American north-west coast, but they constitute the apex of the triangle embracing the strategic ocean area, Alaska-Hawaii-Panama. And the Aleutian Islands give the United States command of the Pacific from their submarine base at Dutch Harbour, Unalaska, to their naval base at San Diego, California.

It may be pertinent to ask, what would be the position of America today if Alaska had remained Russian? And will the sentiments expressed in the *New York Herald* at the time when that territory changed hands, prove to be true in the years to come? This is what the *Herald* said: "Russia and the United States must ever be friendly, the colossi having neither territorial nor maritime jealousies to excite the one against the other. The interests of both demand that they should go hand in hand in their march to Empire." Different was the viewpoint of the contemporary *Novoe Vremya*, which, after the Spanish-American war, wrote: "Russia must be on her guard against the United States, especially in view of the enormous wealth of its Pacific shores, and the strategical position occupied by America in the Sandwich, Philippine, and the Samoan Islands."[2] The

[1] This was established during the war under the personal orders of Stalin.
[2] H. H. Bancroft, *The New Pacific*. (The Bancroft Company, New York 1900); p. 216.

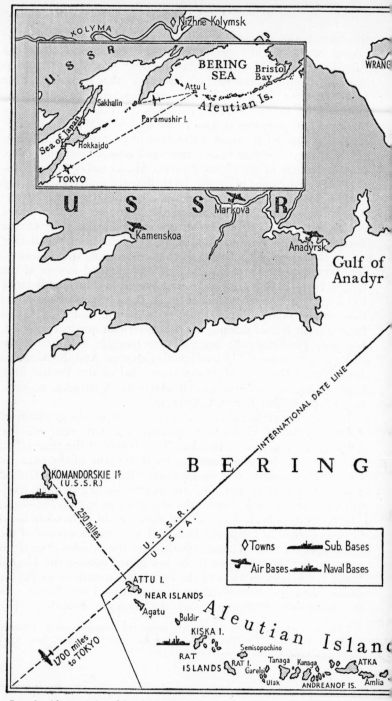

Reproduced by permission of Serial Map Service, from "Serial Maps," Vol. IV, No. 9, p. 81.

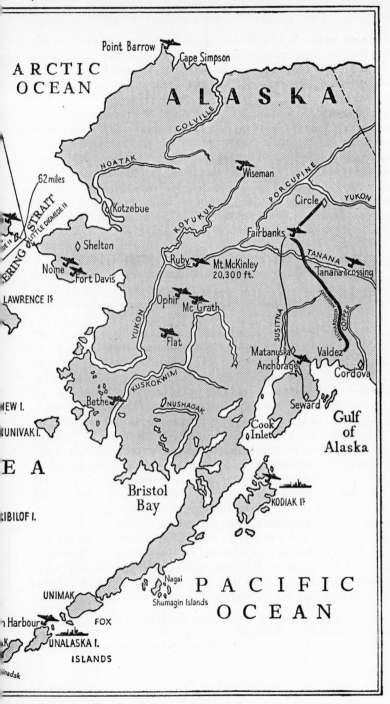

HOWING the strategic importance of the Aleutian Islands, and giving the atum Line between the territories of the United States and the U.S.S.R.

249

reference to the Sandwich Islands (Hawaii) recalls the fact that long before their annexation in 1898 the United States knew of rumours that Russia was prepared to oppose that step, but Secretary of State Marcy "had little fear of interference from that quarter".[1] The independence of the Hawaiian Islands had been guaranteed earlier by the United States, but, being no more than 2,100 miles from San Francisco, it was felt they were too near the American coast to be left to themselves. "It is imperative," declared Mahan, "to take possession, when it can be done righteously, of such maritime positions as contribute to secure command."[2] To annex Hawaii, Mahan averred, would be "a token that the nation in its evolution has aroused itself to the necessity of carrying its life . . . beyond the borders which heretofore have sufficed for its activities".

THE "OPEN DOOR" IN CHINA

A year after the American purchase of Alaska, the United States Navy had ordered Captain Reynolds to occupy Midway Island, with the ultimate object of making a naval station here for the route to China. Meanwhile Russia no less than Japan, had become increasingly anxious about American aims in the Pacific, ever since the visit of Commodore Perry, U.S.N. to Japan in 1853. Perry had stated that he looked forward to a time when there would be on the east coast of Asia a large number of American "commercial settlements", and in one despatch spoke of "the expediency in establishing a foothold in this quarter of the globe, as a measure of positive necessity to the sustainment of our maritime rights in the East".[3] Formosa and the Lu Chu Islands he regarded as the starting point of this expansion westwards. Russian fears may have been based on the realisation of a geographical truth—that migrations which start from the heart of a continent, if they are powerful enough do not stop at the shores of that continent, they surge overseas. Certainly the Russian Government had declined to entertain Muraviev's proposal to attract Americans as settlers in the Far East, bluntly stating that it would be too dangerous. American ships which entered Russian waters for seal fishing were regarded by the Russians in a very unfavourable light. Apart from the fact that this industry was a source of State revenue and

---

[1] J. M. Callahan, *American Relations in the Pacific and the Far East, 1784-1900.* (Johns Hopkins Press, Baltimore, 1901); p. 121.
[2] *The Interest of America in Sea Power.* (Sampson Low, Marston, 1897); p. 52.
[3] S-Ex.Doc.34. 33-2, p. 12.

"poaching" was, therefore, to be discouraged, the Imperial Government suspected other objectives. Therefore "little mercy is shown the pirate schooner, and a few years ago", wrote Wirth Gerrare in 1903, "American citizens might be seen working in chains on the roads of Vladivostock, whilst one of the smartest Russian revenue gun-boats is a confiscated three-masted American sealing schooner, with auxiliary screw."[1] Whaling off the Russian Pacific coast was guarded by the Government as closely as seal hunting, and to revive this industry a State subsidy was given to Count Keyserling who had a monopoly of the Siberian whaling.

When the United States annexed the uninhabited and seemingly unimportant Wake Island in 1899, it was for the purpose of establishing a Pacific cable station. If the eastern arm of the China Sea is included in the Pacific, then Wake Island can be regarded as a mid-Pacific island, and one which offers such wide radius of operations that its strategic importance is at once obvious. It was not then apparent, however that this island and others in the chain from Hawaii to the Philippines would become invaluable for America in a world war nearly half a century later. After the Spanish-American War it was widely believed that Russia aimed at establishing a naval base in the Philippines.[2] America's interest in securing an "Open Door" policy in China, particularly from Manchuli in the north to Kwantung in the south, made it imperative for the United States to gain control of the Philippines before anyone else did. In addition, the fact that the other Powers had strongly entrenched themselves in China—Great Britain in the Yangtze Valley,[3] Weihaiwei, Kowloon; Germany in Kiaochow; France in Kwang-chow-wan; Japan encroaching on Fukien, and Russia on Kwantung—impelled America to retain the Philippines after her victory at Manila in 1898.

By the time that she had acquired those islands it was clear that the United States had abandoned the principle enunciated earlier by Jefferson—that a meridan of partition through an ocean could be regarded as the limits of a State's expansion. From now on it could be said "the ocean is the only absolute boundary." From the days of the China tea trade, when the

[1] *Greater Russia*; p. 194.
[2] See also Tyler Dennett, *Americans in Eastern Asia*. (The Macmillan Company, New York, 1922); p. 623.
[3] Britain by control of the Yang-tse-Kiang could ensure the passage of battleships up to Nanking, and of smaller warships up to Hankow.

Boston and Baltimore clippers crossed the Pacific in the early period of the Chinese Republic, can be traced the American aim to rule the waves of that ocean. "The Power that rules the Pacific is the Power that rules the world," proclaimed Senator A. J. Beveridge[1] just after the United States had acquired the Philippines. These islands had brought his country nearly 7,000 miles west across the ocean right to the coast of Asia. Whereas Russia had reached the Far East via Siberia and Manchuria, America had done so by island-hopping and the Philippines. The latter were America's advance posts to the "Open Door" of China.

The interest of the United States in the China trade can be traced along with the development of the American type of clipper ship in the ocean tea race, but as early as 1784-5 two United States ships, the *Empress of China* and the *Pallas*, had called at Canton and had returned to Boston with a cargo of tea and silks. From that time on, America's trade with the seaports of the Celestial Empire continued to grow, and in 1844 she had obtained from China a treaty providing for Most-Favoured-Nation Treatment for U.S. nationals. In Shanghai, the United States looked ahead to the time when she hoped for a predominating influence in trade with the Chinese. Mr. T. B. King, of the Committee of Naval Affairs, in his report in 1837 to the House of Representatives recommending steam navigation from America to China, said: "The extension of our territorial possessions in the Pacific has placed it in our power ultimately to communicate with China almost as rapidly as we now do with Europe." America's Pacific Mail Steamship Company had been instituted chiefly for this purpose, at a time when Russia was still in possession of Alaska, but the Russians had established no similar trans-Pacific service, though their Government was subsidising shipping elsewhere.

American proposals were made for neutralising the railway system of China by placing it under international control. American engineers also urged the construction of a West Manchurian Railway to connect the Pechili Gulf with Aigun on the Amur. In both instances Russia supported Japan's rejection of the proposals, pointing out that the South Manchurian Railway formed an integral part of the Trans-Siberian system, and that Russia must have unrestricted communication with her Far Eastern seaports.

Japan had already used her position in North China and

[1] Congressl. Records, 56 Congress, 1st Sess.; Vol. 33, 1900; p. 704.

Manchuria to hamper American business, and in her control
of the South Manchurian Railway had held up American
goods shipped to Dairen. One of Japan's "Twenty-One
Demands" to China in 1915 was that the Chinese should not
lease or cede to any Power any harbour, bay or island, along
their coasts. But the Russians too had frequently acted in
a manner contrary to acceptance of the principle of the "Open
Door" in China and Manchuria. At one time they announced
that they would exclude American oil from the port of Dairen.[1]
The proclamations of the Russian Controller at the treaty port
of Newchang were further instances of Russian indifference to
the Hay Doctrine. Newchang was not even a Russian leased
port, it still belonged to China. There was also the case of the
Russian violation of the neutrality of China, when, on the eve
of the war with Japan, Russian ships had taken refuge in
Chinese ports, and among them the *Ryeshitelni* had stayed at
Chefoo beyond the twenty-four hour time limit.[2]

Such attempts at domination in China, whether by Japan or
by Russia, were entirely opposed to American interests in the
Far East, and on 1 February, 1902, the famous Hay Note was
addressed to the Chancelleries of eleven countries, declaring
that: "The attainment by one Power of such exclusive privileges
for a commercial organisation of its nationality, conflicts with
the assurances repeatedly conveyed to this government by the
Imperial Russian Ministry of Foreign Affairs, of the Imperial
Government's intention to follow the policy of the Open Door
in China." Russia had been one of the seven Powers ostensibly
pledged to the principle of the "Open Door" by her reply to the
earlier Hay Note of 6 September, 1899, but later she had
pressed China to refuse to open any new treaty ports in Manchuria. Her reply to that first Hay Note had certainly been
somewhat evasive, and was, in the opinion of the United States
Government, the least satisfactory of those received. One
juridical writer goes so far as to say: "It distinctly failed to
commit the Russian Government to the exact propositions made
by Secretary Hay."[3]

Japan, after her victory in 1906 over Russia, succeeded that
Power in efforts to make an appanage of Manchuria, and in
a supplementary agreement to the Russo-Japanese Treaty for
mutual defence, 1916, she had got Russia to surrender the

[1] *The Times*, 13.9.1901.
[2] See *American State Papers, Foreign Relations, 1904*; pp. 424-25.
[3] W. W. Willoughby, *Foreign Rights and Interests in China*; Vol. I, p. 73.

strategic line connecting the South Manchurian Railway with the Sungari River. The intervention by U.S. forces under General Graves in Manchuria during the Russian Civil War had one motive only—to resist the Japanese penetration into that region and into Siberia. The Americans had therefore specially sent from San Francisco units of their railway corps, to keep open the Chinese Eastern Railway through Manchuria for the transport of supplies shipped to Vladivostock.

The determination of the United States to maintain the policy of the "Open Door" in China was responsible for the agreement made by the signatory Powers to the Washington Treaties, 1922, whereby they agreed to "respect the sovereignty, the independence, and the territorial and administrative integrity of China." At the end of the nineteenth century, Secretary of State John Hay had said: "He who understands China, holds the key to international politics for the next two hundred years." That statement was the basis of American policy in the Far East, particularly as regards the Chinese seaboard. By this time the "Open Door" policy, known as the Hay Doctrine, had come to transcend in importance the Monroe Doctrine, and later, in 1948, American support for General Chiang Kai-shek was not unexpected. In other words, the Pacific now took precedence over the Atlantic. The western Pacific was a zone of supreme concern to a Power with extensive interests in the China trade. The region was one of equal importance to Russia, because that country has always realised she must have access to ports on the Yellow Sea. That is why Russia, once she did gain influence in eastern China, has always been ready to fight to maintain her position there.

The adoption of Mahan's theories of Sea Power, reflected in the U.S. Navy Act of 1890, was another factor in American Pacific policy which Russia viewed with misgiving. Mahan saw that the Hawaiian Islands were necessary for the defence of the Panamanian Isthmus. But he saw far beyond that. He believed that the destiny of America was to become a great world Power. A powerful fleet, he maintained, was necessary for supporting a commercial drive across the Pacific to Asia, and he held that in turn overseas colonies were necessary for maintaining naval power, inasmuch as they provided bases for naval operations. When Mahan's classic study, *The Influence of Sea Power upon History, 1660-1703*, first appeared, American commerce was carried largely in foreign vessels, and partly due to the Government's failure to subsidise shipping at a time when

ALASKA 255

Russia was doing this, America's trade with China declined for a period. The United States also suffered in its lack of the bases which it now possesses. Under the presidency of Theodore Roosevelt however, new establishments overseas were sought, and the theories of Mahan began to be applied to the American navy and mercantile marine, a considerable expansion of both becoming a definite feature of American policy.

In our own time we see in the United States the twentieth century development of the ideas of Mahan, viz., that mercantile imperialism is essential for national prosperity, and expanding foreign commerce is necessary for the maintenance of sovereign power. And to enable such a mercantile service to function freely, a navy must be maintained. With the opening of the Panama Canal, that doctrine of mercantile expansion which Mahan preached became a reality. The trade of eastern America and of the Mississippi Valley flowed out through its locks to the Pacific. A Two-Ocean Navy can now pass its largest battleships through the third set of locks on their way out to the U.S. island bases in the Pacific.

Today, the acquisition of new island possessions by the United States, and of the Kuriles by Russia, has brought the U.S. and the U.S.S.R. nearer to each other geographically. While the Russians strengthen their position on the Asiatic mainland in ports and along littorals, the Americans draw nearer that mainland by acquiring such ex-Japanese island bases as Okinawa and Iwojima, and by control of the Ryukyus. From Vladivostock it is 1,055 miles to Okinawa, which the United States had planned as a giant air base. Japan, by passing under the control of the Allies after the second world war, became the meeting-place of the U.S. and the U.S.S.R.; within the Japanese homeland the United States had considered the maintenance of a naval base, and for this had named Yokosuko, formerly used by the Japanese Fleet. With the disappearance of Japan as a naval Power, the North Pacific (except for the few island stations maintained by the United Kingdom in that area) became a zone in which only two nations had ocean power—America and Russia. The future is pregnant with possibilities.

The doctrine of the inevitability of expansion, so clearly being fulfilled today by America with the aid of her overwhelming naval power, was formulated by Mahan at the beginning of this century. But as long ago as 1868 N. P. Banks, chairman of the Foreign Relations Committee at the time of America's purchase of Alaska, said of the Pacific: "It is on that line that are to be fought the great battles of the hereafter. It is there that the institutions of the world will be fashioned and its destinies decided."[1]

[1] *Congressional Globe*. 40th Congr. 2nd Sess. Part 5. Appendix 377-403. From House debate of 1 July, 1868.

X

THE SIBERIAN SEA ROAD

ONE of the most important maritime trade routes of the future is the Siberian Sea Road. When the latter first came to be regarded as a serious proposition, a Norwegian Syndicate undertook the investigation of its commercial possibilities, and in 1912 the Siberian Steamship Company, with its headquarters at Oslo, was founded on the assumption that expeditions along the Northern Sea Route would prove practical ventures. The Company then embarked on various industrial enterprises in Siberia; sawmills were started along the Yenesei, and plans were made for a shipyard at Krasnoyarsk. With the object of opening up a regular trade connection with the interior of the country via the Kara Sea and the Yenesei, Fridtjof Nansen in 1913 had sailed in one of the Syndicate's vessels, s.s. *Correct*, and his account of that voyage, entitled *Through Siberia, the Land of the Future*,[1] testified to his faith in the use of this sea passage.

The *Correct*, a vessel of 1,550 tons deadweight, and a speed of ten knots in calm weather, set to sea with a cargo of cement from Stettin, destined for the Siberian Railway. Entering the Kara Sea she sailed to the north of Byeli Ostrov and on to Dickson Island, thence south to the Gulf of Yenesei, and anchored off Nosonovski Pesok. After discharging her cargo she started on her homeward voyage, but Nansen, whose eventual destination was the Russian Pacific province of Amursk, went by the steamer *Omul* up the Yenesei to Krasnoyarsk. Here he was impressed with the general desire of the inhabitants to find an outlet for their raw products via the Arctic Ocean, a tradeway through the Kara Sea to the Atlantic countries. It was clear to the Allied Governments early in the first world war, that if the wheatlands of the Yenesei could send their produce to western Europe, this would go far to solve the food problem. The supplies however, as well as the fleets of steamers which the Syndicate had launched on the Ob and Yenesei, were confiscated by the Soviets in 1917.

The favourable report which Nansen had brought back as to

---

[1] Translated by Arthur G. Chater. (Heinemann, 1914.)

the practicability of a Siberian seaway, had led the Imperial Government to increase the number of Arctic wireless stations, one being set up on Dickson Island in 1915, and that year the trading depot of Ustport was founded. Farther west too there was an increase in Arctic voyaging. During the first world war Britain had built for the Russian Government four icebreakers, and five were transferred from Canadian waters for use in the White Sea, where supplies were brought from the Allies to Archangel.

THE KARA SEA EXPEDITION

Efforts to develop the Northern Route as a trade channel continued to be made soon after the Russian Revolution. Boris Vilkitski, the noted Russian explorer, had recently added his name to the list of those who had demonstrated the possibility of using the Arctic Route as a passage for cargo ships, when in 1919 he had organised the Arctic Maritime Expedition from Archangel to the delta of the Ob, for the purpose of bringing supplies to the forces of Admiral Kolchak. The arrival and return of Vilkitski's ships had been duly noted by Krassin, Commissar for Trade and Industry, who tried to start on development of the Great North Way, planned to link up the Siberian waterways with the White Sea and the Baltic ports. The year 1919 also saw the first Kara Sea Expedition. The Kara Sea lies between 70° N. and the Polar Ice-Cap: navigation through its waters is difficult, as parts of that region are affected by magnetic interference, and this had to be taken into consideration in compass reckoning. The entrance to this sea is formed by the Kara Strait "through which the whole of some European countries could pass easily".[1] To overcome the magnetic interference mentioned above, a non-magnetic metal ship was designed for the route, and was effectively equipped for meteorological research in the Kara and the East Siberian Seas. In 1933 the Sudostroi (Ship Designing Trust) had made plans for new steamers to serve the Northern Sea Route, capable of going through the Arctic without icebreakers. Of super-*Cheliuskin* type, though of the same basic dimensions as *Cheliuskin*, they were to be built in the Baltic and Leningrad shipyards.[2]

In the annals of Arctic seafaring the year 1919 is generally

[1] L. K. Brontman, *On the Top of the World*. (Gollancz, 1938); p. 215.

[2] See Moscow correspondent, A. A. Kashintzeff, *British-Russian Gazette and Trade Outlook*. (London); Vol. X, No. 12, p. 236.

referred to as the occasion of "the first Kara Sea Expedition"; in reality that sea was crossed more than half a century earlier by ten convoys which sailed on to the deltas of the Yenesei and the Ob, conducted by that sturdy English mariner, Captain Wiggins. In the 1926 Expedition, one section formed chiefly of vessels sailing under the British flag, went to the Yenesei, and penetrated four hundred miles south of the delta to a point farther up the river than had ever been reached before. At the confluence of the river Kureika with the Yenesei these vessels shipped 1,500 tons of graphite, "this being the first time in the record of the expedition that graphite has been transported from Siberia by these means".[1] The route generally followed takes the convoys via the Barents Sea to the Matochkin Strait and through the Kara Sea to the Gulf of Ob. There the Expedition has usually divided, one section sailing up the Ob, and the other going on east to the Yenesei. But this is only one half of the Northern Route; from ports between Vladivostock and the mouths of the rivers in the Yakutsk district it was found possible to work a regular service without serious risks. Professor Tverskoi has pointed out that in spite of the fact that the ice here is thicker than in the Kara Sea, these voyages are less dangerous than in the western part of the Arctic Ocean "because the ships pass along the coast through a strip of open water with one-year-old broken ice, which is formed as early as the month of July". It remained for the renowned voyage of the *Cheliuskin* to prove that a regular shipping route across the Arctic was possible.

To ensure co-ordination among the ships of different nationals taking part in these expeditions, the Northern Sea Route Bureau (integrated with Komseveroput) was set up in London.[2] The need for keeping to schedule is paramount: there must be no "lagging" among the trade convoys, as the open season is shorter than the closed one. The improvement in the service during the third decade of this century is indicated by the fall in insurance rates. In 1921 the risk on ships going through the Kara Sea was rated at 25s. a ton; in 1932 it was 5s.[3] In 1924 only three ships crossed that sea; in 1930 fifty did so. In 1938 nearly half a million tons of freight was carried through those waters, and in 1940 a hundred cargo vessels and thirteen icebreakers were working on Russia's Northern Sea

[1] *British-Russian Gazette and Trade Outlook*; Vol. III, No. 7, p. 318.
[2] The Bureau was later transferred to Berlin.
[3] Leonard Matters, *Through the Kara Sea*. (Skeffington, 1932); p. 7.

Route. The previous year a return voyage had been made from Anadir Bay (south-west of the Bering Strait) to Murmansk in a single season. These advances on earlier days of navigation had been made possible in the first place by modern hydrographic surveys, in the second by air reconnaissance. After the 1934 Kara Sea Expedition the route was entirely re-charted, but Professor Mason has pointed out[1] that east of Dickson Island charts were unreliable up to 1937. In that year, however, fresh surveys were made off the Taimir Peninsula, among the Nordenskiöld Islands.

Along the Northern Route there are four main shipping lanes, and the choice of route is determined by ice conditions. The voyage is most usually made via the passage of Yugorski Shar (between the Siberian coast and Vaigatch Island) which leads to the Kara Sea. The western entrance to Yugorski Shar is difficult owing to the treacherous rocks; there is a clear approach from the eastern end. The Strait is winding for nearly all its length of ninety-seven miles, and can be blocked even when the ice has melted in June, as the wind from the north will blow floes and small bergs. But of all dangerous areas along the Northern Route, the water by Byeli Island, off the Yamal Peninsula, and well to the east of Yugorski Shar, is the worst.

The second seaway along the Arctic route follows the Strait of Kurskie Vorota which separates the island of Vaigatch from Novaya Zemlya, and the third route takes ships through the Strait of Matochkin, the passage which cuts Novaya Zemlya in half. This is the shortest of all the routes, but it is one little used as it is subject to drifting ice.

The fourth route passes from the Barents Sea to the Kara Sea, by following the northern coastline of Novaya Zemlya and rounding Cape Mavrikaya. This however is used least of all, as it is too often ice-blocked.

From the Kara Sea, all four routes proceed on a north-easterly course through the Vilkitski Strait, past Cape Cheliuskin, across the Laptev Sea, then due east across the East Siberian Sea, thence south of Wrangell Island till they pass through the Bering Strait into the Bering Sea. (See Map, p. 264.)

There are four fairly well-defined sections of Russia's Arctic coast: (1) The Kara Sea to the Yenesei delta. (2) The Yenesei to Cape Cheliuskin. Here the conditions are worse owing to the number of archipelagoes—barriers to the breaking up of the

[1] "Notes of the Northern Sea Route," *The Geographical Journal*, XCVI, No. 1, p. 37.

ice. (3) Cheliuskin to the Kolima. The ice in this section is severe in parts, but warmer conditions prevail near the deltas of the great Siberian rivers, the Lena, Yana, Indigirka. (4) The Kolima delta to the Bering Strait.

Efforts to make the Northern Sea Route a regular channel of communication had been handicapped in the past through lack of knowledge of ice movements, particularly in the Kara Sea, where the chief difficulty is the very short navigational season—nearly always less than three months. By the time that ends, the rivers too begin to freeze, so even though the deep-sea vessels may reach the deltas of the great rivers and return before the ice closes, the steamers which take the trans-shipped cargoes up the rivers to such towns as Obdorsk, Igarka, and Turukhansk, have their own difficulties to face with the ice. Without the service of icebreakers such river routes would not be practicable.

Writing three hundred and thirty-three years after the first English expedition, undertaken by Jackman and Pet, to the Kara Sea, Nansen remarks how little had the general conditions changed there. Plans for surveying the disposition of ice had first been made in 1924-5, but it was not till eight years later that scientific exploration added any outstanding data to the known facts of ice movement. Two-and-a-half months (usually commencing about the middle of July) is the average time when the seas are ice-free in these latitudes; the general drift of the Polar pack-ice is north-west, i.e. from the Bering Strait to the East Greenland Sea, but currents and winds make the course irregular. Hence the need for reconnaissance planes and careful observation for Arctic navigation. In 1927 Soviet scientists engaged on this work had undertaken the first expedition to the shores of Franz Josef Land—territory which Russia formally annexed two years later. Novaya Zemlya was also charted, and reports made on the White Sea currents. And in 1929 these regions were surveyed from the airship *Graf Zeppelin* by scientists of various nationalities.

The first vessel to make the Northern Route from east to west in one navigational season was the Canadian-built ice-breaker *Litke*, which left Vladivostock in June 1934, and reached Murmansk in September. The first cargo ships to succeed in this achievement were the *Anadir* and the *Stalingrad*, which in 1935 carried freights from Vladivostock to Murmansk, a passage which in the case of the *Anadir* took ten weeks and two days. The most hazardous part of the voyage was in the

East Siberian Sea, owing to the accumulation of pack-ice of several seasons. The critical time was in July, when the two vessels became ice-wedged close to Aion Island, where Amundsen had been forced to winter in 1920. "For forty and fifty hours at a stretch Captain Melefsorov sat high in his crow's nest with nothing beside him but a samovar of tea, while the steamer, built to sail through a depth of twenty-one feet of ice, was forced to break through ice twenty-two and sometimes twenty-three feet deep. Suddenly a warm wind returned. The Captain felt his ship lurch, he peered breathlessly again through his binoculars and shouted to the men to proceed, the ice had been broken and his ship was free."[1]

After delivering Siberian ponies at Ust-Kolima on the Kolima River, the *Anadir* called at Igarka, where she was welcomed by the ships of many nations. By the time she reached Murmansk she had opened a tradeway along the top of the world. Her companion vessel *Stalingrad*, arrived at Murmansk six days later.

Not only was the Arctic Route traversed from east to west, but from west to east, that same year. We recall that the icebreaker *Sibiriakov* had voyaged from Archangel to Vladivostock in 1932, but the first cargo ships to make that route in the one sailing season were the *Iskra* and *Vancetti*. (They had been escorted by the icebreaker *Yermak* through the Laptev Sea, and had been taken over by the *Lenin* when they reached the islands of the Nordenskiöld Sea.) The year 1935 was indeed a memorable one in the history of northern navigation. How quickly advantage was taken of its achievements will be realised from the fact that in 1936 no less than fourteen ships made a through passage along the Arctic seaway.

The Northern Sea Route could not have become the important addition to Russia's sea communications which it has, but for the work of scientists and explorers, whose assembled data have enabled Polar stations to be established all along the shores of the Arctic as aids to shipping where navigation is most difficult, especially in the Kara and Laptev Seas. It is however only since 1933 that Soviet administration has done much of its extensive work in this connection. Before then, in the south-western section of the Kara Sea, for about 2,900 nautical miles, there was only one lighthouse for every three hundred miles. By 1934 there was only one lighthouse east of the Yamal

[1] Ruth Gruber, *I Went to the Soviet Arctic*. (Gollancz, 1936); p. 355. Acknowledgments to the Viking Press, New York.

Peninsula, but by 1937 there were ten.[1] In addition to the Russian Government, certain foreign ones had given an undertaking during the conferences of the International Polar Congress at Hamburg, 1879, to establish scientific stations in the Far North. It has been stated by at least one authority on Arctic exploration that 1913 was the year in which the first of such stations was set up in Polar waters. This is not the case. Under the auspices of the Imperial Russian Geographical Society, the Lena delta was carefully mapped during the period 1882-84, and Lieut. Jurgen, who supervised this work, set up a station on Sagastyr Island, latitude 73° 23′ N. The first radio station to be established was on the Strait of Matochkin, and was followed by another on Vaigatch Island, and one on the mainland facing the Yugorski Strait to help the passage of vessels to the Kara Sea. But when Nansen voyaged by this route in the s.s. *Correct*, that ship could not establish wireless connection with any of these stations, for they were not in working order. Others had been planned, but up to the time of the Revolution there were only five Polar stations: by the beginning of the last war there were seventy-two, and after the end of the war work was begun on many more along the whole Arctic region between Norway and Alaska. Within the next decade stations will be constructed on all the larger Arctic islands. From "Radio North Pole", daily weather reports have been issued ever since that memorable day, 23 May, 1937, when Professor Schmidt set up a station at the North Pole. The principal meteorological station in the Arctic is on Dickson Island,[2] which is less than six miles long and only four miles wide—a small place for the very important work carried on there. Baron Nils Nordenskiöld, during his voyage in the *Vega*, foresaw a busy future for Port Dickson, which he described as "the best-known haven on the whole northern coast of Asia". From that station in the Arctic Sea, the agricultural workers of Ukraine and South Russia are warned of coming drought; indeed it is from the Far North that weather warnings are sent out all over the Soviet Union. Even on ice floes drifting westwards through the Kara Sea, robot meteorological stations have been planted by the Russians.

Since the time when Professor Schmidt's North Polar Station

[1] T. A. Taracouzio, *Soviets in the Arctic*. (Copyright 1938 by The Bureau of International Research, Harvard University and Radcliffe College. Reference by permission of the Publishers, The Macmillan Company, New York); p.108.

[2] Discovered by Nordenskiöld in 1873.

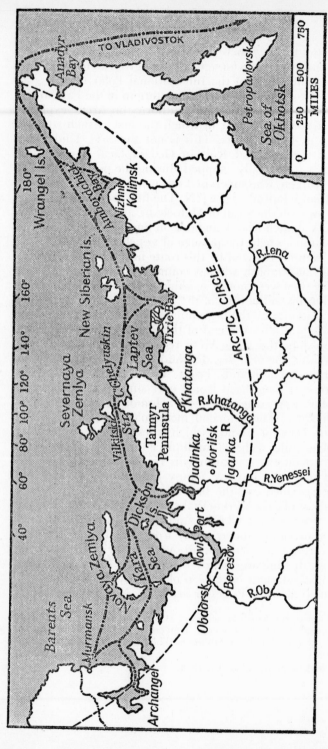

THE NORTHERN SEA ROUTE

(Reproduced by courtesy of George G. Harrap and Co. Ltd., from "The U.S.S.R.: A Geographica Survey," by J. S. Gregory and D. W. Shave, p. 349)

264

WHEN Nordenskiöld, by his voyage in the *Vega*, 1878-79, showed that the North-East Passage could become a practical sea route, he crowned with success the efforts made by adventurers of many different nations for over three hundred years. As far back as 1530, two English merchants in Seville—Robert Thorne and Roger Barlow—had written a treatise, to be presented to Henry VIII, urging that monarch to promote an expedition to Cathay by way of the Arctic seas. "If," they say, the members of such an expedition "will goe toward the Orient they shall injoy the regions of all the Tartarians that extend toward the midday, and from thence they may goe and proceed to the land of the Chinas, and from thence to the land of Cathaio Orientall, which is of all

the main lande most Orientall that can be reckoned from our habitation. And if from thence they do continue their navigation, following the coasts that return toward the Occident, they shall fall in with Malaca, and so with all the Indies, which we call Orientall, and following the way, may returne hither by the Cape of Buona Speransa: and thus they shall compasse the whole worlde".

The chronicle of the efforts made to reach, by a North-East Passage, "the land of Cathaio Orientall", is a saga of northern navigation in which English, Dutch, Russian, Danish, Swedish, and Norwegian mariners have taken a leading part. (The number of Basque seamen who sailed on these voyages in the early part of the quest, is a tempting subject for research.)

was set up, it has been found necessary to establish supplementary stations to allow for the ice-drift round the Pole. During the second world war, seventy-seven scientific stations were maintained by the Arctic Institute, and in 1942 the Soviet Government sent ten expeditions from Archangel to ensure that navigation should be clear along the Northern Route. Even in the last year of the war, three expeditions were sent to the Arctic, one of which was to study the oceanography of the East Siberian Sea.

The efficiency of the radio service, the fact that the harbours of most of the Arctic ports are becoming equipped for expeditious loading, that the Arctic Fleet is adequately served with fuel tenders, and that light railways are being opened up in the Arctic, is due to the zealous work in recent years of the Northern Sea Route Administration (Glavsevmorput), first established in 1932 for the control and economic development of Soviet territory north of latitude 62° N. During one period there were signs that certain elements in the Administration were opposed to the central regime, and in the Moscow Treason Trials of 1938, various members were charged with "wrecking tactics". The hold-up of shipping that year was due to the fact that most of the icebreakers had been left ice-bound in the previous winter, and when this was traced to the work of certain officials, the Administration was purged and re-organised.

THE "CHELIUSKIN"

To gain more information about conditions in the Arctic, the *Cheliuskin* made her renowned voyage in 1933. This 4,000-ton ship, specially designed to withstand ice-pressure, left Murmansk on 10 August with a picked crew. On their way from the Barents Sea, past Cape Cheliuskin and the deltas of the Ob and the Yenesei, the scientific staff, trained in the study of solar radiation, noted the effects of the latter, for the Arctic is one of the chief centres of the earth's meteorological conditions. Plotting currents, marking the drift of bergs, the members of the expedition, which included some women, drifted into the Bering Strait. "Locked now in an ice-field with the frozen ocean behind them, the explorers were driven by currents along the coast of Alaska, and then back to the north. In February 1934 the *Cheliuskin* sank, but the heroes of that voyage, after leaving the ship, set up camp, and in a temperature in which birds dropped dead in the air of cold, they made a landing-ground for a rescue plane. By the time they were finally rescued from the air, they had collected scientific data of the greatest value to the Fatherland."[1]

PAPANIN'S EXPEDITION

It was, however, Papanin's Expedition of 1937 which eclipsed all others up to that time by the results of its discoveries. Starting from Rudolf Island, the most northerly island of Franz Josef Land, and six hundred miles from the North Pole, Papanin, Otto Schmidt, and their scientific companions, landed near the Pole from a plane on 21 May. Three other planes arrived later, bringing more than thirty other members of the expedition with supplies and specialised equipment for the floating camp which was to be the home for the next nine months of Papanin and his three fellow-workers. Their intention was to gain more information about the Polar Basin, in particular about the ice-drift. More than forty years earlier Nansen had come to see that the way to investigate the conditions of the Polar Basin was to make use of the drifting pack—i.e. to drift with it, instead of trying to avoid it. The Soviet scientists, in their efforts to add to the existing knowledge of Arctic air currents and of the physics of the ocean, adopted the same plan as Nansen. These four explorers, leaving their thirty-five companions—headed by Professor Otto Schmidt—at the Pole, settled on a drifting ice-floe which was borne by a Polar current in the direction of Greenland. Four times daily they sent radio reports to Moscow of their weather and water investigations. Papanin and his companions, Peter Shirsov (hydrologist, who had been on the *Cheliuskin* voyage), Eugene Feodorov (magnetologist), and Ernst Krenkel (wireless operator), floated south-west on an average of four-and-a-half miles a day, though on the last part of their course this was sometimes increased to ten or twelve miles. The explorers found that even in calm weather the ice drifts south, i.e. it is independent of local wind.

Till then very little had been known about the direction of the drift of floes in the Upper Polar Basin. "Experience in Arctic navigation has shown that the problems of the Northern Sea Route cannot be investigated satisfactorily unless the central part of the Arctic Basin is studied at the same time. Such seas as the Kara, Laptev, East Siberian, and Chukotsk are no more than gulfs of the Arctic Basin. It is clear therefore that one

[1] M. Mitchell, *The Red Fleet and the Royal Navy*. (Hodder & Stoughton, 1942); pp. 46, 47.

cannot speak of being familiar with the seas on the northern coast of the U.S.S.R. until the whole Arctic Basin has been fully investigated, its hydrological system studied, and the laws of the formation of the ice and its drifts understood."[1]

As they drifted, Papanin's party took soundings through the ice with a weight attached to a steel hawser; these hydrological tests often took three-and-a-half hours, as the weight had to be raised slowly. Such soundings enabled the explorers to trace the contour of the ocean bed from the Pole to the south-east coast of Greenland. In the western part of the channel between Spitzbergen and Greenland the existence of a submarine ridge, first suspected by Nansen, was confirmed. The depth of the ocean at the Pole was ascertained for the first time. The greatest depth recorded by Nansen in his drifting *Fram* had been 3,850 metres, But Papanin's party ascertained it to be 14,075 feet, and by this discovery they also made it known that there could be no land in the neighbourhood of the North Pole. On 7 June, 1937, a wireless message from the Pole was sent by I. Papanin and E. Krenkel: "Our position today is: 88° 54′ North, 20° West. Our hydrological station took the full depth of the water. This depth proved to be 14,075 feet. A sample of bottom was taken —a small column of greenish-dark-grey silt."[2] There is a deep depression in the floor of the ocean from the Pole to 86°, a depression which in some parts is over two miles. At latitude 88° 41′, longitude 10° W., the hydrologist recorded a depth of 4,395 metres—the greatest recorded.[3] But at latitude 81° 53′ and longitude 6° W., "the whole of the cable (of the hardworked winch) then on the drum was paid out but failed to find bottom."

It was revealed that at a depth of 1,500 feet the temperature of the water was 0.48° Centigrade; thus it was established that in the centre of the Arctic Ocean at the North Pole there was a vast layer of warm water. Papanin's team of scientists had found that the Gulf Stream warmed the Arctic Basin from Florida right to the North Pole.

Nansen, drifting in the *Fram* from the Laptev Sea to Greenland, had discovered that throughout the whole course of his

[1] Professor N. Zubov, "The Cherevichny Triangle: Recent Polar Explorations", translated by Z. Schomberg, *The Anglo-Soviet Journal*. (Lindsay Drummond); Vol. III, No. 1, p. 50.

[2] L. K. Brontman, *On the Top of the World*; p. 242.

[3] This is the figure given by P. Shirsov and E. Feodorov, in "Results of the Scientific Work on Drifting North Polar Station," published in *Soviet Life and Work*. April-May, 1938; p. 13.

drift there was warm Atlantic water at a depth of 100-150 metres. This layer of water was found by Papanin's party to have higher salinity. "The general situation seems to be this : at depths of 825 to 1,975 feet there is a warm stream of Atlantic origin with temperatures above zero. At a depth of 2,475 feet the temperature is approximately zero; then the temperature falls gradually until it reaches its minimum at depths of 8,250 to 9,850 feet, where the temperature lies between —0.82° and —0.84°. At greater depths the temperature rises again and near the bottom this rise amounts to two-tenths of a degree."[1]

Since the days of Nansen's voyage in 1893-6, there has been a rise in the temperature of the weather, a change which has made navigation easier. The average thickness of Polar Sea ice has been reduced from 365 cms. at the time of the *Fram*, to 218 cms. as recorded by the *Sedov* (1937-40.) Since then the rise in the weather temperature has continued to increase.

Papanin's explorers found animal life; to their surprise they caught a crab, and so the old idea that the North Polar waters were uninhabited was refuted. Gulls, a guillemot, seals, were found too, and these fed on minute plant life which is fairly abundant in August. Thus it was made clear that sufficient sunlight penetrates the Polar ice in the summer months for the development of vegetable plankton.[2]

When the floe had carried the four scientists nearly nine hundred miles, and they were drifting south of Greenland, the melting of the ice obliged the expedition to be curtailed. Early in February messages were sent out asking for relief, and by that time the little party had had to transfer to a stretch of ice only fifty yards by thirty. They were in a dangerous part of the Greenland current when to their rescue came planes with the icebreakers *Taimir*, *Murman*, and *Yermak*, and the auxiliary motor-ship *Murmanetz*. When the party was finally rescued, they had drifted 1,200 sea miles in 274 days.

Through the expedition, knowledge has been gained of the central Polar Basin over which the movement of masses of cold air influences directly the climate of Europe and Asia, and new weather charts have accordingly been made. Papanin's observations revised the old ideas about North Polar weather; he found that the periodicity of the visitation of cyclones was more regular than had been believed. Also that the weather in the region

---

[1] L. K. Brontman, *On the Top of the World*; p. 266.
[2] See "Expedition to the North Pole," by Rear-Admiral I. Papanin, *Soviet Union News*; Vol. II, No. 10.

of the cold Polar cap is much calmer than on the borders of the
Arctic Ocean. In the former area there is an absence of powerful
winds, but on the other hand, there is an absence of anti-
cyclone elements. On the basis of Papanin's reports, long-term
weather forecasts for shipping have been made possible; vessels
can now be told what will be the position of floes a day or two
later, and Polar fliers have been equipped with more reliable
meteorological data. Discoveries about terrestrial magnetism
near and at the Pole have enabled corrections to be made on
magnetic maps.

Ivan Papanin, whose work has earned him the gratitude of
pilots of the seas and of the skies, has held the post of Chairman
of the State Arctic Navigation Institute, and in 1943 he became
Chief of the Northern Sea Route Administration.

In the history of Polar exploration the name of Professor Otto
Schmidt will rank with that of Papanin. The idea of setting up
a Polar station had been Nansen's in 1933, but the man who
actually carried this out was Professor Schmidt, who with his
team of co-workers had said goodbye to "the floating four" at
the Pole. At the same time they set up the first meteorological
station which was intended to connect with the whole system
of stations along the Soviet Arctic mainland and islands. When
Schmidt took leave of Papanin at the North Pole, "what," asks
L. K. Brontman, "was passing through his mind?" And the
Arctic writer goes on to say: "No doubt he was reflecting that
from here, from the North Pole, a dozen Polar stations would
arise, created by his efforts, on the islands and coasts of the
Polar Basin. Along the Northern Sea Route he no doubt saw
caravans of cargo ships sailing, the forerunners of yet other caravans. The whole map of the Arctic would be criss-crossed by
the routes travelled by this man, whose cold, deep, analytic
mind is linked with the ardent heart of a conqueror and a
Bolshevik."[1]

Let us take the appraisement of another writer from a different angle. Dr. T. A. Taracouzio in his immense work on Soviet
Arctic exploration,[2] speaks of the ability of the Russians to
advance the development of the Arctic "on an unprecedented
scale, to accelerate it with an unheard of vigor, and to support

[1] *On the Top of the World*; p. 185.
[2] *Soviets in the Arctic* (Copyright 1938 by The Bureau of International
Research, Harvard University and Radcliffe College. Reproduction by
permission of the Publishers, The Macmillan Company, New York).
Introd., p. viii.

it with an almost unlimited financial aid". The result of this, he says, is that "the news of human progress beyond the Arctic Circle, which in days gone by would have aroused universal enthusiasm, today may well have a two-fold effect: rejoicing in the scientific world and at the same time grave concern in the world of international politics".

DRIFT OF THE "SEDOV"

Further knowledge of the Polar Basin was gained in the same year as the Papanin expedition began its drift to Greenland. In 1937 the icebreaker *Sedov* (2,360 h.p., 3,056 tons), while surveying the Laptev Sea, was ordered to go to the rescue of the icebreakers *Malygin* and *Sadko* which had become ice-locked in another part of that sea. In attempting the rescue, *Sedov* herself became trapped in the ice off the New Siberian Islands, and after a time began to drift. "Drift as near as you can get to the Pole" came the order from Stalin. (The latter may have recalled the words of Admiral Makarov a generation earlier, who had said that the building of icebreakers "would mean that we could sail through the Kara Sea and reach the Ob and the Yenesei without becoming ice-bound or without loss of ships, we could even get to the North Pole".) And for two years the crew drifted, till on 20 February, 1939, the *Sedov* accomplished a record among ships, for she passed the 86th parallel of latitude, three hundred miles from the North Pole, and nearer to it than any ship had ever got before. *Sedov* however was only drifting, and the record for a ship under her own steam is (at the time of writing) still held by the U.S. vessel *Roosevelt*. More than a hundred years earlier than *Sedov's* venture, the English expedition, under Captain Parry, commanding the sloop *Hecla*, had reached a point only 3° 84.5' farther south than the *Sedov*, for Parry's boats, *Enterprise* and *Endeavour*, had been dragged over ice from the parent ship till they reached latitude 82° 45' N.

Lieutenant Greely of the U.S.N., however, by his excursion into Grinnell Land in 1882, had surpassed all previous records by pressing on to latitude 83° 24' N., and this remained the most northerly point reached until Nansen found latitude 86° 14' in the *Fram*, which had drifted stern foremost to that point.[1] Peary, in 1909, had reached the Pole after leaving his ship the *Roosevelt* two miles beyond Cape Sheridan, in latitude 82° 30',

[1] Captain Cagni, of the Italian Navy, in 1900 had reached 86° 34', the last part of his effort being made on foot.

the last three miles of all being covered on foot. In 1926 the Americans, Admiral Byrd and Floyd Bennett, had flown over the North Pole; three days later this feat was achieved by Amundsen, Ellsworth, and Nobile (with thirteen others) in the dirigible *Norge* in its flight to Teller, Alaska. And in 1928 Nobile had again reached the Pole, this time in the airship *Italia*. The Peary expeditions and that of the aviators, were the only ones which had advanced farther north than the *Sedov* with her record of 86° 39′. (That is, unless we are prepared to accept the report given to the Hydrographer Royal in the time of King Charles I, by a seaman at Amsterdam who had served with the fishing fleet off Greenland. This mariner said that he had sailed on alone, reached the Pole, and got 2° beyond it, without meeting ice. "This, though it sounds like a sailor's yarn, is not impossible, for several polar expeditions sailed in later days on account of the large lanes of water and the softness of the ice."[1] According to certain Hindu and Persian writers, the existence of the Frozen Ocean was known several thousand years B.C.)

The icebreaker *Sedov* began her drift in almost the same part as the *Fram* did, but the *Fram* had thereafter been sent in a more westerly direction. At last a day came in January when the searchlights of the icebreaker *Stalin*, stabbing the Greenland Sea, caught the *Sedov* in their beams. Aided by her rescue-ship, the *Sedov* reached Murmansk after drifting for two years and three months. In her course she had traced the continental shelf in some detail, and she had found that the ocean bed showed more irregular features than had been previously believed. But it is for her discoveries regarding the general circulation of the Arctic that the name of this vessel will be remembered. "It is now quite clear that Nansen's Laws of Arctic Drift are good ones. These state generally that the speed of ice-drift is one-fiftieth that of the wind, and that there is a deflection to the right of thirty to forty degrees, due to the rotation of the earth. The *Sedov* workers have been able to discover, further, that the drift follows the isobars, with high pressure to the right and low to the left; and that it is roughly parallel to the gradient of atmospheric pressure. The ice of the Polar Basin is driven by the wind clockwise round a pole of inaccessibility, and escapes from the Basin into the Greenland Sea (taking all Papanins and *Sedovs* with it) owing to the East Greenland current, which runs southwards along a meridian, and, opposite Spitzbergen, may

[1] W. B. Whall, *The Romance of Navigation*; p. 119.

reach a speed of up to six or seven miles a day."[1] But according to Professor Zubov, it is only a hypothesis that there is a large rotation of ice directed clockwise to the left, with the centre lying near the "Pole of Inaccessibility". Writing in 1942[2] Zubov says that this hypothesis has been neither refuted nor sufficiently confirmed. From observations of the *Sedov's* expedition it is clear, he remarks, that the pressure of the atmosphere in the Arctic Basin changes from season to season. Also that the ice of the Arctic Basin does not drift according to a simple plan from the coast of Alaska into the Greenland Sea. Like any other ocean basin, the Arctic has a complex system of currents which influence the movements of the ice.

"The Pole of Relative Inaccessibility" lies in the eastern zone of the Arctic, and north of Wrangell Island, approximately latitude 83° 4' N. and longitude 175° E. Of all Arctic regions it is the most remote and is more difficult to reach than is the North Pole. About this area much more was known after Cherevichny's flight there in 1941. His expedition is known as the Cherevichny Triangle, from the course of the three landings on the ice which formed an almost equilateral triangle.

It is in the Arctic regions generally that the development of airways will be of special assistance to that of sea transport. In the mastery of the Arctic, Russia's part has been a leading one; her maritime developments in the Far North, as elsewhere, have shown that there is every likelihood of her proving herself able, in the words of Peter the Great, "to conquer the art of the sea."

[1] James Fisher, F.R.G.S., "The Soviets in their Arctic", *The Anglo-Soviet Journal*. (Lindsay Drummond); Vol. II, No. 1, p. 51.
[2] "The Cherevichny Triangle: Recent Polar Exploration," translated by Z. Schomberg. *The Anglo-Soviet Journal*; Vol. III, No. 1, p. 49.

XI

ICEBREAKERS

"THE aeroplane is the eye; the radio station is the ear, and the icebreaker is the fist in this work of ours."[1] Without the icebreakers there would have been no Northern Fleet, no short sea route for ships voyaging from the North Pacific to the North Atlantic. Thanks to the icebreakers attached to the Northern Fleet, the new Arctic freighters can go from the White Sea to the Bering Sea without refuelling. Plans for enlarging the icebreaker fleet were advanced before 1939: "An even larger transport of 16,000 tons, with a cruising radius of 7,500 miles, was projected before the outbreak of war. Likewise super icebreakers of 50,000 horse-power and 24,000 tons displacement are being discussed in order to cope with demands on war-time shipping between the Soviet Far East and European Russia, and between America and Canada and Russia."[2]

Sooner or later Russia was bound to possess a fleet of icebreakers, but these vessels owe their actual origin to Admiral Makarov, who, when on the staff of Kronstadt Naval College, pointed out how "nature has treated Russia badly in giving her ice-bound ports." Russia, he said, "needs icebreakers more than any other country in the world does." Impressed with the achievement of the British-built *Yermak* in 1901, when she salved a cruiser off Hogland Island, Makarov suggested that another *Yermak* should be built. The purpose of this was to prepare a channel through the Arctic so that a naval fleet could be transferred from Murmansk to Vladivostock. The work of the Tyneside-built *Yermak* has been most important, as her share of ice has been principally that in the Vilkitski Strait, the narrow channel which separates Novaya Zemlya from the mainland. Unless that passage is kept ice-free it means that one of the principal straits on the Northern Sea Route is bisected by an ice-barrier, and the full strategic value of that route is lost to

[1] M. Lavrov, President of the North Sea Route Co-operative Development Concession (Komseveroput) to Leonard Matters. *Through the Kara Sea*, p. 38.
[2] Davies and Steiger, *Soviet Asia*; p. 128. Acknowledgments to Miss Viola Cooper for U.S. copyright.

Russia. The *Yermak* was the first icebreaker to accompany freighters through the Kara Sea.

An early type of icebreaker was the *Sibiriakov*, an ex-whaler, built on the Clyde in 1909. Under the Polar explorer Otto Schmidt, and Captain Voronin, this vessel left Archangel in 1932 and, as stated earlier, was the first icebreaker to make the passage through the Arctic seas and the Bering Strait in one navigation season. In achieving this voyage in just over two months, the *Sibiriakov* (1,140 tons) made an advance on Nordenskiöld's *Vega*. Another British-built icebreaker is the *Litke* (3,028 tons, 17 knots), constructed originally for service on the St. Lawrence, between Quebec and Prince Edward Island, when she was known as *Canada*. For her graceful lines she has been called "The White Swan of the Arctic Fleet". The *Litke* was at one time on the Black Sea, clearing the ice passage to the Sea of Azov; later she went to Vladivostock, and in 1934 voyaged thence to Murmansk in the navigation season. In the second world war another Canadian icebreaker, the *Montcalm*, was acquired by Russia.

The *Sedov* (1,140 tons, 12 knots), also built in British yards, set out for the Northern Land in 1930, and in that area made new discoveries among the Sergius Kamenev Islands: October Revolution Island and Red Army Strait were among the new names which the explorers on the *Sedov* added to the map of Arctic Russia. The map that the four scientists of the expedition brought back with them was indeed a very different one from the chart of 1913, with its indeterminate line of Arctic coast and islands. Under the command of Professor Schmidt, the *Sedov* in 1933 set up the first Polar station on Rudolf Land (Severnaya Zemlya), the base from which the 1937 expedition to the Pole was made.[1] The discoveries resulting from the *Sedov's* Polar "Drift," 1937-39, have been noted in the previous chapter.

Of the icebreakers built since the Russian Revolution, the *Lenin* (British-built) was for long the world's most powerful; though constructed as early as 1917 she had the remarkable speed of 19 knots. During the famine after 1920 she conducted a convoy of Siberian grain ships through the Kara Sea to the relief of stricken areas. It was this icebreaker which rescued Nobile's party when after the trans-polar flight the members had landed on an ice-floe. In 1946 the *Lenin* took her place once again in a British shipyard, for that year she appeared in

[1] As a result of the 1933 effort, airfields are now established on high plateaux in the middle of the island.

(Reproduced by courtesy of George Philip and Son Ltd., from "Modern School Atlas", p. 14.)

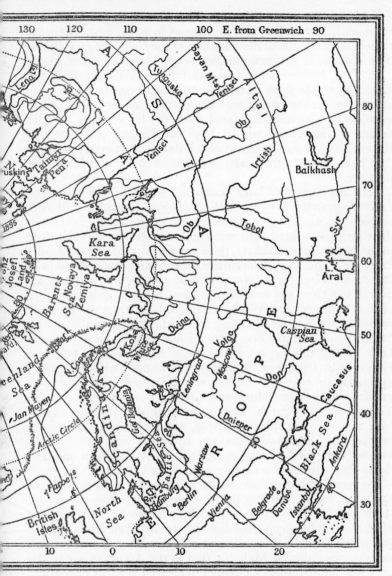

SHOWING, by the black line, the extreme limit of drift ice.
The stippled line indicates the Edge of Ice (Spring).

the Mersey for reconditioning. The *Krassin* (9,300 tons), another early icebreaker, was prominent in 1933, when she went to help in the rescue of the members of the *Cheliuskin* expedition. The *Rusanov* is a much smaller vessel than the others, only 2,600 tons, but competent enough for her task of opening the Kara Sea to the ships which are eastward bound for the ports of Siberia. In the past it was her practice to see all the other ships out of the Kara Sea, and often she herself only left just before the ice closed in. In 1936 the *Rusanov* went west to Rudolf Land to set up there a new Polar station; even that stout ship had to make three attempts before she got through the pack ice.

Five icebreakers of later design are the *Josef Stalin* and the *Lazar Kaganovitch* (1937), *Molotov* (1939), *Levanevski* and *Otto Schmidt* (1940). These 15-knot vessels, of the same class, have their propellers fitted with removable blades. For the first time in the history of icebreakers, these were equipped with catapults for planes. The *Josef Stalin* carries three hydroplanes; flagship of the Arctic Fleet, of 11,000 tons and 10,000 h.p., she has an overall length of 345 feet and a 75-foot beam, and is a product of the Ordzhonikidze Works, Leningrad. In 1939 she beat the record of the *Sibiriakov*, sailing from Murmansk to the Bering Strait, a distance of 3,800 miles, in one month. Another vessel built during this period is the *Sergei Kirov*, a large vessel of 12,000 tons (the average tonnage was 10,000) with a speed of 15 knots. In 1940 the *Dickson* was launched. She made her maiden voyage from Murmansk to Tixii Bay, and called at the Yenesei port of Igarka. That same year the *Mikoyan*, 11,000 tons, and carrying three seaplanes, was completed. All the icebreakers mentioned are specially equipped with strong decks for mounting heavy naval guns. It is believed that in addition thirty-four vessels, of a smaller type, were in existence in 1948.

Russian icebreakers are today built on the principle not of ramming, but of climbing the ice-edge and smashing the ice by sheer weight. The first vessel of this type to be built was the *Pilot*, designed to keep clear the channel between Kotlin Island (on which stands Kronstadt) and St. Petersburg. It was pointed out then by Admiral Makarov that in the Arctic, owing to the very low temperature, a channel so cleared is a free one; there is no broken ice to hinder the movement of the vessel backward preparatory for the next drive forward. But in the Baltic and the Black Sea, where the temperatures are not so low as in the Arctic, fragmentation occurs, and is a serious handicap to the

vessel attacking the ice. Hence in those regions "Russian Fleet
and Merchant Navy icebreakers are designed with power and
not weight as the most essential feature, though, like the Arctic
exploration vessels, they have frames set unusually close together, and more bulkheads than ordinary ships of the same
size. That is why, in addition to the large icebreakers already
described, the Soviet Union possesses many of only moderate
tonnage—some with a displacement of less than 1,500 tons.
Yet in every instance their engines are immensely powerful, so
that broken ice may be swept aside. When extra weight is
needed to break the ice, it is obtained by admitting water into
tanks at the bow, tanks which can be filled at the rate of 250
tons an hour."[1] The difference in principle between the earlier
and later types of icebreakers is illustrated by the *Sedov* and the
Yermak; the former breaks through the ice with her special
prow, but the latter tops the ice. The *Krassin, Yermak, Lenin,
Litke, Sibiriakov, Rusanov, Sedov*, were all built in foreign yards
and, according to Professor Mason,[2] only the first three of these
among the old breakers, are of the ice-crushing type. *Litke*,
though often classed with *Lenin* as an icebreaker, is, in this
writer's opinion, more of the ice-cutting class. (Dr. Taracouzio,[3]
however, thinks that all but the *Litke* can be classed as ice-
crushing types.)

In rare cases where freighters have not been able to have the
service of icebreakers, the crew have resorted to blasting the
ice with explosives, but the danger here is that the ice thrown
up will impede the vessel still further. A passage can sometimes
however be forced by re-blasting, as in the case of the *Artyukh*
which despite a broken engine came through the ice after
repairs, though it took her twenty days to get clear.

Not till 1937 were there any Russian-built icebreakers. The
previous year the Northern Sea Route Administration had
decreed that maritime transport should be given priority over
all other work in the Arctic, and accordingly work on the construction of an icebreaker fleet was intensified.

Since the incorporation of the Baltic States in the U.S.S.R.,
at least two icebreakers have been added to the Soviet fleets.

[1] Arthur Turner, "Icebreakers and the U.S.S.R.", *The Trident*, November,
1941; pp. 407-408.
[2] "Notes on the Northern Sea Route," *The Geographical Journal*; Vol.
XCVI, No. 1.
[3] *Soviets in the Arctic* (Copyright 1938 by The Bureau of International
Research, Harvard University and Radcliffe College. Reference by
permission of the Publishers, The Macmillan Company, New York); p. 117.

One is the Esthonian *Surr Tall*, another the Latvian *Krisjanis Valdemars* (15 knots.) Russian icebreakers sometimes voyage far from home. The *Krassin* in 1941 had voyaged from Archangel along the Northern Sea Route, through the Bering Strait, and docked at Seattle, a distance of 6,000 miles. The *Mikoyan* had arrived (armed) at Montevideo in April 1942, and had cleared for a port in Chile. All of these icebreakers are diesel-propelled vessels. The value of the fuel resources of the Far North is here apparent—the new icebreakers are heavy consumers of oil. Part of their duty is to clear the ice from the deltas of the Arctic rivers up which the steamers bring fuel from the oilfields of the North to the Ice Fleet. Considerable though the oil consumption is for the newer icebreakers, the latter have an advantage over the old coal-burning ships which, according to H. P. Smolka's inquiries, could not be absent from their fuel bases for more than twenty-five days.[1]

The scientific discoveries in the Far North have been made possible by equipping the icebreakers with observatories and laboratories. It has been the practice of the Northern Administration to investigate the Arctic coastline section by section rather than to attempt the work at a single stretch; hence the number of expeditions within recent times. One of the main economic advantages which will derive from these has been mentioned by Smolka[2] who relates how, when he was voyaging in the *Yermak*, her commander, Krastin, "figured out that it costs 1,000 roubles to transport a ton of metal from Moscow to Yakutsk—first by rail through Siberia to Irkutsk and then down the Lena. The cost is only 600 if the load is taken to Murmansk by rail and then by the Northern Sea Route to Port Tiksi and by river craft to Yakutsk". The icebreakers, in shortening the distance from Murmansk to Vladivostock by 8,000 miles (via the Cape or the Panama it is nearly 14,000, but by Cape Cheliuskin only 6,000) have thus, economically and strategically, strengthened enormously the position of the Soviet Union.

[1] *Forty Thousand Against the Arctic* (Hutchinson, 1938); p. 249.
[2] *Ibid.*, p. 250.

XII

ATLANTIC AIMS

"ON the wings of socialism Russia can fly over the whole of Europe and reach the Atlantic," wrote the revolutionary philosopher Herzen in 1850. It has certainly been within the period since the introduction of scientific socialism that Russia has succeeded in linking the Pacific with the Atlantic. In a more literal sense than Herzen's words imply, the western ocean has been reached by an all-Russian route—thanks to the work of Soviet icebreakers.

The aims of Russia in the North Atlantic will be influenced by the fact of her present supremacy in the Baltic. Times have changed since, in the course of the Seven Years War, the Russians in their conflict with Prussia attempted to take Colberg from the sea. Their squadron under Admiral Mishukov appeared on the coast of Prussia, "but did not materially aid the land campaigns, and the possible uses of a navy do not seem to have been realised".[1] Though the Baltic Fleet during the second world war was largely concerned with assisting land forces by coastal action, its submarine attacks on German transports in the Gulf of Finland showed that by this time there did exist in the minds of the naval staff, the conception of the navy as a weapon of offence.

At the most successful periods of their campaigns, both Peter the Great and Catherine the Great had dominated the Baltic, but they were never supreme there, inasmuch as they never controlled the Skagerrak and the Kattegat. Although in international law the Baltic Sea has never been regarded as a closed one, the ships of Peter and of Catherine could, as today, only have passed via the Kattegat into the North Sea and so into the Atlantic, by the goodwill of Sweden. And when, in our own times, Germany cut the Kiel Canal, she offset for Russia much of the work which Peter the Great had achieved for his country in opening the Baltic as a passage to the west. It is significant that in 1945,[2] Copenhagen Radio stated that Russia had

[1] Colonel Sir George Sydenham Clarke, K.C.M.G., F.R.S., *Russia's Sea Power, Past and Present*; p. 27.
[2] 17 July.

demanded at the Potsdam Conference that all the entrances to the Baltic from the North Sea, including the Kiel Canal, should be placed under international control, and that the U.S.S.R. should share in this.

These proposals were, however, a considerable modification of earlier ones, if the statements made by Goering on this subject at the Nuremberg Trials can be accepted, for according to these, in the talks between Molotov and Hitler held in Berlin in November 1940, the Soviet Foreign Minister had told the Fuehrer that Russia required the approaches to the Baltic Sea, the Sound between Denmark and Sweden, and the Skagerrak. Words written by Mackinder may be recalled at this point: "The Islanders of the World cannot be indifferent to the fate either of Copenhagen, or of Constantinople, or yet of the Kiel Canal, for a Power in the Heartland and East Europe could prepare, within the Baltic and Black Seas, for war on the ocean."[1]

The incorporation of the Baltic States in the Soviet Union in 1940 was, as we stress later, a maritime gain of the first importance for Russia. And Polonisation of eastern Germany after the last war, which has brought more of the Baltic littoral to a Slav people now closely knit with Russia, will place the latter in a still stronger position on the Baltic. The Potsdam Conference gave the U.S.S.R. Koenigsberg and other bases on the former Prussian coast, and the Soviet occupation of Prussia brought Russia actually west of Copenhagen at one point, and less than a hundred miles from the North Sea. Upon the outcome of this Slav migration westward, the future history of Europe depends. And the coming decades will reveal whether Napoleon was right when he said that the twentieth century would either be the century of revolutions or of the Cossacks. (Today we might say "both".) Asia is on the Elbe.

This Slav penetration to the west will certainly affect the Atlantic aims of the Soviet Union. During the Napoleonic war the Germans, with the object of detaching Sweden from the Russian orbit, had invented and circulated a story of a will of Peter the Great which purported to charge his successors with the task of obtaining an ice-free harbour for their country on the coast of Scandinavia, thereby bringing Russia on to the Atlantic. Propaganda of the same character was circulated by the Germans just before the first world war, with the result that

[1] *Democratic Ideals and Reality*; p. 224. With acknowledgments to Lady Mackinder.

a certain section of Swedes themselves raised a fund for building a warship to meet the alleged designs of Russia on Swedish waters in the Gulf of Bothnia.

Germany had always been alive to the fact that Russia is vulnerable at this corner of Europe. Foreign control of the northern Baltic would not only threaten Russia's chief trade route, but more than counter the advantage which she would gain from acquiring territory on the North Atlantic seaboard of Scandinavia. In the middle of the nineteenth century, Britain and France, aware that Russia was then definitely seeking to establish herself on the North Atlantic littoral, had come to make in 1855 a treaty with Sweden by which the two Powers promised armed help to the latter (then united with Norway) if Russia made encroachments on Swedish or Norwegian territory. King Oscar I, on his side, agreed not to give up any land to Russia, nor even to allow her fishing or pasture rights. This, says Professor Worm-Müller, "was a complete reversal of the policy of 1813, the reason being the fear that Russia would try to secure access to one of the ice-free harbours of Northern Norway and thus become an Atlantic Power. The territory supposed to be most in danger at this time was Finmark. As a matter of fact, the danger existed, but that danger was chiefly centred in the interest evinced by the Finnish authorities to extend their economic rights (fishing, reindeer-grazing, etc.), into Norwegian territory. The oft-repeated stories of the Russian claim to have ports on the southern shores of the Varanger-fjord were, in reality, Finnish claims supported by historical, ethnological and other reasons."[1] Professor Worm-Müller adds: "Relations between Russia and Norway, and especially Finmark, have always been good, but the question of Finmark and fear of Russia were again to the fore in the 1930's, partly due to German propaganda and even more to the Russian attack on Finland in 1939."

When by the Russo-Finnish peace terms of 1940 Finland ceded to Russia the Finnish part of the Rybachi and Sredni Peninsulas, and when by the Armistice terms of 1944 Finland gave up to the U.S.S.R. the Oblast of Petsamo, Russia was brought nearer the realisation of her long-standing North-Atlantic aims. Advances towards the latter were being made by the Tsarist Government before the Revolution, when negotiations had been opened with Norway for the building of a

[1] "Norway's Foreign Relation and Policy," *The Norseman*. (Lindsay Drummond); Vol. II, No. 2, p. 83.

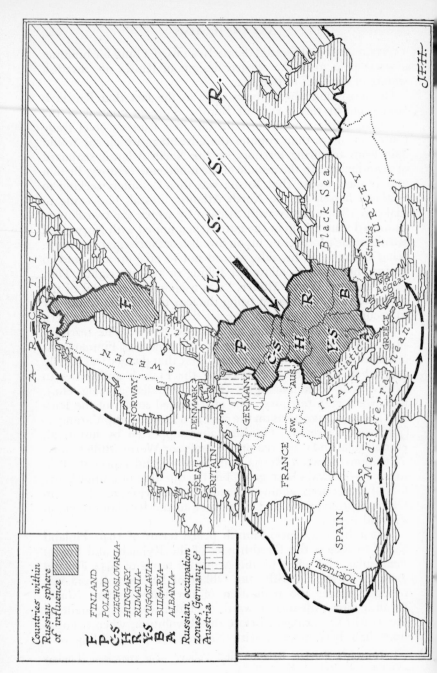

Countries within
Russian sphere
of influence

F. FINLAND
P. POLAND
C-S CZECHOSLOVAKIA
H HUNGARY
R RUMANIA
Y-S YUGOSLAVIA
B BULGARIA
A ALBANIA

Russian occupation
zones, Germany &
Austria

U. S. S. R.

ARCTIC

SWEDEN

NORWAY

DENMARK

Baltic

GREAT
BRITAIN

GERMANY

FRANCE

SW.

AUS.

SPAIN

PORTUGAL

ITALY

Adriatic

Mediterranean

GREECE

Aegean

Straits

TURKEY

Black Sea

J.F.H.

FROM THE ARCTIC TO THE AEGEAN—
BY LAND AND BY SEA

MUCH has been written on the strategic maritime advantage gained for Russia by the construction of the Baltic-White Sea Canal, which has reduced the voyage from Archangel to Leningrad from the former 2,840 sea-miles to a distance of only 674 miles. The linking of the White Sea and the Baltic has indeed been one of the most important changes on the map of Russia since the Revolution.

But equally significant from the point of view of Atlantic strategy, is the short cut from the Baltic to the Mediterranean which the U.S.S.R. can now command through the group of States linked with her politically. From Stettin on the Baltic to Sasseno in the Adriatic, the Republics of Poland, Czechoslovakia, Hungary, Yugoslavia, Albania, run directly north-south from sea to sea, a bloc of Central European States of the Russian nexus. The accompanying map, showing the long sea route from the Arctic to the Aegean, and the short land corridor from the Baltic to the Mediterranean, indicates that the foreign policy of the Soviet Union is one fully alive to the importance of sea power.

(The map also suggests that this may be the century of the Slavs.)

Russian railway through Finland to Narvik. Today, in the development of Petsamo as a naval base by the Soviet Union and in the conception of the Atlantic Pact by other Powers, the importance of the North Atlantic in strategic considerations is apparent.

Indicative of the increasing interest of Russia in Norway, and based on long-term considerations of maritime strategy as well as on her desire for security as regards neighbouring States, was the Soviet Union's opposition to the negotiations for the inclusion of Norway in the Atlantic defence alliance. Today the Soviet Union has a common frontier with Norway.

Extension of interest in the north-western Atlantic seaboard on the part of Russia will inevitably affect Britain at a most sensitive point. As D. J. Dallin observes in his study of the three major World Powers,[1] it has always been a maxim of British policy in Europe to support the small nations on the Atlantic coast, as Norway, Denmark, Holland, Belgium, and Portugal constitute a British line of defence against the strongest Powers on the Continent. (The union of the Netherlands with Belgium in 1815 was the work of Britain who then needed such a buffer against any revival of French aggrandisement. Today it is the Irish seaboard which assumes a new importance in relation to the Atlantic aims of the World Powers.)

But America, even more than Britain, is affected today by Russian aims in the North Atlantic. That ocean merges, in its northernmost waters, with the Arctic one. It is here, above those seas, on the Polar trunk lines of tomorrow, that the geography of today has brought America and Russia closer to each other than they have ever been before. This was sharply manifested when in 1944 the Soviet Union asked the Norwegian Government to agree to a revision of the Spitzbergen Treaty of 1920 by which the recognition of the sovereignty of Norway over the Spitzbergen Archipelago had been affirmed by the major Powers. Russia based her objection to the treaty on the fact that she had not been a party to it; in 1925 she had given *de facto* and in 1935 *de jure* adherence to it. By the terms of the treaty Norway had undertaken "never to build, or permit the building of, naval bases in the territories specified," and not to construct any fortifications or permit the islands to be used for warlike purposes. The reference to naval bases may surprise many who are unaware that part of the coasts of Spitzbergen are affected by the Gulf Stream. The deep fjords in the archi-

[1] *The Big Three.* (Allen & Unwin, 1946); p. 50.

pelago, which can take vessels up to destroyer capacity, will have additional value with the development of super-submarines and their special uses in Arctic warfare.

When in 1947 Russia again opened the question of treaty revision, she stated that she had special interests in the archipelago, and claimed that the treaty disregarded Soviet security. She therefore proposed that Russia and Norway should jointly undertake the defence of Spitzbergen—a proposal which would require a revision of the 1920 treaty.

Although the coal of Spitzbergen is no negligible economic factor—part of Russia's Arctic fleet being supplied by fuel from the Barentsburg mines at Ice Fjord—it was the strategic, far more than the economic advantages offered by Spitzbergen, which made the Soviet Government anxious to secure control over this territory. Spitzbergen is on the edge of the Polar Ice-Cap; the Russian move was to gain a vantage point in the race for the Arctic airways. Air and sea bases on Spitzbergen would counter the American bases on Greenland, from which Spitzbergen is little more than 450 miles. The archipelago is also only 900 miles east of Iceland, while the distance which separates it from Ellesmere Island in Canada's northern territory is less than 1,760 miles. The acquisition of Spitzbergen could thus provide Russia with an offensive base on the North Atlantic, as well as a defensive one for her own Arctic coast and her naval ports of Molotovsk, Murmansk and Poliarnoye.

In the far southern regions of the Atlantic, as well as in those we have been considering in the extreme north, Russia has also shown an interest, though this was more than a hundred years earlier. During the Spanish-American crisis of 1819-20, the Tsar's Government displayed concern lest the United States should acquire Florida.[1] How far the interest which Russia showed as well in Cuba, and in Spain's revolted colonies in South America, was due to her desire for expansion southward on the American seaboard, has not so far been made known. The weakness of his navy at that time forced the Tsar to adopt a vacillating policy towards the issue of Spanish-American relations. But, as the despatches of Pinckney, the American ambassador to St. Petersburg at this time show, the United States was becoming seriously apprehensive about Russian aims on the American mainland.

Still farther south in the Atlantic, Russian ships found their

[1] See Count Nesselrode to P. de Poletica, 27 November, 1819. *Annals of Congress, 16th Congress, 2nd Session, 1820-21*; p. 1,402.

way about this time, when Captain Bellingshausen in the sloop-of-war *Vostok*, and Lieut. Lazarev in the *Mirny*, sailed to Antarctic waters, and reached latitude 69° 52′ S. Bellingshausen, who had sailed as a lieutenant with the Krusenstern expedition, achieved the distinction of circumnavigating the Antarctic Ocean, and thus completing the circle which Cook, in a slightly more northerly latitude, had nearly made. *Within* the South Polar Circle these two navigators between them covered a large sector of the circumference of the Antarctic Ocean.

Bellingshausen's expedition was scientific in purpose, and was conducted throughout with a meticulous regard for detail; soundings were taken wherever possible, and the South Shetlands were surveyed as far as conditions would allow. The sea named after Bellingshausen lies west of Graham Land and south-west of Drake Strait. The Commander's discovery of Alexander I Land (which, however, he mistook for mainland) led him to sight the fringe of the Antarctic Continent, though he failed to recognise it for such.

Belief in the maritime destiny of Russia was almost an article of faith with the Emperor Alexander I, whose instructions to Bellingshausen included a direction that the voyagers should use their stay in foreign possessions and in lands newly discovered, "for the advantage of future Russian navigators".

The expedition was treated characteristically with a considerable amount of secrecy, and not till ten years after his return was Bellingshausen's own account of the voyage made public. He had discovered twenty-nine islands, nineteen of which were in the tropics.[1] His account of a voyage of no less than 57,073½ miles, concludes with a sentence mediæval in its quaintness and at the same time suggestive of his German origins: "One coral reef and one lagoon were also discovered."

---

[1] *The Voyage of Captain Bellingshausen into the Antarctic Seas, 1819-1821*, translated by Frank Debenham. (Printed for the Hakluyt Society, 1945); p. 465. 2 vols.

XIII

THE BALTIC

FOR many centuries the Baltic has been a zone contested by the Great Powers: Sweden and Russia, Germany and Russia, have in turn fought for supremacy there. It is in the Baltic area that Russia meets the West, and this gives it a special importance. "In a political sense the eastern Baltic area forms the frontier line between immense Russia and the western world. The issues do not arise in the Baltic and with rare exceptions are not decided there. But they always find a clear reflection there."[1]

The Baltic Republics form part of the great Russian Plain which—the Urals excepted—stretches from the Baltic to the Yenesei (a fact which favours the development of inland navigation). The non-mountainous nature of these Republics has always made it difficult for Russia to defend her western frontiers. In the thirteenth and fourteenth centuries the Baltic Provinces were largely dominated by the East Prussian Group of Teutonic Knights, and the ports of those Provinces were worked in the interests of the Hanseatic League, of which Germany was virtually head. Even the trade passing through Novgorod the Great was controlled by the German "courts" of Lübeck and the "yards" of Gotland. The Hanse merchant fleets sailed the seas of Europe bringing not only the wares of the West to Russia, but taking from that country its tallow, hides, skins, and oil, to other lands. Never till the time of Peter the Great did a Russian trading fleet take the waters of the Baltic. Cities had grown up along its shores which were German in character (but the hinterland remained Slav); Germany in the twentieth century sought to revive that domination of the Baltic and its coastlands which she had exercised in the fourteenth. For commercial as well as strategic reasons the Third Reich pursued that aim, since Germany's foreign trade before the outbreak of the last war was highest with the Baltic countries. Sweden, Norway, Finland, and Denmark accounted for 10 per cent. of Germany's imports and 12 per cent. of

[1] Gregory Meiksins, *The Baltic Riddle*. (A. A. Wyn, Inc., New York); p. 5.

her exports.[1] (The United Kingdom came next, the figures being 5.7 per cent. of Germany's imports and 7.3 per cent. of her exports.) It will be realised that the lowness of these figures is apparent rather than real, for Germany's trade was widely distributed.

The great German rivers, the Weser, the Elbe, and the Oder, have determined the situation of Germany's ports, and since the construction of the Kiel Canal it was inevitable that Germany should be one of the leading Powers on the Baltic. At a conference held in 1908, efforts to neutralise that sea had resulted in the passing of a resolution by Russia, Germany, Sweden, Denmark, which virtually excluded the influence of non-Baltic countries from that region. But World War I brought the Allies there; later the Anglo-German Naval Agreement of 1935 gave Germany scope for extending her power in the Baltic at the expense of the other countries. World War II saw Russia break that power by regaining the Baltic Republics. The latter, collectively, possess a seaboard on one of the most important zones of the sea. "If either Russia or Germany were to take possession of these countries, the Baltic Sea would be in danger of becoming little more than a Baltic Lake," stated the authors of the Report of the Royal Institute of International Affairs in 1938.[2] Yet only three years earlier the Anglo-German Naval Agreement which gave Germany the right to build submarines (prohibited by the Versailles treaty), had brought the Baltic well within the possibility of its becoming a German lake.

Russia, for her part, had long aimed at supremacy in these waters, and her wars with Sweden in the seventeenth and eighteenth centuries were largely inspired by that aim. Under Catherine the Great a rapid increase in the Russian Baltic Fleet between 1787 and 1789 was designed to this end, and had brought the strength of the flotilla up to more than one hundred and fifty. The Swedish king, Gustav III, hoping to regain Finnish territory, had re-opened the Baltic Wars. The various engagements had culminated in the second battle of Svenskund, Viborg Bay, in 1790, and though the Russian flotilla was defeated, it remained numerically the stronger one —so much so, indeed, after Sweden's total loss of ten battle-ships, that Gustav's navy was no longer in a position to oppose Catherine's. Her Baltic Fleet helped her to get Lithuania, also

[1] Robert Dickinson, *The German Lebensraum*. (Penguin Special, 1943); p. 161.
[2] *The Baltic States*. The Royal Institute of International Affairs. (Oxford University Press, 1938); p. 62. Reproduced by permission of the O.U.P.

Courland (part of Latvia), and with the latter the valuable harbour of Windau (Ventspils), so that Russia had at last gained a warm-water port on the Baltic. Esthonia she had already acquired under Peter the Great by the Peace of Nystadt. But after the Treaty of Brest-Litovsk, 1918, the Baltic States, the Moonsund Islands, and every Baltic port, were occupied by German forces. Brest-Litovsk imprisoned the Russian fleet by denying it access to any harbour except Kronstadt Bay. Before that, Libau (Latvia) and Paldiski (Esthonia) had been Russia's principal naval bases after Kronstadt.

In Imperial times Libau (Liepaja) was a naval arsenal; but it had the disadvantage of being close to the German frontier, which made its evacuation necessary in the first world war, and in 1914 the base was dismantled. The Russian Commander-in-Chief, who was able to retain Helsingfors and Reval, also used Lapvik, near Hangoe, and British submarines too had harbourage here. The value of Liepaja has risen since the acquisition of Memel and Koenigsberg, because until then, Liepaja, 450 miles from the main Baltic base of Kronstadt, was a somewhat isolated naval outpost. As a channel connects the port of Liepaja with the sea, ships here are sheltered, but there is always the danger that the canal mouth can be blocked by enemy action, Kaliningrad (Koenigsberg) would, in an aggressive Reich, threaten Liepaja, seventy-five miles to the north. That is one reason why the Russians took care that Koenigsberg should be theirs after the drawing of the Polish-German frontiers at the end of World War II. The Germans in the past however, have been just as apprehensive of an invasion by sea from Russia, and in 1918 most of what remained of the German navy was kept in the Baltic. But when two years later the Baltic States had gained their independence, it had meant the reduction of Russia's Baltic coast to less than a hundred miles. All that Russia then had was a strip at the head of the Finnish Gulf. And she no longer controlled direct communication from Moscow and Leningrad to the ports of Tallinn, Pärnau, and Paldiski in Esthonia; the Soviets secured however free transit to those ports, and when in that year—1920—their Government made peace treaties with the new Baltic Republics, it may be noted that Esthonia was the first of the Border States with which a treaty was made.[1]

[1] Treaty of Tartu with Esthonia, of Moscow with Lithuania, of Riga with Latvia.

The strategic importance of the Baltic States has constantly
been emphasised by German military as well as naval writers.
After the Treaty of Brest-Litovsk the Germans, in addition to
the Baltic States, had the principal Finnish bases. Ludendorff's
memoirs[1] reveal what the German designs were at that time.
"We now hold positions at Viborg and Narva which would at
any time enable us to advance on Petrograd." In 1918 when
Hindenburg was asked why he needed the Baltic Provinces,
he replied: "to manœuvre my left wing in the next war".
Hitler rated their value no less highly than Hindenburg did.
"Possibly his very first step as Chancellor of the Reich in 1933
was the general fortification of the Pomeranian and Prussian
coasts."[2] So important were the Baltic States to the plans of
"Operation Barbarossa"—Hitler's scheme for his intended
attack on Russia—that at a German naval conference held on
2 January, 1941, Hitler, discussing the forthcoming invasion,
said: "It must be remembered that the main aim is to gain
possession of the Baltic States and Leningrad." Accordingly,
five months later, armed forces of the Reich invaded the Baltic
Republics. Germany, once she regained her status as a Great
Power, had no intention of letting those States remain independent. She had always regarded them as ground for colonising,
and for developing her own Baltic trade. Hitler's seizure of
Memel in 1939 had been an immediate threat to the Baltic
countries: no time had been lost by the Germans in building
a high road from Memel to the Lithuanian port of Palanga,
and in constructing a naval port in Memel with special facilities
for a U-boat flotilla. On the occasion of Hitler's visit there, just
before he seized that city, the need for enlarging the harbour
was demonstrated when the German Fleet was obliged to anchor
outside the port. Plans for this enlargement were regarded by
the Russians as a direct threat. Russia herself, desirous of getting
a warm-water port on the Middle Baltic, had long coveted
ice-free Memel, though when she later acquired Liepaja she
had gained a warm-water port. Her subsequent demand for
Koenigsberg (Kaliningrad), which the Poles had expected
would be theirs after the end of the war, was therefore unnecessary so far as the gain of an ice-free harbour was concerned.
Moreover Kaliningrad is not invariably ice-free. The reasons

[1] *Meine Kriegserinnerungen, 1914-1918.* [Translation taken from the English
edition, *Concise Ludendorff Memoirs, 1914-1918.* (Hutchinson, 1933.)] Acknowledgments also to Albert Bonnier, Stockholm.
[2] W. E. Hart, "Germans' Exposed Flank Along the Baltic Coast." *The
Daily Telegraph.*

why Russia did insist on getting that harbour are strategic
reasons. That base, now used as an advance one for the Red
Navy, is a most important one on the Baltic. Almost exactly in
the middle of the eastern littoral of that sea, naval planes are
within rapid striking distance of all the Russian ports, also of
Copenhagen, and of the Swedish islands of Öland and Gotland.
Half-way between Memel and Danzig, Kaliningrad can, from
its position on the Gulf of Danzig, neutralise the value of the
latter harbour. East Prussia without Koenigsberg (Kaliningrad)
is an emasculation. From that harbour ships can pass up the
Frische Haff through a twenty-nine-mile-long channel to the
port of Pillau. This canal, cut through the sand-bar known as
Frische Nehrung, enables ships to reach the port of Elbing—
once a Prussian but now a Polish port, and connected by a
channel with the Vistula. Kaliningrad ranks as a first-class
naval fortress: it stands four-and-a-half miles from the mouth of
the Pregel where that river enters the Frische Haff, and is fortified on both banks.

The next port of size on the southern shore of the Baltic is
Gdynia, retained by Poland, but used by the Russians for
salving German shipping of every description after the second
world war. Here they commenced work on the intended raising
of the battleship *Gneisenau*, which the Germans had used as
a block-ship at one of the harbour entrances; here too the
Russians salved the ex-battleship *Schleswig-Holstein*.

Opposite Gdynia, across the bay, lies the port of Danzig
which is usually ice-free all the year round. Here there is very
little current, and deep-water vessels can dock in the harbour.
But before the building of Gdynia the port of Danzig was
becoming inadequate for dealing with the growing Polish
trade. The decision made at Potsdam 1945, that the port of
Stettin should be administered by Poland, was designed to
assist the expansion of Polish exports in a new industrial development of that country. Since then however, this port has been
presented to Czechoslovakia, a country so closely contained
within the Russian orbit as to have the effect of giving the
Soviet Union a port much farther west on the Baltic than had
been foreseen at Potsdam. Still farther west, the port of
Warnemünde began to be developed by the Russians in 1946 as
a strongly fortified naval base.[1] This is in line with pre-Revolution policy which aimed at acquiring all East Prussia and its
coastline to Stettin, and establishing Russian naval bases on this

[1] For details see Special Correspondent, *The Daily Telegraph*, 3.9.1946.

littoral. In fact, approximately the same frontier on the south-east Baltic was marked by Russia for herself in the first world war as was actually occupied by her after the second.

By the terms of the Berlin Conference (Potsdam) 1945, it was agreed that, pending the final determination of territorial questions at the Peace settlement, the section of the western frontier of the U.S.S.R. which is adjacent to the Baltic Sea, "should pass from a point on the eastern shore of the Bay of Danzig to the east, north of Braunsberg-Goldap, to the meeting point of the frontiers of Lithuania, the Polish Republic, and East Prussia." Thus Russian Baltic territory was increased by the acquisition of a triangular region, having its apex at Memel, and its base along a line drawn from a point between Brauns-berg and Koenigsberg to a point north-east of Goldap. The inclusion of Koenigsberg in this region, and the fact that the north-eastern shore of the Bay of Danzig passed to the Soviet Union, meant that Russia was now assured of that dominance of the Baltic which had been a main objective of Peter the Great. Truly has it been said that the Baltic is an immovable salient into the heart of western Russia,[1] and the rulers of modern Russia are determined at all costs to safeguard that western region from any penetration of so vulnerable a zone as the north-eastern Baltic.

If we turn now to the economic importance of the eastern Baltic countries, their effect on Russia's trade will be seen from the fact that up to 1920 (when the Border States gained their independence) 30 per cent. of Russia's exports and 35 per cent. of her imports passed through these countries. (As regards the actual foreign trade of the Baltic States however, by far the greatest part was with the United Kingdom. In the period 1937-8 Britain's share of the total foreign trade of the Baltic States collectively was between one-third and one-half. Germany was the best customer of those countries after the United Kingdom. In that same period the Latvian Government instituted a shipping company for carrying cargo to British and German ports. It was the Russian acquisition of Esthonia, Latvia, and Lithuania in 1940 which changed the trade balance in favour of the Soviet Union.) The incorporation in the U.S.S.R. of the Baltic States was, from the Russian standpoint, a change as necessary as it was inevitable. They were a natural outlet for commerce and a gateway to the open seas.

[1] *Cards on the Table: An Interpretation of Labour's Foreign Policy.* (The Labour Party, Transport House, 1947); p. 11.

In 1927, Russia, with a view to augmenting the exports between herself and Latvia, had undertaken to increase her use of the Latvian ports. In this way an impetus had been given to the expansion of these Baltic harbours and to the improvement of their rail communications with Russia. The following figures for shipping entering the Baltic ports in 1938 show that Riga was still the principal port for commerce a year before the outbreak of the second world war:—

Riga	..	..	..	..	.. 1,243,000 tons net
Tallinn ..	..	..	..	..	957,000 „ „
Memel ..	..	..	..	..	845,000 „ „
Ventspils..	..	..	..	..	325,000 „ „
Liepaja ..	..	..	..	..	298,000 „ „

In Lithuania, plans had been made before 1939 to build up a merchant service, a start having already been made by the *Maistas* co-operative society. The Lithuanians had also aimed at developing Sventoji, near the Latvian border, from a small fishing village into a modern port. When the Germans seized Memel in 1940, Lithuania lost her only harbour of any size on the Baltic. The consequences of German control of any port on the eastern shores of that sea had been foreseen much earlier by the Latvian Minister of Foreign Affairs, M. Felix Cielens: "If we permit any state hostile to Russia to establish its political influence in our territory, we can with mathematical certainty, forecast political pressure from the East. If we permit such places as the terminals of Russian sea-bound railways, the harbours of Riga, Ventspils, Liepaja and the strategic islands of Oesel and Dagoe to become bases for operations hostile to Russia, I say emphatically that under such circumstances counter operations from the East are inevitable. Russia will strive to eliminate influences hostile to herself, and seek to establish her own political hegemony."[1] Those circumstances did arise, and accordingly on 28 September, 1939, Russia made with Esthonia a pact, the third article of which shows the importance that the U.S.S.R. attached to the Esthonian ports and islands: "The Esthonian Republic secures to the Soviet Union the right to maintain naval bases and several aerodromes for aviation on lease at reasonable terms on the Esthonian islands of Saaremaa (Oesel), Hiiumaa (Dagoe) and in the town

[1] *The International Situation of the Baltic States and the Tasks of Latvian Foreign Policy.* (In Lettish.) Riga, 1927. Cited by Gregory Meiksins, in *The Baltic Riddle;* p. 111.

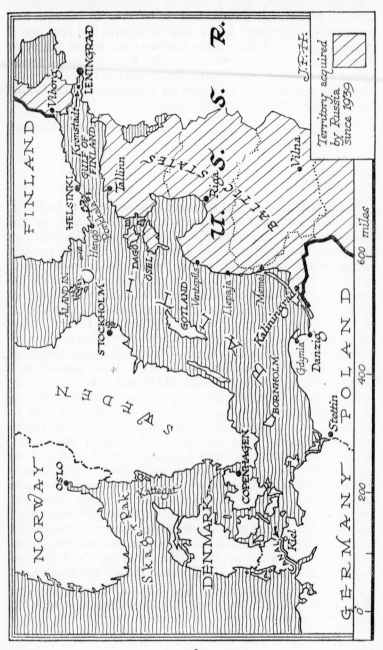

R.

FINLAND

Viborg

Kronstädt
LENINGRAD

HELSINKI

GULF OF FINLAND

Hangö Porkkala

Tallinn

ÅLAND IS.

DAGÖ

ÖSEL

U. S. S. R.

Riga

BALTIC STATES

Vilna

STOCKHOLM

GOTLAND

Ventspils

Liepaja

Memel

Kaliningrad

SWEDEN

Skager Rak

Kattegat

BORNHOLM

Gdynia

Danzig

NORWAY

OSLO

Stettin

DENMARK

KIEL CANAL

Kiel

COPENHAGEN

GERMANY

POLAND

Territory acquired
by Russia
since 1939

J.F.H.

0   200   400   600 miles

FROM the earliest days of European maritime enterprise, the Baltic has been one of the principal tradeways between eastern and western Europe. The rise of the Hanse towns gave a fresh impulse to trade on the Baltic, and under Tsar Boris, towards the end of the sixteenth century Riga, Dorpat, and Reval were open ports to the ships of the Hanse cities. In the same century, agents of the Muscovy Company followed much of the track now taken by the Baltic–White Sea Canal: the route of Sparke and Southam for instance, in 1566, after leaving Solovetski Island in the White Sea, took those travellers to Soroka Bay and up the River Vyg to Lake Voitsk, thence to Lake Onega. From here they sailed on to the River Svir and to Lake Ladoga (then they turned south to strike the old trade route to Novgorod.)[1]

Kronstadt, the principal European naval base of the U.S.S.R., was the creation of Peter the Great; in 1917 it played a leading part in the early scenes of the Russian Revolution. Four years later the sailors of the warships *Sevastopol* and *Petropavlosk* revolted here in sympathy with the workers' strike action against the Petrograd Soviet, and presented their "Fifteen Demands", which included freedom of speech, of assembly, and of elections. In the second world war the Red Banner Baltic Fleet, based on Kronstadt, prevented the Germans from making

a seaward assault on Leningrad; on the coastal side the enemy could get no nearer than Oranienbaum. The fleet was greatly helped here by the Soviet Union's acquisition in 1940 of the Baltic Republics, whose continued existence as independent States after 1939 was an impossibility—either they went to Russia or to the Reich.

Command of Tallinn and of the northern shore of Estonia meant command of the Gulf of Finland's southern approach to Leningrad. The acquisition of Latvia meant the gain of the important harbour of Riga, and of the ice-free ports of Ventspils (Windau) and Liepaja (Libau). These two places also provided bases on the Baltic for Russia's Naval Air Arm. Lithuania brought her another ice-free port in Memel. With the acquisition of Koenigsberg (Kaliningrad) Russia can dominate the Bay of Danzig, and this has become her principal naval base on the southern Baltic. In 1947 the German armoured ship ex-*Luetzow*, sunk in the Baltic, but salved by the Russians, was towed to Kaliningrad, and here too, from Stettin, came the hull of the aircraft carrier ex-*Graf Zeppelin* (2,500 tons, 30 knots.)

Russia's losses in the Baltic in World War II included 56 submarines and the ice-breaker *Sibiriakov* (1,140 tons); the first ship to make the voyage from Archangel to Vladivostok in one navigation season.

[1] See map of their journey, facing p. 190 in Vol. II, *Early Voyages and Travels to Russia and Persia*, by Anthony Jenkinson and other Englishmen. Printed for the Hakluyt Society, 1886.

of Paldiski (Baltiski Port). The exact sites for the bases and aerodromes shall be allotted and their boundaries defined by mutual agreement."

The reference in this article to the islands of Oesel and Dagoe, recalls the fact that they had been specifically mentioned in the treaty made between Russia and Esthonia in 1920. At that time the two countries had agreed to accede to the conditions of any international agreement which might in future be made for neutralising the Finnish Gulf. No such international agreement was made, "although in 1925-6 the Finnish and Esthonian Governments negotiated agreements with the U.S.S.R., relating to the control over the Gulf and assuring free passage of Soviet vessels to Soviet ports."[1] Esthonia had declined to neutralise the islands of Saaremaa (Oesel) and Hiiumaa (Dagoe).

The 1939 Pact with Esthonia included a mutual undertaking to give military assistance in the event of direct aggression or threat of aggression from any great European Power against the sea frontiers as well as the land ones of Russia and Esthonia. (Both Esthonia and Latvia had previously, in the spring of 1939, rejected Moscow's offer of military assistance when the Baltic Republics had been threatened by Germany.) In May 1940 Russian forces entered Lithuania, Latvia, and Esthonia, and in accordance with the terms of the 1939 Pacts, they established naval garrisons at the chief ports—Palanga, Liepaja, Ventspils, Riga, Paldiski. Of the Russian occupation of the Republics, D. J. Dallin, in *Soviet Russia's Foreign Policy, 1939-1942*,[2] asks, how was this venture to be explained to the outside world, undertaken as it was at a time when the Ribbentrop-Molotov Pact was in operation, and moreover at a time when Russo-German relations were closest? Strategically viewed, the Russian occupation of the Baltic States could have one country only in mind—the one dominating the Baltic, and that was Germany. But in view of the Pact, he says, another country must be named, and so England was chosen. Publicity was given to the fact that the British Fleet had sailed up the Baltic in 1919 to attack Kronstadt, and that naval manoeuvres had taken place in the Baltic after the first world war. The question of the purchase by Britain of Oesel Island was, it was stated, being considered by His Majesty's Government.

[1] *The Baltic States.* Information Department of the Royal Institute of International Affairs. (Oxford University Press, 1938); p. 66. Reproduced by permission of the O.U.P.

[2] Yale University Press, 1942; pp. 81, 82.

The Pact of 1939 between Russia and Esthonia was followed by a Trade Agreement which concerned the passage of freight from Russian and from Esthonian territory, and the reciprocal use of ports for this. Russia was expanding her trade with the Baltic. After the incorporation of Esthonia in the U.S.S.R. in 1940, an impetus was given to the shipbuilding industry in the Russo-Baltic yards of Tallinn. Work was also commenced on developing the small Esthonian ports of Narva-Jonsuu and Pärnau. In that year too Soviet engineers began to reconvert the harbour of Paldiski—which for long had been used primarily as a fishing port—into a naval base. Once Russia had acquired this defence location on the southern shore of the Finnish Gulf, and Hangoe on the northern, she could protect Leningrad on both flanks. Paldiski has an entrance free of shoals and has good anchorage. It is easier to defend than the Latvian port of Liepaja, because opposite the latter, in mid-Baltic, is the island of Gotland (highly fortified by the Swedes after the outbreak of war in Europe in 1939); nevertheless Russia by 1946 was maintaining both large and light naval forces at Liepaja. Here too Soviet engineers reconditioned the U-boats which had been assigned to Russia as part of her share of the German Fleet.

The importance of Paldiski was made clear to all students of naval warfare in September 1944, when after the boom in the Finnish Gulf had been cut, this naval base was recaptured from the Germans. Only then did the Russian Baltic Fleet have freedom to move out of the Gulf of Finland into the Baltic, and to cut off a good part of Schoerner's Northern Army from escape by water. The fleet was not yet in full control of the sea however, and a considerable force of Lindemann's army had managed by mid-September to get out of Esthonia and Latvia by sea to Danzig. But with the acquisition of bases at Paldiski and the Moonsund Islands, the Russian Fleet now commanded the whole *northern* coast of Esthonia. The Moonsund Islands, Dagoe and Oesel, had always been, from Russia's point of view, vital to the security of her principal naval base Kronstadt, also to Leningrad; and the incorporation of these islands in the U.S.S.R. was now justified by results. Whoever is in possession of those Esthonian islands and of bases on the southern shore of Finland, can close the entrance to the Finnish Gulf. These islands can also cut the iron ore supply from Sweden. "I know from my trip in the Baltic this year," wrote the Hague Correspondent of *The Manchester*

Guardian,[1] "that it was Germany who advised the Finns to fortify the Aaland Islands and advised Esthonia to fortify the islands of Dagoe and Oesel—a scheme which was in preparation and which was intended by the Germans to bottle up Russia in the Gulf of Finland."

As important to Russia as Paldiski, is Narva, near the famous "Narva Gap" between the Baltic coast and the head of Lake Peipus. This harbour gives the Soviet Union command of Narva Bay; midway between Tallinn and Kronstadt it stands on the line from Tallinn to Leningrad via Rakvere. Formerly the frontier town of the Russian-Esthonian border, Narva was for long the eastern key to the Republic of Esthonia. Its acquisition by Russia strengthened the position of the Baltic Fleet; in the spring of 1942 that fleet, which had for long been imprisoned in the ice, steamed into Narva Bay. Its ships later covered General Govorov's motorised infantry advance across the River Narva; at that time the Germans were reported to have in the Baltic two 10,000-ton pocket battleships, two heavy cruisers, four light cruisers and a small destroyer flotilla.[2]

Until 1940, when Russia had secured the western seaboard of Esthonia, naval action was much restricted for her. And until she had acquired the warm-water ports in Latvia her fleet was virtually imprisoned for several months in the year. The Gulf of Finland, two hundred miles long, to which the Russian Baltic Fleet was formerly confined, is full of shoals and shallows, and there is ice usually from December to April. But now that the Soviet Navy has room to manœuvre, and freedom of action in the Baltic, we may expect to see impressive training displays in those waters.

Almost as important to Russia as the Esthonian harbours and islands, are the ports of Latvia. On 5 October, 1939, Russia and Latvia signed a Pact of Mutual Assistance in which Article III stated: "For the purpose of guaranteeing the security of the U.S.S.R. and consolidating her own independence, the Latvian Republic grants the Union the right to maintain naval bases in the town of Liepaja (Libava) and Ventspils (Vindava) and several aerodromes for aviation on lease at reasonable terms. The exact sites for the bases and aerodromes shall be allotted and their boundaries defined by mutual agreement."

The ports of Liepaja and Ventspils above mentioned, are

[1] 6.11.1939.
[2] Figures given by Commander Oelberg, Swedish Navy, as reported by Special Correspondent, Stockholm. *The Daily Mail*, 31.1.1944.

warm-water ones. The usefulness of the latter, when the Baltic has sometimes frozen to a depth of twenty feet, needs no emphasis. Liepaja (which up to 1940 had a free port) and Ventspils, are deeper than the other harbours along the shallow coast of Latvia, but even so the use of these ports for larger vessels is limited.

The incorporation of the Baltic States with the U.S.S.R. brought within the territory of the Soviet Union the principal Latvian port of Riga, which in Tsarist times ranked as Russia's third largest port in the west, coming after Petrograd and Odessa. Riga is ice-locked from December to March, but under normal conditions it has, as the chief harbour in a gulf one hundred miles long and sixty miles wide, a value which has never been overlooked either by Russians or Germans. Further, its communications with important centres inland make Riga a definite objective in any campaign directed from the Baltic against the Soviet Union. "From a strategic point of view it is interesting to note that both the ports of Riga and Liepaja, via the Latvian junction of Daugavspils (Dvinsk) are on the direct Vitebsk-Smolensk line."[1] Russia, by the incorporation of Latvia, also gained the small, but commercially useful port of Jelgava on the Lielupe, built during the ten-year period 1920-30.

After the signing of the Mutual Pact of Assistance with Latvia, *Pravda* wrote: "Already the Mutual Assistance Pact between the U.S.S.R. and Esthonia, which gave the Soviet Union the right to have in the islands of Oesel and Dagoe and in the town of Baltiski bases for its naval fleet and a number of aerodromes for its aviation, has altered the position in the Baltic. Leningrad and the whole north-west of the U.S.S.R. is now defended, not only on the side of Kronstadt, but also on that of Oesel, Dagoe and Baltiski. And now the security of north-western U.S.S.R. will be further strengthened in the towns of Libava and Ventspils (Vindava) by the establishment of bases for a naval fleet and aerodromes for aviation."

The reference to aerodromes in the foregoing article is of significance, inasmuch as an airfield was completed by the Germans just before the outbreak of the war at Spilves Plava, near Riga. Russia was never under any illusion as to Germany's intentions to dominate the Baltic. In July 1939 the Soviet Baltic Fleet had gone on a three days' cruise, after the Baltic States had declined to accept the Russian guarantee of security.

[1] L. F. Gray, "The Baltic States," *The Trident*; Vol. VI, No. 58.

It was noticeable at the time that the fleet, which sailed round Gotland, had taken a course to the left of the Aaland Islands, to whose proposed re-fortification Russia had stated that she was opposed unless it was undertaken by the Finns without third-party assistance. On 10 October, 1939, Russia completed her efforts to frustrate German designs by making the Third Pact of Mutual Assistance with a Baltic State—Lithuania. In the subsequent incorporation of the Baltic Republics can be seen the logical sequence to the policy of Ivan IV, Alexis, Peter I, and Catherine the Great. There was a reversal of the German-dictated Treaty of Brest-Litovsk, when in the Russo-German negotiations of 1939 it was arranged that Russia should have a free hand with the Baltic States.

But notwithstanding her Pact with Germany, Russia increased her estimates for defence from 27,000,000,000 roubles in 1938 to 57,000,000,000 in 1940, and the need for strengthening her navy, particularly the Red Banner Fleet of the Baltic, was regarded as paramount.

FINLAND

If we look at the map, we shall find that the best approach to Petrograd is from the Baltic, and that the shortest and easiest route is through Finland, whose frontiers are only about thirty miles distant from the Russian capital. Finland is the key to Moscow.

The Times., 17.4.1919.

The quotation above shows the danger to which Russia is exposed if a Power hostile to her threatens Finland, and it shows that such a danger was recognised in Britain a quarter of a century ago. That Russia recognised it in 1939, as she also did earlier, was evidenced by her attack on Finland with whom she had a Pact of Non-Aggression. Writing of the period immediately after the Ribbentrop-Molotov Pact, Maurice Hindus, in *Russia Fights On,*[1] says: "I had heard in Stockholm that Admiral Raeder, chief of the German Navy, on learning of the concessions Ribbentrop had yielded to Russia in the Baltic, raged with fury and threatened to resign from his command. Sailor that he was, he feared that Russia might put herself in a position to sever communications with the ports through which Germany received the Swedish ore she had to have for the manufacture of the higher grades of steel. The haste and clumsiness with which Russia had made her descent on Finland,

[1] Collins, 1942; p. 34.

were inspired by a frenzied wish to build new naval and aerial bases in the Gulf of Finland to be used, not against Finland, a country of three and one half millions, but against a big Power, in the first place against Germany."

With the close of the Russo-Finnish War in 1940, the Peace which was signed between the two countries gave to Russia the lease for thirty years[1] of the Finnish naval port of Hangoe. The waters within a radius of five sea miles to the south and east of Hangoe, and within three miles to the north and west of the peninsula, together with the islands in that area, were also ceded to the Soviet Union. It is only fifty miles across the sea from Hangoe to the Esthonian port of Paldiski, and when Russia acquired the latter it was clearly only a matter of time till she would take steps to lease a base on the other side of the Gulf. The ice-free harbour of Hangoe on the slender peninsula at the mouth of the Finnish Gulf, is ringed by small islands, and the nearby mainland consists of formidable cliffs. Hangoe has an additional importance in that it can cut off the iron ore supplies coming up from the Finnish port of Oulu on the Gulf of Bothnia. Thus its later return to Finland by the Russo-Finnish armistice agreement, 1944, while welcome to the Finns, came as a surprise to many who were unaware of the motives underlying such apparently conflicting moves in terms of Soviet strategy.

The whole Karelian Isthmus, and Viipuri (Viborg) with the bay and its islands—including the strategic ones of Hogland and Björkö which protect Viborg—were ceded to Russia by the Treaty of 1940. "Petersburg is the window on the Baltic, Viborg is the shutter to that window," Peter the Great had said. Viborg, which was the second town of Finland, is not only important as a fortress of the first rank, but as being linked by the Saimaa Canal with Finland's lakes; hence its possessor has direct access to the country's extensive inland waterways system. When Finland ceded Viborg she lost her greatest port for exports, and when she gave up Uuras near the entrance to the Saimaa Canal, she lost the chief port for her timber trade. Viborg, like other Finnish ports on the northern shore of the Gulf of Finland, can in hostile hands, menace the right flank of the Russian naval base of Kronstadt. When the Soviet Union acquired Viborg and its strategic islands, that danger was removed.

The ports of Oulu and Komi, on the Gulf of Bothnia, are

[1] For an annual payment of £30,000.

linked to the northern harbour of Petsamo by the highway running through Rovaniemi. (A railway, commencing at Helsinki, runs to Rovaniemi, and from there the motor road goes to Liinahamari on the shores of the Arctic.) Thus the Bothnian Gulf is connected with the Arctic, a fact which makes it essential both from the Russian and the Finnish point of view, that the Gulf should be kept out of enemy control. Another link with the Arctic is provided by the road from Salmijaervi in northern Finland, which runs to the port of Kirkenes in northern Norway. By the Peace terms signed on 13 March, 1940, Russia was given the right to use the Salla-Kemi railway from the Gulf of Bothnia across northern Finland. Article VI laid down that "As provided by the Treaty of 1920, the Soviet Union and her citizens are granted the right of unrestricted transit across the Petsamo region to Norway and back."

By the same peace terms, as will be remembered, Finland ceded to the U.S.S.R. the Finnish part of the Rybachi Peninsula commanding the entrance to Petsamo harbour; it was land vital to the Finns, and without it the value of Petsamo (which the Russians at that time evacuated), was much reduced. The Peninsula, however, had been Russian territory before the first world war.

Petsamo, which the Finns had acquired from Russia in 1920, was their prized outlet to the North Atlantic, their one ice-free port on the Arctic. In World War I the Germans, just before the Allied intervention, were pressing north through Finland to establish U-boat bases at Murmansk and Petsamo. In World War II Petsamo provided them with a main port of supply for northern Norway as well as for Finland. Between September 1939 and April 1940 (i.e. during part of the period of the Russo-German Pact), the Soviet Union permitted Germany to make use of the anchorage at Poliarnoye, and German merchant ships, particularly those engaged in the nickel trade, availed themselves of harbourage here. According to the publication (issued by the United States Department of State Documents) of records captured in Germany concerning Nazi-Soviet relations, 1939-41, von Schulenberg had received instructions on 5 September, 1940, to inform the Soviet Union that the German Navy "intends to abandon the base on the Murman coast, as such are now available in Norway".

Before they attacked the Soviet Union the Germans had stationed ships between Tromsoe in Northern Norway and Petsamo in Finland, as part of Admiral Raeder's plan was to cripple the Red Navy's Northern Fleet by seizing the Kola Peninsula, in this way depriving the Russians of their only ice-free supply port, Murmansk—used later by the Allied convoys. As early as 1936 the German War Minister von Blomberg had gone, ostensibly for a cruise, but in reality for investigation, round the North Cape. After 22 June, 1941, German troops were stationed in Russian Arctic territory, and threatened the approaches to Murmansk; it was thus not surprising that Petsamo Province was the subject of special attention in the Russo-Finnish Armistice Agreement of 1944. (The nickel mines in that region were one of the most important sources of Finland's capital wealth; unworked deposits had recently been discovered on the Kammikivi Tunturi Fell.) Its proximity to Murmansk, and the fact that this base is situated on a narrow strip of land along the northern frontiers of Russia and Finland, made it inevitably an area of particular concern to the Soviet Union's Northern Fleet.

Another region strategically important to one of Russia's fleets—the Ladoga Flotilla—and ceded by Finland to the U.S.S.R., was the territory surrounding Lake Ladoga, including Kakisalmi and Sortovala. In all, Finland gave up one-tenth of her territory to Russia.

Article V of the 1940 Treaty had laid down that: "Finland undertakes, as provided by the Peace Treaty of 1920, not to maintain in the waters along her coast on the Arctic Ocean naval and other armed ships, excepting armed ships of less than 100 tons displacement, which Finland has the right to maintain without restriction, she also has the right to maintain not more than 15 naval and other armed ships of a tonnage not exceeding 400 tons each.

"Finland undertakes, as was provided by the same Treaty, not to maintain in the said waters any submarines or armed aircraft.

"Finland similarly undertakes, as was provided by the same Treaty, not to establish on that coast military posts, naval bases or heavy repair shops of greater capacity than necessary for the above-mentioned ships and their armaments."

With provisions such as these, added to the loss of Viborg and its islands, Finland had virtually no ability to defend herself at sea. At the same time, the cessions made by the Finns in 1940 and 1944, will, by increasing the defensive power of her stronger neighbour Russia, ensure for Finland the minimum risk of invasion by a third Power.

THE WHITE SEA CANAL

The White Sea Canal has been the means of giving the Northern Fleet direct communication with the Baltic Fleet. Its strategic value was proved in the last war when it enabled Russian warships to make their way from the Baltic to safer waters, and also when it was used to relieve the one hard-pressed railway that connects the supply port of Murmansk with Leningrad. After receiving considerable war damage it was repaired and re-opened for transport in 1946. Known also as the Stalin Canal, this channel is really a system of water-ways linking the Neva, Lake Ladoga, the Svir, and Lake Onega, and in this way connecting Leningrad with the White Sea. This system has also shortened the distance from the White Sea to the Black Sea by over 2,160 miles. And it has provided a waterway from the Baltic to the Caspian, for a branch of this Canal links the southern end of Lake Onega with the Sheksna, a tributary of the Volga, whose delta debouches on the north-west corner of the Caspian Sea. The planned reconstruction of the sytem will enable the largest of the Volga steamers to go right up to the White Sea by 1950.

Today it is no longer necessary for ships sailing from Arch-angel to Odessa to make the long voyage through the Barents Sea and round the North Cape; their route now takes them across the Gulf of Onega, through the Stalin Canal to Lenin-grad, and thence down the Baltic. From the White Sea the Canal follows the Shijnia and the Vyg to Lake Vyg, thence by the Povenchanka River to the northern end of Lake Onega, a total distance of one hundred and forty miles. The actual length of the Canal itself is over seventy-five miles. A waterway linking the Baltic with the Black Sea, which would take larger ships, "is likely to be a *fait accompli* ere many years have passed," wrote F. T. Jane in 1900.[1] The Grand Duke Alexander Mikhail-ovitch was the sponsor of this scheme, but plans for connecting St. Petersburg with the Arctic had been made in the early nineteenth century by an Englishman, Adam Armstrong. His canal, via Lake Onega, would have greatly reduced the dis-tance between the Russian capital and Archangel. But long before this the waterways of the Neva, the Svir, and the lakes had been used by the merchants of old who made their way from Novgorod to the shores of the White Sea in their search for furs, and by this water route went the troops of Peter I who were sent against the Swedish soldiers in Finland. Peter the Great

[1] *The Imperial Russian Navy: Its Past, Present, and Future;* p. 414.

indeed, determined to make St. Petersburg not only a royal but a great mercantile capital, had dreamed of a waterway that would stretch from the Baltic to the Caspian. "This project did not appear to be of very difficult execution, by means of small canals which he caused to be made near Wistchniwoltchkock, between the two rivers of Tzen and of Smila; the first of which is joined to the Tweretz by the Volga, and the second enters into the Insda, which near the great Novgorod, is in confluence with the Wolchowa, that runs into the lake of Ladoga, out of which the River Newa issuing, disembogues into the sea below Petersburgh. But there was no making use of the lake of Ladog, it being subject to storms, and full of rocks and dangerous places."[1] The hazards presented by Lake Ladoga are further described in the same contemporary account: "The navigation on this lake is very difficult by reason of the deep water, few harbours, sorry shipping, and inexperience of the Russian seamen; and great is the danger in passing the three falls, at the entrance into the Neva. So that many vessels are yearly lost, to the exceeding detriment of St. Petersburg in point of merchandise, and especially of provisions, all supplies coming this way. And the accomplishing of the canal of communication betwixt the Volkoff and Neva, on which the Tsar is so intent, is the only expedient to remove these fatal inconveniences."[2]

And so Peter I had the canal made from Schlussellung "where it communicates with the Newa, and continues along the lake of Ladoga, as far as the town of that name, where it joins the River Wolkowa. It is in length about a hundred and four wersts, or twenty-six French leagues. The breadth is seventy feet, and the depth sixteen. The sides are cased with timbers, except a small space that is faced with stone. There are sluices along the canal to raise or fall the water."[3]

The construction of the White Sea Canal has involved the raising of the level of Lake Vyg and the building of a dam of considerable dimensions at Nadvoizy. Describing the construction of the Canal, Dr. V. Tchernavin[4] says: "There is a lock built at the outlet of the River Vyg, and the excess water is taken by canal, 20 km. lower; near Lake Shavan another dam

[1] *Memoirs of Russia, Historical, Political, and Military from the Year 1727 to 1744*; p. 62.
[2] *Ibid.*, pp. 111, 112.
[3] *Ibid.*, p. 62.
[4] *The Trident*, Vol. II, No. 13, p. 181.

has been constructed and a wooden lock obstructs the River Vyg. Farther down, towards the White Sea, the flow of waters of this river is regulated by three successive dykes and locks; these are the Palokorjinskaia, Matkojinenskaia and Vyg-ostrovskaia, the latter near the villages of Vyg-ostrov and Shijnia. The old village of Shijnia has been flooded and exists no longer. Altogether, there are five dams and twelve locks regulating the descent of water from Lake Vyg to the White Sea." Over the whole course there are thirty-two inner canals and in the construction of the waterway more than 200,000 forest acres had to be cleared, yet the work was done in twenty-one months.[1] On 18 May, 1933, a squadron of the Red Banner Baltic Fleet steamed for the first time through the newly opened White Sea Canal.

The strategic value of the latter is, of course, enhanced by the fact that the passage of ships via this waterway to the Arctic is less easily detected than via the route by the Baltic and North Atlantic. The importance of the Canal will increase when the existing plans for a main Arctic railway materialise. Branch lines have already been laid to various towns which will later be joined by means of a trunk line. The White Sea port of Soroka for instance, is now connected by rail with Kotlas on the Northern Dvina, and that line is extended to Siktivar at the confluence of the River Vychegda with the Northern Dvina. (Kotlas is the head of the river navigation, and the town is a centre of steamer building. Siktivar is likely to become an inland port of some importance, for besides its connection with the Vychegda and the Northern Dvina, it has easy water communications with the Kama, the Vyatka, and the Pechora.) The use of the White Sea Canal has made Soroka a port with a future. Situated at the mouth of the Vyg, on the western shore of the Gulf of Onega, it is the chief port on the western coast of the White Sea for the shipment of wood pulp, and of timber from the Karelian forests. South-east of Soroka, and at the White Sea terminal of the Stalin Canal, is the modern port of Byel-morsk. At the extreme end of the north-west arm of the White Sea is Kandalaksha, which exports aluminium as well as canned fish. From here the line is electrified to the naval base of Mur-mansk. Kem, on Popov Island, is a place chiefly concerned with the export of pit-props and plywood. As a port it had done good service during the first world war, for coal shipped by Britain

[1] Figures taken from *Monthly Review*. (Issued by the Moscow Narodny Bank, Ltd., London); Vol. VI, No. 7.

to Russia was discharged here at a high daily average rate.[1] From here in 1918 the steamship *Archangel Michael* had sailed with British troops to capture Onega on the White Sea.

Timber for Peter's Baltic Fleet had been taken up the Volga to the Tver, and up that river to Beonets, twenty-three miles from Novgorod, whence it was conveyed to Ladoga. It took a long time even up to 1933 for timber ships to reach Leningrad from Archangel—nearly two-and-a-half weeks, in fact. But since the opening of the White Sea Canal it has taken only one-third of that time. This advantage was one of benefit to a number of the schooners built in Finland as reparations for the Soviet Union. Two hundred such vessels were constructed and sent out to the principal seaports of the U.S.S.R.[2] At least two of them—three-masted barquentines—were in use as school sailing ships, one of which called at Plymouth in 1948. The building of such a substantial number of these vessels within a short time points to the Soviet Government's emphasis on its plans for mercantile expansion.

[1] C. E. Fayle, *Seaborne Trade*; Vol. III, p. 239.
[2] Most of them have sailed to Vladivostock, either via Suez or Panama. Several put in to San Pedro, California, for repairs, and four barquentines were at Colon early in 1948. *Aktinia, Jemchoog, Kalmar, Korall, Midija, Mercator, Sekstan,* are among the names of these vessels. (See article by John Lyman, *Spindrift*, June 1949. John Anderson, Falkirk.)

XIV

THE NAVIES OF RUSSIA

WE have now in our chronicle of Russia's seaward expansion, arrived at a point where the Soviet Union stands within easy distance of completing her historic march to the oceans. It is time therefore to consider the instruments which have helped her to reach this position, and those which in future will help her to advance beyond it.

THE IMPERIAL RUSSIAN NAVY

It is sometimes claimed that the origins of the Russian Navy are even older than those of the Royal Navy. It is true that a hundred years before Alfred laid the foundations of England's maritime defences, Russian ships had been engaged in desperate sea fights, but it cannot be said that these ships existed as part of an organised fleet in the sense that Alfred's did. In his work on the Imperial Russian Navy, F. T. Jane wrote that "a thousand years ago the foremost sailors of the time were Russians". The historian no doubt had in mind the campaigns of the Kievan and Novgorodian princes against Byzantium in the ninth and tenth centuries, but if so, the sailors to whom he refers were not Russians but were those Scandinavian Varangians of whom an account has been given early in this book. Alfred did not actually start to found the English fleets till after the last Danish dispersal, i.e. about A.D. 897. By that time the Viking Varangians were well established in Russia, having got to Kiev and beyond, before A.D. 860. Long before the ninth century, as W. E. D. Allen in his exhaustive history of Ukraine has pointed out, the inhabitants of the swampy forests along the great rivers were suffering from the depredations of Scandinavian pirates, and the Slavs in general, as the peaceful tillers of the soil, were the natural victims of the raiding Asiatic horseman and the Scandinavian river pirate. Though Slavs had settled along the Dnieper in the seventh century, they were not sailors in the sense that the Varangians were. These Scandinavian seafarers brought their maritime life into the countries they raided, and Russia, like Britain, Ireland, and Northern France, received the waves of those "foremost

 [continued on page 315

THE NAVAL BASES AND THE PRINCIPAL SEAPORTS
OF THE U.S.S.R.

"WE must create a mighty fleet", said a spokesman of the Russian Communist Party broadcasting in November 1948.

Five hundred years earlier the "Little Father of the Russian Navy" had been presented by Elizabeth Tudor to Ivan the Terrible. This small ship passed into the possession of Prince Nikita Ivanovitch Romanov, and it was this boat, by that time in a battered condition, which Peter the Great had been shown in a shed at Ismailov. The Tsar had it repaired by the shipwright Brandt, who had built the *Orel* in the time of Peter's father Alexis, its commander being an Englishman, David Butler. Shipbuilding was revived under Peter, who himself worked at this craft, deserting his bride on their honeymoon for this work on Lake Pleshtcheyevo, hammering and drinking with the Dutch craftsmen Brandt and Kort, and at Archangel, dressed in a Dutch uniform, frequenting the taverns with the Port Pilot. The first ship of Peter's new fleet—the *Apostle Peter*—on which the Tsar himself had worked in Holland as a carpenter, sailed into Archangel on June 29th, 1694, flying the Dutch flag. Peter appointed himself captain, (though he also acted as cabin boy to the master of the vessel). His first "admiral", Romodanovsky, and his first "vice-admiral", Buturlin, had never been to sea, but on July 31st, 1694, at the head of his three ships, the Tsar, "surrounded by his illustrious admirals", escorted four Dutch vessels into the White Sea. "A few cannon fired into the blue filled his cup of joy to the brim".[1]

It was Dutch ships which in those days were seen most often in that sea, but a century earlier it was English seamen who were the most frequent visitors in the White Sea ports; in 1566 a new charter had been granted by the Emperor to the Merchant Adventurers, confirming them in their monopoly of trade in the ports of the north. Today the Northern Sea Route has become a practical means of linking these ports and the modern naval bases of the White Sea, with those of the western Pacific seaboard, and the fact that twelve Russian submarines were lost in Arctic waters in the second world war, points to the possibilities of Arctic undersea warfare on a large scale in any future conflict.

Petsamo, Murmansk, Poliarnoye, and Kandalaksha are the principal Soviet ports in the region of the Kola Peninsula; Archangel on Dvina Bay can also be used by warships in the ice-free months, and Molotovsk on the opposite side of the Bay, is a base for submarines. Eastward along the Arctic Sea Route lies the Kara Sea; beyond it is the Gulf of Ob. If a deep channel were cut across the Yamal Peninsula, this would save the long voyage across the Kara Sea and up much of the long Gulf of Ob. Novy Port and Obdorsk are often used by ships in preference to the much nearer one of Yamal, as the latter, owing to the slow currents in that part of the Gulf, is sometimes frozen for long periods. Eastward again is the Yenesei, which has a fairly good seaport at Golchika, but Igarka, much farther up, is the busiest port on this river.

Siberia, with its great extension both in latitude and longitude, is an area in which the development of port facilities is only to be expected. But eastern Siberia has a poor ocean-face, owing, in the north, to the projection of the Kamchatkan Peninsula, then, farther south, to the situation of Sakhalin Island, and east of this to the chain of the Kurile Islands. In the Maritime Region east of the Amur River, Soviet continental territory is blocked again

[1] Georges Oudard: *Peter the Great*, translated by F. M. Atkins. (T. Werner Laurie, 1930.)

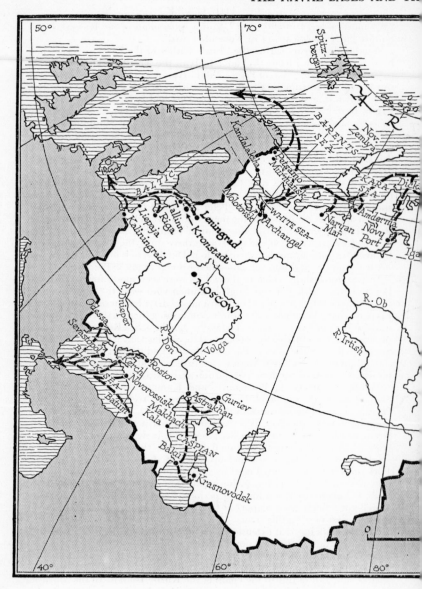

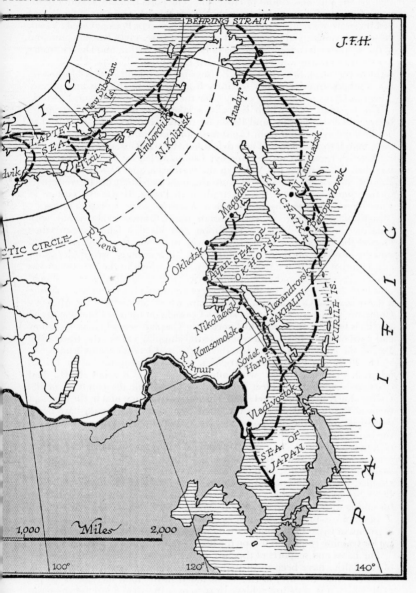

from the ocean, by the long range of Sikhota Alin, and beyond this, to the east, by the Japanese island of Hokkaido. The ports themselves suffer in the north from the foggy conditions in the Sea of Okhotsk, and west of the Bering Sea there are no really good natural harbours except Petropavlovsk. Vladivostock, a commercial port as well as a naval base, gives Russia command of the north-western zone of the Sea of Japan; Port Arthur and Dairen ensure her the use of warm-water ports in the Far East. From Vladivostock, however, right to the Black Sea, the U.S.S.R. (save for her inland seas) is blocked on the southern frontier of her territory from access to the seas and oceans. This is a factor of great importance for the future course of world history.

The Caspian Sea (which is really a lake) was the scene of struggles between Russia, Turkey, and Persia for many centuries. In 1569 a fleet of Turkish galleys set sail from Constantinople for Azov, with troops aboard for a march to Astrakhan. Their defeat here by the Russians, was witnessed by English travellers of the Muscovy Company led by Thomas Bannister, who had sailed down the Volga in the 70-ton barque *Thomas Bonaventura*. English merchant adventurers were the most persistent of the westerners in the efforts to capture the silk trade with Persia. It was the custom in those days to refer to English arrivals as *Korabelnie gosti*—seafaring visitors— "Englishmen " being, in the Russian mind, almost synonymous with "mariners". When Anthony Jenkinson and his two fellow countrymen crossed the Caspian in 1558 on their way to Persia, they took soundings, and explored the northern part of that sea. "It is curious" wrote Alexander von Humboldt,[1] "to see that this same nation, which in the vast ocean has rendered such great and memorable services to astronomical science, should also have been excited by the interests of commerce to survey the coasts of a great basin of Central Asia". Astrakhan, where members of the Muscovy Company were sometimes attacked by Cossacks on their perilous voyage to Persia, is today as then, the chief port of the Caspian Sea, where tankers now call with oil from Baku, and where coastal shipping carries the trade from Persia, the cotton of Uzbekistan, the copper and lead of Kazakhstan.

The Black Sea Fleet was the creation of Alexis Greig, son of the British admiral, Samuel Greig, who, after joining the Russian Navy, had destroyed the Turkish Fleet in 1770, and to whom the conquest of the Crimea for Russia was largely due. His son was instrumental in the development of the princial ports on the Black Sea, ports which today are being developed under the first post-war Five-Year Plan. The latter provides for the building of a new shipyard, and for the construction of passenger vessels of 5,000–6,000 tons. As regards warships, many new submarines are required, for 23 were lost in the Black Sea in the war. Another loss was the seaplane carrier *Stalin*, of 9,000 tons, carrying 22 seaplanes, and with a claimed speed of 30 knots. Improvements are to be made to certain of the Black Sea harbours, where the south-west winds sometimes make it difficult for sailing ships to put to sea. The Russians, who before the last war used the *Tovarishtch* (ex-British *Lauriston*), as a sailing school-ship, acquired from the Germans in 1946–47 the four-masted *Padua* and the auxiliary *Kommodore Johnson* for training ships, and it is on the Black Sea that these vessels will be used.

The bases and seaports of this Sea and of the Sea of Azov, and those too of the Baltic, have been dealt with in detail elsewhere, so it need only be said here that they are, of course, included in the total increase of 70 per cent. which it is aimed to achieve in 1950 over the 1940 figure for the number of deep-water quays to take sea-going vessels.

[1] *Asie Centrale*, II, p. 232.

sailors". (In fairness to some of these invaders of Russia it must be mentioned however that the chiefs among them were merchants rather than looters; the word "Variag"—the Greek rendering of "Varangian"—means a pedlar. In the early days of intercourse between these Scandinavian "Rus" and Byzantium, there were four well-defined trade treaties, two of which were made by Oleg and one by Igor.)

It is difficult to find anywhere that the Russians themselves claimed to have had any real naval power before the time of Peter I. It was not till his reign that they possessed any definite maritime laws, or any formulated principles of naval art. It was Peter who gave the name of "The Little Father of the Russian Fleet" to the sailing boat sent by Elizabeth Tudor to Ivan the Terrible, and it has been said that to this vessel the modern Russian navy owes its origin.[1] Peter himself averred that his passion for navigation dated from the day he discovered this "battered old English boat" in a storehouse at Izmailov, though, indeed, the gift of the astrolabe from Prince Dolgoruki (Russian Ambassador in France) which delighted the Tsar, probably first aroused his enthusiasm for the art of seafaring. In any case, two years before his discovery at Izmailov, we find Peter "sending to the Ordnance Office for 'small ships'", which, Kluchevsky suggests[2] were models preserved by Peter's father for the building of the *Orel* on the Okha. Karsten Brandt who had constructed that ship, was engaged by Peter to repair the Elizabethan one, which, after sailing on the Yausa River at Moscow, was sent to Kronstadt by order of the Tsar, saluted by his ships of war, and returned eventually to Moscow, to be kept as a perpetual reminder of how, from so small a beginning, a fleet could arise.

In 1703 the first Russian squadron (six frigates) ever to be launched on Baltic waters, set sail from Lodeinopolsk Wharf. In 1713, only four years after Peter's great victory over the land forces of his maritime rival Charles XII at Pultowa, his entire fleet had consisted of only four ships of the line and some frigates. For on his defeat by the Turks at Pruth, all he had been able to save from his Azov Fleet was part of the stores, which he sent to Archangel and St. Petersburg. After Pruth he was prohibited from keeping a Black Sea Fleet, and that fact had accounted for a substantial reduction in the navy he had

---

[1] See also F. T. Jane's *The Imperial Russian Navy; Its Past, Present, and Future*; p. 43.
[2] *A History of Russia*; Vol. IV, p. 11.

commenced to build up. But it must not be forgotten that at the time of his death his fleet was a force to be reckoned with. Writing nearly forty years later, Harris, in his *Collection of Voyages*, says of the Russians that "to consider them in the light of a naval and commercial Power, seems a little premature", but by 1791 Pitt had urged an increase in British naval strength to meet the growing maritime power of Russia. Four years later the latter country, which had joined in the war against France, was able to send a large squadron to join the English Fleet in the North Sea, though these Russian vessels actually had no marked influence on the course of the war that year. (One hundred years later Russia could claim to have the third most powerful navy.) Under Tsar Paul the total strength of the Imperial Navy in the Baltic had been eighty-two ships of the line and forty frigates—numbers which had aroused the misgivings of Nelson, who, had he had his way, would have destroyed that entire fleet at Reval. The decision of his commander, Sir Hyde Parker, not to detach part of the British Fleet for this purpose, but to make a concentrated attack on Copenhagen instead, had the result of leaving the Tsar free to continue helping Napoleon for a time by placing an embargo on British shipping.

The practice of officering the Russian fleets with men from Britain, begun under Peter I as mentioned before, had persisted throughout the reign of Catherine, but this did not affect her attitude to England's maritime policy. The Empress continued to oppose in general Britain's claim to the supremacy of the seas, and specifically, the British Maritime Code. (Equally was Catherine opposed to the Continental System of Napoleon, even when allied with him.) A modern historian has rightly shown how her relations with neutrals were affected by the naval policy of Great Britain: "Russia," he says, "was dependent upon the commerce of neutrals and therefore did everything in her power to uphold their rights, whether against Great Britain or France."[1] That was why Catherine had headed the Armed Neutrality League to protect the rights of non-belligerents, at a time when England, France, and Spain were at war. But this Maritime Confederacy, primarily directed against Britain, availed the Russians little, for they could take no action because their ships had so many British officers on board. In the battle of Viborg one in every five of the officers in the Russian

[1] Foster Rhea Dulles, *The Road to Teheran*. (Princeton University Press, 1944); p. 18.

ships was British, notwithstanding the fact that two years previously a considerable number of such officers had resigned
from the Russian navy when Paul Jones had been made an
admiral.

Samuel Greig, one of the most famous admirals who ever
served with the Russian navy, was a Scotsman. He commanded the fleet in the war with Sweden, 1788, and became
Governor of Kronstadt; his son was responsible for the reorganisation and expansion of the Black Sea Fleet. The Russian
battleship *Admiral Greig* was so named in honour of the Scottish
sailor. Other names which figure prominently in Russian naval
history are Elphinstone, Mitchell, Mackenzie, Dugdale, and
Saunders. In the battle of Hogland between Russia and Sweden,
1788, in the twenty-five ships engaged there were no less than
eleven British commanders. "At one time more than half the
entire list of officers were of Anglo-Saxon and Celtic nationality," wrote F. T. Jane.[1] And another naval historian, Sir
George Clarke, says: "The Russian navy may almost be said to
be the creation of British seamen."[2] In the eighteenth century
and in the first half of the nineteenth it was the practice of many
Russian officers to serve for a time with the English navy. Three
of the first four Russian commanders to make a round-the-
world expedition—Krusenstern, Lysiansky, and Golovnin—
received their early training in this way, and Krusenstern,
whose studies in oceanography were later to prove of such
value, had been specially trained in England in various
branches of nautical science. The *Nadezhda* and the *Neva* in
which he and Lysiansky achieved the first Russian voyage of
circumnavigation, 1803-06, were bought in London. The result
of this close association with the British navy as M. A. Sergeyev[3]
has pointed out, was that Russian officers made comparisons
which were unfavourable to the Tsarist navy. Krusenstern was
emphatic in urging naval reorganisation at home, and the subsequent reconstitution of the Naval Cadet School, St. Petersburg, was due to his work there as director, and to him was also
due the nucleus of the Imperial Naval Academy. These institutions derived many of their features from the English models.
During that period the Russian navy was numerically strong.

[1] *The Imperial Russian Navy; Its Past, Present, and Future;* 2nd edition, p. 78.
[2] *Russia's Sea Power, Past and Present.*
[3] Introduction to *Russian Voyages Round the World,* by N. Nozikov. Edited
by M. A. Sergeyev and translated by Ernst and Mira Lesser. (Hutchinson
1945); p. xv.

After the Napoleonic Wars, Dr. Anderson points out "it was soon second only to the English. No less than sixty-five battleships were built in the Baltic between 1815 and 1855, and though most of these had only a short life, the fleet was kept at a high total".[1]

After her defeat in the Crimean War it was to England that Russia turned, as in earlier times, for the rebuilding of her fleet. (Her ships, built mainly of fir, had not been noted for longevity.) But her dependence on foreigners for building up and maintaining her navy decreased when Grand Duke Constantine became head of the Russian Admiralty. He applied himself to the task of enlarging the Imperial Navy. "A turret-ship, two floating batteries, and ten monitors were at once laid down at Cronstadt and the Baltic ports. Between 1864 and 1867 seven ironclads were constructed in Russia by native workmen. A ukase of 1866 forbade the Admiralty, the War Office, and the Ministry of Communications to place orders for material abroad. Three years later the Baltic Fleet included 23 armoured vessels; but, with one exception, they were adapted only to coast defence."[2] The monitors referred to in this passage had been laid down as a result of the impression these vessels had made on Russia in the American Civil War. "Even after the Crimean War," says Dr. Anderson, "the Russian Navy was probably the strongest in the Baltic, but a new Power was shortly to appear."[3] The Prussian navy was before long to out-match the Baltic Fleet of Russia.

Alexander II who was the Tsar at the time of Constantine's ambitious naval programme, had supported the Grand Duke in his work of strengthening the fleet. He saw the need of giving funds for this, and when he died (1881), his navy was armed with 1,400 breech-loading guns[4] and 28,000 sailors. Sevastopol was rebuilt after its shattering in the Crimean War, and Batum was made a modern naval base, strongly fortified—in contravention of the Treaty of Berlin.

Grand Duke Constantine had been responsible for various innovations in naval training, such as the practice of sending crews on long-distance voyages. A squadron had sailed from Kronstadt for Vladivostock, and in 1858 six Russian corvettes had made a round-the-world voyage. Up to the time when

[1] *Naval Wars in the Baltic*; p. 350.
[2] Francis Henry Skrine, *The Expansion of Russia, 1815-1900*; p. 285.
[3] *Naval Wars in the Baltic*; p. 352.
[4] Skrine, as above.

Constantine had begun to press his new naval policy Russia had concentrated mainly on coastal defence craft. It was not till 1863 that she started building ironclads, although her old enemy Turkey, having seen the success of the French with these new vessels at Kinburn in 1855, had gone ahead with the building of armour-clad ships. "It is with the Crimean War that the age of the ironclad may be said to begin."[1] At Sinope, 30 November, 1853, wooden ships for the first time had had to meet "the deadly effect of shell-fire". So the benefit of the armour-plated warships was at once apparent, although the earliest of these flat-bottomed vessels, styled floating batteries, were sometimes so unstable that they heeled over even in calm. The first Russian ironclad was the *Pervenets*, built in England, and her speed was only nine knots. (As the Russians had no Mediterranean bases they had to sacrifice speed for range.) The largest of the armourclads up to 1875 was *Peter the Great* (8,750 tons) for Baltic service.

The disadvantages to Russia of divided fleets was seen in the Russo-Turkish War of 1877-78, when she had not enough ships in the Black Sea and was opposed by a powerful Turkish fleet which included ironclads. The only ships of this type which Russia could muster in the Black Sea were *Novgorod* (2,700 tons), and *Admiral Popov* (3,590 tons). These were circular barbette ships built on the principle that only half the armour is necessary on a round turret compared with that required for a flat surface. Incapable of steering or steaming, they could not be trusted at sea, and were used only for harbour defences. "Add to these a few old and worthless corvettes and sloops, and a dozen or more torpedo launches, many of which had been sent overland by rail from the Baltic, and we have the war fleet of Russia in these waters."[2]

But Russia learnt her lesson. The Russo-Turkish War had taught her the need of a Black Sea Fleet, and of specialised development of torpedo craft. That war too had put to practical test the bold plan of the young naval lieutenant, later to be world-known as Admiral Makarov, who had first conceived the idea of fitting out a fast steamer equipped with launches carrying mine-laying apparatus. The small passenger steamer *Constantine* had been the first to carry out this experiment, and by

[1] H. W. Wilson, *Ironclads in Action*. (Sampson Low, 1898; 6th impression); Vol. I, p. 286B.
[2] Colonel Sir George Sydenham Clarke, *Russia's Sea Power, Past and Present*; p. 118.

daring attacks under cover of night several of the Turkish ships
had been sunk. In these operations by Makarov, torpedoes were
used for the first time. Thus the *Constantine* became such a
menace to the Turkish Fleet that many of the enemy ships were
compelled to remain in their bases.

Twenty years after the war of 1878 Russia was the third
strongest Sea Power, and all the sea-going warships of the new
fleet were built at home. It is instructive to turn to the figures
for the Russian navy at that time, and to see how far the efforts
—started by Grand Duke Constantine—to bring the Imperial
Navy nearer to the strength of Britain's, had succeeded. These
figures are taken from *Ironclads in Action*, Vol. II,[1] where the
author, H. W. Wilson, has given "a comparison of the fleets of
England, France, and Russia, as they stood in August 1897,
including ships built, building, and projected." The author
states that "The battleships which are unquestionably first-
class of the three Powers, are these:—

England	France	Russia
12 *Majestics*	3 *Jénas*	2 *Peresviets*
6 *Canopuses*	3 *Charlemagnes*	3 *Tri Sviatitelias*
1 *Renown*	1 *Henri IV*	3 *Poltavas*
8 *Royal Sovereigns*	4 *Carnots*	3 *Sissoi Velikis*
2 *Centurions*	1 *Jauréguiberry*	1 *Georghi Pobyedonosets*
2 *Niles*	1 *Brennus*	1 *Navarin*
		1 *Dvenadsat Apostolov*

Total 31. Types 6. Total 13. Types 6. Total 14. Types 7.
Ships of each type, Ships of each type, Ships of each type,
     5.16   2.16   2.

"Ready for sea in the above class the numbers were, in 1897,
England nineteen, France four, and Russia eight." Later, after
mentioning other classes, Mr. Wilson says that the three fleets
"stand thus in effective, modern, or modernised battleships:
England forty-nine, France thirty-five, Russia twenty-five."[2]

Battleships could not be constructed in the open air in Russia
as they could in England. Owing to the climate the work had to
be done in a roofed shed having solid walls and ends, one of the
latter being pulled down when the vessel was launched. The
inefficiency of Russian shipbuilding which was marked at the
time of the Russo-Japanese War, was partly due to the moving
of naval engineers from ship to ship.

[1] Sampson Low, 1898; 6th impression; p. 271.
[2] *Ironclads in Action*; Vol. II, p. 273.

Seamanship was adversely affected by the climate, which shortened the period of a Russian sailor's service. At one time naval conscription was carried out only in the maritime provinces of Russia, but later was applied generally. Liability to serve did not apply till the recruit was twenty-one. This handicapped the seaman, who at that age lacked the years of training which a British rating, for instance, possessed, and which had made the latter sea-minded while his Russian opposite number remained land-minded. As regards the study prescribed for cadets, maritime history was much neglected at the Naval School, St. Petersburg, and "the Course of naval tactics had no existence" according to Captain N. Klado, Professor of Mathematics at the Naval Academy, and historian of the Russo-Japanese War. But the Russian Naval Intelligence Department had, at the beginning of the twentieth century, the reputation of being the best in the world. "It is no secret," wrote F. T. Jane in 1904, "that the confidential books issued to the officers in our own and any other important navy, are usually issued to Russian officers" before being issued to those for whose sole consumption they were intended.[1]

"Russian naval ambitions received a crushing blow in the war with Japan, 1904-05.[2] When hostilities began, quite a powerful Russian fleet had been assembled in the Far East, comprising seven battleships, eleven cruisers, twenty-five destroyers and a number of minor war vessels. But political considerations were allowed to prevail over strategical needs, so that four of the cruisers were detached from the main fleet at Port Arthur and stationed at Vladivostock, while another cruiser and a gunboat were sent to the Korean port of Chemulpo, exposing them to inevitable destruction.

"Nor was Russian leadership remarkable in its quality. After the damage done by the initial torpedo attack of the Japanese at Port Arthur had been made good, Admiral Makarov showed a measure of determination and energy which went some way towards restoring confidence; but he lost his life when his flagship was mined and sunk in April, 1904. His successor, Admiral Vitgeft, was killed in the course of a sortie made by the fleet in the following August. After that action, damage suffered by various ships proved beyond the limited resources of the Port

[1] *The Imperial Russian Navy, Its Past, Present, and Future*; p. 449.
[2] The author was favoured by receiving from the late Mr. Francis E. McMurtrie, A.I.N.A., editor of *Jane's Fighting Ships*, this summarised account of the Russo-Japanese War.

Arthur dockyard to repair. In order that the fortress might be able to hold out as long as possible, guns and men were landed to reinforce its defences; thus the fleet was gradually reduced to impotence, all the principal ships being sunk at their moorings or scuttled before Port Arthur fell at the beginning of 1905.

"To the Russian Government it had seemed that the situation might still be retrieved, especially as Japan had been weakened by the loss of two battleships and two cruisers in the course of 1904. A fresh fleet was formed and despatched to the Far East in October, 1904; but its disabilities were such that no one with sea experience could have expected it to accomplish its objects. To begin with, its composition was too heterogeneous, as in addition to seven battleships and six cruisers of fairly modern design which formed the nucleus of the force, there were a number of obsolete units which were nothing but a hindrance to its progress. Paucity of bunkering facilities added to the length of the voyage round the Cape of Good Hope, which occupied over seven months. Calls had to be made at the French ports of Dakar and Libreville, in West Africa, Nossi Bé in Madagascar, and Kamranh Bay in Indo-China. At the last-named port, where coal and supplies were obtained and minor repairs taken in hand, a junction was effected with a number of ships which had proceeded via the Suez Canal.

"In these circumstances it must be conceded that it was a creditable feat for Admiral Rozhdestvenski to have brought his fleet so far without a total breakdown in all departments. Yet the result when it was met by Admiral Togo's smaller but better trained fleet in the Strait of Tsushima in May, 1905, was a foregone conclusion. Almost all the Russian ships were sunk or captured, with little loss to their opponents. Surviving units were three cruisers which took refuge at Manila, where they were interned; and the small cruiser *Almaz* and two destroyers which succeeded in getting through to Vladivostock.

"Apart from questions of defective material, of which there were not a few, the cause of these successive defeats is to be found in the much inferior training of the Russian personnel. Japan, too, had the initial advantages of a strong strategical position and better bases. Japanese staff work was also more efficient than that of the Russians. Naturally, it took many years for the Russian Navy to recover from its loss of prestige, to say nothing of the difficulty of replacing so many lost ships. From the third naval Power in the world—a position she had held for many years—Russia abruptly descended to the sixth place. By the time war broke out with Germany in 1914, six new battleships and four new cruisers had been launched, but the fleet as a whole had scarcely regained confidence in itself."

Among the Russian military leaders who however regarded the Treaty of Portsmouth only as a truce, and believed that renewal of war was inevitable, was General Bashenov. "A strong fleet, with Vladivostock as its base, is an absolute necessity," he insisted. "Orders should be placed at once with shipbuilders all over the world, and premiums offered for delivery before contract date, in order that we may be in possession of a naval arm as soon as possible."[1] In 1912 the "Little Shipbuilding Programme" attempted to bring the Russian fleet up to its earlier position, but as Sir Julian Corbett has stated,[2] reconstruction had not proceeded far enough to make it an effective factor in the situation. At the commencement of the first world war Russia had in the Baltic only four battleships in commission—*Imperator Pavl, Andrei Pervozvanni, Tzesarevich,* and *Slava.* There were also four out of eight projected new battleships, which had been launched in 1911, "but only two of them were approaching completion". In addition there was the *Rurik,* British-built flagship of Admiral von Essen, and four other cruisers. The naval reconstruction programme had fallen so far short of its target that when Russia and Japan were allies in 1916, it was in Japanese ships that Russian troops were transported from Dairen to the Western Front. That year Japan returned to the Russian Navy two of her own battleships, the *Sagami* and the *Tango,* also the armoured cruiser *Soya,* prizes taken in 1905.

THE SOVIET NAVY

Today Russia is conscious of her future as a maritime Power, and the country that could once be correctly called a land animal is now becoming so sea-minded that there is a tendency abroad to forget that she has not always been thus. The position assigned to the navy in Russia as an arm of defence in the 1914-18 war, may be judged from the fact that the Baltic Fleet was under the command of a soldier, Grand Duke

[1] B. L. Putnam Weale, *The Truce in the East and its Aftermath.* (Macmillan & Co., 1907); p. 392.

[2] *History of the Great War.* Based on Official Documents, by direction of the Historical Section of the Committee of Imperial Defence, Naval Operations. (Longmans, Green & Co., 1938, 2nd edition); Vol. I, p. 9. Reproduced by permission of the Controller, His Majesty's Stationery Office.

Nicholas. This was consistent with the tendency to subordinate the Navy to the Army, a procedure which has operated unfavourably for Russia in two of the three major wars in which she has been engaged since the beginning of the century. According to one source[1] the Russian Fleets (1 January, 1913), consisted altogether of twenty-nine large and two hundred and thirty small units, with a complement of 46,300 men. The Baltic Fleet might have given a better account of itself, but for the untimely death of Admiral von Essen, the one senior officer who at the outset showed initiative. At the same time the disparity between the Russian and German Fleets in the first world war had made the role of the former a defensive rather than an offensive one—though, indeed, the defence of the Gulf of Riga and the enforced evacuation of the port of Riga by the Germans was due mainly to the operations of British submarines, a fact which was admitted at the time in an official Russian Order. The Germans never succeeded in reaching Leningrad, nor in their attempts to capture the Russian ships when Kronstadt was ice-bound. The German Fleet, which consisted of two battleships and several cruisers, preceded by the icebreaker *Hindenburg*, had steamed north, but a mine had wrecked the *Hindenburg*, and the German ships got no farther than the Aaland Islands.

In the opening of his Report on operations in the Baltic, during the war of intervention, Rear-Admiral Walter Cowan wrote: "My aim was throughout the year to prevent any Bolshevik warships breaking out into the Gulf of Finland—and the ice has now relieved me of this responsibility—and also to frustrate by every means the most evident design of the Germans to overrun and dominate the Baltic Provinces and then to advance on Petrograd."[2]

After the war of intervention, which lasted fourteen months, what remained of the Red Fleet could not, strictly speaking, be called a navy. Two Russian battleships had been torpedoed by British m.t.b.s, at Kronstadt (the only British loss apart from a couple of mine casualties, was a destroyer.) Several ships had been sunk to prevent the Germans getting them; some had been given by General Wrangel to France. In all, Russia had only three old battleships, two modern and three old cruisers, some flotillas of destroyers (principally only for river use) and

[1] Gregor Alexinsky, *Russia and the Great War;* p. 104.
[2] Published as a Supplement (No. 5) to *The London Gazette*, 6 April, 1920. Extract by permission of the Controller, H.M. Stationery Office.

submarines. There were no Soviet warships in the Arctic or even in the Pacific at that time; indeed, even in 1934 there was, on the word of the Navy Commissar, only one Russian warship in the Pacific, and that was a submarine.

It was from the nucleus of the Baltic Fleet that the modern Russian navy had been built up. Between 1929 and 1937—i.e. during the First and Second Five-Year Plans—the Russians claimed to have built four hundred and eighty warships of 850,000 tons. In that period the number of ships built was stated to have been four times, and their tonnage three times, that of the corresponding ten-year period 1904-14. These figures differ widely from estimates given by some of the British naval authorities, and the increase, whatever its extent, cannot at that particular time be attributed to the naval purge which removed the defensive-minded admirals, as it was only in 1938 that the latter were replaced by men who urged that Russia should possess a navy capable of offensive operations. "We must build, and we are building, a really powerful navy, which includes vessels of all classes," said V. Orlov, chief of the Soviet Navy. In 1940 it was announced that one hundred and sixty-eight large and small surface vessels, including fast m.t.b.s, were added to the Soviet Union's Navy under the Third Five-Year Plan.

The secrecy which always surrounded the number, classes, and disposition of the ships of the Russian Fleets in pre-Revolution days, is well known, and goes back to the eighteenth century (though a curious contradiction to this was the fact that in that century and in the next, the practice as we have observed, was to engage many Englishmen as officers in Russian ships.) The tradition has been maintained in modern Russia; in 1939 the Soviet Union withheld particulars of her naval strength from publication in the British Official Return of the Strengths of the Fleets. That is why the publication known as *Fleets: The British Commonwealth of Nations and Foreign Countries (1939)*,[1] while it gives data concerning the fleets of the British Commonwealth of Nations, Japan, France, Italy, and Germany, gives no information about the navy of the U.S.S.R. According to extracts produced at the Nuremberg trials from the log-book of Admiral Raeder, Chief of the German Navy, despite the retention of British ships, and help in other ways given by the Soviet Union to Germany before Hitler's invasion of Russia,[2] the Russians refused to allow the

[1] H.M. Stationery Office, 1939.
[2] See British United Press Reports, 11.12.1945.

Germans to repair warships or to fit out auxiliary cruisers in their yards. The shroud of secrecy which surrounded the ships of the Soviet Union, was of course inevitably lifted to some extent when those ships came into action in the war, but Russia's subsequent unwillingness to reveal her naval strength was responsible for the editor's remark at the head of the Russian section in *Jane's Fighting Ships* (*1947-48*). "It is extremely difficult," he said, "to secure accurate information regarding the Russian Navy."

The Soviet Union took very little part in international conferences in the inter-war years. She had not been a signatory to the Quadripartite-Pacific Treaty, 1921 (between the United States, Britain, France, Japan), which terminated the Anglo-Japanese Alliance, and laid down that in any disputes concerning the Pacific the matter should be placed before a joint conference of the High Contracting Parties. It is true that the Soviet Government was not at that time recognised by the United States, but the fact of the exclusion of Russia from a treaty which expressly bound its members to respect each others' rights in relation to their Pacific dominions and islands, shows also that Russia was not then regarded as a Pacific Power. She had taken no part in the Washington Naval Conference, 1922. Chicherin, however, as Commissar for Foreign Affairs, had protested to Washington at the exclusion of Russia "from a conference which touches it directly," and against "any intention of any Power whatsoever to adopt decisions touching the Pacific without consulting Russia."[1] Nor was that country a party to the London Naval Treaty of 1930, though in a Note to the British Government dated 16 February, 1937, the Soviet Government declared its acceptance of those clauses in the treaty which concern the action of submarines against merchant shipping in time of war.[2] Nor was the Soviet Union represented at the London Naval Conference, 1936, though to the terms of this Conference—which was open to other Powers by virtue of their bi-lateral Pacts with Britain—Russia acceded.

In 1937 an interesting event occurred which at the time was interpreted by some as suggesting that in future Russia might pursue a less rigidly isolationist naval policy. As a result of the

[1] Crosby to Secretary of State, 22 July, 1921.

[2] Part IV of the 1930 Treaty lays down that submarines must observe the rules of International Law which forbid submarines to sink or put out of action a merchant vessel without first ensuring that all aboard are transferred to a place of safety.

termination of the London Naval Conference and the conclusion of a new Naval Agreement between Britain, America,
and France, an agreement was signed between the respective
Governments of the United Kingdom and the U.S.S.R. providing for "The Limitation of Naval Armaments and the
Exchange of Information concerning Naval Construction."
(How far the latter part of this provision was carried out on the
Russian side was a subject of criticism in some quarters, on
account of the fact that the Soviet Union did not furnish
particulars of the strength of her navy for the British publication
of Returns of the Fleets, 1939.) The Agreement was to remain
in force until 31 December, 1942. Its main provisions will be
found in the Appendix (II) to this book. There too is included
an important provision relating to Russia's Far Eastern Fleet,
a provision which shows that the Soviet Union insists on maintaining her policy of complete freedom of action in regard to
all matters concerning her Pacific Fleet.

During a session of the Supreme Soviet of the U.S.S.R.,
M. Molotov said: "We must take into consideration the
fact that our land is vast, and that for an enormous distance it
is surrounded by seas. This reminds us that our fleet must
always be strong and efficient." If, he said later, "before 1938
the growth of our navy showed itself principally in the addition
of light surface ships and submarines, the Soviet Union, after
1938, was building and is continuing to build, ships of all
classes, including large ones. For the period 1930-39 alone, the
total tonnage increased by 130 per cent., i.e. more than double.
And for the one year 1939 the fleet gained 112 surface ships,
large and small. In 1940 our battle fleet received 50 per cent.
more new surface ships than in 1939, and 300 per cent. more
fighting submarines than in 1939."

Under the First Five-Year Plan relatively more merchant
vessels than warships had been built, as the first need at that
time was transport for heavy freight—machinery for electrifica-
tion, plant for production. All Russia was on the move. It was
the Second Five-Year Plan which saw the expansion of the
navy: the newly-created Pacific Fleet was stated to have
numbered more than one hundred vessels, not counting small
ones, in 1939.[1] And by that year the U.S.S.R. had fourteen
naval stations.

[1] "The Armed Forces of the U.S.S.R." (Condensed from *Малая
Советская Энциклопедия*, вт. изд. Москва. Vol. X, 1940.) *American Review
of the Armed Forces of the U.S.S.R.*, August 1941.

This expansion was not achieved without a purge of personnel. As previously mentioned, radical changes were made in the Commands of the fleets; those members of the Naval Staff and those officers who had advocated a defensive navy, were replaced by men who favoured the building up of a strong one, capable of carrying out major actions on all the seas. The Admiral formerly in command of the naval station at Archangel, was relieved of his command in 1938. He had shown a preference for increasing the number of coastal submarines rather than the building of battleships. Others reported[1] as removed were the Commander-in-Chief and the respective Admirals in command of the Baltic, Black Sea, Pacific, Northern Fleets, and the Amur Flotilla. The Chief of Naval Construction and three chief political advisers were also stated to have been dismissed. This, to many people, was a further reason for belief that the Soviet navy, after a purge which was reported to have removed most of its highest naval men, could hardly be regarded as an efficient one.

There was a good deal of speculation in the foreign press as to the appointments which would follow the reported removal of the Commander-in-Chief and all the Fleet Commanders. Little was known outside the U.S.S.R. of the personnel appointed after the purge, but the latter brought to the front a remarkable man in Admiral Kuznetsov, who in 1939 was appointed Commissar for the Navy, and at the age of thirty-eight was the youngest supreme naval chief in the world.

In 1938 when a Commissariat of Navy was first formed, M. Molotov said: "The mighty Soviet Power must have a navy, both on sea and ocean, commensurate with its interests and worthy of our great cause." In mentioning ocean as well as sea, M. Molotov showed that the Russian Government was aware of a particular deficiency, one to which the English naval historian, Brian Tunstall, has drawn attention in *Ocean Power Wins*. After paying tribute to the work of the Soviet Union's sea-going ships, Mr. Tunstall says: "There is, in fact, no such thing as an ocean-going Red Fleet. Admittedly Red warships have to use the oceans in order to reach their eastern station at Vladivostok, but it would seem that they treat this as a rare and unusual operation, just as the unfortunate Baltic Fleet did in 1904-5 when it met utter and annihilating disaster at the hands of Admiral Togo in the Straits of

---

[1] See *The Times*, 31.8.1938, and *The Yorkshire Post*, 16.5.1938.

Tsushima."[1] Mr. Tunstall, writing in 1944, remarked that Russia had not yet fully appreciated either the value of ocean power or the efforts needed to make it.[2]

But the value of ocean power became clearer to "the land animal" in the second world war, when the Germans advanced right to the Crimea, taking the rich Ukraine, and so cutting drastically the industrial and agricultural resources of European Russia. Then it was that the Soviet Union became dependent on supplies from Britain and America—supplies which could only be delivered by ocean power. And how much Russia did depend on foreign naval power will be realised when it is recalled that by the beginning of March 1945, four million tons of supplies had been brought by Allied convoys to her northern ports[3]—not to mention all that had been sent via the Persian Gulf and Egypt. When the last two routes are included, the total value of supplies sent by Britain to the Soviet Union from 1 October, 1941, to 31 March, 1946, was £308,000,000.

It is in the Far East that Russia's will to ocean power is now most clearly manifest. At the end of the nineteenth century her expansion eastwards had been accompanied by a significant increase in her Pacific Fleet. From the Siberian flotilla created by the pro-Consul Muraviev, the Pacific squadron had shown signs of developing to a strength sufficient to support Russian aims in Manchuria and the Yellow Sea, and when the Russians took Port Arthur, Britain had threatened to build a fleet in the Far East equal to those of France and Russia combined. But Russia's tendency then, and for long after, had been to specialise in small ships—particularly in submarines and in motor torpedo boats—for use in Pacific waters. This policy was partly due to the formation of the Kurile Islands, which makes the Sea of Okhotsk practically an enclosed one—a factor unfavourable to a big fleet of capital ships. If such a fleet had been based on the ports of the Maritime Territory (Primorsk), it could, when operating in the Sea of Japan, have been threatened by the Japanese from Hokkaido. But the strategic situation has altered radically in favour of Russia now that she has acquired the Kuriles.

Another factor has been to her advantage. The effect of the Russo-German Pact was to alienate Japan from the anti-Comintern Alliance. This meant, as Professor Hearnshaw has

[1] *Ocean Power Wins.* (Martin Secker and Warburg, 1944); p. 59.
[2] *Ibid.*, p. 52.
[3] Parliamentary Statement by the First Lord of the Admiralty, 7.3.1945.

pointed out,[1] a reduction of the strain on British sea power in the Pacific; it could then be concentrated on the North Sea and the Atlantic. Hence Russia at that time had no other formidable maritime Power except Japan confronting her in the western Pacific. As Britain has never since regained her naval supremacy in the Far East, and with the transference of the H.Q. of the Commander-in-Chief, Far Eastern Station, weakened her position in the region of Hong Kong, Russia, until the future revival of Japanese sea strength, is faced by no strong naval Power except America, to check her Pacific aspirations.

One interesting development which is likely to arise from the Soviet Union's special concern for its Pacific Fleet, is a concentration upon the building of aircraft carriers. In the Pacific, except for the Kommandorski Islands in the northern part of that ocean, Russia is poorly provided with islands suitable for use as air bases, but this limitation can be overcome at least partially, by a large fleet of carriers. It may not be without significance that it was to Far Eastern waters that the Soviet Government sent its principal aircraft carrier, the *Krasnoye Znamya*, 22,000 tons, carrying sixty planes and mounting twelve 4-inch A.A. guns. Russia's scarcity of island bases caused Moscow to view with disfavour the announcement made by America at the end of the war with Japan, that the United States would increase the number of its naval and air stations in the Pacific. But having occupied the Liao-tung Peninsula, and by agreement with China acquired the joint use of Port Arthur as a naval base, with joint control of Dalny as a free port, and having also recovered southern Sakhalin and acquired all the Kurile islands, Russia had gained access to the ocean which it had always been her aim to achieve. She was now well on her way towards the realisation of that objective thus described by a contemporary Russian writer, "the Soviet Union is determined to breathe fresh air."

The actual strength of Russia's surface navy after the second world war however, was far from commensurate with her strategic maritime advances. "There is no sign of any relaxation of the secrecy in which the affairs of the Soviet Navy have long been enveloped," wrote Mr. Francis E. McMurtrie, in his contribution to *Brassey's Naval Annual, 1946*. It was believed however, he said, that by the end of the second world war only the ex-*Royal Sovereign* had any pretensions to real fighting value. This battleship had been operating with the Russian Arctic

[1] *Sea Power and Empire*. (George Harrap, 1940); p. 265.

Fleet and in 1944 was on loan to the Soviet navy, when she was re-named *Arkhangelsk*. It is curious that this ship of 29,150 tons, with a speed of twenty-three knots, and of the same class as *Revenge*, should have been referred to in more than one British newspaper as the largest unit in the Russian Navy, for *Tretii International* was of greater tonnage. (The armament of *Royal Sovereign* however, was larger than any in the Red Fleet, for it included eight 15-inch guns, twelve 16-inch, eight 4-inch A.A.)[1] *Tretii International* (re-named *Sovietskii Soyuz*) was laid down in Leningrad in 1939: the hull of this battleship was so badly damaged during the war however, that it was believed that construction has been much retarded. "The report that this ship was launched in 1945, should therefore be received with caution," said the editor of *Jane's Fighting Ships, 1946-47,*[2] and in the 1947-48 edition of that annual he stated that "as the material for her construction (with the possible exception of the main engines, said to have been supplied from Germany early in 1941), has to be furnished from Russian sources, early completion is not to be expected." This battleship (estimated at 35,000 tons), mounted with nine 16-inch guns, was reported to be designed as the first of a class.[3] *Gangut* (ex-*Oktiabrskaya Revolutsia*) of 23,606 tons, and *Sevastopol* (ex-*Pariskaya Kommuna*) of 23,256 tons, were the two other battleships of the Soviet navy which were known to have been actively engaged in the second world war. A coast-defence ironclad, *Väinämöinen* (3,900 tons) was the largest of the ships acquired from Finland.

By the tripartite naval agreement made at the Berlin Conference in 1945, Russia's share of the operational units of the German Fleet included ten U-boats, ten destroyers, and the German prize cruiser *Nürnberg*, (re-named *Makarov*). She had also the damaged hulls of the German aircraft carrier *Graf Zeppelin*, and the coast defence ship *Schleswig-Holstein*. Not more than six serviceable Russian cruisers (including *Nürnberg*) were believed to have survived the war.[4] The Soviet Union's deficiency in cruisers had been for some time a weakness in her navy, and it was not surprising that during the Russo-German

---

[1] *Brassey's Naval Annual, 1944.* Edited by Rear-Admiral H. G. Thursfield. (Wm. Clowes & Sons); Pictorial Section I, p. 29.

[2] Sampson Low & Marston; p. 268.

[3] *Les Flottes de Combat, 1947.* (Société d'Editions Géographiques, Maritimes, et Coloniales, Paris, 1947); p. 307. (When the Germans claimed to have captured this ship they gave her tonnage as 45,000.)

[4] *Brassey's Naval Annual, 1946.*

Pact the Russians, according to Admiral Raeder's diary,[1] asked for the hulls of three German cruisers then building. The Soviet Union's best-known cruisers are those of the *Kirov* class, which includes some recent ships. (It was this class which furnished Germany with a pretext for arming certain of her own new cruisers with 8-inch instead of 6-inch guns.) The Russians had for long admired the Italian fast cruisers of the *Condottieri* class—5,000-8,300 tons—with a speed of thirty-seven knots; these however are suitable for calmer waters, they were not designed for rough seas. Consequently, after the surrender of the Italian Fleet to the Allies in World War II, transfers to Russia for purposes of training were made from the navies of Britain and the United States. *Royal Sovereign*, *Milwaukee* (U.S. light cruiser of the *Omaha* class, re-named *Murmansk*), eight American destroyers, four modern American submarines, and forty-nine steel submarine chasers were loaned to the Russian navy. Four British submarines: *Sunfish*, *Ursula*, *Unison*, and *Unbroken* were also transferred. (H.M.S. *Ursula* was one of the most famous British submarines; her operations during the second world war included the negotiation of a minefield off the mouth of the Elbe, when she had dived under a German destroyer to sink a cruiser.) *Sunfish*, after being transferred to Russia, was lost on active service. The British destroyers lent to the Russians were designated by them *Derzki*, i.e. *Audacious* class. They were: *Brighton*, *Chelsea*, *Churchill* (later lost on active service), *Georgetown*, *Leamington*, *Richmond*, *Roxborough*, *St. Albans*. An additional destroyer, *Lincoln*, was handed over to provide spare parts. This fleet of thirteen warships (whose value was about £4,000,000), sailed to Murmansk, and thereafter operated as part of the Arctic Fleet.

According to a report to which allusion is made in the French naval annual *Les Flottes de Combat* (1947),[2] the U.S.S.R. received from America a very considerable number of naval vessels and auxiliaries. These were said to include sixty-two destroyer escorts and twenty-eight frigates. In the case of *Milwaukee*, and also of *Royal Sovereign* and the nine British destroyers and four submarines, a naval protocol in the Italian Peace Treaty stipulated that these should be returned to Britain when the Russians received their share of the Italian Fleet.[3]

[1] See British United Press Reports of Nuremberg Trials, 11.12.1945.
[2] Addenda.
[3] Statement by Admiralty Financial Secretary, in the House of Commons, 26.11.1947.

With certain small exceptions, America and Britain announced that they would waive their own share in that fleet: such ships as they would have received were to be scrapped in Italian shipyards. Russia was to receive one battleship *Giulio Cesare*, (23,622 tons), one cruiser (*Duca d'Aosta*), four destroyers, fourteen torpedo boats, two submarines, the training-ship *Cristoforo Colombo*, three coastal craft, and various small vessels.

In specialising in speedy ships today, the Soviet Union is following the same objective as Peter the Great, whose first aim was to have a fleet capable of rapid mobility. It is their speed as aircraft-carrying ships that is one of the chief characteristics of the *Kirov* cruiser class—*Kirov*, *Kuibishev*, *Molotov*, *Maxim Gorki*, *Voroshilov*, and *Ordzhonikidze* (each of 8,545-8,800 tons.) Their armament includes nine 7.1-inch guns: they were all built between 1936 and 1940, and eight such cruisers would have been in commission by 1941 if the Russians had not blown up *Frunze* and *Kaganovitch* at Nikolaiev to prevent the Germans finding out their latest designs. *Kirov* and *Maxim Gorki* were damaged during the war, but as far as was known, not severely. These two ships, as also *Ordzhonikidze* and *Kuibishev*, have a speed of thirty-four knots, and all were built at Leningrad. The speed of modern Russian shipbuilding is to be noted in connection with the first three of these cruisers; all were completed within two-and-a-half years of launching, and *Kirov* actually made her appearance within a year of launching. *Petropavlovsk* (ex-*Luetzow*) was another addition to Russia's cruiser strength, having been acquired from Germany in 1940. She displaces 10,000 tons, carries four aircraft and includes twelve 7.1-inch guns in her armament. "Originally she was to have mounted eight 8-inch guns, but it is reported from Sweden that she has been re-armed with twelve Russian weapons of 7.1 inch calibre."[1] We have noted that the Soviet Union was also to acquire one Italian cruiser. In the list published by *Brassey's Naval Annual*, *1946-47*, four other cruisers appear: they are *Krasny Kavkaz* (launched at Nikolaiev, 1916, completed 1930, 7,600 tons, 29½ knots, four 7.1-inch guns); *Kalinin* (completed 1942, 7,725 tons, 34 knots, nine 7.1-inch guns); *Kaganovitch* (completed 1944, 7,725 tons, speed not given, nine 7.1-inch guns); *Krasny Krym* (7,200 tons, 29½ knots, fifteen 5.1-inch guns). The *Naval Annual* also lists four other (unnamed) cruisers of 7,725 tons each (building.) Three others of the same tonnage are queried, viz., *Chkalov*, *Chapaev*, and *Kuibyshev*. The A.A. guns on Russian warships are

[1] *The Navy*, March, 1944, p. 77.

as a rule mounted singly, a practice which Russian naval
authorities claim is an advantage, as it enables simultaneous
concentration on more targets than is possible when the guns
are mounted doubly.

Russia's deficiency in cruisers is in marked contrast with her
flotilla strength. Mr. Tunstall in *World War at Sea*,[1] has given
some interesting data in this connection. "First come the new
Leningrad class of torpedo cruisers, extraordinary hybrid ships of
2,900 tons, armed with five 5.1-inch guns, six 21-inch torpedo
tubes, and with a speed of thirty-six knots. . . . All are fitted
for mine-laying. The first was launched in 1935, and according
to a German estimate five were in service in June 1941. Their
design has clearly been inspired by that of the French *contre-
torpilleurs*, which range from 2,100 tons to 2,900 tons." In 1944
Russia had twelve flotilla leaders and fifty-six destroyers, but
her losses in the latter were considerable, and of the *Leningrad*
class only five were thought to remain in existence after
the war.

"Of destroyers proper," says Tunstall, "there are the partly
completed *Stremitelni* class, launched in batches from 1936
onwards, of 1,800 tons, mounting four 5.1-inch guns, and with
a speed of thirty-seven knots. About ten were in service when
the Russo-German war began out of a projected total of thirty-
six.[2] Apart from these there are a large number of fairly obsolete
and completely obsolete destroyers, dating from 1910 to 1918,
several of which however, have been reconstructed, though
with what result it is difficult to imagine."[3] Among the destroyers
acquired by Russia as a result of the Peace treaties of 1947,
two came from Rumania, and three, as we have mentioned,
from Italy. From the Japanese Fleet Russia acquired six
destroyers. Her losses in the war had been thirty.

The creation of a submarine fleet was commenced under the
First Five-Year Plan, and today the Soviet Navy leads the world
in the number of its under-water vessels. "We have," wrote the
Commissar for Shipbuilding, in *Pravda*, "every right to assert
that on all possible marine theatres of war in the Baltic and
Black Sea, in the North, and particularly in the Far East, the
U.S.S.R. has a powerful submarine fleet, capable of assuring

[1] Martin Secker and Warburg, 1942; p. 168.
[2] Ten more are believed to have been almost completed, and of this total
force of twenty recent destroyers, more than half were at Leningrad when
war broke out.
[3] *World War at Sea*. pp. 168, 169.

the security of all the sea frontiers of the Soviet Union." The products of the Russian shipyards, he asserted would surpass in speed and armament anything now on the seas.

It is not improbable that these words were far from being a species of bluff, designed to make Japan and Germany think twice. Russia does have a way of springing surprises on the world. Germany at any rate, was convinced of the superiority of Russia's submarine fleets. Despite the boasts about its U-boats, the German Admiralty, in its official annual, *Nauticus* (1938), stated: "It is necessary to recognise the incontestable fact that the U.S.S.R. possesses at the present time the most powerful submarine fleet in the world. Another incontestable fact is that, in three maritime regions, i.e. in the Baltic and the North Sea, in the Mediterranean, and the Pacific, every consideration of strategy must henceforth count with a factor (which was neglected after the end of the world war, till recently), viz., the modern efficient battleships flying the Soviet Standard."

For security reasons much of the submarine building was transferred to the Asian side of the Urals before the last war. (The practice of siting industrial establishments beyond the Urals was not an innovation of the Soviets, it had been started under Tsar Nicholas II.) A special type of submarine for coastal defence, with a speed of nineteen knots and 21-inch torpedoes, was one of the products of those regions. At Nikolaiev on the Bug, submarines with the *schnorkel* device have been constructed from the designs of those taken by the Russians from the Germans at Elbing. At Odessa and Kronstadt as well as at Nikolaiev, midget submarines similar to the *Seehund* type have been built.

The majority of the Russian submarines built before 1937 were coastal types, designed for defensive work. But most of the later vessels have been built for a different purpose; they can voyage far from their bases, and they have been constructed as much more powerful ships to meet the possibility of Russia being blockaded by sea. These new submarines have been designed to enable the Soviet Navy to break any such blockade. Credit to their long cruising radius was given by the Secretary of the United States Navy, who reported on 25 March, 1948, that "several Russian submarines had been sighted recently off American shores." (This report was repudiated by Tass Agency in a Moscow broadcast, three days later.)

In an article published in *The Navy*, April 1948, on the

contemporary Soviet Navy, Captain Russell Grenfell, R.N.,[1] recalled that the Soviet Union had recently been broadcasting that her submarine strength in the Baltic-Arctic region was 250. And if, he continued, "it is anywhere near that, we ought to know from recent experience what that could portend. The German submarine offensive against our sea communications in the last war constituted the gravest danger of the war; and before it was brought under control, we had to provide 400 to 500 destroyers and escort vessels, together with numerous coastal aircraft, for the protection of our shipping. The condition of security in the Atlantic was numbers". (Since the appearance of that article, the 1948 edition of *Jane's Fighting Ships* gave the estimate of 250 Russian submarines in service, and 100 more believed to be in hand. Plans for 1,000 submarines of all types within the next three years, were stated to have been made.)

The reports that the Russians after the war, had been engaging German crews in the newer class of submarines, indicated their desire to profit by the specialised training possessed by such personnel. What Russia might do with her submarines, said the writer of *The Navy* article, was not a matter for complacency in Britain, and one of the most disturbing aspects of the official silence about the British naval forces, related to the question of anti-submarine defences. Recalling the "reckless reductions" made in the inter-war years, and emphasising the fact that submarine warfare would be a good deal more dangerous in a third world war than in the second, Captain Grenfell referred to the construction by the Russians of the major naval base, Molotovsk, on the Arctic coast. Such a base gave direct access to the Atlantic, and the writer asked, "Against whom but ourselves can its use be intended?" He went on to say:—

"Would the Russians be taking all this trouble if they are relying on atom bombs or rockets to knock us out in the lamentable event of a conflict? I think not. It surely behoves us, therefore, to make quite sure, while there is still time, of the adequacy of our anti-submarine defences. It is by no means impossible that, while our air striking force was dropping its bombs on the Russian vastness (if it could get there), we ourselves could be effectively blockaded by new-type submarines against which we had failed to provide proper counter-measures.

"It would really be rather a pity were we to become so transfixed with fear of atomic explosion as not to realise that an older

[1] *The Navy*, April, 1948. (The Navy League); pp. 120, 121.

form of attack could still bring us down, especially since it has nearly brought us down twice already."

According to a statement made in the spring of 1948 by Admiral Louis E. Denfeld, United States Chief of Naval Operations, the estimated strength of Soviet submarines was then about 260 completed, and a further 110 building. It is not unlikely that by the time this book is completed, the total number of Russian submarines may well be approaching 500. And of these a number will no doubt embody the results of the German wartime development of the engine giving high speed under water. The Mark 21 U-boat, capable of more than fifteen knots, was one of the latest submarines built by the Germans under Hitler; this vessel was acquired by the Americans after the war, but it is likely that the Russians, with the assistance of German technicians, had evolved an under-water vessel of a speed at least equal to that of Mark 21 by the beginning of 1948.

Considerable additions have been made to Russia's fleet of minesweepers. Several of the most modern of these 400-ton vessels were built in Canada towards the end of the war. They have a wide radius of action and have been designed primarily for use in the Pacific. In 1942 a certain number of Norwegian whaling vessels were transferred to the U.S.S.R. for use as minesweepers, and after the war "over 40 fleet minesweepers, some 30 motor torpedo boats, and 50 motor launches fitted for minesweeping"[1] were among the vessels Russia acquired from Germany.

Russian motor-boats have tended to show a preference for carrying mines rather than torpedoes, and in this respect have differed from British vessels of a similar type, in which 18-inch torpedo tubes have been the general rule. "More than 70 per cent. of the known surface ships of the Russian Navy, including all the destroyers, are fitted as minelayers."[2] The Russians first used mines in war in 1854-55, in Baltic waters. But their tradition for efficient minelaying really dates from the time of the Russo-Japanese War, when of Japan's six battleships at Port Arthur, two were sunk by mines, and four cruisers and five other warships were lost in the same way. The tradition was perpetuated in the first and second world wars. In the former,

[1] Francis E. McMurtrie, A.I.N.A., *Brassey's Naval Annual, 1947*; Chapter III, "Foreign Navies," p. 45.
[2] Fletcher Pratt, *Sea Power and Today's War*. (Methuen, 1940); pp. 105,106. By permission of the Publishers.

Russian minelayers, according to Tokarev,[1] laid 47,000 mines in the Baltic and the Black Sea together. In that war the first satisfactory mines which Britain obtained came from Russia; they were sent from Vladivostock to Plymouth.

High claims for the fighting efficiency of their fleets were made by Soviet spokesmen during World War II. But in non-Russian naval circles some of the official Soviet figures have been received with reservation. By 1 July, 1944, according to a broadcast given by Major-General Grigoriev on Red Navy Day, the Baltic Fleet had sunk 1,666 enemy ships and destroyed 5,308 planes.

The Northern Fleet has been called "detski pyatiletok", "the child of the Five-Year Plan", for it dates from the time of the visit made to the Arctic coast by Stalin, Kirov, and Voroshilov in 1933. High too were the claims made for this fleet by Lieut.-Colonel Peter P. Anchersky. During the war, he said, it had sunk more than 500 German transports carrying troops and war material, and had brought down more than 1,000 German planes.[2]

Of the Pacific Fleet, Admiral Kuznetsov, Commissar for the Red Navy, speaking in March 1939, at the Eighteenth Conference of the Communist Party of the U.S.S.R., made this pronouncement: "We now have excellent coast defences, and whereas formerly we had practically no fleet at all in the Far East, during the last five to six years we have succeeded in organising a fleet there fully capable of defending our Far Eastern coasts."

The respective strengths of the Russian and Japanese Navies at the beginning of World War II were as follows:[3]

Russia

Battleships	.. ..	4 (and 2 projected)
Cruisers	.. ..	8
Aircraft carriers ..	..	1 (1 building)
Flotilla leaders ..	..	3 (8 building)
Destroyers	.. ..	28
Submarines	.. ..	109

"There are about thirty-five destroyers and torpedo-boats completed from 1895 to 1912 of very little if any fighting value."

[1] Н. Токарев: *Военно-торской Флот СССР в Отечественной Войне.* Государственное Издательство Политической Литературы, Москва, 1943.
[2] "Under the Red Banner," *The Navy,* April, 1945; p. 120.
[3] *Brassey's Naval Annual, 1939;* p. 300.

Japan

Battleships	.. ..	9
Cruisers	.. ..	37
Aircraft carriers ..	..	7
Seaplane carriers..	..	6
Destroyers	.. ..	119
Submarines	.. ..	62 (and 1 building)

Regarding the Soviet warships of the future, only time will show whether or not M. Tevosyan, Commissar for Shipbuilding, was correct in declaring that the Russian battleships and cruisers would be "among the most powerful in the world in regard to the power of their artillery, their speed, and their fighting capacity".

For the present, it would be rash for anyone outside the inner naval circles of the Soviet Union to make any comment on this statement, for, in the words of R. J. Daniel, contributor to the 1948 edition of *Brassey's Naval Annual*,[1] "News from the Soviet on naval construction has been almost non-existent during 1947".

The real strength of the Red Navy lies in its submarines, about which certain data will be found in the Supplementary Section at the end of this book. Here too is given some account of the part played by the fleets of the U.S.S.R. in the second world war.

[1] p. 502.

XV
MERCANTILE MARINE
THE VOLUNTEER FLEET

"No information has been forthcoming from the Soviet authorities and it is extremely difficult to keep touch with the many changes of name. Many names are held by two or more vessels at the same time." Anyone who has studied the subject of Russia's mercantile marine knows only too well the mass of conflicting statements and statistics accumulated after research among the articles which have appeared in non-Russian papers.

The difficulty of gathering information about the real strength of Russia's merchant navy to which the editor of *Merchant Ships*[1] refers in the passage just quoted, has not prevented his standard work from giving some helpful data on this subject. The latest figures available (at the time of writing) in Mr. Talbot-Booth's book are for 1944, when we are told that Russia had approximately five hundred and sixty steamships of 960,000 tons gross, and one hundred and thirty-nine motor vessels of 346,000 tons gross; in all six hundred and ninety-nine ships of 1,306,000 tons gross. From *Lloyd's Register* (July 1939) the fact emerges that the most striking increase during the inter-war period concerns the average deadweight tonnage, which at the beginning of World War I was 1,150, but at the beginning of World War II was 3,000. It is unfortunate that no returns were available for Russia in *Lloyd's Register Shipbuilding Returns, December, 1946*, though this publication, officially used at the Shipwrights' Exhibition, London, 1947, gives the number and gross tonnage figures for the merchant vessels under construction in sixteen countries. By 1st July, 1947 however, more information was available, for on that date *Lloyd's Register* gave the total number of vessels in Russia's mercantile marine as 952, and the gross tonnage as 2,156,987.

Soviet ports are badly placed in relation to the main trade routes of the globe, and this has been a handicap to Russia's maritime development. Her share in the world's international trade before the second world war did not exceed one per cent. "The volume of Russia's exports and imports was about

[1] *Merchant Ships, 1944.* Edited by E. C. Talbot-Booth, R.D., R.N.V.R. (Sampson Low, 1944.)

one-tenth of Germany's, one-fifth of France's, and one third of Belgium's. Russia's rôle in the world's markets, at a time when its economy was rapidly expanding under the Five-Year Plans, was about the same as the rôle of Finland or Rumania."[1]

The beginning of the nineteenth century had seen some serious efforts to improve the status of Russia's merchant shipping; in 1806 a school was founded at Nikolaiev for training masters and pilots of commercial vessels. In 1832 this was enlarged, and moved to Kherson, while a similar institution was opened at St. Petersburg. Four years later a scheme known as the "Corporation of Free Mariners" was introduced, whereby families devoted to navigation were for the first time incorporated in certain towns along the sea coasts and river banks.[2] In 1856 a Steam Shipping and Trading Company, with the privilege of acquiring land free of charge, was formed for the construction of docks and harbours.

But right up to the middle of the century Russia's shipping was so far from being in a position to meet her trade requirements that her chief exports—flax, pitch, hemp, tallow, hides, timber—were carried mainly in British bottoms. The history of Russia's merchant navy, as an organised institution indeed, may be said to begin only with the year 1876, when the Volunteer Fleet was started with the object of giving Russia maritime power. It was founded by national subscription, but at the outbreak of the Russo-Japanese War it consisted of not more than twenty-five vessels, most of them very antiquated. To this fleet was attached the Black Sea Navigation Company, which even by 1904 only possessed ten ships. The first vessels were *Russia*, *Petrograd*, and *Moscow*. These merchant ships, of which all the earliest were built in England, were controlled by the Russian Admiralty, and were capable of being armed—though, wrote F. T. Jane in 1899[3]—all these vessels' 9-inch and 6-inch guns were stored at Vladivostock or on the Black Sea. From Odessa to Vladivostock Russia had no base from which these ships could be equipped for war. So they were not such a menace as many people in Britain and in America then believed them to be. (Only three of them actually took part in the Russo-Japanese War.)

[1] From an article based on the statistical tables of international trade, *The Observer*, 5.3.1944.
[2] For their privileges see W. S. Lindsay's *History of Merchant Shipping and Ancient Commerce*. (Sampson Low, Marston, Low & Searle, 1874); Vol. III, p. 30.
[3] *The Imperial Russian Navy; Its Past, Present, and Future*; 2nd edition, p. 335.

At the same time this apprehension was based on long-term rather than immediate calculations. One well-known American writer, A. J. Beveridge, was looking beyond his time, when in 1903 he describes a 12,000-ton Russian ship of the Volunteer Fleet, tied up at Port Arthur. "These astonishing ships," he says, "—astonishing when you consider that Russia is a land nation . . . constitute one of the world's fast lines. There is not a modern device which they do not have."[1] They are, Beveridge points out, fitted to be auxiliary cruisers in time of war, and provide complementary communications to those secured by the Trans-Siberian and the Chinese Eastern Railways. The Volunteer Fleet, he continues, "is not only Russia's first adventure in a large way in the fields of maritime commerce; it is also a great practical training school for Russian seamen". Its officers are carefully trained navigators, and its crews chiefly recruited from the shores of the Baltic and the Black Sea. Hence Russia is preparing practical seamen for her navy and mercantile marine *"with which, in the course of time, she expects to become one of the first sea powers of the world".*[2]

If, says Beveridge, the route of these vessels from St. Petersburg is traced on the map, the globe-girdling aspirations of these Russians will be grasped. "For practical purposes this remarkable fleet makes but two ports—Russian Odessa or St. Petersburg in Europe, the port of departure—and Russian Dalni, Port Arthur or Vladivostock in northern Asia, the port of destination. Thus, practically without commerce except at Russian ports, Russia sails almost around the world to complete her circuit of empire."[3]

The Far Eastern ports mentioned in the previous paragraph were linked together when, before the Russo-Japanese War, a steamer service between Vladivostock and Port Arthur was opened by the Volunteer Fleet. By the middle of the first world war that fleet included a certain number of ocean-going steamers; it owned dock and harbour installations and port equipment, and it had offices and agencies in more than fifty places outside Russia. None the less, the Russian mercantile marine was quite unequal to the demands made upon it during the first world war. According to the calculations of the Allied Shipping Control Committee in 1915, Russian shipping could lift only about one-third of the required imports of 3,000,000

[1] *The Russian Advance.* (Harper & Bros., New York, 1903); p. 89.
[2] *Ibid.*, p. 90. [*Italics ours.*]
[3] *Ibid.*, p. 92.

tons,[1] and in 1916-17 it was British ships which carried three-fourths of the supplies to White Sea ports; Russian vessels took only one-fifth of the total cargoes.[2] The Commission had to allocate a hundred ships belonging mainly to Britain and America for the White Sea service, Hudson's Bay Company helping with the French exports to Russia.

As a result of the Civil War many of the Russian ships in the Northern and Black Sea ports were removed by the interventionists. Britain took over about fifty steamers which included more than twelve fair-sized liners of the Volunteer Fleet and of the Russian East Asiatic Company.[3] In Far Eastern waters where it had given most service, the remnants of the Volunteer Fleet were lost when in 1921 the counter-revolutionaries captured Vladivostock. (One of the principal vessels which had patrolled these waters in the Allied operations against the Germans, was the *Ryasan*, converted to an armed merchant cruiser. This had been captured by the enemy in the Strait of Korea, and refitted in their base of Tsingtau.) Foreign trade by sea remained almost negligible after the Revolution till 1921, when the New Economic Policy gave some stimulus to exports.

In 1922 the fleet began to be re-created by the Soviets, who took action in several instances for recovery of their ships and harbour properties. Up to the end of 1924 there had been returned to the Soviet Government all its former property in Russia and many of the ships which had been taken abroad. By that year all the largest vessels of the Volunteer Fleet which remained to Russia were marked A1 at Lloyds, some trading between Leningrad and London, and thence to the Black Sea.[4] The need for a merchant navy had become pressing, for Russia required imports to build up her industries. In the war of intervention she had come to know what a complete blockade by sea could mean. One-third of her total imports had previously passed through the Dardanelles,[5] and there is a good case for the assumption that the blockade of that channel, and of the Baltic Sea, were among the immediate causative factors of the Revolution, as the shortage of imported goods produced a chaotic situation throughout the country.

[1] C. E. Fayle, *Seaborne Trade*; Vol. II, p. 263.
[2] *Ibid.*, Vol. III, p. 239.
[3] *Ibid.*, Vol. III, p. 360.
[4] L. Haden Guest, *The New Russia*. (Thornton Butterworth, 1926); p. 265.
[5] For figures in detail see Gregor Alexinsky, *Russia and Europe*; p. 111.

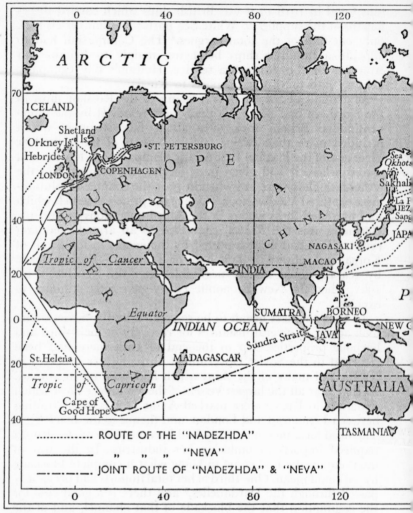

ROUTE OF THE "NADEZHDA"

" " " "NEVA"

JOINT ROUTE OF "NADEZHDA" & "NEVA"

(*Map reproduced by permission of Messrs. Hutchinson from "Russian Voyages Round the World", by N. Nozikov. The book edited by M. A. Sergeyev and translated by Ernstand Mira Lesser.*)

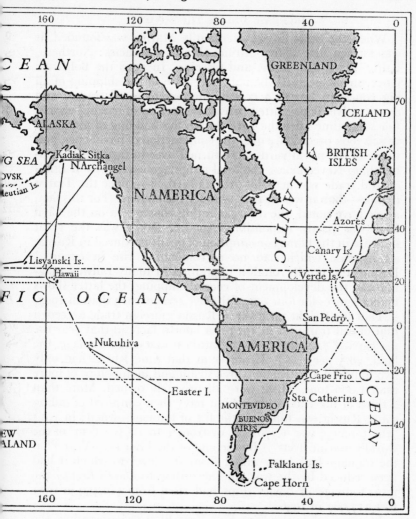

THE first Russian voyage of circumnavigation was undertaken primarily for the expansion of commerce. The great trade routes of the world, familiar for so long to the maritime nations, had been used but little by Russian ships before the beginning of the nineteenth century.

INCREASE UNDER THE SOVIETS

When the State Soviet Mercantile Marine was founded, it was formed first of five distinct shipping agencies: Northern, Baltic, Black Sea, Azov, and Caspian. In 1918 the Bolshevik Government decreed the nationalisation of the shipping of all big concerns, but to a certain number of small traders and co-operatives it permitted private ownership of trading vessels. For some time after the 1918 decree the building of merchant vessels took precedence over the construction of naval ones, and many of the naval yards were turned over to mercantile ship-building. Nevertheless, the total freightage carried by Russia's coastal trade was actually greater in 1913—under the Tsarist régime—than it was in 1927—under the Soviets. (For this fact, as we have noted, the disorganisation consequent on the Civil War was partly responsible. Another factor was the great increase in the home consumption of goods produced in Russia, an increase which had no corresponding rise in exports.) Despite the pre-Revolution opposition of many railway magnates to the development of coastal shipping, the latter shows higher figures for four out of the five seas in 1913 than in 1927.

That the freight turnover of Russia's foreign trade exceeded that of rail transport in 1913 is a known fact; in that year the sea carried 71.5 per cent. of Russia's total cargo tonnage, the land, 28.5 per cent.[1] However at that time Russia had only two hundred and seventy-three steam and motor-ships of more than 1,000 tons. These were all privately owned. More than a third of the Russian merchant navy then consisted of sailing ships. Russia was ninth on the list of tonnage owned; in 1914 "the tonnage was 1,770,000, or from 1 to 1.5 per cent. of the world's marine fleets".[2] By the end of the First Five-Year Plan the tonnage had been raised from the level to which it had been reduced by the war, and according to *Lloyd's Register* the gross tonnage of Soviet ships had risen from 412,459 in 1921 to 1,217,907 in 1936.

In 1931, while the First Five-Year Plan was operating, the U.S.S.R.'s merchant service carried only 4 per cent. of her exports; in 1937 the figure was approximately 50 per cent.[3] This increase was due to the fact that Russia was buying many

[1] *Bank for Russian Trade Review* (*London*) ; Vol. II, No. 6, p. 18.
[2] S. P. Turin, *The U.S.S.R.; An Economic and Social Survey.* (Methuen, 1944) ; p. 24. By permission of the Publishers.
[3] *Monthly Review.* Issued by the U.S.S.R. Trade Delegation in the United Kingdom. Vol. X, No. 12, p. 596.

ships abroad. During the chief period of economic depression between the two world wars, when Russia was able to buy cheaply in many countries, Britain, more than any other, was building ships for the U.S.S.R.'s mercantile marine (whereas she was building considerably less tonnage than many other countries were for Russia's navy.) But later the British embargoes on trade with the Soviet Union during the time of strained political relations, were partly responsible for the loss of shipping orders from Russia. Time charters for British ships on Russian account had been cancelled, thereby increasing the numbers of unemployed workers in the Tyneside yards. Russian orders went to continental shipowners, and Britain ceased to be a competitor for such orders until the trade embargoes were raised in July 1933. In that year representatives of the Soviet Government visited Britain to purchase second-hand steamers for use with the timber trade. They were able to buy cheaply then, as British exports, particularly coal, had declined steeply, and ships were laid up at nearly every port in the United Kingdom. Primarily for the purpose of dealing with her exports, the Soviet Union in 1938 spent twenty-five million roubles on the purchase of ships from abroad. After the second world war Russia (sharing with Poland) received in reparations one-third of the merchant fleet of the Reich. The largest share of the remaining two-thirds was finally allocated to Britain, who received more than 50 per cent. of the total tonnage allotted, making her share approximately 350,000 tons. The Inter-Allied Reparations Agency had previously announced that the division was apportioned on the basis of tonnage lost by each country in the war. It is not clear then why the British Empire, which lost 10,870,000 tons, was, under the *original* Reparations settlement, awarded less than Russia.

The Soviet Union has now taken advantage of her increased Baltic coastline by pressing forward with shipbuilding plans for all the yards she has acquired from Tallinn to Kaliningrad. This maritime expansion shows that the U.S.S.R., no less than the Atlantic Powers, appreciates a fact to which a leading British naval historian gave much point in a recent book: "The future of the world depends more than it ever did in the past on ocean trade, and when once the restrictions created by the war have been removed, ocean trade will be the symbol of the world's political and economic convalescence."[1]

[1] Brian Tunstall, *World War at Sea*; p. 231.

XVI

INLAND WATERWAYS

RUSSIA's system of artificial inland waterways has been planned with a view to enabling units of the different naval fleets to be transferred rapidly, when needed, from one sea to another. Canals have been widened and deepened so as to take warships, and when this process has been completed, units of the Baltic Fleet will have direct communication with the Black Sea Fleet, and the new berthing and repair docks and the shipbuilding yards which are being opened at ports in the south, will not, as in the past, be entirely separated from those in the north. Of the four fleets of Russia, the one to benefit the most from this development is the Black Sea Fleet, for that has always been liable to enforced independence of operations. It was, indeed, its relative isolation which for so long stultified its growth; outlay on warships for this sea was considered to be uneconomic. It was to the Baltic Fleet that main efforts at development were directed.

Peter the Great, like all enlightened Russians, had realised the immense asset that the waterways of Russia were to her, but many of his successors failed to see that such means of transport would inevitably become feeders to, rather than rivals of, the railways which they were anxious to protect. It was not till after the Revolution that the inland waterways were developed as a definite system of communications for the whole country. They would, it was estimated, by the end of the Third Five-Year Plan have increased by 76,015 miles. In 1917 it had been proposed to construct new systems and to double the facilities for inland navigation. The aim then as now was, in the words of a leading Soviet geographer,[1] to link the five seas and create a unified deep-waterway system in the European part of the U.S.S.R.

The increase of waterway traffic in the Soviet Union as compared with that in pre-Revolution times, is due to the vast expansion of industry in the U.S.S.R.; the new industrial economy required radical changes in transport for the despatch

[1] N. N. Mikhailov, *Soviet Land and People*. (Published by *Soviet News*, London, 1945); pp. 72, 73.

348

of material—primarily machinery—to the different parts of the Union. Conversely it may be said that the development of her inland waterways has revolutionised the economic geography of the Soviet Union. Before that development the chief cargoes had been grain and timber; today heavy machinery accounts for the greatest freight turnover. The raised power of towing tugs has led to an increase in the fleets of barges, and except in the timber-floating regions the slow-going rafts are seen much less frequently. By 1941 the number of steamers and motor vessels on inland waterways was 2.2 times as great as in 1929.[1]

Russia is wealthy in her waters;[2] without her great rivers the giant hydro-electric constructions could never have supplied her with the power which they have. Today there are 325,000 miles of navigable waterways in the U.S.S.R. (and many more than that if the timber-floating routes are included.) In 1918, owing to wartime damage and dislocation, the freight carried on the rivers was reduced to 16 per cent. of the total for 1913. But by 1929, through work under the First Five-Year Plan, the figure was 50,000,000 tons as against 48,000,000 for 1913.[3] In 1943 Russia's inland waterways were scheduled to carry 160,000,000 tons of freight. But for the war the entire river transport system would have been re-organised, and many new canals made to link together the cities. The vast hydro-electric station projects—notably the Kuibishev dam—belong to these plans.[4] The Soviet official statement is that the Germans sank or seized 4,280 passenger and cargo vessels and tugboats, and 4,029 barges.[5] But intensive work on re-building the river fleets was quickly started, and by 1944 the shipyards at Kiev were producing motor ships on a pre-war scale. It was estimated that by 1950 the inland water transport system would carry 38 per cent. more freight than before the war.

[1] George Kublitsky, "Inland Water Transport." Published in *Soviet Transport*, by Professor V. Obraztsov and Others. (Issued by *Soviet News*, London, 1946); p. 60.

[2] There are said to be 108,000 rivers in the U.S.S.R.

[3] George Kublitsky, "Inland Water Transport." (See Footnote 1, *Ibid.*, p. 58.)

[4] See also summary made by George Hanna and published in *Soviet War News*, 2.3.1944, of an article in "Transactions of the Academy of Sciences of the U.S.S.R."—Technical Sciences No. 9, 1943—by Professor Obraztsov, a leading Soviet transport engineer.

[5] Extraordinary State Commission for Ascertaining and Investigating Crimes of the German Fascist Invaders, issued September 1945.

THE MOSKVA-VOLGA CANAL

The U.S.S.R. has five principal river flotillas, the Volga, the Don, the Dnieper, the Danube, and the Amur. The construction of the Moskva-Volga Canal enabled units of the Volga flotilla to help in the defence of the Russian capital in the last war; it was fortunate that the Canal was completed four years before the German invasion. It is an essential part of Russia's water transport system; "Volga River water now washes the walls of the Kremlin in Moscow". This means that the products of the chief industrial and agricultural areas of the Volga basin can be brought by water to Moscow: Gorki, Kuibishev, Stalingrad, Astrakhan, can all send their freights to the capital. The oil too of Perm can be sent by the Kama and the Volga to Moscow (and in its own boats, for Perm is a centre of shipbuilding); the Tula coalfields have the services of the Volga and the Don waterways by use of the Moskva-Volga Canal. By the Volga-Kama waterway the Russian capital is connected with the great industrial centres of the Urals.

The Canal has shortened the distance between Moscow and Gorki by sixty-eight miles, and between Moscow and Leningrad the decrease is still more marked. For not only is the Volga now linked with Moscow, but with Leningrad, as a result of the reconstruction of the Volga-Baltic waterway, a work which was among the most urgent on the programme of the Third Five-Year Plan. And the Kama River, a tributary of the Volga, is linked by the canal system with Pechora in the Far North. This gives the Arctic port a waterway connection with the south for the transport of coal from the fields of the Pechora River, and of oil from the fields of its tributary the Ukhta.

"Volga, the good old mare, will carry everything," is a saying whose truth has become more apparent since the making of the Moskva-Volga Canal. That canal, which is one-and-a-half times as long as the Panama, carried—in the first three months after it was completed—400,000 passengers[1]. It was substantially responsible for the figure of 18,112,000 tons, representing the total Volga freightage in the first year of the last war.

Commencing seven kilometres above the mouth of the Dubna, a small tributary of the Moskva River, it passes through the land along which a gigantic glacier once moved, north-south. It is eighty-five metres wide, so steamers (it was planned to take three-deck vessels) can pass up and down at full speed. To enable them to reach Moscow, thirteen new bridges had to be built,

[1] Figures given in *Monthly Review*; Vol. X, No. 11, p. 540.

as the existing ones were too low. (A diagram of the Canal will be found on p. 395 in the Supplementary Section of this book).

An early account of the obstacles to navigation on the River Moskva will be found in the sixteenth-century writings of Baron Sigismund von Herberstein,[1] who records that sailing "is slow and difficult on account of the numerous turnings and windings with which the river is indented". These difficulties had, of course, to be overcome in our own time by Soviet engineers, who worked to increase the speed of vessels by adopting the principle common to all modern canals—that of reducing the number of small locks and replacing these by fewer but more powerful ones. From the fourth and last lock at Vlakhernskaya "the Volga water, its level raised by the dam, flows downhill for only 16 kms., after that it has to be raised by mechanical means to the reservoir on the watershed which lies between the River Volga and the River Moskva, and which is about forty metres high. For this purpose the northern slope of the canal is divided into five sections, forming a series of steps each of which is higher than the preceding one by about eight metres. At each of these steps there is a pumping station furnished with four propeller pumps which raise the water to the next section".[2]

In more pictorial language the author-engineer Komarovsky has thus described the region: "Looking at the green meadows, woods, and pastures on the shores of artificial lakes and observing the flocks of ducks rising noisily from under the very nose of the ship, or the grey gulls circling and screeching overhead, one might think that these lakes, bays and creeks, have been created by nature, and have existed here since time immemorial. Only the stone banks of the canal and the arched bridges spanning it bear witness to the fact that this waterway is the hand of man."[3]

THE VOLGA AND THE DON

Another key-canal in the U.S.S.R.'s transport system is the Volga-Don. Such a channel had been attempted by Peter the Great. He had built Taganrog harbour against the Turks and their fortress at Kerch, and had worked to enable a Volga fleet to transport an army, via a Volga-Don Canal, to the Azov Sea. The canal was to link together two tributaries of the Volga—

[1] *Notes Upon Russia.* (Printed for the Hakluyt Society, London, 1851); Vol. II, p. 2.

[2] *U.S.S.R. in Construction, 1930-39;* Volga Canal, Vol. II. (The State Publishing House of Graphic Arts, Moscow.)

[3] A. Komarovsky, "The Moscow-Volga Canal." *The U.S.S.R. Speaks for Itself.* (Lawrence & Wishart, 1942. Reprinted); Vol. II, pp. 100, 101.

the Kamishinka and the Slovina—then, running through Lake Ivan it was to connect the latter with the Don and the Okha. Some of the ships were "launched, rigged, and sent down to Astrakhan; some they since essayed to bring up the Volga, and by the channels of other rivers, in conjunction with the Ladoga Lake, to St. Petersburg, but the frequent shallows rendering the design abortive, the ships lie rotting near Vishni-Volochkok in the road from Moscow to St. Petersburg".[1] And when Peter the Great was defeated at Pruth in 1711, he had to give up Azov and Taganrog, and so "rendered all his naval armament on the River Don entirely useless."

Today the Volga-Don Canal which joins the Volga near Stalingrad, provides cheap transport for the coal and iron of the Donetz Basin to the north, and of timber to the south. The iron ore of Krivoy Rog is river-borne too. The Canal also irrigates the Trans-Volga region which suffers from periodic drought. And it links Stalingrad to Rostov, so that the former city can, by means of the Manych Canal, export to Azov.

The Manych Canal which has joined the Caspian to the Azov Sea and the Black Sea, presented peculiar difficulties in its construction, owing to the fact that the Caspian is twenty-six metres below the level of the Don. Commencing at Alabu, south of Astrakhan on the Volga, the canal ends just north of Rostov, where the Manych River joins the Don. For the last stage of the four hundred-mile-long Canal, the Sukhov Kuma river-bed has been used. One result of the increased traffic on the Don which has followed the construction of the Manych Canal, has been the growth of Rostov as a port. But the most important gain from the linking of the Caspian and the Black Seas is the fact that ocean steamers can take oil from Baku and grain and cotton from the Trans-Caucasian Republics, to the industrial areas of the Lower Dnieper and the Donetz. The old waterways system—the Marinskaya—which linked the Baltic and the Caspian—was only possible for barges and timber rafts; the Marinskaya system was entirely reconstructed when the Volga-Don and White Sea Canals were laid.

"The straightening of the Volga," at the Samara bend and in the Saraka Luka area, has saved shipping-time. The Greater Volga Plan, as part of the Five-Year Plans, has provided for the construction of a chain of power stations along the Volga from Moscow to the Urals; the industrial area of the south Urals has

[1] *The Russian Fleet Under Peter the Great.* (Publications of the Navy Records Society); Vol. XV, pp. 3, 4.

already been linked with the ports of the Volga and those of the Sea of Azov by the Saratov-Milero Railway.

THE DNIEPER AND THE DANUBE

The third of Russia's River Fleets, the Dnieper flotilla, was able to extend its activities after the erection of the giant dam at Dnieprostroy, which was completed in 1932. Before that, the Rapids of the Upper Dnieper had prevented the use of the river for direct navigation between the Black Sea and the towns in White Russia. The Dnieper, 1,400 miles in length, rises like the Volga, in the Valdai Hills, and winds its way south-east through the Black Earth region till it reaches the stretch between Dniepropetrovsk and Zaporozhye. Here for over fifty miles are rocks and currents which formerly made navigation almost impossible. In 1927 the Dnieprostroy scheme was inaugurated, and a port was built with modern equipment.

For the first time in the history of navigation, on 1 May, 1933, two steamers sailed from Kiev on the Dnieper to Kherson on the Black Sea, passing through the great locks at Zaporozhye. This was made possible only by the mastery of the Dnieper Rapids. After the construction of the hydro-electric station, the Dnieper and the Bug were joined by the Beresina Canal, and by 1940 the Ukraine could by this means ship its peat and wheat to the Black Sea. Products of the metal industry of Melitopol could be taken north for use in the river shipyards, vessels built in the yards of Nikolaiev could be brought under their own power to the ports of the Upper and Middle Dnieper, machinery from Briansk could be exchanged direct with oil from Batum, and Smolensk had an all-waterway communication with Sevastopol. The system is linked with the Vistula, and the change effected by the full use of the Dnieper, meant that the transit trade of such countries as Poland and Germany had now another water route to the Black Sea ports and Turkey. It meant that Russia's own trade with Turkey and Iran was increased. Linked to the Don by the rivers Samara and Torietz, the Dnieper now affords a waterway joining the Baltic to the Azov Sea. The value of the Dnieper as a river route is enhanced by the length of its navigation period: on the Lower Dnieper this amounts to approximately two hundred and eighty days, a longer season than that of any other of the great Russian rivers.[1]

[1] James S. Gregory and D. W. Shave, *The U.S.S.R.; A Geographical Survey*. (Harrap, London, 1944. John Wiley & Sons, Inc., New York); p. 63.

The fourth of the U.S.S.R.'s River Fleets, the Danube flotilla, provided in the second world war several instances of the integral character of Russian land and river warfare, for one of the main functions of this flotilla was to destroy tanks and other armoured weapons within range of the water. Gunboats and armoured cutters operated in this way between Belgrade and Budapest, and crews of the flotilla helped to drive the Germans out of the Hungarian capital. This flotilla was increased when, in accordance with the 1945 armistice terms with Hungary the latter was required to pay reparations which included Danubian river-craft. As a result of her five-year pact of economic co-operation with Hungary, which gave the Soviet Union a substantial interest in the economy of that country, Russia has gained a new share of control in Danubian navigation. She further increased her Danube tonnage when by the armistice terms with Rumania, the latter country, as part-payment of reparations, ceded to the Soviet Union much of her own river-craft. To restore to the Danube its capacity as a free highway under international control, was the aim of the Western Powers, but the Soviet standpoint was that control of the Danube was exclusively the concern of the Riparian States. At the Conference held in August 1948, Russia insisted that only the Danubian countries should have right of navigation for naval vessels. She herself claimed the fleet of the Danubian Shipping Company, of approximately 337,000 tons, formerly the property of Austria.

So important have the inland waterways become to the U.S.S.R. that a British paper during the war seriously suggested that they might have been used to take part of the Black Sea Fleet to the Baltic. "The Russians have secretly transferred part of their Black Sea Fleet—including submarines—to help in the fighting in the north" stated the report. "How the Russians got the submarines from the Black Sea to the Gulf of Finland is not revealed—whether they were navigated for nearly 2,000 miles along Russia's mighty rivers and new giant canals, or brought 4,000 miles round via the Mediterranean, past Britain, past Kiel, and through the narrows between Germany and Sweden". Enlightenment on this matter is not likely to be forthcoming.

THE ARAL SEA

Russia's inland seas, like her lakes and rivers, are now increasing their fleets to meet the needs of growing industries round their shores. East of the Caspian Sea, across the Kirghiz Steppes, lies the Aral Sea, frozen for part of the year not only on most of its shoreline but for some distance inland up the deltas of its rivers. So little known was it less than a hundred years ago, that in the Russian campaign against Khiva in 1873 it was hardly considered in the plan of operations. When a few reconnaissance vessels were sent on the water that year, it surprised many people to learn that the sea was navigable everywhere in the south. The silting up of that shore and the eastern one, and the severe storms and the prevalence of fogs, however, made harbourage impossible except in a few places. In the east it was only between Cape Tiouk Karagan and the Balkhan Gulf that harbourage could be found. From there to Astrabad there was no place where a ship could berth. In the north, only in the Bay of Perovski was there a suitable roadstead, and in the 1873 campaign the ships had to winter at Kasilinsk on the Syr Daria. Thus Aral, until the opening up of navigation on the Syr Daria, was an isolated sea. The first attempt to create a flotilla there had been made in 1847, when two vessels, the warship *Nicholas* (a wooden sailing vessel) and the two-masted trading ship *Michael*, were built in Orenburg and taken in sections to the Aral Sea; they worked at first with the fishing stations. Then came the *Constantine*, in which Admiral Butakov surveyed the whole area, and part of the Amu Daria which flows into the Aral Sea. He found not only that the Amu was navigable as far as Koungrad, but that one of its branches, the Kuk-Uziak, could be used by flat-bottomed vessels for a considerable distance. For nearly forty years Butakov's charts remained the only material for the study of this sea.[1]

In the Khivan campaign the flotilla consisted of one gunboat (*Samarkand*), with one barge, and the *Perovski* with two barges; there was a total complement of two hundred and sixty men.[2] The vessels went some distance up the Ulkun-Daria (an arm of the main river), but navigation for anything but very small vessels was not possible beyond Lake Kara-Kut. The shallow deltas of the Amu and Syr Daria could only be traversed by small, flat vessels—useless for the open sea—so it was found that separate flotillas for the Aral and for the two rivers were necessary. In 1885, when the flotilla had increased to nineteen

[1] See Hugo Stumm, *Russia in Central Asia*. (Harrison & Sons, London, 1885); p. 46.
[2] *Ibid.*, pp. 331, 332.

vessels (more than half of these were barges), the *Samarkand* and *Perovski* still remained the only ones fit for active service on the sea. In addition to the difficulties of harbourage there were those of fuel, the only kind obtainable being that of the saksaul shrub, which burnt very quickly, so that large quantities had to be taken on board. Saksaul is one of the few forms of vegetation which the surrounding desert area does produce. Today part of the sandy waste is being changed to pasturage by artificial grass-sowing from aeroplanes, and in time the work of the Desert Cultivation Bureau will have transformed this region to an important one for sheep-grazing. Vessels for the transport of wool cargoes will be a need of the future.

Into the Aral Sea flows the Syr Daria, whose course Russia in the last century followed in her eastward expansion via Tashkent to the Northern Pamirs. Not only is the Syr Daria now open to shipping, but in yards along its banks tugs and barges are built of pine from the Tien Shan mountains. "Sixty per cent. of the freight formerly carried by the overloaded Tashkent railroad, connecting Central Asia with the southern Urals, can now be shifted to the river—including timber from the Tien Shan mountains, coal from the mines at Shurab and Suliuktin, salt from new diggings near the river, or petroleum from nearby wells via the short pipe-line to be built to the river bank."[1] The Ferghana Canal (170 miles long) in the Uzbekistan Republic, is linked with the Syr Daria to irrigate the surrounding arid lands. Connected with this system too, and joining the Syr Daria, is the Tashkent Canal. Traffic will be increased on these waterways when the mercury mines in the Ferghana Valley— the biggest in the Soviet Union—are fully developed.

THE RIVERS OF SOVIET ASIA

The Amu Daria (Oxus) once flowed across Turkmenistan, and fell not into the Aral, but the Caspian Sea. Anthony Jenkinson, the noted sixteenth-century English traveller, voyaging on the Caspian in 1558, wrote in his letter to the Muscovy Company, "Note that in times past there fell into this gulf the great river Oxus." The intention is to divert the present course to the original bed, so as to provide the Kirghiz desert with a new irrigation system—an idea which had been also in the mind of Peter the Great, who had in fact entered into negotiations

---

[1] William Mandel, *The Soviet Far East.* (The Dial Press, Inc., New York, 1944); pp. 122-123.

with the Turkoman Chief, Khodja Nefes, about this project. Peter knew too of the legends of gold washed from the mountains down to the mouth of the Amu Daria and worked by the Khivans in secrecy. (It was to find out the truth about the rumoured goldfield at Yarkand, as well as to get cotton from Central Asia for his newly created textile industries, that Peter had started his Khivan campaign from the Caspian Sea.) Because of its usefulness in watering the desert lands through which it flows, Amu Daria has been called the Russian Nile. It rises in the Hindu Kush, and its delta is on the southern shore of the Aral Sea. The fact that these two rivers, the Syr Daria (Jaxartes) and the Amu Daria, have been used increasingly for transport, is but the natural development of undertakings commenced a hundred years earlier, when in addition to the Orenburg steamers previously mentioned, two were sent in sections from Sweden. The Russian rulers realised the importance of the Aral Sea and its rivers; the Amu Daria and the Syr Daria, each 1,300 miles long, could, they knew, be used for penetration into Central Asia, and the Aral Sea could become a base for the transport of armies by the riverine routes. Perovski, when he was Governor of this region, had seen the need for getting a fleet on the Aral Sea, and when he created one there, said that he needed it to supply the inhabitants of that area with necessities. When told there were no people there to supply, he replied "then the fleet will bring them".[1]

Fort Kazabusk, on the Lower Syr Daria, was built in 1846; a hundred years later, as the result of the First and Second Five-Year Plans, shipyards can be seen at the port of Charjow on the Amu Daria, and shipment of cargoes makes Leninsk a place of growing importance. Work on the diversion of the Amu Daria to its original channel was begun in 1933, and the course planned will take the river through the Uzboy depression and across the Kara Kum desert.

In Kirghizia, north of the headwaters of the Syr Daria, is the lake of Issik-Kul. This is in the centre of a mountain forest region, and to provide transport for the products of the saw mills and lumber camps, a new fleet has been built to cross the lake. The chief port on Issik-Kul is Rybachi, whence a line runs to Kant, near Firunze. This railway is partly used for the transport of coal from the Salinka field near Issik-Kul.

East of the Syr Daria across the salt steppe and desert lies Lake Balkash with the copper mines at Kounrad, near which

[1] Wirth Gerrare, *Greater Russia*, p. 274.

molybdenum, zinc, and tungsten are also found. On the shore
of the lake ship's armour can now be made. From the Kara-
ganda coalfield a line runs south-east to Port Balkash, near the
copper mines, and to serve the needs of the foundry at Kounrad
new steamers have been built. The development of transport on
Lake Balkash was made profitable with the opening of the
Turk-Sib. Railway: cotton, rice, cattle, wool, sugar, hides,
could find markets when once rail and water communications were made available and worked under a co-ordinated
scheme.

Far to the north of Lake Balkash is Lake Chany, situated
between the industrial cities of Omsk and Novosibirsk; here
too, on Chany, the number of steamers has been increased. The
lake will be linked up with the great Siberian rivers by an
extension of the canal system, and in this way connected with
the principal river routes far to the west. A wide field for
development lies in this work of extending the canal system to
link the rivers of Asiatic Russia with those of European Russia,
since the Russian river system in both continents is mainly
north-south. (Notable exceptions to this are the Ural, the
Upper, Lower, and Stony Tunguska, and the Viluisk—all
Siberian rivers.) "In the Soviet Union, plans are being studied
for joining by canals the rivers Kama, Chusovaya, Tura, Tobol,
Irtysh, Ob, and the Yenesei, and these, in turn, through the
Lower Tunguska, with the Lena River, thus providing a waterway through the heart of Siberia to the top of the world in
Asia, a waterway that will require ships to be effective."[1] Once
more we see the pattern of the pre-revolutionary Russian
designs being worked out under the rulers of Russia today. The
Imperial Government of more than a hundred years earlier
had realised the difficulties of taking its projected Trans-
Siberian Railway across the stormy waters of Lake Baikal by
ferry, so it decided to encourage river transport in that region,
using the tributaries between the Siberian rivers and the Ob-
Yenesei Canal; in 1846 the first steamer service was opened
between Tomsk and Tiumen on the Ob, and another followed
on the Yenesei. Thirty years later, Funtusov, a Siberian merchant, made investigations at his own expense to show that
affluents could be used to connect these two rivers. "By 1895
there were some hundred and twenty steamers on these rivers
and prior to the railway they became the main trade arteries

[1] R. A. Davies and A. J. Steiger, Soviet Asia. (Gollancz, 1943.) Acknowledgments to Miss Viola Cooper for American copyright. p. 201.

and mail routes."[1] It is interesting to recall that the economist Ostrovski had offered as an alternative to the proposal for a trans-Siberian railway the much less costly plan of using the rivers, and of laying lines to cover only the portages between the waterways.[2] This would have saved about four thousand miles of rail track.

The extent to which northerly communication in the U.S.S.R. is effective, depends much on the development of ice-free connections between the Siberian rivers and the Northern Sea Route; particularly it depends on voyages being made in one season. Though, as we said in the White Sea Canal chapter, the Soviet Government has planned to build a great Arctic railway, there are as yet only embryo lines along the Far North. Until railways are much farther advanced in northern Russia, the mineral and timber products of such regions as Siberia will continue to require for their transport the use of river and ocean ways. The coniferous forests of the Siberian Area which provide the river-port of Igarka with timber for its mills, lie far up the Yenesei and make this region of western Siberia the richest timber country in the world. Russia has about 30 per cent. of the world's forest area, and in Siberia there are nine hundred million acres of this.

It is fortunate that the Yenesei, like the Ob and the Lena, flows *north*, as logs can be floated downstream to Igarka and other ports, the long, floating journey being a cheap form of transport. Down the Yenesei too come boats with furs and minerals from the Far North to Igarka for trans-shipment to ocean-going vessels, eastward bound for Vladivostock, or westward for Murmansk.

The Yenesei at its mouth is over twenty miles wide, and the Yenesei Gulf is a hundred miles from shore to shore. The course of the river is often a winding one through narrow passages between rocky islands, and this calls for skilful navigation on the part of pilots; the latter conduct steamers usually as far as the trading depot of Ustport. It was a Norwegian syndicate, directed by Jonas Lied, which had first developed trade along the Yenesei and the Ob, and had planned the shipbuilding yards at Krasnoyarsk. The Civil War retarded these enterprises, but the Soviets realised their value, and also the need for extending the system of water transport, especially as the one line

---

[1] Prince Lobanov-Rostovsky, *Russia and Asia*. (Copyright 1933 by The Macmillan Company, New York. Extract by their permission); p. 217.

[2] See Emil Lengyel, *Secret Siberia*. (Robert Hale, 1947); p. 87.

of east-west communication (the Trans-Siberian Railway) was entirely disorganised by the Civil War. In 1920 the Committee of the Northern Sea Route (Komseveroput) was established to develop not only the Arctic seaway but also the northern river routes of the Union. Up till the time of the Revolution the only Siberian rivers which had been properly surveyed were the Ob and the Yenesei, and the Lena as far as Yakutsk. These were the rivers to which Komseveroput devoted particular attention, owing to their connections with the commercial ventures known as the "Kara Sea Expeditions". Not the least notable part of the work of Komseveroput has been on the Yenesei, for which river special craft has had to be made. (It is a distant day now from the one in 1875 when on this river Nils Nordenskiöld saw dogs towing boats upstream for the Samoyeds.) Owing to its course through the Sayan Mountains, rapids are formed below Krasnoyarsk, and these could not be navigated by ordinary steamers. The Yenesei possesses about two thousand miles of good navigation and in addition about three thousand miles of tributaries which can be used by vessels of various kinds.[1] In this respect the Yenesei has advantages over the Ob, as the latter would require most extensive dredging for the whole of its lower reaches to be clear for navigation. The detritus brought by the spring floods makes it at present impossible for deep-draught vessels to go far beyond the estuary. This is one of the tasks to which Soviet engineers will apply themselves, as the Ob is too vast a watershed, too useful a system, to be left unused by larger vessels. With its tributaries, its navigable mileage is second only to that of the Volga.[2]

With the recent expansion of Russia's Asiatic waterways system, coal can now be sent from the Kuzbas field via the Ob to the new towns arising north of Novosibirsk, and by that river copper can be carried from the Ridder mines. Iron ore from the Urals is unloaded from the railway, shipped down the Kama to Perm, and can be sent via rail to the Irtysh and thence to the towns of the Ob. Ferrous metal products from Sverdlovsk and Perm travel via the Trans-Siberian Railway to Omsk on the Irtysh, and thence can be shipped to the Gulf of Ob, and

---

[1] See also J. B. Gregory and D. W. Shave, *The U.S.S.R.; A Geographical Survey* (Harrap, London, 1944. John Wiley & Sons, Inc., New York); p. 296.

[2] The actual lengths of the above-mentioned rivers are: Volga, 2,305 miles; Yenesei, 2,380; Ob, 2,510; Lena, 2,665. The longest river of all is the Amur, of 2,721 miles. Figures given by N. N. Mikhailov in *Soviet Land and People,* published by *Soviet News,* London, 1945.

SHAVANSK DAM,
ON THE BALTIC—WHITE SEA CANAL

(Photo: Planet News Ltd.)

THE waterway whose construction has reduced the voyage from Archangel to Leningrad to one-fourth of its former length. The huge sheet of water falls with such an even flow, that to an observer this roaring cascade appears to be frozen motionless.

eventually along the Arctic Sea route. The coal of Kuznetsk and Krasnoyarsk finds its way to the sea by the Yenesei, so too the coal of Tunguska; the Yenesei also carries the nickel of Norilsk. (The latter is connected by railway with the port of Dudinka at the head of the Yenesei Gulf, whence the Norilsk metals are taken by freighters into the Arctic, then carried west to Murmansk or east to the ports of Yakutia.) Along the Yenesei are stations used by the flying-boats which take furs from the Far North to Krasnoyarsk, the terminal of the flying-boat service from Dudinka. The Arctic deltas of the Siberian rivers have for long been used by hydroplanes equipped in summer with pontoons and in winter with skis.

In 1942 *Pravda* stated that the amount of grain sent from the Province of Irkutsk by the Lena and Angara rivers, was for the past twelve months about equal to the amount sent by rail. The Lena also takes freights of gold from the Aldan field, which proceed by rail to Sovietskaya Gavan for shipment to other Far Eastern places. New dredging steamers have been allocated to the Vitim River, a tributary of the Lena, as the bed of the Vitim contains the principal gold supply of the Lena field. The rivers of Yakutia have been used increasingly for navigation since 1936, when "for the first time in history two caravans of river ships sailed to the Yakutsk rivers Indigirka and Yana by the sea route".[1] But navigation on the Yana is only possible by the use of a special type of vessel. On the Indigirka boats can take freight as far as the tributary Moma.

Lake Baikal, over four hundred miles long, is the longest and the deepest lake in the world: owing to its depth the volume of water is actually greater than the Baltic.[2] It has a new importance in keeping constant the level of the Angara now that plans for hydro-electrification have materialised on this river. Metallurgical developments have been followed by increased steamer traffic on Baikal: in Mount Khatalson, between the northern border of Outer Mongolia and the southern shore of Lake Baikal, lie the richest wolfram deposits in the world. Important deposits of uranium have been found in the neighbourhood of Baikal. On this remote lake in Buriat Mongolia icebreaker ferries carry truck trains. One of the earliest ferries, the *Baikal*, was built by Armstrong-Whitworth of Tyneside, being commissioned by the Russian Government in order to make possible the construction of the Trans-Siberian Railway

[1] *Monthly Review*; Vol. I, No. 4, p. 125.
[2] N. N. Mikhailov, *Soviet Land and People*; p. 15.

along the southern shore of the lake. Important lead mines lie behind the eastern shores of Baikal, and there are manganese deposits on the opposite side, also on Olkhon Island. "The Russians are not at all anxious to reveal the amount of manganese being extracted at Olkhon, but the deposits are spoken of as 'colossal'."[1]

The importance which the Soviet Government attaches to this region is clear from its intention to connect it by canal system with the Chusovaya (a tributary of the Kama.) The Chusovaya is to be linked via the river Izet with the Ob, and the Ob with the Yenesei and the Angara. In this way these rivers, and consequently Lake Baikal, will be connected with the Volga. This increase of water communications for towns along the Angara river will benefit Cheremkovo, which has the third largest coalfield of the U.S.S.R. It has been computed by the Soviet Academy of Sciences that the Angara, with the erection of hydro-electric stations, can yield ten times the power now produced on the Dnieper.

The Selenga steamship line has enabled increased supplies of food to reach the peoples of Buriat Mongolia. By the Selenga River, cargoes can now go direct from ports on Lake Baikal to Ulan-Ude, capital of Buriat Mongolia, and in this way a saving is effected against the more expensive rail transport. Here, on the Selenga, are shipyards which build vessels for this river and the Angara.[2]

THE AMUR

We have dealt with four of Russia's River Flotillas: the fifth is the one that operates on the Amur, and it plays an important part in the defences of the Soviet Union. When Muraviev, almost a hundred years earlier, gained for his country the right of navigation on the Amur and control of its lower region, he could not have foreseen that he was providing Russia with an alternative means of transport of troops in the ice-free months, in the event of the Trans-Baikal railway system being cut in a second world war. After the Japanese invasion of eastern Manchuria, the Amur flotilla, strong in its numbers of monitors and armed launches, co-operated with land forces of the Second Far Eastern Command (based on Khabarovsk) in repelling enemy counter-attacks in August 1945. Units of the flotilla

[1] R. A. Davies and A. J. Steiger, *Soviet Asia*; p. 144.
[2] For details of freight turnover, see G. D. R. Phillips, *Dawn in Siberia*. (Muller, 1943, 2nd edition); p. 160.

were active when Soviet troops took Aigun, near Blagovyeshchensk on the Amur. Gunboats patrolled the Ussuri River also,
when land forces captured the port of Saodjate. For commercial
cargoes as well as for naval occasions the Amur River has become indispensable in the transport system of the Far East; by
the beginning of this century it had 1,600 steamers,[1] and it was
by this river that the flood of immigration had surged into the
Maritime Province. Today it is by this route that the coal of the
Burei Basin and of the Little Khingan Mountains is sent to the
Pacific.

The fact that priority in the post-war Five-Year Plan is being
given to the area between Lake Baikal and the Pacific, will
speed the development of riparian transport in this region of
the great rivers of Far Eastern Russia.

[1] E. J. Harrison, *Peace or War East of Baikal?* (Kelly & Walsh, Yokohama,
1910); p. 70.

CONCLUSION

THAT we live in the dawn of the atomic age is commonly accepted; that we have arrived at the oceanic age is no less true, but is rarely stated. The light elements, hydrogen and helium, offer greater sources of atomic power than uranium does, and it is to the immense reservoir of the oceans that nations will turn for the inexhaustible supplies of that power. For reasons arising from a new technique of warfare, as well as for reasons geographical, we may expect to see nations looking to the oceans for the conservation of their main sources of strength. The Bikini tests showed that the best defences against atomic attack are dispersal and distance; the seas and oceans which cover three-fourths of the globe offer better prospects than the land does for such defences. And the safest place of all may be under water, for the coming of the futuristically armoured super-submarine, and the deep-level atomic-propelled submersible ship, may provide anti-aircraft shelters, as well as mobile operational bases.

That the atomic age will call for an increase, rather than any decrease in Sea Power on the part of the leading nations, is the opinion of many naval authorities and various national leaders. President Truman in the Navy Day speech, 27 October, 1945, was insistent on the need for maintaining powerful navies. "What the distant future of atomic research may bring to the Fleet we honour today," he said, "no one can foretell. But the fundamental mission of the navy has not changed. Control of our sea approaches and of the sky above them is still the key to our freedom, and to our ability to help enforce the peace of the world." This was also the viewpoint of Admiral King, U.S. Chief of Naval Operations, who believed that the atomic bomb could not prevent fleets from operating; General Marshall too upheld the doctrine of sea power, having pointed out that as it would still be necessary to capture the enemy's base of operations and "seize the site from which he launches his attacks", control of the seas for the transport of troops would remain a factor of primary importance. Fleet-Admiral Chester W. Nimitz, U.S.N., has said : "The Navy is still the first line the enemy must hurdle either in the air or on the sea in approaching our coasts across any ocean. The earliest warning of enemy air attack against our vital centres should be provided by naval air, surface and submarine radar pickets deployed in the vast ocean spaces which surround the continent. . . . Protection of our cities against missile-launching submarines can best be effected by naval hunter-killer groups composed of small aircraft carriers and modern destroyers operating as a team with naval land-based aircraft."[1]

The position of the world's fleets in future will depend on their strength underseas: a new chapter in naval history opens with the Age of the Super-Submarine. Nevertheless the last day of the surface ship is still far from our sight. Britain, like America, is looking to mammoth aircraft carriers to take the place of battleships as the principal striking ships. (In the case of Britain, only time can show whether this transformation is being carried out on an adequate scale.) Mr. Churchill revealed his belief in the fleets of the future as "guardian carriers", when on 26 March, 1947, he said: "The means of destroying aircraft may well keep pace with the destructiveness of the explosives which aircraft can carry. Therefore it is foolish for people who have not given long thought to this matter to dismiss it as if the surface ships which steam across the oceans would no longer play a part in a future war." Speaking at the celebration of Trafalgar Day, 1947, held by the Navy League, its President, Admiral Sir Lionel Halsey, emphasising the need for watchfulness, said: "For we, in these islands, are still the centre of a sea-girt Commonwealth and Empire. Our sea services are still the fundamental basis of our prosperity in peace and our security in war. *Neither the passage of time nor modern weapons have altered that.*"

The balanced conclusion to the chapter entitled "Global Warfare of the Future", contributed by Dr. Herbert Rosinski to *Brassey's Naval Annual, 1947*, should be read by all who are interested in this subject. "Even in atomic warfare global strategy must continue to rest ultimately upon sea power," says that writer. He has the testimony of history to support him. For centuries the seas and oceans have been the primary lines of communication of the globe. No Power can really be a Great Power unless it dominates the main arteries of the world.

Global defence as conceived by the United States and the

[1] From a paper sent to the Secretary of the United States Navy. Reproduced in *The Navy*, May 1948. (The Navy League.)

British Commonwealth today, is based on the belief that ocean zones rather than land masses will determine future strategy. East Africa and South Africa, marked for key regions in the defensive system,[1] are areas commanding the South Atlantic and Indian Oceans and, integrated with the U.S. plans for world defence, they are linked with the American island bases in the Pacific.

Russia's intention to build powerful navies is a proclaimed fact, but, in the view of many people, her understanding of the actual part played by sea power in the last war was for some time, and to some extent still is, limited. This limitation is one in which, as we have shown, Marshal Stalin has not shared, and exceptions are found too in the writings of Admiral Kuznetsov[2], Admiral Isakov, and of Professor Ivanov, Corresponding Member of the Soviet Academy of Sciences,[3] also in M. Maisky's wartime tribute to the men of the Northern Convoys; but in general the extent to which the Russians have realised how much they owed to British sea power has been inadequate. The British campaign in Egypt and Libya was invaluable to the Red Fleet in the Black Sea and the Sea of Azov: by their control of sea communications too the British were able to hold Tobruk for eighteen months and so bar the way to Rommel's march to Egypt, from Egypt to the Levant, and thence to the Caucasus. The Russian winter campaign of 1941 obliged Germany to use up a large amount of her reserve stocks of oil which she had got from the Rumanian wells; a drive to Baku was therefore imperative. The German plan was to make a combined air and sea landing at the Black Sea port of Batum in order to seize the Caucasian oilfields, but as long as British naval and air forces controlled the eastern Mediterranean, the Germans had to face the fact that they must take the difficult overland route for the transport of any oil they might seize.

"We must be prepared to keep the peace by force," declared President Roosevelt. As victims of aggression in the second world war we have all been in the same boat. If we do not pull together, and in a strongly manned boat, worse than shipwreck will be our lot—the world will be engulfed in a maelstrom which may prove the doom of the greater part of mankind.

[1] This however was before the South African elections, 1948, brought to power a party with a very different policy from that of Field-Marshal Smuts. This was likely to have necessitated at the time a revision of strategic plans by the Chiefs of Staff.

[2] Article in *Pravda* on twenty-third anniversary of Red Navy Day, 1941.

[3] "The Power of the British Navy," *Soviet War News*, 29.5.1943.

Is Britain, it has been asked, in danger of ignoring the warning by Admiral Sir Lionel Halsey on Trafalgar Day, 1947? "Sea power," he said, "has made us what we are. Sea power has preserved us in our hours of trial. *If we neglect our sea power we shall assuredly perish.*" Here, in conclusion, we may revert to a notable writer, quoted in the Introduction to this book. It was Mackinder who said that after Trafalgar Britain forgot that East Europe and the "Heartland" would make a mighty sea-base.[1] Writing after the first world war, he asked: "Must we not still reckon with the possibility that the Great Continent might some day be united under a single sway, and that an invincible sea-power might be based upon it? May we not have headed off that danger in this way and yet leave by our settlement the opening for a fresh attempt in the future?"[2] And, had the great geographer been alive today, he would no doubt have underlined the words he wrote after World War I: "No mere scraps of paper . . . are, under the conditions of today, a sufficient guarantee that the Heartland will not again become the centre of a World War."[3]

America in the expansion of her sea power, sees one of her most vital means for the maintenance of her security. This was the motive which impelled her decision to build up a new fleet of fast aircraft carriers, deep-diving submarines, anti-submarine vessels, and guided missile warships. Russia for her part, aware that command of the oceans is for the future even more than it has been for the past, a pre-requisite both for security and for power, will endeavour by every means to acquire new bases. Her Arctic conquests have equipped her for triumphs in Antarctica. She, in common with other nations, will not be uninterested in finding whether the deposits of uranium under the South Polar Ice-cap are not so negligible as at present believed. And in her realisation of her future rôle as a Sea Power, she may play a part undreamt of even by her far-sighted ruler Peter I, who promised his people that they should be great by sea.

[1] *Democratic Ideals and Reality*; p. 7.
[2] *Ibid.*, pp. 91, 92.
[3] *Ibid.*, p. 143.

SUPPLEMENTARY SECTION

THE RUSSIAN FLEETS IN THE SECOND WORLD WAR

In addition to the naval annuals of Messrs. Sampson Low, and of Messrs. William Clowes, to whom acknowledgments have been made earlier, the following publications have been indispensable as sources of reference for this Supplement: *"Flottes de Combat"* (*Societé d'Editions Géographiques, Maritimes et Coloniales*); *"Lloyd's List amd Shipping Gazette"*; *"The Navy"* (*Navy League*); *"Pravda"*; *"Krasny Flot"*; *"Soviet War News"* (*1941-45*); *"Russia Today"*; *"Voyenno-Morskoy Flot U.S.S.R. v Otechestvennoye Voyeene,"* by *N. Tokarev*; *"The Red Fleet in the Second World War,"* by *Admiral I. S. Isakov* (*Hutchinson*); *"News Bulletin"* (*Anglo-Russian Parliamentary Committee*); *"Bank for Russian Trade Review, Ltd."* (*London*); *"Monthly Review"* (*Moscow Narodny Bank, Ltd.*). *"Ports of the World"* (*The Shipping World, Ltd.*) has been consulted for data in the section on the Black Sea ports. Indebtedness is also expressed to the Library of The Society for Cultural Relations between the Peoples of the British Commonwealth and the U.S.S.R. The Library of the Press Association has been a valued guide to reports in daily publications, and to the Department of Naval Information, the Admiralty, the author tenders her appreciation of the loan of material.

STRENGTH OF THE RED NAVY

"The main and most important task carried out by our navy in all Soviet waters has been *to protect the strategic flanks of the Red Army, extending to the coasts, against enemy landing parties and naval operations,* and to direct its own blows against the enemy's flanks and rear." In these words Admiral Isakov[1] has defined the principal function of the Russian navy in the second world war. There were, as he says, "no classic combats between battle forces, or large-scale engagements which in previous wars were generally followed by prolonged periods of inactivity." Naval actions in World War II were "tense and continuous, on the surface, in the air and along the coasts".[2] It was over Russian

[1] *The Red Fleet in the Second World War,* translated by Jack Hural (Hutchinson, 1946); p. 16. [2] *Ibid;* p. 15.

ports that the Luftwaffe launched its first attacks against the
Soviet Union; Kronstadt, Murmansk, Sevastopol and Odessa
were among the earliest targets, and the dropping of mines and
bombing of ships were among the first of the hostile operations.

How far was the Red Fleet at that time prepared to meet the
German offensive? Intensified work on the building of warships
had been a special feature of the Third Five-Year Plan. In the
summer of 1939 Admiral Isakov, Vice-Commissar for the
Russian Navy, came back from the United States after negotiat-
ing for the purchase of machinery for making armour plate;
also for equipment for dockyards.[1] In 1940 there was a spec-
tacular increase in the building of submarines; nearly three
times the number produced for the Russian flotillas in 1939
were added in 1940. Even so, on 24 July that year, Admiral
Kuznetsov declared: "Many countries might envy the number
of ships we annually put into commission. But for us this scale
is still obviously inadequate." And in an article in *Pravda*[2] M.
Tevosyan, Commissar for Shipbuilding, stated that "the rate
of construction of our ships still lags behind that of foreign,
particularly British, shipyards. For instance, the light cruiser
Glasgow took twenty-nine months to construct; the building of
a similar type of ship in the U.S.S.R. took thirty-five months".
The Commissar for Shipbuilding expressed the hope that a
time reduction of 25-30 per cent. would be achieved. The same
year that the Commissar made that criticism, a British newspaper[3] wrote: "In view of the time taken by the Russian shipbuilders to build destroyers—not to mention cargo-ships—it
will be many years before we see a modern Russian-built
capital ship. And the Soviet Naval Spokesman, in a radio
commentary, 6 June, 1940, on the naval expansion plans of
Great Britain for that year, declared that Russia could not get
behind other Powers in shipbuilding: *King George V*, he pointed
out, was one of the most powerful battleships yet built.   So
it was that Admiral Kuznetsov announced soon afterwards that
in order to expedite naval expansion at home, the Soviet Union
had gone over from individual to mass building of warships.
The slogan "From individual Stakhanovite to Stakhanovite
ships" became a reality. Down to the last decade of the nine-

---

[1] *The Daily Telegraph*, 4.7.1939.

[2] Translation from *News Bulletin*, Anglo-Russian Parliamentary Committee, Press Department, 29.9.1939.

[3] "Soviet Naval Ambitions," *Glasgow Herald*, Shipbuilding Correspondent, 31.10.1939.

teenth century the tendency in Russia was to produce ships singly, not in batches. The closing years of the century foreshadowed a change, and today whole classes are produced at a time.

In an Order of the Day, on Red Army Day, 1945, Marshal Stalin said: "The Soviet people wishes to see its navy still stronger and mightier." This desire is one which has increased in the U.S.S.R. since 1939. A search among the earlier files of Russian papers will bear this out, even allowing for the fact that the war naturally gave more publicity to maritime subjects than was previously the case. Even in the first year of the Russo-German fighting, about the fleets relatively little is to be found compared with the material which appeared after 1942. At the end of that year public interest in the navy in Russia had grown so much that over three hundred books and pamphlets dealing with the work of the Red Fleet had been issued. The publications have been collated by a team of writers, and special books have appeared on the defence of such ports as Leningrad, Stalingrad, Sevastopol, Odessa. It is not without significance that when the agreement was signed at the Soviet Embassy in London in 1945 between Mezhdunarodnaya Kniga of Moscow and Hutchinson and Co. (Publishers), London, for the distribution in the U.S.S.R. by Mezhdunarodnaya Kniga of Russian translations of English books, one of the first titles chosen by the Russians was *World War at Sea*, by the naval historian Brian Tunstall. According to the contemporary account of the Russian Fleet given by Tokarev,[1] at the beginning of 1943 a growing popular movement supported the expansion of the Red Navy, and there was widespread approbation of the great increase in the sums devoted to naval development. The new submarines *Yaroslavskii Komsomolets* and *Chelyarbinskii Komsomolets* were built by the voluntary collections of the members of the Young Communist League and of the workers of the Yaroslav and Chelyarbinsk districts.

It was on 18 July, 1935, that Russia's new naval ensign had been hoisted for the first time. "That ensign is white, having the following charges in red: a five-pointed star in the hoist and the hammer and sickle in the fly: the lower edge of the white field has a light blue border. A red flag with a large five-pointed silver star, charged with a slightly smaller five-pointed star in red and having the hammer and sickle badge in silver in the centre, serves in a dual capacity, namely, as the jack when

[1] *Военно-морской Флот СССР в Отечественной Войне.* Редактор Ч-цвик. Художник книги Н. Седельников, Москва, 1943; стр. 9.

afloat and the fortress flag when hoisted on land."[1] (The flag of the Imperial Russian Navy had been white with a blue saltire; in the seventeenth century it had displayed the double-headed eagle.)

In 1939 for the first time, public celebrations and a holiday had marked the observance of Red Navy Day. The following year, on that day (28 July), citizens had taken advantage of the permission given them to visit warships, by going in crowds to the vessels in Leningrad, Sevastopol, Vladivostock. In 1943 the festival included a maritime exhibition in the State Historical Museum, Moscow.

About the actual ships of the four main fleets of the Soviet Union, more, as we have observed, was published in the Russian press during the last war than was formerly the case. In 1928 the *Encyclopædia Britannica*[2] could write of the Russian navy that it was the exception that allusion was made to a ship's name in print. Although for many years Russia had sent information regarding her navy for publication in the *British Official Return of the Strengths of the Fleets*, "the information supplied for publication was frequently exceedingly suspect", to quote the view of a leading British naval writer.[3] (We have noted that in 1939 that information was withheld.) It was not till the arrival of the United Kingdom naval mission in Moscow, August 1939, that much news about the Russian fleets began to appear in the British press.

The real strength of the Russian navy lies in its submarines. As early as 1936 the German Admiralty was aware of Russia's growing strength in these vessels. An official statement from Berlin at that time declared that ninety-six Soviet submarines were in commission and many were building. This was at a time when Germany's submarine fleet was the smallest (twenty-eight); France, with ninety-two, had the highest total after Russia. The figures for 1937, as given in *Jane's Fighting Ships*, show one hundred and twelve with thirty-seven building, as the number of submarines for the U.S.S.R. Japan is shown as having only sixty-eight.

Asserting that the Soviet Union held one of the leading places in the world for submarines, Admiral Isakov, two months

[1] H. G. Carr, M.S.N.R., "Naval Flags of the Allies" (2) U.S.S.R. *The Sea Cadet*, March, 1946. The Navy League.

[2] Vol. XIX, 14th Edtn., p. 705.

[3] Lieut.-Commander Kenneth Edwards, R.N.: *Uneasy Oceans*. (Routledge and Kegan Paul, 1939); p. 117.

before the outbreak of the second world war, announced: "In the event of war we will beat the enemy in his own waters." It was during the period of the building of the *Chuka* class of submarines (1935-1938) that the German Admiralty stated: "Russia has secretly built the mightiest submarine armada in the world."[1] Vessels of the *Chuka* class were larger than those of the *Nalim* class (1937), being 1,080 tons as compared with 650 tons. But the largest of the pre-war submarines were those of the *Pravda* class (1936), of 1,200 tons.

The majority of Russia's submarines built before 1937 were coastal types, designed for defensive work. The later vessels, which have been built for a different purpose, have a long cruising radius. Between 1934 and 1940 the *Schtch* class were built at Leningrad, with a designed speed of 13 knots, and with six 21-inch torpedo tubes. Then came the *S* class, 18 knots, and also having six 21-inch torpedoes. The *Lembit* and the *Kalev* (1937), both ex-Esthonian, were built by Vickers during this period, and have since of course been acquired by the Soviet Union. Of later design are the ex-German submarines: Type VIIB and VIIC (four in number, 1942); IXC (one in number, 1942); XXI (four in number, 1944); XXIII (1944.) Of these, all but Type XXIII have six 21-inch torpedo tubes.[2]

Russian vessels of an earlier class, 1916-17, were engaged in the Baltic in the last war. The following are listed in *All the World's Fighting Fleets:*[3] *Batrak, Bolshevik, Dekabrist, Kommissar, Kommunar, Komsolka, Krasnoarmeyetz, Krasnoflotetz, Krasnoyvardietz, L55* (an ex-British vessel), *Marxist, Metallist, Politrabotnik, Politruk, Proletari, Narodovoletz, Rabotchi, Tovarishtch.* The different types of submarines listed in 1948 will be found in *The World's Warships, 1948,*[4] pp. 88 and 90.

Kronstadt remains the principal submarine base for the Baltic, but Kaliningrad will become an increasingly important station. Of the northern bases, Poliarnoye and Molotovsk, more will be said in the section on the Northern Fleet.

Russia's specialisation in small vessels was well repaid when the testing time came during operations in the Black Sea from June 1941, onwards. Such ships did useful work in landing

---

[1] The Naval Correspondent, *The Daily Telegraph,* 16.3.1936, p. 21.
[2] Particulars as given in *Brassey's Naval Annual, 1947,* edited by Rear-Admiral Thursfield. (Wm. Clowes & Son, 1947); p. 219.
[3] Edtd. by Pay-Lieut. E. C. Talbot-Booth, R.N.R. (Sampson Low, 1944); pp. 593, 595.
[4] Edtd. by F. E. McMurtrie, A.I.N.A. (Sampson Low, 1948.)

operations, co-operating well with larger vessels. Of the M.O. speedboats of 30-60 tons, a Russian naval authority[1] has written: "With their relatively powerful armament and their long range of operation, plus their speed and their great mobility, these small fighting ships are particularly suitable for action along the enemy coast and against enemy bases in fiords and on cliffs." This was demonstrated by the M.O. speedboats of the Northern Fleet in the summer of 1942, when German forces attempted to drive on to Murmansk.

A feature of Russian destroyers and t.b.s is the number of mines they can carry. The minelayer *Marty* is reported to take five hundred mines. This vessel, ex-Imperial yacht, was built at Copenhagen, but was converted to a minelayer in the Leningrad yards in 1937. Improvisation has been claimed by Soviet writers as a characteristic of Russian naval enterprise, and examples of it were noted in the last war; one was provided by the minesweeper *Zashchitnik*, who landed troops in the Crimea for the defence of Feodosia. She survived incessant attacks from the air, and for the courage of her crew she now flies the pendant of the Guards.

Figures showing the strength of the Russian navy at the commencement of the second world war have been given in this book in Chapter XIV. It will be useful to compare these now with the details given for the war-year 1943-44 in *The World's Warships*,[2] in which we find the following: four battleships (*Tretii International, Oktiabrskaya Revolutsia, Pariskaya Kommuna, Marat*); one aircraft carrier (*Krasnoye Znamya*); nine cruisers; forty-six destroyers named, and others of tonnage varying from 1,323 to 2,900, and of speeds from 33 to 37 knots; thirty torpedo boats, all fitted for minelaying; "about one hundred and thirty m.t.b.s, of various types up to 35 tons, armed with two torpedoes"; sixty-eight submarines named (these include ex-British *L55*, of 870 tons, 17.5 knots.)

Pariskaya Kommuna, which was engaged in the Baltic operations, was first in commission as far back as 1915; in 1930 she was commonly said to be unfit for service, but since then she has been reconditioned. *Oktiakbrskaya Revolutsia* (23,606 tons) is another battleship which is more than twenty-five years old, for she made her first appearance in 1914, when she had a reputation for being ill-conditioned and badly ventilated. None

[1] Capt. V. Silayev, Red Navy. *Soviet War News*, 1.6.1942.
[2] (Jane's, 1944), edtd. by Francis E. McMurtrie, A.I.N.A. (Sampson Low, 1944.)

the less, after being reconditioned she did good work in the second world war, among other operations shelling the German forces as they withdrew along the southern shore of the Finnish Gulf early in 1944. These two battleships were equipped with ice-breaking bows some time after they were first launched. Each of them included in the armament twelve 12-inch guns, sixteen 4.7-inch guns, and 18-inch torpedo tubes.[1] *Marat* (23,608 tons) and *Pariskaya Kommuna* (23,356 tons) were laid down at Baltic Works in 1909; like *Oktiabrskaya Revolutsia*, they operated in the Baltic. Their names show the fashion prevalent for a long time in the Soviet Union for christening warships after events and personalities connected with some historical revolutionary period. Of late years this fashion has declined.

The 1944 edition of *Brassey's Naval Annual* includes *Mikhail Frunze* in the list of existing battleships. *Tretii International*, to which reference has been made in Chapter XIV, is one of Russia's modern battleships, having been laid down in the Ordzhonikidze Yard, Leningrad, in 1939. Her tonnage, according to *Jane's Fighting Ships*, is 35,000. (The Germans, when they claimed to have captured her at Nikolaiev, said she was 45,000 tons.) Another battleship of this class is also to be completed at Leningrad; a third was on the stocks at Nikolaiev, but was destroyed by the Russians when the Germans made their southward drive through Ukraine to the northern shores of the Black Sea. Orders for the guns and boilers of this ship were placed abroad, "mostly in Germany and U.S.A."[2] Foreign orders have been responsible in many cases for the completion of Russian warships; *Marat* was built to Italian design; so too were the cruisers of the *Kirov* class and destroyers of the *Stremitelni* type; destroyers of the *Leningrad* class were designed with the assistance of French naval architects. British technicians and shipwrights have in modern times played a greater part in the construction of Russian mercantile ships than naval ones.

Details of Russia's cruiser strength for the year 1946-47 have been given in Chapter XIV in this book; for the war-year 1944 *Brassey's Naval Annual*[3] gives in addition, *Aurora*, launched 1900, completed 1903, 6,730 tons (18 knots); *Marty*, completed 1936, 3,500 tons (25 knots); *Komintern*, completed 1907, 6,675 tons

---

[1] *Jane's Fighting Ships, 1942*, edtd. by Francis E. McMurtrie, A.I.N.A. (Sampson Low, 1943); p. 370.

[2] *Jane's Fighting Ships, 1942*; p. 369.

[3] p. 184.

(23 knots). *Chervonnaya Ukrainia* (1915), 6,934 tons (29 knots), fifteen 5.1-inch guns, was in operation in 1944, but was sunk in the Black Sea.

At the opening of a Navy Exhibition, Moscow, in March 1943, claims were made that the Red Fleet from the beginning of the Russo-German war to 5 March, 1943, had sunk 771 German merchantmen and warships, whose total tonnage was 2,000,000. Damage was said to have been done to 216 other vessels.[1] What proportion of enemy losses was caused by destroyers has not so far been disclosed, but it is known that Russian ships of this class accounted for most of the damage to German troopships in the Baltic. "It is craft such as these, with other modern destroyers of a somewhat smaller type, displacing about 1,800 tons, that have been giving the enemy unwelcome surprises in the Baltic," stated the writer of "Foreign Notes" in *The Navy*.[2] In 1944 there were twelve flotilla leaders and fifty-six destroyers: a list of their names will be found in *Brassey's Naval Annual*.

It is interesting to recall some of the British opinions on the Red Navy before Russia entered the second world war:

"Though on paper it makes a good showing, the efficiency of the Soviet Fleet is a matter of uncertainty. Competent observers are disinclined to rate it highly," said the writer of "Foreign Notes" in *The Navy*, July 1941. The naval writer, Commander Kenneth Edwards, R.N.,[3] comparing the Tsarist Navy with the Soviet one, stated that the former was of no account in the 1914-18 war because the High Command insisted upon its remaining in harbour. The modern Russian navy, he said, was likely to be more virile, and it was well provided with vessels suited to check German naval operations in the Baltic. He also expressed these opinions: "The Russian navy of today is a singularly ill-balanced force according to traditional and oceanic standards. Even in a world where balance between the various categories of warships in several navies is conspicuous by its absence, the navy of Soviet Russia stands out. Yet even in the case of Soviet Russia there are signs of realisation of the fact that the effectiveness of all naval armaments depends, in the long run, upon the support which the light forces can expect from a battle-fleet. Thus Russia is taking steps to rebuild her battle-fleet."

Three months after the commencement of the war, *The*

[1] Reuters, 5.3.1943.   [2] September, 1941.
[3] *Uneasy Oceans;* p. 275.

THE BATTLESHIP H.M.S. *ROYAL SOVEREIGN*

LENT BY BRITAIN TO RUSSIA IN 1944, PASSES UNDER THE FORTH BRIDGE ON HER RETURN HOME ON FEBRUARY 4TH, 1949

(Reproduced by arrangement with Press Association—Reuters.)

SAILING under the Forth Bridge is the battleship H.M.S. *Royal Sovereign*, 29,150 tons, lent by Britain to Russia in 1944, when she was renamed *Arkhangelsk*. At the end of her stormy voyage from Murmansk, she reached her mooring-buoy off Rosyth on February 4th, 1949. The ceremony of transfer took place the following week.

This historic home-coming of a famous British battleship was an event which roused wide interest, but it also had a particular local appeal from the fact that, while entering the Forth, a signal was passed from the Russian captain to the office of the Flag-Officer Commanding Scotland and Northern Ireland, for tickets for the International Rugby Match to be played at Murrayfield the following day.

Evening News[1] stated: "Those who have had the opportunity of observing the Russian fleet at sea have a very poor opinion of it; the material is mostly very old and although it has been modernised, most of the ships have the natural disadvantages of patchwork. Ships which were laid down before the late war for the old Tsarist Navy have been completed this year and last, and the disadvantage of putting new patches into old garments is everywhere apparent. The position is far worse with regard to personnel. The men are keen, and with good officers could be made excellent ratings within the limits of their intelligence. Like the German ratings, they could do their own particular little job coolly and unimaginatively enough if it were thoroughly drilled into them." The article went on to ventilate the opinion that the officer corps was the weakest part of the Russian Navy: that the Revolution having started in the fleet, the Moscow Government was always afraid a counter-revolution would start there too. It added that purges of most efficient officers had not encouraged officers to seek promotion—they wanted to remain unnoticed by the Political Commissar on board.

"What is the strength of Stalin's navy?" asked the *Evening Standard* reporter:[2] "The Russians, who at Geneva demanded that details of the navies of all Powers should be published regularly, have been secretive about their own fleet. The reason, it would seem, was to hide their own weakness. Details of the Russian navy gathered in France show that it is a great deal weaker today than it was before the Revolution in 1917."

Many who took the view that the Soviet navy was but a weak instrument, did so for the following reason. Between the defeat of Russia in her war with Japan, 1905, and the beginning of the 1914-18 war, a lot of talk about the secret expansion of the Imperial Navy had come out of Russia in order to hide the real fact of the fleet's inadequate numbers at a time when it was also inefficient in most other respects. So when once again, between 1936 and 1940, Russia publicised, but with a minimum of detail, the growing strength of her fleets, even informed people outside of the U.S.S.R. were inclined to regard it as another possible piece of bluff.

As regards the efficiency of Russia's battleships and cruisers, the impression widely held before the war that some of them were unseaworthy, was supported by the behaviour of the *Profintern*, when in 1930 on her way to the Black Sea, she had

[1] 5.12.1939.   [2] 11.3.1940.

to put in for repairs at Brest and Naples. "From both places came reports that the ship was in a dreadful state."[1] Nor was this impression weakened by events in the Spanish Civil War; when the Bay of Biscay was assigned to Russia for her sphere of the proposed non-intervention patrol, she withdrew from the organisation.[2] The tradition of obsolescence had persisted from the time when the *Marat*, visiting British waters for the Coronation Review at Spithead, 1911, had been conspicuous for her singular performance. (There may or may not have been unconscious irony in the fact that the Russians sent to the 1937 Review the ship bearing the name of the most anti-Royalist of all the leaders of the French Revolution). Little more enlightenment on the true nature of the Soviet fleets had been gained when on 20 June, 1939, Russian ships once more paid a visit to an English harbour—this time to Plymouth. For the vessels on that occasion were of no higher category than armoured minesweeping trawlers—*Provodnik, Strelia, Podsekatel, Tross*. Nor was the public much more informed when on 18 February, 1944, Russian warships called at Londonderry, for the vessels consisted of only three submarine-chasers, and three minesweepers which had been handed over to the U.S.S.R. at an American base. The occasion marked the first time that any Soviet warships had ever called at Londonderry. A further number of Russian war vessels arrived at this base during November 1944,[3] but news of these visits was not of course released till long after the occasion.

The unfavourable opinion of the Soviet navy which was generally prevalent abroad, drew from the Russian naval spokesman the following pronouncement: "Certain of our capitalist neighbours, who consider themselves great naval powers and harbour antiquated conceptions, think that the U.S.S.R. is Old Russia. They will find that they are greatly mistaken. The new fleet of the U.S.S.R. is carefully studying its neighbours, their strong and weak sides, and will rout the enemy wherever and whenever it will be necessary in the interests of the defence of the Fatherland."[4] Then came this statement in February 1941, from Admiral Isakov, Chief of Staff and Vice-Commissar of the Soviet Navy:

---

[1] Lieut.-Cmdr. Kenneth Edwards, R.N.: *Uneasy Oceans*, p. 119.
[2] *Ibid.*, p. 118.
[3] From Press Association Report, 16.6.1945.
[4] Mr. P. Smirnov, Navy Commissar, at the Joint Session of both Chambers of the Supreme Soviet, Dec., 1937.

"At one time antiquated cruisers and destroyers of the *Aurora* and *Potemkin* vintage formed the nucleus of our navy. Embodying the technical level of the beginning of the twentieth century, these vessels bore the trade marks of various ship-building companies working according to British designs, on French capital and with German equipment. Their place has now been taken by more powerful and faster vessels built according to the last word in steam-turbine, electric and diesel engineering. These new ships, with a larger radius of action and heavier armaments, proudly bear the trade marks of the Sergei Ordzhonikidze, André Marty and other Soviet shipyards. Our sailors and shipwrights are proud of the fact that not only are these vessels completely modern, but that they have been built according to Soviet designs, by Soviet workers and engineers, and from Soviet materials."[1]

A favourable impression of one of Russia's fleets was received from a British source when, writing from Moscow on Red Navy Day, 1943, describing the Review of the Baltic Fleet, the Special Correspondent to *The Times* stated that the appearance of the ships and crews was very good indeed. On that occasion the fleet was lined up between Kronstadt and Peterhof, and on the Neva at Leningrad. Displays by the other Fleets were held at Odessa, Vladivostock and Murmansk.

Naval events in the second world war modified and in many cases changed non-Russian opinion as to the efficiency of certain classes of ships of the Red Fleet. The battleship *Marat*, for instance, belied her reputation for unseaworthiness by taking an active part in operations in the Baltic. Here however she suffered so severely through enemy air action that by the spring of 1943 she lay half sunk in the roads of Kronstadt, where none the less she served a useful purpose by acting as a block-ship, and her guns were still capable of firing. Of other warships which carried out offensive action, mention will be made in the following section on the Baltic.

THE BALTIC FLEET

Of the Red Banner Baltic Fleet which had helped to defend Petrograd in 1919, Marshal Stalin later said: "It can only be welcomed that the Baltic Fleet, which was considered destroyed, is being re-born in the most effective manner. This is acknowledged not only by friends but also by enemies. It is

[1] Quoted by Lucien Zacharoff: *We Made a Mistake*. (The Bodley Head, 1942); pp. 102, 103.

equally comforting that the ulcer of Russian officerdom—its corruption—affected the commanding staff of the fleet least. There were people, despite it, who, to their honour, valued the dignity and independence of Russia higher than English gold. It is still more comforting that the Baltic sailors have again found themselves reviving in their feats the best traditions of the Russian Revolutionary fleet. Without these conditions Petrograd would not have been protected against the most dangerous surprises from the sea." Marshal Stalin's reference to the commanding officers under the former Tsarist régime was substantiated in one well-known instance at least; in 1928 the Commander-in-Chief of the Baltic Fleet was a man who had been an officer in the Imperial Navy.

Nothing is much clearer in matters relating to the sea warfare between the Reich and Russia in World War II than the fact that the German Government (as distinct from the Admiralty) under-estimated the strength of the Soviet's Baltic Fleet— though its alleged concern at the growth of the latter had provided Germany with a pretext for insisting that she must be allowed to build more ships than was permitted by the Versailles Treaty.

At the beginning of the Russo-German war Hitler's transports were only lightly protected by naval vessels. On the opening day of hostilities, ships of the Russian Baltic Fleet were reported to have sunk several U-boats in the Gulf of Finland.[1] Throughout July 1941, the fleet continued to defend Tallinn, second only to Kronstadt in importance as a Baltic naval base. The Germans confidently anticipated the capture of the Russian fleet in its bases, and Goebbels actually announced its destruction before the Germans had launched their main attack.[2] The German Naval Command had declared as a danger area for shipping, the Arctic from the Finno-Russian frontier westwards, also the Baltic—except for Swedish territorial waters and a strip three miles along the German coast. Shipping was warned that within the notified area it was exposed to risk of mines; by use of the latter and by their submarines the Germans hoped to isolate Russia's naval bases on the Baltic. The Gulf of Finland is shallow, submarine ridges are numerous, channels complex, and between Finland and Esthonia the Gulf was strewn with German mines. Russian submarines however maintained their

[1] Reported in *Soviet War News*, 5.8.1941.
[2] Н. Токарев : *Военно-торской Флот СССР в Отечественной Войне;* стр. 28.

attacks on enemy troopships crossing from Germany to Finland, and on enemy vessels carrying iron ore from the Swedish port of Luleaa. As a result of the Russian sinking of Swedish ore vessels, Sweden's naval convoys were strengthened. So strongly did the tradition of British officering of Russian ships persist, that a leading Stockholm paper thought it possible that the submarines which sank these Swedish vessels were commanded by British naval officers, who might have inspired this "revival of the Russian naval offensive spirit". Penetration of Soviet submarines from the Gulf of Finland into the Baltic was admitted by a German naval officer in *Deutsche Allgemeine Zeitung* at the end of December 1943.

To no one more than to Mr. Churchill had the value of the Baltic as a route for striking at Germany early in the second world war been clear. "I sought earnestly," he says, "for a way of attacking Germany by naval means. First and foremost gleamed the Baltic. The command of the Baltic by a British Fleet carried with it possibly decisive gains. Scandinavia, freed from the menace of German invasion, would thereby naturally be drawn into our system of war trade, if not indeed into actual co-belligerency. A British Fleet in mastery of the Baltic would hold out a hand to Russia in a manner likely to be decisive upon the whole Soviet policy and strategy."[1] The menace at that time, Mr. Churchill points out, was not the German Fleet, but the unmeasured strength of a formidable German air force. "If two or three years earlier it had been possible to make an alliance with Soviet Russia," he says, "this might have been implemented by a British battle squadron joined to the Russian Fleet and based on Cronstadt. I commended this to my circle of friends at the time."[2]

Only by command of the Baltic could the British have used Swedish harbours, for Russia was then, in Mr. Churchill's words, "an adverse neutral." Four days after he went to the Admiralty in 1939, Mr. Churchill asked for a plan to be prepared for forcing a passage to the Baltic. This plan was called "Catherine," recalling Catherine the Great, for, says the author of *The Second World War*, he had Russia in his mind all the time. The Admiralty replied that the first requisite for success was that the Soviet Union should not join Germany.[3]

---

[1] *The Second World War*, Vol. I. (Cassell & Co., Ltd., London, 1948. Houghton Mifflin Company, Boston, 1948); p. 363.
[2] *Ibid.*, p. 363.
[3] *Ibid.*, p. 363.

At the time of the German attack on Russia in June 1941, the main work of the Soviet Baltic Fleet was to help the army by bringing in supplies. Operations in the Baltic in the second world war were on the whole rather complementary to land warfare than distinct actions in sea warfare; the chief rôle of the fleet was to support the flank of the Red Army, and later it was to cover the retreat of the latter, and to help in the evacuation of Tallinn. But beyond those immediate tasks there was the duty of preventing the Germans from getting complete control of the Baltic, and also from making a seaward assault on Leningrad. During the early inland advance on that city the enemy reached a point within fifteen miles of it. But on the coastal side their approach halted at twenty-five miles, owing to the defence of Oranienbaum by the Baltic Fleet. That fleet frustrated the attempts of the Germans to take Leningrad from the sea, despite the fact that from Hogland Island to the coast of Esthonia the enemy had spread an anti-submarine net to stop the Russian submarines from leaving Kronstadt. The German occupation of Hogland was serious, inasmuch as the one fairway for shipping in that part of the Gulf runs past Hogland Island. "If Kronstadt is the key to Leningrad, then Hogland is the key to Kronstadt."[1] However, not only did these Soviet vessels succeed in getting down the Gulf of Finland, but in making enough attacks on German shipping to force the enemy to adopt the convoy system for vessels sailing between Germany and Finland. "This in itself was an achievement for the Soviet navy, since it was wasteful both in men and escort ships which Admiral Doenitz so sorely needed elsewhere."[2] Russian submarines were also reputed to have maintained a blockade of the Finnish shore of the Gulf of Bothnia, although mines had been laid by the enemy between the islands in the Aaland archipelago.

Admiral Isakov, with much point, has mentioned[3] the advantage enjoyed by the Russians in the first as compared with the second world war in the Baltic, for in the first case the Imperial Navy had bases on the east and west shores of the Finnish Gulf, and slightly west of a north-south line from Helsinki to Tallinn they were able to stretch a mine belt. And, as he also reminds us, they held the Aaland and Åbo archipelagos. But in

[1] Leonid Sobolev, *The Soul of the Sea*. (Hutchinson, 1945); p. 96.
[2] Ossian Goulding, *The Daily Telegraph*, 11.5.1943.
[3] *The Red Fleet in the Second World War*. Translated by Jack Hural. (Hutchinson, 1946); p. 21.

the last war the Russians only held Hangoe: Helsinki, the principal Finnish naval base, was controlled by the Germans, who could thus directly threaten Leningrad.

Throughout the summer of 1941 units of the Baltic Fleet helped to hold Hangoe, and managed to maintain communications with the garrison at this base for most of the time. Dingdong battles were fought for the islands around Hangoe, some falling to the Germans, but the latter never succeeded in getting more than partial control in the Gulf of Finland. A detailed account of the July engagement in the approaches to the Gulf, when Oesel and Dagoe batteries opened fire on German transports with destroyer and torpedo-cutter escorts, has been given by Captain E. Matveyev, in "Naval Battles in the Baltic," published in *Strategy and Tactics of the Soviet-German War.*[1]

In the winter of 1941 the Baltic Fleet was called upon to play a major part in countering the German attempt to capture Kronstadt. The fortress would have been a prize of the highest value, not only as being the key to Leningrad, but as a first-class arsenal. The naval defences were severely tested, but the base held. In October 1942, Admiral Carls made a determined effort to take Kronstadt and also the islands of Lavansaari and Seiskare in the Gulf of Finland, whose capture would have made it impossible for the Russians to carry on submarine operations in the Gulf. The attempts to land on these islands were repelled.

Among the destroyers of the Baltic Fleet which engaged the enemy were those of the *Stremitelny* class. One which earned distinction was the *Stoiki* (re-named *Drozd*) for its defence of the approaches to Leningrad in the autumn of 1941. In the advance of troops of the Red Army, the destroyers *Gremiaschii* and *Soobrazitelny* gave support, and their crews were the first to receive the title of Guards. Many of the older Baltic destroyers as well as the newer types were in commission in the war. In the former class were the *Kalinin*, laid down 1912, completed 1927, and *Karl Marx*, laid down in the same year as *Kalinin*, and completed 1923. Other destroyers, of which the earliest was completed in 1918, and whose speed was 28 knots, were *Artem, Engels, Gnievni, Gordi, Gromki, Grosiastchi, Grosni, Grosovoy, Karl Liebknecht, Kharkob, Kiev, Lenin, Leningrad, Minsk, Moskva, Perekok, Perekov, Rykov, Stalin, Stalinsk, Sverdlov* (ex-*Yakob,*) *Uritski, Voikov,* and *Volodarski.*[2]

---

[1] Hutchinson, 1942.
[2] *All the World's Fighting Fleets*, edtd. by Pay-Lieut. E. C. Talbot-Booth, R.N.R. (Sampson Low, 1944); pp. 591-593.

"One thing is certain: so long as the Russian Baltic Fleet remains in being, the Germans must either divert U-boats and other warships from the Battle of the Atlantic, or give the enemy a free run. In the latter case, it would be goodbye to the German iron-ore traffic in the Gulf of Bothnia, and it would be difficult for the Germans to send reinforcements to their army in Finland."[1] That the Germans did for a time have to withdraw many of their warships from the northern Baltic was made known when part of their fleet steamed south to Kiel. Here it had to meet the attacks of the Royal Air Force.

The Soviet acquisition of the strategic islands of Oesel and Dagoe, which had resulted from the incorporation of Esthonia in the U.S.S.R. in 1940, had given Russia two valuable bases for her Fleet Air Arm, units of which, co-operating with the Baltic Fleet, defeated a strong assault against Oesel Island on 13 September, 1942. Attempts to land on the following day were also repulsed. In this way the Russians denied the Germans command of the north-east part of the Gulf of Riga. And though in the neighbouring republic of Latvia the enemy succeeded in capturing the warm-water port of Liepaja, it was from the land, not from the sea, that they took it.

But the south-west arm of the Gulf of Riga, and the ports of Liepaja and Ventspils were held by the Germans as late as April 1945. With the Germans commanding the shore batteries in this area, the Russian Baltic Fleet was naturally restricted in its operations. Farther south in the Baltic that fleet was much less successful than it was in the north; it was from the land, not the sea, that the Russians took Danzig and Koenigsberg (though the engagements of their ships in the Bay of Danzig during February 1945, showed that they were not inactive in this area.) The pocket-battleship *Admiral Scheer* had been able to help in the German evacuation of Baltic coastal towns, and also to use Gdynia till the Red Army had threatened that port. Then she was able to withdraw to Kiel, and it was not till the R.A.F. sank her there on 9 April that *Admiral Scheer* was put out of action. No Russian ship had engaged her at sea during that period. Nor was the Baltic Fleet able at any time to pursue German warships through the Skagerrak and Kattegat and up the coast of Norway. Consequently, the *Prinz Eugen*, the *Scharnhorst* and the *Gneisenau* were able to shelter in Norwegian harbours until attacked by the R.A.F. But as we have noted, the Red Banner Baltic Fleet had given proofs of

[1] Lord Strabolgi, *The Star*, 26.7.1941; leader page.

efficiency, and one of the tributes it received came from Commodore Karl Henrick Falkman, who, broadcasting from Stockholm on 22 January, 1942, said: "Though the Red Navy has sustained certain losses, it continues in action on the Baltic Sea—a force inspiring no little respect."[1]

THE NORTHERN FLEET

The main base of the submarines of the Northern Fleet is Poliarnoye. Before the Russians could build this base, they had had to blast the site, and submarine dynamiting had to be undertaken later to widen the port. The growth of this place from a waste of frozen granite to the present Polar port is one of the most remarkable of Russia's achievements in the Far North. During the war period 1942-45, a number of submarine hulls and engines were sent from different parts of the Soviet Union to Poliarnoye and other bases in the Far North, where they were assembled. Torpedo boats for the Far Eastern Fleet were also built in Arctic ports for security reasons.

The submarine fleet based on northern stations consisted of five flotillas, and during the first year in which Russia was at war it was reported in the Soviet press to have sunk 174 enemy ships whose total displacement was nearly 1,000,000 tons. Further high claims were made by the Commander of the Soviet Northern Fleet, Admiral A. Golovko, who said that an additional 171 ships, with a total displacement of 497,200 tons, were sunk during the same period by other branches of the fleet.[2] In two years of war (from the outbreak of hostilities until 1 June, 1943), the ships and aircraft of the Northern Fleet sank 1,500,000 tons of enemy shipping, declared Admiral Isakov.[3] He asserted that the danger to German transports in the north, "in the patrol zones of our motor torpedo boats, submarines, torpedo bombers and Stormoviks", was such that the Germans eventually were "compelled to augment the number of their escort vessels until the latter outnumbered the transports several times over". (One can only say here how profoundly thankful the British convoys would have been for similar protection!)

Only less important than its offensive wartime work was the

[1] Quoted from *The Red Fleet in the Second World War*, Admiral I. S. Isakov. Translated by Jack Hural. (Hutchinson, 1946); pp. 40, 41.

[2] "Defence of the Soviet Arctic," *The Navy*, February, 1945; p. 62.

[3] *The Red Fleet in the Second World War*. Translated by Jack Hural. (Hutchinson, 1946); p. 50.

Northern Navy's protection of the fishing fleets, and of the timber cargoes from the Siberian and Karelian forests. The Arctic has treasures which have only been revealed by recent scientific explorations: among them is the coal north-east of the River Pechora, where the published figures suggest that the deposits may be among the richest in the Union. Until this field was opened, ships and icebreakers in the Far North were fuelled on coal from Spitzbergen and also from the Donbas, which in the latter case was taken to Arctic ports by the White Sea Canal. The coal of the Pechora Basin was a valued contribution to the Arctic Fleet at a time when the Germans were in occupation of the other sites. The opening of a light railway from Vorkuta, the centre of the Pechora coal deposits, to Ustkojva in Komi, has facilitated the transport of fuel north to the fleet, to one of the Pechora ports, and today grimed colliers plough the white seas to Murmansk and Dudinka. The Northern Fleet is also partially supplied by the coal of Khatanga on the Kara Sea, and by the Sangar-Kai fields of Yakutia. Arctic shipping passing through the Bering Strait can also fuel at Providence Bay on the Anadir Gulf. According to *Sovietskaya Arktika*,[1] the Northern Fleet is now fed entirely on Arctic coal. But Papanin, writing in *Pravda* on 6 September, 1939, said that "the problem of coal is still acute for us on the Northern Sea Route". Two months after the publication of Papanin's article, *Pravda* wrote more optimistically: "We have every reason to hope that in the near future big coal and oil industries will grow up along the Northern Sea Route, which will provide fuel not only for the Arctic Fleet, but also for the new settlements and towns arising on the Arctic coast. There should be no reason to import fuel for the Arctic, for the Arctic possesses its own natural resources of coal, oil and rare metals."[2] Of other northern resources many were mentioned in the first chapter of this book, and the Arctic Fleet with its air arm has become one of their principal guardians.

Another reason why the Northern Fleet is necessary for the defence of Russia's Arctic coastline is the fact that all along those shores are the terminals of the air lines to the Far North. When the offensive power of the Red Navy becomes a really formidable factor, its Northern Fleet will be viewed increasingly in the light of a protector of the Polar airports. Ships in the

[1] No. 5, 1940, p. 6.
[2] Quoted by Professor Kenneth Mason, "Notes on the Northern Sea Route," *The Geographical Journal*, July, 1940; pp. 40, 41.

Barents Sea can then guard from seaborne assault the aircraft defences of Murmansk, which is the terminal of the air line from Leningrad: ships of the Arctic Fleet can help to protect the airport at the mouth of the Mezen River, which is linked by air with the port of Archangel. So too, Pechora, terminal for the airway from Ust-Tailma, can be defended by ships at the mouth of the Pechora River; and New Port, with the last air station on the line from Tobolsk, can have support from vessels based on the Gulf of Ob. Dudinka, the end station on the air service from Krasnoyarsk, can rely on the protection of ships stationed near the delta of the Yenesei; so too, the airport on Dickson Island, which is linked with the mainland by a branch air line from Dudinka. Another branch runs east to the air station on Khatanga Bay, whose defences can be strengthened by ships operating in the Laptev Sea. The northerly airline from Yakutsk terminates at Tixii, where vessels of the Lena delta can support the defences of this important section of the East Siberian coast.

In the extreme east of the Arctic region, the Chukchi Peninsula—opposite the shores of Alaska—is ringed by an airway which takes a course from Cape Schmidt to East Cape, thence to Chukotski Cape on the Bering Sea. From Chukotski Cape a line goes south round the Gulf of Anadir via Novo Marinsk to Markovo, both of which airports are on the Anadir River. In the defence of these important air stations, the Soviet ships of the East Siberian and Bering Seas can play their part.

The tenth anniversary of the Northern Fleet was celebrated on Red Navy Day, 1943, and the Military Council of that fleet received a message of congratulation from Marshal Stalin. From Britain too came tributes to the men of the Arctic Fleet. To a group of seamen and pilots King George VI awarded decorations for bravery in action and for repelling enemy attacks on British convoys. "Russian seamen will wear their British decorations proudly as symbols of the growing friendship between our great peoples, and as a sign of comradeship in arms," declared M. Shirsov, People's Commissar for the Mercantile Marine of the U.S.S.R.

THE NORTHERN CONVOYS

The principal aim of the Germans in occupying Norway was to cut off the Russians from Anglo-American aid. The capture of coastal bases in the north of Norway early in the last war gave the German warships a quick striking advantage. They had a small fleet disposed offensively at Kirkenes, heavy forces based at Trondheim, they held Vadso, and the indented coast-line from Finmark to Varanger Fjord with its numerous inlets for U-boats, and they had Petsamo, only seventy miles from Murmansk. From the Bay of Biscay to the North Cape they held 2,000 miles of coast, and the harbours which these shore-lines gave them. The lifeline to Russia was flanked by this enemy-occupied littoral, and for 2,500 miles the British convoys were exposed to attacks from the Luftwaffe and U-boats before they could discharge their precious cargoes at the White Sea ports. First from Trondheim and then, in 1943, from Alten Fjord, they had to reckon with the possibility of attack from the battleship *Admiral von Tirpitz*, the battle-cruisers *Scharnhorst* and *Prinz Eugen*, the cruisers *Admiral Hipper*, *Nürnberg* and *Köln*, and the pocket-battleships *Admiral Scheer* and *Luetzow*; about twenty U-boats also were based on Norway.[1] Elsewhere it has been said that for some time during the war the strategic effect of British sea power in the global struggle against the Axis was, with certain notable exceptions, not fully recognised by the Russians, whose sea-consciousness is only developing. But the immediate help given to the Soviet Union by the men and ships who voyaged from Britain and America with the Northern Convoys did not lack appreciation on the part of the citizens of the U.S.S.R. It was by the northern route that the first of the British convoys to Russia sailed, on 12 August, 1941. It consisted of six ships carrying stores and aircraft. The following list in one ship is typical of the cargoes carried (before the Moscow Conference, held in September, when it was arranged that tanks also should be released by Britain to Russia): boots, 725 tons; rubber, 3,990 tons; mines, 200 tons; depth charges, 750 tons; ethyl fluid, 150 tons; cobalt, 4 tons; aircraft, 20; one radar set. The convoy was escorted by three destroyers and three mine-sweepers, covered by two cruisers, one aircraft carrier and three destroyers.[2] The whole convoy arrived at Archangel without loss on 31 August, and all the supplies which Britain had promised her Ally for the winter of 1941 were delivered on time. It was indeed not till 2 January, 1942, that any loss in a Russian convoy occurred at all. By the end of July 1944, there had been despatched from the United Kingdom to ports in Northern Russia, 3,480 tanks, 3,200 aircraft, 7,800 vehicles of

[1] Department of Naval Information, the Admiralty.
[2] Acknowledgments to the Department of Naval Information, the Admiralty.

all descriptions, and over 500,000 tons of stores.[1] By the beginning of March 1945, 4,000,000 tons of supplies had been delivered in convoy through North Russian ports.[2]

At a meeting of the Joint Chiefs of Staffs Committee in the spring of 1942, a memorandum was drawn up of three main defensive tasks, of which the first was "to keep Russia effectively in the war". This placed the despatch of munitions and aircraft to Russia in the highest priority, and the protection of Russian convoys therefore, became the chief commitment of the Home Fleet. The Admiralty ordered that most of the big ships of that fleet were to be used as covering forces, and destroyers, corvettes and trawlers were transferred from the Atlantic to strengthen the Russian-bound convoy escorts. In the view of one British naval authority, the fate of Russia, "trembling for long in the balance, may well have been determined by the munitions which reached her by Murmansk and the Persian Gulf and Egypt".[3]

For the first time in history men of the Royal and Merchant Navies were honoured as Heroes of the Soviet Union, when on 20 April, 1943, M. Maisky awarded this highest distinction to seamen who had served in the convoys to Murmansk. In his address at the Soviet Embassy on that occasion M. Maisky said: "Little more than a year ago I had the great pleasure, on behalf of the Soviet Government, to bestow Soviet decorations on four British airmen for deeds of gallantry performed by them when fighting on our front. Today I have an equal pleasure to bestow on behalf of my Government, Soviet decorations on a number of officers and men of the Royal Navy and Merchant Navy."

The Order of the Red Banner, the Order of the Patriotic War, and the Order of the Red Star were then presented, though only two of the twelve men so honoured were present to receive the awards. Two of the other ten were dead; the remaining eight were at sea.[4]

M. Maisky, continuing his address, paid the following tribute to the British Navies:

"The Royal Navy and the Merchant Navy of Britain have, in the words of Nelson, 'done their duty' in this war. They have

[1] *Merchantmen at War*, prepared for the Ministry of War Transport by the Ministry of Information. (H.M. Stationery Office, 1945); p. 108.
[2] Statement made in Parliament by the First Lord of the Admiralty, 7.3.1945.
[3] Captain Russell Grenfell, R.N.: *The Navy*, June 1945; p. 168.
[4] In Appendix III A, to this book, will be found the names of the men to whom the awards were made.

shown themselves worthy of their best traditions. It is enough
to mention the names *Graf Spee*, *Bismarck*, *Altmark*, the *Rawal-
pindi* and Narvik to see that the spirit of the Royal Navy fully
preserves the heritage of Nelson, and it is enough to recall the
history of the convoys to Malta and to Murmansk to be sure
that the British Merchant Navy has given us unsurpassed
examples of skill, endurance and bravery.

"Yes, British sea power has done great things in the last
three or four years. It severely blockaded Hitler Germany and
her satellites; and on the other hand it has kept the oceans open
for the United Nations. It made it possible for this country not
only to survive, but also to build a great army and powerful
air force, fully equipped with the most modern appliances of
war. At the same time, British sea power secured a great flow
of supplies from Britain and America to other Allied nations,
and more particularly to the U.S.S.R.

"We all know that these great achievements were bought at
a high price. It is true that the surface raiders have somewhat
receded in this war, but instead, the rôle of the submarine and
aeroplane have tremendously increased. Just at this very
moment the deadly U-boat campaign is the chief menace. This
battle is not yet definitely won by your gallant seamen.

"But let me commit this indiscretion! I have not the slightest
doubt that eventually your country will beat the U-boat now
as completely as it did in the last war. I have continuously held
this conviction all through the various phases of the present
war, with all its ups and downs, and when, in the darkest
moments of the war at sea—and there were such moments—
my Allied friends sometimes anxiously asked me why I felt such
confidence, I always replied: 'These British have the sea in
their blood; they may have losses and difficulties, but the sea
is their element and they are unbeatable in their own element.
Somehow they will conquer not only the U-boats, but any
other devilish device Hitler's crazy mind might try to put into
operation.'

"And I feel that I shall not be disappointed in my confidence. In the great epic of sea war one of the most outstanding
chapters were the Northern Convoys which were carrying all
sorts of arms, munitions and supplies from this country, from
Canada and from the United States to the Soviet Union. They
were magnificent exploits. Your merchantmen, protected by
your navy, were battling their way to Murmansk and Archangel through the dark wintry nights, through heavy Arctic

seas with ice and snow storms, through constant attacks by German submarines and shore-based aircraft, defying dangers and privations, defying death itself.

"It was a Northern saga of heroism, bravery and endurance, and the price had to be paid. Some of the ships and some of the men who went to the North have never come back. This saga will live for ever not only in the hearts of your people, it will live also in the hearts of the Soviet people, who rightly see in it one of the most striking expressions of the collaboration between the Allied nations without which our common victory would be impossible.

"These Northern Convoys played, and are playing, a very important rôle in the history of the war. They helped the Soviet Union in the most difficult moments of the past, they greatly contributed to the recent turn of events in the East. Let me, on behalf of the Soviet Government, the Red Army and the whole Soviet people express our most sincere gratitude to your Royal Navy, to your Merchant Navy, to your gallant seamen for their bravery and courage displayed in performing this important operation. And to give expression to these feelings the Soviet Government bestows its decorations upon those men who have given the most outstanding examples of gallantry and endurance in this battle of supplies."

The heroism of the men who sailed with the Northern Convoys has become one of the immortal sagas of the seas. Through ice, fog, and the northern darkness the "caravans" fought their way with cargoes for Russia. The sea lanes between northern Norway and the Kola Peninsula are particularly dangerous by reason of the ice-cap "which in winter swings south to within 250 miles of North Cape";[1] one west-bound convoy was trapped by ice and did not get clear of the entrance to the White Sea until she was a month behind schedule. In a region of lat. 71°, where an ice-pack covers the decks, and icicles form in men's beards, the crews of the Royal and the Merchant Navies brought their ships through to Archangel and to Murmansk. By the middle of March 1945, seven hundred and thirty-nine loaded cargo ships had sailed for North Russia. And of these, six hundred and seventy-seven had docked at North Russian ports. The loss of sixty-two ships represents only 8.4 per cent., and twenty-four of those sixty-two vessels were lost

[Continued on p. 396.

[1] Jasper H. Stembridge: *The Oxford War Atlas.* (Oxford University Press, 1943); Section 4. Reproduction by permission of the Clarendon Press, Oxford.

MOSCOW—PORT OF FIVE SEAS

THREE canals—the Baltic-White Sea, the Moskva-Volga, and the Volga-Don—have made Moscow a port of five seas. These canals have given a new strategic importance to the capital; in the last war, units of the Volga Flotilla, by use of the Moskva-Volga Canal, helped in the defence of the capital. By the construction of this channel and the Volga-Baltic waterway, Moscow now has direct communication by water with Leningrad, while the Baltic-White Sea Canal has enabled oil from the refineries at Gorki, and the products of the Tula coalfield and of the blast furnaces near Moscow, to be transported north to the ports of the White Sea.

The third waterway, the Volga-Don Canal, shows by its position on this map, how Stalingrad, on the Volga, is now linked with the Don. This Canal has made it possible for craft of the Azov Fleet to support the Volga Flotilla in wartime defence of Moscow. (This map, published in 1936, shows the pre-1940 frontiers with the Baltic States, with Finland, and with Bessarabia. It is reproduced from *Генеральный План Реконструкции Города Москвы. ,,Московский Рабочий.''* Москва, 1936.)

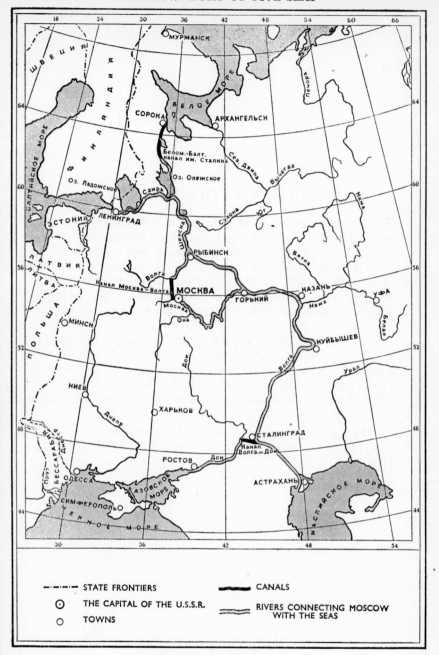

Explanation of Russian Characters :

ВОЛГА = VOLGA

Principal Towns on the Volga :

РЫБИНСК	= RYBINSK	КУЙБЫШЕВ	= KUIBISHEV
ГОРЬКИЙ	= GORKI	СТАЛИНГРАД	= STALINGRAD
КАЗАНЬ	= KAZAN	АСТРАХАНЬ	= ASTRAKHAN

MOSKVA-VOLGA CANAL

THE transformation of Moscow to an inland port has been effected by the Moskva-Volga Canal. By this waterway, units of the Volga Flotilla can transport troops and supplies to the capital in the event of rail communications being cut in time of war. The traffic on this canal was much increased during the war years 1942-44, when special river craft, including rapidly improvised fleets of barges, made their appearance here.

This diagram illustrates the system by which the Moskva River was joined to the Volga. The river port of Khimki, terminal station of the Canal, is indicated by the Russian characters Химки, north-west of Москва. The great reservoirs, shown as the shaded areas, cover the sites of more than 200 villages.

(The diagram is reproduced from *Генеральный План Реконструкции Города Москвы. „Московский Рабочий."* Москва, 1936.)

THE MOSKVA–VOLGA CANAL

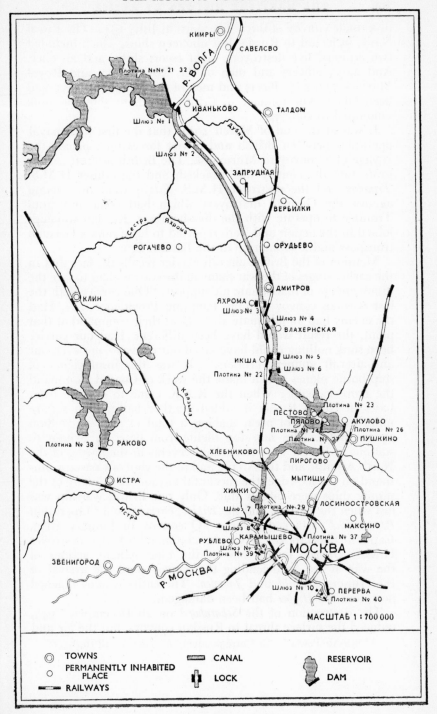

КИМРЫ

САВЕЛСВО

Р. ВОЛГА

Плотина №№ 21 32

ИВАНЬКОВО

ТАЛДОМ

Шлюз № 1

Дубна

Шлюз № 2

ЗАПРУДНАЯ

ВЕРБИЛКИ

Сестра

Яхрома

РОГАЧЕВО

ОРУДЬЕВО

КЛИН

ДМИТРОВ

ЯХРОМА

Шлюз № 3

Шлюз № 4

ВЛАХЕРНСКАЯ

Клязьма

ИКША

Шлюз № 5

Плотина № 22

Шлюз № 6

Плотина № 23

ПЕСТОВО

ПЯЛОВО

АКУЛОВО

Плотина № 24

Плотина № 26

Плотина № 27

ПУШКИНО

Плотина № 38

РАКОВО

ХЛЕБНИКОВО

ПИРОГОВО

МЫТИЩИ

ИСТРА

ХИМКИ

ЛОСИНООСТРОВСКАЯ

Истра

Шлюз 7 Плотина № 29

МАКСИНО

Шлюз 8

Плотина № 37

РУБЛЕВО

КАРАМЫШЕВО

МОСКВА

Шлюз № 9

Плотина № 39

ЗВЕНИГОРОД

Р. МОСКВА

Шлюз № 10

ПЕРЕРВА

Плотина № 40

МАСШТАБ 1 : 700 000

TOWNS

PERMANENTLY INHABITED PLACE

RAILWAYS

CANAL

LOCK

RESERVOIR

DAM

395

in a single convoy of thirty-five ships in July, 1942. The Royal Navy, in its aid to Russia, lost nineteen ships, which included two cruisers, five destroyers, eight escort ships, and an oiler. And 2,055 officers and men of the Royal Navy and Royal Marines, and 525 officers and men of the Merchant Navy had been killed. The tonnage of British merchant shipping sunk amounted to 208,537.

It was at the end of March 1942, that the first joint naval operation between British and Soviet forces took place—the voyage of a convoy to Murmansk. The British aircraft carrier protecting the convoy was attacked, and the cruiser H.M.S. *Trinidad* and the destroyer H.M.S. *Eclipse* went into action against the German destroyers which had come out from Tromsoe to operate with the dive-bombers. Russian warships joined in the action and were reported to have sunk a German transport and a submarine in the Barents Sea.

Mention of the British aircraft carrier recalls the fact that in the earlier stages of the war many of the convoys had to face the disadvantage of inadequate air support. "One carrier with the last Russian convoy—simply tempting Providence . . . Had the enemy had an adequate air force at their command at that point, the result would have been different. Had our carrier been sunk nothing could have saved our convoy—not even our anti-aircraft gunnery cruisers."[1] It was this insufficiency of ship-borne planes which made the work of Coastal Command the more valuable. When the R.A.F. came to operate from bases in North Russia it added another half-million square miles to the patrol area, making a total of over six million square miles. The non-stop flights from bases in Britain to stations in Russia were remarkable events in the battles of the North Atlantic and the Arctic, and to the vigil of Coastal Command on the ice-edge, the successful voyages of so many of the supply ships were largely due. Only one British warship was lost when the *Luetzow* and the *Hipper*, carrying out "Operation Regenboden," attacked a large PQ convoy in January 1943. Captain Sherbrooke, V.C., in command of the destroyer H.M.S. *Onslow*, fought one of the most gallant actions of the war at sea, in defending the convoy until the arrival of the cruisers *Sheffield* and *Jamaica*. The entire convoy reached port, and the *Hipper* had been damaged.

The destruction of the *Scharnhorst* on 26 December, 1943, reduced the surface threat to Russian convoys, but the air and

[1] "Sea-Air Power": Air Correspondent, *The Observer*, 18.10.1942.

submarine menace was unabated.[1] The *Scharnhorst* was sunk sixty miles north-east of the North Cape—the most northerly point at which a naval engagement had ever been fought. Contact had first been made south-east of Bear Island, and south of the ice-pack, by the British cruiser squadron escorting a number of merchant ships. The sinking of the *Scharnhorst*, whose quarry had been the large convoy making for Murmansk, was naturally front-page news in Russia.

The rôle of the heavy cruisers and battleships of the British Home Fleet was to cover the passage of the North Russian convoys, and the Arctic approaches to the Atlantic Ocean. In the Review of Naval Affairs given in the House of Commons on 7 March, 1944, the First Lord of the Admiralty stated that "since the commencement thirteen British warships have been sunk on this duty, and in the same period there were considerable losses of merchant ships. Over all, however, 88 per cent of the cargoes got through". Most remarkable was the achievement of the classic convoy which early in 1945 fought its way through to Russia with large cargoes of supplies, without loss of a single ship, despite repeated assaults by U-boats and by torpedo-bombers. There was a mass attack, first by fifteen Ju.88s, and two days later by thirty of these bombers in the region where the *Scharnhorst* had been sunk off the North Cape. The destroyer H.M.S. *Whitehall*, on her tenth voyage to Russia, beat off an attack by sixteen Ju.88s. On the homeward voyage the convoy had to meet a gale of seventy to a hundred miles an hour, with waves mounting sometimes to sixty feet. The convoy had the protection of ships of the Home Fleet under Rear-Admiral McGrigor, whose flagship was the escort carrier *Campania*. Ju.88s and torpedo-carriers attacked in waves, but aircraft from the *Campania* and *Nairana* beat them off, and although, in the case of the *Nairana*, huge waves were topping her bows, her pilots managed to make flights and deck landings unhurt. The convoy, which had taken railway locomotives and other priority materials for the Russian advance in Germany, and had re-loaded with timber, reached home with a loss of one corvette, H.M.S. *Bluebell*. The weather, stated Rear-Admiral McGrigor, was the worst he had ever known. There were 6,000 officers and men in the escort fleet, but there were also several thousands of merchant seamen, numbers of whom were Americans.

From November 1944, the enemy tended to concentrate their main offensive forces around the approaches to the Kola

[1] Department of Naval Information, the Admiralty.

Inlet, and U-boats in large numbers patrolled this area. Russian submarine chasers and many new anti-submarine devices helped to check this menace, but nevertheless, several ships were lost in this area. When all due acknowledgment has been made to the achievements of the Soviet's Northern Fleet in the second world war, the admission must be made that by itself that fleet was of insufficient strength to ensure that the Northern Approaches were safe for the passage of British and Allied supply ships to Russian ports. This was clear from the extent to which the Soviet Union relied on British escorts and naval aircraft to protect the Allied convoys all the way to the Arctic ports. In July 1942, an important convoy PQ.17, bound for Russia, had been in danger of attack from the 40,000-ton battleship *Admiral von Tirpitz*, and from the cruiser *Admiral Hipper*, also from a large force of enemy destroyers, which were steaming to intercept the convoy. Owing to the imminence of attack from these powerful German warships, (executing "Operation *Roesselsprung*),[1] the convoy received orders to scatter and to make for the Russian ports in independent groups. Six of the British destroyers were ordered to join the First Cruiser Squadron and to seek out the German ships. The fact that U-boats were at that time about in packs, and that they were attacking Soviet ports, suggests that Russian naval forces in the Far North were not as strong as they were officially reported to be during that period in the Soviet press. Of that convoy only eleven of the merchant ships out of the total of thirty-five which had set out for Russia reached their destination. On one occasion a large convoy was in danger of concentrated attack "almost on the North Russian doorstep," where "it was obvious that the enemy had massed a pack of U-boats".[2] When nearing port, U-boats were sighted ahead of the British and American ships. As a result however of Rear-Admiral McGrigor's determination "to hammer a way through the pack for the convoy", and the consequent action of the British aircraft and escorts, the Allied merchant ships arrived without loss at the Russian port. When less than two hours out of port however, the homeward-bound convoy had to face a submarine attack, though "it was obvious that the enemy would expect this convoy".[3]

1 Anthony Martienssen: *Hitler and His Admirals*. (Secker & Warburg, 1948); p. 138.
2 Cmdr. Kenneth Edwards, R.N., Naval Correspondent, *The Daily Telegraph*, 17.2.1945.   3 *Ibid*.

It was in July 1942, that the sinkings reached their highest figure, and at the end of that month in one convoy thirteen ships out of thirty-nine were lost, with another four from the returning convoy.[1] Nevertheless between August 1941, and February 1945, no less than 91.66 per cent. of the war supplies carried to the Soviet Union by the British and Allied convoys had reached Russian ports, and if this achievement was mainly due to British seamanship, Russian naval defence also played a part, inasmuch as Soviet ships in conjunction with the Red Army, had repulsed the German attacks on Murmansk. Soviet seamen had also helped to drive the Germans out of the Norwegian port of Kirkenes, and they had captured the Finnish harbour of Linkomari in the autumn of 1944. Recognition of joint responsibilities in the common struggle was in keeping with the spirit which in 1941 had prompted the foundation of the Anglo-Soviet Shipping Committee, "the first official Anglo-Russian body with joint responsibilities to function since the Russian Revolution".[2]

One convoy each way to and from Russia was run after the cessation of hostilities, 20 May being the date on which the last convoy reached a Russian port. By order of the Admiralty independent sailings were resumed on 25 May, 1945.

The following facts and figures have been supplied by the Department of Naval Information, the Admiralty:

Total number of convoys from the United Kingdom to Russia, 41; from Russia to the United Kingdom, 36; total number of merchant ships in convoys, 775. Value of military supplies sent to Russia, £308,000,000; value of other supplies (raw materials, foodstuffs, machinery, industrial plant, medical supplies and hospital equipment), £120,000,000. Military and civil supplies carried in convoys included the following items: Tanks, 5,218; aircraft, 7,411; vehicles, 4,020; ammunition, over 450,000,000 rounds of all calibres; radar sets, 1,474; telephone equipment, 30,227 miles of cable; guns, over 1,100; aircraft engine spares to the value of £15,981,000.

Civil supplies were as follows: aluminium, 32,000 tons; copper, 40,000 tons; industrial diamonds to the value of £1,424,000; rubber (from Ceylon and Far East), 114,359 tons; foodstuffs to the value of £8,210,000; machine tools, industrial plant and machinery to the value of £45,616,000.

[1] Department of Naval Information, the Admiralty.

[2] *Merchantmen at War*, prepared for the Ministry of War Transport by the Ministry of Information. (H.M. Stationery Office, 1945); p. 52.

Military supplies were made on a Lend-Lease basis, but civil supplies were provided under the terms of the Civil Supplies Agreement, whereby the Soviet Government paid 40 per cent. of the value in gold or dollars and the remaining 60 per cent. out of a credit from His Majesty's Government. The British public also contributed a large proportion of the funds for these supplies under the "Aid to Russia" charity schemes. Since October 1941, this charity spent £5,260,000 on medical items and clothing for the Russian peoples.

Speaking in the House of Commons in April 1946, Mr. Attlee, in presenting the above figures, said:

"The figures given relate to what was despatched. During the war incessant attacks by enemy submarines, warships and aircraft on the Russian convoys took toll of shipments to the extent of some 15 per cent. After 1 April, 1944, in consequence of our growing mastery over the enemy, losses were fortunately negligible. The hazards faced by the Royal Navy and by our merchant ships nevertheless continued, and the fortitude and endurance of all concerned is a matter for high praise and gratitude."

THE BARENTS SEA

Naval operations gave new point to the old description of the Barents Sea as "the Storm Kitchen", for undersea actions in these waters were numerous. According to one Soviet naval writer, Russian submarines were responsible for the loss of thirty-nine German transports in the winter of 1941-42.[1] By the beginning of February 1942, the total number of transports sunk in this way was stated to be forty-five, but again, these figures have not, at the time of writing, been confirmed by British naval spokesmen. Among the most notable of the submarine records was that of the *Malutka* (carrying one machine gun and two 18-inch torpedo tubes.) This vessel was on her way back to her station when she was attacked by an enemy submarine. Several torpedoes were fired at her during an attack which lasted for fifty minutes. When all the German torpedoes had been fired and the U-boat was about to ram, the *Malutka* rose, fired her torpedoes and sank the U-boat. This was one of the longest under-water actions of the war,[2] and one which at the time earned for the *Malutka's* Commander and crew an admiration not confined to the frontiers of the Soviet Union.

[1] Н. Токарев: *Военно-торской Флот СССР в Отечественной Войне.*
[2] The British submarine *H44* was under water for 1 hr. 20 mins. in a minefield.

In the defence of the supply ships making their way from Britain to Murmansk in the Barents Sea, high praise was given to the submarine flotillas by Rear-Admiral A. Frolov, who declared that "more than one-and-a-half million tons of enemy shipping and warships have been sent to the bottom of the Barents Sea",[1] and he affirmed that the submarines under Commander Nikolai Lunin had sunk seventeen enemy ships by the end of June 1944. On 5 July, 1942, in an attack on the *Admiral von Tirpitz*, Commander Lunin's vessel was reported by the Russians to have damaged the German pocket-battleship at a time when, in an attempt to destroy a large British convoy bound for a Russian port, the *Tirpitz* was escorted by more than ten warships. The claim that actual damage was inflicted however, was not endorsed by the British Admiralty.

Writing in December 1942, Captain Sendik of the Red Navy stated that U-boats had only succeeded in sinking $1\frac{1}{2}$ per cent of the cargo vessels carrying supplies to the U.S.S.R. Broadcasting on Red Navy Day, 22 July, 1944, Maj.- General Grigoriev asserted that between 22 July, 1941, and 30 April, 1944, Soviet submarines had sunk four hundred and forty enemy vessels totalling more than two million tons of shipping. These again are high claims; what impresses the average reader most is the endurance which brought victories after trials severe as those described in the *News Chronicle*[2] by officers of a British submarine:

"A British naval officer just home from a Russian submarine base in the Arctic told yesterday of cruises with Soviet sailors in their ice-covered submarines in continual darkness and weather so severe that several times each night they had to dive to melt the ice. This officer is one of a number who have been passing on to Russian submarines their experience of under-sea war against the Germans. The Commander of an-other reported that 'on a cruise in the worst weather of the year . . . it seemed at one time that the submarine became almost top-heavy from the weight of ice on the bridge. A sea-man was constantly on duty beside the conning-tower hatch wiping the exposed rim of the hatch with pure glycerine every few minutes so that the hatch could be slammed to any instant should the submarine have to crash-dive. On this patrol the crew lived and worked in a temperature of forty to fifty degrees of frost. Officers and ratings wore boots two sizes too big for

[1] "The Red Navy at War." *Lloyd's List and Shipping Gazette*, 29.6.1944.
[2] 3.3.1942.

them, to allow for four or five pairs of socks. They had fur caps
and six layers of woollens beneath their special submarine
suits.' " But such conditions were not new to the submarine
crews who got their pre-war training in voyaging to Spitzbergen and Novaya Zemlya.

Surface vessels too did efficient work in the Barents Sea,
where the exploits of the m.t.b. commanded by Lieut. Alexander Shebalin will long be remembered in the annals of the
Northern Fleet.

It was in the Barents Sea that for the first time the flagship
of the British Home Fleet steamed to anchorage in a Soviet
Harbour. In December 1943, Admiral Sir Bruce Fraser,
C.-in.C. Home Fleet, his flag flying in H.M.S. *Duke of York*,
entered a port near the U.S.S.R.'s main Arctic base. Slowly the
mighty British battleship of the *King George V* class passed the
frozen Arctic hills at dawn, and entered the Russian harbour
in the grey light of the northern morning. Aboard the *Duke of
York* to welcome Admiral Fraser came the C.-in.C. of the
Soviet Northern Fleet, Admiral Golovko, and the Royal
Marines formed a guard of honour.

During his stay in port, Admiral Fraser went in "sea hunter"
craft, corresponding to the British anti-submarine m.b.s, to the
principal naval base of the Russian Northern Fleet, where he
boarded and inspected a Soviet destroyer. At a lunch given in
Admiral Fraser's honour, Admiral Golovko gave the toast of
"The people of Great Britain and the British Navy, coupled
with the name of Admiral Fraser," a toast which was justified
very soon afterwards by the British naval victory over the
Scharnhorst, when the German battle-cruiser was sunk by
Admiral Fraser's flagship, H.M.S. *Duke of York*.

MURMANSK

As Russia's one ice-free port on the Barents Sea, Murmansk
is invaluable not only to the U.S.S.R.'s Northern Fleet, which
is based on Kola Bay, but to the Baltic Fleet, based on Kronstadt. The transfer of Baltic warships to Murmansk by the
White Sea Canal, could mean everything to Russia in a naval
engagement in the Arctic or the Barents Sea in which she was
severely pressed. The port is under the direction of the headquarters of the Baltic Sea Fleet in Leningrad.

For the mercantile marine also, Murmansk has a definite
importance. It has often been said that its foundation as a port
dates from the time of Marshal Stalin's visit there in 1933, but

as we shall note in the section on Archangel, it was used as a port by the Allies in the 1914-18 war. Stalin's visit however was quickly followed by developments which changed Murmansk from a fishing port to a town of some size by 1948. It is, like Archangel, a centre of administration of the Central Board of the Northern Sea Route. It is also the chief fishing centre for the Barents Sea and the principal port for trawlers.

The Kola Peninsula, on which Murmansk lies, is rich in minerals; there are deposits of coal, copper and nickel, and there is bauxite in the Khibin Mountain. Its mining and chemical industries are supplied with energy by the Niva hydro-electric station in Karelia, which, till the establishment of the power station at Toulomsk on the shores of the Arctic, was the most northerly hydro-electric plant in the world. The apatite of this region, so valuable for the poor soils of the Arctic, has been of assistance to the Khibinsk Research Station near Lake Imandra, on the Kola Peninsula, where the scientific workers have succeeded in raising on an average "three tons per acre of hardy types of rye, oats, or barley, or twenty tons of potatoes".[1] This promises to be of great assistance for the victualling of ships and for feeding the inhabitants of Murmansk and other White Sea ports. On account of its suspected mineral wealth, the Kola Peninsula was, with Novaya Zemlya, the object of the first expedition sponsored by the Arctic Commission established in 1919. Kola is a region which has to be guarded not only for its economic resources, however, but for its strategic coastline on the sea route that links together the various regions of the northern territories. For quite a long period in the war Murmansk was only fifteen miles from the front line.

The development of Poliarnoye, near Murmansk, as a submarine base, was justified by events in the war. Having the advantage of the influence of the Gulf Stream, this station is open in the winter months. The British submarines *Tigris*, *Trident*, *Sealion* and *Seawolf* were sent here in 1941, one of their chief tasks being to attack German supply ships making for Petsamo and Kirkenes. For the purpose of co-operating with Russian submarines in this work, a British Naval Staff was established at Murmansk.

ARCHANGEL

At the eastern extremity of the White Sea, on the mouth of

[1] Maurice Lovell: *Landsmen and Seafarers*. (Harrap, 1945); p. 45.

the Northern Dvina, stands Archangel, which, though five degrees latitude farther south than Murmansk, is, unlike that port, ice-bound for an average of eighteen weeks in the year. During the war of 1914-18 the Russians had mined the entrance to the Gulfs of Finland and Riga, and the coastal waters of the Aaland Islands; hence the merchant shipping was closed via the Gulf route and had to make the long voyage via the White Sea to Archangel. When that port was ice-bound, Murmansk was used; it was a new port specially developed for this traffic. Archangel at that time was poorly developed; the largest vessel which could make use of it was a light cruiser. Its development would have been more advanced but for the poor railways of the Arctic region.[1] Not till 1915 was the broad-gauge line from Archangel to Vologda begun. The new Swedish-Finnish line from Tornea to Karunki helped when White Sea shipping was closed.

During the first world war up to the time of the Revolution, the larger ships of the Russian Volunteer Fleet, all of which had been built in England, were employed on a regular supply service in the Atlantic under British management. Munitions were transported from America to North Russia, whence timber and pit props would be brought to England. These having been discharged, the ships would sail again in ballast for American ports to load more munitions. After the Revolution most of these ships continued in Allied service as transports, those that survived being ultimately returned to the Russian flag. A number of vessels were transferred from the British flag to Russian ownership during 1914-15. These included the existing icebreakers *Feodor Litke* (ex-*Canada*, ex-*Earl Grey*), *Georgi Sedov* (ex-*Beothic*), *Vladimir Rusanov* (ex-*Bonaventure*), *Sadko* (ex-*Lintrose*), and *Malygin* (ex-*Solovei Budimirovich*, ex-*Bruce*), all of which had been built for service in Canadian waters. With the aid of the *Canada*, as she then was, it was found possible to keep the passage to Archangel open for longer than the normal period, and when she was disabled the *Sadko* took over the task.

With its floating bergs, the Strait of Gorlo, which connects Archangel with the White Sea, is dangerous; a swift-running tide runs the full forty miles of it. Midyug Island guards the approaches to Archangel. This was fortified, but was captured by the light cruiser H.M.S. *Attentive*, and by the seaplane carrier *Nairana*, supported by armed trawlers, gunboats, and

[1] For lack of facilities at so-called "ports" on White Sea, and poor equipment of Archangel, see Fayle: *Seaborne Trade*, Vol. II, p. 122.

French light cruiser. This cleared the seaway to Archangel, and the fall of that city soon followed.

In the summer months Archangel relieves much of the strain on Murmansk, and during the second world war it had the advantage of being more remote from enemy air attack, and so when its harbour was open it was a safer port for Allied convoys. From the United Kingdom to this White Sea port the convoys had to make a voyage of 2,500 miles. The double-track railway which runs from here due south to Vologda gives additional importance to Arkangelsk in time of war, for from Vologda freights can be sent due west by rail to Leningrad. As regards actual area, Archangel is at present the largest of the Soviet ports. Its growth has been as remarkable as that of other Russian seaports, for during the Civil War it suffered widespread destruction. Today it is the principal timber port for the U.S.S.R.

Archangel is the headquarters of the Institute of Marine Fisheries and Oceanography, which undertakes the investigation of ocean foods and new fishing grounds, and has made an extensive survey of the coasts of the White Sea. It is also the headquarters of the Administration of the Northern Sea Fleet in its control of the ports of the White Sea and the Arctic.

LENINGRAD

Leningrad, with a population of over three million, and an industrial output of nearly one-fourth of the whole Union, is the principal port of the U.S.S.R. It is primarily a commercial one, but during the war it became as well a naval base, for within the city, on the Neva, part of the Baltic battle fleet was stationed in the winter of 1942; there it was out of range of the German heavy guns sited near Oranienbaum. But even before the war Leningrad was regarded as a naval fortress-city, and at the beginning of 1938 the announcement was made that it was to be closed to foreign consular officials. Leningrad was being developed as a strong naval base.

The administration of the commercial port is vested in peace time in the All-Union Marine Transport Company. On 26 January, 1930, the Central Executive Committee and Council of People's Commissars had decreed: "That to the All-Union Marine Transport Company be transferred all the mercantile seaports including Leningrad, with all properties belonging to them." In war time the approaches to Leningrad are controlled by the Navy Commissariat. The State dockyards are at Nevski, Galerni Ostrov, New Admiralty, and at Kronstadt. Naval guns are made at the Putilov steelworks. At the mouth of the Neva is Vasili Island, site of the Naval Academy.

Before the Revolution the port of Leningrad was poorly equipped; there were few mechanical appliances. Of the latter there were only eleven before 1914, whereas four hundred had been established by 1936.[1] In 1924 a large new harbour was started on Gladki Island for dealing principally with timber exports. The Leningrad shipbuilding yards were for many years the most important in the Soviet Union; latterly, as a precautionary measure, some of the submarine building formerly undertaken here went to Sverdlovsk beyond the Urals. In 1936 the Uralmashsavod plant was taken over by the naval and military authorities and used for constructing these vessels. Nevertheless, enough work went on at the wharves of the Barotshini Harbour in Leningrad for one war correspondent to assert that the assemblage of submarine parts here was "on a scale hitherto undreamed of in the outside world".[2] In Leningrad too, one of Russia's aircraft carriers, the *Krasnoye Znamya*, was laid down in 1939. The Elling yards were responsible for the 8,700-ton refrigerator ships, of which the *Felix Dzerzhinski* and the *Siberia* were the first. The wartime type of armoured gunboat popularly known as the "sea tank", was a product of the city. A canal fifteen miles long connects the latter with the rocky fortress of Kronstadt, ice-locked in winter. Its harbour faces the South Channel, across which lay the ancient Peterhof (reduced to ruins by the Germans); the island batteries north of the dockyards afford additional protection to Leningrad.

The loss of Leningrad would have meant the capture of Kronstadt and the fall of the fleet in the Baltic. It would also have meant the cutting of the railway to Murmansk, and the consequent loss to Russia of her northern link with the Atlantic Allies. (This line runs south of Lake Ladoga, crosses the Svir, skirts the western shores of Lake Onega, proceeds due north through Karelo-Finnish S.S.R. to Kandalaksha on a deep inlet of the White Sea. It then turns east of Lake Imandra up the Kola Peninsula to Murmansk.) "A wounded warrior standing guard on the Baltic coast at the Gateway to Russia's northern territories" was Zhdanov's wartime description of the second city of the Soviet Union. Its canals divide it into a city of eight islands, and these waterways, together with the Neva, afford

[1] *U.S.S.R. Handbook.* (Gollancz, 1938); p. 359.
[2] Ossian Goulding: *The Daily Telegraph*, 11.5.1943.

obstacles to tank invasions. In Leningrad we are never far from the sea; the maritime character of the city has been graphically presented in the words of Ilya Ehrenburg: "Leningrad entered history like an enormous ship cutting through the night."[1]

On 21 August, 1941, 300,000 Germans under the command of von Leeb, made their first attack on the city. Leningrad which, according to the enemy, was to have fallen after a short fight, withstood a close siege of seventeen months, and a total siege period of over two years, and in the end drove back the attackers. Ice-bound and shell-shattered, ringed by the German armies, the citizens of Leningrad faced their first winter of the siege. Sailors of the Red Banner Baltic Fleet supported the garrison, and sailors of the *Marat* acted as shore spotters.

Despite the urgency of defence at sea, numbers of Baltic sailors had been ordered to shore defences round Leningrad and along the Finnish Gulf, as soon as war started. (In the same way the seamen had rallied to the call of Lenin, twenty years earlier, when he appealed for sailors to fight ashore.) In September 1941, the Germans nearly got through the outer defences, and it was largely due to the Baltic Fleet holding the right flank that Leningrad was saved at that time. On the testimony of Admiral Galler, "naval artillery fire proved one of the most important factors in the defence of the city. Baltic artillerymen helped to break the Leningrad blockade".

Leningrad is ice-bound for an average of five months in the year. During the ice-free season supplies were brought to the city by the Ladoga Flotilla. In the frozen months Leningrad's port could not be used for the reception of supplies. But its citizens were daunted neither by nature nor by the arc of steel that enclosed them on all but the seaward side. Across the frozen water of Lake Ladoga they made the famous ice-road, which enabled food and ammunition to be brought in to the beleaguered city. That ice-road passed the granite fortress of Oreshek which, known in old days as "the key to the Neva", stands on the island of Orekhevo in the middle of the river. "Oreshek" means a "nut", and the Germans found it a hard one to crack, guarded as it was by sailors of the Baltic Fleet for over twelve months. Though the place crumbled about them, they, like the Marines of Sevastopol, stayed to the end and fired their last shot from the shell of their "nut". The sailors' stubborn defence of their naval battery prevented the Germans from

[1] "Breaking the Blockade": *The Defence of Leningrad*. (Hutchinson, 1943); p. 82.

crossing to the right bank of the Neva. And their fire also kept the way open for supplies to reach the fortress.

Sailors never seem far from the city of Leningrad: "It is night once again, with drenching rain, and Leningrad listens to the downpour and wonders how things are going with the sentries at the front who never close their eyes, with the sailors on patrol plunging in their motor boats through the dark waves, with the pilots scorning the night and the dirty weather."[1] Nikolai Tikhonov wrote the above in his *Leningrad Calendar* for October 1942. The maritime side of the city's life is constantly in his mind; of the siege during December he wrote this:

"Powerless to capture the city, the enemy is driven to a frenzy of rage. He fails to realise that every inhabitant looks on his house as a warship, in which he has his regular duties, and as a sailor keeps his ship spick and span, carries coal for his boilers, and keeps his watches on deck, so the Leningrader, although there is no surging sea around him, but now for the second year quiet shores of granite and the snowy lines of the houses on the embankment, devotes himself to the daily routine as though he were in the strictest service. . . . There are even wardrooms in this enormous battleship Leningrad. 'Red Corners' have been arranged in the air-raid shelters."

Countless citizens will never forget their sailors of the Baltic Fleet. When on 14 January, 1943, the long siege of Leningrad was raised and the Russians counter-attacked, proudly the spire of Rastrelli's Admiralty still rose above the Neva, proudly it looked down on the men who had saved it, who walked beneath it, with the black and gold ribbon round their caps, and with the streamers flying in the wind. They were the sailors of the Baltic Fleet who had been honoured with the title of "The Naval Guards". They had shared with the citizens of Russia's northern capital the ordeal of one of the longest and most terrible sieges in history. They had faced and fought blockade and bombardment till finally the "steel ring" of the Germans was smashed. In the ultimate victory of Leningrad no men played a finer part than the sailors of the Baltic Fleet.

THE BLACK SEA FLEET

The Black Sea Fleet is much more recent than the Baltic one, for it was not till 1926 that its first battleships under the Soviet

---

[1] Nikolai Tikhonov: "Leningrad Calendar, 1942": *The Defence of Leningrad*. (Hutchinson, 1943); p. 65.

régime appeared on its own sea. Not the least important task of this fleet in the second world war was to guard the tankers which crossed in convoy, a task competently carried out by the destroyer flotilla, in which force lay the real strength of the Russian fleet in the Black Sea. During the war the Germans aimed at linking the Rumanian and Caucasian oilfields by the sea route; that they failed in this objective was due to British sea supremacy in the eastern Mediterranean as well as to the work of the Black Sea Fleet. The enemy had to use their over-worked land routes for transport of men and materials, and they were compelled to keep many of their vessels immobilised in the Rumanian port of Constanza, and in the Bulgarian ports of Burgas and Varna.

For a considerable time Russia lost all her naval ports on the Black Sea. Yet as long as she kept command of the water, she prevented the Germans from transporting troops by sea in numbers sufficient to help their land campaigns. Russia retained at least one battleship and one aircraft carrier (*Stalin*); on 23 November, 1942, the London *Times* reported the Black Sea Fleet as consisting of one battleship (*Pariskaya Kommuna*), three cruisers, twelve destroyers,[1] and a large submarine force.[2] Against this the Axis possessed only two or three Rumanian destroyers out of an original five, one Rumanian submarine, and a few small Italian submarines built in Rumania. There were, however, a large number of German and Italian m.t.b.s at that time, and U-boats had entered the Black Sea early in the war. On 31 December, 1942, an Associated Press report stated that the *Krasnaya Kommuna*, the *Stalin*, one heavy and three light cruisers, four destroyers, and thirty submarines, had bombarded several German-occupied ports, to give protection to the left flank of the Russian Caucasian Army.

The use of the lesser ports, after the loss of the main ones, enabled the Red Fleet not only to retain command of the Black Sea, but to carry out offensives. The latter usually took the form of assaults by M.O. speedboats, with Marines making forced landings, and the cruisers *Krasny Krim*, *Krasny Kavkaz* and *Chervonnaya Ukraiina* covering these raids. *Krasny Kavkaz* (8,000 tons) was built at Nikolaiev in 1916; her speed is 30 knots, and her complement is 600. *Chervonnaya Ukraiina* (6,700

[1] Other sources have been inclined to put the number of destroyers as higher.

[2] The estimated number given for the spring of 1942 has appeared elsewhere as fifty.

tons) was sunk during the war; she carried 100 mines, had a speed of 30 knots, and a complement of 600. Of all the Black Sea ships, *Krasny Krim* was the best known, for up to the beginning of 1943 not one ship in the convoys which she protected was reputed to have been lost. Claims have been made that by June 1942, she had repelled over two hundred enemy attacks. Her guns gave effective support in the defence of Sevastopol, to which base she had brought at different times so many of the Marines. The Germans asserted they had sunk her off that naval base in June 1942, a claim which was never confirmed by the Russians. Her crew were given the title of "Guards".

The flagship of the Black Sea destroyer flotilla was the high-speed *Tashkent*, built to Italian design in 1937. Constructed at the Ansaldo works at Leghorn, with a tonnage of 2,800 and speed of 39 knots, she had been delivered at Odessa on 3 May, 1939. Delivery had been delayed owing to a dispute between Russia and Italy over the Russian supply of oil for Italian warships. When the *Tashkent* steamed through the Straits, she was manned by an Italian crew. This destroyer later brought into Sevastopol equipment and ammunition for the troops defending the city. It was said[1] that she once had to stand up to an attack of ninety-six enemy planes. She was scuttled at Novorossisk, but is thought to have been salved. In another class, the minesweeper *Arseni Raskit* earned a reputation for her Black Sea exploits. From Soviet sources it was claimed that by March 1944 this vessel had covered over 50,000 miles and escorted two hundred transports since the war began.

Russian operations in the Black Sea and on its shores were greatly helped by the Naval Air Arm. The latter was reported to have destroyed five enemy convoys on 27 April, 1944. High claims for this Service have been made by Tokarev,[2] who says that "during three months of operations only, in the height of the autumn battles of 1942, our Naval Air Arm sank five Fascist minesweepers, nineteen coastal ships, six torpedo-boats, four transports, and a number of other ships. In air battles, two hundred enemy planes were destroyed".

Crews of the Black Sea Naval Air Arm also played a part in the attacks on Constanza, and again in the attacks on Novorossisk after its fall to the Germans. The Rumanian ports of Sulina and Galatz—used by the Germans for the building of U-boats —did not escape considerable damage from Russian naval air

[1] *Военно-морской Флот СССР в Отечественной Войне.* Стр: 50
[2] *Так же,* стр. 58.

attacks. At the beginning of the war Rumania's diminutive mercantile marine consisted of about forty vessels, but the Russian warships were said to have destroyed most of them.

The Bulgarian ports of Varna and Burgas, where Admiral Schuester had established a naval transport staff, proved to be useless for Germany's intended purpose of immobilising the Russian Fleet. Indeed the tables were now turned, mainly owing to raids made by Russian submarines. Burgas as a port is useful, for it can take light cruisers, but as late as 1944 it had no repairing docks. Constanza suffered badly from Russian naval guns; oil barges and oil storage depots were destroyed, and as a port it was to become practically unusable by the Germans. On 29 August, 1944, its capture was announced after a combined attack by tank and motorised forces, in combination with ships and landing parties of the Black Sea Fleet.

Useful work was done by the *Malutka* class of submarines, a special type of small submarine, built 1928-30, with a maximum of 200 tons surface displacement. These vessels have two 18-inch torpedo tubes and a speed of 8-13 knots.[1] In the work of evacuating the wounded from Sevastopol and Odessa, the submarines took part.

The evacuation of Odessa was carried out under conditions not much better than those at Sevastopol. The garrison was small; it had defended itself for over two months against eighteen German and Rumanian divisions. The withdrawal was completed on 16 October, 1942. On 10 April, 1944, Odessa was recaptured after a one-day assault. The Russians, when they entered the city, found two-thirds of the port and all the wharves destroyed. But they now once more had a principal base in the western part of the Black Sea, and the Germans were prevented from making a seaward escape. For their lack of ships the enemy paid dearly; with such disparity in numbers they could not hope to hold the ports indefinitely. Their seizure of the Perekop Peninsula brought home to them as much as anything else did, how much they needed a navy in the Black Sea.

<h2 align="center">THE BLACK SEA PORTS</h2>

Because the oil centres of the Caucasus lie behind the eastern shores of the Black Sea, it is the eastern coastline which is strategically the most important to the U.S.S.R., though the chief naval port, Sevastopol, and the largest commercial one,

Odessa, are on the western side. Sevastopol, about which more will be said later, was closed to foreign visitors three months before the outbreak of the second world war. It is the training station of the Black Sea Fleet, has a good harbour and extensive repair facilities, but it suffers from south-westerly gales. From Sevastopol it is 200 miles to Constanza, 260 to Varna, and 170 to Sulina.

The Administration of the Black Sea Fleet, which controls all the Russian ports of the Black Sea except Tuapse, has its head-quarters in Odessa. This port is 344 miles almost due north from Constantinople, and 164 north-west from Sevastopol; primarily a commercial seaport, it is also used by naval vessels, and ice-breaking ships for the Black Sea and Azov are kept here. For two to three weeks in the year, usually, Odessa is closed by ice though some years it is entirely ice-free; its subsidiary port, Khor, is frozen from December to March. Odessa, whose road-stead gives good anchorage, is of great importance to the U.S.S.R., as it can take imports when Leningrad is closed. Its prosperity in the first half of the nineteenth century was due to the fact that it was, between 1817 and 1857, a free port. The closing of the Dardanelles both in the first world war and in the Civil War, ruined it. Like Novorossisk and Nikolaiev, Odessa after 1920 handled less than half the amount of cargo it did before the Civil War. But by 1924 the harbour had been nearly cleared of wreckage, and was able to deal with a considerable grain export. Grain from the agricultural regions is loaded at the Odessa wharves by floating elevators, which were first installed in 1932. Two years later Odessa was a busier port still, as the first regular steamship line between here and New York was opened, sailings being made by the steamers *Komsomol*, *Stary Bolshevik* and *Kalinin*. In March 1937, the 5,000-ton floating dock, built in the Odessa shipyards, left for Vladi-vostock, to be used for timber-floating in the Far East.

Novorossisk, which had been developed as a complementary base to Sevastopol, is also the great granary port of the Kuban, and a centre of marine engineering. Situated on the north-eastern shore of the Black Sea, it is an open port on a bay which is four miles long; the foothills of the Caucasian ranges are not too far off to provide natural defences on the north side, and additional ones are afforded by the marshes and lakes of the Kuban. The harbour of Novorossisk suffers from the *bora*, the north-east wind from the Caucasian hills, which makes anchor-age sometimes unsafe. Ships can be repaired at the Sudostal works. "Not even a single German launch ever entered or emerged from Novorossisk Harbour or Bay, let alone enemy warships and supply ships," wrote Admiral Isakov.[1] Supplies for the German garrison in this port had to come overland. The garrison withdrew after Russian Black Sea troops had landed, and on 16 September, 1943, Novorossisk was liberated from the German and Rumanian divisions.

Nikolaiev, which is reached by the Ochakov Channel, is frozen from December to March. It is too far from the open sea to become a first-class naval port, and when enlarged it required dredging to a depth of thirty feet. Icebreakers are necessary to keep open for all the year the estuary of the Dnieper and the channel of the Bug which connects Nikolaiev with the Black Sea. Founded as a port by Catherine II, Nikolaiev is fifty miles from the sea, on the east bank of the estuary of the Bug, where that river is joined by the Ingul. Ships are built here for the Far Eastern Fleet, also tankers, icebreakers, timber barges. It is a port for the export of grain, the iron ore of Krivoy Rog and the manganese of Nikopol.

After being occupied by the Germans, Nikolaiev was re-captured on 28 March, 1944, by the troops of General Malinovsky's Third Ukrainian Army. Its recapture not only meant that the German army was cut off in the Crimea, but it enabled the Russians to deprive the enemy of his already slender sea communications with Rumania. This much good the Germans did by their occupation of Nikolaiev—they built from the north-west a new single-track railway to Odessa, from which the former is seventy-four sea miles distant.

Kherson, which first rose under Potemkin to a position of any importance, has been called the twin port of Nikolaiev, from which it is thirty-seven miles to the south-east. Situated near the mouth of the Dnieper, on the right bank, it was developed to take the increased traffic which followed the completion of Dnieprostroy. The Dnieper is now an all-way navigation river, and a canal has been constructed at Kherson to enable ships of moderate draught to reach the open sea, but most of the unloading of any but the smaller vessels is done by floating elevators. The chief cargoes handled are grain exports. In October 1930, work was commenced at Kherson on shipbuilding works designed to be the largest in Ukraine.

The Russians, who for a time in the last war lost all their

[1] *The Red Fleet in the Second World War.* Translated by Jack Hural. (Hutchinson, 1946); pp. 87, 88.

main ports on the Black Sea, showed considerable adaptability
in making use of their lesser ones. When the naval ones fell
they were under the disadvantage of having to fall back on
mercantile harbours such as Poti, Batum, Tuapse. Batum is the
principal mercantile port on the eastern shore of the Black Sea ;
it is situated four hundred miles south-east of Novorossisk. The
largest oil port of the U.S.S.R., Batum is the terminal of the
pipeline from Baku, and here the ships of the fleet are fuelled.
It is ice-free, and has a roadstead which could accommodate
a considerable number of ships. But it is handicapped by south-
westerly winds, and ships are often unable to anchor here for
fear of collision. As late as 1945 its docking facilities were insufficient for its traffic. The harbour is shallow and requires constant
dredging. Sand-drifts from Chorokh River are kept in control
by the Burun Tabisk mole. Batum is important for Russia's
trade with Iran; it is cheaper for the Soviet Union to ship goods
for the Middle East and for the Republics of the Trans-Caucasus
via the Black Sea Route to Batum, than to use the Armavir-
Tbilisi Railway.

Tuapse and Poti were ports also used by the smaller ships
of the fleet when Novorossisk fell to the Germans, but neither
can be compared with that naval base. Poti exports manganese,
and Tuapse is an oil port fed by a branch of the pipeline which
runs from Makhach-Kala on the Caspian. It is under the
direction of the Black Sea Oil Fleet, whose headquarters are at
Tuapse. Poti, on the River Rion, has a harbour which is often
difficult of approach, owing (as in the case of so many of the
Black Sea ports) to the south-westerly gales. From Poti the
Trans-Caucasian Railway runs to the oil port of Baku. Another
port which has grown rapidly under the Five-Year Plans is
Sukhum-Kaleh, between Tuapse and Poti. It lies on the Bay of
Sukhum, is free from ice, and is sheltered by mountains, but the
harbourage is not good, and the marshy nature of the ground
makes for poor communications between the port and the
interior.

During the last war the Russians also had recourse to such
small ports as Feodosia. This has the advantage of being
situated between two fortresses—those of Sevastopol and Kerch
—and it has a mountain barrier behind it. So long as Sevastopol remains in Russian hands, Feodosia is a port easily defended.
By 15 April, 1944, nine divisions of Germans and Rumanians
in the Crimea were driven into the south-west corner of the
peninsula. After capturing Kerch, General Yeremenko's

Maritime Army, advancing from the east, joined with General Tolbukhin's forces which had advanced across the Sivash Sea; Feodosia, which had for a time been occupied by the enemy, was once more in Russian hands. South of Feodosia, and thirty miles away, on the eastern tip of the Crimean Peninsula, is the small seaport of Sudak, from which, as also from the little port of Alushta, twenty miles from Yalta, the Germans tried to make a seaward escape in light vessels. Another Crimean port used (but for small ships only) by the Russians in their Black Sea operations, was Eupatoria. This port, which has an open roadstead of considerable area, has only a poor anchorage; it is not deep enough for large vessels. It is used chiefly for cargo—principally livestock. Much of its trade is with Turkish ports.

Ochakov, built on a tongue of land at the confluence of three rivers, the Bug, Dnieper and Berezan, is a port also used by small ships. Its fortress of Kara-Kerman, on a steep cliff, commands the seaward approach to the Dnieper-Bug estuary. From the Kinburn Spit, two miles from Ochakov, sailors and marines of the Black Sea Fleet made a surprise attack on the German troops who had invested the port. Using rafts to get up channel by night, they succeeded in making a landing. The town was taken by General Malinovsky's troops on 31 March, 1944.

One of the most remarkable facts about the naval operations during the war was that though the Russians lost Odessa, Sevastopol, Novorossisk, Nikolaiev,[1] their four principal naval ports of the Black Sea, they never allowed their ships to be trapped in their bases. The lesson of Port Arthur had been well and truly learnt. The Black Sea Fleet retained its mobility as a sea-going force instead of trying to function "as a series of pill-boxes for harbour defence".[2]

SEVASTOPOL

Sevastopol, "The August City", bears a title whose tradition was maintained in the second world war. It was the great Russian General, Suvorov, who first saw the possibilities of Sevastopol as a naval citadel, and pressed for its development. Had he been alive in the last war he would have echoed the words of Ilya Ehrenburg: "Throughout the world the immortal name is repeated: Sevastopol. It has become a symbol of

[1] When the Germans took this they used the repairing yards for submarines.

[2] Naval Correspondent, *The Manchester Guardian*, 1.12.1942.

resistance, of the grandeur of human achievement, of proud courage."[1] This is the tribute which Ehrenburg has paid to the City of the Black Sea sailors, and in the defence of Sevastopol none played a prouder part than the men of the Black Sea Fleet. From the opening day of the attack on their city, 22 June, 1941, till its fall in July 1942, the Marines and naval gunners combined to support the efforts made by the Red Army to keep the enemy from capturing the principal naval base on the Black Sea. That base, up till the time of its fall, was a secret as closely guarded as in the days of Catherine the Great; its harbour, half a mile wide, was never open to ships of commerce. It was the bastion of the Black Sea, the key to the Crimea, and as such to be defended to the death. On the day that the first German bomb fell on Sevastopol, naval planes and A.A. gunners succeeded in driving off the air attacks. Not till 30 October, 1941, did the battle for the city begin in earnest. By that time the Germans had got to the Perekop Isthmus, and regarded the fall of Sevastopol as imminent. Yet, in the words of Vice-Admiral Oktiabrski, "for over eight months our heroic marines, infantrymen, pilots, gunners, mortar crews, and tankmen defended the naval fortress with a bravery and endurance unexampled in the history of war".

The defenders of Sevastopol had set up a floating battery at the spot where, in the Crimean War, Admiral Kornilov had ordered his men to sink their ships to avoid capture. An unfinished warship removed for safety from Nikolaiev, provided the platform for the machine-guns and anti-aircraft artillery. Boris Voyetekhov, in *The Last Days of Sevastopol*,[2] describes how, through the bitter winter and the spring storms, "this square steel fortress which was gripped by enormous anchors, poured fire at German bombers, E-boats, torpedo-carrying planes, and even at submarines which were trying to attack Soviet transports".

In December 1941, Sevastopol had to endure one of the fiercest periods of its bombardment, when even the Germans were amazed that anything could still live in the city, but warships continued to bring up troops and supplies, and to evacuate wounded and civilians. The difficulty of doing this was increased by two factors. The first was the presence of the

[1] *"City of Courage": Sevastopol. November 1941-July 1942.* (Hutchinson 1943); p. 9.
[2] Cassell and Co., 1943. Acknowledgments also to Alfred A. Knopf, Inc., New York.

Germans in hill positions above Balaclava, whose harbour was at the south-east end of Sevastopol's outer line of defence. From those dominating positions the enemy was able to attack Russian withdrawals from the perimeter of Sevastopol to the sea. The second adverse factor was the insufficiency of airfields, which prevented the Russians ashore from sending aircraft to help the ships. Never was the value of aircraft carriers more clearly proved to the Russians; at that time, when Sevastopol was surrounded on three sides, and the airfields in the hands of the enemy, a larger number of sea-based aircraft would have made a great difference to the defence of the city.

The siege of Sevastopol is above all the story of the Marines. It was they who in the early days of the assault successfully challenged the German boast that the city would fall in three days. It was they who helped the famous Drapushko Battery in the epic defence of the granite fortress erected to guard the harbour entrance. That naval battery came into fierce action on 15 November, 1941, when the enemy was said to have fired over three hundred shells at the citadel. But the Black Sea gunners and the Marines held the enemy back. As Sobolev has pointed out, the defenders were aided by the fact that whereas their original coastal guns had been intended for seaward defence only, their new long-range batteries could be trained landwards. And so, throughout that winter of 1941, the fort still held. And "during the second defence of Sevastopol, the great-grandchildren of Admiral Nakhimov's Marines again hoisted the proud flag of Black Sea fame over the old fort".[1]

The story of the seventy-four Marines who took a vow to hold that fort and to keep the way clear to the sea for those who had to leave the city, is an imperishable one. There they manned the citadel and held it for three days, though the walls fell about them. On the fourth day they were ordered to leave the ruins and board the last boat. "They went down to the harbour-side in silence, without any hurry, uniforms in tatters, covered with dust, wounded; they made a solemn procession of heroes, a terrible and wonderful vision of the Black Sea glory, the great-grandchildren of the Sevastopol sailors who once upon a time built this old fort."[2]

Immortal too is the story of the five Marines who went to stop an enemy tank column hurling incendiary containers. Two

---

[1] Leonid Sobolev: "In the Old Fort": *Sevastopol, November 1941-July 1942.* (Hutchinson, 1943.)
[2] *Ibid.*

of the men fell; the other three kept up the fight and finally tied grenades to their bodies, ran under the tanks, and were blown up with them. The last defence of the naval citadel was kept up from a lighthouse, and one of the last three naval men to leave the ruins of Sevastopol was Admiral Oktiabrski, Commander of the Black Sea Fleet. The fall of the city was inevitable, for the defenders were outnumbered on an average of four to one. But Sevastopol, city of the sailors, port of pleasant squares and parks, with the chestnut trees that shade its boulevards, the acacias giving green to its streets, the white houses with gaily painted shutters, and the balconies bright with flowers—Sevastopol has risen from her ruins with a splendour brighter than she knew of old, because of this thing that happened on the heights of Malakov:

"Gathering round him his Marines of Captain Alexander's 35th Battery on the Malakhov Kurgan, the political commander spoke these words: 'I know that every one of you would a hundred times rather fight the most desperate sea battle than be dive-bombed once you are ashore. But the Germans have forced us to fight on shore. Eighty-two years ago a Russian Admiral ordered his men to sink their vessels in this Bay of Sevastopol. Those orders were obeyed and the guns were brought ashore to defend the city, as these our guns do today. Twenty-four years ago Lenin ordered our ships to be sunk at Novorossisk—these orders were obeyed. Last year Stalin ordered us to blow up the Dnieper Dam and we did. Now we have to die. We have to die for those who, one day, will return to Sevastopol; we have to die for those who one day will build another Dnieper Dam. We have to die for those who will go on fighting at sea.'

"The men removed their caps and stood silent for a short time and then swore an oath to conquer or die. They returned to their guns wearing under their Red Army blouses their striped sailor jerseys 'for luck' and twisted round their forage caps hat-bands bearing the names of their ships. A few days later they were surrounded, and thousands of bombs fell on the Malakhov Kurgan; they fought till the last shell had been fired and then blew up themselves and their guns. No white flag ever flew at Sevastopol!"[1]

Though Sevastopol was officially evacuated on 3 July, it

[1] Boris Voyetekhov: *The Last Days of Sevastopol;* pp. 143, 144. Acknowledgments to Cassell & Co., London, and to Alfred A. Knopf, Inc., New York.

was not till the 14th that the group of sailors, holding the Khersonese lighthouse, ceased fighting. It was not unfitting that the last act of defiance of those sailors should have come from that last spit of land on Sevastopol Bay.

The story of the siege of the city has been told in an unforgettable way in the film called *The Glory of Sevastopol*.[1] Sailors are marching past the monument to the seamen of 1905 who revolted in the *Potemkin*.[2] Dawn breaks over unruffled waters; the scene quickly changes to a black smoke screen and a rush to action stations. Again a sudden contrast from a scene of warm sunshine to one of ice-covered decks: the Black Sea too has many moods, and like most large land-locked ones, is subject to storms without warning. Submarines are shown lying off Sevastopol, and we are given a glimpse of the Council of the Black Sea Fleet under Vice-Admiral Oktiabrski, working over the final details of a plan of attack. A submarine is sent to a position off-shore to scout enemy dispositions on a nearby beach. They must find out those dispositions or it will not be safe for their own submarines to surface. Landing from an inflated rubber boat, the Russian sailors destroy the enemy communications ashore, and signal to the flagship "Coast clear". Motor launches churn through the foam to the shore; aboard them are picked men, the Commandos of the Black Sea Fleet. "On across the bay charges this cavalry of the sea", the barrage from the big ships providing cover for the landings.

When the Germans took Sevastopol after its siege of two hundred and fifty days, they only got the ruins of that city. The fight for its recapture lasted from 14 April until 9 May. By that time the enemy had lost all the Black Sea ports, and when the Russians retook Sevastopol they completed the liberation of the Crimea, which the Germans had described as their "aircraft carrier in the Black Sea".

Tribute to the work of the Black Sea Fleet was paid in the message sent on 5 November, 1944, by the British First Lord of the Admiralty: "We rejoice that enemy naval power has been extinguished in the Black Sea."

THE SEA OF AZOV, AND THE AZOV FLOTILLA

The Sea of Azov is usually frozen from the end of November to the middle of April, and it has no port that is not ice-bound

---

[1] English version prepared by the Soviet Film Agency. Shown in London 1943, 1944.

[2] Sevastopol was the home port of *Potemkin*.

for some period: even the principal up-river port Rostov is ice-locked for an average of three months in the year, and the many mouths of the Don are frozen on an average for fourteen weeks. These mouths are shallow—the greatest depth does not exceed thirteen metres—and only two of them are used for navigation, one by ships, the other by rafts. Rostov is the headquarters of the administration of the ports of the Azov Sea. The place is important as the junction of three railway systems, one running north-west, the other south-east to the Caucasus, and the third up the basin of the Volga. The ship-building yards of Rostov give this river-port a close connection with the Sea of Azov, but the principal *sea* ports for Azov are Taganrog and Mariupol. Taganrog suffers from being on a very shallow gulf of that name, from which the water is driven away by the north and north-east winds, and the water level "falls two metres or more so that ships are unable to ground".[1] From Taganrog, freight from Rostov is conveyed in local steamers to seagoing ships.

Mariupol, situated within easy access of the great industrial and agricultural regions of Ukraine, has direct communication with the Donetz basin, and so has an important coastal trade for grain, coal, and the iron ore of Krivoy Rog. Mr. S. P. Turin, in his detailed work, *The U.S.S.R.: An Economic and Social Survey*,[2] puts Mariupol among the five principal seaports of the Union. Like Taganrog, it suffers from being ice-locked, though only as a rule for two-and-a-half months in the year. Towage in and out of the harbour is always necessary. During the Civil War after 1917, Mariupol, like many other ports, had become derelict, its harbour was choked, and no dredging had been done. Intensive repairing was begun in 1924, and eight years later a contemporary journal stated that "the construction of what is intended to be the largest shipyard in Europe will shortly begin at Mariupol".[3] But since that time the development of this port as a centre of shipbuilding has not fulfilled as yet, those earlier expectations. Mariupol consists of three independent sections: (1) The principal port. (2) Kalmius River port, used by smaller vessels. (3) Novo-Azov, opened in 1932, under the First Five-Year Plan, to take vessels of deeper draught than (2), particularly for cargoes of ore obtained from

[1] *Encyclopædia Britannica*, Vol. II, 14th edtn., p. 830.
[2] Methuen, 1944; p. 26.
[3] *Monthly Review*, Vol. V, No. 12, p. 10. (Issued by the Moscow Narodny Bank, Ltd., December 1932.)

the Kerch Peninsula. After discharging ore, the ships load Donetz coal for the harbour of Kamysh-Burun on the Azov Sea.

Ships leaving Mariupol for the Black Sea pass through the Kerch-Yenikobsk Canal, which requires continual dredging. Plans for making Kerch a first-class naval fortress were made at the end of the nineteenth century; the port, which handles the iron ore of the neighbourhood, is only ice-bound for an average of six weeks in the year, whereas the ports of Berdyansk and Yeisk are frozen for two and three months respectively.

The Strait of Yenikale, which leads via the Kerch Strait from the Sea of Azov to the Black Sea, is the narrowest passage of water between the Crimea and the Kuban. Provided it is well guarded from the air, this tideless Strait of Yenikale can ensure protection for the Azov Fleet against a sea-borne attack from the Black Sea. Through that strait passed the Azov Sea Flotilla when it came to help the Black Sea Fleet in the assaults on the Crimea. The Azov ships had to run the gauntlet of the Kuban islets on which the Germans had machine-gun sites. They also had to pass the Taman Peninsula, whose loss to an enemy force at any time is a serious matter for the Russians, as it means that Novorossisk is threatened. The small size of the peninsula bears no relation to its strategic value as the land-wedge commanding the Kerch Strait. That strait separates the Crimea from the Kuban, and no enemy, holding the latter, will be content till he has the former.

The northern shores of the Sea of Azov demand strong defences, where, by the delta of the Don, passage can be made to the industrial and shipbuilding port of Rostov, and, by the Don-Volga Canal, the Volga can be reached near Stalingrad. In the autumn of 1942 the defences of those northern shores were tested when the Germans advanced towards the coast. It was the sailors and marines of the Azov flotillas who routed the enemy detachments. Naval aircraft from the Black Sea attacked the columns moving down the coast, and destroyed the bridges across the Don.

The Azov Sea Flotilla took part in the landing operations on the Kerch Peninsula in December 1941, transporting forces of the Red Army from the Taman Peninsula to the northern shore of Kerch. The difficulty which confronted the Allied armies before they could undertake a "Second Front" on the European mainland should, in the opinion of some British strategists, have been clearer to the Russians—at any rate in the Black Sea area —than it was, for it took them fourteen weeks to establish a small bridgehead in the Crimea, north of Kerch. It has been pointed out[1] that in their case there were only a few miles of intervening water, not the open sea, and they had air bases nearer at hand than the British had when they made the Anzio bridgehead. But, we remember too, the weather conditions were severe in the winter of the Russian assault, and the achievement, when it did take place, was a well-earned success for the Azov Sea Flotilla, whose operations supported those of the Black Sea Fleet. An account of those operations has been given in *The Navy*[2] by a Red Navy captain, who has told us how units of the fleet effected a landing north of Feodosia, and by holding that part of the coast prevented the Germans from bringing up reinforcements from the Crimea; it was no light task, as the Germans had seventeen divisions in the Caucasus. The first landings took place on 26 December, when the temperature of the air was below zero, the sea stormy, and part of the coast was ice-bound. "The passage and landing were effected during a storm of five degrees. Some of the means of disembarkation were cast ashore, men were washed off and carried away by the waves, and the ships were torn from their anchors." But the main forces were carried through the Strait of Kerch, principally near the point of Kamysh-Burun, and various diversionary landings were made; the vessels managed to bring in tanks and heavy artillery, but the bridgehead held by the Marines was less than a square mile, and was under concentrated fire. The men however held their position till Russian reinforcements were landed north of the peninsula.

THE CASPIAN SEA

The Caspian Sea was given a new strategic value when plans to link it with the Black Sea by a canal system were first made. Peculiar problems arose in work over the canal, owing to the low level of the Caspian, but now destroyer flotillas in that sea are linked with those on the Black Sea. The fulfilment of these plans by the construction of the Don-Volga Canal will give an importance to the Caspian Sea Flotilla which it has not held in the past.

The port of Krasnovodsk on the Caspian Sea has become of greater value since subterranean water was found on the Krasnovodsk Peninsula. Formerly this port—the only one of

---

[1] "The Strategy of Anzio: Pinning Down an Army"; *Serial Maps*. (Serial Map Service, Letchworth); Vol. V, No. 7, p. 68.

[2] Captain Krylov: "Landing Operations": *The Navy*, pp. 294, 295.

any size on the east Caspian shore—was almost entirely devoid of fresh water, which had to be brought from Baku across the Caspian, a voyage of nearly two hundred miles. The provision of new shipyards at Krasnovodsk was the work of the First and Second Five-Year Plans. Another Caspian port enlarged under these plans was Makhach-Kala, completely modernised for the reception of oil supplies. The sea routes crossing the Caspian from Astrakhan and from Baku, with tankers and grain ships, are an essential part of the transport system for supplies to and from Central Asia.

The State Caspian Boat Company has linked Baku with the Volga, and Trans-Caucasia with the Central Asian Republics, and the construction of the deep channel linking Karabugaz Bay with the Caspian Sea has made it possible for cargoes destined for Turkmenistan to be shipped direct to Karabugaz. At the north-western extremity of the Caspian Sea is Astrakhan, the principal centre of shipbuilding for the Republic of Kazakhstan in Asiatic Russia. On the left bank of the Volga, and fifty feet below sea level, Astrakhan is frozen sometimes for four months in the year, but in its ice-free period it receives oil from Baku, cotton from Turkestan, and rugs and wool from Persia. Its chief exports are grain and salt.

The shores of the Caspian Sea are valuable economically as well as strategically. Makhach-Kala, on the western coast, is the port for the great oilfields of Grozni; Karabugaz, on the eastern gulf of the Caspian, yields the world's largest supply of sodium sulphate (Glauber salts.) And the Caspian is the richest inland sea in the world in fish; in particular the fishing grounds at the mouths of the Volga, Ural, Terek, and Kara yield prodigious supplies. For the protection of these deltas, river gunboats of the *Krasny Azerbaijan* type were originally built. The vessel which gave its name to this class was constructed at Leningrad in 1909, but has been reconditioned. Much later river gunboats are *Choriok, Kunitza, Laska, Vidra,* built 1936-37, with a speed of 12 knots.[1] Destroyers of the Caspian Sea Flotilla include *Altvater, Bakinski, Rabotchi, Markin,* each with a speed of 20 knots.

STALINGRAD

Stalingrad is, after Astrakhan, the chief port of the Lower Volga, and in defence of "the City of Steel" the Volga Flotilla played an indispensable part. On 3 August, 1942, began the siege that was to last till 3 February, 1943. The army of

[1] Particulars from *Jane's Fighting Ships, 1944-45;* p. 394.

von Bock was confidently awaiting its triumphal entry into the bastion of Bolshevism. But Stalingrad stood, even under the staggering weight of steel hurled against it till after the dawn of the new year, 1943. The world knows the story of the battle clash of the German Sixth Army and the Sixty-Second Army of General Chuikov, of the storming by the Russians of the Kurgan heights, the keypoint of the enemy. From those ancient towers of the Tartars, where the Russian hero Dmitry Donskoy routed the Tartars in 1380, the Russians of 1943 looked down on their port of the Lower Volga and saw the shining river flowing past the city whose ruins stretched for ten miles along the waterside. On 19 November the battle tide had turned, and the surrounded Russians became the surrounders; on 31 January von Paulus and his fellow generals surrendered to Stalingrad.

<h3 style="text-align:center">THE FAR EASTERN FLEET</h3>

Speaking in March 1939 at the Eighteenth Conference of the Communist Party of the U.S.S.R., Admiral Kuznetsov, Commissar for the Red Navy, declared: "We now have excellent coast defences, and whereas formerly we had practically no fleet at all in the Far East, during the last five to six years we have succeeded in organising a fleet there fully capable of defending our Far Eastern coasts."[1] That fleet, he added, now had "a large number of warships, in addition to numerous small boats such as motor torpedo boats, etc., as well as a strong submarine fleet. All those vessels were constructed in Soviet yards and equipped with arms of Soviet manufacture. In addition, the Pacific Fleet also has attached to it a strong air fleet".

Four months later, on Red Navy Day, 24 July, the Admiral gave an address of an even more minatory nature. "We have in the Pacific," he said, "more than a hundred fighting vessels, and in view of the turbulent character of our Far Eastern neighbour, this fleet has to be on the alert and ready to defend the Fatherland at any moment. In order," he continued, "to avoid any misapprehensions, I have to declare the U.S.S.R. possesses a larger number of submarines than any other country in the world. I can say more—we have a larger number of submarines than Germany and Japan combined." That the Admiral's words should not be regarded by Japan as mere bluff, reviews of their flotillas were held by the Russians at

[1] According to *The Statesman's Year Book*, *1944*, there were at Vladivostock sixty submarines, thirty being ocean-going, and there were thirty fast m.t.b.s.

Khabarovsk on the River Amur. For economic no less than strategic reasons the Amur Valley has formidable defences. Writing in 1937, the Japanese naval authority, Lieut.-Commander Tota Ishimaru, said: "Russia . . . has more than 1,200 up-to-date forts along the River Amur to the west of Pogranichnaya, Tung-Ning, and Hei-Ho, west of Vladivostock; and she has manned these forts and stations with 240,000 men and 900 aeroplanes."[1]

Though Russia's participation in the war against Japan in 1945 was of only six days' duration, certain operations were performed by units of her Far Eastern Fleet. Mention has already been made of the work of the Amur River Flotilla; among the best-known of its gunboats are *Krasnoye Znamya*, *Rabotchi* and *Proletari*, whose average speed is 11 knots. Older vessels are *Lenin*, *Krasny-Vostok*, *Chicherin*, and *Sverdlov*, whose speed is slightly less than that of the river gunboats of the Caspian Sea. The Northern Pacific Flotilla was engaged too. Under command of Vice-Admiral Andreyev, these warships were responsible for the landing of troops of the Second Far Eastern Command on the southern half of Sakhalin Island and on the islands of Shumshu and Paramushiro in the Kurile group. And it was ships and units of the Pacific Fleet, under Admiral Yumashev, which occupied in Northern Korea the ports of Rashin, Seishin, and Gensan. Port Arthur and Dairen, however, were captured as the result of airborne and not seaborne landings.

NAVAL AIR ARM

"Naval aviation has been supplemented by new planes of modern design." This statement formed part of the Report to the Central Committee of the U.S.S.R., January 1936,[2] and events since that time would appear to have substantiated this part of the report. Up to the summer of 1945 the most recent of all Russia's vessels, except her new destroyers, were those of her Naval Air Arm, chiefly to be found on the Black Sea. "The air arm of the Black Sea Fleet has prevented other German attempts to land from the sea, by successfully raiding invasion concentrations in the Crimea," said Admiral Oktiabrski, commanding the Russian forces responsible for the landing operations on the Kerch Peninsula. Naval airmen in this

[1] *The Next World War*, translated from the Japanese by B. Matsukawa. (Hurst & Blackett, 1937); p. 283.

[2] Quoted by Capt. Sergei N. Kournakoff in *Russia's Fighting Forces*. (International Publishers, New York, 1942.)

theatre of war operated far inland as well as over sea, attacking the naphtha region of Ploesti.

One of the principal aircraft carriers in the Black Sea was the *Stalin*, an ex-cruiser (1914) formerly known as the *Krasnaya Bessarabia* and later as *Admiral Kornilov*. The *Stalin* was a vessel of 9,000 tons, and was said to have been constructed to carry twenty-two aircraft; a larger carrier, the *Voroshilov*, completed in 1940, was built to carry many more aircraft than the *Stalin*.

In the Baltic the Fleet Air Arm took part in one of the principal naval actions in that sea, when towards the end of 1942 the Russians defeated the German attempt to seize Kronstadt. In that engagement naval planes protected the warships and sank two large transport vessels. The work of the Naval Air Arm in the Baltic was one of the decisive factors in the destruction of the German forces withdrawing from Esthonia in October 1944. Among the principal aircraft carriers in this sea is the *Krasnoye Znamya*, 12,000 tons, which is generally believed to have twenty-two aircraft, though some authorities place the number higher. It has a speed of 30 knots and carries twelve 4-inch guns. From the Baltic, naval airmen bombed Koenigsberg early in the Russo-German war, and in July 1942, Fleet airmen again raided that base, also the ports of Stettin, Danzig, Memel, and they attacked German aerodromes in northern Norway and Finland, in this way helping to keep open the sea lanes of the convoy route from Britain.

Airmen of the Northern Fleet were not behind the others in achievements. The name of Boris Safonov may grow legendary in the years to come. For this man, who brought down twenty-six enemy planes in twelve months, was twice a Hero of the Soviet Union, thrice decorated with the Order of the Red Banner, a holder of the Order of Lenin, and of the British-awarded Distinguished Flying Cross. As was the case with several crews of Russian ships, and with various detachments of Marines, a number of Fleet Air Arm regiments were honoured with the title of "Guards". These "Sea Guards" were some of the most recently formed units of the Fleet Air Arm, but their work earned them high reputation.

COMMANDERS OF THE FLEETS

"Our task is to raise still higher the defence of the land frontiers and sea coasts of the Soviet Union," declared M. Molotov. "We trust that our sailors will fulfil this task with honour, and the People's Commissariat of the Navy will work persistently and indefatigably for the creation of a strong Soviet Navy."[1]

The growing tasks of the Red Army in the second world war increased the work of the Commissariat of Defence, so that a separate Commissariat of the Navy had become necessary. Hitherto the navy had been part of the single command, and all the armed forces had been under the Commissar for Defence, Marshal Voroshilov. The command of the fleets had been lodged in the Military Councils, which included the Commanders and the ships' Political Commissars. But on 12 August, 1940, a decree cancelled the order which had been in force for some years, that "Political Commissars in ships must personally participate in elaborating all orders given by the naval officers". The post of Political Commissar in the Red Navy was abolished. It was reported that the work of such officials was considered to have been accomplished, and it was stated that the cancellation decree was issued in order to "strengthen the authority of commanding officers" and to unify leadership. Deputy commanding officers were to be attached to warships to carry on the political education of the seamen.

The first decree of the Council of Peoples' Commissars to be signed by Marshal Stalin in his capacity as Premier (in which office he succeeded M. Molotov in May 1941) was the appointment of two Vice-Admirals and nine Rear-Admirals, which brought the total number of these ranks in the first case to ten, in the second to fifty-four. The appointment of Admiral Kuznetsov as Commissar for the Navy was followed by an expansionist policy among the fleets. In July 1939, Kuznetsov declared that the Northern Fleet was increasing even more rapidly than the Pacific one; that in the Baltic more than fifty warships had taken part in recent manœuvres, though these did not comprise the total number of ships in that fleet. He stated also that some of the old warships in the Black Sea could now be used as training-ships, owing to the completion of a number of modern vessels. The Black Sea was destined to receive a foreign capital ship ten years later, for the battleship *Giulio Cesare*, which the Russians gained as part of their post-bellum share of the Italian Navy, was sent to Odessa.

SEAMEN OF THE SOVIET UNION

When a man joins the Russian Navy, he takes this oath:
I, a citizen of the U.S.S.R., entering the ranks of the Workers' and

[1] *Moscow News*, 5.2.1938. Abridged from *Pravda*.

Peasants' Red Navy, do take the oath and solemnly swear to be an honourable, brave, disciplined and watchful fighter, to keep strictly all naval and state secrets, to fulfil obediently all naval regulations and the orders of commanders, commissars, and chiefs.

I swear to apply myself conscientiously to acquiring knowledge of naval affairs, to guard unsleepingly the naval and national possessions, to remain devoted to my last breath to my people, to my Soviet Father-land, and to the Workers' and Peasants' Government.

I shall ever be ready at the command of the Workers' and Peasants' Government to go forward for the defence of my Fatherland—the U.S.S.R., and as a fighter of the Workers' and Peasants' Red Navy, I swear to defend her with courage, with skill, with dignity and with honour, sparing neither my blood nor my life to achieve victory over the enemy.

If of malice I betray this my solemn oath, then let me be visited with the strict punishment of Soviet law, general hatred, and the contempt of all working people.

Marshal Stalin, as head of the Russian Defence Forces, had a high opinion of the Red Navy men. Visiting a Soviet warship, on being asked to give his impressions in the Distinguished Visitors' Book, he wrote: "Remarkable people; bold and cultured comrades, ready to perform anything in our common cause. It is a pleasure to deal with such comrades; it is a pleasure to fight the enemy side by side with such fighters." It was on his personal orders given in May 1939 that the period of naval service was raised from four to five years. That for the Naval Air Arm however was four years.

In the summer of 1943 the ranks of officers serving in the Russian Navy became more sharply defined. Hitherto personnel holding the equivalent of officer rank had been known as members of the "Commanding Staff", which consisted of junior, middle, and senior categories. But the status of the officer class became more clearly determined two years after the outbreak of war, as the following Order will show:

"By a decree of the Presidium of the Supreme Soviet, the personnel of the Red Navy will henceforth be differentiated into officers, petty officers, and rank and file. Officers will be divided into the following groups: (a) Junior officers, including the ranks of Junior Lieutenant, Lieutenant, Senior Lieutenant, and Captain-Lieutenant. (b) Senior officers, including the ranks of Captain of the Third Rank, Captain of the Second Rank, and Captain of the First Rank. (c) Officers, including the ranks of Rear-Admiral, Vice-Admiral, and Admiral of the Fleet."

Early in March 1944, Marshal Stalin created two new

Russian naval Orders, the Order of Ushakov, and the Order of Nakhimov, both of them named after Russian admirals.[1]

The achievements of the men of the Red Fleets have made their uniform—the black caps with the flying ribbons, and the jersey with the blue and white stripe—an emblem of pride to citizens of the U.S.S.R. "In our country," said *Pravda*,[2] "the name of the Soviet sailor has become a symbol of supreme bravery, unshakable staunchness and boundless loyalty to military duty."

THE MARINES

"The Black Devils"—the title which the Marines, by their daring, earned from the Germans—have inherited a strong fighting tradition from the days of the Civil War, when they came ashore to storm the Winter Palace in the October Revolution in 1917. In the second world war they fought with a reckless valour which it would be hard to match in the history of warfare. Sevastopol and Odessa, Feodosia and Novorossisk, have seen their exploits. Unforgettable the courage of the Third Regiment of Popatov's unit of Marines, and that of the First Marine Regiment, formed of sailors of the Black Sea Fleet, who took part in the fighting during the siege of Odessa. Led by Colonel Osipov, an ex-officer of the cruiser *Rurik*, these Marines drove the Rumanians from the outlying parts of the city.

In the north these sea-soldiers helped in the defence of the Baltic islands, and of Leningrad; they also played a part in the defence of the inland port of Moscow. It was natural that the sight of those flying ribbons in the black sailor caps should have inspired the citizens of Russia's seaports with pride. The attachment of the Marines to their distinctive caps has become a tradition: it is their custom to wear them when going in to attack, and the ribbons as much as the bayonets of "the Black Devils" have become a symbol of Russian resistance.

THE GUARDS

The award of the title of "Guards" as a mark of honour in the case of certain ships' crews, was a wartime innovation and one which seemed to have been popular among Red Navy men.

[1] Ushakov was the founder of the Black Sea school of naval warfare, of which Nakhimov was one of the most famous exponents. Nakhimov was commander in the Russian naval victory at Sinope, and was the defender of Sevastopol.

[2] 1.3.1944.

Among the ships so honoured was the Black Sea cruiser *Krasny Krim*, commended for the work of her A.A. gunners. The destroyer *Gremiaschii*, for her work in escorting convoys, and the destroyer *Soobrazitelni*, were two other ships which, as mentioned in the Baltic section, flew the pendant of the Guards. The same distinction was conferred on certain armoured cutters of the Volga Flotilla, the First and Second Squadrons of which were held in special esteem by the citizens of Stalingrad for their work in ferrying troops and supplies across the Volga under fierce ordeal of battle.

MERCANTILE MARINE: UNDER THE FIVE-YEAR PLANS

Russia's merchant navy, notwithstanding its growth under the first three Five-Year Plans, had no margin for wartime losses. Since the war however, every effort is being made to build a merchant fleet commensurate with the country's needs. Under her post-war Five-Year Plans the Soviet Union is also developing her existing ports and is building new ones. "It has," says the Editor of *Ports of the World*,[1] "been impossible to obtain any reliable up-to-date information for some German, and for any Japanese or Russian ports." Up to the outbreak of the last war Russia was represented as exporting from twenty-eight ports—a small number indeed for a country comprising over nine million square miles, compared with the 89,041 square miles of the United Kingdom, whose ports of export were more numerous than Russia's. (Anyone who wishes to ascertain the number of those British ports must have a lot of time at his disposal before he can count them up in *Ports of the World*.) But when so much of Russia's coastline is Arctic, frozen earth makes drainage and pipe-laying a problem, and the difficulties of building harbours in that terrain are apparent.

When the State Soviet Mercantile Marine was founded, it was formed of five distinct shipping agencies: Northern, Baltic, Black Sea, Azov, and Caspian. During 1923 the Caspian shipping agency was absorbed by the oil industry, since 90 per cent. of its work was concerned with oil transport and it had no connection with other lines.[2]

On 5 January, 1918, the Bolshevik Government had decreed the nationalisation of the shipping of all big concerns, but to a

[1] Edited by Sir Archibald Hurd, A.I.N.A. (The Shipping World, Ltd., London, 1947); 2nd edtn.

[2] "Soviet Mercantile Marine": *Bank for Russian Trade Review*, Vol. II, No. 6, p. 18.

certain number of small traders and co-operatives, private ownership of trading vessels was permitted. In 1935 Russia was the only country in the world which both owned and operated its entire merchant fleet.[1]

For many years after the Revolution the U.S.S.R. had exported little but agricultural, dairy, and timber products, but the expansion of industry began to reveal itself with the export figures during the First Five-Year Plan period. In 1929 for example, machinery was exported to the value of 1,849,000 roubles; in 1935 to the value of 6,826,000 roubles.[2] Following the second world war, Russia's need for imports of certain categories is pressing, but as time goes on the need of shipping for such will decrease—if past results are any pointer to future ones—for whereas in 1913 over 43 per cent. of machinery used in Russia came from abroad, in 1937 less than 1 per cent. was imported. Nearly one-fifth of the coal consumed in Russia was foreign coal in 1913, but in 1938 the U.S.S.R. was exporting coal. Over 46 per cent. of cotton was sent abroad by the U.S.S.R. that year. According to Mikhailov[3] the freight turnover of the ports of the Soviet Union was increased by 92 per cent. under the First Five-Year Plan. Under the Second and Third Five-Year Plans both trade expansion and ship-building development were bringing Russia along the road to self-sufficiency, but the war placed an enormous strain on the industrial economy of the Soviet Union. The work of re-building her depleted, and in some cases shattered, industries has called for an increase of such imports as machine tools from abroad. But it is also for the increasing *exports* of timber, coal, cotton, metals, canned fish, and hides that Russia will need an enlarged mercantile marine. It may be long before her own needs permit her to export oil in any quantity, but additions will have to be made to her tanker fleets for her increasing use of petroleum products a home. Baku is the greatest oil-bearing region, so it is on the Caspian Sea that the chief increase will be made to the oil fleet.

The increase already achieved in the U.S.S.R.'s merchant navy was not reached without severe struggles and many set-backs: it would be a great mistake to think that all went

[1] See also *International Sea Transport:* Brig.-Gen. Sir Osborne Mance, K.B.E., C.B., C.M.G., D.S.O., assisted by J. E. Wheeler. (Issued under the auspices of the Royal Institute of International Affairs, Oxford University Press, 1945); p. 131. Reproduced by permission of the O.U.P.
[2] M. Zhirmunski, *Soviet Export.* (Mezhdunarodnaya Kniga, 1936.)
[3] *Soviet Geography*; p. 192. By permission of Messrs. Methuen.

according to Plan. Scandals and disorder prevailed in the merchant fleets not long before the second world war. Purges followed, affecting some members of the Transport Commissariat. In April 1938 M. Yezhov became head of the Soviet merchant fleets—ocean-going as well as inland.

If we look at the figures for the Russian mercantile marine before the outbreak of the last war, we find that the year 1938-39 is the one period for which a clear summary of the position can be obtained. A comprehensive survey is to be found in the *Register of Shipping of the U.S.S.R., 1938-1939,* which was issued from the head office of the Soviet Shipping Bureau in Leningrad. "This Register," said *Shipbuilding and Shipping Record,*[1] "has been carefully compiled. No criticism can be levelled at the amount of information which is published. The compilers have gone to great pains to see that every possible detail has been included. In this respect the Register is therefore somewhat superior to other shipping registers."

Separate columns were given for hull, main engines, main boilers, electrical and refrigerating machinery, holds, winches and derricks, and for dimensions, draught, cargo and passenger capacity. The text is in English and Russian. The Register showed that, of the total number of six hundred and sixty-four vessels of all types and classes, the great majority were small cargo ships— three hundred and three were of 1,000-5,000 tons, and fifty-six of these were motor-ships; and there were "no large ocean-going ships as we understand the term in this country". It was the opinion of the writer of the analysis of the Russian Register (published in *Shipbuilding and Shipping Record*) that out of the six hundred and sixty-four vessels on the Register, only half could be of use as ocean-going shipping. Nearly one-third of these vessels were built in Britain, before the Russian Revolution, and the oldest of these sea-going ships was nearly thirty years old. "Above 5,000 tons, the number of ships on the Register shows a rapid and surprising decline. Between 5,000 and 8,000 tons there are only thirty-three vessels, of which twenty are motor ships. Six of the thirty-three were built in British yards. There are no vessels over 8,000 tons, except one— a converted British Cable ship."

Nevertheless under the Five-Year Plans much attention has been paid to the building of new types of vessels. All motor-ships launched since the commencement of the First Five-Year Plan were equipped with new type diesel engines. The majority

[1] 12.10.1939 [Transport (1910), Ltd.]; p. 405.

of the most recent vessels owned by the U.S.S.R. have been
built in Russia, of which the Baltic Shipbuilding and Engineering
Works have constructed most; next come the Leningrad yards,
which have specialised in diesel engines, then come the Sormovo
Works at Gorki. The first passenger steamer to operate on
Russia's Trans-Atlantic service, opened between Leningrad and
New York in 1945, was the *Viacheslav Molotov*, flagship of the
Baltic Merchant Fleet. She was the first Russian passenger ship
to dock in Britain after the war. Built in the Netherlands, she
is one of the steamers engaged on the regular service between
the Soviet Union and Britain.

In the Appendix to *Lloyd's Register Book, 1947-48*, Statistical
Tables for 1947,[1] we find the following data: total number of
steamers of 100 tons and upwards belonging to the U.S.S.R.,
778, total gross tonnage, 1,742,162; motor-ships, 174, total
gross tonnage, 414,825 (including sailing vessels and barges,
grand total 964, tonnage 2,164,467); steam and motor trawlers
and other fishing vessels, 126, tonnage 62,738. (It is remarkable
that Great Britain and Northern Ireland, with coastlines so
much shorter than Russia's, and devoid of inland seas, have
1,124 vessels listed in this class, with a total gross tonnage of
297,236.)

Figures for oil tankers of 1,000 tons and upwards are given
for the U.S.S.R. as follows: steamers, 14, total gross tonnage,
94,031; motor-ships, 23, total gross tonnage, 99,435. (These
figures may be compared again with those for the United
Kingdom, in which the total number of oil tankers is 434. It is
even more striking to note that, while the U.S.S.R. possesses,
as we have seen, a total of 37 oil tankers—of 1,000 tons and upwards—Sweden has only 2 less. Norway's total is 194, and that
for America 864.) It must be borne in mind that "owing to the
difficulty experienced in obtaining precise information in the
case of Soviet Russia the figures given for that country may
not be comprehensive."

Although, as we have said, Russia's ports have been and to
a great extent still are, badly placed as regards the main trade
routes of the world, the fact that her coasts are adjacent to her
fast-developing new industrial regions, offsets to some extent
the former disadvantage. For her trade expansion a strong
mercantile marine has become a necessity. Despite its increase
under the Five-Year Plans, the Russian merchant navy was
still far from equal to the needs of the U.S.S.R. during the

[1] Table I, Lloyd's Register of Shipping.

second world war. It was British, not Soviet ships, which brought back to Murmansk in August 1941, the 2,000 Russian miners who had been working at the Barentsburg mines on Spitzbergen. During the last phase of the war in Europe, complaints were made that numbers of Soviet citizens released by British and American forces from German camps on the Continent, were being detained in England. The explanation probably lay in the fact that Russia lacked the ships to bring her citizens home. On 31 October the *Empress of Australia* and the *Scythia* sailed from Liverpool, carrying the first contingent of Russian ex-prisoners of war back to the Soviet Union. Between October 1944, and 4 May, 1945, 42,421 Soviet citizens had been repatriated from Britain and the Mediterranean, and, except for one U.S. vessel, all the shipping which took these people home had been British. It was only British vessels too which transported to Russia 14,565 Soviet citizens liberated on the Continent by U.S. troops. Again, the British subjects who had been liberated by Russian forces in Europe had been brought home from Odessa not in Soviet but in British ships. And it was in a British convoy which left the Kola Inlet on 28 October, 1944, that about 5,000 Russian naval officers and men sailed for a United Kingdom port to take over British warships transferred to the Soviet navy.[1]

But, if the official figures[2] are correct, eighty-nine of Russia's shipbuilding yards had been destroyed in the last war. Hence the Soviet Union pressed for shipbuilding facilities in her claims for advance reparations from Germany. It was arranged by the Allied Control Council that Russia and Poland should have the Deschameg-Weser shipyards at Bremen.

Though the Tsarist Government had spent annually about one-and-a-quarter million roubles on chartering foreign vessels for Russia's exports and imports, there existed in those times no official institution of shipping brokers.[3] But the period following 1921 saw the creation of bureaux for co-ordinating the export work of specialised trade bodies; the central organisation which was set up to deal with the transport of outward cargoes and with forwarding agencies was known as *Sovfrakht*, and today it is one of the most important Corpora-

[1] Department of Naval Information, the Admiralty.
[2] Extraordinary State Commission for Ascertaining and Investigating Crimes of the German Fascist Invaders, issued September 1945.
[3] *Foreign Trade in the U.S.S.R.:* J. D. Yanson. (Gollancz, 1934. New Soviet Library, No. 8); p. 160.

tions in the U.S.S.R. Part of its function is to carry out, on a State monopoly basis, operations connected with chartering foreign tonnage both in the U.S.S.R. and abroad. *Sovfrakht* is a Corporation under the Commissariat of Foreign Trade, upon whose annual plans the work of the Export Corporations is based.[1]

A "Committee of Standards" for exports forms part of the People's Commissariat of Foreign Trade, designed to ensure satisfactory quality of exports. In view of the one-time British embargo on trade with Russia, it is interesting to note that in 1938 Soviet exports to the United Kingdom were higher than to any other country, the value being 375,124,000 roubles. No less than 40 per cent. of Russia's timber exports were taken by Britain. The second highest customer was Belgium, to whom Russia sent goods to the value of 116,803,000 roubles. But from the last country Russia imported goods totalling 405,858,000 roubles in value; from Britain the figure was only 240,309,000 roubles.[2]

The Soviet Maritime Code is based on the International Conventions on Salvage and Collisions at Sea, which Conventions it adopted in March 1926. In February 1931, the Government approved of a Marine Arbitration Committee to be set up in Moscow. "Hitherto, owing to the absence of any Marine Court of Arbitration in the U.S.S.R., salvage disputes have had to be referred to foreign arbitration, as for instance, to Lloyd's, even if both ships, the salvaging and the salvaged, had been sailing under the Soviet flag."[3] Henceforth all disputes relating to the salvaging of foreign vessels in Russian waters could be adjudicated in the U.S.S.R. The form of contract of the commission was identical with Lloyd's form of salvage agreement, except that the former provided that arbitration should be in Moscow instead of in London.[4] The awards of the Maritime Arbitration Commission might, "on application of the interested party or on the intervention of the Public Prosecutor of the Supreme Court of the U.S.S.R., be set aside by the Supreme Court of the U.S.S.R. and referred back to the Maritime Arbitration Commission for reconsideration".[5]

[1] See also M. Zhirmunski: *Soviet Export*. (Mezhdunarodnaya Kniga, 1936.)
[2] See Table 60, *The U.S.S.R.: An Economic and Social Survey*, p. 207. By permission of Messrs. Methuen.
[3] *Monthly Review*, Vol. IV, No. 2, p. 10.
[4] *Ibid*, Vol. IX, No. 10, p. 554.
[5] *Ibid*, Vol. IX, No. 5, p. 283.

Marine insurance of Soviet exports and imports is controlled by *Gosstrakh* (State Insurance Department), and by the Black Sea and Baltic Insurance Company. Different routes require in many cases different types of vessels, and provision for these special requirements is ensured by *Gosstrakh*. This State company has thus to deal with passage through the Dardanelles, where there have been occasional strandings, causing trouble for the Black Sea ships. "The cost of insuring a cargo of grain shipped in the summer from the Black Sea to the Continent is 50 per cent. more than for insuring a similar cargo from the River Plate. Whilst for a winter voyage from the Black Sea the insurance costs about two-and-a-half times that from the Plate."[1]

The improvement in navigational aids along Russia's Arctic coasts—radio and meteorological stations—and the better work of her icebreakers, is reflected in the insurance rates for Arctic shipping. In 1924 the rates for a voyage to Murmansk were considerably higher than those to ports in northern Norway. But by 1929 the risk rates were not much higher.[2]

In Chapter XVI in this book, details have been given of the inland water transport system. In this section on the Mercantile Marine it will suffice therefore, to make only the briefest general remarks. In October 1925, the Soviet Government, which had previously nationalised river shipping, decided to allow private ownership of commercial craft for internal water transport without special permission. The crew was limited to twelve per boat: there was no restriction as to the number of boats which could be owned privately, but the number was of necessity small, since the total crew under individual ownership was limited to fifty. An exception to this, however, was made in the case of Volga boats, which were permitted to have a crew of sixteen per boat and a total crew of seventy.

The administration of all shipping on inland waterways is undertaken, within defined limits, by the All-Union River Transport Companies. This was fixed by decree of 26 January, 1930, when the Central Executive Committee and Council of People's Commissars, U.S.S.R., declared: "That to the All-Union River Transport Companies be transferred all the river shipping which is within the authority of the People's

[1] *Monthly Review.* (Issued by the Moscow Narodny Bank, Ltd.); Vol. V, Nos. 8, 9; pp. 6, 7.

[2] For more details regarding freight insurance, see "Marine Insurance in connection with Soviet Trade": *Monthly Review*; Vol. V, Nos. 8, 9; pp. 6,7.

Commissariat for transport. And all the property which was within the administrative authority of the internal waterways."[1]

On 15 April, 1943, by Decree of the Presidium of the Supreme Soviet, martial law was extended to the People's Commissariat of Marine Shipping, to the Central Administration of the Northern Sea Route, and also to the People's Commissariat of River Shipping.

[1] *U.S.S.R. Handbook*, p. 351.

ANNEX

For the privilege of making the following extracts and references from *Fuehrer Conferences on Naval Affairs, 1939-1945*, my sincere thanks are expressed to The Controller, His Majesty's Stationery Office; also to Messrs. William Clowes and Son, Ltd., for their kindness in permitting me to copy this material from *Brassey's Naval Annual, 1948.*—M.M.

The Preface to the 1948 edition of *Brassey's Naval Annual* (edited by Rear-Admiral H. G. Thursfield) states that:

"The bulk of this year's issue is occupied by a reprint of a number of documents, issued by the Admiralty at various dates during 1947, which have attracted great interest but which have hitherto not been available *in extenso* to the general public. These documents have been selected, as being of outstanding interest, from the great mass of German naval archives which fell into Allied hands in the closing stages of the war. They have been summarised, perforce very briefly, in the press—starved of newsprint—as they appeared; but this is the first occasion, as far as is known, that they have been made available in full to the public. . . . They afford a comprehensive picture of the war at sea, as viewed on the highest German plane from beginning to end; and they illustrate once again in the most convincing manner, the disasters that have ever overtaken the would-be world dictator who fails to understand the significance and potency of sea power.—H. G. T."

FUEHRER CONFERENCES ON NAVAL AFFAIRS

INTRODUCTION

"In the later stages of the Allied advance into Germany in 1945, a team of British and American Intelligence Officers kept a special look-out for German official records and archives, removed from Berlin for safety when the capital became the obvious objective of the Allied chief effort. Most of those of the German Naval Headquarters were found, and captured intact, by this team at Tambach in Bavaria. According to the evidence of Grand Admiral Doenitz at his trial at Nuremberg, he, conscious that the German Navy had nothing to hide or to be ashamed of, in the record of its part in the war, had given orders that they were to be preserved. There is no means of checking that statement, but even if those orders were given, it is quite probable that they would not have availed to preserve the archives had an inveterate Nazi amongst those who had charge of them considered that he would be carrying out the Fuehrer's wishes in destroying them. Their preservation is due chiefly to the competence and promptitude of the Allied Intelligence officers, who found and seized them before anyone could make away with them.

"Amongst the mass of records thus captured, one series stands out as of particular interest and importance, and has been translated and issued by the Admiralty—that of the minutes of conferences which the C.-in-C. of the Navy, or his deputy, had with Hitler. It was Hitler's practice to hold regular Conferences with his various commanders and Ministers, to hear reports of the military situation, and to issue rulings, decisions, or orders on every sort of subject. The C.-in-C. of the Navy—Raeder up to January 1943, and Doenitz from then on—was not always summoned to these Conferences, but only to those at which naval affairs were discussed. He was usually to be found at the Naval Headquarters in Berlin—except when visiting naval bases or establishments—while the Conferences were held at one of the places where Hitler had his own Headquarters. It was Raeder's custom, also followed by Doenitz when he succeeded, to take rough notes at the Conferences of what took place, and during his journey back to Berlin to draw up from them a record in minute form to be entered in the archives. These are the minutes which have been translated and issued by the Admiralty.

"It must be realised that these minutes, though they form what is probably the most authentic epitome of the war at sea as seen on the highest German official plane, have nothing in common with the private diary of an individual. They are not necessarily either complete, entirely accurate, or wholly ingenuous; nor do they necessarily record what their compiler actually saw and heard of the events and discussions with which they deal. Under Nazi rule, any subordinate might be a political informer on his superiors, if he considered them to be insufficiently thorough-going in their Nazism. These records, therefore, are what the C.-in-C. of the Navy was willing to have entered in official archives rather than what he might have written in a private diary intended for no other eye than his own. That limitation must be borne in mind in drawing any historical conclusions from a study of them.

"In issuing the translated minutes, the Admiralty remarked that the originals were verbose and often filled with minor technical details which, in order not to obscure the main picture, have been either summarised or omitted altogether. On the other hand, the Admiralty added a running commentary —printed in small type in the pages which follow—describing the general situation at the time, and the sequence of main events of the war, so that the background of each conference is presented to the reader. The information on which this commentary is based was drawn from Admiralty records as well as German sources, so that it is sometimes more complete than that which was available to the Germans at the time. This background commentary will be found most useful to the general reader in enabling him to grasp the relevance—or irrelevance—of what took place at the Conferences.

"The matter contained in the records was released simultaneously in Great Britain and the United States—the actual translation was also a piece of team-work—but the "background commentary" was a British contribution only. The American release consisted of the translated minutes themselves only, unabridged, with all their technical detail. The British version was issued, in typescript form, only to the Press and to certain University libraries in seven instalments, each covering one year of the war; these were issued, at intervals of some three weeks, not in chronological order but in the order in which they happened to be completed. It was thus only when the last of the instalments—that for 1941—was issued that it became possible to view them as a whole; and in the meanwhile, as a result of the severe shortage of newsprint, the Press were able to print only the briefest summaries of them. This is the first time, as far as is known, that the whole of the documents issued by the Admiralty have been printed.

"They are here reproduced as issued, except that here and there a few minor misprints, or errors in spelling, translation, or construction, have been corrected, or English usage substituted for American.—H. G. T."

Extracts from FUEHRER CONFERENCES ON NAVAL AFFAIRS, 1939-1945.

Note: The page numbers in all the following references in brackets under the Chapter titles, apply to text in *The Maritime History of Russia, 848-1948.*

For CHAPTER VII. The Soviet Far East.

(Page 200. Refer the Russo-Japanese Pact, 1941.)

The Report of the C.-in-C., Navy, to the Fuehrer, on April 20, 1941 (relative to the Russo-Japanese Neutrality Pact): It is stated that the Fuehrer values this Pact "because Japan is now restrained from taking action against Vladivostock and should be induced to attack Singapore instead". (*Brassey's Naval Annual, 1948*, p. 193.)

For CHAPTER XII. Atlantic Aims.

(Pages 283, 286. Refer the cession of Petsamo by the Finns to the Russians in 1940.)

(a) In the *Report of the C.-in-C., Navy, to the Fuehrer, on December 30, 1939*, it is stated that in high military circles in Norway, one section is of opinion that Russia will occupy Tromsoe, and that the division of Norway has also been agreed on by Russia and Germany. (*Brassey's Naval Annual, 1948*, p. 70.)

(b) *The C.-in-C., Navy, in his Report to the Fuehrer on March 9, 1940*, stresses that above all, Britain must not be allowed to occupy Norway; that Germany must forestall this by occupying Norway herself. The C.-in-C. recommends that after the Germans have invaded Norway, the Russians should be informed that Tromsoe has not been occupied. "This could be interpreted by the Russians as constituting some considerations for their interests. It is better to have the Russians in Tromsoe than the British". Admiral Raeder adds however, that "The Fuehrer does not wish to have the Russians so near, and is of

the opinion that Tromsoe will also have to be occupied by us".
(*Brassey's Naval Annual, 1948*, p. 86.)

(c) *Minutes of the Conference at Fuehrer Headquarters, August, 11
1943*. Hitler gives indications of growing differences between
the Anglo-Saxons and the Russians. The former, he says, 'do,
not wish to see Russia in Finland, nor, under any circumstances,
to have Russia improve her sea communications with the
Atlantic in the North". (*Brassey's Naval Annual, 1948*, p. 357.)

For CHAPTER XIII. The Baltic.
(Page 292. Refer Hitler's early intention to gain control of
Baltic States.)

> Commentary by the British Admiralty.   "Raeder in a private memorandum
> to the German Naval Historian in 1944 had stated that in his opinion
> Hitler had decided as far back as 1937 to eliminate Russia at least as a
> Baltic power."   (*Brassey's Naval Annual, 1948, p. 168*.)

For CHAPTER XIII. The Baltic.
(Page 292. Refer Hitler's seizure of Memel, 1939.)

(a) *Conference of the C.-in-C., Navy, with the Fuehrer on December 10,
1944*. The C.-in-C., Navy, emphasises the importance of Memel
and says its loss would endanger the Navy's bases, training
areas, and convoy lanes. (*Brassey's Naval Annual, 1948*, p. 421.)
(Page 293. Refer harbours on the Gulf of Danzig.)

(b) *Conference of the C.-in-C., Navy, with the Fuehrer, January 21,
1945*. Admiral Doenitz again stresses the great importance of
the Gulf of Danzig, the only submarine training area. "He
emphasises that the loss of this area would paralyse submarine
warfare". (*Brassey's Naval Annual, 1948*, p. 429.)
(Page 293. Refer decision regarding Stettin at Potsdam Conference, 1945.)

(c) *Conference of the C.-in-C., Navy, with the Fuehrer, on February
3, 1945*. Admiral Doenitz states that Stettin and Swinemuende
"are of decisive importance, and from a strategic point of view
the enemy made a mistake in attacking Berlin rather than these
harbours". (*Brassey's Naval Annual, 1948*, p. 429.)

(d) *Conference of the C.-in-C., Navy, with the Fuehrer, on February
20, 1945*. The C.-in-C., Navy, points out that it is of the utmost
importance to naval warfare to hold the Stettin area. To hold
Stettin and Swinemuende means that the deep seas east of
Bornholm can be used for submarine training. The ports of the
western Baltic are shallower. (*Brassey's Naval Annual, 1948*,
p. 449.)

For CHAPTER XIII. Finland.
(Page 302. Refer report in Stockholm of Admiral Raeder's reactions to Ribbentrop's concessions to the Soviet Union on the Baltic.)

(a) *Report of the C.-in-C., Navy, to the Fuehrer, on December 12, 1939* (relative to the Russo-Finnish conflict): "The C.-in-C., Navy, recommends accommodating Russia, for example in the matter of oil supply for submarines, as Russia also offers us practical advantages, e.g. holding foreign ships for three days after the departure of the *Bremen*". (*Brassey's Naval Annual, 1948*, p. 67.)

(b) *Minutes of the Conference of the C.-in-C., Navy, at Fuehrer Headquarters, Wolfsschanze, July 9, 1944.* The C.-in-C., Navy, stresses the importance of German control of the Baltic for the importation of Swedish ore, and points to the serious consequences which would follow a Russian break-through in the Baltic. If this should occur even further south, i.e. in Lithuania or East Prussia, then the German position on the Gulf of Finland—including the Baltic islands—would be worthless. Such a break-through would make it impossible to supply the Northern Army Group and Finland by sea, because of attacks from Russian air bases in Lithuania. (*Brassey's Naval Annual, 1948*, p. 501.)

For CHAPTER XIII. Finland.
(Page 304. Refer use of anchorage at Poliarnoye permitted by Soviet Union to Germany during Russo-German Pact.)

(a) *Report of the C.-in-C., Navy, to the Fuehrer, on October 10, 1939.* Admiral Raeder reports that auxiliary cruisers detailed to operate in the Indian Ocean are being equipped—one in Murmansk: "The Russians have offered the bay east of Murmansk as a base; this will be investigated". (*Brassey's Naval Annual, 1948*, p. 46.)

(b) *Report of the C.-in-C., Navy, to the Fuehrer, on October 16, 1939:* "The C.-in-C., Navy, reports that the Russians have placed at our disposal a well-situated base west of Murmansk. A repair ship is to be stationed there". (*Brassey's Naval Annual, 1948*, p. 52.)

For CHAPTER XIII. Finland—White Sea Canal.
(Pages 303-05. Refer cession of Finnish ports to Russia.)
(Page 306. Refer use of White Sea Canal by Russian warships in World War II.)

Report of the C.-in-C., Navy, to the Fuehrer, February 4, 1941.
This describes the measures which will be taken for closing the
entrance to the Baltic Sea. Surprise attacks are to be made by
the German Air Force against Russian bases and ships in the
Baltic, Arctic Ocean, and Black Sea. The western entrance to
the Gulf of Finland is to be blocked by mine barrages laid from
Finland. Mine sweeping on a large scale must be undertaken
once the Russian Fleet is eliminated. An agreement should be
reached with Finland for obtaining the use of Finnish bases.
"The locks of the White Sea Canal must be destroyed in order
to prevent the escape of ships to the north". (*Brassey's Naval
Annual, 1948*, p. 176.)

For CHAPTER XIV. The Soviet Navy.
(Page 338. Refer claims made in Russian broadcast on Red
    Navy Day, 1944, regarding German ships sunk by Russian
    Baltic Fleet.)
    (a) *Report of the C.-in-C., Navy, to the Fuehrer at Wolfsschanze,
November 13, 1941* (relative to the war in the Baltic): "Up to ten
Russian submarines are still at sea, but have achieved no
successes so far, unless it was a submarine torpedo which hit
U144. . . . The cruiser *Marty* and some destroyers are evidently
still fully capable of operating, but the report concerning
battleships is that 'they are still heard in radio traffic but are
no longer able to operate' ". (*Brassey's Naval Annual, 1948*,
p. 236.)
    (b) *Conference of the C.-in-C., Navy, with the Fuehrer, at Wehr-
wolf, August 26, 1942:* "The particular type of warfare in the Gulf
of Finland permits only the use of very small vessels. The most
effective weapon for this region has proved to be the mines.
Actions of the Russian Fleet, which were expected on a larger
scale, did not materialise due to mines. Only two or three
submarines broke through into the Baltic, compared to at least
twenty which were destroyed in trying to reach it. The conquest
of Leningrad would terminate naval warfare in that region".
(*Brassey's Naval Annual, 1948*, p. 289.)
    (c) *Conference of the C.-in-C., Navy, with the Fuehrer, on February
17, 1945.* The admiral on special duty states: "With the exception of a few successful operations by Russian submarines the
danger to our convoys from Russian naval forces is less serious"
than the danger the Russians could inflict by air attack on
German convoys in the Baltic. (*Brassey's Naval Annual, 1948*,
p. 447.)

For SUPPLEMENTARY SECTION. Strength of the Red Navy.

(Pages 376-79. Refer non-Russian opinions of the Soviet Navy before, and during early part of, World War II.)

According to *Admiral Raeder's Report of November 22, 1939*, Hitler thought that the Russian ships were in poor condition, and refused the suggestion that Russia should be asked to give submarines to Germany. And he was of the opinion that the Russians would not give them. (*Brassey's Naval Annual, 1948*, p.58.)

For SUPPLEMENTARY SECTION. The Baltic Fleet.

(Page 292. Refer the importance of the Baltic States to the plans of "Operation Barbarossa".)

Hitler in *Directive No. 21, "Operation Barbarossa"*, outlining his intended attack on the Soviet Union, says that the Russian Baltic Fleet will rapidly lose its bases, and therefore its use as a battle force will be lost too. (*Brassey's Naval Annual, 1948*, p. 159.)

(Page 382. Refer Ossian Goulding's report of drain on German escort ships, owing Russian attacks on enemy convoys sailing between Germany and Finland.)

Report of the C.-in-C., Navy, to the Fuehrer, December 22, 1942. Reporting on the situation in the Baltic, Admiral Raeder says: "Since we have so few escort vessels, and these are so heavily taxed, we must review once more the advantages to be gained from an occupation of the islands of Laansaari and Seiskar and of the Schepel-Oranienbaum strip before the spring of 1943. Only a really effective blockade of the eastern part of the Gulf of Finland, close to the enemy's key bases, could give us hope of saving fighting forces and mines. Even if Leningrad were completely destroyed by artillery fire, the submarine danger would still exist because Kronstadt remains a base. Every submarine, however, that gets through the blockade is a threat to the entire Baltic Sea and endangers our shipping which is already barely sufficient". (*Brassey's Naval Annual, 1948*, pp. 302, 303.)

(Page 382. Refer anti-submarine net spread by the Germans from Hogland Island to the Esthonian coast.)

Minutes of the Conference of the C.-in-C., Navy, with the Fuehrer at Headquarters, Wolfsschanze, July 8, 1943. Admiral Doenitz emphasises the importance of capturing the Oranienbaum basin. "However, no Russian submarine has succeeded so far in getting out of Leningrad harbour." (*Brassey's Naval Annual, 1948*, p. 384.)

(Page 384. Refer the command of the South Baltic by the German Navy, and the part played by *Admiral Scheer* in evacuation of coastal towns.)

Conference of the C.-in-C., Navy, with the Fuehrer, on February 9, 1945. The Fuehrer highly commends the achievement of the Navy in transferring the 3rd S.S. *Panzer* Corps from Libau to Stettin. (*Brassey's Naval Annual, 1948*, p. 441.)

For SUPPLEMENTARY SECTION. The Northern Convoys.
Page 396. Refer insufficiency of British aircraft carriers protecting the Northern Convoys early in 1942.)

Report by the C.-in-C., Navy, to the Fuehrer at Headquarters, Wolfsschanze, March 12, 1942. In the Arctic Ocean the German Air Force must wage relentless war against enemy carriers. "Elimination of the aircraft carriers would basically improve our chances". (*Brassey's Naval Annual, 1948*, p. 266.)

(Page 389. Refer meeting of Allied Joint Chiefs of Staffs Committee, 1942, when it was stated that the first of the three main defensive tasks was "to keep Russia effectively in the war".)

Conference of the C.-in-C., Navy, with the Fuehrer at Wehrwolf on August 26, 1942. "Supplies to the northern ports of Russia remain decisive for the whole conduct of the war waged by the Anglo-Saxons". (*Brassey's Naval Annual, 1948*, p. 289.)

For SUPPLEMENTARY SECTION. Leningrad.
(Page 406. Refer shipbuilding industry of Leningrad.)

Report of the C.-in-C., Navy, at Conference with the Fuehrer at Wehrwolf, August 26, 1942. The C.-in-C. "requests a directive that the shipyards in Leningrad be spared shelling and air attacks and not be destroyed with the city for obvious reasons. The Fuehrer declares that such systematic sparing of the shipyards is possible in the case of artillery, but not in connection with air raids; however, air raids never achieve complete destruction of docks in any case. The Fuehrer will take the Navy's request into account although he is of the opinion that the Russians will destroy the docks themselves". (*Brassey's Naval Annual, 1948*, p. 289.)

For SUPPLEMENTARY SECTION. The Black Sea Fleet.
(Page 409. Refer *The Times* report, 23.11.1942, of the Axis warships in the Black Sea.)

(a) *Conference of the C.-in-C., Navy, with the Fuehrer at Wehrwolf, August 26, 1942.* Admiral Raeder says: "We hope that the

Russian Black Sea Fleet will be put out of action by October or November. Submarines will remain important in the future when the Black Sea is used as a training area. . . . The Fuehrer considers the submarines in the Black Sea important because they will have a very favourable political influence on Turkey. He suggests that six submarines for this reason be transferred there. The C.-in-C., Navy, agrees". (*Brassey's Naval Annual, 1948*, pp. 289, 290.)

(b) *Minutes of the Conference of the C.-in-C., Navy, with the Fuehrer at Headquarters, Wolfsschanze, December 19 and 20, 1943.* The Fuehrer expresses his intention of utilising the Danube monitors not only on the Danube, but especially in the Black Sea and the Kerch Strait. (*Brassey's Naval Annual, 1948*, p. 374.)

For SUPPLEMENTARY SECTION. Sevastopol.

(Page 419. Refer description of the Crimea by the Germans as their "aircraft carrier in the Black Sea".)

The Commentary of the British Admiralty on the situation October 25, 1943, concerning the Russian advance on the southern sector of the Eastern Front : " Hitler saw his hold over the Ukraine slipping. . . . The Black Sea, however, was perhaps the only area where Germany's sea power was undisputed, and Hitler turned to Doenitz to see how this sea power could be used offensively, or, in the last resort, to secure the safe evacuation of the Wehrmacht. The Crimea was the key position, and at a conference on October 27, plans were discussed for making the Crimea an unassailable stronghold". (*Brassey's Naval Annual, 1948*, p. 370.)

For SUPPLEMENTARY SECTION. The Sea of Azov.

(Page 421. Refer German attack on defences of northern shores of Sea of Azov.)

Conference of the C.-in-C., Navy, with the Fuehrer at Wehrwolf, August 26, 1942. Admiral Raeder reports: "Considerable losses in the Sea of Azov were caused specially by Russian mines. Further losses would be incurred in trying to put the ports acquired into navigable condition, always keeping in mind the fighting tenacity of the Russians". (*Brassey's Naval Annual, 1948*, p. 290.)

(Page 422. Refer help given by Azov Sea Flotilla to Black Sea Fleet in the Russian assaults on the Crimea.)

Minutes of the Visit of the C.-in-C., Navy, at Fuehrer Headquarters, Berghof, February 26 and 27, 1944. "Plans for establishing a base for naval forces . . . in the Sea of Azov" are explained to the Fuehrer, who says he fears the Russians will land in the

Crimea by way of the Sea of Azov. (*Brassey's Naval Annual, 1948*, p. 385.)

For SUPPLEMENTARY SECTION. The Caspian Sea.
(Page 423. Refer destroyer flotillas on Caspian.)

Conference of the C.-in-C., Navy, with the Fuehrer at Wehrwolf, August 26, 1942. Admiral Raeder reports: "The only vessels which can be sent to the Caspian Sea at the moment are coastal minelayers (*KM-Boot*) and Italian units of the type used in the Black Sea. No final conclusions on how to transport the vessels have been reached. In the Caspian Sea we will be confronted with an enormous Russian superiority, since all our equipment must be brought by land". (*Brassey's Naval Annual, 1948.* p. 290.)

APPENDIX I

"*The Limitation of Naval Armaments and the Exchange of Information Concerning Naval Construction.*" *Agreement signed by the Governments of the United Kingdom and of the U.S.S.R., 17 July, 1937.*[1]

Under Part II the main provisions are contained in Article 4: (i) No capital ship was to exceed 35,000 tons standard displacement. (ii) No capital ship was to carry a gun with a calibre exceeding 16 in. (A Protocol modifying the Agreement of 17 July, 1937, was signed in London on 6 July, 1938. It was then laid down that the figure of 35,000 tons in Article 4 (i) should be replaced by the figure of 45,000 tons.)

Article 5 of the 1937 Agreement laid down that no aircraft carrier was to exceed 23,000 tons or to carry a gun with a calibre of more than 6.1 in. Under the terms of Article 7 no submarine was to exceed 2,000 tons standard displacement, or to carry a gun exceeding 5.1 in. in calibre.

[1] Published as Cmd. 5679 by H.M. Stationery Office. Reproduction by permission of the Controller.

APPENDIX II

Agreement signed on 17 July, 1937, between the Government of the United Kingdom and the U.S.S.R. providing for "The Limitation of Naval Armaments and the Exchange of Information concerning Naval Construction." [1]

This Agreement contains an important provision concerning Russia's Far Eastern Fleet. Under Part II, the 2nd Clause of Article 2 relating to limitation, states:—

"It is understood, however, that the Soviet Government shall not be bound by the limitations and restrictions of this part of the present Agreement in so far as the Soviet Far Eastern naval forces are concerned, so long as there shall not be concluded a special agreement between the U.S.S.R. and Japan on this subject. Nevertheless, the Soviet Government will not construct or acquire any vessels exceeding the said limitations and restrictions except in the event of such construction or acquisition by Japan or any other Power in the Far East."

Russia's insistence on freedom of action wherever her Pacific Fleet was concerned, arose from the fact that Japan had repudiated the Washington Naval Agreement of 1922, and had refused to be bound by its limitation clauses. Clause (3) lays down that

"Should the Soviet Government, as the result of such construction or acquisition by Japan or any other Power in the Far East, decide to construct or acquire vessels exceeding the said limitation or restrictions, a notification to that effect shall be made to the Government of the United Kingdom, and the vessels concerned shall not be laid down or acquired until after this notification has reached the Government of the United Kingdom."

Under Clause (5) it is laid down that

"Nothing in paragraph (2) above shall entitle the Soviet Government to construct or acquire any vessel exceeding the limitations or restrictions prescribed by this Pact of the present Agreement for service, or to employ such a vessel on service, elsewhere than in the Far East, wherever the vessel may be constructed or acquired. The Soviet Government shall equally not be entitled by anything in paragraph (2) above to transfer from the Soviet Far Eastern to the Soviet Baltic or Black Sea Fleet any vessel constructed or acquired in the exercise of the right conferred by that paragraph."

[1] See also this book, p. 327.

Part III of this 1937 Agreement is headed *Advance Notification and Exchange of Information.* Article 2 lays down:—

(1) (a) "Each Contracting Government shall communicate every year to the other Contracting Government information as hereinafter provided, regarding its annual programme for the construction and acquisition of all vessels of categories and sub-categories specified in the Agreement, and periodical information giving details of such vessels and of any alterations to vessels of the said categories or sub-categories already completed.

(b) It is understood, however, that the Soviet Government shall not be under any obligation to furnish the Government of the United Kingdom with any information regarding any vessels coming within the said categories or sub-categories which may be constructed in the Far Eastern territories of the Soviet Union, for service in the Far East, so long as there shall not be concluded between the Soviet Government and the Japanese Government a special agreement on this subject; and this Part of the present Agreement shall be read subject to this understanding."[1]

[1] *Treaty Series No.* 17 (1938) :—

Agreement between His Majesty's Government in the United Kingdom and the Government of the Union of Soviet Socialist Republics providing for the Limitation of Naval Armament and the Exchange of Information Concerning Naval Construction (with Protocol of Signature and Exchange of Notes of November 12-19, 1937, regarding the Russian text.)

Quotations by permission of the Director of Publications, His Majesty's Stationery Office, London, 1938. Command Paper 5679.

APPENDIX III

A

Recipients of the medals awarded by the Soviet Government to officers and men of the Royal and Merchant Navies, for their work with the Northern Convoys:—

Order of the Red Banner:
Captain Maxwell Richmond, R.N.
Captain Richard Onslow, R.N.
Captain Eric Percival Hinton, R.N.
Captain John Lawrie, D.S.O., D.S.C. (Merchant Navy.)

Order of the Patriotic War (First Degree):
Chief Petty Officer Cornelius Stephen Collins, R.N.
Chief Engineer Officer William Kelly S. Robinson (Merchant Navy.)
Chief Officer William Prance (Merchant Navy.)

Order of the Patriotic War (Second Degree):
Able Seaman Henry James Woodward, R.N.
Boatswain Frederick John Kendle (Merchant Navy.)
Sailor Anthony Martucci (Merchant Navy.)

Order of the Red Star:
Steward Robert Quick (Merchant Navy.)
Ship's Cook Benjamin Thompson Coffey (Merchant Navy.)

B

Names of Russian members of crews of the Northern Fleet, who received decorations from H.M. King George VI:—

Awarded the D.S.O.:
Captain Vladimir Izotov, of the tanker *Azerbaidjan*, (Holder of the Order of Lenin)
Captain Mikhail Pavlov, of the tanker *Donbas*.

Awarded the O.B.E.:
Captain Ivan Afanasyev, of the motor ship *Stary Bolshevik*.
Captain Kiril Kasyanchuk, of the motor ship *Engels*.

C

(i) Message from the Board of Admiralty, London, 31.12.1941, to Admiral Kharlamov, Soviet Naval Attaché in London:—

"The Board of Admiralty send to you and through you to all officers and men of the Soviet Navy, their greeting and good wishes for the New Year. With increasing confidence in the triumph of the common cause they look forward to the day of final victory, which is being brought so much nearer by the heroic achievements of the Soviet forces."

(ii) Message from the defenders of Kronstadt to the defenders of Malta, 5.5.1942 :—

"We, the marines of the fortress of Kronstadt, congratulate you on your recent award. We are watching with most sincere sympathy your heroic struggle against our common enemy and are full of admiration for your courage and tenacity. We are completely confident that you will be strong and brave enough to beat off all the many and varied attacks of the Nazi and Fascist hordes, and to hold your island fortress until victory comes. Blow for blow! No mercy for the enemy!

"On behalf of the marines of the fortress of Kronstadt:

"Vice-Admiral Tribuz; Members of the Military Council Smirnov and Verbitsky."

(iii) Message to the pilots of the Fleet Air Arm of the Royal Navy, sent on behalf of the Naval pilots of the Soviet Union. :—

"In the days of the great fight against the Hitlerite hordes, the naval pilots of the Soviet Union warmly greet the naval pilots of Great Britain.

"Comrades-in-arms, the historic task of freeing humanity from Hitlerite tyranny has fallen to the lot of the peoples of the Soviet Union and Great Britain. In the fight against Hitlerism, which seeks to drown the whole world in blood, naval pilots have shown fearlessness and great military ability. We record with admiration the operation carried out by you at Taranto, the devastating blows on the battleship *Bismarck*, and your courageous fight for the destruction of military objectives and bases of the hated enemy.

"The unshakable will of our peoples to wage the fight until complete victory over the enemy, binds us naval pilots mercilessly to exterminate the Hitlerite monsters on sea, on land and in the air. Our cause is a just cause. We are defending the liberty and happy future of all humanity. Victory will be ours.

"On behalf of the naval pilots of the Soviet Union:

"(Signed)—

"Lieutenant-General of Aviation, Zhavoronkov.

"Major-General of Aviation, Korobkov.

"Major-General of Aviation, Kuznetzov.

"Naval Pilots, Heroes of the Soviet Union, Preobrazhensky, Ubenov, Torakev, Brinko and Krohalev."[1]

(iv) Message in reply to (iii) sent to *Soviet War News*, 29.9.1941, by Rear-Admiral A. L. St. G. Lysky, Fifth Sea Lord and Chief of Naval Air Service:—

"Sir,—Please allow me through you to reply to the message to the pilots of the Naval Air Service from the pilots of the Soviet Naval Air Force, which we read in the *Soviet War News* yesterday.

[1] *Soviet War News*, 27.8.1941.

"We welcome the spirit of friendship shown to us by our valiant comrades of the Soviet Naval Air Force, and we look forward to the day when our combined efforts may bring that victory which we both so ardently desire. The Naval Air Service reciprocates warmly the greetings and good wishes of the Soviet Naval Air Service, and wishes them good hunting and happy landings."

BIBLIOGRAPHY

GENERAL

Большая Советская Энциклопедия. (Государственный Научный Институт). Энциклопедическое Издательство «Советская Энциклопедия». Москва, 1947.

Об отношениях Новгорода к Великим Князьям : С. М. Соловьев.

Chronique dite de Nestor : Louis Léger. (École des langues orientales vivantes, Paris, 1884.) [This is the French translation of *Pervonachalnaya Letopis,* the Kiev Chronicle, generally attributed to Nestor.]

Rerum Moscoviticarum Commentarii : Sigismund von Herberstein. (Antwerp, 1557.)

Notes Upon Russia: Baron Sigismund von Herberstein. Translation of the Earliest Accounts of that Country. Entitled *Rerum Moscoviticarum Commentarii.* (Printed for the Hakluyt Society, London, 1851 ; 2 vols.)

The Relations Between Ancient Russia and Scandinavia : Dr. Vilhelm Thomsen. (James Parker, Oxford and London, 1877.)

L'Empire Grec au dixième Siècle : Constantin Porphyregénète : Alfred Rambaud. (A. Franck, Paris, 1870.)

The Vikings : Allen Mawer. (Cambridge University Press, 1913.)

Rorik of Jutland and Rorik of the Russian Chronicles : Colonel N. I. Belaiev, C.B. (Reprinted from the Saga Book, Vol. X, of the Viking Society for Northern Research, 1929.)

A History of the Vikings : T. D. Kendrick, M.A. (Methuen, 1930.)

The Anglo-Saxon Version, from the Historian Orosius : Aelfred the Great. Together with an English translation from the Anglo-Saxon. (S. Baker, G. Leigh, T. Payne, B. White, London, 1773.)

König Aelfred und seine Stelle in der Geschichte Englands : Dr. Reinhold Pauli. (Wilhelm Hertz, Berlin, 1851.)

Петр Великий : Героическая Поэма: Михаил Ломоносов. Ст. Петербург, 1770. [?]

Discours sur le premier voyage de Pierre le Grand, principalement en Hollande : J. Meerman. (Debure, Paris, 1812.)

Passages from the Life of Peter the Great : Eugene Schuyler. (Sampson Low, Marston, Searle & Rivington, 1881.)

Peter the Great and His Pupils, 1689-1730. Cambridge Modern History, Vol. V. Edited by A. W. Ward, Litt.D., G. W. Prothero, Litt.D., S. Leathes, M.A. (Cambridge University Press, 1908.)

Histoire des Relations de la Russie avec la Chine sous Pierre le Grand (1689-1730): Gaston Cahen (Librairie Félix Alcan, Paris, 1912.)

Peter the Great: Alexei Tolstoi. Translated by Edith Bone and Emil Burns. (Gollancz, 1936.)

Memoirs of Russia, Historical, Political, and Military, from the Year 1727 to 1744 : Translated from the original manuscript of General Manstein (officer in the Russian Service). Edited by David Hume. (T. Becket and P. A. De Hondt, London, 1770.)

Memoirs of Peter Henry Bruce, Esq., A Military Officer in the Service of Prussia, Russia, and Great Britain : PETER HENRY BRUCE. (London, 1782.)

Contemporary Memoirs of Russia from the Year 1727 to 1744 : GENERAL CHRISTOPHER HERMANN V. MANSTEIN (an officer in the Russian Service). First edited by DAVID HUME. (Longman, Brown, Green, & Longmans, 1856.)

Russia : W. R. MORFILL. (Sampson Low, 1880.)

История России с Древнейших Времен: С. М. СОЛОВЬЕВ. (С. Петербург, 1894; 5 том.)

A History of Russia : V. O. KLUCHEVSKY. Translated by C. J. HOGARTH (Dent & Sons, 1911.) 5 vols.

The Comedy of Catherine the Great: FRANCIS GRIBBLE. (Eveleigh Nash, 1912.)

Russia : G. DOBSON, H. M. GROVE, H. STEWART. (A. & C. Black, 1913.)

La Russie et L'Europe : GREGOR ALEXINSKY. (Flammarion, Paris, 1917.)

Histoire de la Russie : ALFRED RAMBAUD. Histoire Universelle, sous la direction de M. V. DURUY. (Hachette, Paris, 1918.)

Russia from the Varangians to the Bolsheviks : RAYMOND BEAZLEY, NEVILL FORBES and G. A. BIRKETT. (Oxford University Press, 1918.)

A History of Russia : GEORGE K. VERNADSKY. (Yale University Press, 1930.) Revised edition.

The Life of Peter the Great: G. OUDARD. Translated from the French by F. M. ATKINS. (T. Werner Laurie, 1930.)

Pierre le Grand et son Oeuvre : V. O. KLUCHEVSKY. Translated by H. DE WITTE. (Payot, Paris, 1930.)

A History of Russia : BERNARD PARES. (Cape, 1937.) Third edition.

The Ukraine: A History: W. E. D. ALLEN. (Cambridge University Press, 1940.)

U.S.S.R. : Her Life and Her People : MAURICE DOBB. (University of London Press, Ltd., 1943.)

Survey of Russian History : B. H. SUMNER. (Duckworth, 1944.)

POLITICAL

International

Recueil d'Actes Internationaux de l'Empire Ottoman: GABRIEL NORADOUNGHIAN. (Pichon, Paris, 1897-1902.) 3 vols.

Tilsit : France et Russie sous le Premier Empire : EDOUARD DRIAULT. (Librairie Félix Alcan, Paris, 1917.)

Concise Ludendorff Memoirs, 1914-1918. (Hutchinson, 1933.)

A History of Europe, from 1815-1923 : SIR J. A. R. MARRIOTT. Methuen's History of Mediaeval and Modern Europe, Vol. VIII. (Methuen, 1931.)

The World Crisis, 1915 : THE RT. HON. WINSTON CHURCHILL, M.P. (Odhams Press Ltd., 1923.) 2 vols.

The Lausanne Conference on Near Eastern Affairs, 1922-1923. Cmd. 1914. (London, 1923.)

The Conduct of Foreign Relations Under Modern Democratic Conditions : DE WITT CLINTON POOLE. (Yale University Press, New Haven, 1924.)

A Short History of International Affairs : 1920-1939 : G. M. GATHORNE HARDY. Issued under the auspices of the Royal Institute of International Affairs. (Oxford University Press, 1942.)

The Road to Teheran : FOSTER RHEA DULLES. (Princeton University Press, 1944.)

Speaking Frankly : JAMES F. BYRNES. (Copyright, Donald Russell, Trustee of the James F. Byrnes Foundation. 1947.)
Keesing's Archives, Vols. I-VII. (Keesing Ltd., London and Keysham 1931-1948.)
The Second World War: THE RT. HON. WINSTON CHURCHILL, M.P. (Cassell and Co., Ltd., London, 1948. Houghton Mifflin Company, Boston 1948.)

America

American State Papers, Foreign Relations, Vol. V.
Annals of Congress : 16th Congress, 2nd Session, 1820-21, p. 1402—Russia's attitude to U.S. and Florida.
American Diplomacy and the Furtherance of Commerce : EUGENE SCHUYLER. (Sampson Low, Marston, Searle & Rivington, 1886.)
The United States and Russia : Their Historical Relations : OSCAR J. STRAUS. (*The North American Review, 1905.*)
Early Diplomatic Negotiations of the United States with Russia : JOHN C. HILDT. (The Johns Hopkins Press, Baltimore, 1906.)
America as a World Power, 1897-1907: JOHN H. LATANÉ, Ph.D. "The American Nation" Series, Vol. XXV. Edited by ALBERT B. HART, LL.D. (Harper Bros., New York.)
Russia as an American Problem : JOHN SPARGO. (Harper Bros., New York, 1920.)
Russo-American Relations, 1815-1867 : BENJAMIN PLATT THOMAS, Ph.D. *Johns Hopkins University Studies in Historical and Political Science,* Series XLVIII, No. 2. (The Johns Hopkins Press, Baltimore, 1930.)
American Policy Towards Russia since 1917 : FREDERICK LEWIS SCHUMAN, Ph.D. (Martin Lawrence, 1928.)
The Origins of American Intervention in North Russia (1918) : LEONID I. STRAKHOVSKY, D.Hist.Sc. (Princeton University Press, 1937.)
A Diplomatic History of the United States : SAMUEL FLAGG BEMIS. (Cape, 1937.)
The Story of the American People : C. P. STRONG, M.A., Ph.D. (Hodder and Stoughton, 1942.)
A Diplomatic History of the American People : T. A. BATLEY. (F. S. Crofts, New York, 1944.) Second edition.

Russia

Despatches, Russia. II, No. 53. August, 1816. United States State Department Archives. (Washing, D.C.)
A Lecture on the Treaty Relations of Russia and Turkey from 1774 to 1853 : THOMAS ERSKINE HOLLAND, D.C. (Macmillan & Co., 1877.)
Russia and the Great War : GREGOR ALEXINSKY. Translated by BERNARD MIALL. (Fisher Unwin, 1915.)
L'Europe devant Constantinople : MAX HOSCHILLER. (Rivière et Cie, Paris 1916.)
The Memoirs of Alexander Iswolsky (formerly Russian Minister of Foreign Affairs and Ambassador to France) : ALEXANDER ISWOLSKY. Edited and translated by CHARLES LOUIS SEEGER. (Hutchinson, 1926.)
Die Petersburger Mission Bismarcks, 1859-1862 : PROF. BARON BORIS E. NOL'DE. Einzige vom Verfasser genehmigte und durchgesehene Übersetzung, Dr. jur. BERNARD SCHULZE. (Rudolf Lamm, Leipzig, 1936.)

458 THE MARITIME HISTORY OF RUSSIA

The Eclipse of Russia : E. J. DILLON. (Dent, 1918.)
Les Documents Secrets des Archives du Ministère des Affaires Etrangères de Russie: EMILE LALOY. Publiés par les Bolcheviks. (Bossard, Paris, 1919.)
Un Livre Noir ; Diplomatie d'avant-guerre d'après les documents des archives Russes. Edited by RENÉ MARCHAND. (Paris, 1922-34.) 3 vols.
Russia's Foreign Relations During the Last Half Century: S. A. KORFF. (Macmillan, 1922.)
The Foreign Policies of Soviet Russia : ALFRED L. F. DENNIS. (Dent, 1924.)
Soviet Russia's Foreign Policy, 1939-1942 : DAVID J. DALLIN. Translated by LEON DENNEN. (Yale University Press, 1942.)
Russia and Post-war Europe : D. J. DALLIN. Translated by F. K. LAWRENCE. (Yale University Press, New Haven, 1944.) Third impression.
Raymond Robins's Own Story: WILLIAM HARD.(Harper Bros., New York,1920.)
The Murmansk Venture : MAJOR-GENERAL SIR C. MAYNARD. (Hodder and Stoughton, 1928.)
Intervention at Archangel : LEONID I. STRAKHOVSKY. (Princeton University Press, 1944.)
Британская Хроника. Сборник статей из британской печати и официальных документов. Министерство Информации Великобритании, Лондон, 1944.
Anglo-Russian Relations, 1689-1943 : SIR J. A. R. MARRIOTT. (Methuen, 1944.)
"Norway's Foreign Relations and Policy": PROF. WORM-MÜLLER. *The Norseman,* Vol. II, No. 2. (Lindsay Drummond.)

GEOGRAPHICAL AND GEOPOLITICAL

General

Босфор и Дарданеллы : С. ГОРИЯНОВ. С. Петербург, 1907.
Le Bosphore et les Dardanelles: SERGE GORIANOW. (Plon-Nourrit et Cie., Paris, 1910.)
Parliamentary Debates, 3rd Series, Vol. 297 : Report of debate on Black Sea : HANSARD.
La Question du Danube : G. DEMORGNY. (Société du Recueuil Sirey, 1911.)
La Question du Bosphore et des Dardanelles : NICOLAE DASCOVICI. (Georg et Cie., Geneva, 1915.)
The Question of the Bosphorus and the Dardanelles : COLEMAN PHILLIPSON, LL.D., Litt.D., and NOEL BUXTON, M.P. (Stevens & Haynes, 1917.)
La Question d'Orient depuis ses Origines jusqu'à la Paix de Sèvres : EDOUARD DRIAULT. (Félix Alcan, Paris, 1921.) Eighth edition.
L'Ultima Fase della Questione Orientale (1913-1932) : AMADEO GIANNINI. (Istituto per l'Oriente, Rome, 1933.)
Danube et Adriatique : G. DEMORGNY. (F. Loviton et Cie., Paris, 1934.)
Turkey at the Straits: J. T. SHOTWELL and F. DEAK. (The Macmillan Company, New York, 1940.)
Democratic Ideals and Reality : HALFORD J. MACKINDER, M.P. (Constable and Co., 1919.)
We Can Keep the Peace : MAIRIN MITCHELL. (Grout Publishing Company, 1945.)

Russia

Khiva and Turkestan : Translated from the Russian by CAPT. H. SPALDING, F.R.G.S. (Chapman & Hall, 1874.)

Russia in Central Asia : Translated by J. W. OZANNE and CAPT. H. SACHS. (Harrison & Sons, London, 1885.)

La Doctrine Panslaviste d'après N. J. Danilevsky : Résumé par J. J. SKUPI-EWSKI. (Bureau de la "Liberté Roumaine," Bucarest, 1890.)

Russland und Europa : N. J. DANILEVSKY. Übersetzt und eingeleitet von KARL NÖTZEL. (Deutsche Verlags. Anstalt, Stuttgart und Berlin, 1920.)

Asiatic Russia : GEORGE FREDERICK WRIGHT, LL.D., F.G.S.A. (McClure, Phillips & Co., New York, 1902.) 2 vols.

The Russian Advance : ALBERT J. BEVERIDGE. (Harper & Bros., New York and London, 1903.)

The Expansion of Russia, 1815-1900 : FRANCIS HENRY SKRINE, F.S.S. (Cambridge University Press, 1903.)

The Russian Conquest of the Caucasus : JOHN F. BADDELEY. (Longmans, Green and Co., 1908.)

Стратегическое Дальнего Востока: V. VILENSKII (Москва, 1921).

Russia and Asia: PRINCE LOBANOV-ROSTOVSKY. (The Macmillan Company, New York, 1933.)

Морское Соперничество Империалистических Держав: Л. Н. ИВАНОВ. (Москва, 1936).

Soviet Geography : N. N. MIKHAILOV. Translated by NATALIE ROTHSTEIN. (Methuen, 1937.)

Soviet Land and People : N. N. MIKHAILOV. (Published by *Soviet News,* London, 1945.)

The U.S.S.R. : A Geographical Survey : JAMES S. GREGORY, B.A., and D. W. SHAVE, M.Sc. (Harrap, 1944.)

Landsmen and Seafarers : MAURICE LOVELL. *The Soviets and Ourselves* Series. Edited by JOHN MCMURRAY. (Harrap, 1945.)

Notes d'économie et de politique de la pré-guerre d'Espagne à la pré-guerre de Grèce : R. LOUZON. *La Révolution Prolétarienne :* No. 311, Nouvelle Série, Janvier, 1948, No. 10. (Revue Syndicaliste Révolutionnaire, Paris.)

America

American History and Its Geographic Conditions : E. C. SEMPLE and C. F. JONES. (Houghton Mifflin Co., New York, 1933.)

The Ramparts We Watch : GEORGE FIELDING ELIOT. (Regnal & Hitchcock, New York, 1938.)

America's Strategy in World Politics : NICHOLAS JOHN SPYKMAN. (Harcourt, Bruce, Inc., New York, 1942.)

The Big Three : DAVID J. DALLIN. (Allen & Unwin, 1946.)

Germany

Weltpolitik, Imperialismus u. Kolonialpolitik : ERNST HASSE. (Munich, 1908.)

Grossdeutschland, die Arbeit des 20. Jahrhunderts : OTTO RICHARD TANNENBERG. Bruno Volger, Leipzig-Gohlis, 1911.)

Welche Strafe soll die treffen, die Schuld am Weltkrieg tragen ? E. V. MAYER. (Leipzig, 1915.)

The Pan-German Plot Unmasked : ANDRÉ CHÉRADAME. Translation by LADY FRAZER. (Murray, 1916.)

Das Annexionistische Deutschland : S. GRUMBACH. (Payot et Cie., Lausanne, 1917.)

L'Allemagne Annexioniste : S. GRUMBACH. *Recueuil de documents publiés ou répandus secrètement en Allemagne depuis le 4 août, 1914.* (Librairie Payot et Cie., Paris, 1917.)

Germany's Annexationist Aims : J. ELLIS BARKER. Translated and abbreviated from the work of S. GRUMBACH. (John Murray, 1917.)

Der Weg völkischen Wirtschaft und zur europäischen Grossraumwirtschaft: WERNER DAITZ. (Deutsche Technik G.M.B.H., München, 1938. Holle, Berlin, 1938.) 2 vols.

Geopolitik des Pazifischen Ozeans : KARL HAUSHOFER. (Vowinckel, Berlin, 1938.) Second edition.

The Roots of National Socialism, 1783-1933 : R. D'O. BUTLER. (Faber and Faber, 1941.)

The Treaty of Brest-Litovsk and Germany's Eastern Policy : JOHN W. WHEELER-BENNETT. Oxford Pamphlets on World Affairs, No. 14. (Oxford University Press, 1940.) New edition.

German Strategy of World Conquest : DERWENT WHITTLESEY. (F. E. Robinson and Co., 1943.)

"The Rumanian Ports": L. F. GRAY. *The Trident,* Vol. VI, No. 60.

Article on the Treaty of Unkiar-Skelessi. *Encyclopædia Britannica,* Vol. XXIII, 11th edition. (Encyclopædia Britannica Co., London, 1929.)

The German Lebensraum : ROBERT DICKINSON. *A Penguin Special, 1943.*

NAVIGATION

(*see also* THE ARCTIC, THE PACIFIC, and other regions)

Divers Voyages Touching the Discoverie of America and the Islands Adjacent unto the Same : RICHARD HAKLUYT. (Thomas Woodcocke, London, 1558.)

The World Encompassed by Sir Francis Drake : FRANCIS FLETCHER. (Nicholas Bovine, London, 1628.)

An Account of several late Voyages and Discoveries to the South and North towards the Streight of Magellan, the South Seas . . . also towards Nova Zembla, Greenland, or Spitzberg. . . . By Sir John Narborough, Captain J. Tasman, Captain J. Wood, and F. Marten of Hamburgh. (London, 1694.) 2 pts.

Navigantium atque itinerantium Bibliotheca, or A Complete Collection of Voyages and Travels : JOHN HARRIS, D.D., F.R.S.

A Collection of Voyages and Travels, some now first printed from Original Manuscripts, With an Account of the Progress of Navigation from its first beginning : Compiled by AWNSHAM and JOHN CHURCHILL. (London, 1704.) 4 vols.

The Principal Navigations, Voyages, Traffiques and Discoveries of the English Nation : RICHARD HAKLUYT. Edited by DOUGLAS S. JACKSON. (Jackson, Son & Co., Glasgow. J. M. Dent & Sons, London, 1907.) 10 vols.

Hakluytus Posthumus, or Purchas His Pilgrimes : SAMUEL PURCHAS, B.D. Edited by S. DOUGLAS JACKSON. (James MacLehose & Sons, Glasgow, 1905, and Jackson, Son & Co., Glasgow.) 20 vols.

The Discovery of Muscovy: From the Collection of RICHARD HAKLUYT. (Cassell & Co., Ltd., 1886.)

Early Voyages and Travels to Russia and Persia: ANTHONY JENKINSON and OTHER ENGLISHMEN. Edtd. by E. DELMAR MORGAN and C. H. COOTE. (Printed for the Hakluyt Society, 1886.) 2 vols.

The Original Letter of the English Pilot William Adams: Reprinted by special permission from the papers of the Hakluyt Society. Published in *More Queer Things About Japan:* By DOUGLAS SLADEN and NORMA LORIMER. (Anthony Treherne & Co., 1904.)

William Adams, The Pilot-Major of Gillingham: J. BATE. (Mackay's Ltd., Gillingham, 1934.)

The Romance of Navigation : W. B. WHALL. Edited by FRANCIS E. McMURTRIE, A.I.N.A. (Sampson Low, Marston & Co., 1925.)

"The Cartography and Observations of Bering's First Voyage": A. W. GREELY. *National Geographical Magazine* Vol. III, pp. 205-230.

The Voyage of La Pérouse Round the World, in the Years 1785, 1786, 1787, and 1788, with the Nautical Tables : GALAUP DE LA PÉROUSE. (John Stockdale, London, 1798.) 2 vols.

A Voyage Round the World Performed During the Years 1790, 1791 and 1792: ETIENNE MARCHAND. Translated from the French of C. P. CLARET FLEURIEU. (Longman, Rees, Cadell & Davies, 1801.) 2 vols.

Voyage Round the World in the Years 1803, 1804, 1805, and 1806, by Order of His Imperial Majesty Alexander the First, on Board the Ships "Nadezhda" and "Neva" : CAPTAIN A. J. VON KRUSENSTERN. Translated from the German by RICHARD BELGRAVE HOPPNER. (John Murray, 1813.) 2 pts.

Voyages and Travels in Various Parts of the World During Years 1803, 1804, 1805, 1806, and 1807 ; G. H. VON LANGSDORF. (Henry Colburn, London, 1813.)

A Voyage Round the World in the Years 1803, 1804, 1805, and 1806. Performed by Order of His Imperial Majesty Alexander the First, Emperor of Russia, in the Ship "Neva" : UREY LISIANSKY, Captain in the Russian Navy. (John Booth, London, 1819.)

The Voyage of Captain Bellingshausen into the Antarctic Seas, 1819-1821. Translated from the Russian by FRANK DEBENHAM, O.B.E. (Printed for the Hakluyt Society, London, 1945.) 2 vols.

Путешествие Вокруг Света Флота Капитана Головина ; С. Петербург, 1822. (2 ч.)

Опыты над постоянным маятником произведенные в Путешествие Вокруг Света на военном шлюпе «Сенявине» в 1826, 1827, 1828 и 1829 годах; Ф. Литке, С. Петербург, 1833 (3 ч.)

Voyage Pittoresque autour du Monde: LOUIS CHORIS. (Firmin Didot, Paris,1822.)

Bibliotheca Americana Nova : A Catalogue of Books relating to America, in Various Languages, including Voyages to the Pacific and Round the World, and Collection of Voyages and Travels printed since the year 1700 : OBADIAH RICH. (Rich & Sons, London, 1846.)

Narrative of a Journey Round the World, During the Years 1841 and 1842: SIR GEORGE SIMPSON (Henry Colburn, London, 1847.)

Histoire Universelle des Voyages: DUMONT D'URVILLE.(B. Renault, Paris,1860.)

Beiträge zur Kenntnis des Russischen Reiches und der angrenzenden Länder Asiens : K. E. VON BAER. (St. Petersburg, 1872.)

Tudor Geography, 1485-1583: E. G. R.TAYLOR, D.Sc., F.R.G.S. (Methuen,1930).

Late Tudor and Early Stuart Geography, 1583-1650 : E. G. R. TAYLOR, D.Sc., F.R.G.S. (Methuen, 1934.)

The Great Age of Discovery: ARTHUR PERCIVAL NEWTON. (University of London Press, Ltd., 1932.)

The Maritime History of Massachusetts, 1783-1860 : SAMUEL ELIOT MORISON. (Houghton Mifflin Co., Boston, 1941.)

The Ocean in English History : JAMES A. WILLIAMSON. (The Clarendon Press, Oxford, 1941.)
Russian Voyages Round the World : N. NOZIKOV. Edited by M. A. SERGEYEV and translated by ERNST and MIRA LESSER. (Hutchinson, 1945.)
A Study of the Oceans: JAMES JOHNSTONE, D.Sc. (Edward Arnold, 1930; 2nd edtn.)

NAVAL

British and General

The Navy of Britain: PROFESSOR MICHAEL LEWIS, M.A., F.R.Hist.S. (Allen and Unwin, 1948.)
The Royal Navy: A History from the earliest times to the death of Queen Victoria: WILLIAM LAIRD CLOWES. (Sampson Low, Marston & Co., 1903.) 7 vols.
Jane's Fighting Ships (1947-1948) : Edited by FRANCIS E. McMURTRIE, A.I.N.A. (Sampson Low, 1948.)
The World's Warships, 1948 (Jane's) : Edited by FRANCIS E. McMURTRIE A.I.N.A. (Sampson Low, 1948.)
Brassey's Naval Annual, 1947-1948 : Edited by REAR-ADMIRAL H. G. THURS-FIELD. (William Clowes & Sons, Ltd., 1948.)
All the World's Fighing Fleets : Edited by PAY-LIEUT. E. C. TALBOT-BOOTH, R.N.R. (Sampson Low, 1944.)
Flottes de Combat, 1947 : Edited by HENRI LE MASSON. (Société d'Éditions Géographiques, Maritimes et Coloniales, 1947.)
The Influence of Sea Power Upon History, 1660-1783 : REAR-ADMIRAL A. T. MAHAN,D.C.L., LL.D., U.S.N. (Sampson Low.)
Histoire de la Marine de tous les Peuples: A. J. BOUVET DE CRESSÉ. (A. André, Paris, 1824.) 2 vols.
Ironclads in Action : H. W. WILSON. (Sampson Low, 1898.) Sixth impression. 2 vols.
Naval Wars in the Baltic, 1521-1850 : R. C. ANDERSON, F.R.G.S. (C. Gilbert-Wood, London, 1910.)
England in the Mediterranean, 1603-1713 : SIR JULIAN S. CORBETT. (Longmans, Green & Co., 1917.) Second Edition. 2 vols.
Report of Rear-Admiral Cowan on naval operations in the Baltic, spring of 1919. Published as a Supplement (No. 5) to *The London Gazette,* 6 April, 1920.
The Naval Side of British History : GEOFFREY CALLENDER, M.A. (Christopher's, 1927.)
Great Sea Stories of All Nations : Edited by H. M. TOMLINSON. (Harrap, 1930.)
A History of Sea Power: PROFESSOR WILLIAM OLIVER STEVENS and PROFESSOR ALLAN WESTCOTT (Doubleday Doran, New York, 1937.)
Fleets : The British Commonwealth of Nations and Foreign Countries. British official return of the strength of the fleets. (H.M. Stationery Office, 1939.)
Sea Power and Empire : PROF. F. J. C. HEARNSHAW. (Harrap, 1940.)
The Destiny of Sea Power : JOHN PHILIPS CRANWELL. (Allen & Unwin, 1942.)
A Short History of the Royal Navy, 1805-1918 : CHRISTOPHER LLOYD. (Methuen, 1942.)

History of the Great War : Sir Julian S. Corbett. Based on official documents, by direction of the Historical Section of the Committee of Imperial Defence, Naval Operations. (Longmans, Green & Co., 1938.) Second edition ; five volumes.
Sea Power and To-day's War : Fletcher Pratt. (Methuen, 1940.)
World War at Sea : Brian Tunstall. (Martin Secker and Warburg, 1942.)
Ocean Power Wins : Brian Tunstall. (Martin Secker and Warburg, 1944.)
"The Power of the British Navy": Prof. Ivanov. Article in *Soviet War News,* 29 May, 1943.
The Naval Heritage : David Mathew. (Collins, 1944.)
Fuehrer Conferences on Naval Affairs, 1939-1945. (H.M. Stationery Office, 1948.)
Hitler and His Admirals: Anthony Martienssen. (Secker and Warburg, 1948.)

America

The Interest of America in Sea Power, Present and Future : Captain A. T. Mahan, U.S.N. (Sampson Low, Marston, 1897.)
Manifest Destiny : Albert K. Weinberg. (The Johns Hopkins Press, Baltimore, 1935.)
Mahan : The Life and Work of Captain Alfred Thayer Mahan, U.S.N. : W. D. Puleston, U.S.N. (Cape, 1939.)
The Rise of American Naval Power, 1776-1918 : Harold and Margaret Sprout. (Princeton University Press, Princeton, 1939.)
A Navy Second to None ; the Development of Modern American Naval Policy : George Theron Davis. (Harcourt, Brace & Co., New York, 1940.)
United States Naval Expedition to Japan, 1852-54 : F. A. Parker. (Author, 5653, Post Road, New York 63 ; 1945.)
Towards a New Order of Sea Power. American Naval Policy and the World Scene, 1918-1922 : Harold and Margaret Sprout. (Princeton University Press, 1940.)
Ships of the Fleet : E. M. Conger. (Henry Holt, New York, 1946.)
Japan's Influence on American Naval Power, 1897-1917 : O. J. Clinard. (University of California, 1947.)
History of the Modern American Navy from 1883 Through Pearl Harbor : D. W. Mitchell. (Knopf, New York, 1946 ; John Murray, London, 1947.)
The Influence of Sea Power in World War II: Captain W. D. Puleston. (Yale University Press. London, Cumberlege, 1948.)

Russia

Летопись крушений и пожаров Судов Русского Флота от начала его до 1854 года: М. Соколов. С. Петербург, 1855.
История Севастополя как Русского Порта : В. Ф. Головачов. С. Петербург, 1872.
Материалы для Истории Русского Флота : (Балтийский Флот, 1702-1725): С. Элагин. Санктп., 1865-1867. В типографии Морского Министерства в Главном Адмиралтействе.
История Русского Флота. Период азовский, 1696-1712 : С. Элагин. Имп. Акад. Санктп., 1864 (2 том).
Морской Сборник. (ч. 1-7, 1898). Издаваемый под наблюдением Главного Морского Штаба. (Редактор Полковник Мордовин.) Том ccclxxxiii, ч. 1-12, 1898. Санктп. Типография Морского Министерства в Главном Адмиралтействе, 1898.

Разсуждения по Вопросам Морской Тактики: Вице-Адмирал С. О. Макаров. (Редактор. Ст. Лейт. К. Житков). Типография Морского Министерства в Главном Адмиралтействе. Петроград, 1916.

История Войны на Море с Точки Зрения Морской Тактики: Альфред Штенцел. (Редактор Капитан 2-го Ранга К. Житков.) Типография Морского Министерства, в Главном Адмиралтействе, Петроград, 1916-1917. (3 том.)

Русская История в Самом Сжатом Очерке: М. Н. Покровский. Государственное Издательство, Москва, 1920 (2 ч.)

Боевое Снабжение Русской Армии в Мировую Войну: А. А. Маниковский. (Переработал и дополнил З. Барсуков.) Государственное Издательство, Москва, Ленинград, 1930. (Вт. издание; 2 ч.)

Свеаборг, Военное Восстание в 1906 году: В. Н. Соколов. Старый Большевик, Москва, 1933.

Царский Флот под Красным Стягом. Документы и воспоминания об участии матросов в революционном движении. (Под редакцией В. А. Плескова и Н. Ф. Цужака.)

Чорноморці в Революції: М. Адамович. Видавництво Всеукраинського Т-ва по политкаторжан и засланцев. Друкарня им. В. И. Ленина, Миколаив, «Шляхи Революции», 1931. Видавництво «Шляхи Революции», Харків, 1931.

Флот. Русские Моряки во время Великой Войны и Революции. Том I, II: А. П. Лукин. Журнал «Иллюстрированная Россия», 1933.

Кронштадт в 1917 году: И. Н. Колбин. Партийное издательство, Москва и Ленинград, 1932.

Издательство Всесоюзного Общества Политкаторжан и сс. Поселенцев, Москва, 1931.

Февраль и Октябрь в Черноморском Флоте: А. П. Платонов. Крымское Государственное Издательство, 1932

Военно-торской Флот СССР в Отечественной Войне: Н. Токарев. Государственное Издательство Политической Литературы, Москва, 1943.

Красный Флот. (Орган Народного Комиссариата Военно-Морского Флота СССР), Москва.

The Russian Fleet Under Peter the Great: By A Contemporary Englishman (1724). Edited by Vice-Admiral Cyprian A. G. Bridge, K.C.B. *Publications of the Navy Records Society,* Vol. XV. (Printed for the Navy Records Society, 1899.)

Russia's Sea-Power, Past and Present: Colonel Sir George Sydenham Clarke, K.C.M.G., F.R.S. (John Murray, 1898.)

The Imperial Russian Navy: Its Past, Present, and Future: Fred T. Jane. (W. Thacker & Co., London, 1904.) Second edition.

The Russian Navy in the Russo-Japanese War: Captain Nicolas Klado, I.R.N. Translated from the French text of René Marchand by L. J. H. Dickinson, D.Litt. (Hurst & Blackett, 1905.)

The Battle of the Sea of Japan: Captain Nicolas Klado, I.R.N. Translated by J. H. Dickinson, D.Litt., and F. P. Marchand. (Hodder and Stoughton, 1906.)

From Libau to Tsushima: Eugen S. Politovsky. Translated by Major F. R. Godfrey, R.M.L.I. (John Murray, 1906.)

The Revolt of the "Potemkin": Constantine Feldmann. Translated by Constance Garnett. (Heinemann, 1908.)

The Epic of the Black Sea : ANDRÉ MARTY. (Modern Books, 1919.)

Statements on Strength of Russian Navy, 1914. *Soviet War News,* 6 March, 1943.

Reports of Naval "Purge" in the Soviet Union. *The Times,* 31 August, 1938; *The Yorkshire Post,* 16 May, 1938.

Report on the Decree Raising the Period of Naval Service in the U.S.S.R. Moscow Correspondent, *The Times,* 19 May, 1939.

Article on increase in shipbuilding: M. TEVOSYAN, Commissar for Ship-building. *Pravda,* 21 and 23 July, 1939.

Translations of statements by M. TEVOSYAN in *Pravda* of 21 and 23 September, 1939, published in *News Bulletin.* (Anglo-Russian Parliamentary Committee, Press Dept., 29 September, 1939.)

Treaty Series No. 17 (1938). Agreement between His Majesty's Government in the United Kingdom and the Government of the Union of Soviet Socialist Republics providing for the Limitation of Naval Armament and the Exchange of Information Concerning Naval Construction (with Protocol of Signature and Exchange of Notes of 12-19 November, 1937, regarding the Russian text). London, 17 July, 1937. Command Paper 5679. (His Majesty's Stationery Office, 1938.)

Treaty Series No. 39 (1939). Protocol modifying the Anglo-Soviet Agreement of 17 July, 1937, for the Limitation of Naval Armament. London, 6 July, 1938. (With Exchange of Notes regarding the Russian text.) (His Majesty's Stationery Office, 1939.)

The Soviets' Fighting Forces: Compiled by THE RT. HON. ARTHUR GREEN-WOOD, M.P. (The Anglo-Russian Parliamentary Committee, 1939.)

Account of Russia's Pacific Fleet. *The New York Times,* 19 September, 1941.

The Red Fleet and the Royal Navy : MAIRIN MITCHELL. (Hodder & Stoughton, 1942.)

Why Russia Will Win: W. P. and ZELDA K. COATES. (Eldon Press, Ltd., 1942.)

Russia's Fighting Forces : CAPTAIN SERGEI N. KOURNAKOFF. (International Publishers, New York, 1942.)

"The Armed Forces of the U.S.S.R." Condensed from the *Malaia Soviet Encyclopedia,* Vol. X, 1940; second edition. (American Review of the Armed Forces of the U.S.S.R., August, 1941.)

"Naval Battles in the Baltic": CAPTAIN E. MATVEYEV. Article in *Strategy and Tactics of the Soviet-German War.* (Hutchinson, 1942.)

Extracts from secret German naval diary referring to Murmansk. *The Daily Telegraph,* 11 December, 1945.

The Soul of the Sea: LEONID SOBOLEV. (Hutchinson, 1945.)

The Red Fleet in the Second World War : ADMIRAL-OF-THE-FLEET I. S. ISAKOV. Translated by JACK HURAL. (Hutchinson, 1946.)

"Naval Flags of the Allies"—(2) *U.S.S.R.:* H. G. CARR, M.S.N.R. *The Sea Cadet,* March, 1946.

Account by ADMIRAL SIR HOWARD KELLY of passage of Russian ships through Straits in World War II. *The Sunday Times,* 3 November, 1946.

Мои Воспоминания: A. N. KRYLOV. (Moscow, 1945.)

Description of cruiser *"Petropavlovsk"; The Navy,* March, 1944. Report of SIR LIONEL HALSEY's speech on Trafalgar Day, 1947; *The Navy,* November, 1947. "The Russian Navy", article by CAPTAIN RUSSELL GRENFELL, R.N.; *The Navy,* April, 1948. "Reproduction of paper" by FLEET-ADMIRAL CHESTER W. NIMITZ, U.S.N., "on the function of the U.S. Navy"; *The Navy,* 1948. (The Navy League.)

Report of Russians and Albanians building submarine base on Sasseno; *The Daily Telegraph*, 8 January, 1947.

MERCANTILE

History of Merchant Shipping and Ancient Commerce : W. S. LINDSAY. (Sampson Low, Marston, Low, and Searle, 1874.) 3 vols.

Frontiers and the Fur Trade: SYDNEY GREENBIE. (The John Day Company, Inc., New York, 1929.)

Seaborne Trade : C. ERNEST FAYLE. History of the Great War based on Official Documents by direction of the Historical Section of the Committee of Imperial Defence. (John Murray, 1920.) 3 vols.

Foreign Trade in the U.S.S.R. : J. D. YANSON. New Soviet Library, No. 8. (Gollancz, 1934.)

Soviet Export : M. ZHIRMUNSKI. (Mezhdunarodnaya Kniga, 1936.)

British Russian Gazette and Trade Outlook. Vol. III, No. 7 ; Vol. X, No. 12. (London.)

Bank for Russian Trade Review, Ltd. Vol. II, No. 6. (London.)

Monthly Review. Vol. I, No. 4; Vol. IV, No. 2; Vol. V, Nos. 8, 9, 12; Vol. VI, No. 7; Vol. IX, Nos. 5, 10, 12; Vol. X, Nos. 8, 11, 12 (Moscow Narodny Bank, Ltd., London.)

Facts concerning shipping losses in Mediterranean during Spanish Civil War. *Labour Research*, Vol. XXVI, No. 10. (Labour Research Dept.)

"Russia's Mercantile Marine." *Shipbuilding and Shipping Record*, 12 October, 1939. (Transport (1910), Ltd.)

Lloyds Register of Shipping, July, 1939.

Russian mercantile tonnage in 1914. Statement in *Pravda*, 12 July, 1939.

The Shipping World Year Book and Port Directory of the World, 1940. (The Shipping World, Ltd., London.)

Article on Russia's exports and imports. *The Observer*, 5 March, 1944.

Merchant Ships, 1944. Edited by E. C. TALBOT-BOOTH, R.D., R.N.V.R. (Sampson Low, 1945.)

Account of losses in Finland's Merchant Navy. *Helsingin Sanomat*, 20 February, 1945.

Merchantmen at War. Prepared for the Ministry of War Transport by the Ministry of Information. (H.M. Stationery Office, 1945.)

Ports of the World. Edited by SIR ARCHIBALD HURD, A.I.N.A. (The Shipping World, Ltd., London, 1947.) Second edition.

Appendix to Lloyd's Register Book, 1947-48. (Lloyd's Register of Shipping, 1948.)

ECONOMIC

The New Russia : L. HADEN GUEST, M.P. (Thornton Butterworth, 1926.)

The Principles of Economic Geography : PROFESSOR R. N. RUDMOSE BROWN, D.Sc. (Sir Isaac Pitman & Sons, Ltd., London, 1936.) Third edition, revised.

U.S.S.R. Handbook. (Gollancz, 1936.)

The Economic Development of the Far East : E. RAIKHMAN and B. VVEDENSKY. (Institute of Pacific Relations, New York, 1936.)

The U.S.S.R. : An Economic and Social Survey : S. P. TURIN, D.Sc. (Econ.). (Methuen, 1944.)

Soviet Economic Development: MAURICE DOBB. (Routledge and Kegan Paul, 1948.)

THE BALTIC

The Baltic States : INFORMATION DEPARTMENT OF THE ROYAL INSTITUTE OF INTERNATIONAL AFFAIRS. (Oxford University Press, 1938.)

German designs in Baltic. Reported by Hague Correspondent, *The Manchester Guardian*, 6 November, 1939.

Problems of the Baltic : F. REDDAWAY, F.R.Hist.S. (Cambridge University Press, 1940.)

The Baltic Riddle: GREGORY MEIKSINS. (A. A. Wyn, Inc., New York.)

Statements on German Fleet in Baltic: COMMANDER OELBERG, Swedish Navy. Reported by Stockholm Special Correspondent, *The Daily Mail*, 31 January, 1944.

Germany's Exposed Flank Along the Baltic: W. G. HART. *The Daily Telegraph.*

Cards on the Table : An Interpretation of Labour's Foreign Policy. (The Labour Party, Transport House, 1947.)

Statement on "Finland as the Key to Moscow." *The Times*, 17 April, 1919.

"White Sea-Baltic Canal": DR.V. TCHERNAVIN. *The Trident*, Vol. II, No.13.

"The Baltic States": L. F. GRAY. *The Trident*, Vol. VI, No. 58.

Statement on cession of Finnish ships to Russia, following Armistice of 1944. *Helsingen Sanomat*, 20 February, 1944.

Article on Russia's development of Warnemünde as naval base: Special Correspondent, *Daily Telegraph*, 3 September, 1946.

THE ARCTIC

Relation of a Voyage for the Discovery of a Passage by the North-East, to Japan and China; Performed in his Majesties Ship the "Speedwel" and "Prosperous" Pink, Anno Domini 1676: CAPTAIN JOHN WOOD. Published in *An Account of Several Late Voyages and Discoveries to the South and North.* (Samuel Smith and Benjamin Walford, London, 1694.)

The Possibility of Approaching the North Pole: Hon. Daines Barrington, F.R.S. (T. & J. Allman, London, 1818, second edition.)

Четырекратное Путешествие в Северный Ледовитый Океан (совершенное по повелению Императора Александра I, на военном бриге «Новая Земля», в 1821,1822,1823 и 1824 годах, флота Капитан-Лейтенантом Федором Литке). Ф. Т. Литке, С. Петербург, 1828, (2 ч.).

An Account of the Arctic Regions, and of the Whale Fishery : W. SCORESBY, Jun., F.R.S.E. (Archibald Constable & Co., Edinburgh, 1820.) Three volumes.

Voyage of Discovery and Research within the Arctic Regions : SIR JOHN BARROW, F.R.S. (Murray, 1846.)

Narrative of the Voyage of H.M.S. "Herald" During the Years 1845-51 : BERTHOLD SEEMAN, F.L.S. (Reeve & Co., London, 1853.) 2 vols.

Admiral Sir P. B. V. Broke, Bt.: REV. J. G. BRIGHTON. (Sampson Low, Son, and Marston, 1866.)

The Arctic Voyages of Adolf Erik Nordenskiöld : ALEXANDER LESLIE. (Macmillan, 1879.)

Vega-Expeditionens Vetenskaphga Iakttagelser : A. E. NORDENSKIÖLD. Bearbetade af Deltagare i Resan och Andra Forskare. (F. & G. Beijers Förlag, Stockholm, 1882.) 5 Bd.

The Voyage of the "Vega" Round Asia and Europe : NILS A. E. NORDENSKIÖLD. Translated by ALEXANDER LESLIE. (Macmillan & Co., 1883.)

Handbook of Arctic Discoveries : BRIGADIER-GENERAL A. W. GREELY. (Sampson Low, Marston & Co., 1866.)

Farthest North : FRIDTJOF NANSEN, G.C.V.O., D.C.L., D.Sc., Ph.D. (George Newnes, 1898.) Two volumes.

Nearest the Pole : COMMANDER ROBERT E. PEARY, U.S.N. (Hutchinson, 1907.)

In Northern Mists: FRIDTJOF NANSEN. (Heinemann, 1911.) 2 vols.

Report of the Swedish Expedition to Spitzbergen, 1890 : GUSTAF NORDENSKIÖLD. Translated by R. DUNN-GARDINER, F.R.G.S. (The Eastern Press, Ltd., London, 1933.)

"Nouvelles Terres et Nouvelles Routes de Commerce dans l'Arctique": CHARLES RABOT. *L'Illustration,* No. 4614, p. 513.

"The Siberian Sea Road": N. A. TRANSEHE (late Commander, Russian Navy.) *The Geographical Review,* Vol. XV, No. 3.

"Russia's Northern Seaway": RICHARD C. STONE. *The Trident,* Vol. VII, No. 72.

"Notes on the Northern Sea Route": PROFESSOR KENNETH MASON. *The Geographical Journal,* Vol. XCVI, No. 1.

Arctic Exploration : T. DOUGLAS HOARE. (Methuen, 1906.)

Nordvest-Passagen. Beretning om Gjöa Ekspeditionen, 1903-1907 : ROALD AMUNDSEN. (H. Aschehoug & Co.; W. Nygaard, Kristiania, 1907.)

Nordost-Passagen: ROALD AMUNDSEN. (Gyldendalske Boghandel, Kristiania, 1921.)

The Northward Course of Empire : VILHJALMUR STEFANSSON. (Harrap, 1905.)

The Adventure of Wrangel Island: VILHJALMUR STEFANSSON with the collaboration of JOHN IRVINE KNIGHT. (The Macmillan Company, New York, 1925.)

The North Pole: ROBERT E. PEARY. (Hodder & Stoughton, 1910.)

The Polar Regions: PROFESSOR R. N. RUDMOSE-BROWN, D.Sc. (Methuen, 1927.)

My Life as an Explorer : ROALD AMUNDSEN. (Heinemann, 1927.)

The Polar Regions in the Twentieth Century : MAJOR-GENERAL A. W. GREELY, U.S. Army. (Harrap & Co., 1929.)

The First Flight Across the Polar Sea : ROALD AMUNDSEN and LINCOLN ELLSWORTH. (Hutchinson.)

Through the Kara Sea : LEONARD MATTERS. (Skeffington, 1932.)

British Polar Explorers: ADMIRAL SIR EDWARD EVANS. (William Collins,1933.)

Fifteen Years of Arctic Exploration : R. L. SAMOILOVICH. Extract from *The Bulletin of the Arctic Institute,* No. 3-4, p. 112, Leningrad. Published in *The Hydrographic Review,* Vol. XIII, No. 1. (International Hydrographic Bureau, Monte Carlo, May, 1937.)

The Voyage of the "Cheliuskin" : By MEMBERS OF THE EXPEDITION. Translated by ALEC BROWN. (Chatto & Windus, 1935.)

Soviets in the Arctic : T. A. TARACOUZIO, Ph.D. Issued under the auspices of the Bureau of International Research, Harvard University and Radcliffe College. (The Macmillan Company, New York, 1938.)

" Results of the Scientific Work on Drifting North Polar Station": P.SHIRSOV and E. FEDOROV. *Soviet Life and Work,* April-May, 1938. (Society for Cultural Relations with U.S.S.R.)

"The Cherevichny Triangle: Recent Polar Explorations"; PROFESSOR N. ZUBOV. Translated by Z. SCHOMBERG. *The Anglo-Soviet Journal,* Vol. III, No. 1. (Lindsay Drummond.)

"The Soviets in Their Arctic": JAMES FISHER. *The Anglo-Soviet Journal*, Vol. II, No. 1. (Lindsay Drummond.)

" Expedition to the North Pole ": REAR-ADMIRAL I. PAPANIN. *Soviet Union News*, Vol. II, No. 10.

Life on an Ice-floe : IVAN PAPANIN. Translated by FANNY SMITHAM. (Hutchinson.)

"The Scientific Value of Expeditions". Leading article on the Papanin Expedition. *Nature*, 26 February, 1939.

On the Top of the World: L. K. BRONTMAN. Edited by Academician OTTO J. SCHMIDT. (Gollancz, 1938.)

Forty Thousand Against the Arctic : H. P. SMOLKA. (Hutchinson, 1938.)

I Went to the Soviet Arctic: RUTH GRUBER. (Gollancz, 1939. The Viking Press, New York.)

Ultima Thule : VILHJALMUR STEFANSSON. (Harrap, 1942.)

Plowing the Arctic : G. J. TRANTER. (Hodder & Stoughton, 1944.)

"The Conquest of the North-West Passage: The Arctic Voyages of the *St. Roch*, 1940-44": HENRY A. LARSEN. *The Geographical Journal*, Vol. CX, No. 1. The Royal Geographical Society. (John Murray, 1948.)

SIBERIA AND KAMCHATKA

Noord en Ost Tartarye : NICOLAES WITSEN. (F. Halma, Amsterdam, 1705.) Two parts.

Travels in Kamchatka During the Years 1787 and 1788 : M. DE LESSEPS. Translated from the French. (J. Johnson, London, 1790.) 2 vols.

Воспоминания о Сибири, 1848-1854: Б. В. Струле. «Общественная Польза», Б. Под'яч, № 39. С. Петерб. 1889.

Narrative of a Pedestrian Journey Through Russia and Siberian Tartary, from the Frontiers of China to the Frozen Sea and Kamchatka : CAPTAIN JOHN DUNDAS COCHRANE, R.N. (Charles Knight, London, 1825.) Third edition; 2 vols.

Narrative of an Expedition to Siberia and the Polar Sea in the Years 1820, 1821, and 1823: LIEUT. FERDINAND VON WRANGELL. Edited by LIEUT.-COL. EDWARD SABINE, R.A., F.R.S. (James Madden, London, 1944.) Second Edition.

Through Siberia, the Land of the Future : FRIDTJOF NANSEN, G.C.V.O., D.Sc., D.C.L., Ph.D. (Heinemann, 1914.)

The Far Eastern Republic of Siberia : HENRY K. NORTON. (Allen & Unwin, 1923.)

The Continent of Asia: LIONEL W. LYDE, M.A., F.R.G.S. (Macmillan and Co., 1933.)

Soviet Asia : R. A. DAVIES and A. J. STEIGER. (Gollancz, 1943.)

Siberia: EMIL LENGYEL. (Random House, New York, and The Macmillan Company of Canada, Ltd.)

Dawn in Siberia : G. D. R. PHILLIPS. (Frederick Muller, 1943.) Second edition.

The Conquest of Siberia : YURI SEMYONOV. Translated from the German by F. W. DICKES. (Routledge, 1944.)

Soviet and Tsarist Siberia : GEORGE BORODIN. (Rich & Cowan, 1944.)

Secret Siberia: EMIL LENGYEL (Robert Hale, 1947.)

THE FAR EAST
General

North Eastern Asia: A Selected Bibliography: PROFESSOR R. J. KERNER. (University of California Press, 1939.) 2 vols.

The Far East : ALEXIS KRAUSSE. (Grant Richards, 1900.)

The Awakening of the East : PIERRE LE ROY-BEAULIEU. (Heinemann, 1900.)

The Reshaping of the Far East: B. L. PUTNAM WEALE. (The Macmillan Company, New York, 1905.) 2 vols.

The Eastern Question : A Study in Diplomacy : STEPHEN PIERCE HAYDEN DUGGAN, Ph.D. The Columbia Studies in History, Economics and Public Law, No. 39. (The Columbia University Press, New York, 1902.)

The Truce in the East and Its Aftermath : B. L. PUTNAM WEALE. (Macmillan and Co., 1907.)

Empires of the Far East : LANCELOT LAWTON. (Grant Richards, 1912.) 2 vols.

Europe and the Far East, 1506-1912 : SIR ROBERT K. DOUGLAS. (Cambridge University Press, 1913.)

Contemporary Politics in the Far East : STANLEY K. HORNBECK, Ph.D. (D. Appleton & Co., New York, 1916.)

The Mastery of the Far East : ARTHUR JUDSON BROWN. (Bell & Sons, 1919.)

The Conflict of Policies in Asia : THOMAS P. MILLARD. (The Century Co. New York and London, 1924.)

A History of the Orient : G. N. STEIGER, H. O. BEGER and C. BENITEZ. (Gunn & Co., Boston, 1926.)

Occidental Interpretations of the Far Eastern Problem : H. G. WOODHEAD, JULEAN ARNOLD, HENRY KITTREDGE NORTON. (University of Chicago Press, Chicago, 1926.)

America, Europe, and the Manchuria Question : THOMAS F. MILLARD, LL.D. (Geneva, 1932.)

Manchoukuo, Child of Conflict: KIYOSHI K. KAWAKAMI. (The Macmillan Company, New York, 1933.)

The Far East : PAYSON J. TREAT, Ph.D. (Harper Bros., 1935.)

The Twentieth Century in the Far East : PERCY HORACE BRAUND KENT. (Edward Arnold, 1937.)

A History of the Far East in Modern Times : HAROD M. VINACKE, Ph.D. (F. E. Crofts & Co., New York, 1942.) Fourth edition.

Asia Unbound ; A Pattern for Freedom in the Far East : SYDNEY GREENBIE. (Appleton-Century Co., Inc., New York, 1943.)

Pacific Charter : HALLETT ABEND. (The Bodley Head, 1943.)

Japan

Narrative of My Captivity in Japan During the Years 1811, 1812, 1813, With Observations on the Country and the People : CAPTAIN GOLOWNIN, I.R.N. (Henry Colburn, London, 1818.)

Recollections of Japan : CAPTAIN GOLOWNIN, I.R.N. (Henry Colburn, London, 1819.)

Japanese Trade with China, 1903. U.S. Consular Reports, 24 February, 1903. Nichi-Ro, Dispatch No. 38, 1904.

The Russo-Japanese Conflict: K. ASAKAWA, Ph.D. (Archibald Constable and Co., 1904.)

American-Japanese Relations : KIYOSHI K. KAWAKAMI. (Fleming H. Revel Co., London and Edinburgh, 1912.)

The Menace of Japan : FREDERICK McCORMICK. (Little, Brown & Co., Boston, 1917.)

Japan and World Peace: KIYOSHI K. KAWAKAMI. (The Macmillan Company, New York, 1919.)

Le Japon et la Paix Mondiale : KIYOSHI K. KAWAKAMI. (Librairie P. Roger et Cie., Paris, 1921.)

The Influence of the Sea on the Political History of Japan : VICE-ADMIRAL C. A. BALLARD, C.B. (John Murray, 1921.)

Japan Must Fight Britain : LIEUT.-COMMANDER TOTA ISHIMARU, I.J.N. Translated by INSTR.-CAPTAIN G. V. RAYMENT, C.B.E., R.N. (Hurst and Blackett, 1936.)

The Next World War : LIEUT.-COMMANDER TOTA ISHIMARU, I.J.N. Translated from the Japanese by P. MATSUKAWA. (Hurst & Blackett, 1937.)

"Tokyo's Inner Ramparts": J. L. FORSTER. *The Trident*, Vol. VII, No. 70.

Article on Japanese declaration against entry of U.S. oil to Manchuria through Dairen. *The Times*, 13 September, 1901.

Article on Japanese attack on Pearl Harbour. *Soviet War News*, 13 December, 1941.

China

Ma Mission en Chine, 1893-1897 : M. A. GÉRARD. (Plon Nourrit, Paris, 1918.)

Treaties and Agreements with and Concerning China, 1899-1919. Compiled and edited by JOHN V. A. MACMURRAY. (Oxford University Press, American Branch, New York, 1921.) 2 vols.

Railway Enterprise in China : PERCY HORACE KENT. (Edward Arnold, 1907.)

Recent Events and Present Policies in China : J. O. P. BLAND. (Heinemann, 1912.)

Foreign Financial Control in China: T. W. OVERLACH. (The Macmillan Company, New York, 1919.)

A Short History of China : DEMETRIUS CHARLES BOULGER. (Gibbing & Co., Ltd., London, 1900.)

China, Japan, and Korea : J. O. P. BLAND. (Heinemann, 1921.)

The Truth About China and Japan : W. B. PUTNAM WEALE. (G. Allen and Unwin, 1921.)

The Foreign Relations of China : MINGCHIEN J. BAU, Ph.D. (Nisbet & Co., 1922.)

The Open Door Doctrine in Relation to China : MINGCHIEN J. BAU, Ph.D. (The Macmillan Company, New York, 1923.)

China Today : Political : STANLEY K. HORNBECK. *World Peace Publication Pamphlets*, Vol. X, No. 5. (Boston, 1927.)

Foreign Rights and Interests in China : WESTEL W. WILLOUGHBY. (The Johns Hopkins Press, Baltimore, 1927.) 2 vols.

China's Foreign Relations, 1917-1931: ROBERT T. POLLARD, Ph.D. (The Macmillan Company, New York, 1933.)

Russia

Le Fleuve Amoûr: C. DE SABIR. (Georg Kugelman, Paris, 1861.)

The Russians on the Amur: E. G. RAVENSTEIN, F.R.G.S. (Routledge & Kegan Paul Ltd., 1861.)

Greater Russia : WIRTH GERRARE. (Heinemann, 1903.)

The Tragedy of Russia in Pacific Asia : FREDERICK McCORMICK. (Grant Richards, 1909.) 2 vols.

Russia in the Far East: LEO PASVOLSKY. (The Macmillan Company, New York, 1922.)

Russia and the Soviet Union in the Far East : VICTOR A. YAKHONTOFF. (Allen and Unwin, 1932.)

A History of the Far East : G. NYE STEIGER. (Ginn & Co., Boston, 1936.)

Russia, Japan and Mongolia : G. D. R. PHILLIPS. (Muller, 1942.)

The Soviet Far East and Central Asia : WILLIAM MANDEL. Institute of Pacific Relations Inquiry Series. (The Dial Press, Inc., New York, 1944.)

Soviet Sakhalin : VLADIMIR KANTOROVICH. (Co-operative Publishing Society of Foreign Workers in the U.S.S.R.)

Article on Vladivostock fortifications. *Parade,* November, 1938.

Article on Vladivostock. *Trud,* 22 March, 1941.

Article on Sakhalin concessions. *The Evening Standard,* 3 April, 1944.

Spotlight on the Far East : J. M. BERNSTEIN, with chapters by MARIE KEESING and HARRIET MOORE. (American Council, Institute of Pacific Relations, and Webster Publishing Co., St. Louis, Dallas, and Los Angeles, 1945.)

Soviet Far Eastern Policy, 1931-1945 : HARRIET LANE MOORE. Issued under the auspices of International Secretariat, Institute of Pacific Relations. (Princeton University Press, 1945.)

America

The United States in the Orient : CHARLES A. CONANT. (Houghton Mifflin Co., Boston and New York, 1900.)

American Relations in the Pacific and the Far East, 1784-1900 : JAMES MORTON CALLAHAN, Ph.D. *Johns Hopkins University Studies in Historical and Political Science,* XIX, Nos. 1-3. (The Johns Hopkins Press, Baltimore, 1901.)

America and the Far Eastern Question : THOMAS F. MILLARD. (Moffat, Yard and Co., New York, 1909.)

Our Eastern Question: THOMAS F. MILLARD. (Appleton-Century-Crofts, Inc., New York, 1916.)

America's Aims and Asia's Aspirations: PATRICK GALLAGHER. (Appleton-Century-Crofts, Inc., New York, 1920.)

Americans in Eastern Asia : TYLER DENNETT. (Macmillan, 1922.)

Roosevelt and the Russo-Japanese War : TYLER DENNETT. (Doubleday, Page and Co., New York, 1925.)

The Far Eastern Policy of the United States : A. WHITNEY GRISWOLD. (Harcourt, Brace & Co., New York, 1938.)

THE PACIFIC

На Востоке. Поездка на Амуре (в 1860-1861 годах): С. Максимов. С. Петербург, 1864.

Наши Задачи на Тихом Океане : А. Максимов. С. Петербург.

Russia on the Pacific: VLADIMIR (VOLPICELLI).(Sampson Low, Marston,1899.)

The Mastery of the Pacific : ARCHIBALD R. COLQUHOUN. (Heinemann, 1902.)

La Lutte pour le Pacifique : Origines et Résultats de la Guerre Russo-Japonaise : RENÉ PINON. (Perrin et Cie., Paris, 1906.)

Russian Expansion on the Pacific, 1641-1850 : F. A. GOLDER. (The Arthur Clark Co., Cleveland, 1914.)

Life of Captain Cook : HUGH CARRINGTON. (Sidgwick & Jackson, 1939.)

The Napoleon of the Pacific, Kamehameha the Great : HERBERT H. GLOVER, D.D. (Fleming H. Revell Co., New York, 1919.)

Congressional Records : *56th Congress, 1st Session.* Vol. 33, 1900. Speech by Senator Beveridge on the future role of America in the Pacific.

Problem of the Pacific in the Twentieth Century : GENERAL N. GOLOVIN, in collaboration with ADMIRAL A. D. BUBNOV. Translated by C. NABOKEFF. (Gyldenal, London, 1922.)

America in the Pacific : FOSTER RHEA DULLES. (Houghton Mifflin Co., Boston and New York, 1932.)

Problems of the Pacific. Proceedings of the Second and Third Conferences of the Institute of Pacific Relations, 1927, 1929. Edited by J. B. CONDLIFFE, M.A., D.Sc. (University of Chicago Press, Chicago, 1928, 1930.)

The Restless Pacific: NICHOLAS ROOSEVELT. (Charles Scribner, New York, 1928.)

Russian Expansion to America: Its Bibliographical Foundations : ROBERT J. KERNER : *Papers of the Bibliographical Society of America*, Vol. XXV, pp. 111-129. (University of Chicago Press, 1931.)

Sea-Power in the Pacific : HECTOR C. BYWATER. (Constable, 1934.)

The Struggle for the Pacific : GREGORY BIENSTOCK. (Allen & Unwin, 1937.)

Cook and the Pacific : JAMES A. WILLIAMSON. (Hodder & Stoughton, 1946.)

Pacific Horizons : *The Exploration of the Pacific Before Captain Cook* : CHRISTOPHER LLOYD. (Allen & Unwin, 1946.)

The Exploration of the Pacific : J. C. BEAGLEHOLE, M.A., Ph.D., (A. and C. Black, 1947.) 2nd edtn.

The Pacific Ocean : FELIX RIESENBERG. (Museum Press, 1947.)

The Background of Eastern Sea Power : F. B. ELDRIDGE, M.A. (Phoenix House, London. Georgian House, Melbourne, 1948.)

THE NORTH PACIFIC

The Worldes Hydrographical Discription : JOHN DAVIS. (London, 1595.) (Reprinted by the Hakluyt Society, 1880.)

Account of the Russian Discoveries Between Asia and America : WILLIAM COXE. (T. Cadell, London, 1780.)

Историческое обозрение образования Российско-Американской Компании и Действии Ее до Настоящего Времени: И. Тихменев. С. Петербург, 1861-63. (2 ч.)

Vitus Bering : The Discoverer of Bering Strait : PETER LAURIDSEN. (Griggs and Co., Chicago, 1889.)

Early Expeditions to the Region of Bering Sea and Strait: From the Reports and journals of VITUS IVANOVICH BERING. Translated by WM. HEALEY DALL. United States of America Coast and Geodetic Survey ; Appendix No. 19. Report for 1890. (Washington, 1891.)

Bering's Voyages : F. A. GOLDER. Translated by LEONHARD STEJNEGER. *American Geographical Society*, Vol. I, 1922 ; Vol. II, 1925.

Voyage of the "Senora": *The Second Bucarelli Expedition:* FRANCISCO ANTONIO MOURELLE. Translated by THE HON. DAINES BARRINGTON. (Thos. C. Russell, San Francisco, 1920.)

The Tracks and Landfalls of Bering and Chirikof on the North-West Coast of America, 1741 : GEORGE DAVIDSON, President of the Geographical Society of the Pacific. (Private publication, 1901.)

Открытия Камчатской Экспедиции Беринга: Л. С. Берг. Москва и Петроград, 1924.

Voyages from Asia to America, for Completing the Discoveries of the North-West Coast of America : THOMAS JEFFERYS. Translated from the Dutch by S. MULLER. (London, 1764.) Second edition.

A Voyage to the Pacific Ocean. Vol. I and II by CAPTAIN JAMES COOK, F.R.S.; Vol. III by CAPTAIN JAMES KING, LL.D., F.R.S. (Nichol & Cadell, London, 1784.)

Voyages Made in the Years 1788 and 1789 from China to the North-West Coast of America : JOHN MEARES. (J. Walter, London, 1790.)

A Voyage of Discovery into the South Sea and Beering's Straits, for the Purpose of Exploring a North-East Passage, Undertaken in the Years 1815-1818 at the Expense of His Highness the Chancellor of the Empire, Count Romanzoff, in the Ship "Rurick," Under the Command of the Lieutenant in the Russian Imperial Navy OTTO VON KOTZEBUE: L. C. A. CHAMISSO DE BONCOURT. (Longmans, Hurst, Rees, Orme, and Brown, 1821.) 3 vols.

Entdeckungs-Reise in die Süd-See und nach der Berings-Strasse . . . in den Jahren 1815, 1816, 1817, und 1818 : OTTO VON KOTZEBUE. (Hoffmann, Weimar, 1821.) 3 pts.

Travels and Adventures of John Ledyard : JARED SPARKS. (Henry Colburn, 1834.)

Early Northern Pacific Voyages : PETER CORNEY. (T. G. Thrum, Honolulu, 1896.)

Лоция Северо-Западной части Восточного Океана: Е. Максимов. (Издание Главного Гидрографического Управления Морского Министерства). С. Петербург, 1912. Русские открытия в Тихом Океане и Северной Америке в xviii-xix веках. (Edited by A. I. ANDREEV.) Academy of Sciences, Moscow and Leningrad, 1944.

The Hawaiian Islands : Early Relations with the Pacific North-West : JUDGE F. W. HOWRY, F.R.S.C. Edited by A. P. TAYLOR and R. S. KUYKENDALL. (Archives of the Hawaii Commission, No. 5, 1930.)

The New Pacific : HUBERT HOWE BANCROFT. (The Bancroft Co., New York, 1900.)

Lines on Russian claims in North Pacific. Niles's Register, 10 May, 1823.

ALASKA AND THE NORTH-WEST COAST OF NORTH AMERICA

History of the Pacific States of America: HUBERT HOWE BANCROFT. (A. L. Bancroft & Co., San Francisco, 1882-90.) 34 vols.

Francis Drake on the North-West Coast of America in the Year 1579 : GEORGE DAVIDSON. (Transactions and Proceedings of the Geographical Society of the Pacific, 1908.)

Voyage Pittoresque : LUDOVIC CHORIS. (Paris, 1822.)

North-West Coast of North America : ROBERT GREENHOW. (Wiley & Putnam, New York, 1840.)

Замечания о Камчатке и Русской Америке в 1809, 1810 и 1811 годах: В. М. Головнин.(С. Петербург, 1848.)

Die Russisch-Amerikanische Handels Kompanie, bis 1825 : HANS PILDER, Ph.D. (G. J. Göschen'sche Verlagshandlung, G.m.b.H., Berlin und Leipzig, 1914.)

Memorial of Percy McDonough Collins, Upon the Subject of an Intercontinental Telegraph, Connecting the Eastern and Western Hemispheres, by Way of Behring's Strait. (Government Printing Office, Washington, 1864.)

Congressional Globe : 40th Congress, 2nd Session. Part 5, Appendix 377-403. From House debate of 1 July, 1868, on purchase of Alaska.

Guide-Book to Alaska and the North-West Coast : E. R. SCIDMORE. (Appleton and Co., New York, 1889.)

Harriman Alaska Expedition : JOHN BURROUGHS, JOHN MUIR, GEORGE B. GRINNELL. (Doubleday & Page, Ltd., London, 1901.)

The American Fur Trade of the Far West : HIRAM MARTIN CHITTENDEN. (New York, 1902.) 3 vols.

History of the Pacific North-West : JOSEPH SCHAFER. (Macmillan, 1905.)

Inside Passage to Alaska : 1792-1920 : WILLIAM W. WOOLEN. Edited, PAUL L. HAWORTH. (Arthur H. Clark Co., Cleveland, 1924.) 2 vols.

History of Alaska Under Rule of United States : JEANNETTE PADDOCK NICHOLS. (Arthur H. Clark Company, Cleveland, 1924.)

The Story of Alaska: C. L. ANDREWS. (Lowman & Hanford Co., Seattle, 1931.)

Fur Trade and Empire: Sir George Simpson's Journal, 1824-25: Edited by FREDERICK MERK. Harvard Historical Studies, Vol. XXXI. (Harvard University Press, 1931.)

Lost Empire: HECTOR CHEVIGNY. (The Macmillan Company, New York, 1937.)

The Annexation of Russian America to the United States : VICTOR J. FARRAR. (W. F. Roberts, Inc., Washington, D.C., 1937.)

Российско-Американская Компания : С. В. Окун. Moscow, 1939.

The Californian Sea Otter Trade, 1784-1848 : ADELE OGDEN. (University of California Press, 1941.)

Alaskan Back Door to Japan : PHILIP PANETH. (Alliance Press, 1943.)

Here is Alaska: EVELYN STEFANSSON. (Charles Scribner's Sons, New York, 1943.)

From Wilderness to Empire : ROBERT GLASS CLELAND. (Knopf, New York, 1944.)

The Letters of John McLoughlin from Vancouver to the Governor and Committee. Edited by E. E. RICH, M.A. (Vols. IV, VI, VII, of the Hudson's Bay Record Society, published for the latter by the Champlain Society 1941-44.)

Report of a Russian base on north-west American mainland during World War II. *Post Intelligence,* 30 September, 1944.

Report of a Russian base on north-west American mainland during World War II. *News Chronicle,* 2 October, 1944.

INLAND WATERWAYS

Ukraine and Its People : HUGH P. VOWLES. (W. R. Chambers, 1939.)

U.S.S.R. in Construction, 1930-1939, Vol. II. (The State Publishing House of Graphic Arts, Moscow.)

The Unified Transport System of the U.S.S.R.: K. N. TVERSKOI. The New Soviet Library, X. (Gollancz, 1935.)

The Urge to the Sea: The Course of Russian History. ROBERT J. KERNER. (University of California Press, Berkeley, Los Angeles, 1942.)

Waterways and Water Transport: A. BLIDMAN. "The Moscow-Volga Canal": A. KOMAROVSKY. Published in *Agriculture and Transport.* *U.S.S.R. Speaks for Itself.* Vol. II. (Lawrence & Wishart, 1942.) Reprinted.

Речной Транспорт. Москва.

Soviet Transport: PROFESSOR VLADIMIR OBRASTSOV. With chapter on Inland Water Transport by GEORGI KUBLITSKY. *Soviet News,* 1946.

The Mighty Volga : FRANK MOSS. *Ice-breakers and the U.S.S.R. :* ARTHUR TURNER. Published in *The Trident,* Vol. IV, No. 37, November, 1941.

Summary of an article by PROFESSOR OBRASTSOV in "Transactions of the Academy of Sciences of the U.S.S.R." Technical Sciences No. 9, 1943; GEORGE HANNA. *Soviet War News.*

"Will the Danube again be a Free International Highway?": R. H. C. STEED. *The Daily Telegraph,* 28 July, 1948.

MAPS, and ESSAYS IN CARTOGRAPHY

Imago Mundi: A Periodical Review of Early Cartography: Edtd. by LEO BAGROW and EDWARD LYNAM. Henry Stevens, Son, and Stiles, London. (Pt. I. pubd. Bibliographikon, Berlin; Pts. II, III, pubd. Henry Stevens, Son, and Stiles, London, 1937-1939. Pt. IV. pubd. Kartografiska Sällskapet, Stockholm.)

Orbis Imago: Mappemunde de Gérard Mercator de 1521. (Annales de cercle archéolog. du pays de Waas. Saint-Nicholas, 1886.)

The book of the Ser Marco Polo, the Venetian, concerning the Kingdom and marvels of the East. (Charles Scribner's Sons, 1926.) 2 vols.

Origin of the Strait of Anian Concept: GEORGE E. NUNN. (Privately printed, Philadelphia, 1929. Copyright George H. Beans, 1929.)

Map of the World by Waldsemüller made in 1587, the first in which the name "America" was used to designate the Western Hemisphere. (Monthly Bulletin, International Bureau of the American Reports, Washington, 1904, pp. 625-31.)

An Early Sixteenth-Century Map of the World. (Geog. Jnl., Vol. XXXVI, pp. 199-201. London, 1908.)

Ortelius World Map of 1587. (Reproduced in "The Early Cartography of the Pacific" by LAWRENCE C. WROTH. Published in *The Papers of the Bibliographical Society of America,* Vol. XXXVIII, pp. 87-268. New York, 1944.)

The Manuscript Atlases of Battista Agnese: HENRY R. WAGNER (*Papers of the Bibliographical Society of America,* Vol. XXV. University of Chicago Press, 1931.)

Die ältesten Karten von Russland, ein Beitrag zur historischen Geographie: H. MICHOW u. ANTON WIED. (Hamburg, 1884.)

Nachricht über einige ältere Karten von Russland: F. ADELUNG. (St. Petersburg, 1818.)

The Discovery of North America; a critical, documentary, and historic investigation, with an essay on the Early Cartography of the North West, including Descriptions of Two Hundred and Fifty Maps or Globes existing or lost, constructed the year 1536: H. HARRISSE. (London, 1891; Paris, 1892.)

Les Corte-Real et leurs voyages au Nouveau-Monde: H. HARRISSE. (Mem. Academ. des inscrip., Vol. XII. Paris, 1883.)

Marinus of Tyre's Place in the Columban Concepts: GEORGE E. NUNN. (*Imago Mundi,* Vol. II, p. 27.)

Un Atlas inconnu de la dernière expédition de Drake. (Bul. Géog. hist. et descriptive, Vol. XXIV, No. 3, pp. 396-404. Paris, 1909.)

The Silver Medal, or Map of Sir Francis Drake. (Numismatic Chron., SER. A, Vol. VI., London 1906.)

О Географических Сведениях в древней Руси: И. Д. Беляев. *(Запис.
Р. Геогр.,* том VI, стр. 1-264. Стпбг. 1852).

Географическия Карты России XV-XIX столетий: Н. Бокачев.

Подлинная Карта Сибири XVII в.: А. Григорьев. *(Жур. Мин. Народ.,
Проев,* окт. 1907).

Sparwenfeld's Map of Siberia: LEO BAGROW. Describing Sparwenfeld's copy
of the 1672 Russian Map of Siberia. Copy (made in 1689) preserved
in "Renats Kartas", Univ. Bibl. Uppsala. Published in *Imago Mundi,*
IV (facing p. 66), with L. Bagrow's paper. (Kartografiska Sällskapet,
Stockholm.)

Original-Karte Sibiriens aus dem 17. Jahrhundert: H. MICHOW und ANTON
WIED. (Geogr. Gesellschaft in Hamburg, Bd. XXII.)

Zur Geschichte der Bekanntschaft mit Sibirien vor Jermak: H. MICHOW und
ANTON WIED. (Mitteil. d. Anthropologischen Gesellschaft; Bd. XL.,
Wien, 1910.)

Древнейшия Карты Сибири: А. Миддендорф. (Изд. 1860).

Географический Атлас 1722-1730 года, хранящийся в библиотеке Иркутской
Духовной Семинарии, 1872.

Les cartes de la Sibérie au XVIII-s Siècle: GASTON CAHEN. *(Nouv. Archives des
Missions Scientifiques;* fasc., 1, Nouv. Série, Paris, 1911.)

*Nouvelle Carte des Découvertes faites par des Vaisseaux Russes aux Côtes inconnues
de l'Amérique Septentrionale . . . Dressée sur des Mémoires authentiques de
ceux qui ont assisté à ces Découvertes, et sur d'autres Connaissances, dont on
rend raison dans un Mémoire séparé A St. Petersbourg à l'Académie Impériale
des Sciences, 1754:* GERHARD FRIEDRICH MÜLLER. (Reproduced in
Voyages from Asia to America, by THOMAS JEFFERYS, London, 1761.)

*Nachricht von Land und Seekarten, die das Russische Reich und die zunächst angrän-
senden Länder-betreffen:* GERHARD FRIEDRICH MÜLLER. *(Sammlung Russ
Geschichte,* Vol. VI, pp. 1-108, St. Petersburg, 1761.)

*Прибрежья Ледовитого и Белого Морей с их Притоками по Книге Большого
Чертежа.* Санктп. 1877.

The Cartography and Observations of Bering's First Voyage: A. W. GREELY.
(National Geog. Magazine, Vol. III, pp. 205-230, Washington.)

*Notes on an Original Manuscript Chart of Bering's Expedition of 1725-1730, and
on an Original Chart of his Second Expedition, together with a Summary of
a Journal of the First Expedition kept by Peter Chaplin, and now first rendered
into English from Berg's Russian Version:* W. H. DALL. *(Rep. U.S. Coast
and Geodetic Survey, 1890;* No. 2, pp. 759-74.)

*Chart showing the Tracks of the Ships employed in Captain Cook's Last Voyage to
the Pacific Ocean, in the Years 1776, 1777, 1778, 1779:* JOHN LEDYARD.
(Pubd. in *A Journal of Captain Cook's Last Voyage to the Pacific Ocean.*
Hartford, 1783.)

*Carte des Nouvelles Découvertes au Nord de la Mer du Sud . . . Dressée sur les
Mémoires de Mr. De l'Isle . . . par 1750 . . . avec les Cartes de Guillaume
Delisle et de Philippe Buache:* JOSEPH NICOLAS DELISLE and PHILIPPE
BUACHE. (Paris, 1752.)

*A Chart of the Southern Hemisphere, shewing the tracks of some of the most distin-
guished Navigators:* CAPTAIN JAMES A. COOK. (Pubd. in *James Cook.
A Voyage towards the South Pole and Round the World . . . 1772, 1773,
1774 and 1775.* Wm. Strahan; Thos. Cadell, London, 1777.)

История Географической Карты: Л. С. Багров. Вестник Археологии и
Истории Издаваемый Петроградским Археологическим Институтом.,
Выпуск XXIII, Петр. 1918.

Краткий Исторический Очерк Нашего Гидрографическаго Знакомства ι Водами и побережьями Севернаго Тихаго Океана: С. А. Баргин. «Газета Владивосток», ч. 11, 12, 13, 14, 16, 17, 18, 19, 20; 1889).

Берег Чернаго Моря между Днепром и Днестром, по Морским Картам XIV-го и XV-го столетия: Ф. Врун. (Одесса, 1879).

Перипл. Каспийскаго Моря по Картам XIV в.: Ф. Врун.
  1. Запиь Нов. Унив., том VIII.
  2. Черноморье, том II. *(Записки Одесск. Общ. Истории.* Одесса, 1888).

Иностранные Карты и Атласы XVI и XVII в.в. относящиеся к южной России. (Киев, 1898).

Пояснительная Записка к Карте Аральскаго Моря и Хивинскаго Ханства с их Окрестностями: Я. В. Ханыков. *Записки И. Р. Геогр. Общ.* кн. 5 ; 1851).

The Early Cartography of Japan: G. Collingridge. *(Geog. Jnl.* Vol. III, pp. 403-09. London. 1894.)

The Evolution of Cartography in Japan: M. Ranning. *(Imago Mundi,* II, pp. 17-21.)

The Cambridge Modern History Atlas, Edtd. by A. W. Ward, Litt.D., G. W. Prothero, Litt.D., S. Leathes, M.A. (The Cambridge University Press, 1924.)

An Atlas of the U.S.S.R. : Jasper H. Stembridge. *Oxford Pamphlets on World Affairs No. 61.* (Oxford University Press, 1942.)

Map into Globe : Professor E. G. R. Taylor. *World Review,* January, 1944.

The Oxford War Atlas, Vols. I-III : Jasper H. Stembridge. (Oxford University Press, 1941-1944.

Soviet Russia in Maps. (George Philip & Son, Ltd., 1943.)

Serial Maps. (Serial Map Service, Ltd., Letchworth.) 1939-1948.

SUPPLEMENTARY SECTION

References have been made in this section to the following :—

Annuals

The World's Warships, 1948. Edited by Francis E. McMurtrie, A.I.N.A. (Sampson Low, 1948.)

All the World's Fighting Fleets, 1948. Edited by Pay-Lieut. E. C. Talbot-Booth, R.N.R. (Sampson Low, 1948.)

Brassey's Naval Annual, 1947-1948. Edited by Rear-Admiral H. G. Thursfield. (William Clowes & Sons, Ltd., 1948.)

Jane's Fighting Ships, 1947-1948. Edited by Francis E. McMurtrie, A.I.N.A. (Sampson Low, 1948.)

Miscellaneous

Encyclopædia Britannica, Vol. XIX, 14th edition.

Seaborne Trade : C. Ernest Fayle. History of the Great War based on Official Documents by direction of the Historical Section of the Committee of Imperial Defence. Vol. II. (John Murray, 1920.)

Foreign Trade in the U.S.S.R. : J. D. Yanson. (Gollancz, 1934.)

U.S.S.R. Handbook. (Gollancz, 1936.)

Soviet Export : M. ZHIRMUNSKI. (Mezhdunarodnaya Kniga, 1936.)
The Next World War : LIEUT-COMMANDER TOTA ISHIMARU. Translated by
  B. MATSUKAWA. (Hurst & Blackett, 1937.)
Uneasy Oceans : COMMANDER KENNETH EDWARDS, R.N. (Routledge, 1939.)
The Oxford War Atlas, 1943 : JASPER H. STEMBRIDGE. (Oxford University
  Press, 1943.)
The U.S.S.R. : An Economic and Social Survey : S. P. TURIN. (Methuen, 1944.)
Landsmen and Seafarers : MAURICE LOVELL. (Harrap, 1945.)
Merchantmen at War. Prepared for the Ministry of War Transport by the
  Ministry of Information. (H.M. Stationery Office, 1945.)
International Sea Transport : BRIG.-GEN. SIR OSBORNE MANCE, K.B.E., C.B.,
  C.M.G., D.S.O., assisted by J. E. WHEELER. Issued under the auspices
  of the Royal Institute of International Affairs. (Oxford University
  Press, 1945.
Ports of the World. Edited by SIR ARCHIBALD HURD, A.I.N.A. (The Shipping
  World, Ltd., 1947.) Second edition.

Publications on Russo-German War, 1941-45

M. Molotov's speech on creation of strong navy in U.S.S.R. *Moscow News*,
  5 February, 1938.
Naval Battles in the Baltic: CAPTAIN E. MATVEYEV. Published in *Strategy
  and Tactics of the Soviet-German War*. (Hutchinson, 1942.)
Russia's Fighting Forces : CAPTAIN SERGEI N. KOURNAKOFF. (International
  Publishers, New York, 1942.)
We Made a Mistake : LUCIEN ZACHAROFF. (The Bodley Head, 1942.)
"Breaking the Blockade": ILYA EHRENBURG. Published in *The Defence of
  Leningrad*. (Hutchinson, 1943.)
"Leningrad Calendar, 1942": NIKOLAI TIKHONOV. Published in *The
  Defence of Leningrad*. (Hutchinson, 1943.)
"City of Courage": ILYA EHRENBURG. Published in *Sevastopol, November,
  1941-July, 1942*. (Hutchinson, 1943.)
"In the Old Fort": LEONID SOBOLEV. Published in *Sevastopol, November,
  1941-July, 1942*. (Hutchinson, 1943.)
The Last Days of Sevastopol : BORIS VOYETEKHOV. (Cassell, 1943.)
Voyenno-Morskoy Flot, U.S.S.R. v Otechestvennoy Voyeene : N. TOKAREV.
  (State Publications, Political Literature, Moscow, 1943.)
The Soul of the Sea : LEONID SOBOLEV. (Hutchinson, 1945.)
The Red Fleet in the Second World War : ADMIRAL I. S. ISAKOV. Translated by
  JACK HURAL. (Hutchinson, 1946.)

Periodicals, Newspapers and Press Agency Reports

German Admiralty statement on Russian submarine building: NAVAL
  CORRESPONDENT, *The Daily Telegraph*, 16 March, 1936.
Report of Admiral Isakov's return from America. *The Daily Telegraph*,
  4 July, 1939.
Work of Russian submarines in the Baltic. *The Daily Telegraph*, 24 June,
  1942, 11 May, 1943.
Translation of article in *Pravda* on rate of shipbuilding in U.S.S.R. *News
  Bulletin*, 29 September, 1939. (Press Dept., Anglo-Russian Parlia-
  mentary Committee.)

"Soviet Naval Ambitions": SHIPBUILDING CORRESPONDENT, *The Glasgow Herald*, 31 October, 1939.

Views on condition of Soviet navy. *The Evening News*, 5 December, 1939. *The Evening Standard*, 11 March, 1940.

"Notes on the Northern Sea Route". PROFESSOR KENNETH MASON. Published in *The Geographical Journal*, July, 1940. (The Royal Geographical Society, 1940.)

Value of Russian Baltic Fleet. LORD STRABOLGI. *The Star*, 26 July, 1941.

Account of Russian submarines in Arctic. *The News Chronicle*, 3 March, 1942.

Sea-Air Power: AIR CORRESPONDENT, *The Observer*, 18 October, 1942.

Notes on M.O. Speedboats: CAPTAIN V. SILAYEV, *Soviet War News*, 1 June 1943.

Account of tonnage sunk by Russian submarines in the Baltic: D. SPRINGHALL. *Russia Today*, July, 1943.

"The Red Navy at War": REAR-ADMIRAL A. FROLOV. *Lloyd's List and Shipping Gazette*, 26 June, 1944.

"Arctic Coal": ALEXANDER KARPOV. *Soviet War News*, 13 July, 1944.

"Account of Baltic destroyers": *Foreign Notes. The Navy*, September, 1941. (The Navy League.)

"Defence of the Soviet Arctic": ADMIRAL A. GOLOVKO. *The Navy*, February, 1945.

"Report on Northern Convoys": NAVAL CORRESPONDENT, *The Daily Telegraph*, 17 February, 1945.

Article on supplies to Russia: CAPTAIN RUSSELL GRENFELL, R.N. *The Navy*, June, 1945.

Russian warships at Londonderry. Press Association report, 16 June, 1945.

"Naval Flags of the Allies" (2), U.S.S.R.: H. G. CARR, M.S.N.R. *The Sea Cadet*, March, 1946. (The Navy League.)

"Landing Operations": CAPTAIN KRYLOV. *The Navy*, November, 1942.

"The Strategy of Anzio: Pinning Down an Army": MAJOR HAMISH WILSON, *Serial Maps*, Vol. V, No. 7. (Serial Map Service, Letchworth.)

Notes on the Caspian Shipping Agency. *Bank for Russian Trade Review, Ltd.*, Vol. II, No. 6 (London.)

Articles on the Soviet Maritime Code. *Monthly Review*, Vol. IV, No. 2; Vol. IX, Nos. 5, 10. (Moscow Narodny Bank, Ltd.)

Notes on Mariupol. *Monthly Review*, Vol. V, No. 12. (Moscow Narodny Bank, Ltd.)

Notes on Marine Insurance. *Monthly Review*, Vol. V, Nos. 8, 9. (Moscow Narodny Bank, Ltd.)

INDEX

(For Russian Fleets in World War II, Areas of Sea Warfare (1941-1949), Inland Waterways, Mercantile Marine, Northern Convoys, Principal Ports, Submarines, *see also* Index to Supplementary Section.)
The letter ' **n** ' refers to Footnote.

Centurione, Paulo, Genoese merchant prince, 76
Cetatea Alba, 148
Chamberlain, Rt. Hon. Joseph, 173
Chancellor, Richard, 59, 60, 92, 93, 95
"Chancery of the Military Marine" (Peter I's), 73
Changchun, 181
Chang-ku-feng, 188
Channel, the English, 4, 67
Chany, Lake, 358
Chapaev, Russian cruiser, 334
Charjow, 357
Charlemagne-class battleship (1897), 320
Charles I, Hydrographer Royal to, 272
Charles II of England, 110
Charles IX of Sweden, 65; Charles XI, 72; Charles XII, 13, 67, 71, 72, 116, 315
Chater, Arthur G., 257 n.
Chatham raided by Vikings, 45
Chefoo, 253
Cheliuskin, Cape, see Capes; Semeon Ivanovitch, 12, 101
Cheliuskin, icebreaker type, 258
Cheliuskin, voyage of, 108, 112, 259, 266, 267, 278
Chelsea, British destroyer, 332
Chemulpo, 180, 321
Chéradame, André, 136 n.
Cheremkovo, 198, 362
"Cherevichny Triangle, The", 268 n., 273, 273 n.
Chernaiev, 171
Chevigny, Hector, 223
Chhongjin, 191
Chiaturi, 145
Chicago, 37
"Chichagof" Island, 220
Chichagov, Captain, 109
Chicherin, George V., 137, 138, 325
Chichoff, brig of Russian-American Fur Company, 241
Chile, 280; trade with, 229
Chin-Kiang, 182
China (see also Cathay), 54, 55, 73, 83, 110, 166, 171, 173, 183, 184, 187, 189, 190, 198, 201, 219, 228, 230, 230 n., 236, 250, 253, 265;

Eastern Railway, 174, 176, 181–183, 183 n., 186, 191, 194, 202, 254, 342; Maritime Customs, 177; Nationalist Army, 182; Navy, see Navies; "Open Door" policy, 172, 173, 204, 250–254; opposes Russia on the Amur, 165, 166; ports, 22, 87, 171, 172, 178, 182, 219, 224, 252; Republic, early years of, 182, 252; tea trade, 22, 230, 251, 252
China, North, 182, 252; South, 186, 197, 231, 238
China Concessions, British, 174, 176, 182, 192, 251; French, 251; German, 251
China Sea, 230, 251; East, 182; South, 29
China trade, with America, 21, 22, 224, 229, 230, 251–253, 255; with England, 173, 177, 222, 231; with Japan, 185: with the Netherlands, 230, 231; with Portugal, 230; with Russia, 22, 229, 231, 253; with Russian colonists in America, 224; with Spain, 230; with Spanish colonists of California, 215
Chinchow, 174
Chirikov, Lieut., 55, 83, 210, 212, 214, 218
Chirikov, Russian coastal survey ship, 84, 227
Chishima-Kaikyo Strait, 202
Chita, 175, 193
Chkalov, Russian cruiser, 333
Choris, Ludovic, 21, 27
Christendom, 38
Christmas Island, 20
Chukchi Cape, see Capes; Peninsula, 31 n.
Chukchis, 21, 31 n., 80, 86, 196
Chukot Peninsula, 79, 103, 107, 198, 200
Chukotsk, 29, 267
Chukotski Noss, 84, 86
Churchill, Awnsham, 98 n.; John, 98 n.: Rt. Hon. Winston, 4, 134, 134 n., 135, 141, 366
Churchill, British destroyer, 332
Chusovaya, the, 358, 362
Cielens, Felix, 297
Cipangu (see also Japan), 84, 184

INDEX

Early Maps of N. E. Asia and of the lands around the North Pacific: controversy between G. F. Müller and N. Delisle, 82 **n.**, 232
East Cape (*see also* Cape East), 32, 79, 84
East India Company, 54 **n.**, 184, 222, 229, 230
East Indies, the Netherlands, 28
Easter Island, 20 **n.**
Eastern Question, The, 124 **n.**
Eclipse, American seal-hunting vessel, 224
Eclipse of Russia, The, 178 **n.**
Economic Development of the Far East, The, 200 **n.**
Edmonton, Canada, 209
Edward Bonaventure, Richard Chancellor's ship, 92, 93
Edward VI, King, 76, 94
Egypt, 115, 126; British campaign in World War II, 367; Khedive (Mehemet Ali), 129; supply routes to Russia, 329
Eira, British Arctic exploration ship, 106
Elbe, the, 45, 290, 332
Elbing, 30, 292, 335
Eldridge, F. B., 214 **n.**
Eliot, George Fielding, 33
Elizabeth, Queen, 14, 60, 69, 93, 230 **n.**, 311, 315
Ellesmere Island, 287
Ellsworth, Lincoln, 272
Elphinstone, Admiral, 114, 317
Emden, German light cruiser, 162
Empire Grec au dixième siècle, L', 47 **n.**
Empires of the Far East, 175 **n.**
Empress of China, U.S. cargo vessel (1784), 252
Encounter, English warship (1855), 238
Endeavour, 102; boat used in Parry's Polar expedition, 271
England (*see also* Britain), 3, 5, 59, 63, 92, 125, 126, 128, 159, 237, 298; maritime history of, 10; merchants from, in Muscovy, 14, 53, 54, 58–60, 92, 93, 96, 314; nautical instruments from, 19; war with American colonies, 114

England in the Mediterranean, 1603–1713, 15 **n.**
English Channel, the, 113, 180
English sea sense, 79, 80; seamen, *see* Seamen
"Englishman's Streight", the, 211
Enterprise, of McClure's expedition, 111; boat used in Parry's Arctic expedition, 271
Equator, first Russian crossing of, 19
Erik, son of Harald the Fair, 94 **n.**
Eritrea, 118
Eskimos, 17, 31 **n.**, 112
Essen, Admiral von, 323
Esthonia, 40, 59, 67, 144, 291, 291 **n.**, 297, 298, 300; incorporation in U.S.S.R., 294, 299, 300; Pact with U.S.S.R. (1939), 294, 295; Treaty with U.S.S.R. (1920), 295
Esutoru, 205
Ethiopia, Russian aims in, 116
Eudoki, in which Novodchik is said to have discovered Aleutian Islands, 212
Euphrates, the, 159
Europe, 6, 34, 46, 54, 103, 110, 126, 153, 178, 252, 269, 281, 282, 286, 289, 342; Eastern, 282, 297, 368; Great Plain of, 12, 30, 52; Western, 58, 257, 297
Europe devant Constantinople, L', 137 **n.**
Euxine Sea, 145
Evers, boats on Turkish model, built by Peter I, 66
Expansion of Russia, 1815–1900, The, 128 **n.**, 171 **n.**, 318 **n.**
Expedition, Russian ship reached Ob delta (1734), 101
Expedition to the North Pole (by I. Papanin), 269 **n.**
Express, Swedish sloop, 103
Extraordinary State Commission for Ascertaining and Investigating Crimes of the German Fascist Invaders, 349 **n.**

Fairbanks airport, 32, 209, 247
Famous Voyage of Sir Francis Drake, The, 211
Famous Voyages and Navigations of the English, The, see Voyages
Far East, The, 173 **n.**

expedition, 55, 80–82; relations
with Persia, *see* Persia; scheme for
a Volga-Don Canal, 145, 351;
shipbuilding, 61–64, 81, 315, 316;
wars with Persia, *see* Persia; wars
with Sweden, *see* Sweden
Peter the Great (life by Georges
Oudard), 91, 311 n.; (poem by
Lomonosov), 72; (novel by Alexei
Tolstoi), 60, 61, 62 n., 64; Russian
ironclad, 319
Peter the Great Bay, 170
Peter I Land, 21
Peter Martire, map of, 76, 83
Petrograd, 292, 301, 302, 324;
Soviet, 149, 297
Petrograd, vessel of Russian Volun-
teer Fleet, 341
Petropavlovsk, 28, 41 n., 86, 171,
195, 201, 202, 226, 238, 314, 333
Petropavlovsk, Russian battleship,
297; Russian cruiser (*see also*
Luetzow), 297, 333
Petsamo, 286, 304, 311; ceded to
Russia (1940), 304; German
occupation in World War II, 304;
Oblast, 283, 305
Philip II, King of Spain, 59
Philippine Islands, 40, 84, 228, 230,
247, 251, 252
Phillips, G. D. R., 362 n.
Phillipson, Coleman, 128 n., 131 n.
Philosophy of History, 43
Phipps, Captain J. C., 106
Phoenix, Boston trading ship (early
19th century), 224; members of
McClure's expedition return in,
111; Russian-American Fur Com-
pany's vessel, 223
Photus, Patriarch, 46
Pilder, Dr. Hans, 222 n.
Pillars of Hercules, 94
Pillau, 293
Pilot, Russian icebreaker, 278
Pinckney, Thomas, American Am-
bassador, 287
Pinon, René, 191 n.
Pinto, Fernao Mendes, 184, 184 n.
Pitt, William, 130, 316
Platonov, Professor, 95
Pleshtcheyevo, Lake, 61, 311
Plowing the Arctic, 112

Plymouth, Russian mines sent to,
338; school-sailing ship visits, 309
Podolia, 144
Pohai, Gulf of, 195
Point Speedwell, 100
Pola, 119
Poland, 13, 40, 59, 135, 144, 285,
293, 294, 353; frontier with Ger-
many after World War II, 291;
frontier with Russia, 294; parti-
tions of, 30; people of, 13, 30, 292;
rising (1863), 245; Sigismund II,
King, 14
Polar air routes, 7, 31, 35–37; Basin,
267, 270; Circle, South, *see* South
Polar Circle; Congress, Inter-
national (1879), 263; "Drift",
267, 273; Ice-Cap, 258, 270, 287
Polar Regions in the Twentieth Century,
101 n.
Polar Sea, 37, 88, 269; Eastern,
29
Pole, North, *see* North Pole
"Pole of Inaccessibility", 273
Poletica, P. de, 241, 287 n.
Poliarnoye, submarine base, 311;
used by Germans during Russo-
German Pact, 109, 304
Politovsky, Eugen S., 33 n.
Poltava-class battleship (1897), 320
Polypheme, Russian survey ship, 110
Pomerania, fortification of coast,
292
Ponape, 40
Pontanus, geographer, 73
Poole, Captain Jonas, 98
Popov, Rear-Admiral (1860), 246;
Russian agent, visits Chukchi
Peninsula (1711), 31 n., 80
Popov Island, 308
Poros Harbour, 142
Porphyrogenitus, Emperor Con-
stantine, 47, 123
Port Arthur, 7, 28, 29, 31, 33, 118,
171, 174–176, 179, 182, 189–192,
202, 321, 322, 329, 330, 342; fall
of (1905), 180, 322; leased to
Russia (1898), 27, 172–176, 178;
transferred to Japan, 181, 181 n.,
202; Treaty with China (1945),
gives Russia use of naval base, 7,
29, 118, 182, 314, 330

Seaports—*continued*
160, 162, 167, 175, 193–195, 200, 204, 206, 245, 252, 255, 258, 259, 266, 274, 278, 305, 306, 309, 314, 318, 340, 342, 343, 361; South American, 227
Searchthrift, English pinnace, Stephen Burrough's voyage in, 93
Seattle, 34, 280
Secret Siberia, 42 n., 359 n.
"Sector Theory, The", 35
Sedov, Georgi, 106
Sedov, Russian icebreaker, 106, 269, 271–273, 275, 279
Seeburg, 45
Seegerd, C. L., 172 n.
Seehund-type submarines, 355
Segal, Dr. Louis, 13
Seishin, 192
Selection of Curious, Rare, and Early Voyages, and Histories of Interesting Discoveries, Chiefly Published by Hakluyt, A, 110 n.
Selenga, the, 87, 362; steamship line, 362
Selifontov, Russian Arctic explorer, 101
Selim II, 145
Semes, Rock of, 75
Semipalatinsk, 193
Senyavin, Russian sloop commanded by Feodor Litke, 231
Seoul, Convention of, 189,
Serajevo, murder of Austrian Archduke at, 133
Serbia, 119, 133; Serbs, 133
Serebrennikov, Siberian merchant, 87
Sergei Kirov, Russian icebreaker, 278
Sergeyev, M. A., 18, 18 n., 19 n., 223 n., 228 n., 229 n., 231 n., 284 n., 317, 317 n.
Sergius Kamenev Islands, 275
Serial Maps, 143 n., 167 n.
Sevastopol, 124, 129, 130, 130 n., 131, 132, 134, 143, 150, 353; rebuilt after Crimean War, 318; siege of (1942), 130
Sevastopol, Russian battleship, 297, 331

Seven Years' War, the, 30, 281
Severnaya Zemlya (*see also* Rudolf Land), 106, 275
Seville, 265
Seward, William Henry, U.S. Secretary of State, 41, 246
Seward Harbour, 209; Peninsula, 32
Seya, the, 15
Shadrin, Andreya, 66
Shangch'wan Island, 230
Shanghai, 174, 186, 203, 252
Shannon, English whaling ship, at Spitzbergen, 106
Shantung, 187, 197; Province, 173, 187
Shavan, Lake, 307
Shavansk Dam, facing p. 360
Shave, D. W., 52, 353 n., 360 n.
Sheksna, the, 306
Shelikov, Gregor, 87, 213, 213 n., 222, 226; Natalie, 213
Shell-fire, first use of, 129, 319
Shestakov, Governor in Siberia, 86
Shetland Islands, 94
Shields, James, 223, 224
Shijnia, 306, 308
Shimoda, 185
Shimonoseki, Treaty of, 189
Shipbuilding, British, 61–64, 275, 341, 347, 361; Danish, 63; Dutch, 58, 61, 63, 64, 71, 311; Finnish, 309; Imperial Russian (*see also* Peter the Great; Catherine II; Grand Duke Constantine), 14, 58, 61–65, 71, 72, 81, 82, 185, 223–225, 257, 258, 311, 316, 317, 320, 325, 333–335, 359; Japanese, 185; Soviet, 18, 67, 166, 193, 194, 199, 200, 204, 278, 299, 308, 310, 314, 327, 340, 346, 347, 350, 362; Venetian, 62, 65
Shipwrights, British, 61–64, 70, 70 n.; Dutch, 58, 62–64, 311
Shipwrights' Exhibition, London (1947), 340
Shirsov, M., Commissar for Soviet Mercantile Marine (1943), 267, 268 n.
Shoalwater Bay, 221
Shogun, the, 184
Short History of International Affairs, 1920–1939, A, 139 n.

INDEX 525

Tretii International (*see also Soviet-skii Soyuz*), Russian battleship, 331
Tri Svyatitelya-class battleship (1897), 320; sailing vessel on Golikov-Shelikov expedition to Aleutian Islands, 222, 223
Trident, The, 279 n., 301 n., 307 n.
Trieste, 119
Trinidad Bay, 211
Tripartite Agreement (1940), 39
Tripoli, 117
Tromsoe, 103, 107, 304
Tropic of Cancer, 19
Trotsky, Leon, 136, 150, 150 n.
Truce in the East and its Aftermath, The, 191 n., 323 n.
Trud, Russian paper, 204
True discourse of the late Voyages of Discoverie, etc., 74
Truk, 40
Truman, President, 119
"Tsargrad", 123
"Tschrikof's" Islands, 220
Tschugatsch, Gulf of, 220
Tsesarevitch, Russian battleship, 180, 323
Tsingtau, 343
Tsugaru Strait, 175, 200
Tsushima Island, 188, 189; Strait, 28, 33, 181, 322, 329
Tuapse, 145
Tula, 58
Tunat Island, 103
Tunguska, the, 87, 193; Lower, 57, 358; Stony, 57, 358; Upper, 57, 77, 358
Tunguz, coal of, 36
Tunstall, Brian, 328, 329, 334, 347 n.
Tura, the, 57, 358 n.
Turcomans, 153
Turin, S. P., 346 n.
"Turk-Sib." Railway, 358
Turkestan, 153, 156, 193; Railway, 161, 162
Turkey (*see also* Dardanelles; Straits), 38, 61, 65, 66, 108, 115, 117, 119, 122, 123, 125, 127–133, 136–140, 160, 179, 353; Convention with Russia (1798), 125; helped by France to fortify Straits, 126;

projected naval attack by Allies (1915), 135; Russia's wars with, *see* Russo-Turkish wars
Turkish-Armenian conflicts, 133; -German squadron, World War I, 150
Turkish Fleet, 114, 115, 129–132, 134, 135, 147, 314, 319, 320
Turkmenistan, 156, 356
"Turnagain River", 218
Turner, Arthur, 279
Turukhansk, 57, 77, 104, 261
Tusko, ship of Russia-Finland Whaling Company, 22
Tuyl, Baron de, 242
Tver, the, 309
Tverskoi, Professor, 259
"Twenty-one Demands", Japan's, 253
Tweretz, the, 307
Tyneside, Soviet ships built on, 347, 361
Typhoon, Russian tug, 202
Tzen, the, 307

U-boats (*see also* Submarines), 304, 335; acquired by Russia, 331; in Black Sea, 148; flotilla base at Memel, 292; *Mark 21,* 337; reconditioned by Russians at Liepaja, 299
Ukhta, the, 35
Ukraiintsov, Emilien, 124
Ukraine, 117, 143, 144, 200, 263, 310; German march through (1942), 57, 329
Ukraine and Its People, 45 n.
Ulan-Ude, 362
Ulkun-Daria, the, 355
Ulrich, Captain (in navy of Charles XII), 116
"Ultima Thule", 94
Ultima Thule (by V. Stefansson), 109 n.
Umea, 69
Unalaska Island, 21, 41, 88, 112, 208, 213, 218, 219, 221, 223, 225, 247
Unbroken, British submarine, 332
Under the Red Banner, 338 n.
Unison, British submarine, 332

SUPPLEMENTARY INDEX

Åbo Islands, 382

Åland, Islands, 382, 404

Admiral Hipper, German battle-cruiser, 388, 396, 398

Admiral Kornilov, Russian ex-cruiser (*see also Krasnaya Bessarabia*, and aircraft carrier *Stalin*), 426

Admiral Scheer, German pocket-battleship, 384, 388, 446

Admiral von Tirpitz, German pocket-battleship, 388, 398, 401

Admiralty, British, 401; Churchill goes to (1939), 381; Commentary on German naval documents, 442, 447; Department of Naval Information, 369, 388 n., 397 n., 399 n., 434 n.; First Lord's message to Black Sea Fleet (1944), 419; greetings to Admiral Kharmalov (1941), 452; issue of documents from captured German naval archives, 438, 440

Afanasyev, Captain, 452

"Aid to Russia" (*see also* Anglo-American aid; Northern Convoys), 400 (World War I); 404, 446 (World War II)

Air Routes, Russian Arctic, 386, 387

Aircraft carriers, British, 396–398, 446; limitations on tonnage laid down by Agreement (1937), 449; Soviet carriers, 379, 406, 409, 426

Airports, Polar, 386

Alaska, 387

Alexander, Captain, defender of Malakov (1942), 418

All the World's Fighting Fleets, 373, 383 n.

All-Union Marine Transport Company, 405

Allied Joint Chiefs of Staffs Committee, meeting of (1942), 389, 446; Shipping Control Committee (1915), 434

Alten Fjord, 388

Altmark, German "prison-ship," 390

Altvater, Russian destroyer, 423

Alushta, 415

America (*see also* United States), Intelligence Officers, 439

Amur, the, 425; Flotilla, 424, 425; Valley, 425

Anadir, the, 387; Gulf, 386, 387

Andreyev, Admiral, 425

Anglo-American aid to Russia (*see also* "Aid to Russia"; Northern Convoys), 390, 398, 399

Anglo-Soviet Shipping Committee, 399

Ansaldo Works, Leghorn, 410

Anzio, 422

Archangel, 387–390, 403, 404, 404 n., 405

Arctic bases, 385, 387, 401, 402, 444; coasts, 386, 436; Fleet, *see* Northern Fleet; meteorological stations, 436; Ocean, 386, 396, 402, 446; ports, 385, 386, 396, 402–405; seas, 391

Armavir-Tbilsi Railway, 414

Arseni Raskit, Russian minesweeper, 410

Artem, Russian destroyer, 383

Asia, Central, 423

Astrakhan, 393, 423

Atlantic, the, 404; Battle of the, 384; North, 396, 442

Attentive, British light cruiser, 404

Attlee, Rt. Hon. Clement Richard, 400

Aurora, Russian cruiser, 375, 379

Azerbaidjan, Russian tanker, 452

Azov Flotilla, 392, 419, 421, 422, 447; ports, 447; Shipping Agency, 430

Azov Sea, 412, 419–421, 447, 448; northern shores of, 447

Babinski, Russian destroyer, 423

Baku, 414, 423; oil, 423